MARKETING
COMMUNICATIONS

To Caroline, Arthur, Dan and Becky

MARKETING
COMMUNICATIONS
JOHN EGAN

Australia • Canada • Mexico • Singapore • Spain • United Kingdom • United States

THOMSON

Marketing Communications
John Egan

Publishing Director John Yates	**Publisher** Jennifer Pegg	**Development Editor** Tom Rennie
Production Editor Lucy Mills	**Manufacturing Manager** Helen Mason	**Marketing Executive** Leo Stanley
Typesetter Newgen, India	**Production Controller** Maeve Healy	**Cover Design** www.mulcaheydesign.co.uk
Text Design Design Deluxe Ltd, Bath, UK	**Printer** Rotolito Lombarda S.p.A. Italy	

BRIEF CONTENTS

CONTENTS

ABOUT THE AUTHOR

John Egan is a Principal Lecturer at Middlesex University Business School. He is a member of the Academy of Marketing Executive and co-chaired the Academy's Conference in 2006. He is a member of the Institute of Direct Marketing Educator's Panel and a Chartered Marketer. Prior to entering full-time academia in 1997 he had worked in UK and overseas retailing with organizations such as Associated Merchandising Corporation, Mappin and Webb and Garrard. He is author of *Relationship Marketing: Exploring Relational Strategies in Marketing* and co-author of *Public Relations: Contemporary Issues and Techniques*. He has authored several journal articles and is on the editorial panels of the *European Journal of Marketing* and the *Journal of Political Marketing*.

PREFACE

Marketing communications is one of the most exciting and stimulating areas in modern marketing. Its popularity as an area of study has grown consistently over the years and the number of texts dedicated to the subject has multiplied in parallel. So why another book on marketing communications? The answer lies in the rapidly changing marketplace.

All areas of marketing have been affected by the technological advances of the past ten or so years. The means by which we communicate with each other have changed radically and this is reflected in the commercial world. These advances, particularly the Internet and World Wide Web have enabled interaction on a scale that could not have been dreamed about a few decades ago. This is not, however, the only or possibly the most important transformation. Indeed some would argue that the 'e-revolution' has been more about providing additional channels of communication rather than a re-invention of marketing. What has changed more than anything else is the consumer. Bombarded with hundreds of messages every day they are more selective in their attention. Mass advertising, while it will always have a place in the communications mix (see Chapter 9), no longer has the influence it had over previous generations. Marketers are looking to other 'below the line' tools to gain the attention of potential customers. Not only that but organizations are using consumers themselves as the medium with tactics variously known as buzz marketing, or viral marketing. It is these changes that this text looks to accommodate.

Despite the importance of looking at the present and anticipating the future this should not be at the expense of ignoring past experience. Indeed this text begins with a look at how commercial communications have developed over the centuries and why this set the pattern for the modern day industry (see Chapter 1). The book discusses communications theory (Chapter 2), how this has developed and how this is currently operationalized. Subsequent chapters analyse the consumer buying process (Chapter 3), image and brand management (Chapter 4), marketing communications planning (Chapters 5 and 8), marketing research (Chapter 6) and target marketing (Chapter 7). The individual aspects of the marketing communications mix are examined (Chapters 9 to 14) before critically analysing (in Chapter 15) the contribution of theories and concepts surrounding integrated marketing communications (IMC). It is a contention of this text that internal marketing is an area of growing importance and a chapter has been dedicated to this (Chapter 16). Marketing channels and business-to-business communications are examined (Chapter 17) and ethical and regulatory issues, an area of increasing concern, reviewed (Chapter 18). The communications industry, which in many ways reflects albeit sometimes unwillingly, the changes in modern communications is discussed (Chapter 19) and the implications of an increasingly global industry considered (Chapter 20). In the final chapter an attempt is made to summarize current changes and predict a course for the future. The hope is that the reader will find the text comprehensive, interesting and stimulating.

If you have any comments on any aspect of this book I would be delighted to hear from you at j.egan@mdx.ac.uk.

John Egan

October 2006

ACKNOWLEDGEMENTS

As with any book it was unlikely to see the light of day without the help and support of many people. My sincere thanks go to everyone at Thomson Learning who have been involved but particularly Jennifer Pegg and Tom Rennie whose enormous support and occasional cajoling have been invaluable. My thanks also go to the reviewers whose experienced and practical advice was so important. Special thanks go to Andy Cropper at Sheffield Hallam University whose contributions are acknowledged as an important addition to this text. I would also like to thank Nik Mahon at Southampton Solent University for contributing a number of case studies used in the text. My colleagues at Middlesex University Business School including those who have left to take up other appointments deserve a special mention for their genuine friendship over the years. Last but certainly not least my family Alison, Tom and Alice for their unselfish support.

The publisher acknowledges the contribution of the following lecturers who provided numerous reviews of the manuscript:

Nik Mahon – Faculty of Media, Arts and Society, Southampton Solent University

Peeter Verlegh – Department of Marketing Management, RSM Erasmus University

Emma H. Wood – The UK Centre for Events Management, Leeds Metropolitan University

Connie Nolan – The Business School, Canterbury Christ Church University

Mirjami Lehikoinen – Helsinki School of Economics

The following lecturers are acknowledged for their role in reviewing the proposal:

Paul Copley – University of Northumbria

Chris Hackley – Royal Holloway College, University of London

John Goodfellow – London Metropolitan University

Kitty Koelmeijer – Tilburg University

John May – University of the West of England

Richard Scullion – University of Bournemouth

Anne Torres – University College Galway

The following lecturers are acknowledged for their role in the pre-proposal market research:

George Angelopulo – University of South Africa (UNISA)
Roger Bennett – London Metropolitan University
June Dennis – Leeds Metropolitan University
Debra Harker – University of the Sunshine Coast
Howard Jackson – University of Huddersfield
Mirjami Lehikoinen – Helsinki School of Economics
Rita Martensen – Gothenburg University
Pierre McDonagh – Dublin City University
Caroline Oates – University of Sheffield
Lisa O'Malley – University of Limerick
Andrea Prothero – University College, Dublin
Rob Townsend – University of Bedfordshire
Anne Torres – University College Galway
Peeter Verlegh – Erasmus University Rotterdam

Thank you to Kim Roberts at London South Bank University for kindly providing extra case studies used on this textbook's companion website.

We would also like to thank the following for permission to reproduce copyright material and for their kind efforts in assisting this publication:

Haymarket Business Publications Limited
Dominic Curran, Director, Karen Earl Sponsorship
Jon Claydon
Derek Holder
Cunning
Nikon UK Limited
Team Saatchi
The Chartered Institute of Marketing
Canon (UK) Limited
Corbis
Alamy
ISBA
Red Bull Photofiles and Andi Schaad
The Advertising Archives
Nielsen Media Research
Innocent Drinks
FDS Field Marketing
Republic PR
BtoB Magazine, Crain Communication Inc.

In some instances we have been unable to trace the owners of copyright material, and we would appreciate any information that would enable us to do so.

SUPPLEMENTS

Thomson Learning offers various supplements for lecturers and students who use this book. All of these supplements (with the exception of the ExamView® disk) can be found on the companion website: www.thomsonlearning.co.uk/egan.

For the lecturer

- **Solutions Manual** – The Solutions Manual, downloadable as a PDF document, includes solutions to all exercises that accompany the textbook.

- **ExamView®** – Using thousands of questions created specifically for this textbook, this test bank and test generator allows lecturers to create online, paper and local area network (LAN) tests. This CD-rom based product is only available from your Thomson Learning sales representative.

- **PowerPoint® Presentation Slides** – A full set of PowerPoint Slides for every chapter, can save lecturers valuable time in classroom preparation.

- **Extra Case Studies** – This powerful set of Extra Case Studies also contains indicative answers, making then ideal for classroom discussion or assessment.

- **Web Links** – Carefully selected by the authors, dozens of Web links provide valuable guidance on useful websites.

For the student:

- **Multiple Choice Questions** – Dozens of practice questions for every chapter provide students with a valuable revision tool.

- **Glossary** – An electronic glossary provides useful definitions of all key terms.

- **Learning Objectives** – Listed for each chapter, they help the student to monitor their understanding and progress through the chapter.

- **Web Links** – Carefully selected by the authors, dozens of Web links provide valuable guidance on useful websites.

Other supplementary resources:

- **Virtual Learning Environment** – All of the web material is available in a format that is compatible with virtual learning environments such as Blackboard and WebCT. This version of the product is only available from your Thomson Learning sales representative.

- **TextChoice** – TextChoice (www.textchoice.com) is the home of Thomson Learning's online digital content. It provides the fastest, easiest way for you to create your own learning materials. You may select content from hundreds of our best-selling titles to make a custom text. Please contact your Thomson Learning sales representative to discuss further.

WALK THROUGH TOUR

LEARNING OBJECTIVES appear at the start of every chapter to help you monitor your understanding and progress through the chapter. Each chapter also ends with a summary section that recaps the key content for revision purposes.

LARGE PHOTOGRAPHS are reproduced in full colour to fully convey the strong visual element of marketing communications.

WEB LINKS are provided in the margin next to relevant sections to allow you to integrate your learning with robust online resources.

KEY TERMS are highlighted with an explanation in the margin when they first appear in the text to reinforce important terms and concepts.

MINICASES are provided throughout which illustrate how marketing communications is applied in the real world.

SUMMARIES at the end of each chapter provide a thorough re-cap of the key issues to help you assess your understanding and revise key content.

REVIEW QUESTIONS are provided at the end of each chapter to help reinforce and test your knowledge and understanding.

DISCUSSION QUESTIONS are provided at the end of each chapter to provide a platform for classroom discussion.

FURTHER READING and **CHAPTER REFERENCES** are provided to allow you to explore the subject further and act as a starting point for projects and assignments.

CASE STUDIES are provided at the end of each chapter to show how each chapter's main issues are applied in real-life marketing situations. Each case is accompanied by questions to help you test your understanding of the issues.

A companion website accompanies

MARKETING COMMUNICATIONS

JOHN EGAN

Visit the *Marketing Communications* website at www.thomsonlearning.co.uk/egan to find valuable teaching and learning material including:

For lecturers:

- Solutions Manual
- PowerPoint® Presentation Slides
- Extra Case Studies
- Web Links

For students:

- Multiple Choice Questions
- Glossary
- Learning Objectives
- Web Links

CHAPTER ONE

MARKETING COMMUNICATIONS: PAST AND PRESENT

LEARNING OBJECTIVES

Having completed this chapter you should be able to:

- Understand the reasons behind the growth of marketing communications.
- Be aware of the main developments in the marketing communications industry.
- Have a general understanding of marketing communication's tools and their part in an integrated campaign.
- Recognize the part played by different media in the communications process.

INTRODUCTION

When the question 'what is marketing communications?' is asked the likelihood is that there will be as many answers as there are respondents. One of the most common responses is likely to be that it is simply advertising, because this is the most visible of the marketing communications (marcoms)[1] mix and there is little doubt that for many years the promotional function was dominated by mass advertising. Indeed, prior to the twentieth century the term advertising was used for what might contemporaneously be called marketing (in its widest sense). Even today commentators frequently use the terms interchangeably.

Over the past two decades, however, the term marketing communications has eclipsed that of advertising and promotion when describing how an organization presents itself and its brands to its audience, whoever that audience might be. This text will, therefore, take in the first instance a simple working definition of marketing communications as: 'the means by which a supplier of goods, services, values and/or ideas represent themselves to their target audience with the goal of stimulating dialogue leading to better commercial or other relationships'.

This simple definition serves to emphasize the idea of reaching out to an audience whether the organization is a commercial, not-for-profit, government

Marketing communications
The means by which a supplier of goods, services, values and/or ideas represent themselves to their target audience with the goal of stimulating dialogue leading to a better commercial or other relationships.

Advertising
A paid-for, non-personal form of mass communication from an identified source, used to communicate information and influence consumer behaviour with a high degree of control over design and placement but potentially a low degree of persuasion and credibility. It is never either neutral or unbiased.

Marcoms
A frequently used short-form for marketing communications.

[1]Marcoms is a frequently used short-form for marketing communications.

or other type of collective and trying to establish a dialogue. Its construct being designed to reflect the underlying communications objective and either specifically or indirectly inform, differentiate, remind reassure and/or persuade the target audience to act. Alongside this, it is also important to acknowledge that marketing communications is an evolving medium, in a state of constant and dynamic flux. Influenced by both wider environmental influences and, more directly, media development, budgetary demands and, most of all, consumer attitude.

MARKETING COMMUNICATIONS HISTORY

Marketing communications activities were practised long before they were analysed and defined in the twentieth century. Box 1.1 notes some of the marketing communication milestones throughout its long history of development and innovation. Nevett (1982: 3), in his review of advertising history, urges us to 'not indulge in speculation as to whether prehistoric cave paintings, Babylonian inscriptions, the ten-commandments or the writings on the wall at Balthazar's feast constitute advertising', and yet, in their own way they all represent communication of one kind or another. In commercial terms early examples of publicity included the Babylonian tablets bearing inscriptions of various craftsmen including an ointment maker, a scribe and a shoemaker. Ancient Greece provides clear evidence of what today would be recognized as advertising or sales promotion. Criers, whose main occupation was the proclamation of new laws, were also available for hire by traders. Someone who availed himself of this service was Aesclyptöe, an Athenian cosmetics vendor whose advertisement (a forerunner of today's jingles) ran (Nevett 1982):

> For eyes that are shining, for cheeks like the dawn,
> for beauty that lasts after girlhood has gone,
> for prices in reason, the woman who knows,
> will buy her cosmetics at Aesclyptöe.

By Roman times advertising was in widespread use. The best preserved examples of this come from the ruins of Pompeii, destroyed by the eruption of Vesuvius in AD 79, where there are not only numerous example of signs (e.g. a mill for a baker, a boot for a shoemaker, a ham for a butcher, a goat for a dairy etc.) but actual advertisements written on walls. For example one of the earliest known tourism advertisements was on the walls of Pompeii (Russell and Lane 2002) and read:

> Traveller
> Going from here to the Twelfth Tower
> There Sarinus keeps a tavern
> This is to request you to enter
> Farewell

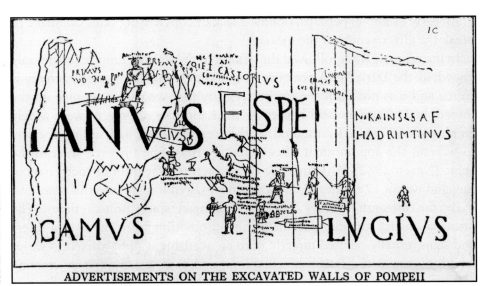

ADVERTISEMENTS ON THE EXCAVATED WALLS OF POMPEII

SOURCE: © BETTMANN/CORBIS

Advertisements on the excavated walls of Pompeii, Italy.

@

Explore advertising history at: **www.hatads. org.uk/**.

Box 1. 1 Historical development of marketing communications

circa

3000 BC	Babylonian tablet bearing inscription of an ointment maker, a scribe and a shoemaker
400 BC	Criers in ancient Greece
AD 79	Poster advertisements preserved following Vesuvius eruption
1140	Criers widely employed in France
1441	Moveable type invented (Guttenberg)
1477	First English advertisement (William Caxton)
1525	The first advertisement printed in a news sheet (Germany)
1610	Newspapers circulating in Germany and the Netherlands
1614	Earliest known law restricting advertising prohibited shop signs from extending more than eight feet (UK)
1622	The first English newspaper
1625	First English newspaper advertisement
1655	The use of the term 'advertising' becomes established
1657	The first English language publication devoted entirely to advertising (*The Publick Advertiser*)
1740	The first printed outdoor posters (hoardings) appeared in London
1786	The first known advertising agent (William Taylor)
1841	First advertising sales agency in the USA (Volney-Palmer)
1871	First known research into advertising effectiveness (*A Guide to Advertising*)
1891	First account executive (J. Walter-Thompson, USA)
1917	Association of British Advertising Agents (ABBA) formed which later became the Institute of Incorporated Practitioners in Advertising and is now the Institute of Practitioners in Advertising (IPA)
1926	Commercial radio introduced (USA)
1930	Radio Normandy broadcasts advertising to UK market
1947	Commercial television introduced (USA)
1955	Commercial television introduced (UK) First advertisement Gibbs SR toothpaste

Sources include Nevett 1982, Wells *et al.* 1995, Russell and Lane 2002.

An early example, perhaps, of how a lack of copywriting skills can make or break the effectiveness of the message!

In the centuries that followed the demise of the Roman Empire (commonly known as the Dark Ages) evidence of marketing communications activity is scarce and it is not until the twelfth century that we can again pick up the thread. In 1140 criers (still known by the Latin title of Praeco) were widely employed in France. By the end of that century Paris had sufficient criers to warrant the appointment of two master-criers, one for each bank of the Seine (Nevett 1982). Although the earliest written mention of such criers in England was in 1299 they almost certainly existed long before this date.

By the fifteenth century little had changed since Roman times. The principal media for announcements and promotion were the use of criers and signs, usually painted directly onto an available wall or affixed to shops or other commercial establishments. Inns vied with one another by creating conspicuous illustrated signs to advertise their services to a largely illiterate audience. This accounts for many of the unique public house names that have survived to the present day (e.g. Hole in the Wall, the Green Man, etc.). In England in 1614 the first law in restraint of such advertising prohibited signs from extending more than eight feet (2.44 metres) from a building (Russell and Lane 2002).

One of the forerunners of modern advertising were the 'siquis', handwritten bills common in England in the sixteenth and seventeenth centuries. Originally these were used to advertise clerical positions and set out the requirements for the post. They were in Latin and usually began *si quis* (if anybody). The name stuck and soon these notices were taking a variety of subject matter including lost-and-found, runaway apprentices etc. (Russell and Lane 2002).

The first really modern innovation came with the invention of the printing press. This opened up a range of possibilities for advertising to be displayed, taken away or kept for further reference. The earliest example of a printed poster advertisement in English was a 3 by 5 inch bill, promoting the 'Pyes of Salisbury' a set of rules for the clergy. It was printed by William Caxton around 1477 about 40 years after Guttenberg's original invention. The poster included the plea 'Pray do not pull down this advertisement.'

Printing was also a major part of the evolution of newspapers, which themselves were to play such an important part in the development of advertising over the succeeding centuries. Although the Romans posted daily government newsletters known as *acta diurna* as early as 59 BC, the forerunner to the newspaper was probably the manuscript newsletters, copies of which were circulated in the Middle Ages by banking houses. The first example of a printed advertisement was probably in such a German news pamphlet around 1525. By 1610 records show that newspapers were beginning to circulate widely in Germany and the Netherlands. Although principally news-bearing mediums, advertising soon became the principal means by which production and distribution costs could be offset. The first English language newspaper was *The Weekly Newes of London* first published in 1622 and the earliest example of an advertisement in an English newspaper can be traced to 1625. The first publication in the

'New World' of North America was *Public Occurences Both Forreign and Domestick*, which appeared in 1690 but for only one edition! The first American newspaper to carry advertising (in this case advertising a reward for the capture of a thief) was the *Boston Newsletter* in 1704 (Wells *et al.* 1995).

The roots of modern marketing communications are, however, firmly associated with the Industrial Revolution. Prior to this the vast number of producers each made a limited number of products and delivered them for consumption locally. Traders would bring their goods to market and sell them according to local supply and demand. Between 1740 and 1821 a major transformation took place in UK manufacturing that would ultimately spread to many parts of the world. The Industrial Revolution saw a major switch from individual artisans to mass production in huge custom-built factories. Mass produced goods manufactured in one location required wide distribution to sustain production levels. New distribution channels were developed (railways, canals etc.) to cope with this expansion of traffic but how was consumer demand to be generated? Mass production was all very well but it also required mass consumption!

Manufacturers identified the mass media as the vehicle to stimulate demand and began to make use of advertising in two distinct ways[2] (Nevett 1982). The first was to offer retailers advertising space as an inducement to buy more stock. For example in 1780 William Jones, a London Chemist and Druggist, offered a free advertisement in selected local newspapers to stockists who bought a dozen bottles of his Tincture of Peruvian Bark. The second strategy was to promote direct to the consumer with a view to informing the public about the product and building up confidence in its benefits. This was an example of what today would be called 'brand-building'.

Such was the growing proliferation of advertising in the eighteenth century that in 1759 Samuel Johnson wrote that they 'are very negligently perused, and it is therefore necessary to gain attention by magnificence of promise and by eloquence, sometimes sublime and sometimes pathetick'. Yet Johnson appeared to have a sense of advertising's growing appeal when in 1760 he wrote: 'the trade of advertising is now so near to perfection that it is not easy to propose any improvements' (*Idler*, issue 40, 20 January).

During this period the principal mass media were newspapers and magazines. In the UK the number of newspaper titles rose from 25 in 1700 to 258 in 1800. UK annual paper production, between 1800 and 1860, rose from 11 000 tons to 100 000 tons. In the USA the number of newspapers more than doubled between 1830 and 1860 (from 1200 to 3000) and the number of magazines increased by over 250 per cent between 1850 and 1880 (from 700 to 2400). The platform for mass advertising had arrived and the increased levels of choice placed before consumers had the inevitable impact of stimulating demand and driving the growth of mass consumption.

Poster advertising too continued to increase during the period such that it was becoming a problem akin to that of **fly-posting** today. Daniel Defoe, in

Fly-posting
Posters randomly affixed to walls rather than licensed hoardings.

[2]In later times these would be called 'push' and 'pull' strategies (see Chapter 5)

A Journal of the Plague Year, described the proliferation of poster advertising by the middle of the seventeenth century:[3]

> *it is incredible, and scarce to be imagin'd, how the Posts of Houses and Corners of Streets were plastered over with Doctors Bills, and Papers of ignorant fellows; quacking and tampering in Physick, and inviting the People to come to them for Remedies; which was generally set off, with such flourishes as these, (viz) INFALLIBLE preventive Pills against the Plague. NEVER FAILING Preservatives against the infection. SOVERAIGN Cordials against the corruption of the body ... I take notice of these by way of Specimen: I could give you two or three dozen of the like, and yet have abundance left behind.*

Patent medicine suppliers were, during this period, major sponsors of advertising on both sides of the Atlantic with an importance akin to that of cigarette advertisers in the twentieth century. In an age where the threat of serious, even fatal disease, was ever present such 'magic remedies' were in great demand. In the USA by the 1870s patent medications were the largest single category in advertising and continued to dominate this medium until the end of that century. On the downside the fraudulent claims of the quack remedies was an early example of how one sector can give the whole of advertising a bad name (Russell and Lane 2002).

Patent medicines affected marketing communications in other ways too. Because of the (supposed) qualities of these medicines it was desirable that each unit should be packaged separately so that it could carry a notice about the patent and warning against infringements and imitators. According to Nevett (1982: 24) as 'sordid though this form of enterprise unquestionably was, the medicine vendors may well be regarded as the pioneers of modern marketing, branding their products, advertising them widely and distributing them over large areas of the country'.

The term advertising, which prior to the mid-nineteenth century referred to any and all promotional activity, came to be more narrowly defined in this period as 'paid for mass media communication' and was the tool that led the significant development of brands and markets from the late nineteenth century through to the 1950s. Even as early as the nineteenth century leading advertisers, such as Schweppes, Crosse & Blackwell and Lea & Perrins, were running campaigns that covered wide areas of the UK. In the USA large-scale advertising during the second half of the nineteenth century helped lay the foundations for the growth of such present-day companies as American Express, American Tobacco, Campbell's Soup, Carnation, Coca-Cola, Colgate-Palmolive, Eastman-Kodak, Sears, Roebuck & Co., Quaker Oats, Heinz, Libby, Pillsbury, Procter & Gamble and Nabisco to name but a few (Sivulka 1998).

Although as early as 1630 an advertising agency model was said to be operating in France (Varey 2002), little detail is known. The claim to be the first known and recognizable advertising sales agency is often credited to

[3]Quoted in Nevett 1982: 12.

Volney-Palmer in the USA in 1841 but, despite the rather diverse definitions of the term agency, the title probably goes to William Taylor who, in the *Maidstone Journal* of 1786, described himself as an advertising agent. James White was another UK pioneer who founded his agency in 1800 and Charles Barker another who established his business in Birchin Lane, London in 1837. By this time it was probable that many leading agents were offering all the services that might be required in the preparation and execution of a campaign (Nevett 1982). By 1880 advertising agencies were common in most of the UK's principal towns and cities.

By the turn of the century the marketing communications industry was entering its more modern phase. The advances in printing technology were creating formats that could be used creatively by advertisers and catalogues that were to become the means by which small towns and rural communities were to become part of the consumption machine. As the twentieth century progressed the introduction of, first commercial radio stations and, later in the century, television was to see broadcasting taking over from printed

Box 1.2 Radio advertising

Not everyone was convinced that new technology was the way forward in advertising. When asked about the new medium of radio an anonymous potential investor was said to have retorted 'The wireless music box has no imaginable commercial value. Who would pay for a message sent to nobody in particular?' Although he or she evidently got this wrong from an investment perspective, later generations of potential advertisers were to use the same argument against the mass media!

Figure 1.1 Enterprise

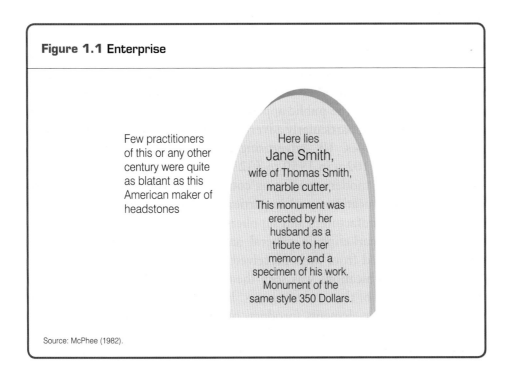

Few practitioners of this or any other century were quite as blatant as this American maker of headstones

Here lies
Jane Smith,
wife of Thomas Smith, marble cutter,

This monument was erected by her husband as a tribute to her memory and a specimen of his work. Monument of the same style 350 Dollars.

Source: McPhee (1982).

messages as the dominant advertising media. This period also saw the recognized growth of other marketing communications tools such as public relations and sales promotion. As early as 1900 powerful business interests employed public relations professionals to 'defend their special interests against muckraking journalism and government regulation' (Cutlip *et al.* 1994: 2). Sales promotion grew with the fast developing retail industry and in particular with the advent of the department store and variety chain grocery stores and, later in the twentieth century, supermarkets.

Although the history of marketing communications is ongoing the informality, and perhaps naiveté, of earlier times was, by the middle of the twentieth century, being replaced by increased creativity and developing best practice. Marketing education was coming to the fore as the provider of professionals for this growing industry. The advertising industry in particular saw huge growth in the second and third quarters of the twentieth century. By the end of it, however, it was the 'newer' marketing communications tools that were coming to prominence. By 2000 two-thirds of marketing communications spend was below the line (i.e. marketing communications tools excluding advertising, see Figure 1.4) a reversal of the situation 50 years before (Varey 2002).

Below the line
The marketing communication tools excluding advertising.

MARKETING COMMUNICATIONS EDUCATION

It was during the period between 1920 and 1950 that marketing education developed (initially out of the study of economics), spread through schools and colleges around the world and became an important adjunct to business life. By 1950 business education was firmly established in the USA and there were signs of activity in other western markets. During the 'golden age of marketing' (1950–70) the public appetite for new goods and services was at its height. Marketing, particularly advertising, became an important stimulant to growing economies. UK advertising expenditure (in real terms) rose significantly from £102m in 1950 to £323m in 1960 and £554m in 1970. It would appear that modern marketing could sell anything and that modern marketing communications, and in particular advertising, could deliver the customers that manufacturers and suppliers required.

The study of marketing in general and marketing communications in particular developed from their perceived importance to economic growth. Marketing communications was seen then, much as it is seen today, as the most visible aspect of the marketing mix. In this regard it is seen to combine with the three other elements (product, place and price) to create a unique marketing profile for a particular product or brand. For the marketer, the basic challenge was seen to be the combination of these four elements into a marketing programme that would bridge the gap between the company and the consumer and ensure it could compete effectively in the marketplace. The 4Ps (product, place, price and promotion) model developed by McCarthy (1960), was, however, itself a distillation of Borden's (1964) '12 elements of a marketing programme' many of which were recognizable themselves as marketing communication's tools as shown in Figure 1.2 below.

4Ps
A model of marketing which incorporates product, place, price and promotion.

Figure 1.2 Borden's 12 elements of a marketing programme

Product Planning	Personal Selling	Display	Pricing
Advertising	Servicing	Branding	Promotions
Physical Handling	Channels of Distribution	Packaging	Fact Finding and Analysis

Source: Borden (1964).

It was the simplified 4P marketing framework rather than the more comprehensive 12 elements that were quickly adopted by students, teachers and practitioners alike, as a straightforward, easy to remember and intuitively rational marketing model. The so-called 'golden era of marketing' (1950–70) was a time of high consumer trust, effective mass advertising, growing prosperity, homogeneous demand, poorly developed distribution channels and, above all, dominant manufacturing power (O'Driscoll and Murray 1998: 396) and the 'brand management model' or 'toolbox approach' (Grönroos 1994) of the marketing mix appeared to be working very effectively indeed.

In the late 1960s the favourable conditions that had seen the rapid growth of western markets began to change dramatically. During this period North American, Western European and Pacific Rim markets started to become saturated. Population growth, a feature and major driver behind the rise in consumer purchasing, was declining. Branded goods in general showed little growth and markets were becoming dominated by oligopolies (e.g. Coca-Cola–Pepsi Cola, Procter & Gamble–Unilever, etc.). Branding, originally conceived to provide customers with quality assurance evolved into a segmentation tool with different brands for each, ever smaller, segment. As segments proliferated so did brands contributing further to marketing's increased productivity problems (Sheth and Sisodia 1999: 78).

Oligopolies
A market situation in which there are few sellers in the market and where the marketing action of one firm will have a direct effect on the others.

Mature markets, as these economies were rapidly becoming, exhibited characteristics that differentiated them from growth markets (Christopher 1996: 55). In particular consumers, faced with a surfeit of goods and services, were to become much more demanding. Marketing communications functions such as advertising, public relations, sales promotion and direct marketing were becoming more sophisticated but this only resulted in commercial clutter which made it 'more difficult for brands to be seen or heard' (Duncan 2002: vii). In this buyer's market customers began to realize the attractiveness of their spending power and began to take advantage of it. Customers were growing much more sophisticated and less easily persuaded by marketing messages.

During this period it was becoming evident that the perceived benefits of marketing communications tools, particularly advertising were in decline, as the media market (television, radio and magazines in particular) fragmented causing the **cost-per-thousand**[4] rates of most media to increase substantially. Other major changes included the development of own brands from dominant **FMCG** (Fast Moving Consumer Goods) retailers. Increasingly these retailers were looking not for brand-building advertising to support their businesses but 'below the line' (see Figure 1.4) in-store promotions as an incentive to stock branded lines. The main casualty at this time was the advertising industry (see Minicase 1.1). During the period 1966 to 1974 the number of people involved in UK advertising (as opposed to other forms of marketing communications) fell by almost a third from 20 000 to 14 000.

Cost-per-thousand

A measure for comparing the cost effectiveness of media calculated by dividing the cost of an advertisement in one particular medium by the circulation.

FMCG

Fast moving consumer goods (such as those sold in supermarkets).

Views on the marketing function are discussed further at: **www.urbino.net/bright. cfm?specificBright=The%20Marketing %20Function.**

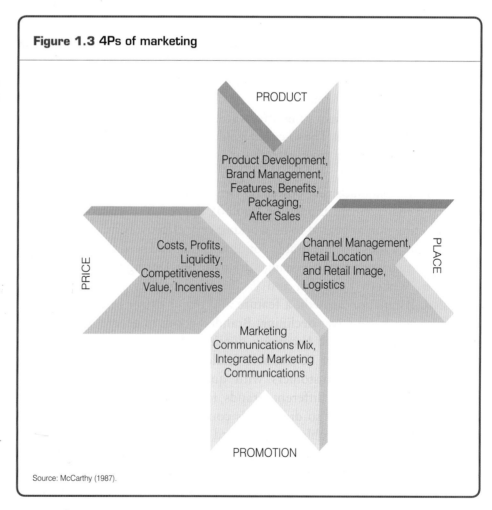

Figure 1.3 4Ps of marketing

PRODUCT

Product Development, Brand Management, Features, Benefits, Packaging, After Sales

PRICE

Costs, Profits, Liquidity, Competitiveness, Value, Incentives

PLACE

Channel Management, Retail Location and Retail Image, Logistics

Marketing Communications Mix, Integrated Marketing Communications

PROMOTION

Source: McCarthy (1987).

[4]Cost-per-thousand (CPT) is a frequently used ratio comparing the costs between different media.

The changing face of marketing communications

Although it is dangerous to generalize on the basis of one set of figures there is an indication of the long-term changes that are taking place in the industry in the first quarterly Agency Barometer survey conducted in September 2003. The survey, from the Communications Agencies Federation, the joint forum of the Institute of Practitioners in Advertising (IPA), the Marketing Communication Consultants Association (MCCA) and the Public Relations Consultants Association (PRCA), questioned senior executives from all three trade organizations. The survey reflects structural changes in the business and how clients are choosing to promote their products and services.

The survey noted that whilst media, public relations, multi-discipline, direct marketing/sales and promotion/interactive agencies all revised their forecasts upwards, the advertising and creative agency forecasts were static. Increased forecasts were most marked among smaller agencies. It also noted that over 60 per cent of agencies said they were more optimistic than three months ago. The weakest levels of confidence were in the advertising and creative sectors where fewer than half the agencies expressed optimism.

In an article reporting these results Emiko Terazono (2003) noted that an increasing number of companies regarded traditional media as expensive. The article quoted Matthew Hooper, Chairman of MCCA, who, commenting on this change, remarked that 'As a result, creative brand agencies are struggling.'

On the optimistic side over a quarter of agencies wanted to increase their graduate recruitment but recruiting activity in advertising/creative agencies is expected to remain sluggish.

Source: Terazono, E., 'Feeling a little bit better', *Financial Times*, September 29, 2003 (used with permission).

Figure 1.4 Above and below the line

@

Sample agency in 'new media' at:
www.theiq-group.com.

The various marketing communications tools are frequently referred to as 'above the line' (advertising) or 'below the line' (all other marketing communication tools). This has a historical foundation and is based on the way that agencies (which for most of the twentieth century were principally advertising agencies) invoiced their clients. Advertising was placed with the media at an agreed rate. The agency would invoice this total amount to their clients. When paying the media owner for the space the agency would deduct an agreed percentage of 10 per cent or 15 per cent. Other services of the agency (sales promotion, public relations activities, etc.) were additional costs added on after the main charge for advertising space. The invoice might look like this:

INVOICE	
6 insertions *Evening Globe*	£ 12 000
6 insertions *Daily Globe*	£ 12 000
3 insertions *Sunday Globe*	£ 4 000
Subtotal	£ 28 000
In-store promotional literature	£ 5 000
New product launch event	£ 5 000
Total	£ 38 000

Thus advertising was referred to as 'above the line' (i.e. included in the main media costs) and other tools 'below the line'. In addition, some marketers refer to direct marketing (which in theory overlaps both advertising and promotion) as 'through the line'. This terminology may eventually fade away as many agencies have moved away from commission-based earnings to fee-based earnings.

The pressure to change still continues. Increased sophistication, technological developments and a move towards consolidation has seen a rise in smaller agencies, who now have to compete creatively in a crowded marketplace. For example, the development of digital media based solutions has created a new market in the in-house television advertising sector for companies such as The IQ Group.

Perhaps the biggest changes of all are the consumers who, it would appear, no longer respond as readily to traditional forms of advertising and promotion as they did decades before. Clients too are much more demanding requiring better results from their communications. Marketing communications is being driven towards greater accountability and the increasing favouring of a database approach by many organizations who seek to measure effectiveness through their ability to 'count them out and count them back in again' (Evans 2003: 257).

In the business education field marketing and marketing communications were seen to be changing yet the concepts and theories that were still promulgated by the communications industry were from the bygone age of the 1950s and 1960s (McKenna 1991; Christopher and Baker 2000). The 4Ps approach promoted the image of a 'tool box' (Grönroos 1994: 5) of science-orientated marketing that was heavily criticized as 'a neglect of process in favour of structure' leading to a 'lack of study into many of the key variables' (Christopher et al. 1991: 8). As Varey (2002: 10) notes, marketing communication is nearly always presented in texts as the promotion of producer and product to a predetermined audience to elicit desired responses – if only it were that easy! In reality everything an organization does communicates something about the firm and its goods and services regardless of whether the marketer accepts this and acts upon it (Grönroos 2000).

It seems clear that marketing communications is moving in a more 'sophisticated and eclectic direction' than was previously the case (Evans 2003). As well as questioning of the marketing mix orthodoxy there are evident changes in how marketing communications are perceived and practised. Marketers are being forced, by ever-turbulent market conditions, to find new or outstanding ways to communicate with their customers. None are complete replacements for previous practice, which continues in parallel. Indeed part of the new communications paradigm is the greater variety of tactical approaches now being used.

DEVELOPMENTS IN MARKETING COMMUNICATIONS

Marketing in general and marketing communications in particular are always adapting and changing to accommodate changing market circumstances. There are currently three major developments that have permeated all sectors of the industry. These perceived developments are as shown in Box 1.3 below.

Box 1.3 Developments in marketing communications

Perceived Movement from		Perceived Movement to
Mass Communication	> > > >	Targeted Communication
Selective Communications Tools	> > > >	Integrated Marketing Communications
Dominated by Consumer Goods	> > > >	Recognition of importance of Service and Business-to-Business (B2B) sectors

---

MASS vs TARGETED COMMUNICATION

Mass communications, as we have noted, was at the heart of marketing communications from the Industrial Revolution through until the last quarter of the twentieth century. The challenge to this dominance has come from two principal directions:

Philosophically	The development of relationship marketing
Technologically	The ability to analyse and target individual customers (sometimes called **one-to-one marketing**)

One-to-one marketing
A concept that proposes that customers can be individually targeted.

These developments do not sound the death-knell of mass communications (it would be difficult to imagine companies such as Coca-Cola or Kellogg's wholly giving up mass advertising) but it is no longer automatically assumed that, for example, television adverting is the most effective tool and medium to reach all customers. A distinction is being made between broad, untargeted communications and more personal, targeted communication. Both types have, needless to say, their own particular strengths and weaknesses. De Pelsmacker *et al.* (2001: 6) looked at the advantages and disadvantages of targeted (personal) communications in comparison with mass communications and the contrasting results are shown in Box 1.4.

The developments in data collection and processing, the increased sophistication of the Internet and other electronic media together with the growing urbanity of the consumer, seem to indicate that this movement from mass to targeted communication will continue into the future.

Box 1.4 Personal versus mass communications

	Personal Communications	Mass Communications
Reach Big Audience		
• Speed	Slow (PS) Fast (DM)	Fast
• Cost per Customer	High	Low
Influence on Individual		
• Attention Value	High	Low
• Selective Perception	Relatively Lower	High
• Comprehension	High	Moderate/Low
Feedback		
• Direction	Two-Way	One-Way (generally)
• Speed of Feedback	High	Low
• Measuring Effectiveness	Accurate	Difficult/Impossible
	DM = Direct Marktg	PS = Personal Selling

Source: *Marketing Communications*, De Pelsmacker et al., © Pearson Education Limited 2001 (used with permission).

SELECTIVE vs INTEGRATED MARKETING COMMUNICATIONS (IMC)

A second feature in the development of modern marketing communications is a shift towards an integrated communications approach. Integrated marketing communications (IMC) is, in theory, the process of using promotional tools in a unified way so that communications' synergy is created (Semenik 2002: 8). According to Paul Simons,[5] Chairman and Chief Executive of Ogilvy and Mather UK: 'marketing communications must become more integrated... the various elements of promotion devoted to informing, persuading and inducing action from a range of target audiences must be studied, analysed, planned and implemented in a co-ordinated and effective manner'. The fundamental principle of IMC is that it takes a holistic approach to communications and drives an organization to consider the total impact of all of their communications activities at any one time. Directly impacting upon marketing planning by acknowledging that all aspects of organizational communication have the potential of influencing all stages of the customers' buying process.

An IMC approach should influence all brand messages, not just those regarded as traditional marketing communications (Duncan 2002). This is regarded by many as an important concept as it recognizes that non-marketers[6]

[5]Quoted in Smith and Taylor (2002: viii).
[6]Sometimes referred to as 'part-time marketers' (PTM).

are also transmitting important messages and that many of these messages are not directly under the control of a traditional marketing department (e.g. packaging). As a consequence, it is important that any individuals working within marketing have a very broad appreciation of the various marketing communications' tools available to them, whether or not they fall within their particular specialist field.

Despite its seeming advantages integrated marketing communications (IMC) is not fully accepted in academia nor fully adopted in the communications industry, largely because of its supposed difficulty to implement. Indeed, some authors would question whether or not integrated marketing communications is even a new concept. They argue either that it is simply the basis under which organizations have always wanted to operate, but for a variety of reasons have been unable to fully operationalize it, or that this is the traditional way that companies act anyway, but it has just been reinvented as a concept. The concepts and tactics suggested by an integrated marketing communications approach are covered in more detail in Chapter 15.

CONSUMER GOODS ORIENTATION vs TOTAL MARKET ORIENTATION

Another major change, closely associated with relationship marketing, is the movement away from the domination of consumer goods marketing and, in particular, American consumer goods practice of the 1950s (O'Driscoll and Murray 1998: 409), towards a more holistic model that incorporates business-to-business (B2B) and services, both very substantial sectors in their own right. These latter categories were frequently regarded as 'exceptional', in relation to consumer goods marketing because they did not seem to quite fit the existing marketing models. In many traditional marketing books services and business-to-business (or industrial marketing) were covered by largely unconnected chapters at the end of the text which simply noted the differences between them and consumer goods.

In the business-to-business area, researchers[7] observed the existence of lasting buyer–seller relationships in business markets and pointed out the severe shortcomings of traditional marketing theory to capture and explain this phenomena (Håkansson and Snehota 2000). The relative importance of the marketing communications tools was also an issue. This was never a sector that invested heavily in mass advertising whereas personal selling was prevalent because it was seen to have a greater influence given the characteristics of this market.

Relationship marketing
To 'identify and establish, maintain and enhance and, when necessary, terminate relationships with customers and other stakeholders, at a profit so that the objectives of all parties involved are met; and this is done by mutual exchange and fulfilment of promises' (Grönroos 1994).

---

[7]These researchers mainly belonged to what became known as the Industrial Marketing & Purchasing Group (IMP).

In the service sector, an area that was rapidly becoming dominant[8] in many western markets, the traditional marketing models again appeared to be a poor fit. New models were proposed based on the original marketing mix. To the original 4Ps (product, place, price and promotion) it was suggested adding people, physical evidence, processes (Booms and Bitner 1981), political power, public opinion and other Ps to fill the perceived gaps. But even these were not quite enough. A new perspective on marketing was growing based on relationships and, in particular, that point (or points) where the customer interacts with the employee – the so-called 'moment of truth' when business is lost or won.

This relationship marketing perspective (as it became known) emphasized the importance of all the organization's relationships (employees, suppliers, etc.) not just the customer–supplier dyad. This perspective has a number of implications for marketing communications strategy. As well as the obvious need to communicate at, as well as before, the point of sale, this emphasizes the importance of internal marketing and training of staff (see Chapter 16), as well as an organization's corporate relationships. In addition, the external communications take on an important role in both the fostering, development and maintenance of long-term relationships between organizations and between organizations and consumers. The concept, however, is not altruistic but an adaption to modern marketing conditions. As Foxall *et al.* (1998: 4) note: 'consumer-orientated management (is not) an optional extra. It is an essential corporate outlook in affluent, competitive societies in which consumers enjoy unprecedented levels of discretionary income and the power of choice that makes that happen.' The importance of these themes will be developed further in later chapters.

MARKETING COMMUNICATIONS TOOLS AND MEDIA

A clear distinction should be made between marketing communications tools and the media that may carry their messages.

Marketing communication tools	The processes by which marketers develop and present an appropriate set of communication's stimuli (e.g. advertising, public relations, etc.).
Media	Those channels through which the communications are carried (e.g. television, Internet, etc.).

It is important not to confuse 'tools' and 'media' as they have differing characteristics and serve different roles. It is also important to make the

---

[8]By the middle of the 1990s over 75 per cent of the working populations of the UK and USA were in service industries.

distinction because aspects surrounding electronic media (e.g. the Internet) are frequently posited as processes set apart from other aspects of marketing (e.g. e-marketing, Internet marketing, etc.). From the perspective of marketing communicators the Internet, and other electronic channels, are additional mediums of communication. Like all other media they have their strengths and weaknesses (see Chapter 8).

Marketing communications tools

A simple way of conceptualizing marketing communications options is to use the analogy of a toolbox. Thus the various elements of communications delivery, sometimes referred to as the **marketing communications mix** or promotional mix, are often referred to as marketing communications tools. It is the use and manipulation of this mix, to varying degrees, that can dictate the effectiveness of communications to a target audience.

There is far from total agreement as to what constitutes the finite list of marketing communications tools, nor is there full agreement as to the definitions of each tool. As a general rule the larger the number of tools proposed the narrower the defined boundaries of each is supposed to be. As an indication of the different perspectives the views of some notable writers on marketing communications are shown in Box 1.5.

This text tries to chart its way through this forest of definitions by first concentrating upon those that most (but certainly not all) agree are central tools of marketing communications (namely advertising, sales promotion, public relations, personal selling) and using this as a base upon which to explore those tools with specific characteristics (e.g. direct marketing,

Marketing communications mix
The tools used in marketing communications such as advertising, sales promotion, public relations, personal selling, direct marketing, etc. (also referred to as the **promotional mix**).

SOURCE: © TEAM SAATCHI (REPRODUCED WITH PERMISSION)

A bus shelter advertisement for the 'Recycle for London' campaign – just one element of the marketing communications mix.

sponsorship, etc.). An indication of the close association and overlapping nature of the tools can be seen in Figure 1.5.

The major characteristics of the major marketing communications tools are as shown in Box 1.6. The different tools, as one might expect, have different strengths and weaknesses, which will be discussed in greater detail in later chapters, but there are a number of other critical considerations that also need to be taken into account when planning activities which include:

1 The amount of time available to develop the communication message and format.

2 How much control is required over its delivery.

3 The extent of financial resources available for its production.

4 The skills and expertise available for its creation.

5 The respective levels of credibility that each tool and its delivery media add to the organization/brand.

6 The relative size and geographic scale of the target audience.

Box 1.5 Marketing communications tools

Author (date)	Marketing communications tools
Lancaster and Massingham (1993), and Lane and Russell (2001),	Advertising, Sales Promotion, Public Relations, Personal Selling.
Fill (2002)	Advertising, Sales Promotion, Public Relations, Personal Selling, Direct Marketing.
Belch and Belch (2001)	Advertising, Sales Promotion, Publicity/Public Relations, Personal Selling, Direct Marketing, Interactive/Internet Marketing.
Smith and Taylor (2002)	Advertising, Sales Promotion, Publicity/Public Relations, Personal Selling, Direct Marketing, Sponsorship, Exhibitions, Packaging, Point of Sale/Merchandising, Word-of-mouth, E-marketing, Corporate Identity.
Smith (1998)	Advertising, Sales Promotion, Publicity/Public Relations, Personal Selling, Direct Marketing, Sponsorship, Exhibitions, Packaging, Point-of-Sale/ Merchandising, Word-of-mouth, Corporate Identity.
Shimp (2003)	Mass Media Advertising, Online Advertising, Sales Promotion, Store Signage (Point-of-Sale), Packaging, Direct Mail, Opt-in E-mail, Publicity, Event and Cause Sponsorship, Personal Selling.
Duncan (2002)	Mass Media Advertising, Sales Promotion, Public Relations, Personal Selling, Merchandising, Point-of-Purchase (Point-of-sale), Packaging, Speciality Adverting (Premiums), Licensing, Direct (Response) Marketing, E-commerce, Internal Marketing, Events and Sponsorship, Trade Shows (Exhibitions), Customer Service.

Figure 1.5 The overlapping nature of marketing communications tools

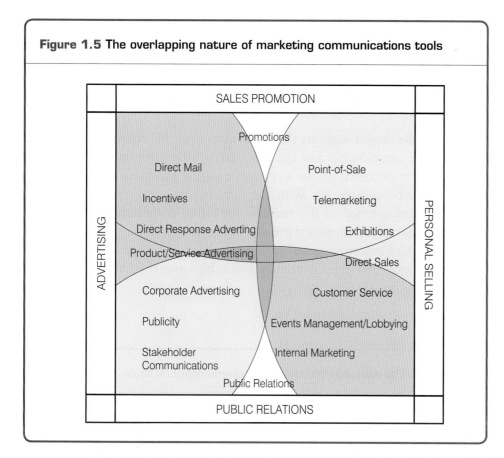

[9]Cause-related promotions are those associated with benefiting some charitable or other socially responsible cause.
[10]Quoted in Baines, Egan and Jefkins 2004.

Because of their different strengths and weaknesses these tools are seen to serve different purposes. In Chapter 2 there is a discussion regarding the 'hierarchy of effects models' and in Chapter 3 a fuller discussion regarding buyer behaviour. Suffice at this time to note that a rational model of buyer behaviour suggests that consumers pass through various stages before purchase.

In effect the model suggests that customers must be aware and interested before desire can develop and the purchase is ultimately made. In addition there is the importance of the experience of the purchase itself on future behaviour to be considered. With the differing objectives in mind we can predict the importance of the various marketing communications tools at different stages in the supposed process.

As the model below suggests (as a generalization) advertising and public relations are tools that develop brand relationships over time, whereas personal

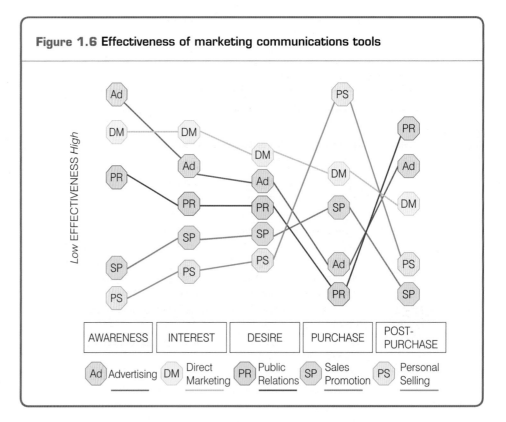

Figure 1.6 Effectiveness of marketing communications tools

selling and sales promotion are seen as shorter-term stimuli to purchase. Again as a generalization advertising and sales promotion are seen to be under the editorial control of the marketer whereas public relations and personal selling (because of the fickleness of human beings) are seen as less controllable. These characteristics are illustrated in the matrix in Box 1.7.

Box 1.7 Control/time matrix

High	Long	Term	Short

Degree of Control

Advertising	Sales Promotion
Public Relations	Personal Selling

Low

The choice of which marketing communications tools to use are determined by the characteristics associated with each tool. These are summarized in Box 1.8 and this will be discussed further in the relevant chapters.

Box 1.8 Key characteristics of major marketing communications tools

Communications	Advertising	Sales Promotion	Public Relations	Personal Sales	Direct Marketing
Ability to deliver personal message	Low	Low	Low	High	High
Ability to reach large audience	High	Med	Med	Low	Med
Level of interaction	Low	Low	Low	High	High
Credibility given by target audience	Low	Low	High	Med	Med
Costs					
Absolute costs	High	Med	Low	High	Med
Cost per contact	Low	Med	Low	High	High
Wastage	High	Med	High	Low	Low
Size of investment	High	Med	Low	High	Med
Control					
Ability to target particular audiences	Med	High	Low	Med	High
Ability to redeploy as circumstances change	Med	High	Low	Med	High

Source: *Marketing Communications*, Fill, © Pearson Education Limited 2002 (used with permission).

Media

Some marketing managers and agencies consider 'media' to include communication tools (e.g. sponsorship, point-of-sale, etc.) as well as mainstream media (television, press, etc.). In this text media is defined as the medium through which the message is channelled rather than the strategy behind the message delivery. As such, it relates to any medium capable of carrying a message to one or more people, but this does not mean that all media are a form of hollow pipe capable of carrying all types of messages to all types of audiences. Each again has its own particular strengths and weaknesses, a concept that will be expanded upon in later chapters.

The list of different media never stands still. Just as the twentieth century saw the introduction of broadcast media, current technological developments are helping differentiate brands from the crowd. For example, stimulated by the need to counter the growing ambivalence, particularly to advertising by increasingly sophisticated consumers, marketers are looking beyond traditional media to find new and better ways of communicating with their customers. This has culminated in a growing number of spectacular campaigns involving light projection onto famous landmarks (see Case Study 1.1 The Art of Guerrilla War), huge poster-like messages on building sites, giant representations of products, public service vehicles transformed and all singing, all dancing e-mails. Known collectively by the term **alternative** or **ambient media,**[11] it is best described as communications with a 'wow' factor (see Box 1.9 for alternative terms). That is advertising that is *not* in a traditional media and is clever, witty or daring and which causes consumers to stop and pay attention. Needless to say, once the medium for these messages becomes too commonplace (and no longer 'wow' us) they cease, by definition, to be ambient media.

The changing viewpoints and new opportunities are challenging many of the traditional thinking on media selection. Traditionally, textbooks and the advertising industry considered media selection on the basis of measurements such as **opportunities-to-see** or response rates. Today, however, we are faced with a much greater challenge of establishing an understanding of how people use the various media. This challenge too will be followed up in Chapter 10.

Ambient media
Often associated with outdoor media and best described as anything that introduces a 'wow factor' capable of attracting attention and curiosity (also referred to as alternative media).

Opportunities-to-see (OTS)
A measure used by media buyers to estimate how many times the target audience may see the message.

> **Box 1.9 Alternative marketing vehicles – future of marketing**
>
> A.C. Nielsen (2003) *Consumer Insight Magazine* note the confusing number of terms for those alternative attempts to reach the consumer bypassing traditional media vehicles. They include **buzz marketing**, **street marketing**, **guerrilla marketing**[12] (see Case study 1.1), **renegade marketing**, **virtual marketing**, **ambush marketing**, **vanguard marketing**, **ambient marketing**, **covert marketing**, **under-the-radar marketing**, **diffusion marketing** or **viral marketing**. All refer to new mediums often aided significantly by **word-of-mouth** and developed to bypass the consumer's growing apathy to traditional forms of communications.

DISPUTED TERRITORIES

With most business and marketing texts there are areas of disagreement and marketing communications is no exception and three such issues are shown

[11]A term first termed by the Concord Agency.
[12]Guerrilla marketing is a term coined by Jay Conrad Levinson and is used to describe unconventional marketing intended to get maximum results from minimum outlay.

below. Although these will be discussed in their respective sections, it is doubtful that this will be to everyone's satisfaction. The three include:

- *Whether personal selling should be part of the marketing communications mix.* Many would argue not. The perspective taken in this text is that it is an important means of communicating with the customer, particularly in the retail and business-to-business (B2B) sectors and as such should be included.

- *Whether public relations (PR) has become, as suggested by Dolphin and Fan (2000: 197), 'debased' and replaced variously by corporate affairs, corporate communications and/or public affairs.* Although there is evidence in the marketplace that job titles are changing away from public relations towards those noted, this text maintains public relations as a core area whilst discussing the implications of corporate communications.

- *Whether the Internet should be regarded as a new type of marketing or whether it is just another communications medium.* Whilst recognizing the importance of e-communications, particularly in relation to direct marketing, this text chooses to regard it as an important medium of communication rather than a new marketing approach.

Summary

This chapter introduced a simple definition of marketing communications and presented a short history of such communications over the centuries. It reviewed the twentieth-century marketing mix approach to marketing as well as more current thinking and related this to the changing nature of markets that are driving these trends. The chapter noted authors' different views on the promotions mix and the overlapping nature of communication tools. In particular it looked at the moves from mass to target marketing communications and the move away from the narrow consumer goods perspective to a total market orientation. It also reviewed the different communications tools and the media, old and new, associated with them.

Review questions

1 How would you define marketing communications?

2 Explain the principle of integrated marketing communications.

3 What are Borden's '12 elements' of a marketing programme?

4 What is the difference between 'above the line' and 'below the line'?

5 How would you define a 'moment of truth'?

6 What would you consider to be the main challenge of an integrated marketing communications approach to a company?

7 Define 'marketing tools' and 'media'.

8   List the tools you might find in the marketing communications toolbox.

9   What are the main characteristics of sales promotion?

10   Give an example of 'alternative' media.

Discussion questions

1   The art of marketing communications goes back a long way. How do you think the way in which advertising has been used and constructed will have evolved over that time and why?

2   What do you believe is the danger to a company in simply seeing marketing communications as 'advertising'?

3   What are the main perceived shifts in the development of marketing communications and what might their implications be?

Further reading

Balmer, M.T. and Greyser, S.A. (2006) 'Corporate marketing: integrating corporate identity, corporate branding, corporate communications, corporate image and corporate reputation', *European Journal of Marketing*, 40 (7): 730. Drawing on the key literature relating to the history of marketing thought, this study reiterates the case that corporate identity, corporate branding, corporate communications, and corporate reputation should be integrated under the umbrella title of corporate marketing.

Leahigh, A.K. (1993) 'The history of – quote, unquote – public relations', *Public Relations Quarterly, Fall*, 38 (3): 24–5.

O'Barr, W. M. (2005) 'A brief history of advertising in America', *Advertising and Society Review*, 6 (3).

Shapiro, S.J. (2005) 'Looking backward – and ahead', *Journal of Public Policy & Marketing*, Spring, 24 (1): 117–20. Exploring the origin of advertising and public relations.

Sivulka, J. (1998) *Soap, Sex and Cigarettes: A Cultural History of American Advertising*, Belmont, CA: Wadsworth Publishing.

Swain, W. (2004) 'Perceptions of IMC after a decade of development: who's at the wheel, and how can we measure success?', *Journal of Advertising Research*, 44 (1): 45–65. An overview of the understanding of integrated marketing communications within industry following a period of integrated marketing communications being seen as the saviour of marketing communications.

Thomas, C. and Guinn, O. (2006) 'How nothing became something: white space, rhetoric, history, and meaning', *Journal of Consumer Research*, 33 (1): 82. An attempt to advance visual theory in the domain of commercial rhetoric (advertising) by demonstrating how objects and symbols derive meaning from their histories.

Chapter references

Baines, P., Egan, J. and Jefkins, F. (2004) Public Relations: Contemporary Issues and Techniques, Oxford: Elsevier Butterworth-Heinemann.

Belch, G.E. and Belch, M.A. (2001) Advertising and Promotion: An Integrated Marketing Communications Perspective, 5th edn, New York: McGraw-Hill.

Booms, B.H. and Bitner, M.J. (1981) 'Marketing strategies and organisation structures for service firms' in J. Donnelly and W.R. George (eds), Marketing of Services, Chicago, IL: American Marketing Association.

Borden, N.H. (1964) 'The concept of the marketing mix', Journal of Advertising Research (June): 2–7.

Christopher, M., Payne, A. and Ballantyne, D. (1991) Relationship Marketing, Oxford: Butterworth Heinemann.

Christopher, M. (1996) 'From brand values to customer values', Journal of Marketing Practice, 2 (1): 55–66.

Christopher, M. and Baker, S. (2000) 'Relationship marketing: tapping the power of marketing' in Cranfield School of Management Marketing Management: A Relationship Marketing Perspective, Basingstoke: Macmillan.

Cutlip, S.M., Allen, H.C. and Broom, G. (1994) Effective Public Relations, Upper Saddle River, NJ: Prentice Hall.

De Pelsmacker, P., Geuens, M. and Van den Bergh, J. (2001) Marketing Communications: A European Perspective, London: Prentice Hall.

Dolphin, R.R. and Fan, Y. (2000) 'Is corporate communications a strategic function?', Management Decision 38/2: 99–106.

Duncan, T (2002) Using Advertising and Promotion to Build Brands, New York: McGraw-Hill.

Egan, J. (2004) Relationship Marketing, 2nd edn, Harlow: Pearson Education.

Evans, M.J. (2003) 'Marketing Communications Changes', in S.Hart (ed.), Marketing Changes, London: Thomson.

Fill, C. (2002) Marketing Communciations: Contexts, Strategies, and Applications, 3rd edn, Harlow: Financial Times, Prentice Hall.

Foxall, G.R., Goldsmith, R. and Brown, S. (1998) Consumer Psychology for Marketing, London: International Thomson Business Press.

Grönroos, C. (1990) 'Relationship approach to the marketing function in service contexts: the marketing and organization behaviour interface', Journal of Business Research, 20: 3–11.

Grönroos, C. (1994) 'From marketing mix to relationship marketing: towards a paradigm shift in marketing', Management Decision, 32(2): 4–20.

Grönroos, C. (1995) 'Relationship marketing: the strategy continuum', Journal of the Academy of Marketing Science, 23, 4: 252–4.

Grönroos, C. (2000) 'Creating a relationship dialogue: communication, interaction and value', The Marketing Review, 1: 5–14.

Håkansson, H. and Snehota, I.J. (2000) 'The IMP perspective: assets and liabilities of business relationships', in J.N. Sheth and A. Parvatiyar (eds), *Handbook of Relationship Marketing*, Thousand Oaks, CA: Sage, 69–93.

Kelman, H. (1961) 'Processes of opinion change', *Public Opinion Quarterly*, (25) Spring: 57-78.

Lancaster, G. and Massingham, L. (1993) *Marketing Management*, New York: McGraw-Hill.

Lane, W.R. and Russell, J.T. (2001) *Advertising: A Framework*, Upper Saddle River, NJ: Prentice Hall.

McCarthy, E.J. (1960) *Basic Marketing: A Managerial Approach*, Homewood, IL: Irwin.

McCarthy, E.J. (1987) *Basic Marketing: A Managerial Approach*, 9th edn, Homewood, IL: Irwin.

McKenna, R. (1991) 'Marketing is Everything', *Harvard Business Review*, Jan.–Feb.: 39–45.

McPhee, N. (1982) *The Complete Book of Insults*, London: Chancellor Press.

Nevett, T.R. (1982) *Advertising in Britain: A History*, London: Heinemann.

Nielsen, A.C. (2003) 'Alternative marketing vehicles: future of markets', *Consumer Insight Magazine*, June, www.marketingpower.com, accessed 31 October 2005.

O'Driscoll, A. and Murray, J.A. (1998) 'The changing nature of theory and practice in marketing: on the value of synchrony', *Journal of Marketing Management*, 14 (5): 391–416.

Russell, J.T. and Lane, W.R. (2002) *Kleppners' Advertising Procedure,* Upper Saddle River, NJ: Pearson Education.

Schramm, W. (1955) *How Communication Works in the Process and Effects of Mass Communications*, Urbana, IL: University of Illinois Press.

Semenik, R.J. (2002) *Promotion and Integrated Marketing Communications*, London: Thomson Learning.

Sheth, J.N. and Sisodia, R.S. (1999) 'Revisiting marketing's generalisations', *Journal of Academy of Marketing Science*, 17 (1): 71–87.

Shimp, T.A. (2003) *Advertising, Promotion and Supplemental Aspects of Integrated Marketing Communications*; 6th edn, London: Thomson Learning.

Sivulka, J. (1998) *Soap, Sex and Cigarettes: A Cultural History of American Advertising*, Belmont, CA: Thomson Learning.

Smith, P.R. (1998) *Marketing Communications: An Integrated Approach*, 2nd edn, London: Kogan Page.

Smith, P.R. and Taylor, J. (2002) *Marketing Communications: An Integrated Approach*, 3rd edn, London: Kogan Page.

Terazono, E. (2003) 'Feeling a little bit better', *Financial Times*, 29 September.

Varey, R.J. (2002) *Marketing Communications, Principles and Practice*, London: Routledge.

Wells, W., Burnett, J. and Moriaty, S. (1995) *Advertising Principles and Practice*, Upper Saddle River, NJ: Prentice Hall.

The Art of Guerrilla War

The British consumer is now bombarded with around 700 sales and marketing messages each day. Communications success is about cutting through this brand babble. The fragmentation of media and a dearth of 'event' TV shows mean high spending ad campaigns are not the answer they once were. So we must look down new avenues, one of which is using so-called 'guerrilla' techniques to grab a slice of limited attention spans. This increasingly popular approach sprung from illegal bill stickers used to create what we would now call a 'word-of-mouth' effect.

Guerrilla marketing can be hugely successful. But equally it can stink. An example of the guerrilla genre at its best was *FHM*'s decision to project a huge image of Gail Porter's buttocks on to Big Ben in 1999. This was appropriate for an irreverent lads' mag brand. Other attempts, however, have fallen on their face. In the mid-1990s Cadbury's tried similarly projecting an image of its Wispa Gold chocolate on to St Paul's Cathedral, the tenuous link being St Paul's 'whispering gallery'. It was a damp squib due to lack of originality of the stunt, but, moreover, because it is difficult to pretend a chocolate bar has attitude. If guerrilla attitude doesn't fit your brand you're in danger of looking like your drunk uncle dancing at a wedding. My experience is that it works best when igniting dry tinder.

In 1999 my company acted for the Consumers' Association, which wanted to bring down the artificially high car prices paid by the British consumers. On press day at The Motor Show that year we transformed a tame CA stand on car safety into a colourful protest against 'The Great British Car Rip-Off'. For just a £10 000 public relations and poster campaign, 'rip-off Britain' became a media buzzword, culminating in questions to Parliament. Car prices fell by 9 per cent within six months.

Guerrilla tactics also work for ballsy, challenger brands. In 1998, facing competition from British Airways' entry into the low-cost airline sector, easyJet founder Stelios bought nine tickets to GO's inaugural flight. Wearing Orange jumpsuits, his staff sat in the back of the plane giving interviews to journalists and handing out easyJet tickets.

But, of course, guerrilla warfare requires audacity. Marketing directors more concerned about keeping their job than taking a risk should probably steer well clear.

After their successful Gail Porter/Big Ben stunt in 1999, 'ideas company' Cunning provided further extensive public relations coverage for their client, FHM, by devising a new 'spoof' marketing medium: foreheADS™.

SOURCE: © CUNNING (REPRODUCED WITH PERMISSION)

Finally never patronize your consumer.

We increasingly find ourselves talking to a marketing savvy generation brought up on a diet of Nike and PlayStation. So good guerrilla marketing means letting consumers in on the joke. Stimulate them and entertain them and they may pay you back with their loyalty.

Case study questions

1 How appropriate was the FHM stunt for an irreverent lads' magazine?

2 How was it that the later FHM stunt was successful but the Cadbury's Wispa campaign failed?

3 Are there any lessons to learn from the Consumer Association or easyJet examples?

Source: Jon Claydon, The Art of Guerrilla War, *Financial Times*, 13th October 2003 (reproduced with permission).

CHAPTER TWO

COMMUNICATIONS THEORY

LEARNING OBJECTIVES

Having completed this chapter you should be able to:

- Understand the theories and concepts behind the practice of marketing communications.
- Appreciate the importance of message source characteristics.
- Describe the important elements of a successful message and the effects of message repetition.
- Recognize the importance of opinion formers and opinion leaders in the wider communications process.
- Understand the concepts associated with 'hierarchy of effects' models and their application to campaign strategy.

INTRODUCTION

Communication is a word that that is not wholly without controversy. Most dictionary definitions suggest that it can mean *either* the giving *or* the exchange of information, yet the traditional marketing viewpoint was that the marketer produced and communicated messages whilst consumers received and consumed them. A distinctly one-way process, but in a changing consumer environment the validity of this traditional viewpoint is being challenged and most marketers today define marketing communications as a two-way exchange.

COMMUNICATION MODEL

Early models of the communication process reflected the one-way communication approach. Klapper's (1960) term **hypodermic effect** or **magic bullet** encapsulated the notion that communication was the transfer of ideas, feelings, knowledge and/or motivation from one mind to another.

Hypodermic effect
An early model of marketing communications that inferred communication was one way (also referred to as **magic bullet**).

Source
The originator of the message (also refers to the person delivering the message).

Message
The vehicle by which an idea is transmitted via a medium.

Encode, encoded (messages)
Putting the idea into a format (e.g. speech, print, etc.) using a combination of appropriate words, pictures and symbols so that it can be transmitted via a medium (e.g. television).

It was Wilbur Schramm (1955), however, who developed what is now accepted as the basic model of mass communication (see Figure 2.1). As a demonstration of the communications process it is wonderfully simplistic in its imagery, but in interpreting it the one really vital element you have to overlay is the unstated need for quality in the linkages between each element. It is these that will have a significant impact upon the success of the communication. Schramm's communications model implies two-way correspondence as there are response and feedback mechanisms built in. The sender or the source may also alter or adapt messages and/or the media as necessary.

Figure 2.1 is an adaptation and development of Schramm's original model. Here the **source** identifies the need to transmit a **message**. The message is made up (or encoded) into a format (e.g. speech, print, etc.) using a combination of appropriate words, pictures, symbols (see Box 2.1), music, etc. It is important to note the importance of communications other than words to

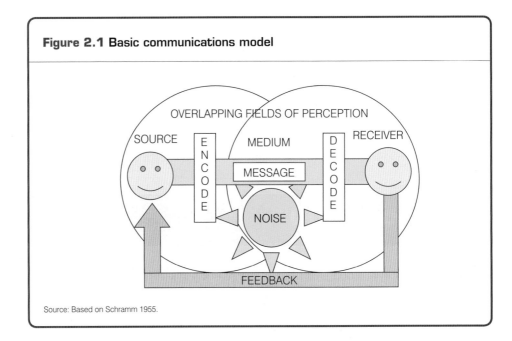

Figure 2.1 Basic communications model

Source: Based on Schramm 1955.

Box 2.1 Silent communication methods

Method	Implication
Letters/Numbers	Progression and/or status (e.g. XJ6, XJ8), size (1500, 2000)
Space	Freedom, space
Artefacts	Status (e.g. quality watches)
Movement (kinetics)	Emotion, body movements (e.g. shrug of shoulders, folded arms, etc.)
Smell	Atmosphere, desire (e.g. coffee, fresh bread, etc.)
Touch	Quality (e.g. furniture, fabric, etc.)
Colour	Feature (e.g. white = purity, red = danger, etc.)

our understanding of messages. It is estimated, for example, that only around 30 per cent of communication uses words and that people communicate the majority of the time using other **silent communication** methods (see Box 2.1).

It should be noted that much 'silent communication' changes from culture to culture. Indeed poor understanding of cultural differences leads to 'ethnocentrism' – the practice of assuming that others think and believe as you do, and cross-cultural differences can easily lead to communications being misunderstood or even totally rejected. This will be developed further in Chapter 20 but examples of the impact of silent language can also be found on the Internet (see weblink).

Although words themselves are only a minor part of any communication they evidently play an important part in the message being understood. The meaning of words can be:

- **Denotative** (having meaning for everybody) or
- **Connotative** (having meaning unique to the individual).

The inevitable impact of the latter being that the same communication might be interpreted in different ways by different people and thus it is vital for marketers to both understand and have an empathy with their target audience. In terms of the basic communications model this means overlapping fields of perception. This perceptual understanding should include the effect of

- **Semiotics**: the study of signs and symbols in a language (see Box 2.2).
- **Syntactics**: the grammatical arrangement of words.
- **Semantics**: the branch of linguistics concerned with meaning.

The definition of a word or phrase, for example, is not always the same for every audience. The term 'wicked' is one illustration of this. According to most dictionary definitions it means 'sinful, iniquitous, given to or involving morality' (OED 1996). To most young people, however, it means formidable, remarkable and excellent. The words, therefore, not only need to be in a language that the receiver understands but ascribed cultural meanings need to be taken into account too. Further examples of the importance of syntactics and semantics to understanding is indicated by the story of Pedro Carolino in Minicase 2.1.

Silent communication
A non-verbal communication such as a shrug of the shoulders.

Learn more about silent communication at: **http://home.arcor.de/be/bethge/nonverbaleng.htm.**

Denotative
Words having meaning for everybody.

Connotative
Words having meaning unique to the individual.

Semiotics
The study of signs and symbols in a language.

Syntactics
The grammatical arrangement of words.

Semantics
The branch of linguistics concerned with meaning.

Box 2.2	**Semiotics (the study of signs, symbols and meanings in communication)**	
		Example
1 Icon	*a sign that looks like an object or represents it visually, in a way that most people could relate to*	No Smoking sign Wheelchair access
2 Index	*a sign that relates to the object by some form of causal connection*	Yawn *equates* to boredom sweat *equates* to thirst
3 Symbol	*an artificial sign created for a purpose or meaning*	Olympic rings London Underground Symbol

Medium
A means of carrying the message (also referred to as **media channel**).

Direct marketing
Seeks to target individual customers with the intention of delivering personalized messages and building a relationship with them based on their responses to direct communication.

Word-of-mouth (WoM)
Marketing messages that circulate around a marketplace without the aid of marketing communications.

Viral marketing, buzz marketing or street marketing
Marketing spread by word of mouth. Alternatively marketing materials created by the brand owner that are passed on and spread 'virus-like' around the Internet.

@

An example of a leading viral marketing agency: **www.theviralfactory.com.**

Mass media
Largely untargeted media including newspapers, television, radio, etc.

Slice-of-life
Advertising that uses simulated 'real-life' situations and where the viewer is encouraged to get involved with the action.

Brand values
Those values associated with a brand (e.g. status, youth, etc.).

Source attractiveness
How attractive and persuasive the source is and how much the source identifies with them.

Decoding
Translating the message into understandable concepts.

Field of perception
An individual's range of understanding. Overlapping fields of perception enable understanding (also referred to as **realm of perception and realm of understanding**).

Clever use of the language can also add to the effectiveness of the message. In particular communicators use:

- Simile: a figure of speech involving the comparison of one thing with another (e.g. 'like Murphys I'm not bitter').
- Metaphor: the application of a name or phrase which is imaginatively but not literally applicable (e.g. 'Lenor is like a breath of fresh air').
- Allegory: where the meaning or message is represented symbolically (e.g. the Irishness of Caffries).

The message from the sender to the receiver travels via some sort of **medium** (or media channel), which may be personal or non-personal. Personal mediums include face-to-face communications and certain media associated with **direct marketing** (telemarketing, electronic mail, etc.). Word-of-mouth (WoM) is a particularly powerful personal medium although the transmission of accurate or even positive messages, travelling through a chain of individuals, cannot be guaranteed. In recent years, however, marketers have begun to concentrate their minds on how to promote word-of-mouth through strategies variously known as **viral marketing, buzz marketing** or **street marketing**. These strategies encourage the spread of positive messages (virus-like) through the community. For example, the film *The Blair Witch Project* used viral marketing to build up word-of-mouth for the documentary-like realism of the film. Hotmail could never have expanded its network without the viral-like effect of messages on every e-mail despatched through their system. Companies (for example Ford) are producing short online videos especially created to be copied and circulated around the World Wide Web. Volvo have also used the Web to encourage word-of-mouth having first attracted potential customers (or the simply curious) to their site using a widespread television and newspaper campaign. In May 2001 McKinsey and Co. reported that word-of-mouth influenced as many as two-thirds of all consumer products sold.

Non-personal mediums are characterized by, what has become known as, **mass media**. This term includes newspapers, television, radio, etc. Information received directly from a non-personal source is, generally, less persuasive than information obtained from a personal medium. The mass media is not, however, above attempting to increase credibility by 'personalizing' the messenger(s). This may be done by creating around the message a homely or familiar situation (e.g. a family eating a meal). This so-called slice-of-life advertising encourages the receiver to imagine themselves in that particular situation (see Chapter 9), thus encouraging them to feel comfortable and at ease with the images and messages presented, identify with them and recognize the associated **brand values** that accompany it (see **source attractiveness** below).

Decoding (effectively the recognition of the meaning presented by the words, pictures, symbols, music, etc.) is affected by the receiver's **field of perception**[1] which encompass the perceptions, experiences, attitudes and

---

[1]Also called the realm of perception or realm of understanding.

values of the receiver. The more the source understands about the receiver (and visa versa) the easier it will be to decode the message successfully. To put this another way, the greater the overlap between the source's and the receiver's 'fields of perception', the more likely it is that they will understand each other (see Figure 2.1 and Minicase 2.1).

Effective communication, therefore, is where the recipient receives and comprehends the message that the sender sends. Ineffective communication is where the message is:

- misunderstood and/or
- misinterpreted and/or
- rejected.

Communication is an inter-personal activity which is highly dependent upon the social context in which it takes place. Therefore:

- The sender needs to identify in advance the target audience and how they will receive it.
- The sender will need to persuade the receiver that the message is worth listening to.
- There needs to be a clear, and as far as possible, unobstructed route or channel (medium) through which the message can be sent, received and understood.
- The sender needs evidence (feedback) that the message is not only received but is understood and having the desired effect.

Feedback
The reaction of the receiver having received the message.

Clarity of understanding (created by overlapping fields of perception) is, therefore, also required if feedback is to be interpreted by the source in the right way (see Figure 2.1). Feedback is the reaction (or reactions) of the receiver having received the message. These are important to the source as they

MINICASE 2.1

Pedro Carolino

An example of the concept of the realm of perception and the importance of syntactics and semantics is given by the story of Pedro Carolino who, in 1883, decided to produce a handy Portuguese–English phrase book. This was despite the fact that his English was poor and he didn't have a Portuguese–English dictionary to help him. Undaunted, and armed with an English–French dictionary and its French–Portuguese equivalent Carolino produced his book. Some examples from the section headed 'Idiotisms (idioms) and Proverbs' gives a flavour of the result with the best guess at what he meant in brackets:

- A take is better than two you shall have   (A bird in the hand is worth two in the bush)
- The stone as roll not heap up not foam   (A rolling stone gathers no moss)
- The dog than bark not bite   (His bark is worse than his bite)
- Nothing some money, nothing some Swiss   (Nothing ventured, nothing gained).

can verify whether the message has been received correctly (e.g. favourable reaction, etc.) and whether the receiver has acted upon it (increased sales etc.). As communication and greater understanding develops over time, feedback may become more complex and include **complaints** (also called customer 'voice') or **suggestions** that may benefit the company and its relationship with its customers in the longer term. Feedback is also, generally, better utilizing personal than non-personal mediums. Feedback is, for example, likely to be clearer and more immediate in a personal (face-to-face) selling situation than some other form of response (letter, e-mail, etc.). At the other extreme feedback from mass media advertising (brand building rather than direct-response) can be unclear and/or only become clearer over time.

SOURCE CHARACTERISTICS

The accurate transfer and acceptance of messages is highly influenced by the characteristics of the source of the message. As a consequence, the source needs to be seen both as a composite element of communications effectiveness and an important part of any communication process; and not simply regarded as just the generator of the message. Kelman (1961) suggests that **source credibility**, **source attractiveness** and **source power** are the three factors that most define the source characteristics of the messenger (see Box 2.3).

Source credibility is associated with recognized objectivity and includes two additional important constructs **trust** and **expertise**.

Complaints
Negative reaction reported back to the source (also called **customer voice**).

Suggestions
Constructive feedback from customers.

Source credibility
How much confidence the receiver has that the source can provide an expert and/or objective opinion.

Source attractiveness
How attractive and persuasive the source is and how much the source identifies with them.

Source power
Where compliance with the request involves a real or perceived reward or actual or apparent avoidance of punishment.

Trust
A confidence in someone or something. There are three forms of trust: institutional trust, character-based trust and process-based trust.

Expertise
Expertise includes aptitude, required training and experience and is domain specific.

Box 2.3 Source characteristics

Characteristic	Description	Example
Source Credibility	How much confidence the receiver has that the source can provide an expert and/or objective opinion.	Former police officer endorsing security system.
Source Attractiveness	How attractive and persuasive the source is and how much the source identifies with the receiver[2].	A celebrity or, at the other extreme, an ordinary person like the receiver.
Source Power	Where compliance with the request involves a real or perceived reward or actual or apparent avoidance of punishment.	Aggressive sales person, threat to well-being, etc.

Source: Kelman 1961.

[2]A good example of which would be the recruitment of sales staff who have a strong connection with target customers.

Trust itself can take one of three basic forms that focus upon the institution and the individual.

- **Institutional trust:** based on the rule of law (trust based on minimum standards legislation) or qualification (e.g. doctors, lecturers, etc.).
- **Character-based trust:** trust in individuals (particularly important in personal selling).
- **Process-based trust:** trust built up over time (i.e. **reputation**).

Whatever combinations of these forms of trust are present will determine the way the message is received and ultimately believed.

Source expertise includes aptitude, required training and experience and is domain specific. For example you may trust a former Police Commissioner to tell you about home-security equipment but not necessarily about holidays abroad. A famous footballer may successfully endorse sportswear but is less likely to be as influential in the financial services market.

Source attractiveness is associated with identification or relationship seeking behaviour. This may be aspirational or simply identifiable with an everyday situation. An example of the latter is 'slice-of-life advertising' where the target audience is easily identifiable attending to some everyday problem (e.g. blocked drains, high credit card bills, etc.). Aspiration also relates to situations in which we might dream of seeing ourselves taking part (e.g. an opening night party, at the Ambassador's reception). This association between the aspiration and the product or service may change the receiver's perception of it. Another important example of the importance of attractiveness relates directly to the celebrity endorsement. Ever since Lillie Langtry appeared on a pack of Pears soap in 1893, stars have lent their names to the promotion of branded products (Mistry 2006). Communicators have always found that messages from stars of stage, screen and television are generally received well and it is believed that their influence may even have increased in recent years with the growth of the so-called 'cult of celebrity' where famous (or infamous) and/or broadly recognizable characters compete for appearances in magazines and broadcast media. So powerful is the 'pull' of some celebrity names that a sportsman like David Beckham, who currently has deals with Gillette, Coty, Adidas, Police and others has now earned around £60 million from product endorsements and advertising alone to add to his not inconsiderable football salary (Mistry 2006).

The credibility of the celebrity is important in creating a believable link between the meaning(s) associated with that celebrity and the product or service they are promoting (Pickton and Broderick 2001). For example, Charlotte Church was chosen to front a Walker's Sensation crisp campaign. According to the company 'the Welsh singer was selected because she is a real women, with a luxury lifestyle' which they felt 'fitted perfectly with the Sensations brand' (Mistry 2006). Such is the growth of the 'cult of celebrity' that it is calculated that at least one-in-four television advertisements now use celebrities, up from one-in-eight ten years ago (*ibid.*).

When source credibility is called into question, however, companies will frequently attempt to dissociate themselves as quickly as they possibly can.

Institutional trust
Trust that is based on the rule of law (e.g. minimum standards legislation) or qualification (e.g. doctors, lecturers, etc.).

Character-based trust
Trust in individuals (particularly important in personal selling).

Process-based trust
Trust built up over time (i.e. reputation).

Reputation
Trust and confidence built up over time.

Michael Jackson's parting from Pepsi Cola was one such example and, more recently, Kate Moss, the face of several cosmetic and fashion houses, was publicly dropped by several sponsors following a drugs allegation (only to be re-employed by, for example Calvin Klein once the initial bad publicity had died down).

Source power is where the source of the message has the power to punish or reward and where influence is largely sought through compliance. This may be associated with sales promotions (buy now – offer ends soon), penalty warning (e.g. reminders to get in tax returns by a certain date) or promotions largely based upon developing feelings of guilt (e.g. are your children protected?).

Not only is clarity and source credibility important but anything else that is happening as the message is 'transmitted' can affect its reception. When considering **noise**, therefore, it is not just the volume of interference that is a factor but the slightest nuance risks influencing both the quality of message reception, its interpretation and the resultant feedback. This may be because the number/content/attraction of other messages both within and outside of the channel distracts the receiver(s). Noise may be deliberately introduced for example in so-called '**spoiler-campaigns**' where the competition deliberately introduces a competing, conflicting or denigrating messages to counter the message from the source (tabloid newspapers frequently run spoiler-campaigns against one another's promotions and politicians regularly denigrate opponents' messages).

Brand confusion is one outcome of indistinct communication. Suppliers of products or services with very similar names, characteristics or benefits may find it difficult to distinguish their message from others. In this situation the more unique the message in terms of content and execution the less likely that brand confusion will occur (see Minicase 2.2). At the other end of the scale if the presentation of the message is so unique and memorable that it overshadows the product or service itself it is equally detrimental. This is known as **vampire creativity** and it occurs primarily when the communication is *too* original, *too* entertaining or *too* involving (Wells *et al.* 1965) and where the creativity of the agency is remembered ahead of the product or service it is seeking to promote.

Repetition is seen as beneficial to the reception of the message. Research by Mano (1996) suggests that respondents who have been exposed to an advertisement once before (as compared to respondents who were exposed for the first time) appear to evaluate the message as more favourable and less dull. Wells *et al.* (1965) note that psychologists maintain that you need to hear a message a minimum of three times before it crosses the threshold of perception and enters into the memory. Gary Lineker's 11-year relationship with Walkers reveals how repetition can strengthen the association for consumers who are already aware of the endorsement (Mistry 2006).[3] Jingles and catchy tag-lines also aid memorability.

Noise
Anything that interferes with the proper delivery of the message (e.g. competing messages).

Spoiler-campaigns
Where the competition deliberately introduces competing, conflicting or denigrating messages to counter the message from the source.

Brand confusion
Any misunderstanding concerning brand values and benefits, an outcome of indistinct communication.

Vampire creativity
Occurs when the communication is *too* original, *too* entertaining or *too* involving such that it distracts the consumer from the brand message.

Repetition
Repeat exposure to the brand message (also called frequency)

[3]According to an Institute of Practitioners in Advertising submission in 2002, Lineker's endorsement was delivering an immediate return on investment of £1.7 million, building to £5.1 million in the long term.

The case of the 118s

In 2003 the UK telecommunications watchdog (Oftel) ended British Telecommunications' (BT) monopoly of Directory Enquiries and a number of services (each beginning with the prefix 118 followed by 3 further digits) entered the market to challenge BT. BT itself was forced by the regulator to change its number from 192 and it adopted the number 118 500. In hindsight this was perhaps not the most memorable of possible numerical combinations. The marketing problem for all these new services was how do you make a number attractive and memorable particularly when the public appeared confused by the array of providers and saw little difference in what they were offering.

118 118 was launched by The Number in December 2002 and in March of the following year commenced a series of advertisements, devised by agency WCRS, featuring two 1970s style athletes (each bearing the numbers 118) who bore a striking resemblance to David Bedford the former 10 000 metres world record holder (who later successfully took legal action against the company). The popularity of the advertising and, above all, its memorability (they regularly made it to *Marketing*'s AdWatch recall rankings) seemed to be putting them ahead of the field such that by 2004 they were claiming to have 50 per cent of the UK Directories market. In March 2004 they were forced (as a result of the Bedford judgement) to drop the trademark 1970s runners but chose to retain the same actors (Colin Carmichael and Darren McFerran) in a new role as 'seventies retro cops' dressed in yellow jumpsuits who were 'out to help the public through life's varied challenges'. The new commercials were to be part of a £10 million campaign to promote additional services from 118 118 such as unlimited numbers and cinema listings. Rival company Conduit, who operated as 118 888 used dancing numbers (11, 88 and 88) in a campaign that was perceived as memorable in a different way. According to Ben Bold (*Marketing*, 15 January 2004) 'Conduit has run some memorable work, but it has irritated rather than engaged… (they need) to develop a cohesive strategy to compete with 118 118'. In January 2004 Conduit suspended all advertising through Euro RSCG as the company sought a merger with rival operator Telegate who operated the 118 666 service.

Yell, owners of *Yellow Pages* and operators of the 118 247 launched late in 2003 developed its service as part of a £2 million above the line campaign created by Abbott Mead Vickers BBDO and featuring popular actor James Nesbitt. 118 800 meanwhile hired direct marketing agency 23red to handle its business-to-business customers.

So what about BT. They were certainly noticeable initially by their absence from mass media advertising. Instead they developed during 2003 a poster campaign that utilized their public call boxes together with giant post-it notes on the sides of city buildings. Around half their budgeted expenditure for the 118 500 service was, however, below the line including leaflets sent out with bills. According to a report in *Marketing* (1 April 2004) this low key approach may be working. BT admit they arrived late and that it has spent less than half as much as 118 118. Nevertheless it now claims to have regained top spot in directory market share.

Launched in March 2003, the 118 118 campaign featured highly in advertising recall rankings.

SOURCE: IMAGE COURTESY OF THE ADVERTISING ARCHIVES

Decay
Corruption of a message over time.

Wearout
Consumer boredom and/or irritation at a repeated communication.

Transformational
Image-dominant, brand building messages.

Selective attention
The process of screening out information that does not interest us and selectively processing the information that does. Messages that successfully bypass 'selective attention' are likely to be perceived positively.

Researchers have also found that information **decays** at a 'negatively decelerating rate' with 60 per cent of the initial yield of information (from, for example, an advertisement) having decayed within six weeks (Fill 2001: 74). On the other hand showing a message too often can also lead to consumer boredom or **wearout**. Wearout is essentially a point at which a level of exposure has been reached, after which continued exposure results in negative rather than positive feelings. Effectively the communication becomes irritating. Reasons for this irritation include:

- they are unbelievable, exaggerated and over-dramatized situations
- they include unsympathetic characters
- continuous brand comparison and brand repetition
- they include information orientated messages (as opposed to **transformational** or image-dominant messages)
- they are hard-sell (as opposed to soft-sell)
- they include satire, provocation and eroticism (versus music, sentimental situations and warmth).

Wearout is thought to cause individuals to use **selective attention** and switch-off after a certain number of exposures and/or to use counter-argument against both the message and the medium monotony (Petty and Cacioppo 1979).

It would appear that wearout appears more for some types of message than for others. For example, complex messages, minor changes in advertisement execution, short or slow commercials and non-food *do not* seem to experience the negative effects of a high exposure rate whereas humorous, long, fast-paced, image dominant and transformational commercials *do* suffer from high repetition levels (De Pelsmacker *et al.* 2001).

It is important to note that all of the above are generalizations because every consumer reacts differently due to their individual attitudes and values as will be discussed in Chapter 3.

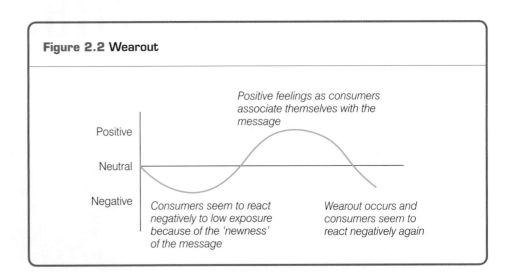

Figure 2.2 Wearout

Positive

Neutral

Negative

Positive feelings as consumers associate themselves with the message

Consumers seem to react negatively to low exposure because of the 'newness' of the message

Wearout occurs and consumers seem to react negatively again

TWO-STEP COMMUNICATIONS MODEL

The simple communications model shown in Figure 2.1 assumes that the message travels direct to the intended recipient. This 'one-step communications' model does not, however, reflect the way many commercial and other messages are received in the real world. When a customer wants to buy something where the features are complex or expenditure is high (or both) and/or where that purchase affects our self-image, the consumer may seek advice on the potential purchase or follow the perceived trend(s) in the market. Alternatively they may be recommended by others to take some purchasing decisions they had not previously considered.

The two-step model, therefore, introduces the concept of **opinion formers** and **opinion leaders** (defined in greater detail below) as shown in Figure 2.3. Opinion formers are people with influence or authority over our lives. They might be journalists, broadcasters, analysts, politicians, scientists or anyone with some real or imagined status who can be trusted (rightly or wrongly) to impart good advice. An example of this, sometimes covert, influence is the BBC's Food Programme. A recommendation on that television show for a household gadget can lead to substantially increased sales for that item in the days following the programme. So-called **advertorials** (where an advertisement is designed to look like newspaper or magazine copy) also seeks to take advantage of this phenomenon. Here 'paid-for' advertising is made to look

Opinion formers
People with influence or authority over our lives, for example journalists, broadcasters, analysts, politicians, scientists or anyone with some real or imagined status who can be trusted (rightly or wrongly) to impart good advice.

Opinion leaders
May not be formal experts. They do not necessarily provide advice but consumers are prone to follow them. They are often, but not always, from a higher social status than their immediate contemporaries and frequently more gregarious.

Advertorials
Advertising in the format of magazine or press editorial.

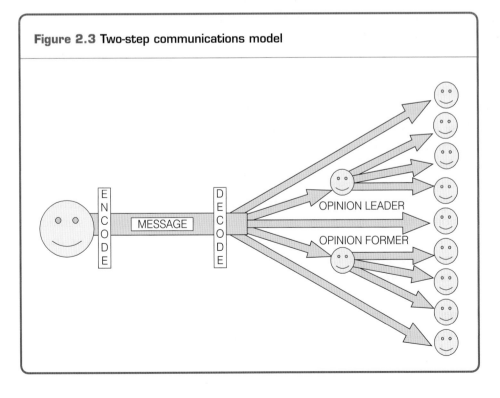

Figure 2.3 Two-step communications model

Fashion icons
Celebrity fashion leaders (e.g. David Beckham or Madonna).

Diffusion of innovation
The way that new developments (e.g. mobile telephones) enter the market. Rogers' (1983) theory of diffusion suggests that various consumers enter the market at different times and he called them innovators, early adopters, early majority, late majority and laggards.

Connectors
Collective name for opinion formers and opinion leaders and others (e.g. family) who help to carry the message to the consumer (also referred to as **influentials**, **carriers**, **trendsetters** and **evangelists**).

Reference groups
Groups with whom consumers associate themselves, e.g. faith groups, social groups, etc.

Learn more about influentials at: **www. brandchannel.com/features_effect. asp?pf_id=196.**

Innovators
Those customers who are at the forefront of trends particularly in technical innovation. They are likely to have a higher disposable income and willing to pay a high price for being first in the market.

Early adopters
Frequently the opinion leaders. Their entry into the market is significant. They are generally younger with above average education and/or income.

Early majority
Entry of the early majority of customers represent the first move towards general acceptance. The speed of adoption can be seen to have increased considerably.

Late majority
Sceptical of new ideas but eventually take up innovations.

Laggards
Sometimes technophobic, the last group to take up an innovation.

like editorial copy in the knowledge that the latter will carry considerably more influence than the former.

Opinion leaders are also influencers but may not be formal experts. They do not necessarily provide advice but consumers are prone to follow them. They are often, but not always, from a higher social status than their immediate contemporaries and frequently more gregarious. Their opinion is regularly sought on one or more different subjects and they may be asked to endorse many different products. In the world of clothing they are often called **fashion icons**, examples of which include celebrities such as David Beckham or Madonna. Opinion leadership can be stimulated in a number of ways, for example through the use of testimonials in advertising or by creating backdrops (e.g. a laboratory) that signify professionalism or status. Opinion leaders will frequently take risks and be amongst the first to adopt new styles, visit exotic places and purchase new products. The rest of the society may then follow but not all at once (see **diffusion of innovation** below).

Collectively opinion formers, opinion leaders and any others that help to 'pass on the message' might be called **connectors**. Marketers also know them variously as influentials, carriers, trendsetters and evangelists (Nielsen 2003). Alternative (or ambient) media (see Chapter 1) often relies on the influence of connectors who have mastered what sociologists call 'weak-tie' or 'social ambience' (Nielsen 2003). The larger their network of social acquaintances, the more 'power' connectors wield in society and the better positioned they are to trigger trends. Indeed any source of social influence can be considered as a potential audience for marketing communication including social and cultural groupings often called **reference groups** (Pickton and Broderick 2001). These could include family, work colleagues and social and religious groups.

As noted above opinion leaders frequently take risks and be amongst the first to adopt new products or services whereas the rest of the society will only follow in time. This process of staggered adoption (of new products, fashion, etc.) over time, by different sections of society, is called diffusion (Rogers 1983).

Diffusion of innovation over time is said to follow a pattern as illustrated approximately in Figure 2.4. The first into the market are seen as the **innovators**. These are those customers who are at the forefront of trends particularly in technical innovation. They are likely to have a higher disposable income and be willing to pay a high price for being first in the market. Innovators are estimated to represent 2.5 per cent of the (eventual) total market. The next group are known as the **early adopters**. This group are frequently the opinion leaders noted above and their entry into the market is significant. They are generally younger with above average education and/or income and represent around 13.5 per cent of the market. The **early majority** (34 per cent) represent the first move towards general acceptance and the speed of adoption can be seen to have increased considerably. The **late majority** (34 per cent) are more sceptical of new ideas but, as the saying goes 'the luxuries of one generation become the necessities of the next' and they eventually come aboard. By now the majority of the market have adopted the innovation. The last 16 per cent are called the **laggards** and these are often technology averse.

Ultimately, however, as in the case of radios, televisions, refrigerators, and perhaps latterly mobile telephones, they too adopt the innovation.

The **product life cycle** (PLC) is another concept that emerged from research on adoption and diffusion of information. In marketing the life cycle concept has been applied primarily in the sense of product, market and brand life cycles (Bruhn 2003). A typical life cycle (see Figure 2.5) could be hypothesized as consisting of an introductory period, a period of growth, a maturity phase and ultimately decline unless the product brand can be reinvented (as for example Harley Davidson or Brylcreem). The importance of the life-cycle concept has been challenged significantly over the years largely from the perspective that

Product life cycle
Concept that suggests products go through a cycle that includes a period of introduction and growth, a maturity phase and ultimately decline unless the product brand can be reinvented.

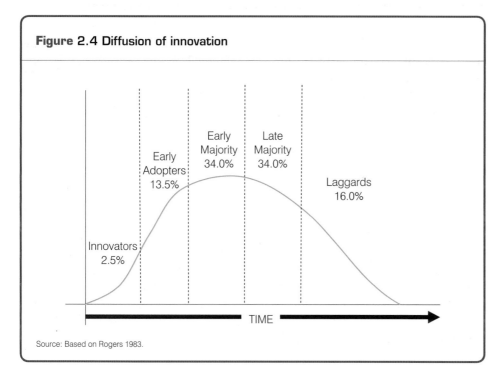

Figure 2.4 Diffusion of innovation

Source: Based on Rogers 1983.

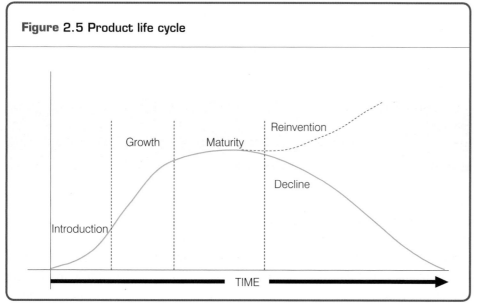

Figure 2.5 Product life cycle

it is difficult to know where on the life cycle a product/brand is at any one time. Even if its scientific application is doubtful it is, however, useful in explaining the rationale behind differences in marketing communications strategy at different stages of a company's and/or brand's evolution. The implication of this is that not only do the tools and strategies change depending on whether the communicator wishes to gain attention, create interest, stimulate desire or generate action (see hierarchy of effects models in Figure 2.6) but that the particular life-cycle characteristics of the product or service need be taken into account. Box 2.4 shows how a brand's perceived position on the product life cycle may be seen to determine its marketing and marketing communication objectives and the strategies and marketing communications tools used to achieve them.

Box 2.4 Life cycle effects on marketing communications strategy

	Introduction	Growth	Maturity	Decline
Marketing Objectives	Help early adopters adopt	Quickly gain market share	Expand market share and build customer/ distributor loyalty	Maintain dominant market position and consider brand extensions
Marketing Communications Objectives	Create awareness, create interest/ desire among innovators	Strengthen brand preference (with customers and distributors). Encourage wider trial and use	Increase frequency of use and/or suggest possible new uses	Minimize promotion but retain brand values. Perhaps create specialist niche
Marketing Communications Strategy (tools in order of priority)	Public relations/ publicity, personal selling, advertising, sales promotion	Advertising, personal selling, sales promotion, public relations/ publicity	Advertising, dealer promotions, sales promotions, public relations/ publicity	Reduced media expenditure

Source: Based on Smith *et al*. 1997.

HIERARCHY OF EFFECTS MODELS

Hierarchy of effects models
Models that purport to show how marketing communications can help the buying process. AIDA and DAGMAR (see Glossary) are amongst the best known.

From the earliest days of consumer research it was seen that it was rare for consumers to make instant unsupported decisions. Instead it was proposed that consumers went through a number of stages prior to purchase. The many models developed to show this concept have become collectively known as **hierarchy of effects models**. These represent some of the oldest marketing communications models to appear, with the earliest being published in 1898.

They continued to have prominence until the 1980s and despite subsequent revisions of thinking they arguably still have important resonance today. As with all models they should be recognized for what they are – attempts to simplify complex processes and not truths. They are, however, useful in explaining the theory behind marketing communication strategy.

Proponents of the traditional hierarchy framework suggest that audiences respond to messages in a very ordered way that is firstly **cognitively** (thinking), then **affectively** (feeling) and thirdly **conatively** (doing) (Barry and Howard 1990). Cognition is typically defined as 'mental activity' as reflected in knowledge, beliefs or thoughts that someone has about some aspect of their world (Barry and Howard 1990). Advertisers have historically relied on measures of memory (such as recall) to gauge cognition. So, for example, in *Marketing*'s 'Adwatch Survey' respondents are asked by the pollster 'Which of these TV commercials do you remember seeing?' The affective component is any degree of feeling and emotion, in a general sense, which can be attributed to the brand. This is often associated with what is known as **brand personality** (see Chapter 4). Conation refers to either intension to perform a behaviour (e.g. purchase) or the behaviour itself.

One of the earliest attempts to model the effect of marketing communications was the **AIDA** model generally attributed to Strong in 1925 but which actually originated with E. St. Elmo Lewis around 20 to 30 years earlier. Initially designed to qualify the stages a salesperson would take a prospect through a sale, this later became the basic framework against which persuasive communication, particulary advertising, was thought to work. AIDA stood for **attention**, interest, desire and action and represented the stages the rational consumer was supposed to pass through before the ultimate purchase. This can be superimposed on the hierarchy model as shown in Figure 2.6. Later models similar in construction were also developed to explain the communications process. They included

Cognitive
The process of thinking.

Affective
Feeling processes.

Conative
Doing/action processes.

Brand personality
The character and essence of a brand. The perceived lifestyle associations and values (e.g. status, fashion, quality, etc.).

AIDA model
Generally attributed to Strong (1925) the model was designed to represent the stages through which a salesperson should take a prospect but was later adopted as a basic framework to explain how persuasive communication (mainly advertising) worked. AIDA stands for attention, interest, desire and action.

Attention
In communications theory attention must be gained before a message can be delivered.

Figure 2.6 Hierarchy of effects models

Hierarchy of Effects Models

	KNOWLEDGE	FEELING	MOTIVATION →ACTION
AIDA Strong 1925	Attention Interest Desire		Action
DAGMAR Colley 1961	Awareness Comprehension	Conviction	Purchase
Lavidge and Steiner 1961	Awareness Knowledge	Liking Preference	Conviction Purchase
Wells *et al.* 1965	Awareness Perception Understanding		Persuasion
	COGNITIVE	AFFECTIVE	CONATIVE

DAGMAR
DAGMAR (defining advertising goals for measuring advertising results) was Colley's (1961) formula for setting communications orientated objectives.

AIDAS
AIDA model with the addition of after-sales service (S).

DAGMAR (defining advertising goals for measuring advertising results) which was Colley's (1961) suggested formula for setting communications orientated objectives. Lavidge and Steiner (1961) and Wells *et al.* (1965) were also trying to represent the communication process in their hierarchy models.

What is most evidently missing from the above models is the post-purchase effect. That is the effect on future decision making having experienced consumption. Evidently a good consumption experience is likely (but not certain) to lead to other purchases. As early as 1911 Sheldon included 'permanent satisfaction' as the final step in the Lewis/Strong model to create **AIDAS**. This was an early recognition of the now recognized importance of post-purchase (Barry and Howard 1990). Rogers (1983) as part of his theory of adoption suggested that there were various stages including knowledge, persuasion, decision (adopt/reject), implementation and confirmation (continued adoption, discontinuance, continued rejection). Bovée *et al.* (1995) took this further by suggesting that this post-purchase period is the point when advertising (and the other marketing communication tools) should be used to bolster the customers' sense of satisfaction about the action or purchase and that this phase represents the beginning of a new cycle in the communication process.

In their review of hierarchy of effects models Barry and Howard (1990) noted that while there was general agreement among researchers on the three stages in the hierarchy, there was significant disagreement as to the order of the stages.

The traditional hierarchy of effects model makes the assumption that consumers always go along the rational path of [learning] → [feeling] → [doing]. Although this might be considered logical and rational our knowledge of the way people work suggests that rationally is not always a human strongpoint. Box 2.5 shows examples of where alternate paths (B to D) to consumption can be seen to be taking place. Although there are in theory six combinations

Figure 2.7 Extended hierarchy of effects models

Extended Hierarchy of Effects Models

	KNOWLEDGE	FEELING	MOTIVATION → ACTION	POST-PURCHASE
AIDA(S)	*Attention Interest*	*Desire*	*Action*	*(Satisfaction)*
Rogers	*Awareness*	*Persuasion*	*Decision Implementation*	*Confirmation*
Bovée et al.	*Awareness Acceptance Comprehension Preference*		*Ownership*	*Reinforcement*
	COGNITIVE	AFFECTIVE	CONATIVE	CONATIVE

of the three elements A–D represent the most persuasive matches. It also introduces the concept of **involvement** as a measure of how important (in monetary and/or other terms) the consumer regards the purchase to be.

Involvement
The degree of perceived relevance and personal importance attached to the purchase.

Box 2.5 Alternative effects hierarchy

	Involvement	Description	Examples
A: [learning] ➜ [feeling] ➜ [doing]	High	*Informative* Classic Hierarchy	High ticket items e.g. Jewellery
B: [feeling] ➜ [learning] ➜ [doing]	High	*Affective* Self-esteem, Ego	e.g. Sports car, Perfume
C: [feeling] ➜ [doing] ➜ [learning]	Low	*Social* Personal Taste	e.g. Pizza, Inexpensive gift
D: [doing] ➜ [learning] ➜ [feeling]	Low	*Habitual* Routine Behaviour	e.g. Shampoo, Newspaper

Matches are:

A The classical hierarchy discussed previously and frequently referred to as the 'extended problem solving' model. Purchase decisions are characterized by their importance (high involvement) and rational decision making. Examples include the purchase of high ticket items such as jewellery.

Extended problem solving
Model where purchase decisions are characterized by their importance (high involvement) and rational decision making.

B High involvement again but where less information may be required, perhaps because the brand image is strong. It is associated with status items such as sports cars or quality watch brands.

C Often characterized as 'limited problem solving' this might be described as 'life's little pleasures' or impulse purchases. These are affected by personal taste and include, for example, a gift for a friend.

Limited problem solving
Known and familiar purchases (modified or straight re-buys) with medium involvement in the purchase.

D Habitual and routine behaviour for example the purchase of a newspaper.

These alternate means of consumer decision making relate directly to involvement and **experience**. Involvement, as noted previously, is the degree of perceived relevance and personal importance attached to the purchase. Experience is the extent to which the consumer has accumulated prior knowledge of the product or service concerned (see Figure 2.8). Looking

Experience (in relation to purchasing)
The extent to which the consumer has accumulated prior knowledge of the product or service.

Figure 2.8 Problem solving

	High	Involvement		Low
High	Extended Problem Solving	A	C	Limited Problem Solving
Low	Status Seeking or Brand Loyalty	B	D	Habit or Variety Seeking

at decision making in this way enables a matrix to be created that has direct connections with those factors discussed as A to D above.

A key advantage of considering hierarchy of effects models, irrespective of any debates around accuracy, is their recognition that brand awareness is important. Another benefit is that they again help distinguish between the likely objectives at each stage of the model. Although the hierarchy of effects models were largely used to explain characteristics of advertising, they are useful as a predictor of the relative importance of all the marketing communications tools at various times during the process (see Figure 2.9). Differing objectives mean different strategic approaches which in turn means use of the most effective tool for the situation. Advertising and public relations are, for example, tools most effectively used for learning and developing feelings over time. Sales promotion and personal selling are more immediate 'action' tools. This is illustrated in Figure 2.9 below.

Not withstanding the contribution the classical hierarchy models have made, and continue to make, they have a number of shortcomings:

- There is no empirical support that suggests consumers actually go through each stage.
- Hierarchy models do not take account of the potential for interaction between stages.
- Post-purchase experience is often not considered.

Hierarchy of effects models and related frameworks see **brand awareness** as a prerequisite for **brand attitude** formation and subsequently conclude that affective responses cannot be formed or purchases made without having an existing awareness of the brand. Most companies, therefore, strive for what is frequently known as **front-of-mind-awareness**, in effect establishing their brand before all others in the mind of the consumer.

Despite their evident shortcomings the models discussed in this chapter present a framework for concepts and theories that can be examined and challenged in the light of observed consumer behaviour.

Brand attitude
How the consumer feels about the brand.

Front-of-mind-awareness
Maintaining awareness of the brand in the consumer's mind.

Figure 2.9 Hierarchy of effects and relevant marketing communications tools

Learning	Feeling	Doing
Advertising		Personal Selling
Public Relations		Sales Promotion

Summary

This chapter reviewed those concepts and theories associated with marketing communications research and practice. It introduced the 'simple communications model' and described the important elements of it. It reviewed the characteristics of the 'source' and the 'message' that are associated with message clarity and those characteristics that restrict effective communication. The 'two-step model' introduced the concepts of 'opinion leaders' and 'opinion formers' and their influence on message management. The associated concepts of 'diffusion of innovation' and the 'product life cycle' were explained and their connection with marketing communication strategies explored. Returning again to the 'hierarchy of effects' models, versions were analysed and alternatives were suggested.

Review questions

1 How would you illustrate the basic process of communication?
2 What would you consider to be the problems associated with ethnocentrism?
3 Explain the difference between semiotics, syntactics and semantics.
4 What do you consider are the key determinants of ineffective communication?
5 Why might the source of a piece of communication be important?
6 Define 'noise'.
7 What is the principle of 'wearout'?
8 To what extent can hierarchical effects models incorporate the impact of post-purchase behaviour?
9 What do you consider to be the main advantages of using hierarchy of effects modelling?
10 Would you consider David Beckham to be an opinion former or an opinion leader and why?

Discussion questions

1 Viral marketing is a phenomena of Internet advertising. What do you think the dangers might be for companies adopting this medium and under what circumstances do you feel this form of advertising might be inappropriate?
2 Repetition is an important aspect of message receipt and acceptance. To what extent do you feel this works and what would you need to consider if you were building this into a communications plan?
3 How valuable are hierarchy of effects models and to what extent can you use them in your communications planning?

Further reading

Berglind, M. and Nakata, C. (2005) 'Cause-related marketing: more buck than bang?', *Business Horizons*, Sep., 48(5): 443–53. The concept and practice of cause-related marketing and its social-ethical complexities.

Menord, V.I. and Menord, M. (2006) 'No longer lost in translation', *Quality Progress*, Aug., 39(8): 27–32. Exploring the use of language in marketing communications.

Rucker, D.D. and Petty, R. (2006) 'Increasing the effectiveness of communications to consumers: recommendations based on elaboration likelihood and attitude certainty perspectives', *Journal of Public Policy & Marketing*, Spring, 25(1): 39–52. Looking at methods available to effectively communicate potential risks associated with products and services to purchasing consumers. Includes several theories on the psychology of persuasion.

Shapiro, S.J. (2005) 'Looking Backward – and Ahead', *Journal of Public Policy & Marketing*, Spring, 24(1): 117–20. This article focuses on the intellectual history of the marketing discipline.

Wang, S. (Alex) and Nelson, R.A. (2006) 'The effects of identical versus varied advertising and publicity messages on consumer response', *Journal of Marketing Communications*, Jun., 12(2): 109–23. This study argues that varying messages in advertising and publicity about a product or service intelligently could be an effective technique in integrated marketing communications.

Chapter references

Barry, T. and Howard, D.J. (1990) 'A review and critique of the hierarchy of effects in advertising', *International Journal of Advertising*. 9: 121–35.

Bovée, C.L., Thill, J.V., Dovel, G.P. and Wood, M.B. (1995) *Advertising Excellence*, Englewood Cliffs, NJ: McGraw-Hill.

Bruhn, M. (2003) *Relationship Marketing: Management of Customer Relationships*, Harlow: FT Prentice Hall.

Colley, R.H. (1961) *Defining Advertising Goals*, New York: Association of National Advertisers.

De Pelsmacker, P., Geuens, M. and Van den Bergh, J. (2001) *Marketing Communications: A European Perspective*, London: Prentice Hall.

Fill, C. (2001) 'Essentially a matter of consistency: integrated marketing communications', *The Marketing Review*, 1 (4): 409–25.

Fill, C. (2002) *Marketing Communciations: Contexts, Strategies, and Applications*, 3rd edn, Harlow: Financial Times Prentice Hall.

Kelman, H. (1961) 'Processes of opinion change', *Public Opinion Quarterly*, (25) Spring: 57–78.

Klapper, J.T. (1960) *The Effects of Mass Communication*, New York: Free Press.

Lavidge, R. and Steiner, G. (1961) 'A model for predictive measurements of advertising effectiveness', *Journal of Marketing*, Oct.: 61.

Mano, H. (1996) 'Assessing emotional reactions to TV ads: a replication and extension with a brief adjective checklist', *Advances in Consumer Research*, 23: 63–9.

Mistry, B. (2006) 'Star spotting', *Marketing*, 7 June: 33–4.

Nielsen, A.C. (2003) 'Alternative marketing vehicles: future of markets', *Consumer Insight Magazine*, June, www.marketingpower.com, accessed 31 October 2005.

OED (1996) *Concise Oxford Dictionary of Current English*, 9th edn, London: BCA.

Petty, R.E. and Cacioppo, J.T. (1979) 'Effects of message repetition and position on cognitive responses, recall and persuasion', *Journal of Personality and Social Psychology*, 37 (January): 97–109.

Pickton, D. and Broderick, A. (2001) *Integrated Marketing Communications*, Harlow: Prentice Hall.

Rogers, E.M. (1983) *Diffusion of Innovations*, 3rd edn, New York: Free Press.

Schramm, W. (1955) *How Communication Works in the Process and Effects of Mass Communications,* Urbana, IL: University of Illinois Press.

Smith, P., Berry, C. and Pulford, A. (1997) *Strategic Marketing Communications: New Ways to Build and Integrate Communication*, London: Kogan Page.

Strong, E.K. (1925) *The Psychology of Selling*, New York: McGraw-Hill.

Varey, R.J. (2001), *Marketing Communication: Principles and Practice*, London: Routledge.

Wells, W., Burnett, J. and Moriaty, S. (1965) *Advertising Principles and Practice*, Upper Saddle River, NJ: Prentice Hall.

CASE STUDY 2.1

Mickey Mouse Fruit?

A growing problem identified within western countries at the end of the twentieth century was a marked increase in obesity, grounded, it was felt, in poor eating habits and a more docile and inactive population.

Children no longer spent their days playing outside but preferred the latest video game, pausing only to snack on crisps or grab a quick can of pop. Eating habits had become generally erratic and the meaning of a 'balanced diet' had long since been forgotten.

Indications of the extent of the problem are easy to find. For example, one piece of US research concluded that in 1960 around 4 per cent of American children were considered obese but by 2004 it was 15 per cent. In Australia a 2006 survey identified a 5 per cent increase in overweight/obese children since 1999 and a 2006 UK Trading Standards Institute study prompted Ron Gainsford, their Chief Executive, to conclude that 'if current trends continue, a third of adults, one fifth of boys and a third of girls will be obese by the year 2010'.

Concerns were also being raised by consumers and perhaps the most visible were the 2004 Morgan Spurlock *Super-Size Me* documentary, when he lived for 30 days on McDonald's products, and the 2005 Jamie Oliver *School Dinners* series, which highlighted the general poor diet of British youngsters and their passion for 'fast food'.

▶

The effect? Well for McDonald's, the youth market is a very important sector and retaining both its young customers and their parents is critical for long-term survival. Andrew Taylor, UK Chief Executive, admitted that childhood obesity concerns influenced the decision to introduce salads, but the commercial reality was that its traditional menu item, the burger, was in decline. With five-year sales growth figures up to 2003 barely reaching 1 per cent p.a. across its major US market alone they clearly had to find alternative meal solutions.

Press reports were not kind though. In March 2004 a news article at www.timesonline.co.uk announced that a 'McDonald's Salad is more fattening than a burger', and this was not untypical of other coverage. McDonald's attempted to counter the bad image, for example by launching www.supersizeme-thedebate.co.uk to try and put a reasoned position behind the criticism. Dropping the 'super-size' campaign and developing the menu to include more healthy items, for example launching organic semi-skimmed milk in 2003. They also worked hard at improving their image, one result being the RSPCA 'Alternative Award' for its commitment to animal welfare. But the perception with consumers appeared to remain: McDonald's = unhealthy.

The importance to them of the youth market cannot be underestimated. Over the previous ten years Disney imagery and promotions typified their children's marketing activities which, for Disney, generated around $100 million per year in licence fees. The value to McDonald's can only be speculated, but the benefits of association to Disney are clear. Good wholesome entertainment, good wholesome fare.

But consider this from the perspective of Disney.

Their statement on corporate responsibility (www.corporate.disney.go.com) includes the words 'acting responsibly in all our professional relationships'. Being seen as contributing to a rising wave of health problems amongst the young, therefore, is hardly in line with this policy and it is not surprising that in June 2006 it announced that it was ending its relationship with McDonald's and forming a new association in the UK with Tesco.

A television advertisement featuring McDonald's new focus on healthy eating.

SOURCE: IMAGE COURTESY OF THE ADVERTISING ARCHIVES

What might be surprising though was the nature of that association – Disney branded satsumas. With Winnie the Pooh collectible stickers on the skin of the fruit that could be transferred into a sticker book. Largely unnoticed in the UK, Disney had already begun licensing fresh fruit in European supermarkets, with baby tomatoes in France and mini bananas in Germany. Targeting healthy foods, seeking to disassociate itself from products that could be linked to childhood obesity and clearly distancing itself from McDonald's.

This UK move actually followed a 12-month programme of around 300 new food product launches across Europe with a Disney licence, from pastas to pizzas and beef burgers in the shape of Mickey Mouse.

Andy Mooney, chairman of Disney Consumer Products, explained that they were trying to develop 'better ranges for kids', confirming that the Company wanted to be associated with 'healthier' areas of the food business.

So what comes next, Mickey Mouse apples or Goofy bananas?

Case study questions

1. McDonald's are clearly faced with a tough communications challenge, to reposition themselves in the eyes of both consumers and the opinion formers within society. What are the challenges they face in communicating their new 'healthy' identity?

2. What is the fundamental message that Disney is trying to convey with this new venture and how might it be incorporated into future communications activities?

3. Why would European supermarkets feel that Disney branding on a piece of fruit will make it more appealing to consumers?

Case study written by Andy Cropper, Senior Lecturer, Sheffield Hallam University.

CHAPTER THREE
BUYING BEHAVIOUR

LEARNING OBJECTIVES

Having completed this chapter you should be able to:

- Understand the different schools of thought on consumer decision making.
- Recognize the factors that affect decision making and the ways researchers classify them.
- Understand the importance of attitudes, perception, learning and motivation on buying behaviour.

INTRODUCTION

What makes buyers buy? This question has troubled marketing scholars for over a century. What is certain is that the answer is not straightforward. Every consumer is different as a result of their own unique characteristics and the effect society has upon them. These all-powerful drivers are frequently referred to as **nature** (i.e. those characteristics we inherited) and **nurture** (i.e. the effect of society upon those characteristics). Marketing communicators, whilst recognizing this complexity, need to be aware of what stimulates audiences and what does not. This is very far from being an exact science.

Theories of decision making generally fall into two schools of thought: the cognitive paradigm and the behavioural paradigm.

THE COGNITIVE PARADIGM

The cognitive paradigm is so-called because it focuses on an individual's thought processes and sees consumer choice as a problem-solving and decision-making series of activities the outcome of which is determined principally by the buyer's intellectual functioning and rational goal-orientated processing of information (Pickton and Broderick 2001). This makes the rather rash judgement that consumers are highly rational, willing to put themselves

Nature
Those characteristics we inherit from our forebears.

Nurture
The effect of society upon the characteristics we are born with.

Cognitive paradigm
Focuses on an individual's thought processes and sees consumer choice as a problem-solving and decision-making series of activities the outcome of which is determined principally by the buyer's intellectual functioning and rational goal-orientated processing of information.

Behavioural paradigm
Proponents of this paradigm believe it is not possible to study what goes on in the consumer's mind because it is too complex. Instead output is measured following a given stimulus. In effect it is a 'black box' into which stimuli flow and out of which behaviour occurs.

Routinized problem solving
Repeat behaviour with low involvement, usually low cost and often limited external knowledge.

Problem recognition
Recognition that a purchase must be made to fulfil a need or want (also referred to as **problem definition**).

Information search
Where the customer collects information on a range of products or services prior to purchase.

Evaluation
Evaluation of information collected prior to purchase.

Decision (in terms of buyer behaviour)
The decision to purchase.

Purchase
The act of exchange of one commodity for another (usually money).

Post-purchase evaluation
Evaluation of a product or service which may lead to repurchase.

Straight re-buy
Business-to-business (B2B) term for re-buying a product without changing the supplier or the specifications.

Total set
All of the products available in a category.

Awareness set
Those products in a category that the consumer is aware of.

Evoked set
Those products in a category that the consumer has 'front-of-mind' and will make the purchase choice from.

Brand salience
The importance and prominance of a brand.

out of their way, problem solvers. It also makes the assumption that most product choices are **routinized problem solving** (see Chapter 2) characterized by habitual behaviour with little thought going in to the purchase and largely based on previous buying experience. The simple buying model (Figure 3.1) is an example of this perceived rational process.

Most cognitive models, however complex, are generally based on a model similar to Figure 3.1. Models involve a **problem recognition** (or problem definition) stage which acts as the trigger for the process. This *may* lead to an **information search** where the potential customer collects information on a range of products or services, and which aids their subsequent **evaluation**. A **decision** is made which *may* lead to a **purchase**. Post-purchase evaluation *may* mean that the next time it will be a **straight re-buy** if everything has been to the customer's satisfaction. Alternatively it might end up in a further search for information if the experience was not a satisfactory one. The continual use of the word *may* emphasizes that the model is not a straightforward linear model and that iteration can and does occur at every stage.

There are limitations that have been identified by a number of authors. In particular:

- Consumers do not have perfect knowledge of all alternative products (the **total set**).
- They are only aware of a percentage of the products (the **awareness set**).
- They reduce this to a smaller, more manageable group (the **evoked set**) from which a decision is made.

The major management implication of this is that achieving awareness, although an important prerequisite, is not in itself enough. A key objective of any brand holder should be to get their brand into the evoked set (see Chapter 4 **brand salience**). The term front-of-mind (as discussed in Chapter 2)

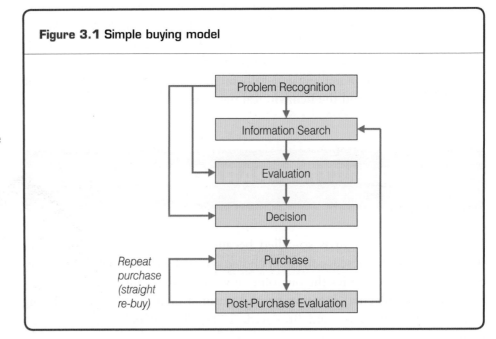

Figure 3.1 Simple buying model

is frequently used by marketers to emphasize that it is a principal objective of brand owners and their communications teams to aim for a prominent place in an evoked set.

Closely associated with the simple buying model is the concept of a **problem solving** hierarchy. As discussed in Chapter 2, this suggests that there are various levels of problem solving and that the level affects how much care, attention and involvement we are prepared to undertake when making buying decisions. They are labelled the **extensive problem solving, limited problem solving** and **routinized problem solving** models and are described as follows:

- Extensive problem solving (high involvement)

  Important decisions warrant greater deliberation
  Usually higher expenditure

- Limited problem solving (medium involvement)

  Known and familiar (modified or straight re-buys)
  Usually moderate pricing

- Routinized problem solving (low involvement)

  Repeat behaviour often limited external knowledge
  Usually low pricing

Problem-solving models
Extensive, limited and routinized problem-solving models.

Extensive problem-solving models
Model that reflects important purchase decisions (e.g. higher expenditure) warrant greater deliberation and higher involvement.

Limited problem-solving models
Known and familiar purchases (modified or straight re-buys) with medium involvement in the purchase.

Routinized problem solving
Repeat behaviour with low involvement, usually low cost and often limited external knowledge.

THE BEHAVIOURAL PARADIGM

The behavioural paradigm is derived from operant behaviouralism research by Skinner, discussed in more detail on page 68. Proponents of this paradigm believe it is not possible to study what goes on in the consumer's mind because it is so complex. Instead, it is proposed, output is measured following a given stimulus. In effect the consumer is a 'black box' into which stimuli flow and out of which behaviour occurs, with the consequence that this behaviour might then influence or reinforce future behaviour and thus increase its occurrence. An illustration of the process as conceived by behaviouralists is shown in Figure 3.2 below.

Behavioural theorists believe that marketing communications activity should be based on creating the correct environmental cues for the individual and monitoring the responses to these cues as a guide to future activity.

Figure 3.2 The behavioural paradigm

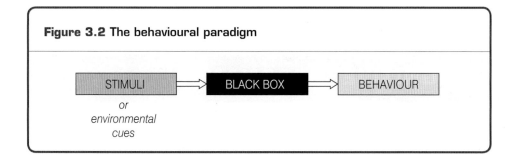

According to Foxall (1993), for example, the behavioural paradigm makes two assumptions. These are that:

- The frequency with which the behaviour is performed is a function of the consequences of such behaviour in the past. That is the success of previous outcomes are likely to determine the number of times that the stimulus is repeated.

- The determinants of behaviour must, therefore, be found in the environment rather than the individual. The triggers to that behaviour can, therefore, be applied by the marketer.

ALTERNATIVE MODELS OF PROBLEM SOLVING

Although eminently logical most decision-making models relate to **high involvement purchases** and are extensive problem solving types, most product or service choices are, however, **routine problem solving** characterized by habit with little thought given to the range of alternatives (including, at times, price). Ehrenberg and Goodhardt (1979) suggest that the greater part of the buying experience is rooted in past experience as indicated in the **ATR model** (see Figure 3.3).

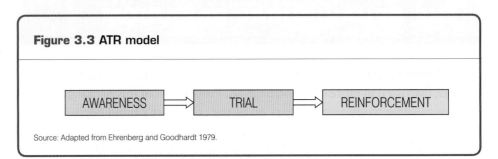

Figure 3.3 ATR model

AWARENESS → TRIAL → REINFORCEMENT

Source: Adapted from Ehrenberg and Goodhardt 1979.

The important thing here is to gain trial as there is a natural reluctance to try something new. This reluctance explains why so many new consumer products are introduced through **trial packs** and **giveaways**. The trial is a considerable barrier which, once overcome, can lead to repeat purchases in the future.

It is also quite common behaviour for normally brand loyal customers to shop around occasionally. A practice which may or may not eventually lead back again to the original brand.

COGNITIVE DISSONANCE

This theory was developed by Festinger (1957) and remains somewhat controversial. It is based on the presumption that if an individual holds two

High involvement purchases
See extensive problem-solving model.

Routine problem solving
See routinized problem solving model.

ATR model
Awareness, Trial and Reinforcement. Ehrenberg and Goodhardt (1979) suggest that the greater part of the buying experience is rooted in past experience.

Trial packs
New product, frequently in smaller than normal quantity and at a special price to encourage trial.

Giveaways
Products distributed (in-store or elsewhere) without cost as a means of encouraging trial.

conflicting cognitions (or views) he or she will experience mental discomfort (**cognitive dissonance**). In this event individuals will seek to reduce or eliminate this dissonance by either changing one or the other viewpoint or by introducing a third view that will account for and reduce the dissonance. In marketing terms this cognitive dissonance is most likely to show up after a purchase (**post-purchase dissonance**) because any purchase involves some form of self-justification particularly if high costs (monetary or emotional) are involved in the purchase. Blythe (2000) suggests that there are four general approaches to reducing dissonance and these are:

- Ignore the dissonant information (e.g. accept a car's poor performance as one of those things!).
- Distort the dissonant information (e.g. pretend the car works well in certain circumstances such as in the rain).
- Play down the importance of the issue (e.g. look for the positive features and benefits such as comfort).
- Change the behaviour or situation (e.g. get rid of the car!).

It is frequently proposed that brand building communications (e.g. advertising) helps reduce cognitive dissonance by emphasizing to existing consumers the positive attributes of the purchase reinforcing the view that they have made the right decision. In automobile advertising, for example, it is suggested that many of the viewers are existing customers looking for such reassurance.

FACTORS AFFECTING BUYING BEHAVIOUR

It is probable that the best approach to understanding buying decision behaviour is through a combination of cognitive and behavioural decision making, augmented by other factors including internal and external influences, mediated through individual and unique personalities. The wide range of different factors affect our reception of information, what we do with that information and, consequently, our buying behaviour.

Race, religion and culture set the tone for our particular values as modified by our membership of primary (e.g. family) or secondary (e.g. work colleagues) groups. Internally our **attitudes**, **perceptions**, **learning** and capacity for memory, and **motivations** are considerable strong influencers. To these our individual characteristics, such as age, gender, income, personality and family situation are seen as further determinants of what we choose to pay attention to and ultimately purchase. External factors such as our personal situation (e.g. health), the prevailing fashion, the availability of disposable funds, the legal position, time associated factors (e.g. time to search), the power of the media and communication messages, the weather or even the current stock position act as further moderators to our behaviour. These diverse influences are shown graphically in Figure 3.4.

Cognitive dissonance
The mental discomfort that an individual feels if they hold two conflicting cognitions (or views). Individuals will seek to reduce or eliminate this dissonance by either changing one or the other viewpoint or by introducing a third view that will account for and reduce the dissonance.

Post-purchase dissonance
Dissonance (mental discomfort) felt after purchase regarding whether or not the buyer has made the right decision (e.g. is it value for money?).

Attitudes
Strongly felt, not easily changed views. Attitudes form an important part of consumer theory because it is believed to be the link between what consumers think and what they buy in the marketplace.

Perceptions
Perception is how we interpret and make sense of the world. The way an individual perceives a situation may be different from how others perceive the same situation.

Learning
The human capacity to know and act upon a situation based on some prior experience.

Motivation
Inner drives which cause human beings to strive for some level of satisfaction.

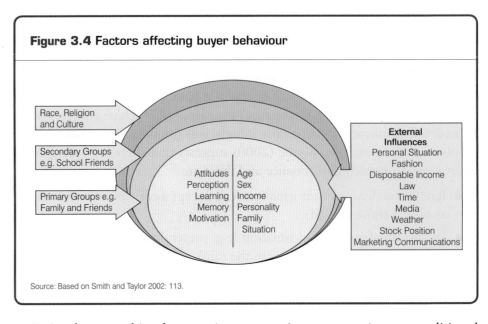

Figure 3.4 Factors affecting buyer behaviour

Source: Based on Smith and Taylor 2002: 113.

Basic demographic factors (age, sex, income, etc.) are traditional discriminators as they are seen to have an effect on purchase decisions. Other aspects (employment, motivation, etc.) are used as the traditional basis for creating 'groupings' of consumers. Perhaps the oldest such classification in the UK is the National Readership Survey's (NRS) socioeconomic groupings much beloved of newspaper and magazine circulation managers. The NRS social grade definitions are shown in Box 3.1 below.

The NRS socioeconomic groupings have considerable failings. They were developed at a time when the class structure was more pronounced than it is today. It was also based on the occupation of the head of the household with no consideration for the partner/spouse or other influencers. In 2001 a new classification was introduced based on the way people work. The classifications distinguish between employers, the self-employed and employees who are further segmented by the nature of their job conditions including career prospects, the length of notice required, whether paid a salary or a wage and the standard of pension and insurance provision. The seven new classifications are shown in Box 3.2.

Box 3.1 Socioeconomic groupings

Social Grade	Social Status	Occupation
A	Upper Middle Class	Higher managerial, administrative or professional
B	Middle Class	Intermediate managerial, administrative or professional
C^1	Lower Middle Class	Supervisory or clerical, junior managerial, administrative or professional
C^2	Skilled Working Class	Skilled manual workers
D	Working Class	Semi-skilled or unskilled manual workers
E	Lowest level of subsistence	Pensioners or widows/ers, casual or lowest grade workers

Box 3.2 Seven classifications of social class

Class	%*	Description
One	8.5	Large employers and higher managerial and professional occupations
Two	19	Lower managerial and professional occupations
Three	9.4	Intermediate occupations (e.g. medical/legal secretaries)
Four	7	Small employers and 'own account' workers (e.g. hotel manager)
Five	7.2	Lower supervisory and technical occupations (e.g. traffic wardens)
Six	12	Semi-routine occupations (e.g. sales assistants, taxi drivers)
Seven	9.1	Routine occupations (e.g. waiters, packers, couriers)
	29	Unclassified are those who have never worked, the long-term unemployed, full-time students and others not covered

*Because of rounding up the total does not make 100.

It remains to be seen if this new classification will eventually take over from the old. Given the traditional nature of the magazine and newspaper industries it is unlikely to happen overnight.

Lifestyle is also seen as an important discriminator. Researchers investigate consumer **VALs** (values, activities and lifestyles) and will frequently give distinct groupings a name that describes these broad characterizations. NRS, for example, use a table of descriptors that each represent a particular lifestyle (see Box 3.3 below).

VALs
Values, activity and lifestyle analysis.

Box 3.3 NRS profiles

Class	Descriptor	Class	Descriptor
A	Affluent achievers	G	Senior citizens
B	Thriving greys	H	Producers
C	Settled suburbs	I	Hard-pressed families
D	Nest builders	J	Have-nots
E	Urban ventures	K	Unclassifiable
F	Country life		

An individual's life-stage is seen as a particularly important discriminator. Box 3.4 is a typical list of descriptors showing the changing circumstances experienced during a typical lifetime. At each stage consumers have different needs and (given the cost of rearing children) different levels of disposable income with which to satisfy them.

Even more detailed profiles are available in developed markets around the globe. For example CACI Ltd produce **Acorn profiles**. These describe residential neighbourhoods and are based on the approximately 1.7 million postcodes in the UK. The full Acorn profile comprises of 17 distinct categories containing 54 Acorn neighbourhood types. It is **geodemographic** (i.e. combining both geographical and demographic features) and has been used by marketers to target consumers with particular characteristics. The Acorn classifications are shown in Box 3.5.

Test your VALS score at: **www.sric-bi.com/VALS.**

Acorn profiles
Describes residential neighbourhoods and are based on the approximately 1.7 million postcodes in the UK. The full Acorn profile comprises of 17 distinct categories containing 54 Acorn neighbourhood types.

Geodemographic profiles
Combining both geographical and demographic features to provide a profile.

Box 3.4 Family life cycles

Life-stage	Description
Single	Living alone. No dependents
Single Parent	Alone with dependent child/children
DINKS	Double Income No Kids
Full Nest 1	Youngest Child under 6
Full Nest 2	Youngest Child over 6
Full Nest 3	Dependent Children
Empty Nest 1	Children moved out but still working
Empty Nest 2	Retired Couple
Solitary Survivor 1	Still working widow/er
Solitary Survivor 2	Retired widow/er

Box 3.5 CACI Acorn profile

Wealthy Achievers	Wealthy Executives	01 – Affluent mature professionals, large houses
		02 – Affluent working families with mortgages.
		03 – Villages with wealthy commuters
		04 – Well-off managers, larger houses
	Affluent Greys	05 – Older affluent professionals
		06 – Farming communities
		07 – Old people, detached houses
		08 – Mature couples, smaller detached houses
	Flourishing Families	09 – Larger families prosperous suburbs
		10 – Well-off working families with mortgages
		11 – Well-off managers, detached houses
		12 – Large families & houses in rural areas
Urban Prosperity	Prosperous Professionals	13 – Well-off professionals, larger houses and converted flats
		14 – Older professionals in detached houses and apartments
	Educated Urbanites	15 – Affluent urban professionals, flats
		16 – Prosperous young professionals, flats
		17 – Young educated workers, flats
		18 – Multi-ethnic young, converted flats
		19 – Suburban privately renting professionals
	Aspiring Singles	20 – Student flats and cosmopolitan sharers
		21 – Singles and sharers, multi-ethnic areas
		22 – Low income singles, small rented flats
		23 – Student terraces
	Starting Out	24 – Young couples, flats and terraces
		25 – White-collar singles/sharers, terraces

Box 3.5 (Continued)

Comfortably off	Secure Families	26 – Younger white-collar couples with mortgages
		27 – Middle income, home-owning areas
		28 – Working families with mortgages
		29 – Mature families in suburban semis
		30 – Established home-owning workers
		31 – Home-owning Asian family areas
	Settled Suburbia	32 – Retired home owners
		33 – Middle income, older couples
		34 – Lower income people, semis
	Prudent Pensioners	35 – Elderly singles, purpose built flats
		36 – Older people, flats
Moderate Means	Asian Communities	37 – Crowded Asian terraces
		38 – Low income Asian families
	Post Industrial Families	39 – Skilled older family terraces
		40 – Young family workers
	Blue-Collar Roots	41 – Skilled workers, semis and terraces
		42 – Home owning, terraces
		43 – Older rented terraces
Hard Pressed	Struggling Families	44 – Low income larger families, semis
		45 – Older people, low income, small semis
		46 – Low income, routine jobs, unemployment
		47 – Low-rise terraced estates of poorly-off workers
		48 – Low incomes, high unemployment, single parents
		49 – Large families, many children, poorly educated
	Burdened Singles	50 – Council flats, single elderly people
		51 – Council terraces, unemployment, many singles
		52 – Council flats, single parents, unemployment
	High-Rise Hardship	53 – Old people in high-rise flats
		54 – Singles and single parents, high-rise estates
	Inner-City Adversity	55 – Multi-ethnic purpose built estates
		56 – Multi-ethnic, crowded flats

@ Explore 'Acorn' at: **www.caci.co.uk/acorn/**.

A number of factors similar to those above are used to create composites of a brand's target audience. Known as **trait theory** it is where an individual is viewed as a composite of several behaviour traits or characteristics (Sheth *et al*. 1999). These traits are of particular interest to marketing communicators who are interested in the relationship between broad personality traits and general types of behaviour. There are very many examples of this consumer typology indeed some major brands have their own typologies describing in some detail the types of consumer of their product or service. A typical

Trait theory

A theory that suggests individuals should be viewed as a composite of several behaviour traits or characteristics.

example of a typology was that introduced by Young and Rubicam in the 1980s called the 4Cs (consumers). They are shown in Box 3.6 below.

Using these traits as guides, marketers establish target groups of customers who hold most promise for the brand. As Minicase 3.1 suggests this does not always work.

MINICASE 3.1

Trait theories

The danger of subjective profiles are outlined by the Former Marketing Director of a major UK FMCG (fast moving consumer goods) manufacturer interviewed as part of a research project in December 2003. He stated that 'most of our brands had more off-strategy eating than on-strategy eating going on'. He went on to explain that they 'would very carefully target a brand at an archetypal consumer with a particular need…the classic cube of who, why, when and frankly, when you analyse the numbers an awful lot more was getting eaten by the wrong people, at the wrong time, for the wrong reasons, than you would care to admit'. Although perhaps not a ringing endorsement the same executive went on to say that it could be helpful, 'It can help you at least to have clarity, to have a clear view, of which customer you have in mind.'

ATTITUDES

Personal attitude plays a central part in consumer behaviour. Attitudes are what drives a human being to act in a certain way. Attitudes form an important part of consumer theory because it is believed to be 'the crucial link between what consumers think and what they buy in the marketplace' (Foxall *et al.* 1998: 102). The experiential combination of perception and the learning process can help influence the creation of predisposed attitudes, for example to imagery, situations or circumstances, which might influence the way in which consumers react, creating a bridge between the way people think and the way they behave. Attitude is a learned tendency to respond and react to

Box 3.6 Young and Rubicam 4 consumers typology

Name	Description	Tendency to purchase
Aspirers	Seeking status and self-esteem	Symbols of achievement
Succeeders	Successful but need to control their lives	Quality (actual or perceived)
Mainstreamers	Basic need for security and belonging	Established products/brands
Performers	Self-fulfilment rather than status	Own brands, natural products

something in a consistent (favourable or unfavourable) way (Onkvisit and Shaw 1994). Put more simply a predisposition to respond in a consistent manner to a stimulus; a tendency to act or behave in some predictable way. Attitudes are difficult to change. Even when change is affected this is usually over a long period of time.

Attitudes (and in particular cultural attitudes) may be characterized as stereotypes which are very useful to marketers targeting particular groups (see Chapter 6). The effect of individual cultures (or sub-cultures) are very strong. They are not those features we are born with (nature) but those we derive from the society around us (nurture). Culture is everything a person learns and shares with members of a society including ideas, norms, morals, values, knowledge, skills, technology, tools, material objects and behaviours (Sheth *et al.* 1999). These unique characteristics will define acceptable patterns of behaviour within a society and are usually visualized through:

- a society's values
- a society's norms or rules of behaviour
- a society's rituals and symbols
- a society's myths (stories describing key societal values) (Sheth *et al.* 1999).

Despite the importance of attitude in buying behaviour a positive attitude is not, however, necessarily a good predictor of purchase behaviour. For example an individual may have an excellent attitude to Ferrari as a brand but other factors (e.g. finance) may inhibit purchase. From the perspective of repeat business it is also incorrect to assume that satisfaction with a product or service at any point in time will necessarily ensure re-purchase or longer-term loyalty. Research by Reichheld (1993) and Mittal and Lasser (1998) suggest that satisfaction is not a surrogate for customer retention or loyalty. They note that high levels of customers who defected to other brands had declared themselves satisfied or very satisfied immediately before the defection. What becomes more relevant, therefore, is the relationship between a change in attitude and that individual's actual intent to act in a particular way.

PERCEPTION

Effective marketing management rests on two fundamentals (Foxall *et al.* 1998):

- Consumers act on their perceptions and these come from the information they receive.
- Managers need to understand the nature of the perceptions their customers and potential customers have.

Perception is how we interpret and make sense of the world. A fundamental part of the function of marketing communications, therefore, is to ensure that the product or service finds the right place in the consumer's 'field of perception' or real world view/'world-view' (see Chapter 2). Not everyone perceives the same thing. When two opposing football fans see a referee award a penalty one may (genuinely) see it as a definite penalty award while the other (genuinely) will see it as unjust.

We each create our own 'cognitive map', therefore, which is essentially an imaginative construct that will be influenced by:

- subjectivity: determined by each individual's own world-view;
- categorization: how each individual develops information;
- selectivity: how much the brain selects from the environment (see selective attention);
- expectation: what leads individuals to interpret later information in a specific way (e.g. seeing only part of a familiar label enables the brain to complete the picture);
- past experience: what leads us to interpret current experiences (e.g. sometimes sights, sounds or smells trigger appropriate responses).

The human brain is good at assembling evidence from less than complete information. The presentation of only part of a label or image in the knowledge that the viewer's brain will complete the picture is a common advertising ploy. In the **gestalt approach** to perception this is known as **closure**. In effect, the mind acts as the communications medium as it is only here that the image becomes visible. Gestalt (German for 'whole' or 'entirely') and gestalt psychology stresses the fact that perception of a stimulus takes place within a known context and that the individual's reaction is crucially affected by his or her 'world-view' (Foxall *et al.* 1998: 61).

Before perception can even occur attention has to be gained. Indeed the greater the attention paid the greater the likelihood that the receiver will perceive the right message. There are a number of concepts that are directly associated with perception. These include:

- Selective attention: all consumers are each day exposed to hundreds of competing messages. Selective attention is the process of screening out information that does not interest us and selectively processing the information that does. Messages that successfully bypass selective attention are likely to be perceived positively.
- Selective exposure: that consumers selectively expose themselves to certain messages as opposed to other messages (e.g. by ordering a catalogue).
- Selective distortion: the tendency to hear what we want to hear. Distortion may occur because of prejudice or stereotyping.

The basic principle, according to Foxall *et al.* (1998), is that consumers pay attention to stimuli they deem relevant to their needs, wants, beliefs and attitudes. Once attention is gained the information is interpreted and stored in the memory so as to enforce and enhance existing attitudes and behaviour.

World-view
The consumer's view of the world (see field of perception).

Gestalt approach
Gestalt (German for 'whole' or 'entirely') and gestalt psychology stresses the fact that perception of a stimulus takes place within a known context and that the individual's reaction is crucially affected by his or her 'world-view'.

Closure
Effectively the completion (based on past experience) of something that is incomplete (e.g. part of a name).

Selective attention
The process of screening out information that does not interest us and selectively processing the information that does. Messages that successfully bypass 'selective attention' are likely to be perceived positively.

Selective exposure
Where consumers selectively expose themselves to certain messages as opposed to other messages.

Selective distortion
The tendency to hear what we want to hear. Distortion may occur because of prejudice or stereotyping.

Distortion frequently takes place because of attitude and prejudice. For example, if an individual is a supporter of a particular political party he or she is unlikely to be persuaded by the positive messages of an opposing party at least in the short term. Another distortion is associated with the halo effect. This is when the attributes of one factor are transferred to another in such a way as it affects our judgement. This is the effect sought through brand extension (the halo effect of the original brand), cause-related marketing (the halo effect of the cause or charity) and sponsorship (the halo effect of the event).

LEARNING

According to Foxall *et al.* (1998: 75) Learning is conceptually related to perception. Both involve the individual customer's response to environmental and psycho-social stimuli; both can be explained theoretically in terms of either a stimulus response or a cognitive paradigm; both processes are intrinsically connected with and shaped by an individual's attitude, personality and motivation; both are important in explaining several aspects of consumer behaviour and hence are of practical concern to the marketer.

Most of what consumers know about products or services are gathered through learning. Researchers suggest there are two main types of learning, behavioural (or experiential) learning and cognitive learning, where the former sees learning as largely unconscious and the latter as a conscious mental activity.

Behavioural learning

Three factors are important to behavioural learning: association, reinforcement and motivation. Behavioural learning theory suggests that an individual develops a pattern of behavioural responses because of the rewards and punishments offered by his/her environment (Sheth *et al.* 1999). For learning to occur, therefore, it is generally accepted that what is required is a time-space proximity between the stimulus and response. Learning (or conditioning) takes place through the establishment of a connection between this stimulus and the response. There are two forms of conditioning:

- Classical (or respondent) conditioning originally identified by Ivan Pavlov. It describes a largely unconscious process through which we acquire both information and feelings about stimuli (see Box 3.7).
- Operant (or instrumental) conditioning largely based on the work of B.F. Skinner with pigeons and rats (see p. 68).

Halo effect
Those aspects of the brand that are portrayed to the outside world through marketing communications. It involves image management and the building up of benefits, brand personality and associations. It is the halo characteristics consumers use to distinguish one brand from another.

Brand extension
Extension of the brand. Using an existing brand name in a different category.

Cause-related marketing
An activity in which commercial organizations join with charities or other good causes to market a product, service or the image of the organization, for mutual benefit.

Sponsorship
A commercial activity whereby one party permits another an opportunity to exploit a situation with a target audience in return for funds, services or resources.

Behavioural learning
Suggests that an individual develops a pattern of behavioural responses because the rewards and punishments offered by his/her environment (also referred to as experiential learning).

Cognitive learning
Cognitive learning theory suggests that humans store information for different periods of time (see sensory storage, short-term memory and long-term memory).

Time-space proximity
The time between a stimulus and a response.

Classical conditioning
Originally identified by Ivan Pavlov. It describes a largely unconscious process through which we acquire both information and feelings about stimuli (also referred to as **respondent conditioning**).

Operant conditioning
Where reinforcement follows a specific response. For example do this (e.g. push a button) and you will receive a reward such as food (also referred to as **instrumental conditioning**).

Classical conditioning

Unconditioned stimulus
Something that is naturally stimulating (e.g. smell of food).

Conditioned stimulus
Something that is associated with something else that is naturally stimulating (e.g. ringing of bell means food is coming).

Conditioned response
The outcome of a conditioned stimulus. For example the ringing of a bell (conditioned stimulus) means food (unconditioned stimulus) is coming which may cause salivation (conditioned response).

Ivan Pavlov was a Russian psychologist who experimented on dogs. He began by presenting food to the animals that made them, on sight of the food, begin to salivate. He then noticed that, over time, they began to salivate before the food was presented to them. The reaction was triggered on hearing the footsteps of his assistants who brought the food to them. He began to experiment with a bell being rung as food was presented. After some time the dogs began to salivate just upon hearing the bell. The salivating response to the food itself did not have to be learned as it existed as an instinctive response. The food, therefore, was the **unconditioned stimulus**. In effect the bell became the **conditioned stimulus** and the salivating the **conditioned response**. This can be described diamagramatically as in Box 3.7 below.

The psychology of conditioned response was popular in the early twentieth century and then fell out of favour but is, according to Foxall *et al.* (1998), once again creating interest. The basic process is, according to these authors (p. 90) as follows:

a stimulus either well understood or viewed favourably produces a response in the consumer: for example feelings of pride are elicited upon seeing a nation's flag or feelings of warmth and love upon seeing a baby. In these examples the flag or baby are termed the unconditioned stimulus, and the feelings they evoke are the unconditioned response. Pairing or associating some other neutral stimulus, called the conditioned stimulus, such as a brand name, with the unconditioned stimulus will over time cause the consumer to feel the same feeling when only the brand name is encountered.

For advertisers, the ability to associate their product/services with those specific elements, such as images, emotions or perceptions that will provoke a positive response in consumers can have obvious benefits. An example, suggested by De Pelsmacker *et al.* (2001: 76) is shown in Figure 3.5 below. This suggests that a popular piece of music that produces a happy feeling

---

Box 3.7 Classical conditioning

Pavlov Research

Unconditioned Stimulus	→→→→	*Unconditioned Response*
Food	→→→→	Salivation
Conditioned Stimulus	→→→→	*Conditioned Response*
Bell	→→→→	Salivation

In marketing communications such associations are built up over time. For example:

Unconditioned Stimulus	→→→→	*Unconditioned Response*
Advertising Commercial	→→→→	Positive attitude or feeling
Conditioned Stimulus	→→→→	*Conditioned Response*
Brand	→→→→	Positive attitude or feeling

Figure 3.5 Conditioning

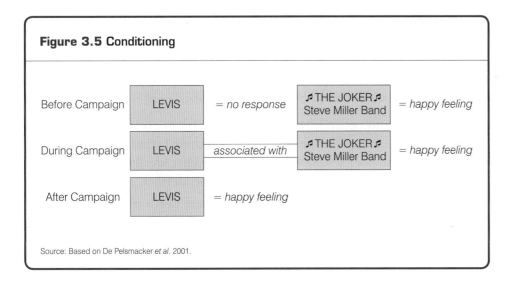

Source: Based on De Pelsmacker *et al*. 2001.

Classical conditioning

Batra *et al*. (1996) describe an experiment used to try and establish whether classical conditioning works. The research was carried out amongst 200 students who heard music being played whilst looking at an illustration of an inexpensive pen. Half the group heard familiar and popular music whilst the other half listened to music that was both unfamiliar and had previously been established was unpopular with this audience. Half of each of the two groups were exposed to a beige pen and the other half a blue pen. A total of 79 per cent picked the colour associated with the popular music. When asked why 62 per cent said they had no reason for their particular choice.

Source: Batra *et al*. (1996).

SOURCE: IMAGE COURTESY OF THE ADVERTISING ARCHIVES.

The AA Car Loans advertisements identify the benefits of the service with a successful, highly-organized couple.

when played, which is then associated with a brand during a campaign, will itself attract a positive response (happy feeling) after the campaign ends.

Marketers are not averse to using popular music (e.g. take my breadth away) or film pastiches (e.g. Thelma and Louise) as stimulants to these feelings of happiness or contentment.

- For learning to occur, however, it is necessary to create an association between the unconditioned and the conditioned stimulus and for this to be over a relatively short timeframe, ideally occurring simultaneously or in close proximity to one another.
- In order for conditioning to take place, there needs to be a relatively high repetition of the association. The more this happens, the stronger the association will be.

Operant conditioning

B.F. Skinner worked with rats that had learned to press levers in order to receive food and who later learnt only to press the lever when a light was switched on (**discriminative stimulus**). This aspect of reinforcement following a specific response is an essential feature of operant (or instrumental) conditioning. The response of the individual is likely to be affected by **positive reinforcement** (reward) or **negative reinforcement** (punishment), although the affect is likely to cease when these reinforcements are taken away.

At its simplest operant conditioning is represented by A:B:C (Blythe 2000), where A is the antecedent (or prior) stimuli, B is behaviour and C is the consequences or outcomes. (Note: the colons indicate that A does not automatically lead to B but is, however, likely to do so.) In commercial terms organizational reinforcement is created by stressing the benefits and/or rewards that the customer will receive on buying this product or service.

Marketers use this learning mechanism most effectively when they make the product its own intrinsic reward. However, when a product or service is a **parity brand** (i.e. with little or no intrinsically superior rewards compared with the competition) marketers offer extrinsic rewards (e.g. coupons, gifts, etc.) to attract patronage (Sheth *et al.* 1999).

Discriminative stimulus
This is a particular stimulus (e.g. light being switched on) that suggests if you do this (e.g. push a button) you will receive a reward (e.g. food).

Positive reinforcement
Reward which reinforces the behaviour that led to the reward.

Negative reinforcement
Punishment which reinforces the avoidance of behaviour that led to the punishment.

Learn more about cognitive experiments with rats at: **http://psychclassics.yorku.ca/ Tolman/Maps/maps.htm.**

Parity brand
A product or service with little or no intrinsically superior rewards compared with the competition, typically leaving marketers to offer extrinsic rewards to attract patronage.

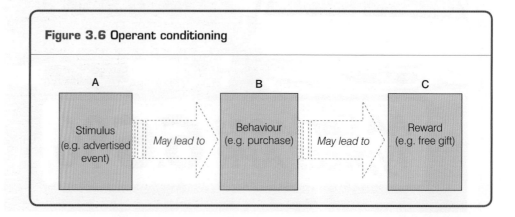

Figure 3.6 Operant conditioning

COGNITIVE LEARNING

Cognitive learning theory suggests that humans store information for different periods of time in order to manage their memory to greatest effect and have three basic levels of access:

- Sensory storage: information that is sensed for a split-second. If an impression is made this will be transferred to the short-term memory.
- Short-term memory: maximum number of items stored (perhaps four or five) for short periods of time (perhaps 8 seconds).
- Long-term memory: information stored for extensive periods of time although constant reorganization and re-categorization takes place as new information is received.

Four functions of memory increase the likelihood that information will be transferred from the short-term to the long-term memory (Foxall *et al.* 1998):

- Rehearsal: by mentally repeating the information the individual increases the chance that it will be linked to other stored information (i.e. learning by rote).
- Encoding: the process by which information is symbolically or verbally represented so that it can easily be stored and retrieved (e.g. jingles, tag lines, etc.).
- Storage: the way the memory is organized.
- Retrieval: the process where information is returned from the long-term to the short-term memory so that it can be used to make evaluations and decisions.

Evidently every consumer has differing learning capabilities so there are no hard and fast rules. A marketer can, however, assist this transfer through unique presentation, repetition, jingles, etc.

Cognitive learning is about processing information. In general information processing is a 'generic term used to describe the series of stages or steps by which information is encountered in the external world, attended to by the consumer, interpreted, understood and stored in memory for future use' (Foxall *et al.* 1998: 79). The learning takes place though three main processes:

- Iconic: developing an association between two or three concepts when there is an absence of stimulus. For example advertisers of certain products that are low-value but frequently purchased will try and remind their target audience, repeatedly, of the brand name in an attempt to help consumers learn. This is again, effectively, learning by rote.
- Modelling approach: (also called **observational learning** or **vicarious learning**.) This involves the consumer in the observation and imitation of others and the application of this to their own lives. An attractive

Sensory storage
Information that is sensed in our minds for a split-second. If an impression is made this will be transferred to the short-term memory.

Short-term memory
Maximum number of items stored (perhaps four or five) for short periods of time (perhaps 8 seconds).

Long-term memory
Information stored for extensive periods of time although constant reorganization and re-categorization takes place as new information is received.

Rehearsal
Aids memory. By mentally repeating the information the individual increases the chance that it will be linked to other stored information (i.e. learning by rote).

Encoding
The process by which information is symbolically or verbally represented so that it can easily be stored and retrieved (e.g. jingles, tag lines, etc.).

Storage
The way the memory is organized.

Retrieval
The process where information is returned from the long-term to the short-term memory.

Iconic
Developing an association between two or three concepts when there is an absence of stimulus.

Modelling approach
Where the consumer through observation and imitation of others (for example in an advertisement) associates it with their lifestyle. Also called observational learning and vicarious learning.

model wearing a particular range of clothing (for example the male model in the Levi's 501 advertisements) generates a need to pattern future behaviour. In other words the same effect (the rapt attention of on-lookers) is promised to those who do the same (purchase 501s).

Reasoning
Where consumers take the information they have about a brand and deduce their own conclusion regarding the brand's suitability for purchase and use. Individuals need to restructure and reorganize information already held in long-term memory and combine this with new information. Thus quite complex associations build up (e.g. Silk Cut cigarettes and silk ribbon).

- **Reasoning**: reasoning takes place where consumers take information they have about a brand and deduce their own conclusion regarding the brand's suitability for purchase and use (Foxall *et al*. 1998). Individual's need to restructure and reorganize information already held in long-term memory and combine this with new information. Thus quite complex associations build up (e.g. Silk Cut cigarettes and silk ribbon).

With such activity going on one might expect a degree of mental overload. Overload is, however, avoided because our mind has only the capability to process certain levels of information. To help limit and prioritize the input, consumers expose themselves to a limited number of messages (see selective attention and selective exposure).

MOTIVATION THEORY

Motivation is what moves people. It is the driving force for all human behaviour or, more formally, it is 'the state of drive or arousal that impels behaviour toward a goal objective' (Sheth *et al*. 1999). Motivational research attempts to discover the underlying motives behind consumer activity. Maslow (1954) developed a model that suggested that different needs drive each of us and

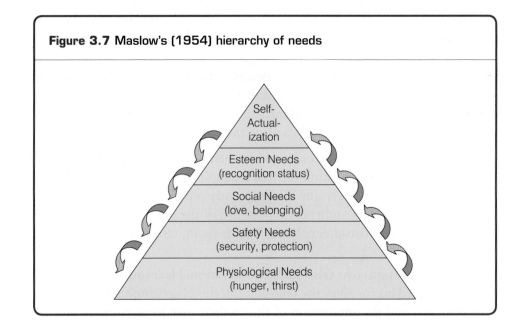

Figure 3.7 Maslow's (1954) hierarchy of needs

Self-Actual-ization

Esteem Needs
(recognition status)

Social Needs
(love, belonging)

Safety Needs
(security, protection)

Physiological Needs
(hunger, thirst)

that when a particular level of need is satisfied a higher, more aspiring need or want becomes dominant. Thus at the most basic level it is our **physiological needs** (hunger, thirst, etc.) that require satisfying. Once these are attended to **safety needs** (security, protections, etc.) become dominant. Having satisfied both physiological and safety needs **social needs** (love, belonging, etc.) and then **esteem needs** (recognition, status, etc.) come to the fore. Finally a **self-actualization** (or self-development) stage is reached where the drive for self-fulfilment is most obvious. The direction is not just in an upward direction. If disaster strikes (e.g. natural disaster or war) and the lower-order needs become once more apparent then the motivation will resort to that level. The motivational process begins when a stimulus engenders arousal or drive which is '**autonomic**' (i.e. felt physiologically and involuntarily) when faced with danger; **emotive** when, for example, you feel lonely; or **cognitive** when, for example, you are negotiating a particular situation (Sheth *et al.* 1999).

Later research suggested limitations in Maslow's theory. This included Clayton Alderfer's (1972) **ERG theory** which like Maslow describes motivational needs but unlike his model is not 'stepped' in any way. These needs are:

- Existence: physiological and safety needs (approximating Maslow's levels 1 and 2).
- Relatedness: social and external esteemness (approximating Maslow's levels 3 and 4).
- Growth: self-actualization and internal esteem needs (approximating Maslow's levels 4 and 5).

In addition to reducing the number of factors the ERG theory differed from Maslow in three ways.

1 It allows for different levels of need to be pursued simultaneously.
2 It allows the order of needs to be different for different people.
3 It acknowledges that if higher needs remain unfulfilled that the person may regress to lower levels (known as the **frustration–regression principle**).

An alternative model of persuasion is based upon **MAO factors** (Petty and Cacioppo 1986). This model suggests that it is not only motivation but ability to process information and the opportunity to make it happen that have a role to play in successful communications. The MAO factors are:

- Motivation: a willingness to engage in behaviour, make decisions, pay attention and process information.
- Ability: refers to resources needed to achieve a particular goal.
- Opportunity: the extent to which the situation enables a person to obtain his/her goal.

If MAO factors are high the consumers are willing to elaborate on the information they have been given to evaluate the argument and what is on offer. If MAO factors are low, central information processing is very

Physiological needs
(Maslow's hierarchy of needs) hunger, thirst, etc.

Safety needs
(Maslow's hierarchy of needs) security, protection, etc.

Social needs
(Maslow's hierarchy of needs) love, belonging, etc.

Esteem needs
(Maslow's hierarchy of needs) recognition, status, etc.

Self-actualization
(Maslow's hierarchy of needs) the need for self-fulfilment and a desire to achieve one's own potential.

Autonomic
A motivation or drive felt physiologically and involuntarily.

Emotive
Strong mental or instinctive feeling (e.g. love, fear, etc.).

ERG theory
(Existence, Relatedness and Growth) Clayton Alderfer's (1972) theory of motivation.

Frustration–regression principle
Suggests Clayton Alderfer's (1972) ERG theory (unlike Maslow's hierarchy of needs) if higher needs remain unfulfilled the person may regress to lower level motivations.

MAO factors
Petty and Cacioppo's (1986) model suggests that it is not only motivation but ability to process information and the opportunity to make it happen that have a role to play in successful communications. The MAO factors are Motivation (a willingness to engage in behaviour, make decisions, pay attention and process information), Ability (refers to resources needed to achieve a particular goal) and Opportunity (the extent to which the situation enables a person to obtain his/her goal).

Heuristic evaluation
Where evaluation is made based upon
extraneous factors such as price.

Arousal seeking
The motive underlying hedonic consumption
is the need to seek arousal. Hedonic
consumption refers to the use of products
or services for sheer enjoyment rather than
problem or need driven.

Hedonic consumption
The use of products or services for sheer
enjoyment rather than problem or need driven.

Need for cognition
A need to understand the world such that
it develops curiosity for further information
(see cognition).

unlikely to occur and consumers are likely to process the communication
peripherally. Decisions are made instead on the basis of certain characteristics
known as **heuristic evaluation**. Heuristic evaluations include, for example,
the perception that the higher the price is the higher the quality will be (e.g.
Stella Artois 'reassuringly expensive'), the use of celebrities to reflect on the
brand (e.g. David Beckham with Nike). Examples of heuristic evaluations are
shown in Box 3.8.

Marketing scholars have also identified some specific needs that are
especially influential in marketing. These are (Sheth *et al.* 1999: 351):

- **Arousal seeking:** the motive underlying **hedonic consumption** is the
  need to seek arousal. Hedonic consumption refers to the use of products
  or services for sheer enjoyment rather than problem or need driven.
- **Need for cognition:** a need to understand the world such that it
  develops curiosity for further information.
- **Need for attribution:** attributions are the inferences that people draw
  about events, other people and their own behaviour and include such
  factors as consistency, consensus and distinctiveness.

Box 3.8 Heuristic evaluation

Feature	Example of Heuristic Evaluation
Country of Origin	Signifies certain characteristics (e.g. French quality, Italian style, German precision, etc.)
Price	The higher the price the higher the quality and the lower the price the lesser the quality
Celebrity	The more famous the celebrity that endorses it the better the quality
Design	The more attractive the product is the better the quality
Status	The higher the perceived status (e.g. Cartier, Rolls Royce) the better the quality will be

---

Summary

This chapter reviewed those concepts and theories associated with consumer
decision making. It reviewed the cognitive and behavioural theories associated
with buying decisions and reviewed alternative suggestions. It looked at the
geodemographic and lifestyle characteristics that affect consumers and the ways
that these are used to build up consumer typologies (or buyer types). It illustrated
the importance of attitudes, perceptions, learning and motivation and their effect
on the buying process.

Review questions

1 Define the term 'front-of-mind' in relation to brand objectives.

2 If consumer products can be introduced through trial, what kind of behaviour can this lead to?

3 How can brand building behaviour reduce cognitive dissonance?

4 Identify two external factors that may influence or have an effect on purchase decisions.

5 What is the term given to the discriminator used to identify consumer needs?

6 Explain 'VALs'.

7 Describe the two main types of consumer learning.

8 In commercial terms, how is organizational reinforcement created?

9 Describe the concept of heuristic evaluation.

10 What is the 'ATR' model?

Discussion questions

1 What influences an individual's buying behaviour and do you believe it it is possible to categorize the factors in any way?

2 How might 'trait theory' influence the way in which you approached market segmentation?

3 What are the challenges faced as a consequence of the 'field of perception'?

Further reading

Andersen, P.H. and Kumar, R. (2006) 'Emotions, trust and relationship development in business relationships: A conceptual model for buyer–seller dyads', *Industrial Marketing Management*, May, 35 (4): 522–35.

Bruce, M. and Daly, L. (2006) 'Buyer behaviour for fast fashion', *Journal of Fashion Marketing & Management*, Jul., 10 (3): 329–44.

Lancastre, A. and Lages, L.F. (2006) 'The relationship between buyer and a B2B e-marketplace: cooperation determinants in an electronic market context', *Industrial Marketing Management*, Aug., 35 (6): 774–89.

Lybeck, A., Holmlund-Rytkönen, M. and Sääksjärvi, M. (2006) 'Store brands vs. manufacturer brands: consumer perceptions and buying of chocolate bars in Finland', *International Review of Retail, Distribution & Consumer Research*, Oct., 16 (4): 471–92.

McFarland, R.G., Challagalla, G.N. and Shervani, T.A. (2006) 'Influence tactics for effective adaptive selling', *Journal of Marketing*, Oct., 70 (4): 103–17.

Reinhard, M.A., Messner, M. and Ludwig, S. (2006) 'Explicit persuasive intent and its impact on success at persuasion – the determining roles of attractiveness and likeableness', *Journal of Consumer Psychology*, 16 (3): 249–59.

Chapter references

Alderfer, C.P. (1972) *Existence, Relatedness and Growth: Human Needs in Organizational Settings*, New York: The Free Press.

Batra, R., Myers, J.G. and Aaker, D.A. (1996) *Advertising Management*, Upper Saddle River, NJ: Prentice Hall.

Blackwell, R., Miniard, P.W. and Engel, J.F. *Consumer Behavior*, 10th edn, Cinncinnati: Thomson Learning.

Blythe, J. (2000) *Marketing Communications*, Harlow: Pearson Education.

De Pelsmacker, P., Geuens, M. and Van den Bergh, J. (2001) *Marketing Communications: A European Perspective*, London: Prentice Hall.

Ehrenberg, A.S.C., Goodhardt, G.J. (1979) *Essays on Understanding Buyer Behavior*, New York: J. Walter Thompson Co. and Market Research Corporation of America.

Festinger, M.J. (1957) *A Theory of Cognitive Dissonance*, Stanford, CA: Stanford University Press.

Fill, C. (2001) 'Essentially a matter of consistency: integrated marketing communications', *The Marketing Review*, 1 (4): 409–25.

Fill, C. (2002) *Marketing Communciations: Contexts, Strategies, and Applications*, 3rd edn, Harlow: Financial Times Prentice Hall.

Foxall, G.R. (1993) 'Consumer Behaviour as an Evolutionary Process', *European Journal of Marketing*, 27: 46–57.

Foxall, G., Goldsmith, R. and Brown, S. (1998) *Consumer Psychology for Marketing*, London: Thomson Learning.

Maslow, A. (1954) *Motivation and Personality*, New York: Harper & Row.

Mittal, B. and Lassar, W.B. (1998) 'Why do customers switch? The dynamics of satisfaction versus loyalty', *The Journal of Services Marketing*, 12(3): 177–94.

Onkvisit, S. and Shaw, J.J. (1994) *Consumer Behaviour, Strategy and Analysis*, New York: Macmillan.

Petty, R. and Cacioppo, J. (1986) *Communication and Persuasion: Central and Peripheral Routes to Attitude Change*, New York: Springer-Verlag.

Pickton, D. and Broderick, A. (2001) *Integrated Marketing Communications*, Harlow: Prentice Hall.

Reichheld, F.F. (1993) 'Loyalty-based management', *Harvard Business Review*, Mar–Apr, 71(2): 64–73.

Sheth, J.N., Mittal, B. and Newman, B.I. (1999) *Customer Behavior: Consumer Behavior and Beyond*, Cincinnati: Thomson Learning.

Smith, P.R. and Taylor, J. (2002) *Marketing Communications: An Integrated Approach*; 3rd edn, London: Kogan Page.

Has TV had its day?

From the initial satellite TV transmission in 1962, it was 27 years before the first UK commercial transmission by Sky in 1989 – with just four channels. The following year, BSB launched five and by 1999, following their merger, there were 60. Transferring from analogue to digital saw this figure grow to 200 a few months later. Coupled with the growing cable market and terrestrial channels, the market had exploded.

For advertisers looking to the TV as a media platform this changed their world. No longer would viewing figures of 4–6 million per programme be regularly seen. The overall number of viewers had continued to increase, but the viewing figures for individual programmes were falling as viewers exercised their choice and spread themselves across the channels. The era of mass advertising had clearly reached its peak.

Thankfully, for the advertisers, this change in the marketplace occurred alongside another revolution in daily lives; the personal computer. From the 16, 32 and 64kb machines of the early 1980s, these evolved into the 3 and 4 GHz machines of the 'noughties'. This drove the development of sophisticated modelling and database software that allowed much more accurate customer profiling and targeting.

Alongside this, and drawing on techniques from another communications discipline, direct marketing, advertising evolved into direct response advertising and became more selective in media placement and more focused upon target groups.

The new challenge, though, was accurate customer profiling and this demanded accurate customer data. In the banking industry during the

Google says the benefits of dayparting for their AdWords advertising service enables retailers to exploit intra-day and intra-week cycles of buyer behaviour.

SOURCE: © VARIO IMAGES GMBH & CO.KG/ALAMY.

1980s this was a major challenge. Long-standing customers were reluctant to divulge even simple personal facts such as date of birth.

By the mid 1990s though, this had started to change. The rise in mobile phone usage, the increase in personal computers and initiatives such as the Tesco 'clubcard' scheme in 1995 began to make people less resistant to sharing personal facts. To the extent that by the turn of the century it seemed that most inhibitions had gone.

In 2004 the BBC carried out a survey, questioning commuters passing through Liverpool Street station in London. Remarkably, when asked, many simply divulged their login and password information for their personal computers. With over 70 per cent of people being tempted to do so in exchange for a bar of chocolate!

Some 34 per cent of respondents even volunteered their password before the chocolate was offered and a similar survey also found that 79 per cent of people readily gave away personal information that could be used to steal their identity.

So gathering data on consumers had clearly never been easier. As TV channels continued to expand, technology started to give users the chance to bypass advertising or avoid it altogether and the frequency of repeats meant that even if you could profile certain viewers, identifying when they watched the target programme remained difficult.

Yet another 'revolution' occurred at the same time. The Berlin Wall 'fell' in 1989 and over the course of the 1990s not only did world markets become much more open, but the rise of the Internet made them easily accessible, for individuals and businesses alike.

The Internet as a trading platform then began to come into its own. The first wholly Internet transaction occurred in November 1994. As the medium became more and more popular, by the end of 2004 some 20 million British adults were using the Internet to shop and by 2005 it was estimated that 22 million (35 per cent of the total population) bought Christmas presents online, spending £5 billion.

The impact upon the retail high street was clear, as was the need to recognize that online buying was more than a short-term phenomenon.

British Computer Society research then identified that nearly 20 per cent of people were choosing to shop online in preference to the high street and that:

- 61 per cent of British adults claimed to have access to a home computer;
- 92 per cent of these were under 65 (21 per cent of British adults).
- The top four reasons for using the Internet were: research/fact finding (36 per cent), online purchasing (35 per cent), information/news (30 per cent), online banking (25 per cent).
- Of those purchasing online, 53 per cent purchased CDs/DVDs, 52 per cent booked holidays, 45 per cent bought clothes, 39 per cent bought insurance; and 38 per cent bought household appliances.
- 71 per cent had purchased goods or services in the past month, with 48 per cent buying at least twice, and 22 per cent at least four times.

For advertisers, the growing online shopping trend provided an attractive platform for future campaigns, yet early attempts at Web advertising, such as 'banner-ads', proved as equally difficult to quantify as TV advertising. However, June 2006 saw an announcement from the Internet search engine, Google, about the introduction of a scheduling service for advertisers, designed to allow different adverts to be shown to Web users depending on the time of day or week they surfed.

Called 'dayparting', this enabled advertisers to automatically adjust their offer or pause and resume campaigns depending upon the time of day or day of week. Allowing them to go beyond customer profiling and incorporate aspects of real-time buyer behaviour into their media planning.

For example, small businesses and local advertisers might choose to schedule their adverts to run only during business hours, when they believed that their customers might be surfing. Advertisers could potentially exploit intra-day and intra-week cycles of buyer behaviour by adjusting their campaigns in real time; and retailers could run additional adverts at lunchtime periods, reflecting the generally higher than average time for consumer purchases.

Now that the Internet is attracting such a significant proportion of the buying public and is beginning to offer relatively sophisticated targeting options, might this now become a future replacement for the TV as an advertising medium?

Case study questions

1 With reference to the buyer behaviour model, how might the changes in the TV sector have impacted upon consumer buyer behaviour?

2 Which consumer products do you believe have the most potential to attract buyers to the Internet and why, how would you categorize those buyers and why might they choose the Internet providers as their retailers of choice?

3 We live in a rapidly evolving world. What current market developments do you believe might affect future patterns of consumer buyer behaviour?

Source: Case study written by Andy Cropper, Senior Lecturer, Sheffield Hallam University.

CHAPTER FOUR

IMAGE AND BRAND MANAGEMENT

LEARNING OBJECTIVES

Having completed this chapter you should be able to:

- Recognize the importance of brands in the marketing communications process.
- Understand the factors and characteristics that contribute to the development of brands.
- Recognize the importance of branding to both the supplier and the consumer.
- Understand the theory behind brand naming, brand extension and multi-brand strategies and comprehend the importance of brand equity in the management of brands.
- Understand the importance of brand-associations to the building of brand image and personality.
- Recognize the part played by positioning in successful brand management.

INTRODUCTION

Branding is essential to marketing communications and the successes of individual brands owe much to how effectively brand owners communicate with the public. Essentially, brands are the product of an organizational intent to distinguish themselves from their competition by augmenting their products and services with values and associations that will be recognized by and have a positive meaning for customers.

There are many definitions of branding although invariably each author selects those aspects that they see as important rather than an all encompassing definition. Some prominent definitions of brands and branding are show in Box 4.1.

As can be seen from the above definitions there is little overlap in the definitions of branding other than as an identifier. By way of clarity the following is offered as a short but comprehensive working definition of branding. Branding is:

A collection of actual and emotional characteristics associated with a particular identified product or service that differentiates that product or service from the rest of the marketplace.

This definition recognizes both the tangible and intangible nature of brands and the important part that branding plays in product and service differentiation.

Box 4.1 Definitions of branding

Wells, Burnett and Moriarty (1995)	Branding: the process of creating an identity for a product using a distinctive name or symbol.
De Chernatony and McDonald (1998)	A successful brand is an identifiable product, service, person or place augmented in such a way that a buyer or user perceives relevant, unique added values which matches their needs quite closely.
Kotler (2000)	(A brand is) a name, term, sign, symbol or design or a combination of these intended to identify the goods and services of one seller or group of sellers to differentiate them from their competitors.
Pickton and Broderick (2001)	Branding is not just a case of placing a symbol or name onto products to identify the manufacturer, a brand is a set of attributes that have a meaning, an image and produce associations with the product when a person is considering that brand of product.

BRAND CHARACTERISTICS

Core
Functional characteristics such as basic product/service, shape/texture, performance and physical capacity. Any changes in the core aspects would directly alter the generic product or service. Also called 'intrinsic' part of a brand.

Augmented
Augmented aspects of a brand include packaging/presentation, price/terms, guarantees, extras (for example built-in software) and after-sales support. Any change in augmented characteristics does not alter the basic function or performance but may affect competitive advantage, trust and other subjective measures of the brand's value.

Although very much a simplification it is useful to visualize a 'brand' as a halo around a product or service offering. Beneath the halo is the **core** (also called 'intrinsic') and **augmented** (also called 'extrinsic') aspects associated with a product or service as represented in Figure 4.1. Core aspects of the brand include functional characteristics such as basic product/service, shape/texture, performance and physical capacity. Any changes in the core aspects would directly alter the generic product or service. Augmented aspects include packaging/presentation, price/terms, guarantees, extras (for example built-in software) and after-sales support. Any change in augmented characteristics does not alter the basic function or performance but may affect competitive advantage, trust and other subjective measures of the brand's value. The 'halo' is that aspect of the brand that is portrayed to the outside world through marketing communications. It involves image management and the building up of benefits, brand personality and associations. It is the halo characteristics consumers use to distinguish one brand from another.

In communicating the brand halo characteristics marketers choose those elements of the brand that will be most attractive to the target audience and which satisfies the current marketing communication objectives

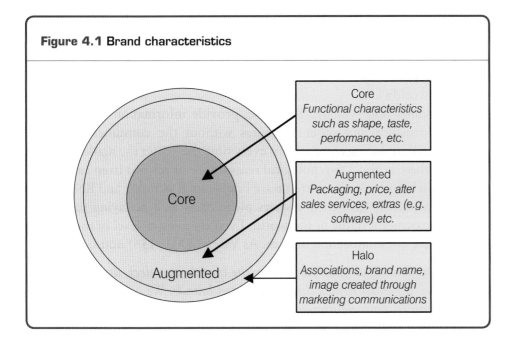

Figure 4.1 Brand characteristics

Core

Augmented

Core
*Functional characteristics
such as shape, taste,
performance, etc.*

Augmented
*Packaging, price, after
sales services, extras (e.g.
software) etc.*

Halo
*Associations, brand name,
image created through
marketing communications*

(awareness, trial, etc.). These factors may include (Biel 1997):

- Brand skills/benefits: What the brand will do for you (e.g. relieve headache, help grass grow greener, etc.).

- Brand personality: The perceived lifestyle associations and values (e.g. status, fashion, quality, etc.).

- Brand interaction   Brand's relationship with customer (e.g. loyalty, closeness, habit, etc.).

- Brand experience   Providing other brand related experiences (e.g. Tango Roadshow, Pepsi Charts, Red Bull Soap Box Derby, etc.).

BENEFITS OF BRANDING

Customers and organizations both benefit from branding. From the customer perspective recognition is an important feature. With experience a customer learns to recognize preferred (as well as non-preferred) brands. For the consumer, once they have experienced the brand (which may be through consumption or 'virtually' through communication) they are likely to be more comfortable with that brand and this tends to lower perceived risk. If for example a business man or woman is travelling for the first time in the Far East they might choose to stay at a branded chain of hotels such as Holiday Inn or Hilton. This is not necessarily because these hotels offer better value

Brand promise
The promise(s) (e.g. safety, comfort, etc.) associated with a particular brand. Broken brand promises may lead to a reassessment of the brand.

or additional comfort but because the traveller has a good indication what to expect from any of their hotels worldwide. This reduces the risk of any unpleasant surprises during the trip. In affect the **brand promise** of these groups are that they will deliver a level of service that consumers would recognize worldwide.

Brand names and symbols, therefore, provide information about quality, taste, performance and other attributes without the consumer having to undertake risk-reducing comparisons every time they enter the market. For the consumer there is also a psychological reassurance or reward from association with certain brands. At one extreme are brands such as Rolex and Rolls Royce which undoubtedly give their owners pleasure as well as saying something about their owner's status in the world. Even on a lesser level brands can be very effective communication devices. As Varey (2002: 156) notes:

> we say something about ourselves by the brands we select, discard and consume. We enact rituals through selected brands. We can also read other peoples' personalities and make judgements about relationships and situations that will make us feel good. Some brands can even help us communicate something to ourselves.

Differentiation
The process of making the organization's brand different from other brands through marketing.

Differentiation from the competition is important in brand building. The origin of the commercial usage of the term branding came from the practice of branding cattle with marks that distinguished ownership. Commercial branding (name, symbols, etc.) also denotes ownership and that the brand is the property of the brand owner. This allows for a certain level of legal protection against **brand pirates** who might seek to pass-off brand characteristics as their own. It was this protection that United Biscuits sought for its Penguin chocolate snack bar against a similar supermarket brand Puffin. Commercial branding also became a means of distinguishing an owner's 'superior product' in comparison to generic product or other brands. In 1924, for example, the New Zealand Dairy Company started to pre-package butter under the Anchor brand. For retailers this was welcomed as a time-saving exercise (as they did not have to cut, weigh and wrap the product) but, importantly, it developed a relationship between the customer and the brand (Brierley 2002).

Brand pirates
Those who seek to pass-off brand characteristics (e.g. package design) as their own.

Where risk reduction is a factor in choice successful brand owners are often able to obtain premier pricing over and about the competition from other branded and non-branded competitors. In the days when IBM was the world's leading computer brand, for example, there was a common saying in the computer purchasing industry that 'you would never get sacked if you bought IBM'. In other words buying IBM was the safe option. You knew the standard to expect and that the purchase was relatively risk-free. You could buy cheaper brands but would you take the risk of it going wrong?

@

See advertising the 'brand' in action at:
www.brandpower.com/.

Branding also offers other benefits to the brand owner. As will be discussed later it also offers opportunities for cross-product development (see brand extension) and encourages thematic consistency supporting **integrated marketing communications** as well as strengthening corporate identity.

Integrated marketing communications
A concept of marketing communications planning that recognizes the added value of a comprehensive plan, that evaluates the strategic roles of a variety of communication disciplines and combines these disciplines to provide clarity, consistency and maximum communications impact.

A summary of the perceived consumer and organizational benefits of branding are shown in Box 4.2.

Box 4.2 Brand benefits

Customer Benefits of Branding	Organizational Benefits of Branding
Assists in the identification of those products and services preferred	Helps differentiate the product or service from the competition
Reduces level of perceived risk	Enables premium pricing (e.g. in situations of perceived reduced risk)
Makes it easier to assess product or service quality	Enhances cross-product promotion and assists the development and use of integrated marketing communications
Reduces the time taken in making product or service selection	Provides for greater thematic consistency and uniform communications
Can provide psychological reassurance and/or reward	Encourages customer loyalty/retention and/or repeat-purchase behaviour
Gives clues about the source and any associated values	Contributes to corporate identity and provides some legal protection

BRAND IDENTITY

Brand identity is a composite of those features of a brand that make it recognizable and it essentially forms the trigger for those 'light bulb' moments in the mind. These identity features include brand names, which can be vocalized or written, and symbols, colours, shapes, etc. that are recognized through sight. Key aspects in a brand identity programme are:

- Design element
- Statements
- Application

Design elements include the logo, graphic features, typeface, symbols and colours that stimulate the recognition and remembrance of a brand. Examples of strong design characteristics include the McDonald's 'golden arches' and the Coca-Cola traditional bottle design. Both are twentieth-century icons recognized around the world.

Statements refer to how the brand is promoted and to copy style and slogans (or tag lines). Slogans can become as distinctive as the brand itself. Thus British Airways was 'the world's favourite airline', Carlsberg is 'probably the best lager in the world' and Stella Artois is 'reassuringly expensive'. In this last example the slogan, which makes clever use of human psychology, turned an obscure Belgian beer in to one of the UK's biggest beer brands. Stella Artois do not claim that their beer is any better than any other rather it lets the customer make the connection with quality. 'Reassuringly expensive' flatters the Stella Artois drinker prepared to pay for this quality.

Application refers to corporate advertising, stationery, signage, livery, etc. and is not so much a separate category of design as a reminder that all

Design elements (of a brand)
Include the logo, graphic features, typeface, symbols and colours that stimulate the recognition and remembrance of a brand.

Logo
An emblem or device used to distinguish an organization or brand.

Graphic features
Those features that distinguish a brand (e.g. McDonald's 'golden arches').

Typeface
The style of letters used within an advertisement or other communication.

Statements
What is said about the brand and how it is promoted, such as copy style and slogans.

Slogans
Memorable phrases that sum up an important characteristic of the brand, such as 'the world's favourite airline' (also referred to as tag lines).

Application
Attention to other aspects of branding such as corporate advertising, stationery, signage, livery, etc.

Corporate advertising
Advertising designed to promote and enhance the image of the company amongst its target publics.

Signage
The identity applied to buildings, vehicles etc. denoting the organization or its brand(s).

Livery
See signage. Particularly relates to vehicles.

organizational messages affect the image of the company/brand not just the planned communications associated with advertising, public relations, etc.

BRAND TRUSTWORTHINESS

Hand in hand with risk reduction goes trust in a brand. As trust grows perceived risk is shown to diminish. Trust in a brand (whether it is a supplier's distributor's or retailer's brand) is important in everyday retail situations but is particularly important when buying through direct response, mail order or over the Internet. If you know the brand (even though you may not know the retailer) and you are confident enough to purchase from this unknown source (particularly if there an Internet trust mark or credit card guarantee against Internet fraud), the risk may appear limited. In the reverse case a consumer may trust an unknown brand from a reputed (bricks or clicks)[1] retailer. Research by Hoddleston and Cassil (1990) confirm that consumers use a brand name as a cue to assess quality and that this is used, where appropriate, to justify a higher price. Ideally both retail and supplier brands would be trusted (e.g. Rolex at Goldsmiths, Sony at Harrods) and you would have what is referred to a **double-header**.

Nationally some brands are trusted more than others. Box 4.3 shows the results of the 2006 Reader's Digest survey of the most trusted brands in the UK. There is a strong correlation between trusted brands and those in a consumer's evoked set (see Chapter 3). As an earlier *Marketing* survey noted:

> *Trust is a cornerstone of any successful brand. It reassures the customer that the product or service they are buying will live up to expectations. It's a basic deal: if the brand delivers, it's rewarded; if it falls short, the customer will almost certainly take their business elsewhere. (Curtis 2004: 28)*

Double-header
Quality brand on sale in a quality outlet (e.g. Rolex in Harrods).

@

Useful industry insights into current brand activities can be found at:
www.brandrepublic.com/magazines/campaign.

BRAND SALIENCE

A desired outcome of brand marketing communications is to make a brand salient (i.e. important, prominent, noticeable) in its **consideration set** (Ehrenberg *et al.* 1997) or evoked set (see Chapter 3). A consideration set might be visualized as a basket of brands in a particular category from which the consumer's selection(s) are made. Consistency of quality and satisfaction over time may lead buyers to trust a brand, which in turn may raise it in their minds to a position of priority in their product choice set. Thus positively influencing their repeat purchase activity. Research indicates that few consumers stick loyally to one brand, however, and over time they

[1]The term 'bricks and clicks' is used to distinguish between off-line (i.e. premises situated) retailers and online retailers.

Box 4.3 *Reader's Digest* trusted brands survey 2006

Category	Brand	Category	Brand
Airline	British Airways	Kitchen Appliance	Hotpoint
Analgesic	Nurofen	Margarine/Butter	Flora
Bank	Lloyds/TSB	Mobile Handset	Nokia
Breakfast Cereal	Kellogg's	Mobile Network	Orange
Camera	Canon	Mortgage Lender	Halifax
Car	Ford	Motor Organization	AA
Car Hire	Hertz	Optician	Specsavers
Coffee	Nescafe	Personal Computers	Dell
Cosmetics	Boots	Pet Food	Whiskas
Cough/Cold Remedy	Beechams	Petrol Retailer	Tesco
Credit Card	Visa	Shoe Retailer	Clarks
Food Retailer	Tesco	Skincare	Nivea
Haircare	Pantene	Soap Powder	Persil
Hayfever Remedy	Piriton	Suncare	Boots/Nivea
Holiday Company	Thomson Holidays	Tea	PG Tips
Household Cleaner	Cif	Toothpaste	Colgate
Indigestion Remedy	Rennie	Utility Company	British Gas
Insurance Company	Norwich Union	Vitamins	Seven Seas
Internet Company	AOL		

Source: *Marketing*, 12 April 2006.

will purchase from a number of brands in the consideration (or evoked) set. Even if a consumer is largely loyal to one particular brand they may consider substituting this for another brand for a short or extended period when:

- the favourite brand is out of stock;
- the competitive factors tip the balance towards a competitive brand (e.g. promotional price offer);
- a new offer (new or updated product) promises more than the existing offer;
- the customer wants variety or acts spontaneously (i.e. impulse buying).

This brand salience is more than just **brand recall** (i.e. the ability to recall from memory brands in a particular category) and may indeed be largely subconscious on the part of the buyer. Brand salience requires, on the part of the consumer (Varey 2002: 159):

- Awareness (of the product or service).
- Interest (to a larger or lesser degree).
- Assurances (as to quality, service, price, etc.).
- Familiarity and acceptance.
- Consistency (of product or service attributes).
- Habitual choosing (building up over time).

It is the responsibility of the marketer to convey these salient points to potential consumers.

DETERMINANTS OF SUCCESSFUL BRANDS

A successful brand is one that develops and sustains over time a strong, positive image in the minds of consumers. Dibb *et al.* (1997) suggested that there are certain determinants of brands that are regarded as successful:

- They are invariably good quality. It is easier to build distinctiveness through quality than price.
- They frequently offer additional, superior services that are less easy to replicate.

MINICASE 4.1

It only takes one

In June 2006 the insurance company, Norwich Union, published the results of research into drivers' bad road habits, based on the views of 300 fleet managers in the UK. For any UK driver the catalogue of problems highlighted, from speeding to a lack of consideration for other road users, is probably unsurprising, but concerns over alcohol and drug abuse by drivers, coupled with insufficient checks on vehicles probably are.

Vehicle branding is a crucial marketing feature for Eddie Stobart, with a 2006 revamp described by the company as utilizing "the latest sign making technology . . . to present a powerful new image in our highly competitive market."

SOURCE: © EDDIE STOBART LIMITED.

For the companies who own the vehicles there are wider consequences. Put simply by Lindsay Guy, Norwich Union fleet underwriting manager, 'How can businesses ensure that their drivers are driving safely while their company name is often visible on the side of the vehicle?'

Branded vehicles are every bit as important in the integrated communications mix as TV adverts or shop displays. They are almost constantly in view and their appearance and activities are seen by a wide range of stakeholders. How can companies ensure, therefore, that brand investment is not undermined by this most visible medium?

Minicase written by Andy Cropper, Senior Lecturer, Sheffield Hallam University.

- Pioneers (or first-movers) often become leading brands.
- Good brands have unique benefits that differentiate them from the competition.
- Successful brands adopt consistent and integrated marketing communications strategies.
- Good brands are not built overnight.

A successful brand will have several facets, and a useful mnemonic for identifying these is VIEW (Twedt 1968). These are:

- **V** Visibility (implying exposure to the target audience)
- **I** Informative (concerning brand benefits)
- **E** Emotional appeal (building up the personality of the brand)
- **W** Workability (how the brand package functions)

Undoubtedly successful brands appear to have these characteristics but will still require constant monitoring. No brand is totally safe and the fall from top brand status may be the first step in a downward spiral unless action can be taken to halt the decline. What causes brands to become unpopular is often more to do with fickle factors such as fashion trends although quality again seems to be an important determinant (see Box 4.4). A hated brand may also be highly popular with some of the population (for example Manchester United also appears on the most popular football brands list). An unpopular brand can resurrect itself. Eastern European vehicle manufacturer Skoda was in the 1990s derided for their poor quality and because they were extremely difficult to resell (even though they were relatively cheap). The purchase of the company by Volkswagen has led to a renaissance in design and quality. The legacy of the 1990s, however, is still there as the company in its advertising asks consumers to believe that the car really is a *Skoda!* (see Minicase 15.1).

Box 4.4 The top-twenty most hated UK brands 2006

1	Pot Noodle (snack)	11	Lidl (supermarket)
2	QVC (TV direct sales channel)	12	Manchester United (football team)
3	Novon (Sainsbury's washing powder)	13	Sky Sports (TV channels)
4	McDonald's (fast food)	14	Snack-a-Jacks (snacks)
5	Tiny (computer supplier)	15	TK Maxx (clothing retailer)
6	Fiat (motor company)	16	Pifco (electricals)
7	3 (mobile phone operator)	17	Allders (department store)
8	*The Star* (newspaper)	18	Kwik Save (supermarket)
9	Sunny Delight (drink)	19	Ferrero Rocher (chocolate)
10	*The Sun* (newspaper)	20	MFI (furniture store)

Source: *Marketing*, 17 May 2006/Josua Consumer Check.

BRAND COMMUNICATION STRATEGIES

Stand-alone brands or master brands?:
**www.honeywell.com/sites/brandM/
standb2mb.htm.**

Brand associations
Those associations built in the consumer's
mind between the brand and something else
that is important and/or enjoyable
(e.g. football).

Line extension
Using an existing brand within a category to
introduce new lines within that category (e.g.
Persil tablets).

Brand extension
Extension of the brand. Using an existing
brand name in a different category.

Brand communication strategies start with a decision as to whether or not to put a brand name on a product and of what sort. The success rates for new brand introductions, however, are not good. A Boston Consulting Group study in the USA showed that in 19 of 22 consumer goods categories the brand leader in 1925 was still the brand leader in 1985 (Varey 2002). However, if a new brand is introduced there are a number of brand naming strategies designed to fulfil different brand objectives. These are shown in Box 4.5 below (also see **brand associations**).

New brands, if they are to be successful, require considerable investment. If the investment is considered too high to launch an entirely new brand a company may decide to use an existing brand name in one of two ways:

- Line extension: using an existing brand within a category for new lines within that category (e.g. Persil tablets).
- Brand extension: using an existing brand name in a different category (e.g. Mars ice cream).

Normally brand extension is in complementary categories, for example the move by confectionery brand owners Mars, Cadbury and Nestlé into the ice cream market. In some instances the brand extension is much more

Box 4.5 Brand naming strategies	
Stand-alone brands	Brands that are not directly associated with a particular manufacturer or retailer for the purpose of communication (e.g. Persil).
Corporate brands	Brands that rely heavily on the corporate name, whether or not a sub-brand is used (e.g. Mercedes 320, Renault Clio).
Own label	Carries the name of the retailer (e.g. Sainsbury's coffee) or the retailer's exclusive brand name (e.g. Dunne's Stores – St Bernard).
Super own label	Exclusive brands created for emphasis or thematic purposes (e.g. Blue Harbour at Marks & Spencer, George at Asda).
Generic brands	Basic own label range with limited packaging (e.g. Tesco's value range).
Exclusive brands	Brands that, although theoretically independent, trade on an exclusive basis with a single retailer (e.g. Ladybird at Woolworth).
Component brand	Where a brand is incorporated into another product (e.g. Intel, Nutrasweet).
Complementary branding	Where two brands combine to strengthen an offer (e.g. Braun and Oral B electric toothbrush).
Co-operative branding	Joint venture schemes (e.g. Ryanair with MBNA on the Ryanair.com credit card).

dramatic. One of the best examples of this kind of brand extension is Virgin whose brand name has adorned, at various times, everything from trains to insurance and records to trans-Atlantic passenger planes.

In normal circumstances brand extension requires some sort of fit with the existing brand although not necessarily in an associated category (Virgin is again an obvious exception to this maxim). Thus most consumers would question the company's strategy if a cereal company such as Kellogg's were to enter the dog-food market, whereas snack bars are quite an acceptable and rational extension. Bic's entry into the perfume market made sense to them because they perceived a gap in the perfumery market for inexpensive fragrances. They failed to realize that it was not just the scent that the consumer was buying but a lifestyle choice and not one associated with Bic's brand image. On the other hand for Harley-Davidson and Guinness to produce clothing ranges does not raise too many eye-brows.

The advantages of line and brand extension to the communication process are manyfold. Communication costs are lower if a consumer already holds a positive image of a brand. Retailers are more prone to using limited shelf space for an existing brand rather than an unknown one. To the consumer the brand name contains a promise of quality that reduces the purchase risk associated with new, untried, products or services. An obvious downside lies in the possibility that the brand or line extension may damage the brand's image. The problems associated with introduction of the Mercedes A-series was nothing short of highly embarrassing for the company and without doubt affected the brand's formerly unblemished reputation for reliability.

Multi-branding is in many ways the opposite of line and brand extensions and is where different names are used in the same product category. An example of a producer who uses a multi-branding strategy is Procter & Gamble. Box 4.6 shows that, in the detergent category alone Procter & Gamble have 11 brands in North America, 16 in Latin America, 12 in Asia and 17 in Europe. In some markets this proliferation of brands is historical. As noted in Chapter 1, as markets became more saturated segments were 'sliced' even thinner with brands created for each, ever smaller segment. In other situations these brands were introduced as **flanker brands** (Clow and Baack 2004), taking advantage of a supplier's market strength to compete against competitor brands for shelf space.

Given the difficulties, multi-brand owners have looked to rationalize the number of brands in their portfolios, particularly where the same product was being sold under different brand names in different markets. Thus in the UK Marathon became Snickers, Opal Fruits became Starburst and Jif became Cif. In other instances takeovers have led to brand changes, for example when One-2-One became T-Mobile. In these situations investment in the original brand names (considerable in the case of One-2-One) is effectively lost and the brand owner must invest further resources in communicating the name change and the personality and associations allied to it. In some instances the brand name(s) are the reason for acquiring established businesses (e.g. Nestlé's takeover of Rowntree). In NCL's agreed takeover of Virgin Mobile it was the latter's brand name that was retained as it was seen to be more in tune with the

Multi-branding
Where different brand names owned by one company are used in the same product category (e.g. Procter & Gamble soap powers Dreft, Daz and Bold).

Flanker brands
Where a supplier takes advantage of its market strength to introduce additional brands which compete against the competition brands for shelf space.

Box 4.6 Procter & Gamble detergent brands

	North America	Latin America	Asia	Europe		North America	Latin America	Asia	Europe
Ace		◆		◆	Ivory Snow	◆			
Alo				◆	Lanxiang			◆	
Ariel		◆	◆	◆	Lenor				◆
Azurit				◆	Limay		◆		
Bold	◆	◆		◆	Magna Blanca		◆		
Bonus			◆		Maintax				◆
Bonux				◆	Myth				◆
Bounce	◆		◆	◆	ODD Fases		◆		
Cheer	◆		◆		Oxydol	◆			
Dash				◆	Panda			◆	
Daz				◆	Perla			◆	
Doll			◆		Pop		◆		
Downey	◆	◆			Quanto		◆		
Dreft	◆			◆	Rapido		◆		
Dryel	◆				Rei				◆
Duplex		◆			Rindex		◆		
Era	◆				Romtensid		◆		
Ezee			◆		Supremo		◆		
Fairy				◆	Tide	◆	◆	◆	◆
Gain	◆				Tix				◆
Gaofuli			◆		Trilo			◆	
InExtra		◆							

Source: Based on Clow and Baack 2004: 44, Table 2.1.

joint company's target audience. It is perhaps most difficult to change names when the 'old' and the 'new' brand personalities seem to be in conflict. This situation demands a degree of creativity if it is to be pulled off. Thus when Freeserve, whose advertising was based on free-spirited, tree-hugging hippies, became Wannadoo,[2] whose brand aspirations were those of a solid citizen and mainstream, a creative approach was called for. In the advertising that announced the brand change the Freeserve hippies were seen shaving off their beards and abandoning their 1960s lifestyle to rejoin the mainstream.

Another reason for brand rationalization in the fast moving consumer goods (fmcg) category is the growing strength of grocery retailers. Whereas in the period 1950–70 it would be commonplace to see as many as four or five brands from one category on a retailer's shelves, today it is more common place to see, alongside the retailers own brand or brands, the **brand leader**, and perhaps the second brand in the category.

Brand leader
The leading brand in a particular category.

[2]Wannadoo has since become Orange which involved yet another image change.

In the 1990s there has been a noticeable trend towards corporate branding particularly (but not exclusively) in the high-technology categories where product turnover is high. It also reflects the high cost of launching new brands often without a guarantee of long-term success. One estimate of the scale of financial involvement towards the end of the twentieth century was that the cost of both launching a brand in Europe or North America and then supporting it in its early years would leave little change out of £1 billion/€1.5 billion (Mottram 1998).

BRAND LIFE CYCLE

The brand life cycle is an adaptation of the product life cycle discussed in Chapter 2. Just as product life cycles predict that a product or service has a natural (but immeasurable) life span so brands are supposed to go through a process as indicated in Figure 4.2.

The **brand life cycle**, quite reasonably on the surface, suggests that brands have different life-stages through which they pass (as has the product life cycle which it mirrors). The introduction of a brand involves investment and starting from scratch in a market can be a slow process. It can take time for a brand to build up the level of confidence (and, therefore, reduce the level of risk), which is a prerequisite to purchase. The growth stage represents a period of growing popularity and acceptance and, perhaps, greater competition. There then comes a point where growth levels off. When this occurs, brand loyalty can suffer and brand awareness decline. To recover from this can

Brand life cycle
Suggests that brands have different life-stages through which they pass (also see product life cycle).

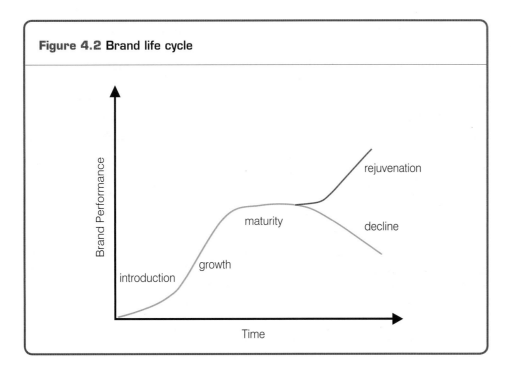

Figure 4.2 Brand life cycle

often require a significant effort on behalf of the organization, drawing on exceptional levels of creativity and rejuvenation. At some point, however, a decision has to be made as to whether to let a brand naturally decline or to invest in its revival. With brands such as Harley-Davidson and Brylcreem investment (driven by changes in fashion) have reversed what appeared to be the terminal decline of these brands. Old abandoned brands have also been brought back to life. In November 2004 it was announced that the Huntley & Palmer biscuit brand, founded originally in 1822, was to be re-launched after a ten-year absence.

The problem with product or brand life cycles is that they are disconnected from time. One brand may last less than a year whereas there are many examples of brands over a century old that, un-rejuvenated, show little sign of decline. As noted in Chapter 2 brands at differing points in the brand or life cycle will have differing marketing and marketing communications' objectives and strategies (see Box 2.4).

BRAND EQUITY

An alternate way of expressing the strength and duration of a brand is through the concept of brand equity. Accountants have argued for years about the value of brands (i.e. the value of owning a particular brand name compared to a generic brand), with all its history, associations and personality. The equity is an important indication to the marketer of the return on investment of marketing and in particular marketing communications. It is this 'added value' that accumulates through investment over time. This 'added value' used to be termed 'goodwill' and was the disparity between the firm's basic asset value and the true worth of the business (with its brands). Thus when an organization was sold it was valued as the sum of its assets plus a figure for goodwill that represented that business' appeal in the marketplace over and above a company starting in that marketplace from scratch. This added value was most dramatically illustrated by Nestlé's takeover of Rowntree. The value of the assets of the company (estimated to be £2.5 billion) paled into insignificance compared with valuations put on brand names such as Kit-Kat and After Eight. Nestlé reportedly paid around six-times the asset worth to secure ownership of these brands.

This goodwill value is now more often called **brand equity**. In economic terms this brand equity might be regarded as the sum of future profits associated with the brand discounted over time.[3] The valuation is not fixed, however. A purchasing company may think that it can increase the brand equity by managing the brand in a different way. Thus when Ford Motor

Goodwill
The disparity between the firm's asset value and the true worth of the business.

Brand equity
The value of owning a particular brand name compared to a generic brand of the same type in the same category.

---

[3]Other types of valuation such as cost-based valuation, market-based valuation and income-based valuation are used to value brands but the intricacies of these methodologies are beyond the remit of this text.

Company acquired Jaguar the consensus at the time was that the purchase cost would never be recouped. Ford, however, believed that they could lever additional value under their ownership.

Brand valuations are produced for various reasons including budget allocation, brand portfolio review, performance benchmarking, balance-sheet calculations and other company valuations. Different methodologies will produce different valuations. Rather than using a simple discounted rate of return Interbrand, the brand development agency which annually produce valuations of the world's biggest brands, uses four criteria for their valuation:

1 **Financial analysis:** a review of the business earnings.

2 **Market analysis:** the percentage of earnings attributed to the brand (branding index).

3 **Brand analysis:** the strength of the brand as perceived by consumers (brand strength score).

4 **Legal analysis:** how well the brand is legally protected.

A change in any of the financial, market, brand or legal factors can dramatically affect brand equity and, if it is owned by a quoted public company, that company's share price.

In Box 4.7 is Interbrand's valuation of the world's top ten brands for 2006.

Financial analysis
A review of the business earnings contributing to a brand's equity.

Market analysis
The percentage of earnings attributed to a brand.

Brand analysis
The strength of the brand as perceived by consumers.

Legal analysis
How well a brand is legally protected.

Box 4.7 World's most valuable brands 2006 vs 2003

Rank	Brand	Value $Bn	Rank	Brand	Value $Bn
1	Coca-Cola	67.00	11	Citi (Citigroup)	21.46
2	Microsoft	56.93	12	Marlboro	21.35
3	IBM	56.20	13	Hewlett-Packard	20.46
4	GE	48.91	14	American Express	19.64
5	Intel	32.32	15	BMW	19.62
6	Nokia	30.13	16	Gillette	19.58
7	Toyota	27.94	17	Louis Vuitton	17.61
8	Disney	27.85	18	Cisco	17.53
9	McDonald's	27.50	19	Honda	17.05
10	Mercedes	21.80	20	Samsung	16.17

Source: Interbrand's 100 Best Global Brands 2006, *Business Week*, 7 August 2006.

Coopers and Simons (1997: 42) have taken the concept of brand equity one stage further with the brand equity lifestyle model as shown in Figure 4.3.

As with the brand and product life cycles the equity model proposes that a brand's value goes through life stages. These stages are indicated on the model and are represented as follows:

● P1: The rapidly rising brand equity of a relatively new brand. This does not apply to all new brands but for those with flair. Often associated with entrepreneurial brands. Examples of P1 companies currently might be Virgin Direct, Goldfish, Egg and MoreThan.

- P2: Mature brands. Major concerns here are brand maintenance and defence against competition. Examples might include British Airways, Dixons and Barclays.
- P3: Perceived to be waning brands (e.g. Woolworth) or those which seem to have disappeared (Smedleys).
- S1: Formerly declining brand that is experiencing or has managed its own resurgence (e.g. BHS, RAC, Brylcreem and Harley Davidson).
- S2: A brand whose equity continues to fall without or despite efforts to turn it around.

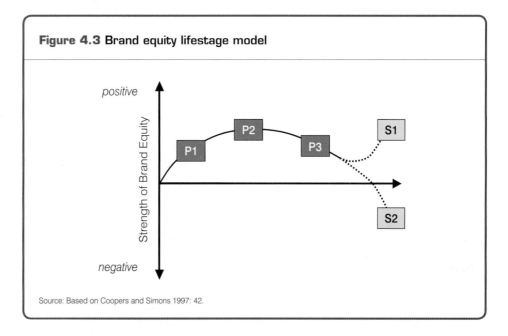

Figure 4.3 Brand equity lifestage model

Source: Based on Coopers and Simons 1997: 42.

BRAND ASSOCIATIONS

The building of brand associations is critical to developing the image and personality of a brand. As will be discussed in Chapter 8 this is normally through the development of a **creative platform** for the brand. There are strategies that can be used to further develop positive brand associations:

- Sponsorship
- Co-branding
- Geographical identifiers
- Ingredient brands
- Support services
- Award symbols

Creative platform
The creative idea on which a campaign is built.

Sponsorship is one of the major ways that companies build brand associations. Beer companies (e.g. Heineken, Ansells, Tetleys, Carling, and Stella Artois) for example, frequently sponsor sporting events. They see their target customers as those audiences most closely linked with each particular sport and the sponsorship is a means of building that association in the consumer's mind. Sponsorship will be covered in more detail in Chapter 15.

Co-branding takes two distinct forms. The first involves joint marketing of products or services such that both (or more) brands benefit in terms of exposure (e.g. Hotpoint and Persil). The second, more commonly known as cause-related marketing, involves a charitable partner (e.g. NSPCC with Microsoft). Research (e.g. Webb and Mohr 1998) suggests that, given the choice between purchasing a product or service from a company that supports a charity and one that does not, unsurprisingly most consumers would choose the one that was charity associated. It may also help those brands that wish to be associated with caring and/or community.

Geographical identifiers can help the building of positive associations with a place. Caffrey's beer exploits its Irishness, Walker's shortbread, in its distinctive tartan packaging, leaves the consumer in no doubt about its Scottish origins. On the other hand McDonald's North American heritage makes it the target for anti-globalization demonstrations. A brand's heritage can be powerful and should be protected if it provides distinct advantage. British Airways sought to distance itself from its British origins by redesigning its livery to reflect cultures from around the world. The decision was reversed when it became apparent that British passengers saw it as a form of betrayal whilst overseas passengers saw the airline's 'Britishness' as part of the brand's personality.

Ingredient brands capitalize on the use of quality ingredients or components to enhance the value of both brands. Intel processors, for example, are regarded almost as a requirement in any brand of personal computer as is Dolby sound in any quality sound system.

Support services are frequently used to develop a distinct brand image. Indeed in many product categories it is frequently the only thing that differentiates one brand from another. In the highly competitive carrier market, for example, UPS offer customers an Internet accessible tracking system that most of the competition cannot match, and that positions them as an efficient and trusted organization.

Award symbols give credibility to a brand and set quality benchmarks. This has proved to be particularly important in situations where some form of guarantee is required to reduce purchase risk (e.g. Internet purchases). In the highly intangible field of education, where status is an important asset, award symbols represent an important differentiator. In Europe many business schools and other institutions offer Masters in Business Administration (MBA) programmes. Of these only a limited number are accredited by the Association of MBAs (AMBA) who maintain rigorous standards through formal validations and inspections. This AMBA accreditation is seen as the quality benchmark by potential MBA students.

Co-branding
Appears in two forms: (1) involves joint marketing of products or services such that both brands benefit in terms of exposure (e.g. Hotpoint and Persil) (2) involves a charitable partner (e.g. NSPCC with Microsoft).

Geographical identifiers
Signs and symbols that suggest a particular geographical location.

Ingredient brands
Where a branded ingredient or component is incorporated in another brand.

Award symbols
Symbols that represent that a certain level of status has been gained by the brand (e.g. accreditation, awards, etc.).

BRAND POSITIONING

Positioning
The process of creating a perception in the consumer's mind regarding the nature of the company and its products relative to the competition.

Benefit positioning
Positioning on the basis of brand benefits. These can be both functional and emotional.

User positioning
User benefits relate to the specific profile of the target audience and is commonly accomplished with the aid of demographic and psychographic variables which denote specific lifestyle characteristics.

Competitive positioning
Focuses on the relative advantages of the brand relative to its competition. This type of positioning is often used to establish the profile of a new brand or to distinguish an existing brand in a highly competitive marketplace.

Multi-dimensional skills map
Matrix used to establish a customer's view of the organization relative to its competitors (also referred to as a perception map).

Positioning may be described as 'the act of designing the company's offering and image so that they occupy a meaningful and distinct competitive position in the target customers' minds' (Kotler 1967). Positioning may be considered on various different levels:

● Benefit positioning

● User positioning

● Competitive positioning

Benefit positioning takes account of the positive outcomes of using the brand. These can be both functional (e.g. cures headaches) and emotional (e.g. shows status). User benefits relate to the specific profile of the target audience. User positioning is commonly excercised through the use of demographic and psychographic variables which denote specific lifestyle characteristics. Competitive positioning focuses on the relative advantages of the brand relative to its competition. For example Hertz may be 'number one' in car rentals but Avis 'try harder' in direct response to this claim. This type of positioning is often used to establish the profile of a new brand (e.g. Ryanair 'we fly for less') or to distinguish an existing brand in a highly competitive marketplace (e.g. Tesco price comparisons with competitors).

Any attempt to reinforce or change what consumers think about the brand is frequently done through marketing communications. Often consumer perceptions are visualized in the form of a **multi-dimensional skills map (or perception map)** as illustrated in Figure 4.4 below. The particular example

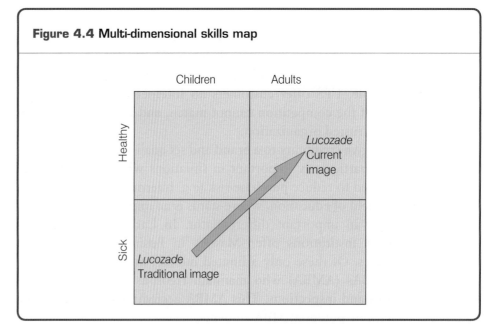

Figure 4.4 Multi-dimensional skills map

used in the illustration shows how Lucozade, a mature, perhaps even matronly brand was successfully repositioned as a trendy, energy enhancing, drink. The messages associated with the brand from its introduction until the 1980s was of a product designed to provide energy for the sick and sick children in particular. Those of a certain age in the UK will remember that Lucozade was a favourite gift for people convalescing at home or in the hospital. Advertising frequently showed a sick child being nursed back to health with the help of the drink and even the packaging (yellow plastic wrap around a severely shaped bottle) exuded institutional care. In more recent years Lucozade have re-positioned their product as a healthy, energy inducing, drink for sporty adults. This is backed up not only through their advertising, but with product placement at major sporting fixtures around the world. It is common to see footballers and athletes leaving the field of competition clutching a Lucozade container.

Summary

This chapter emphasized the importance of branding to marketing communications. It reviewed the characteristics of product and services brands and the concept of the 'brand halo'. The chapter clarified why branding was not only important to the brand owner but that also it reduced search-time and risk for the consumer. It reviewed the determinants associated with successful brands and the differing strategies adopted to build or maintain them. The chapter reviewed the 'brand life cycle' and the relevance of 'brand equity' to modern organizations. It noted the importance of 'brand associations' to developing the image and personality of the brand and of 'brand positioning' as a way of expressing it.

Review questions

1 How would you define 'branding'?
2 What are the 'augmented' aspects of a product or service?
3 What is a 'brand pirate'?
4 Salience is an important aspect of brand communications. Why?
5 What factors determine the success of a brand?
6 Explain the mnemonic 'VIEW'.
7 Describe the elements of the brand life cycle.
8 When might 'cause-related marketing' be appropriate?
9 Define 'positioning'.
10 When might perception maps be of use?

Discussion questions

1 The costs of both launching and supporting a new brand in Europe and North America towards the end of the twentieth century were very high. How do you think this cost will have changed since 2000 and what might be the main factors influencing this change?

2 Consider a well-known brand. In what way has the brand contributed to the development of the brand owner?

3 Using current market examples, under what circumstances would you consider developing an existing brand name through either brand extension or line extension.

Further reading

Caruana, A., Cohen, C. and Krenter, K.A. (2006) 'Corporate reputation and shareholders' intentions: an attitudinal perspective', *Journal of Brand Management*, Jul., 13 (6): 429–40.

Cataluña, F.R., García, A. and Phau, I. (2006) 'The influence of price and brand loyalty on store brands versus national brands', *International Review of Retail, Distribution & Consumer Research*, Oct., 16 (4): 433–52.

Chu, Singfat and Keh, Hean (2006) 'Brand value creation: analysis of the Interbrand-Business Week brand value rankings', *Marketing Letters*, Oct., 17 (4): 323–31.

Ha, Hong-Youl (2006) 'An exploratory study and consumers' perceptions of e-reverse bundling price in online retailing', *Journal of Strategic Marketing*, Sep., 14 (3): 211–28.

Herstein, R. and Gamliel, E. (2006) 'Striking a balance with private branding', *Business Strategy Review*, Fall, 17 (3): 39–43.

Rekom, J., Jacobs, G. and Verlegh, P. (2006) 'Measuring and managing the essence of a brand personality', *Marketing Letters*, Jul., 17 (3): 181–91.

Chapter references

Biel, A. (1997) 'Discovering brand magic: the hardness of the softer side of branding', *International Journal of Advertising*, 16: 199–210.

Brierley, S. (2002) *The Advertising Handbook*, 2nd edn, London: Routledge.

Clow, K.E. and Baack, D. (2004) *Integrated Advertising, Promotion and Marketing Communications*, 2nd edn, Upper Saddle River, NJ: Pearson/Prentice Hall.

Coopers, A. and Simons, P. (1997) *Brand Equity Lifestage: An Entrepreneurial Revolution*, London: TBWA Simons Palmer.

Curtis, J. (2004) 'Brands we trust', *Marketing*, 28 April: 28–30.

De Chernatony, L. and McDonald, M. (1998) *Creating Powerful Brands in Consumer Service and Industrial Markets*, Oxford: Butterworth Heinemann, CIM Association.

De Pelsmacker, P., Geuens, M. and Van den Bergh, J.V. (2001) *Marketing Communications: A European Perspective*, London: Prentice Hall.

Dibb, S., Simkin, L., Pride, R. and Fernell, B.R. (1997) *Concepts and Strategies*, 3rd edn, Boston, MA: Houghton-Mifflin Company.

Ehrenberg, A., Barnard, N. and Scriven, J. (1997) 'Differentiation or Salience', *Journal of Advertising Research*, 37 (6): 7–14.

Fill, C. (2002) *Marketing Communications: Contexts, Strategies and Applications*, 3rd edn, Harlow: Financial Times Press, Prentice Hall.

Hoddleston, P. and Cassil, N.L. (1990) 'Female consumers' brand orientation: the influence of quality and demographics', *Home Economics Research Journal* 18 (3): 255–62.

Kotler, P. (1967) *Marketing Management: Analysis, Planning, Implementation and Control*, Englewood Cliffs, NJ: Prentice Hall.

Kotler, P. (2000) *Marketing Management, Analysis, Planning, Implementation and Control*, Englewood Cliffs, NJ: Prentice Hall.

Mottram, S. (1998) 'Branding the corporation', in S. Hart and J. Murphy (eds), *'Brands': The New Wealth Creators*, London: Macmillan Press, pp. 1–12.

Pickton, D. and Broderick, A. (2001) *Integrated Marketing Communications*, Harlow: Financial Times, Prentice Hall.

Semenik, R.J. (2002) *Promotion and Integrated Marketing Communications*, Cincinnati: Thomson Learning.

Shimp, T.A. (2003) *Advertising, Promotion and Supplemental Aspects of Integrated Marketing Communication*, Cincinnati: Thomson Learning.

Twedt, D.W. (1968) 'How much value can be added through packaging?', *Journal of Marketing*, 32: 61–5.

Varey, R.J. (2002) *Marketing Communication, Principles and Practice*, London: Routledge.

Webb, D.J. and Mohr, L.A. (1998) 'A typology of consumer responses to cause-related marketing from skeptics to socially concerned', *Journal of Public Policy & Marketing*, 17 (2): 226–38.

Wells, W., Burnett, J. and Moriarty, S. (1995) *Advertising: Principles and Practice*, 3rd edn, Englewood Cliffs, NJ: Prentice Hall.

All change at Coca-Cola

Coke Australia is experimenting with new ways to reach its young target audience. It has embarked on an ambitious event and reality TV-based programme to connect with its key 16–24-year-old target group. Shifting its marketing budget away from traditional advertising. Coke's Live 'n Local rock-and-roll tour swung through Australia during March and April this year (2004) with 14 regional and city concerts featuring hot, signed and unsigned bands.

The core marketing concept behind the event was to 'invite the kids into our world rather than intruding into theirs', says Gary Williams, managing director of Coca-Cola Australia. 'We want to provide them with experiences rather than interrupt them, and by doing so integrate the Coke brand into their lives. We want to be music, rather than just supporting it.'

Williams recognizes music's role in the youth scene, and that Coke should become an integral part of it without being viewed as an interloper. As a result, the branding of the concerts was kept low key, focusing on the Live 'n Local tag line on the Coca-Cola brand.

Coke labels exchanged for tickets

'We wanted to avoid "painting it red" and making it so corporate that we turned the audiences off', says Williams. 'The idea was to "paint it real".'

Keen teens got free tickets to the events by trading in 20 Coke labels per ticket, and in return were treated to performances by well-known Australian rockers including 28 Days, Jebediah, Magic Dirt and Betchadupa, plus four unsigned bands.

A nationwide search for unsigned talent was judged by a panel of music industry professionals, journalists and programme managers. The eight finalist bands were featured in a 90-minute special edition of *Video Hits,* a terrestrial Channel 10 programme, called 'Live 'n Local' in early February. Viewers were asked to vote over the following four weekends on which bands they wanted to see in the concerts, and *Video Hits* followed the progress of the concert series as it unfolded across the country.

Fifty thousand tickets available for the six city concerts were mostly sold out. 'The feedback we received from punters has been excellent', says Coke spokesman Joanna Ryan. 'The atmosphere at many of the gigs was electric, with the bands jumping down off the stage after their performances and signing the kids' jeans and stuff. We are really pleased.'

Making a connection

John Roberts, professor of marketing at the Australian Graduate School of Management and the London Business School, says Coke's initiative is part of the broader trend towards creating a buzz around a brand. He says: 'The concert idea is part of the overall movement towards experimental marketing from product placement – starting with the BMW X3 in James Bond to the Microsoft Xbox and its attempts to get kids to become opinion leaders, and Paypal's online chatroom experiments.'

Integrating the brand with a concert experience is appropriate for Coke, says Roberts. 'It's about a sense of belonging. You'll never see a Coke ad with just one person.' At Coke, Ryan agrees: 'The core concept is product engagement, how warm customers feel towards the brand, how engaged and intimate their relationship has become through the events.'

There remains a question of cost effectiveness. Coke won't say how much the events have cost but marketing, ticketing, staging and managing the events, plus the bills for the reality TV series will be equal to a mountain of traditional advertising spend.

Whether the company has got value for money will remain a mystery, but it is doing what it can to measure results. 'It is to do with measuring the strengthening of our customer relationships', says Roberts. 'Measuring the effectiveness of marketing spend is difficult even with fairly direct activities, but its complexity multiplies as you move along the spectrum to traditional advertising and towards this kind of buzz marketing.'

Still, Coke is happy with Live 'n Local and is thinking of turning it into a regular feature of the Australian music scene. The UK, Europe and the US markets are watching with interest.

Desmond Llewelyn presents the BMW Z3 roadster which featured as a product placement within the 1995 James Bond film 'GoldenEye'.

Case study questions

1 What communications advantages does a brand such as Coca-Cola have over lesser known brands?

2 Why does Coca-Cola want to create a 'buzz' around the brand?

3 What other types of promotion might Coca-Cola consider to help achieve their objective of building relationships.

Reproduced with kind permission of The Chartered Institute of Marketing. First published in *the Marketeer*, July/August 2006. Article by Mike Hanley.

CASE STUDY 4.2

Chocolate heaven*

Chocolate Heaven is a small handmade confectionery company based in Tottenham, North London. The company was established in 1996 by Albert Segar and his partner Caroline Trent initially on a trading estate owned and operated by the local council. They have, however, recently (July 2006) moved to a purpose-build facility based in a major industrial regeneration site. Their move was part-funded by a government grant specifically designed to encourage industries with growth potential to expand their production capabilities and, through this expansion, offer worthwhile jobs to local residents.

Albert was born in Belgium and had served an apprenticeship with one of the finest chocolate factories in that country before meeting Caroline, moving to England and setting up Chocolate Heaven. Caroline's background was in accountancy and she handled the growing amount of paperwork that was associated with the business. Having initially started on their own they soon needed extra personnel. At the time of the move Albert and Caroline employed six staff but their business plan anticipated doubling this number within three years. In the same period turnover was forecast to grow from £250,000 to £600,000.

Chocolate Heaven's business to date had largely been with a limited number of department stores in the London area. They specialized in luxuriant cream and liqueur fillings which, for quality and taste, ranked alongside the finest

*Please note this case study is based on a fictional example.

in the world. The perishable nature of the ingredients, however, meant that shelf life in-store was at best three days so stores had to be frequently re-stocked often on a daily basis. This restricted the geographical area to which the company could supply wholesale quantities to approximately 25 miles around their North London base. On the positive side there were a growing number of specialist confectionery shops in the London area and this was seen as an area of significant growth that justified the forecast expansion. In addition Chocolate Heaven had invested in packaging that would safely carry up to 2kg of chocolates via 'next-day delivery' carriers, opening up the opportunity of developing a mail-order business.

Albert and Caroline both realized that, to expand the business, they needed to invest in the Chocolate Heaven brand. Although the potential was excellent they were not the only luxury chocolate maker in London and there was even competition from a well-known Belgium manufacturer who flew in supplies on a daily basis. The priority was to establish, in the minds of its target audience, the quality and particular features of the Chocolate Heaven brand and to encourage trial of the products.

Case study question

1 Assume you are Albert and Caroline. Prepare a marketing communications plan for Chocolate Heaven. At this stage a detailed budget is not required although account should be taken of the likely implications of expenditure. Assumptions may be made about information not included in the case study but these should be justified in the context of the scenario outlined.

Hotel Chocolat prides itself on having a distinctive brand of real, authentic chocolate and this is reflected in the sophisticated branding of their stores.

SOURCE: © HOTEL CHOCOLAT LTD. (REPRODUCED WITH PERMISSION).

CHAPTER FIVE
MARKETING COMMUNICATIONS PLANNING

LEARNING OBJECTIVES

Having completed this chapter you should be able to:

- Understand the importance of developing a marketing communications plan.
- Recognize the value of the situational audit.
- Be able to describe the relationship between objectives, strategies and tactics.
- Understand the concept of positioning.
- Be familiar with the way budgets are created and allocated.
- Recognize the importance of control mechanisms.
- Understand the various levels of customer knowledge and suggest strategies for improvement.

INTRODUCTION

This chapter introduces the concept of marketing communications planning. In this chapter the marketing communications plan itself is introduced and objective and strategy setting discussed. In addition budgeting and control and evaluation measures are reviewed at an early stage in recognition of their importance in the overall plan. In subsequent chapters marketing research and target marketing are discussed before returning to the tactical and operational aspects of the plan in the chapter on campaign planning.

MARKETING COMMUNICATIONS PLAN

The purpose of a marketing communications plan is to systematically set out an organization's communications objectives and devise strategies and tactics regarding how these might be achieved. Most marketing and marketing communication plans follow a pattern which involves elements of analysis, design, implementation and control (see Figure 5.1). Various formats exist and no particular form is proposed as necessarily greatly superior to any other. The plan presented in Figure 5.1, for example, is represented by the acronym SOSTCE (Situation, Objectives, Strategies, Tactics, Control and Evaluation) and, approximately, follows this well tried and tested format. One difference from many linear plans is that the model recognizes that marketing plans are not 'one-off' but need to be continually revisited. Rather than a linear model Figure 5.1 is seen as a continuous circle of activities.

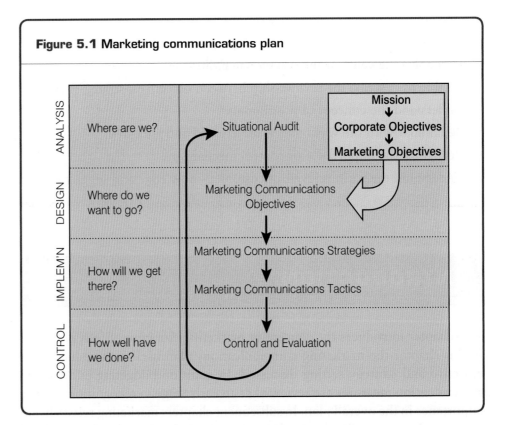

Figure 5.1 Marketing communications plan

SITUATION (SITUATIONAL AUDIT)

Mission
The core business of an organization and its ambitions usually set out in the company's mission statement.

Scope (or reach)
The boundaries of an organization's operation.

The old adage rings true; how can you possibly decide which way to go if you do not know where you have come from? Many organizations begin (or resume) the planning process by establishing (or reiterating or adapting) their **mission** and **scope** (or **reach**). The mission and scope relate to the 'attitudes and expectations within the organisation with regard to the business that the organisation is in, how the organisation rates against competition and how it fits into its environment' (O'Malley *et al.* 1999: 37). These attitudes and expectations are often framed in the form of a **mission statement**.

The **situational audit**, upon which decisions will be based, is a comprehensive assessment of the organization and its competitive and macro environment. Analysts have commonly used versions (both simple and complex) of PEST(L), SWOT and competitive market models to develop such analyses.[1] As we concentrate here on the marketing communications plan this organizational analysis is likely to be reflected in the organizational and marketing objectives which should cascade down through the company. Elements of the PEST(L) model, however, may be a practical tool in a number of specific marketing communications situations, for example:

- Political: e.g. threat of restrictive communications legislation (see Chapter 18)
- Economic: e.g. major job redundancies in proposed campaign area.
- Sociological: e.g. public concern regarding advertising to children.
- Technological: e.g. new technologies (e.g. texting) revising media utilization.
- Legal: e.g. legislation restricting cigarette advertising and sponsorship.

The identification and profiling of target markets is an important prerequisite to any plan (see Chapter 7). For 'customer acquisition' purposes this may still require the use of socio-demographic, geodemographic and/or lifestyle (including propensity to buy) data, whether exercised through rented 'lists' or communications media audience classifications. From the customer retention and development perspective the company's customer database is of paramount importance as it is a means of indicating customers' preferences and profitability. These can be analysed in a number of different ways. Direct marketers, for example, use recency, frequency and monetary value (RFM) models that incorporates data on customers' most recent purchases and the frequency and value of previous purchases to target potential **cross-selling** and **up-selling** (see Chapter 13) opportunities.

Another way to assess the organization's current situation is to visualize it in the form of a multi-dimensional skills map (or perception map) as illustrated in Figure 5.2. Generally known as positioning such analysis seeks to establish the brand's position in the competitive marketplace comparative to its main rivals. This positioning (or any necessary repositioning) will be highly significant in establishing the **brand proposition** and is central in any campaign. In the simple example illustrated 'OurCo' sees its position as a supplier of largely basic, modern furniture in an existing competitive market. It is, however, considering repositioning itself to achieve its corporate

---

Mission statement
A statement that asserts the core business of an organization and its ambitions.

Situational audit
An audit of the current state of the organization often using SWOT and PEST(L) analysis.

Cross-selling
Selling other items (sometimes from different categories) to existing customer base.

Up-selling
Selling higher quality (and, therefore, higher price) items to existing customer base.

Brand proposition
The brand's central proposition, the focus of the brand campaign.

---

[1]PEST (or STEP) stands for elements of the macro environment: political, economic, sociological and technological, to which legal is frequently added. SWOT stands for: strengths, weaknesses, opportunities and threats.

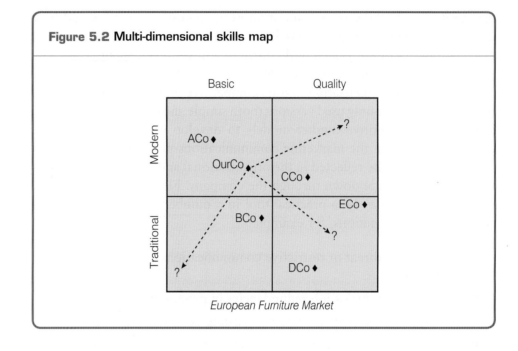

Figure 5.2 Multi-dimensional skills map

expansion objectives. The multi-dimensional skills map suggests three 'gaps' in the market where the company might be more profitably trading. However, just because there is a gap in a particular sector does not mean that a profitable marketplace exists. The sector may not be big enough to sustain and/or the potential customers may be difficult (and therefore expensive) to reach. In this situation the absense of competitors may be an indicator that such repositioning may fail. On the other hand changes in fashion and/or technological advances can rapidly change a sector's profile and repositioning may lead to renewal of vigour and present **first-mover advantages**. Examples of this include the HSBC's move into telephone-only banking through its specially created subsidary First Direct, Royal Bank of Scotland's entry into telephone-based insurance through Direct Line and Amazon's move into Internet book retailing.

The organization's 'position' in the market may be visualized based on a number of attributes and benefits (determined by the sector) including, but not restricted to:

- Quality (e.g. Stella Artois)
- Style (e.g. Apple)
- Status (e.g. Rolls Royce)
- Cost (e.g. Ryanair)
- Originality (e.g. Palm)

Alternatively organizations can be positioned by users or usage, breadth of offering, differentiation or indeed any descriptive variable relevent to the company and the marketplace.

First-mover advantage
Advantage associated with being the first organization in the marketplace and which may include experience, distribution channels, etc.

OBJECTIVES

Objectives are what drive an organization. They are the 'where we want to be' of any business. Objectives should be SMART (strategic, measurable, actionable, realistic and timely), communicable and aspirational. Corporate and/or business objectives play an important role in the activities of individuals, groups and organizations within the organization because (Fill 2002):

- They provide direction and an 'action focus'.
- They provide a means by which decisions, relating to an activity, can be made in a consistant way.
- They determine the time period within which the activity should be completed.
- They communicate the 'values' and scope of the activity.
- They provide a means by which the success of an activity can be evaluated.

Traditionally marketing objectives are derived (or cascade down) from the organizational corporate/business objectives and the marketing objectives and these, in turn, inform the communication objectives (see Figure 5.3). Top level (corporate/business) objectives are usually financial and marketing objectives frequently (but not always) related to sales. Certain marketing communication tools, including sales promotion, personal selling and point of sale, are of a

Figure 5.3 Cascading objectives

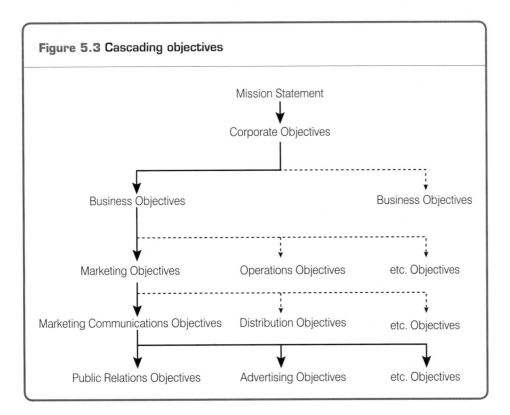

direct action nature (i.e. they call upon the customer to make an immediate response). In such cases sales objectives may be appropriate. Other tools, such as advertising and public relations, are not directly measurable in the short term by sales and may rely on proxy measures for evaluation purposes such as recall (see Chapter 12). It may, however, also be the case that in certain mature markets companies have accumulated knowledge over time of investment in marketing communications and can model the current effect of past investment and predict the future effects of current campaigns.

Albeit that communications objectives cascade down through the company two models can help sharpen the focus of marketing communication objectives. These are the hierarchy of effects and product life cycle models.

Hierarchy of effects models were discussed extensively in Chapter 2. Among the models discussed was DAGMAR introduced by Russell Colley in 1961 in a report to the American Association of National Advertisers entitled 'Defining Advertising Goals for Measured Advertising Results' (whose initials gave the incorporated model its name). DAGMAR was specifically designed to help the setting of objectives and was built on the premise that consumers passed various hurdles on their way to purchasing.[2] The DAGMAR model suggested that these were awareness, comprehension, conviction and action (other similar hierarchy models highlight similar terms) and that these were the primary goals of advertising.

In terms of DAGMAR, AIDA and other models these objectives fell into three broad fields. They may either be knowledge based (e.g. awareness, comprehension, etc.), feelings based (e.g. interest, desire, liking, etc.) or action based (e.g. sales).

- Knowledge-based communication objectives look to stimulate awareness and gain interest and may require creative attention-seeking strategies, involve demonstrations, scientific evidence, and/or celebrity or technical endorsement to achieve the desired outcomes.

- Feeling-based objectives involve developing the 'aura' and 'personality' of the brand through growing reputation and prestige, developing associations and strengthening brand preference and may involve seeking a change in attitudes and opinions to the brand.

- Action-based objectives may be sales oriented but also include the building of competences in areas such as database management.

Marketing communication objectives may also be conceived in relation to a product's or service's perceived position in its life cycle. Notwithstanding the danger of investing too much in such models (not least because of the difficulty in establishing an organization's position in the life cycle) it is a useful aid to developing marketing and communication objectives.

A newly launched product or service is looking initially for awareness and to inform potential customers that there is another alternative in the existing

---

[2] As noted in Chapter 2 the traditional hierarchy of effects models make the assumption that consumers always go along the rational path of [learning] ➔ [feeling] ➔ [doing] (see Box 2.5). Although this might be considered logical our knowledge of human beings suggest rationality is not always the observed response.

marketplace and/or that the newcomer offers something competitors do not (traditionally referred to as its USP – unique selling proposition). There are, however, very few introductions that are truly innovative and most introductions are 'me too', copycat products and services or incremental improvements. Significantly new and unique products or services require considerably greater investment in marketing communications not only to gain awareness but to provide understanding in the marketplace. When, for example, Microsoft launched Windows 95 $200 million was spent to raise awareness and develop interest in this innovative product. Such was the success of this campaign that customers queued to get into stores to buy it and it quickly gained an 85 per cent market share.

During the growth phase of the life cycle brand-building may be the major objective particularly as and when other competitors enter into direct competition or develop new features attractive in the marketplace. Channel development (through distributor targeted campaigns) may also be a priority (see 'push strategies' page 118) at this stage as the brand seeks extra sales outlets.

In the maturity phase there is little or no growth in the total market and, therefore, increased (or at least maintained) market share may be the principal objective. It is interesting to note that the cigarette industry, faced with a complete promotional ban argued that, in a stagnant and/or declining cigarette market, their communication objectives were not the attraction of new smokers to a brand but to improve market share at each other's expense. In the maturity stage it may be beneficial to promote other uses (e.g. Kellogg's Cornflakes as an evening snack) or expand the scope of the brand (e.g. Tesco's introduction of clothing). Brand extension and/or category extension are also potential considerations in a mature market.

Unique selling proposition (USP)
The proposition which sets the brand apart from any other brand.

Channel development
The development of distribution channels.

Market share
The brand's share of the market sector as a percentage of the whole sector.

Figure 5.4 Hierarchy of effects models

	KNOWLEDGE	FEELING	MOTIVATION → ACTION
AIDA Strong 1925	Attention Interest	Desire	Action
DAGMAR Colley 1961	Awareness Comprehension	Conviction	Purchase
Lavidge and Steiner 1961	Awareness Knowledge	Liking Preference	Conviction Purchase
Wells et al. 1965	Awareness Perception Understanding		Persuasion
	COGNITIVE	AFFECTIVE	CONATIVE

In the decline stage the level of communication expenditure supporting the brand may be minimal (e.g. concentrating on point-of-sale materials) or sufficient to keep it going as a niche or secondary brand or it may herald its eventual withdrawal.

As noted previously marketing communication's objectives are frequently more troublesome to evaluate than higher level objectives as they often relate to highly subjective consumer behaviour measures (awareness, interest, desire, etc.). Whereas targets can be set for aspects of the communications mix such as sales promotions and personal selling the measurable affect of advertising or public relations may not be known for some time (if at all). Known as the **lagged** (or **carryover**) **effect** the immediate objective may be to establish the brand at the front-of-mind of the consumer, ready for when the purchase decision will be made, rather than immediate purchase. A review of econometric studies which examined the duration of cumulative advertising effects found that, for mature, frequently purchased, low-priced products the marketing communications' effect lasted up to nine months (Belch and Belch 2001). At the other end of the price scale motor manufacturers do not expect all potential customers to rush out to buy a new car on the basis of one campaign. Rather they are hoping that, when the customer is ready to buy, their brand will be front-of-mind and will be a strong contender for purchase. Where there is a lagged effect **proxy measure** are used such as **advertising recall** or in public relations **media evaluation** (see Chapters 9 and 11). These, however, measure 'awareness' of a campaign rather than interest or commitment. An example of the use of recall measurements appears regularly in the pages of *Marketing* magazine (see page 111). In this analysis 1000 adults (aged 16 to 64) are asked which of the following television commercials do they

Lagged effect
The time between when a consumer sees an advertisement and when they are ready to purchase.

Proxy measures
Measures used when the marketing communication effect on sales cannot be directly measured.

Advertising recall
Unprompted awareness of recent advertising.

Media evaluation
Evaluation of an organization's media coverage over a specific time period.

Industry news can be found at:
www.marketingweek.co.uk and **www.brandrepublic.com/magazines/ marketing**.

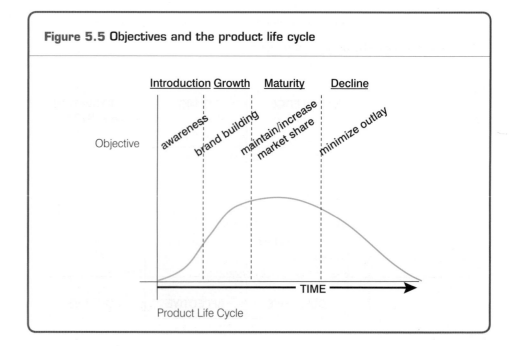

Figure 5.5 Objectives and the product life cycle

ADWATCH

The weekly analysis of advertisement recall

Q: Which of the following TV commercials do you remember seeing recently?

	Last week	Brand	Agency/TV buyer	%
1	(–)	DFS	Uber/Brilliant Media	63
2	(–)	Lynx Dry	VegaOlmosPonce Buenos Aires, Lowe London/MindShare	62
3	(3=)	Weetabix Oatibix	WCRS/Walker Media	58
4	(–)	Tiscali	MWO/Zed Media	55
5	(–)	Tesco	The Red Brick Road/Initiative	53
6	(–)	DoH – Tobacco Control	Abbott Mead Vickers BBDO/PHD	49
7	(–)	Niquitin CQ	WCRS/MediaCom	48
8=	(–)	Clearblue Digital	Amalgamated New York/Initiative	44
8=	(–)	HSBC	JWT London/MindShare	44
10	(16=)	L'Oréal Telescopic Mascara	McCann-Erickson/ZenithOptimedia	43
11=	(–)	Abbey	WCRS/Carat	41
11=	(–)	Nivea Visage DNAge	TBWA\London/Carat	41
13	(–)	Pringles Gourmet	Grey Dusseldorf/Starcom	40
14	(–)	Hellmann's Squeezy Light	Lowe London/MindShare	37
15=	(–)	Del Monte	Leo Burnett Belgium/Starcom	34
15=	(–)	Kellogg	Cartoon Network/MindShare	34
17=	(–)	Sensodyne	Grey London/MediaCom	32
17=	(–)	Poligrip Comfiseal Strips	Grey London/MediaCom	32
19	(–)	Cow & Gate	Ogilvy & Mather/PHD	29
20	(–)	Finish/Hoover	Euro RSCG London/OMD UK	28

Adwatch research was conducted from 28 September-2 October by TNS as part of its twice-weekly OnLineBus omnibus among 1000 adults aged 16-64. For details of the survey, contact sue.homeyardStns-global.com (020 7868 6602). Advertisements were selected by Xtreme Information (020 7575 1800) and Mediaedge:cia UK (020 7803 2000).

2. Lynx Dry

4. Tiscali

11. Abbey

14. Hellmann's Squeezy Light

Sector awareness
Consumer awareness that a sector (e.g. palmtops) exist.

Generic communications
Communications designed to expand the sector rather than any individual brand in it.

Brand awareness
How aware a consumer is of a particular brand (also referred to as brand recognition).

Brand knowledge
Knowledge of the benefits, features, positioning etc. associated with the brand.

Trial
Buying a product for the first time.

Loyalty
Loyalty in behavioural terms is repeated selection of a brand. Loyalty in attitudinal terms incorporates consumer preferences and disposition towards brands.

remember seeing recently? However, simply being aware of the advertisement does not necesarilily imply an intention to purchase. On the other hand unless you are aware of a product or service you are highly unlikely to buy it! This relationship between awareness and ultimate purchase is an interesting and observable one involving perceived stages of involvement with the brand as illustrated in Figure 5.6.

The model proposes[3] that, for a particular existing brand in a particular marketplace, and when prompted by a researcher, sector awareness is highest (and may be close to or at 100 per cent). If this sector awareness is not high it may benefit all competitors banding together to produce generic communications which may benefit the sector as a whole. Prompted brand awareness (or recognition)[4] is measured in relation to sector awareness. Unaided brand awareness (or recall)[5] is lower as is relevent brand knowledge (e.g. benefits, features, positioning etc.) about the product or service. Rather less are perceived to have a positive attitude to the brand and fewer still might trial it. Ultimately the brand owner is looking for loyalty as indicated by repeat purchases and/or high positive attitude but this is likely to be a fraction of those measures that went before. For a new, relaunched or existing brands, therefore, there may well be multiple communication objectives for a campaign. For example:

1 Within 4 months 75 per cent of the target market aware of the brand unprompted.

2 Within 6 months 10 per cent of the target market has trialled the product or service.

3 Within 12 months 5 per cent of the target market are repeat purchasers.

Figure 5.6 Awareness to loyalty scale

Sector Awareness x%

Brand Awareness (prompted)

Brand Awareness (unprompted)

Brand Knowledge

Attitude

Trial

Repeat Purchase and Loyalty

This model is not drawn to scale and is indicative only

---

[3]The model is not drawn to any form of fixed scale. It is the relative reduction between each level and not the exact scale that is a useful.
[4]See Chapter 9.
[5]See Chapter 9.

In a later campaign the objectives may be set higher. There is also an expectation that increasing the numbers at one level leads to greater repeat purchases in the longer term as illustrated in Figure 5.7. If consumers are aware of a number (or **portfolio**) of brands, brand attitude may be a deciding factor and the priority may be to improve this in the target market.

Portfolio of brands
A consumer's basket of brands from which buying decisions are made.

The setting of communication objectives may be, therefore, derived from the marketing objectives but given impetus and meaning through the consideration of hierarchy, life cycle and awareness models.

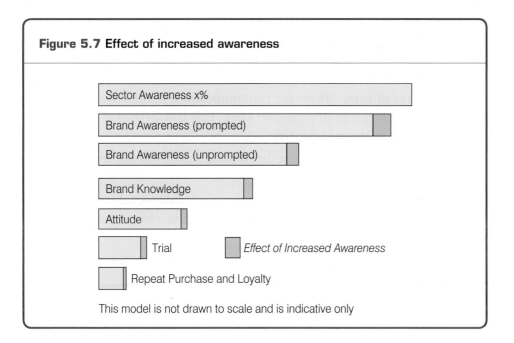

Figure 5.7 Effect of increased awareness

Sector Awareness x%

Brand Awareness (prompted)

Brand Awareness (unprompted)

Brand Knowledge

Attitude

Trial   Effect of Increased Awareness

Repeat Purchase and Loyalty

This model is not drawn to scale and is indicative only

BUDGETING

Budgeting is introduced at this point although the form of budget setting used by an organization determines where in the process itself it is considered. Too often marketing communications are regarded as costs and are frequently the first to be cut when things are not going well. Yet these communications investments play a major part in what will determine the brand's value in the future.

Budgeting 'processes' include everything from the ubiquitous 'back-of-an-envelope' calculation to major planning proposal exercises. These include (Smith 1998):

**Objective and task
(for budgeting)**
Establishing what needs to be achieved and setting the budget on the basis of achieving these objectives.

- **Objective and task** (or **task**) approach: establishing what needs to be achieved and setting the budget on the basis of achieving these

Budget modelling
Various econometric and simulation techniques which seek to model investment and subsequent performance.

Pay-back period (for budgeting)
Where budget decisions are made based upon the time taken to repay the investment.

Profit optimization (for budgeting)
Suggests that investment continues as long as the marginal revenue exceeds the marginal cost.

Percentage of sales (for budgeting)
Where the communications budget is set at a certain percentage of projected sales.

Competitive parity (for budgeting)
Spending determined relative to the spending of the organization's major competitor(s).

Affordable
Where costs and profit margin are deducted from turnover and the balance invested in marketing and marketing communications.

Arbitrary (for budgeting)
A build-up budget approach where senior management arbitrate between different organizational priorities.

@

Look at the Italian Mediaworld website at:
www.mediaworld.it.

Control and evaluation
The means by which a plan is monitored, controlled and measured.

objectives set by the organization. Effectively it is a 'build-up' approach to budgeting that relies on setting the objectives, determining the strategies to achieve them and estimating the costs associated with these tasks.

- Budget modelling: various econometric and simulation techniques which seek to model investment and subsequent performance. This is prevalent in the direct marketing industry where testing is an important indicator of future action (see Chapter 13).

- Pay-back period: where decisions are made based upon the time taken to repay the investment.

- Profit optimization: suggests that investment continues as long as the marginal revenue (i.e. each additional unit generated) exceeds the marginal cost (i.e. each additional unit invested to achieve that extra unit generated).

- Percentage of sales: where the communications budget is set at a certain percentage of projected sales. This is widely used as a benchmark in many industries.

- Competitive parity: spending determined relative to the spending of major competitor(s).

- Affordable: where costs and profit margin are deducted from turnover and the balance invested in marketing and marketing communications.

- Arbitrary: another 'build-up' approach where senior management arbitrate between different organizational priorities.

Budgeting is more than just purely financial. Organizational resources (both physical and in human terms) determine how this finance can be leveraged to achieve the marketing communication objectives. Does enough in-house expertise exist to manage a campaign or does the organization need to look outside to agencies for professional support? Time restrictions too may determine whether additional resources are employed.

CONTROL AND EVALUATION

Although **control and evaluation** appear in the latter stages of the communications plan (see Figure 5.1) the means by which the success of the plan will be monitored, controlled and measured needs to be established at an early stage. Control of the budget is critical and costs, particularly those associated with external agencies, should be closely monitored. Action plans should be established to determine what takes place and when and the resources (human and financial) involved. Given the long lead times in some

Mediaworld: predicting the future

The World Cup presents a massive opportunity for retailers as support for national teams stimulates sales. In 2006, the product of the moment was seen to be plasma and LCD TVs, and sales predictions were high. But so was competition between retailers.

Now the best sales promotion campaigns are those that stimulate high response levels with low redemption rates and Pierluigi Bernasconi, MD of Mediaworld in Italy, felt he had identified the perfect campaign: 'Buy a TV and if Italy win the World Cup you win the TV.' Predictions were that Italy was unlikely to get past the first round, so budget demands would be restricted to the extensive communications campaign planned.

The company prospered, with over 12,000 sales of top of the range TVs at an average of £1,000 per unit. £12 million worth of sales. But then, against all odds, Italy won…

Fortunately for Carlsberg, their World Cup promotion did not encounter the same problems as Mediaworld's.

SOURCE: IMAGE COURTESY OF THE ADVERTISING ARCHIVES.

Minicase written by Andy Cropper, Senior Lecturer, Sheffield Hallam University.

media (e.g. television) plans should be subjected to 'what if' interrogation, for example 'What if the product launch falls behind schedule?' Measurable objectives are the basic evaluation tools. Some measures may be on the basis of pre- and post-campaign research (for example into brand awareness) or **rolling research** (see Chapter 6) to determine the effectiveness.

Rolling research
Research that takes place on a regular basis and asks the same questions so that response comparisons can be made.

STRATEGIES

Strategies
The 'how we are going to get there'. Communication strategies are the ways an organization chooses to communicate with its customers and other stakeholders.

Tactics
The operational element of the communications plan and, by definition, short term. The choice may be between different media (including the Internet) or techniques (e.g. direct marketing).

If the objectives are 'where we want to be' then the **strategies** are 'how we are going to get there'. Communication strategies are the ways an organization chooses to communicate with its customers and other stakeholders. Although the tactical dimension of marketing communication planning will be discussed in more detail in Chapter 8 it is worth distinguishing between strategies and tactics at this point albeit the terms are frequently used interchangeably. Tactics are the operational element of the communications plan and, by definition, short term. The choice may be between different media (including the Internet) or techniques (e.g. direct marketing) or tactical decisions. The potential danger here is confusing the tactical with the strategic. For example despite its influence on business in general, the Internet is a tactical tool (although it may support strategic intent). The Internet is part (certainly not all) of a company's communications armoury. It may promote different approaches but it is, in strict terms, just another media channel.

Marketing communication strategies may include sub-strategies based on the marketing communications tools (e.g. advertising strategies, public relations strategies, etc.) or cross discipline (e.g. media strategy, creative strategy). These should, in the final analysis, blend into one plan.

Communications strategy setting requires knowing or establishing the:

- Target audience (and the ways of communicating with them).
- Positioning of the brand (or where it might be repositioned).
- Distribution channels (and/or the quality level of re-sellers).
- Competition (and their communication strengths and weaknesses).

Strategies relate directly to objectives and also cascade down through the organization (see Figure 5.8). Thus the marketing objectives and strategy relate directly to the marketing communications objectives and strategies so that, for example:

Marketing Objective	e.g. increase sales by 5 per cent ⤵

determines the

Marketing Strategy	e.g. increase awareness of the brand ⤵

determines the

Communications Objective	e.g. increase awareness by 20 per cent ⤵

determines the

Communications Strategy	e.g. develop advertising campaign and leverage through public relations campaign.

By definition marketing communication strategies should be customer orientated and not media orientated. In other words the focus is on reaching particular target audiences rather than media selection *per se*. The media tactics (see Chapter 8) should evolve based on strategic decision making.

Where objectives are derived from hierarchy of effects or life cycle models these may suggest relevant campaign strategies as noted in Box 5.1 below.

Figure 5.8 Cascading objectives and strategies

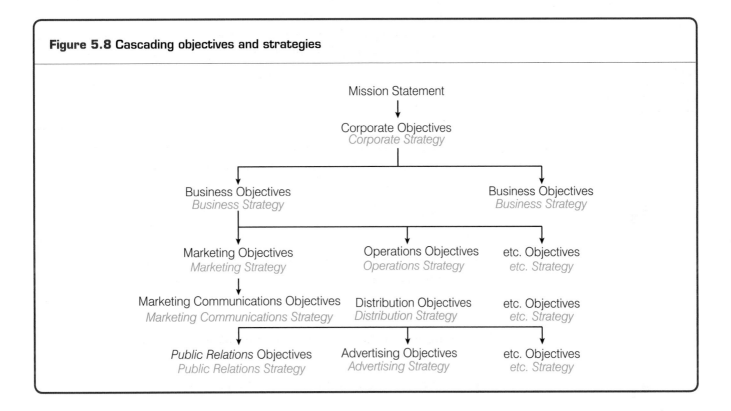

Box 5.1 Objective and strategy development

			Objectives	Example of Possible Strategies
Hierarchy of Effects		Knowledge based	awareness, comprehension	advertising campaign
		Feelings based	interest, desire, liking	increased sponsorship
		Action based	purchase	direct marketing campaign
Life cycle		Introduction	awareness, trial	advertising and point-of-sale
		Growth	brand building, distribution	sponsorship, cause-related promotion, push strategies
		Maturity	market share	sales promotion
		Decline	manage costs	point-of-sale

Push strategies
Strategies designed to influence re-sellers or trade channel intermediaries (e.g. wholesalers, dealers, agents, retailers, etc.) to carry and promote particular brands (i.e. they are 'pushed' into the distribution system).

Pull strategies
Strategies which look to influence the end-user and attract these customers (through marketing communications) 'over the heads' of retailers direct to the individual brand.

Re-sellers
Wholesalers, dealers, agents, retailers, etc. (also referred to as trade channel intermediaries).

Trade promotions
Promotions designed to develop the brand through the trade (e.g. competitions, demonstrations, etc.).

Buying allowances
Cash discounts, increased margins, etc. against goods purchased.

Advertising or sales promotion allowances
Contribution to retailers for advertising.

Joint advertising
Cost of advertising shared between retailer and supplier.

Slotting allowances
Payment in consideration of 'slotting in' a new product into the retailer's merchandise mix.

Point of sale
In-store materials displayed at the time the customer is making buying decisions.

Own brand
A retail brand that carries the retailer name and/or logo.

Cooperative strategy
Retailers and suppliers working together to develop the business through distribution and other efficiencies.

So, for example in the growth phase of the product life cycle strategies to aid brand building may include sponsorship and/or a cause-related promotion or other brand building tools (e.g. advertising, public relations). If, however, the objective is to develop the distribution channels then push strategies (see below) would be appropriate.

Another way of differentiating between marketing communications strategies, particularly in the fast moving consumer goods (fmcg) sector, is between push strategies and pull strategies. Push strategies are those designed to influence re-sellers or trade channel intermediaries (e.g. wholesalers, dealers, agents, retailers, etc.) to carry and promote particular brands (i.e. they are 'pushed' into the distribution system). Push strategies include:

- trade promotions (competitions, demonstrations, etc.),
- buying allowances (cash discounts, increased margins, etc.),
- advertising or sales promotion allowances (including joint advertising),
- slotting allowances (i.e. a payment in consideration of 'slotting in' a new product into the merchandise mix),
- point of sale materials,
- training (to encourage information flow to the consumer and promote good practice at the point of sale).

Pull strategies are those which look to influence the end-user and attract these customers (through marketing communications) 'over the heads' of retailers direct to the individual brand. Customer expectations are raised such that they expect promoted items to be available for them at their local store. By driving customers to purchase they are 'pulling' merchandise through the distribution network. Pull strategies include;

- Brand building (e.g. through advertising, etc.)
- Consumer promotions
- Consumer competitions

For most of the twentieth century 'pull strategies', determined by the major fast moving consumer goods brands, were dominated primarily through mass media advertising but also promotions and competitions. Towards the end of that century this dominance began to wane as the power of major fast moving consumer goods retailers grew in most developed markets. Brand communication budgets were cut as manufacturers vied for shelf space with their competitors and the retailers' own brands. In recent years, in these fast moving consumer goods markets another, less combative, relationship has begun to develop between suppliers and retailers. This cooperative strategy involves a close relationship between retailer and supplier such that the latter knows almost instantly when a product has been sold, at what price, from which location in the store and with what promotional support. Communication plans relating to the brand, by both supplier and retailer, can, therefore, be 'dovetailed' to provide the most effective response. The change in the balance of power has, however, seen a considerable shift away from advertising to 'below the line' tools.

Summary

This chapter introduced the concept of a marketing communications plan and proposed a model within which to frame it. A situation audit was proposed and the importance of target markets emphasized. Objective and strategies were described as flowing down through the company in a cascade effect. Objectives should provide direction and focus and a means by which decisions can be made in a consistent way. They should be timely, communicate the scope of the activity and provide a means by which the activity can be evaluated. The hierarchy of effects and life cycle models were re-introduced as a guide to objective and strategy development. The importance of budget setting and the variety of different budget setting methods were discussed as was the means by which control and evaluation are built into the communications plan. Other strategy models such as 'push' and 'pull' distinguished between campaigns designed for the distribution channel or direct to the customer. The relationship between awareness and other levels of consumer knowledge was also proposed as an aid to strategy development.

In subsequent chapters marketing research and target marketing will be developed before returning to the communications plan to discuss campaign planning.

Review questions

1   How would you describe the 'SOSTCE' circle of activities associated with a marketing communications plan?
2   What do you understand by the term 'first mover advantage'?
3   Explain the terms 'pay-back period', 'competitive parity' and 'profit optimization' in relation to budgeting.
4   What is the difference between strategies and tactics?
5   Define both 'push' and 'pull' strategies.
6   What do you believe 'point of sale' materials will include?
7   What is the purpose of a marketing communications plan?
8   Objectives should be SMART. What does this stand for?
9   Who are the 'trade channel intermediaries'?
10   What is a 'slotting allowance'?

Discussion questions

1   Marketing objectives are traditionally seen as cascading down from above. Using examples to illustrate the relationship between the various levels, how might corporate objectives evolve into communications objectives?

2   How do communications objectives relate to stages of the product life cycle?

3   Using examples, what techniques can be used for evaluating the effectiveness of advertising and how reliable do you think these might be?

Further reading

Anantachart, S. (2006) 'Integrated marketing communications and market planning', *Journal of Promotion Management*, 11 (1): 101–25. Linking the integrated marketing communications (IMC) concept to the planning process in marketing.

Bauman, A., Smith, B.J., Maibach, E.W. and Reger-Nash, B. (2006) 'Evaluation of mass media campaigns for physical activity', *Evaluation & Program Planning*, Aug., 29 (3): 312–22.

Jenkinson, A., Sain, B. and Bishop, K. (2005) 'Optimising communications for charity brand management', *International Journal of Nonprofit & Voluntary Sector Marketing*, May, 10 (2): 79–92.

Piercy, N.F. (2006) 'Exploring the impact of sales upon the planning process: the strategic sales organization', *Marketing Review*, Spring, 6 (1): 3–28.

Schimmel, K. and Nicholls, J. (2005) 'Segmentation based on media consumption: a better way to plan integrated marketing communications media', *Journal of Applied Business Research*, Spring, 21 (2): 23–36.

Sinickas, A. (2006) 'Tailoring campaigns by audience', *Strategic Communication Management*, Dec 2005/Jan 2006, 10 (1): 12–13.

Chapter references

Belch, G. and Belch, M. (2001) *Advertising and Promotion: An Integrated Marketing Communications Perspective*, New York: McGraw-Hill.

Colley, R.H. (1961) *Defining Advertising Goals for Measured Advertising Results*, New York: Association of National Advertisers.

Fill, C. (2002) *Marketing Communications: Contexts, Strategies, and Applications*, 3rd edn, Harlow: Financial Times Prentice Hall.

Lavidge, R. and Steiner, G. (1961) 'A model for predictive measurements of advertising effectiveness', *Journal of Marketing*, Oct.: 61.

O'Malley, L., Patterson, M. and Evans, M. (1999) *Exploring Direct Marketing*, London: Thomson Learning.

Smith, P.R. (1998) *Marketing Communications: An Integrated Approach*, 2nd edn, London: Kogan Page.

Strong, E.K. (1925) *The Psychology of Selling*, New York : McGraw-Hill.

Wells, W., Burnett, J. and Moriarty, S. (1965) *Advertising Principles and Practice*, Upper Saddle River, NJ: Prentice Hall.

Ecover – what next?

Globally, the laundry detergent market is huge and Western europe alone accounts for several billion euro in annual sales. However, despite its size the market has been stagnating since 2000 and this has stimulated aggressive competition between the major operators.

For Procter & Gamble, downward price pressures from retailers and a weakening economy affected US market growth and increased consumer price sensitivity hit sales of its premium products. In addition, anti-American feelings worldwide hit sales in markets such as Africa and the Middle East.

In response, they followed a policy of acquisition and in the Western European market systematically acquired a number of smaller operators, adding around (€107 million in sales from products such as Axion and Gama (France), Dinamo (Italy), Ajax (Sweden) and Dynamo (Denmark); giving them over a third of Western European market share. They also extended their core brands, Ariel, Bold, Daz and Fairy, through innovative formats and formulations to defend existing market share.

Innovation allowed them to stay one step ahead of major rival, Unilever. For example, by getting to market first with Ariel Liqui-Tabs and reducing the potential impact of Unilever's comparative product, Persil capsules. However, they still faced a general decline in world sales of powder detergents coupled with intensifying competition. So their next logical step would be to look closely at the market structure and identify profitable niches.

The largest single market in Europe is the UK, and, like a number of its European cousins, there has been a 'detergent niche' emerging over the last 20 years. A niche currently dominated by the Belgian company, Ecover, who supplies ecological detergents across Europe and America.

Founded in 1980, their ethos has been around 'pioneering', for example they marketed a phosphate-free washing powder even before phosphates were considered an environmental problem. They have now developed into the world's largest producer of ecological detergents and cleansing products, marketing products in 22 countries.

Ecological concern is an integral part of their operation. They created the world's first ecological factory and have been widely recognized for their contributions to environmental sustainability; being placed on the UN 'Environment Global 500 Roll of Honour' in 1993.

This ethos is enshrined in their mission, which is to provide effective, sustainable solutions for the hygienic needs of people. This places an emphasis on both operational processes and ongoing environmental research, with the inevitable financial implications. They also see job performance as a means of assisting the social well-being and personal development of its employees, suggesting that profitability is not at the core of its operation.

The factory is made from sustainable wood and recycled bricks, with a living, grass roof. Management drive the eco-friendly Toyota Prius and the rest of the staff receive financial rewards for using public transport, cycling or joining car-share schemes.

But whilst profitability might not be at the core of its operation, shrewd investment and sound business sense are.

Originally the product was only found in health food shops, purchased by hardcore green enthusiasts. Now, it competes for space in most leading supermarkets. Sales increased 30 per cent in 2005 and by 2006 it was claiming 90 per cent of the UK green cleaning market.

Around 34 per cent of people now use at least some green cleaning products and both Unilever and Procter & Gamble no longer see this as a small niche but as an attractive, viable and growing sector; particularly when you consider that Ecover is sold at a premium price when other segments are increasingly becoming price sensitive. Having been relatively protected from major competitors, Ecover may now be facing a serious challenge.

The approach adopted by Ecover to marketing communications activities has been one of minimalism, thrift, consistency of message and building up a growing 'word of mouth' campaign; avoiding the large costs of mass advertising.

eat organic
clean ecological

Fruit & vegetables grown organically do not have unnecessary chemicals & pesticides over their skin. Similarly, people who clean with **ECOVER** do not have unnecessary chemical ingredients over their skin or put unnecessary chemicals into the environment. The message is simple, for spotless cleaning and a healthy lifestyle -

Eat Organic - Clean Ecological.

25p
off any one
Ecover product
INCLUDING THE NEW LAUNDRY TABLETS

TO THE CUSTOMER: This coupon entitles you to 25p off any Ecover product. Only one coupon per product purchased. Please do not try to redeem this coupon against any other brands as refusal may cause embarrassment and delay at the checkout.
TO THE RETAILER: Ecover will redeem this coupon at face value only if it has been accepted in part payment for Ecover products - Ecover will refuse payment if mal-redemptions is proven. **Please send coupons to:**
NCH DEPT 1190. Ecover FREEPOST
SEA10878, CORBY. NN17 1BR.
VALID UNTIL 30.11.01   1226-00372   SM/04

SUPPORTING THE WORK OF THE SOIL ASSOCIATION
Look for an introductory Soil Association membership offer on ECOVER promotion packs, or for an information pack
telephone: 01635 574553   Soil Association

ECOVER®

This advertisement shows Ecover matching the benefits of their products with those of organic food.

Partnership promotions have proven effective, and cheap. For example, a joint promotion with the Soil Association in 2001 recruited 1000 new members for the association and access to an attractive target market for Ecover. In the same vein, their 2006 campaign saw them combining with Organic Holidays to offer Organic Breaks, again inexpensive to execute but highly targeted.

Having established themselves in mainstream supermarkets, they also adopted low-cost, point of purchase techniques such as bottle-neck fliers offering money-off coupons and competition offers. An example being the spring 2006 on-pack promotion, which offered a first prize of 'having your home professionally spring cleaned from top to bottom, using Ecover products'.

One of the keys to this type of campaign is that the offer attracts people to purchase, but very few actually get around to redeeming offers or entering competitions and, if they do, the costs of fulfilment are relatively low.

Throughout, the core messages are around the ecologically sound nature of the product. They might highlight the irritable residue that can often be left by ordinary products, but point to the non-irritable properties of the plant extract-based Ecover which conditions skin rather than harms it. Or they counter the price premium by focusing on the fact that it is highly concentrated, requires very little to give an adequate wash and actually works out cheaper than other brands. They even focus on the fact that the packaging is 100 per cent recyclable.

All of these elements can be copied though. So, if large organizations such as Procter & Gamble were to consider trying to develop this segment, how can Ecover defend themselves?

Case study questions

1 How would you summarize the market threats and opportunities facing Ecover?

2 What do you believe will be the major challenges faced by Ecover should either Unilever or Procter & Gamble decide to enter into direct competition?

3 In anticipation of more aggressive competition, how would you advise Ecover to develop their marketing communications activities within: (a) the UK and (b) Europe as a whole? What would be the implications of your recommendations?

Case study written by Andy Cropper, Senior Lecturer, Sheffield Hallam University.

CASE STUDY 5.2

Musuem marketing *

The Hendon Local History Museum (HLHM) is a newly established enterprise based in a former warehouse within five minutes walk of Hendon Central Underground Station. The initial funding for the project came in part from the European Unions' Local Initiative Fund and partly from a grant from the National Lottery Heritage Fund. The Museum is to get a small annual grant from the local authority in recognition of the potential educational contribution it will make to schools in the Borough but in general it is planned to be self-financing through a mixture of entrance fees to the museum, the holding of special events and, it is hoped, commercial sponsorship. The opening date for the Museum itself has been set for 18 June 2007, that is in approximately five months time.

Stephanie Quinn is the Marketing Director for the HLHM and took up her appointment four weeks ago. She has spent most of her marketing career with theme park companies but she was very well qualified and managed to convince the interview panel of the many similarities between this and the job she has since undertaken. She has spent most of the past four weeks visiting similar operations in the British Isles and Europe as well as using her network of marketing contacts to 'get to know' the business. Her next most important job is to create a marketing communications (MC) plan for the Museum covering, in some detail, the next 12 months but extending out, more generally, over the next five years. Because of time restrictions due to the impending launch this is taking precedence over the development of the full marketing plan which will be completed later in the year. The marketing communications plan needs to be completed quickly as it is due to be presented and, hopefully approved, by the HLHM Council (the Museum's equivalent of a Board of Directors) during February.

*Please note this case study is based on a fictional example.

▶

The Museum Council has adopted a Mission Statement that reads:

The Hendon Local History Museum will provide the people of the Borough, Londoners in general and the population as a whole with a detailed insight into the commercial and cultural history of the locality. It will be the principal source of such information in the area which it will present in interesting and innovative ways.

Even museums as large as the British Museum typically have limited marketing budgets to operate from.

Overall company objectives have not yet been set but Stephanie knows that, with the time restrictions, she will have to make a number of assumptions as it would not be practical to wait for them to be formalized by the HLHM Council. She has drawn up her own list of probable objectives based upon the Mission Statement and conversations she has had with other members of the Executive, notably the Managing Director. These include the evident aim to make HLHM the number one public attraction in the Borough and to attract a significant number of visitors from other parts of London (the figure of 30 per cent is a suggested target) as well as visitors from other parts of the British Isles (10 per cent) and overseas (10 per cent).

Case study question

1 Assume you are Stephanie Quinn. Prepare an outline marketing communications plan in preparation for the presentation to the HLHM Council. At this stage a detailed budget is not required although you should take account of the probable high cost of certain media in your recommendations. Assumptions may be made where information is not included in the case study but should be justified within the context of your answer.

Small business planning*

Mike Smith lived in Richmond in West London. He had noticed for some time that many of his friends were complaining that they just didn't have enough hours in the day to get housework done. Whether single or living with partners work commitments often meant they arrived home late and, quite frankly, were not in the mood to begin the daily chores of washing, ironing, cleaning, etc. Mike saw an opportunity to offer a cleaning service to these mainly 'thirty-somethings' who were relatively 'cash-rich' but 'time-poor'.

In 2005 Mike established AtHome. His aim was to build up a comprehensive range of cleaning services utilizing local labour that he would pay on a job-by-job basis. His first task was to advertise for potential cleaners in his local area. Although the pay was not great the hours were flexible and this appealed to people who had family commitments or who already worked but needed some extra cash. Within 12 months he was employing up to 30 cleaners on a part-time basis and had also brought in administrative help.

Business was brisk. Originally he has approached his personal contacts but 'word-of-mouth' had brought him many more customers. In addition he had more and more offers of potential cleaners from his own and neighbouring areas. Mike felt that he had the labour and administrative resources to safely expand his business outside of the immediate area initially to neighbouring boroughs but perhaps, eventually, London-wide.

Mike realized that he would need to spend money on such a campaign. He had sufficient funds to spend up to £30 000 over a six-month period. Before he went any further he arranged to see Alice Moore at his local council Small Business Development Office who suggested that, together, they draw up a marketing communications plan.

* Please note this case study is based on a fictional example.

Small businesses need to be innovative to stand out from the crowd – when starting out Innocent Drinks created distinctive product branding and used informal marketing copy to establish a unique dialogue with their customers.

Case study question

1 Assume you are Alice Moore. Draw up a marketing communications plan for AtHome. Although a six-month time period is indicated you may wish, for planning purposes, to extend this to a year or more. At this stage a detailed budget is not required although account should be taken of the likely implications of expenditure. Assumptions may be made about information not included in the case study but these should be justified in the context of the scenario outlined.

CHAPTER SIX

UNDERSTANDING MARKETING RESEARCH

LEARNING OBJECTIVES

Having completed this chapter you should be able to:

- Understand the marketing research process and the factors which determine its importance.
- Distinguish between secondary and primary data collection, probability and non-probability sampling methods and quantitative and qualitative research techniques.
- Recognize the distinction between testing and research and the various testing methods in the communications industry.

INTRODUCTION

Samuel Johnson once observed that knowledge comes in two kinds: we either know about a subject ourselves or we know where we can find information about it. **Marketing research** is a means of developing the latter. It is, in basic terms, a collection of 'tools' of assessment, evaluation and measurement which seeks to reduce the knowledge 'distance' between the product's or service's manufacturer or supplier and the consumer, primarily by gathering relevant, pertinent data. Importantly it is an aid to decision making but is *not* a decision-making method in itself. Regardless of the quality of the data collected judgement will *always* play a part in the final analysis and will *always* determine the final decision.

Marketing research
A collection of 'tools' of assessment, evaluation and measurement which seek to reduce the knowledge 'distance' between the product's or service's manufacturer or supplier and the consumer, primarily through the supply of pertinent information concerning the customer.

MARKETING RESEARCH PROCESS

In simple terms the marketing research process might be illustrated by the diagram shown in Figure 6.1. As with most simplifications, however, it hides a number of variations in approach and complexity that have come to signify modern marketing research. This chapter concentrates on an overview of

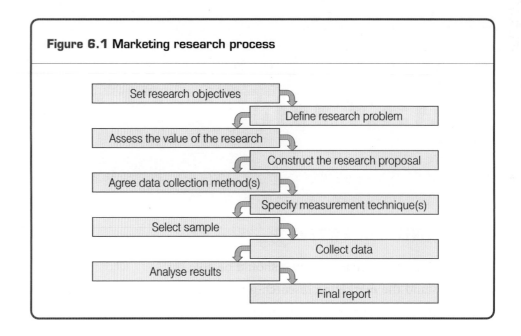

Figure 6.1 Marketing research process

Set research objectives

Define research problem

Assess the value of the research

Construct the research proposal

Agree data collection method(s)

Specify measurement technique(s)

Select sample

Collect data

Analyse results

Final report

research as it affects the marketing communications industry, however, apart from differences in the research problems and specialist research associated with the marketing communications industry, much parallels the more general marketing research processes.

Research should not be a haphazard process. The objectives of the research should be clear and fulfil a defined need. Research objectives should be derived directly from the organizational and marketing objectives and may refer to an existing or potential product or service or, specifically in relation to marketing communications, existing or potential campaigns and/or media. Defining the research problem is a critical step as it designates the areas of research and the types of data required to satisfy the research objectives. Whether the research is conducted internally or using a research agency it is invariably the problem definition stage that is the most difficult. In practice much of the information required may be available in-house. Sometimes, however, and particularly where new markets and/or new campaigns are considered it may be necessary to carry out **exploratory research** to try and establish the parameters of the research problem.

The importance of research assessment is growing within marketing communications as well as marketing in general. This is in recognition of the costs associated with research and that these costs have to be justifiable. The research assessment normally takes the form of a cost–benefit analysis; effectively the cost in monetary terms and in personnel and other resources against the expected benefits derived from the research. Not every company regards research as a viable option. A recent article in *Marketing* magazine suggests that 'while big companies use consumer research...smaller firms tend to go with gut instinct' (Dowdy 2004: 39). Brands launched without the benefit of research include Amé, herbal drink, and Clipper Teas. Other companies have used less than conventional research methodologies. For

Research objectives
Derived directly from the organizational and marketing objectives they may refer to an existing or potential product or service or, specifically in relation to marketing communications, existing or potential campaigns and/or media.

Research problem
What the research is designed to solve.

Exploratory research
Initial research designed to establish the parameters of the research problem.

Research assessment
Assessing the value of research against the benefits derived from it.

Cost–benefit analysis
Ratio of cost to benefit used to establish whether a project, research, campaign, etc. should proceed.

example the three founders of Innocent, the manufacturers of 'smoothie' fruit drinks, restricted their research to a music festival. Having bought £500 of fresh fruit they asked customers: 'Do you think we should give up our jobs to make these smoothies?' They provided a 'yes bin' and a 'no bin' for votes (empty bottles) to be registered and by the end of the festival the majority verdict was that they should go into business making the drinks (see case study Chapter 14).

Most major companies and agencies, however, will look for valid reasons for their research. Factors that determine the value of desired information include (Webb 2002: 17):

- The degree of 'newness' and, therefore, uncertainty in a particular environment.
- The degree of complexity in the environment.
- The strategic importance and cost of making the wrong decision(s).
- The degree of importance the company attaches to the decision(s) being made.

The more the uncertainty and complexity and the higher the costs associated with making the decision the more important it is to consider in-depth research.

At the other end of the scale too much data can confuse and hide clear meaning. As Advertising Planning Consultant Chris Forrest notes:

It is amazingly easy to waste lots of time just swimming aimlessly in data. Don't collect it for its own sake. When developing advertising strategy you are not the uniformed police constable who collects and files information, you are the detective who has to make a case out of it.
(Forrest 1999)

In some sectors **time-to-market** has become an important factor as to how much (or indeed whether) marketing and marketing communications research is carried out. In highly volatile and fast developing technological markets research frequently takes place in the marketplace itself (to the annoyance of 'innovators' who feel they are being used as guinea pigs). Given the need for speed and message dissemination to particular consumer groups marketing communicators frequently use word-of-mouth techniques such as viral marketing or guerrilla marketing (see Chapter 1) in such markets to communicate the benefits and obtain reaction and critical feedback.

Once the need for the research is established and costed a **research proposal** should be drawn up. In constructing the research proposal marketers should concentrate on the precise information needs of the organization. This is particularly important when an external organization is carrying out the research as not only does it aid accurate **briefing**, but it can also help management focus attention on the problem itself. In the course of a long and complicated research project the research proposal can act as a guide and reference point that will keep all the involved parties on track and within mutually agreed limits.

Time-to-market
The amount of time it takes an organization to get a product to market from its original inception.

Research proposal
Costed proposal for a particular research problem.

Briefing
Explanation of the marketing problem either internally or externally.

Conclusive research
Provides accurate and valid descriptions of the variables (descriptive research) or by determining the relationships between them (causal research), for example between advertising and sales.

Qualitative research
Looking to answer the 'why?' and the 'what?' type of questions qualitative research places greater emphasis on understanding consumer behaviour through insights.

Data collection
The collection of data for a particular research project.

Secondary data
Data which is already available from one or more sources. Secondary data may include internal company data or come from external agencies including research agencies, analysts, omnibus surveys, syndicated research or audit data, trade association reports or departments of local, national and supranational government.

Primary data
Data that is collected specifically for a particular research project.

Omnibus surveys
Surveys covering a wide range of interests including those of specific interest to the sponsoring company, are sent to a pre-selected panel of respondents. This type of research enables the costs to be shared with other companies participating in the survey.

Syndicated research or audit data
Carried out by specialist agencies who collect and analyse data on a regular (rolling research) or one-off basis. Clients normally pay a subscription for these services which are available for both retail (e.g. Nielson) and specialist markets.

Outdoor advertising
Posters, billboards, transport and other advertising that is located outside.

Online survey options at **http://web-online-surveys.com.**

Traditionally research has been characterized under two main headings: exploratory research and **conclusive research**, with the latter subdivided into **descriptive** and **causal** (Shao 1998). Exploratory research (often associated with **qualitative research** see page 135) is frequently seen as non-scientific and characterized by a large degree of flexibility and with no insistence on precise measurement. As the name implies this type of research was seen as useful in the exploratory phase, where different variables are defined so that the 'real work' of measurement can begin. Conclusive research would take this further by providing accurate and valid descriptions of the variables (descriptive research) or by determining the relationships between them (causal research), for example between advertising and sales.

Data collection methods can be sub-divided into two principal types: **secondary data** and **primary data**. Secondary data is data that is already available from one or more sources, whereas primary data is undertaken specifically for the project concerned. Secondary data may include internal company data or come from external agencies including research agencies, analysts, **omnibus surveys, syndicated research** or **audit data,**[1] trade association reports or departments of local, national and supranational government. There is often a fine line between what is regarded as secondary or primary data. Omnibus surveys, for example, may be an inexpensive way of gathering primary research. In these surveys forms, covering a wide range of interests including those of specific interest to the sponsoring company, are sent to a pre-selected panel of respondents. This type of research enables the costs to be shared with other companies participating in the survey. With a good knowledge of the market a specialized research company, such as MORI, can bring together co-sponsors for the survey thus saving costs for each participating organization. Syndicated research or audit data are carried out by specialist agencies who each collect and analyse data on a regular (rolling research) or one-off basis. Clients normally pay a subscription for these services which are available for both retail (e.g. Nielson) and specialist markets. In the UK various organizations gather data on the effectiveness of media, for example. The National Readership Survey examines the readership of over 200 publications whilst the Audit Bureau of Circulation (ABC) validates circulation claims by national and local press. Poster Audience Research (POSTAR) uses statistical modelling to assess the effectiveness of **outdoor advertising** on billboards and other sites. The Broadcasters Audience Research Board (BARB) produces estimates of television viewing on the various available terrestrial, satellite and other digital stations, whilst The Radio Joint Audience Research (RAJAR) does a similar job for audio-only transmissions.

Strictly speaking primary data is that which is specifically collected to answer the research objectives, although much of the above falls in to a grey area between secondary and primary research. In general, primary research data is required to answer specific marketing problems rather than for general management information.

---

[1]It should be noted that none of these terms are mutually exclusive and there are considerable overlaps in definitions.

Primary data may be collected in many different ways, and these include:

- **Questionnaire or survey research**: through structured or semi-structured personal, mail, telephone and (increasingly) e-mail and Web-based interviews.

- Discussion: Generally structured or unstructured **depth interviews** or group interviews (often called **panel interviews** in the communications industry). These techniques are used where direct questioning is unlikely to be informative and meaningful. Such interviews are used to generate ideas or investigate feelings and attitudes.

- Observation: used as a means of examining actual as opposed to predicted behaviour. There may, for example, be observation of consumers by a researcher interested in the effects of an in-store promotion. **EPoS (electronic point of sale)** technology has, however, revolutionized in-store monitoring particularly where the retailer shares information, in real-time, with the brand supplier. There is also a growing trend to electronic observation through set-top boxes (in the case of television audits) and the Internet (through **cookie** technology).

Whilst discussing data collection it should be noted that some unscrupulous companies misrepresent themselves as researchers when their principal objectives are selling product/services or fundraising. These practices, specifically prohibited by research associations, are known as **sugging** (selling under the guise of research) and **fugging** (fundraising under the guise of research) respectively.

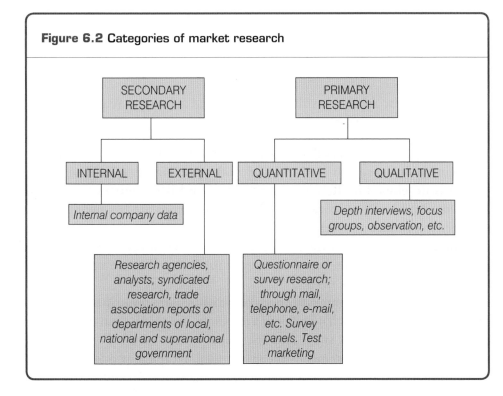

Figure 6.2 Categories of market research

Questionnaire or survey research
Surveys which use structured or semi-structured, personal, mail, telephone and (increasingly) e-mail and Web-based interviews.

Depth interviews
In-depth interviews with a limited number of respondents.

Panel interviews
Group interviews or focus groups.

Observation
Examining actual as opposed to predicted behaviour. For example an observation of consumers by a researcher interested in the effects of an in-store promotion.

Electronic point of sale (EPoS)
Technology at the point of sale that enable transactions to be tracked on a merchandise and customer level.

Cookie
A small text file left on the user's PC that identifies their browser so that they are 'recognized' when they revisit a site.

Sugging
Selling under the guise of research.

Fugging
Fundraising under the guise of research.

@ See online data source examples at: **www.cia.gov/cia/publications/factbook/index.html** and **http://smallbusiness.dnb.com/**.

Measurement techniques
Those techniques (largely quantitative) that are used when collecting data.

Quantitative research
Seeking to answer the questions 'how many?' or 'who?' Research that is looking to measure something.

Attitude scales
Scales that measures a respondent's attitude to predefined statements. Examples include nominal scales, ordinal scales, interval scales and ratio scales.

Content analysis
Used to attempt to quantify the results of unstructured (qualitative) data. This is a technique for making inferences (or recognizing patterns) from the data.

Factor analysis
Systematic review of the correlation between research variables which groups together those that are highly correlated to reduce a large number of variables to a smaller set that are not correlated.

Read about the Likert scale at: **http://ourworld.compuserve.com/homepages/jsuebersax/likert.htm.**

Summated scale
Where the scores for individual responses are added together to produce an overall result (e.g. Likert scale).

Image study
A study of the organization's image in relation to its competitors.

Sample selection
Determines the body of individuals involved in a research project.

Population
In marketing research terms population is the group (demographic, geodemographic, users, former customers, etc.) of interest to the marketer.

The selection of measurement techniques is largely but not exclusively associated with quantitative rather than qualitative research. Measurement is a means by which a property's characteristics may be quantified and should be appropriate to fulfil the research objective. The two main methods used in marketing are questionnaire analysis and attitude scales.

When analysing questionnaires structured questions provide answers (e.g. yes, no, don't know) that can be tabulated to produce meaningful information on a wide range of marketing communications situations. *Marketing*'s Adwatch column, for example, is based upon research by NOP Research Group who interview around 500 adults per month. The advantage of such a methodology is that it produces precise, easily readable information. The down-side is that accuracy may be lost in favour of simplicity and expediency (see Chapter 9 on advertising).

Whereas structured, closed questions (e.g. yes, no, don't know) produce simplified information, unstructured questions produce 'messy' answers that often defy categorization. This is, however, the 'rich information' that cannot be obtained through simplified questioning. In some qualitative research content analysis is used to attempt to quantify the results of unstructured data. This is a technique for making inferences (or recognizing patterns) from the data. Here some counting can be done, and some researchers go on to use factor analysis on the data although this does run the risk of substituting numbers for rich description (Goulding 2002).

As noted in Chapter 3 consumer attitudes are believed to be a crucial link between what consumers think and what they buy. Attitude scales come in a variety of forms:

- Nominal scales: where variables are categorized and used for classification, e.g. age, sex, place of birth, etc.
- Ordinal scales: where objects are ranked in order.
- Interval scales: usually positive or negative values about an arbitrary zero point.
- Ratio scales: are those with a predetermined zero point (e.g. percentage of satisfied customers).

An example of an interval scale widely used in marketing and marketing communications research is the Likert scale (see Figure 6.3). The Likert scale was developed by Rensis Likert in 1932 and is sometimes referred to as a summated scale, as scores for individual responses are frequently added together to produce an overall result.

Another example of an interval scale is the image study, which seeks to make image comparisons between an organization and its competitors. An example is shown in Box 6.1.

Sample selection determines the body of individuals involved in the research. To conduct a census of each member of a population would be extremely costly unless that population is small (e.g. local club membership). Population, in marketing research terms, means the group (demographic, geodemographic, users, former customers, etc.) of interest to the marketer. An alternative term, more often used in the marketing communications industry, is target audience. Normally a sample group is used that reflects, as closely as possible, the population as a whole. This sample stands as a proxy for those situations or populations with which they share one or more characteristics of target audiences. Sampling can be described under two headings: probability techniques and non-probability techniques. Some of the most popular of these techniques are shown in Box 6.2.

Target audience
A defined group of consumers (demographic, geodemographic, users, former customers, etc.) targeted by the marketer.

Probability techniques
Those techniques of selection that are independent of human judgement producing a known and non-zero probability of any one particular case in the population of cases being included in the sample. They are representative of (but never an exact match with) the population as a whole and a determination is made of their statistical accuracy.

Non-probability techniques
Techniques which do not adhere to the law of probability and, therefore, the results cannot be generalized across the population. Rather the sample is chosen at the convenience of the researcher or to fulfil the demands of some predetermined purpose.

Box 6.1 Example of an image study

Company	Number of respondents	Average score	Standard deviation
Lufthansa Technic	42	7.95	0.88
SR Technic	28	7.89	1.07
BA Engineering	34	6.72	1.70
Air France Industries	29	6.59	1.32
TEAM Aer Lingus	43	6.48	1.10
Sabena Technics	27	6.40	1.21
FLS Aerospace	49	6.38	1.15
Sogerma	25	6.26	1.54
ARL	6	5.50	1.66

Fifty-five respondents (maintenance service decision makers) from the European Airline Industry were asked to rate various aspects of aerospace maintenance services in January 1998 on a score of 1 to 10, where 1 was very poor and 10 was excellent. This table summarizes those views.

Source: Baines 1998.

Figure 6.3 Example of a Likert scale

	Strongly agree	Agree	Neither agree or disagree	Disagree	Strongly disagree
XYZ is the brand I prefer most					
If XYZ was not available in my local store I would go elsewhere					
XYZ is a quality brand					
XYZ reminds me of having fun					

Simple random sampling
Sampling based on the chance selection from the target population.

Systematic random sampling
An anonymous sample selection based on a sampling interval.

Sampling interval
When undertaking systematic random sampling the interval between respondents.

Sample error
Inherent in all research quantified, through the application of statistical formulae.

Stratified random sampling
Sample based on the variable percentages as they appear in the population as a whole. Variables may include demographics, income, geography, etc. and should be appropriate to the research taking place.

Cluster sampling
Where the population is divided into mutually exclusive, distinctly separate, subgroups (or clusters). A random selection of clusters is made and a random sample of units taken from these clusters.

Area cluster sampling
Where the population is divided into mutually exclusive, distinctly separate, subgroups (or clusters) on a geographical basis. A random selection of clusters is made and a random sample of units taken from these clusters.

Multistage sampling
A form of cluster sampling used where the subgroups, especially geographical location, are widely dispersed. As with cluster sampling the population is divided into subgroups but a further stage is involved before final sample selection. Techniques may vary but commonly subgroups are selected on a weighted (i.e. proportional to the population of that subgroup) basis and further subdivided, for example on an area (county, city, etc.) basis. The final sample selection is made from these sub-subgroups on a random basis.

Probability sampling includes those techniques of selection that are free from personal influence producing a known and non-zero likelihood of any one particular subject of the research being included in the sample (Kent 1999). They are representative of (but never an exact match with) the population as a whole and a determination is made of their statistical accuracy.[2] **Simple random sampling** is the most basic of techniques and works on the chance selection from the target population. **Systematic random sampling** again uses anonymous selection but based on a **sampling interval**. If, for example, 200 people are required from a population of 19 000, the sampling interval would be 95 (19 000 ÷ 200). In this example a random starting point (between 1 and 95) is chosen and from that point every 95th unit would be sampled. Both simple and systematic random samplings are carried out obeying the laws of probability and estimates can be made of the probable **sample error**. The disadvantage of these techniques is that they may produce unrepresentative samples particularly if the population has a wide degree of variability. **Stratified random sampling** tries to overcome this problem by choosing a sample based on the variable percentages as they appear in the population as a whole. Variables may include demographics, income, geography, etc. and should be appropriate to the research taking place. If, for example, age was an important variable then the sample would need to include in each age category a number of people in ratio to the population as a whole. Researchers would then look to fill the quota for each category. In the technique known as **cluster sampling** the population is again divided into mutually exclusive, distinctly separate, subgroups (or clusters). A random selection of clusters is made and a random sample of units taken from these clusters. In **area cluster sampling** geographical location is the variable. In the UK the locations frequently paralleled the Independent Television (ITV) regions so that the effect of supporting communications campaigns could be measured.[3] **Multistage sampling** is a form of cluster sampling used where the subgroups, especially geographical location, are widely dispersed. As with cluster sampling the population is divided into subgroups but a further stage is involved before final sample selection. Techniques may vary but commonly subgroups are selected on a weighted (i.e. proportional to the population of

[2]The statistical aspects of marketing communications research are outside the scope of this book. For further details on probability sampling see Baines and Chansarkar (2003).
[3]With the growth of digital stations and the drop in viewing figures to under 40 per cent this is much less effective than in the past.

that subgroup) basis and further subdivided, for example on an area (county, city, etc.) basis. The final sample selection is made from these sub-subgroups on a random basis.

However the probability sample is chosen it has to be large enough to be statistically valid. Sampling errors are inherent in all research of this type but can be minimized, or at least quantified, through the application of statistical formulae.[4] **Non-sampling errors** are all those other aspects of research that can seriously affect the outcome. These include such factors as misunderstanding and **interviewer bias**. Non-response is also a factor as it is difficult to know whether those who responded to a particular research programme were in any small way different from those who refused to take part.

Non-probability sampling techniques do not adhere to the law of probability and, therefore, the results cannot be generalized across the population. Rather the sample is chosen at the convenience of the researcher or to fulfil the demands of some predetermined purpose (Webb 2002: 56). **Convenience sampling** is usually a low cost 'straw poll' often used in the exploratory stages of a research programme. As the name suggests the researcher approaches an easily reachable group (e.g. work colleagues) to get a feel for the subject matter. In the technique known as **Judgement sampling** the sample selection is made (by the researcher with or without the advice of experts) based on their relevance to the research project. For example, research into European television advertising may suggest that the sample is made up of executives from that industry. **Purposive sampling** aims to select samples based on certain criteria associated with the research. Therefore, if the research is aimed at gauging the potential impact of a media campaign targeted at, for example, doctors, a purposive sample of doctors may be selected. **Quota sampling** makes more of an attempt to mirror the characteristics of the population by selecting on a proportional basis. For example, researchers investigating a new product launch might base their sample on the demographics (age, sex, etc.) of the target population in proportion to their presence in that population. In **snowball sampling** the respondents are initially selected at random and their views sought. Interviewees are then asked to nominate other people who are part of that population and so on.

Both probability and non-probability sampling have their advantages and disadvantages in terms of cost, speed, sample error, and, ultimately, judgement. In practice, the estimation of sample size and definition is frequently on the basis of previous experience.

QUALITATIVE VS QUANTITATIVE RESEARCH

According to Robson (1993) there are basically two approaches to research. There is the one variously labelled as positivistic, natural science based,

Non-sampling errors
Those aspects of research (other than sampling errors) that can seriously affect the outcome. These include such factors as misunderstanding and interviewer bias. Non-response is also a factor as it is difficult to know whether those who responded to a particular research programme were in any way different from those who refused to take part.

Interviewer bias
Where the bias views of the interviewer corrupts the data collection.

Convenience sampling
A low-cost 'straw poll' often used in the exploratory stages of a research programme.

Judgement sampling
Where the sample selection is made (by the researcher with or without the advice of experts) based on their relevance to the research project.

Purposive sampling
Samples based on certain criteria associated with the research. Therefore, if the research is aimed at gauging the potential impact of a media campaign targeted at, for example, doctors, a purposive sample of doctors may be selected.

Quota sampling
Attempts of researchers to mirror the characteristics of the population by selecting on a proportional basis. For example, researchers investigating a new product launch might base their sample on the demographics (age, sex, etc.) of the target population in proportion to their presence in that population.

Snowball sampling
Where respondent are initially selected at random and their views sought. Interviewees are then asked to nominate other people who are part of that population and so on.

[4]For further details on probability sampling errors see Baines and Chansarkar (2003).

hypothetico-duductive, quantitative or simply 'scientific' and that which is variously called interpretative, ethnographic, phenomenological or qualitative amongst other labels.[5] In simple terms the positivist seeks to explain patterns of behaviour whilst the interpretativist seeks to establish the motivations and actions that lead to these patterns of behaviour (Baker 2001). Simpler still would be to describe quantitative research as seeking to answer the questions 'how many?' or 'who?' and qualitative research for answering the 'why?' and the 'what?' type of questions. As previously noted qualitative marketing research was seen as of practical use only in the exploratory phase, before the 'real work' of quantitative measurement began. This viewpoint, although not completely eradicated, is changing. As Goulding (2002: 9) notes:

> *Even the realm of marketing research, once so heavily reliant on the survey instrument as the main source of data collection, is starting to place greater emphasis on understanding consumer behaviour through qualitative insights, rather than rushing to measure and predict actions before such insights are established.*

Despite the growth in qualitative research quantitative research still dominates amongst the largest research agencies. This is illustrated in Box 6.3 below which shows a breakdown of research types by those agencies in the 'top 20 UK research agencies' who reported this information (those not listed did not report the breakdown).

As noted qualitative research is principally used to answer the 'why' and the 'what' rather than the 'how many' or the 'who' type questions best answered

---

Box 6.3 Research agencies quantitative versus qualitative research

Rank◆	Company	Quantitative research (%)	Qualitative research (%)	Other research* (%)	Turnover 2003 (£m)
1	Taylor Nelson Sofres	58	7	35	159.5
5	Ipsos UK	60	5	35	47.0
6	Synovate	48	32	20	46.9
9	MORI	73	13	14	39.4
11	Incepta Marketing Intel	51	43	6	19.6
12	Martin Hamlin GfK	83	17	0	18.3
17	Maritz Research	30	2	68	11.6

*Other includes those aspects which, in the survey, were not considered as falling under the quantitative or qualitative headings including continuous/syndicated research, mystery shoppers and other specialist research.

◆Rank refers to the company's position in the *Marketing* research league table. Other companies did not disclose the breakdown of their activities.

Source: *Marketing*, 14 July 2004.

---

[5] This two-way division is not strictly accurate as it is possible to have positivist/qualitative and interpretivist/quantitative methodologies. The above, however, represents the more common approach.

through quantitative research. The different characteristics of qualitative and quantitative research as described in Box 6.4.

Box 6.4 Qualitative vs quantitative

Qualitative research
- Open ended, dynamic, flexible
- Depth of understanding
- Taps consumer creativity
- Database – broader and deeper
- Penetrates rationalized or superficial responses
- Richer source of ideas for marketing and creative teams.

Quantitative research
- Statistical and numerical measurement
- Subgroup sampling or comparisons
- Survey can be repeated in the future and the results compared
- Taps individual responses
- Less dependent on research executives' skills or orientation.

Source: Webb 2002.

Focus groups
Normally consist of a small number (eight to ten) target consumers brought together to discuss elements of a campaign from the initial concept stage to post production.

Consumer juries
A collection of target consumers who are asked to rank in order ideas or concepts put to them and explain their choices.

The differences appear significant but then again the outcomes are designed to be different. Whereas quantitative research techniques such as surveys emphasize theory testing and measuring, qualitative techniques are looking for meaning and understanding. Some techniques are less obviously one method or the other. There are numerous (perhaps, in theory, unlimited) research techniques on the continuum between the highly quantitative and highly qualitative research some of which are shown on the continuum in Figure 6.4 below.

Figure 6.4 Continuum of research techniques

<<<<<< Quantitative/Positivist Research Techniques					Qualitative/Interpretavist >>>>>> Research Techniques		
Surveys and other multivariate techniques	Causal modelling and structural equation modelling	Experiments	Instrumental case studies	In-depth interviews	Focus groups / Consumer juries	Action research	Ethno-graphic studies

In the marketing communications industry the most familiar qualitative techniques are in-depth interviews, **focus groups** and **consumer juries**. The objective of in-depth interviewing is to discover 'feelings, memories and interpretations that we cannot observe or discover in other ways' (Carson *et al.* 2001: 73). They can range from an informal conversation to highly structured interviews. They might be used to seek an interviewee's perspective on a new campaign or to develop customer profiles covering a wide range of needs and preferences.

Concept stage
The period when campaign concepts are being developed.

Story-boards
Artistic impressions of a campaign.

Direct opinion measurement
Research that directly asks target consumers about aspects such as message clarity, interest, feelings and attitudes.

Ethnography (ethnographic research)
Where researchers submerge themselves in consumer culture to view consumer dynamics. Photography and video diaries are used by market researchers to delve into consumers' minds.

Focus groups have been used extensively in the marketing communications industry for many years. They normally consist of a small number (eight to ten) of target consumers brought together to discuss elements of a campaign from the initial **concept stage** to post production. At the concept stage of an advertising campaign for example, the target sample are presented with rough outlines or **story-boards** giving an idea of the campaign or campaigns under consideration. A professional moderator aims to understand the thoughts, feelings and attitudes of the group towards a product or service, media or message.

Consumer juries also consist of a collection of target consumers who are asked to rank in order, ideas or concepts put to them and to explain their choices. This type of research is also known as **direct opinion measurement** which, as it implies, asks jurors directly about aspects such as message clarity, interest, feelings and attitudes.

In addition to these common qualitative techniques there is growing use of, what some observers might consider, more esoteric techniques. For example Goulding (2002: 10) describes Semiotic Solutions as a company that 'specialises in cultural qualitative research, drawing upon techniques borrowed from linguistic philosophy, cultural anthropology and the systematic study of signs and codes'. The company's research has formed the basis of many national and international television campaigns and brand repositioning for organizations such as British Telecommunications, Tesco and Coca-Cola. The article in Minicase 6.1 below describes how Link Consumer Strategies are using qualitative techniques to discover from consumers 'genuine insights into subconscious motivations'. **Ethnography**, is currently a marketing research buzzword although it is unlikely that many research agencies submerge themselves in consumer culture as deeply as might be expected by the term. According to David Iddiols,[6] a partner at HPI Research: 'Nearly every agency out there claims to be doing it…but in reality, many are not getting close enough to view the consumer dynamics, which is where the value of ethnographic research resides.' Sanjay Nazerali,[7] Managing Director of research agency The Depot sees ethnographic techniques as a solution to 'the problem of artificial focus groups' but that to 'be of true value, ethnography needs to be about getting deeper, not closer'. The arguments against ethnographic research are less to do with its validity and more to do with the standard of its execution (Barrand 2004). The discipline's base in social anthropology gives a benchmark for future research which, currently, appears to fall well short of this standard.

TESTING

Testing
Unlike marketing research testing measures actual behaviour but does not answer the 'why' and 'how' questions.

Strictly speaking a distinction should be made between marketing research and **testing** (aspects of direct marketing testing will be covered in more depth

[6]Quoted in Barrand (2004: 48).
[7]Quoted in Barrand (2004: 49).

How to dig deeper into the consumer mind

Anthropologists who observe people shopping – 'streetologists' – are among some innovative methods, including cameras and video diaries, being used by market researchers to delve into consumers' minds.

Frustrated by a lack of new insights into product or service categories such as food, drink and banking, research company Link Consumer Strategies, whose clients include Diageo, Kraft and Tesco, is asking consumers to take a more active part in product development.

'It used to be enough to show a consumer a new brand of milkshake, say, and to record that he or she liked the packaging simply because pink had always been their favourite colour', says Louise Southcott, chairman of Link. 'Today though, with so many of our basic needs already met by marketers, it is necessary to go beyond the standard superficialities and tap into people's subconscious. If pink is their favourite colour because it reminds them of a happy childhood, that is something marketers can work with.'

Rita Clifton, chairman of the Interbrand branding agency, agrees that psychology is playing an increasing role in market research and predicts that pure observation will become more important. 'The popularity of reality TV has shown that the public enjoy being filmed in their homes, or on the street, and this is a major boon for market researchers', she says.

Link asks its research subjects to complete complex 'self-investigative' or homework assignments before they attend research sessions, in order to gain greater insight into consumer behaviour than traditional market research provides. Ms Southcott says: 'Increasingly pernicious marketing problems require more in-depth, powerful tools

Recording shoppers on the street or asking them to keep video diaries are increasingly popular approaches for market researchers.

to unlock them and while consumer dialogue is important, it needs to be made to work much harder. By asking consumers to really think about their lives, we can get genuine insights into subconscious motivations.'

Link cites Hovis Crusty White, launched by British Bakeries three years ago. 'We established early on that most people thought white sliced bread was tasteless, nasty stuff and then asked them for the sorts of things that would make them feel better about white sliced bread. 'Many of them came up with words like "love", "comfort" and "homeliness" and some showed a beautiful crusty loaf. The feeling of homeliness associated with the crust was an important hook and the resulting product has done very well in a crowded marketplace.'

Link is also deliberately recruiting more 'creative' and 'early adopter' research subjects. A broader mix of backgrounds and occupations leads to more stimulating debate and encourages participants to reveal more about themselves. Creative types are identified by their ability to answer challenging questions quickly. Link's other techniques include asking respondents to decorate and fill a box of treasured mementos and accompanied shopping trips, when researchers assess the impact of store promotions on shopping decisions.

While the initial work is to find out what really motivates consumers, says Ms Southcott, the really important part is 'to come up with practical answers for our clients about what they should do to give their launch its greatest chance of success, or how they can recapture the power of an established but tired brand. The stuff about what motivates consumers is really interesting but it needs to be backed up with firm business conclusions.'

By Virginia Matthews, *Financial Times*, 8 October 2003 (used with permission).

in Chapter 13). Marketing research is used to reveal attitudes to a campaign, brand or some other aspect of the exchange process. Testing, by comparison, measures actual behaviour. Attitude, as discussed previously, does not determine action. A consumer may respond very positively to the launch, for example, of a new, top-of-the-range sports-car. Family circumstances or lack of funds may mean that this positive attitude will never result in ownership. On the other hand testing will not tell you why a customer has made one choice over another which may affect future planning. As with other aspects of marketing communication the use of one or more measurement techniques will probably result in better overall results.

Testing is also the term used for research into existing or modified factors associated with the marketing of a product or service. Marketing communicators will frequently use **test markets** to carry out controlled experiments before exposing the 'new feature' (product, service, campaign, distribution, etc.) to a full national or even international launch. Technology is such that national television, radio and newspapers have regional editions which may be supplemented by local media to create a test market inside which the new feature can be exposed. Depending on the feature involved, another region or the rest of the market may act as the **control sample** against which results can be measured.

When an advertisement is developed it may be subjected to a number of tests. In the print industries **dummy** magazines may be prepared and distributed to the target audience. These magazines contain normal **editorial** material alongside test advertising. Current advertising is also included as a control against which the new advertising can be measured. Readers are asked questions relating to both the advertising and the editorial in an attempt to establish the impact of the planned campaign and/or the setting of the material.

Test markets
Geographically controlled testing before fully exposing the 'new feature' (product, service, campaign, distribution, etc.) or new brand to a full national or even international launch.

Control sample
The sample which is unaffected by change against which altered variables can be tested.

Dummy
Uncirculated, trial editions of magazines sent to target advertisers or target audiences.

Editorial
Although the term should strictly only be applied to copy written by a newspaper or magazine editor it is frequently used to describe all newspaper or magazine copy.

Previews of finished advertising is common. In the case of television commercials they are often given a **test-screening** prior to final transmission. Following the screening the views of the audience are sought. In certain instances views are sought before and after the screening so that any **persuasion shift** (i.e. changes in preferences) can be monitored. Although this adds to the perceived effectiveness of the advertising, persuasion shift is not, however, a good indicator of actual performance. For example, one of the key observations of a major evaluation of 400 individual advertising tests in the USA was that there was no clear relationship whatsoever between measures of persuasion shift and eventual sales performance (Lodish and Lubetkin 1992).

Post-testing of advertising is common with a number of techniques being used as proxy measures (i.e. not direct measures but subjective indicators) for advertising effectiveness. These include recall tests, or advertising awareness tests, which are designed to measure the impression that particular advertising has on the memory of the target audience measured on a nominal **Awareness Index (AI)**, and recognition tests, which measure the level of attention paid to such advertising and its affect on the consumer (see Chapter 9). Neither test is perfect although its supporters claim 'ad awareness, or recall, is a metric that has stood the test of time and is viewed worldwide as the best means of assessing advertising effectiveness' (Miles 2004a: 57). Its detractors point out that awareness and recall are not good indicators of ultimate purchase intentions. Robert Heath[8] founder of The Value Creation Society cites the example of Stella Artois. Its initial UK press campaign, as measured by a competitor's tracking study, showed that it achieved a claimed ad awareness of just 4 per cent in 1990 compared with 29 per cent for the leading TV-advertised lager brand Castlemaine XXXX. Stella's rating for quality on the same survey was, however, 45 per cent (compared to Castlemaine's 19 per cent). When all the other factors involved were studied, the advertising proved to have been given a star rating. This reinforced the view that Stella Artois had the ability to develop strong brand values without necessarily performing successfully on memory-based evaluative measures.

Test-screening
Screening of an advertisement to a sample audience prior to final transmission.

Persuasion shift
Changes in preferences which occur having seen an advertisement.

Post-testing
Testing after a campaign.

Awareness Index
A measure of advertising awareness.

ONLINE MARKET RESEARCH

With all the hype concerning the Internet and electronic communications it should be remembered that 'online' is, basically, just another medium and many of the techniques and concepts using lesser technology also apply here. There is no doubt, however, that online research has and will have an effect on marketing research in the future. According to *Inside Research*,[9] which has been tracking the medium, spending was predicted to rise to £515m in the USA and £73m in Europe in 2004. There are two types of panel used in

[8]Quoted in Miles (2004a: 57).
[9]Quoted in Miles (2004b: 39).

Access panels
Provide respondents for survey-style information and are made up of targets who have been invited by e-mail to take part with a link to the web survey.

Proprietary panels
Online surveys set up or commissioned by a client firm usually made up of customers of that company.

online research. **Access panels** provide samples for survey-style information and are made up of targets who have been invited by e-mail to take part with a link to the Web survey. **Proprietary panels** are set up or commissioned by a client firm and are usually made up of the customers of that company. To encourage participation in these surveys the researchers often use incentives such as the chance to win a substantial prize. According to Miles (2004b) there are both pros and cons involved with online research and these are shown in Figure 6.5 below.

Figure 6.5 Online panels

The pros of online research	The cons of online research
1 Clients and analysts can see results being compiled in real time.	1 Online panels' demographic profile can differ from that of the general population.
2 Online surveys save time and money compared with face-to-face interviews.	2 If questionnaires take longer than 20 minutes to fill in quality can suffer and they may go uncompleted.
3 Consumers welcome surveys they can fill in when they want to and often need no incentive to do so.	3 Poor recruitment and badly managed panels can damage the data.
4 A more relaxed environment leads to better quality, honest and reasoned responses.	4 Technical problems, such as browser incompatibility, can mean panellists give up.
5 Panellist background data allows immediate access to key target audiences unrestricted by geography.	5 Programming costs are higher than for off-line questionnaires.

Source: Miles 2004b: 40.

POSTSCRIPT

An example of online research at: **www.nielsen-netratings.com** and Internet gateways at: **www.intute.ac.uk/socialsciences** and **www.hero.ac.uk.**

For some considerable time researchers have been concerned about the public's growing unwillingness to take part in marketing research (Nancarrow *et al.* 2004). One reason is most probably associated with the growing, some might say excessive, amount of research by mail, through newspapers or in response (usually by telephone, e-mail and text messaging) to radio or television polling. Another reason may be the growing consumer-literate population who, in return for information, demand more and more incentives before parting with what they know is valuable information. A third reason may be the growth in the number of organizations supplying details to other organizations and the barrage of marketing material that results. Consumers are apparently becoming more selective about who should benefit from their valuable data.

Summary

This chapter considered the marketing research process. It noted the importance of setting research objectives and defining the research problem before constructing the research proposal. It reviewed data collection methods and sampling types and the differences between secondary and primary methods. It also discussed quantitative and qualitative techniques and the growth of more esoteric techniques such as ethnography. Testing was also defined and testing techniques reviewed. The growth of online marketing research was also examined. A postscript to the chapter noted the growing unwillingness of the public to take part in research.

Review questions

1 Describe the marketing research process.

2 In deciding on what data to seek, what factors might determine the value of the information to be gathered when making an assessment of worth?

3 Why would you draw up a research proposal?

4 Explain 'sugging' and 'fugging'.

5 What is the difference between a nominal and an ordinal scale?

6 How would you classify 'judgement sampling'?

7 Explain the difference between qualitative and quantitative research approaches.

8 What do you understand by the term 'consumer jury'?

9 Why would you undertake a test before fully rolling out a market research exercise?

10 What are the pros and cons of online research?

Discussion questions

1 If you were only able to gather research via the Internet, what are the challenges this might pose both in terms of data gathering and the value of the data gathered?

2 What is the difference between exploratory research and conclusive research and how might your approach to these differ, if at all?

3 What is the difference between probability and non-probability sampling and when might you use them?

Further reading

Agafonoff, N. (2006) 'Adapting ethnographic research methods to ad hoc commercial market research', *Qualitative Market Research: An International Journal*, Apr., 9 (2): 115–25. Delving into the nature of ethnography to evaluate its potential as an applied qualitative research method in commercial *ad hoc* market research.

Agafonoff, N. (2006) 'Exploring the privacy implications of addressable advertising and viewer profiling', *Communications of the Acm*, May, 49 (5): 119–23. Looking at the practice of collecting consumer viewing habits on the Internet by advertising companies.

McDougall, J. and Chantrey, D. (2004) 'The making of tomorrow's consumer', *Young Consumers*, Quarter 3, 5 (4): 8–18. Presents the result of Millward Brown's international study of the youth generation's relationship with brands.

Wyner, G.A. (2006) 'Coping with media fragmentation', *Marketing Research*, Summer, 18 (2): 6–7. Looking at the ever-increasing outlets for marketing, including mobile phones, the Internet, product placement and new media technologies.

Chapter references

Baines, P. (1998) 'Consultancy Report FLS Aerospace Advertising Effectiveness Study', Middlesex University Business School.

Baines, P. and Chansarkar, B. (2003) *Introducing Marketing Research*, Chichester: John Wiley.

Baker, M.J. (2001) *Critical Perspectives on Business and Management*, London: Routledge.

Barrand, D. (2004) 'Promoting change', *Marketing*, 6 October: 43–5.

Carson, D., Gilmour, A., Perry, C. and Gronhaug, K. (2001) *Qualitative Marketing Research*, London: Sage Publications.

Dowdy, C. (2004) 'Customer knows best', *Marketing*, 2 September: 39–40.

Forrest, C. (1999) 'Quantitative Data and Advertising Strategy Development', in L. Butterfield (ed.), *Excellence in Advertising: The IPA Guide to Best Practice*, Oxford: Butterworth Heinemann.

Goulding, C. (2002) *Grounded Theory: A Practical Guide for Management, Business and Marketing Researchers*, London: Sage.

Kent, R.A. (1999) *Marketing Research: Measurement, Method and Application*. London: International Thomson Business.

Lodish, L.M. and Lubetkin, B. (1992) 'General Truths?', *Admap* (February): 9–15.

Miles, L. (2004a) 'Recall vs recognition', *Marketing*, 21 April: 57–8.

Miles, L. (2004b) 'On-line, on tap', *Marketing*, 16 June: 39–40.

Nancarrow, C., Tinson, J. and Evans, M. (2004) 'Polls as marketing weapons: implications for the market research industry', *Journal of Marketing Management*, 20 (5/6): 639–55.

Robson, C. (1993) *Real World Research: A Resource for Social Scientists and Practitioner-Researchers*, Oxford: Blackwell.

Shao, A.T. (1998) *Marketing Research: An Aid to Decision Making*, Cincinnati: South Western College Publishing.

Webb, J.R. (2002) *Understanding and Designing Market Research*, 2nd edn, London: Thomson Learning.

CASE STUDY 6.1

'That's no way to treat a lady'

Marketers have an unfortunate tendency to stereotype women. Some 91 per cent of women say advertisers do not understand them and 58 per cent of women are annoyed by marketers' approaches. Marketers tend to ignore or generalize women's circumstances and place them in demographic categories that are no longer relevant or applicable to today's female consumer – the perfect mum, the alpha female, the fashionista, the beauty bunny or the great granny have nothing, or very little, to do with real women's lives, aspirations and needs.

In general, people, and especially women, are adopting a more individualistic approach to living and lifestyle. They marry much later, if at all, and children and marriage are no longer intrinsically linked. The number of UK marriages has fallen from 300 000 to 200 000 each year. The average age for women to marry in Britain today is 28, and by 2005 less than half of the female population were married.

Currently, 28 per cent of British households are single households. The percentage of first-time mothers in their forties has doubled since 1950 and figures within the nuclear family structure are in meltdown, with the number of children dropping from the 2.4 standard to just 1.3. Greater financial independence has seen more women becoming SMCs (Single Mothers by Choice), and almost 50 per cent of women now have a child outside marriage, compared to just 17 per cent 20 years ago. The average age for having a first child in Britain has changed from 26 to 29. And more and more women are not just putting off childbirth, they are cancelling it completely. If these trends continue some 25 per cent of British woman born after 1973 will be childless at 45.

Career opportunities

Most women now participate in the workforce – 76 per cent of all US woman aged 25 to 54 work full or part time. They also work longer hours – twice as many women than in 1979 work 49 hours or more per week. They are earning higher salaries than ever before and more businesses than ever are set up by women. Women are also beginning to outnumber men in the younger age groups in the creative professions, media and marketing – plus medicine, public sector management and accountancy.

Single women make up a fifth of all mortgage applications, and the spending power of women in the USA and Western Europe is predicted to rise from $980 billion in 2002 to $1400 billion by 2007.

The result of these social shifts is not only that a large number of single working women are earning lots of money and are highly influential consumers and tastemakers, but that women pride themselves on their business acumen and value the financial independence and the freedom it gives them. Their hard work means they can afford to play hard and they feel free to spend and consume as they wish.

Women's high disposable income makes them an attractive market and prime candidates for the sort of brands that pay real attention to their specific needs and encourage and allow relationships. Getting women's attention is hard: they are media-literate, recognize a sell when they see one – and they don't like to be told what to do.

Changing attitudes

Women are becoming increasingly intolerant of the lack of insight and attention being paid to their needs. They are no longer attracted by the classic stereotypes and are rebelling against the dictates of perfect mother/wife/executive roles. Women want brands to see their 'other lives' and respect and acknowledge them.

To many, media people still view women through male eyes, alienating rather than encouraging them. Women want to be addressed on their own terms and with products that they can develop a relationship with. Women don't want to be marketed at or solicited. They want non-invasive peripheral selling.

brush it, blow-dry it,
let the weather at it;
if there's light damage,
make sure the solution
isn't too heavy-handed.

We all enjoy expressing ourselves through our hair. But the things our hair goes through every day, can weaken it, causing slight dryness, flyaways and a few split ends.

New Dove Essential Care, helps strengthen it again, without overdoing it and weighing your hair down, leaving hair soft and silky to the touch.

New Dove. Give your hair just the right level of care.

campaignforrealbeauty.co.uk 🕊 *Dove*

New Dove Essential Care.

Dove has launched a sophisticated marketing campaign that plays against the traditional marketing stereotypes of women and fashion.

Women are very different from men. They are more complex and multifaceted – they operate in a highly personal way and are concerned with everything a brand does and says. Men buy on the spot, women gather information, look at all options and talk and network until they make a brand decision. Women resonate with messages focused on values, relationships and win-win mutuality, not competitive, hierarchical ideas. In fact, women are already the dominant consumer force, making 92 per cent of all purchasing decisions and recommending a good experience 21 times versus men's 2.6 times.

Advertisers and marketers have been slow to recognize that woman don't buy brands but join them. Adding a splash of pink or a touch of 'female values' doesn't change the fact that women still want marketing messages to reflect the reality of their lives – lives that are fuller and increasingly complex.

Women are not a homogeneous group, they are divided by age, lifestage, wealth, family status and education, so not only is it time for marketers to realize that women are different from men, but that in fact, women are different from any brand or advertiser targeting one stereotype over another will be penalized.

Female consumers demand brands and products that reflect their individual status. They expect to be treated fairly, not marginalized or charged extra because they are perceived as being a lucrative market segment.

The advertising industry has not always been quick to pick up on the changing expectations of women. Far too often those creating the advertising material are male, and it is all too easy for them to fall back on the old stereotypes – the housewife preoccupied with the whiteness of her wash, the young woman who only wants to get married, the granny who longs for a stairlift and a telephone call from her grandchild.

In an increasingly fragmented society, brands that allow individual relationships with the female consumer will succeed. It is time for marketers to realize that women have many lives and lifestyles and to target them accordingly.

Case study questions

1 What challenges does this article raise for future consumer research?

2 What is meant by the comment that 'advertisers and marketers have been slow to recognize that women don't buy brands but join them' and how might this affect marketing research?

3 Give examples of stereotyping in advertising.

Source: Rebekka Bay, 'That's no Way to Treat a Lady' *The Marketer*, 7 November 2004: 13–15.

CASE STUDY 6.2

Imbibe Drinks*

Imbibe Ltd is a manufacturer of non-alcoholic drinks largely distributed via a select number of off-licences and public houses across the UK. Their range consists of all the standard products (tonic water, lemonade, etc.) as well as a few that are more exotic (e.g. kiwi juice). Although they are ranked a lowly sixth in terms of UK soft-drink suppliers they have a loyal customer base and had managed in the financial year 2006/2007 to increase turnover by 7 per cent to a figure approaching £3 million.

The future, however, does not look quite so bright. Competition is becoming more intense as the overall numbers of public houses and off-licences fall and the supermarkets increase their share of the business. The company had responded initially by targeting the supermarkets but this had not been overly successful. Imbibe had the capacity

* Please note that this case study is based on a fictional example.

▶

to produce own-branded goods in limited quantities and had hoped that this volume would replace any branded business lost. The margins, however, were much tighter than the company felt it could afford and so other ideas were considered.

Following a period of research and development Imbibe are ready to launch a new product that they hope will recover their position in the market. 'Imbibalite' is a high-energy drink with a strong, almost coffee-like, taste. Although there are other successful high-energy products available (e.g. Red Bull) 'Imbibalite' seeks to differentiate itself on the basis of its unique flavouring. Research has suggested that this taste is not to everyone's liking but that it did score highly with a significant minority of the population who were said to have 'more mature tastes'. Indeed this minority group were vividly described by the agency that carried out the research as in the 25 to 35 age range, often single but with extensive social lives.

Imbibe plan to launch 'Imbibalite' in October 2007. They recognize that the marketing communications experience they have in-house is limited and have appointed Adara a local marketing communications agency to help them in this part of the launch process.

Case study question

1 Assume you are the Adara consultant working with Imbibe. Prepare a marketing communications plan for the launch of Imbibalite. At this stage a detailed budget is not required although account should be taken of the likely implications of expenditure and in particular the likely financial limitations of a small company. Assumptions may be made about information not included in the case study but these should be justified in the context of the scenario outlined.

The first Red Bull Air Race 2006 in Abu Dhabi – Red Bull's Air Race World Series is just one part of an incredibly sophisticated marketing strategy for the energy drink company.

CHAPTER SEVEN
TARGET MARKETING

LEARNING OBJECTIVES

Having completed this chapter you should be able to:

- Understand why segmentation, targeting and positioning are seen as fundamental to marketing.
- Explain the major ways in which a market can be segmented.
- Describe ways in which a segment might be targeted.
- Recognize the place of loyalty in the target marketing process.
- Understand the concepts behind positioning and repositioning in target markets.

INTRODUCTION

Successful marketing campaigns are said to be dependent on the answers to three basic questions:

- Who is my customer?
- What do they buy?
- Where can I find them?

In an attempt to answer these questions marketers have developed various tools that enable them to establish potential customer profiles and target those consumers whose profile matches this most closely. Target marketing or segmentation, targeting and positioning (sometimes shortened to STP) is claimed to be one of the 'absolutely fundamental approaches to marketing' (Smith and Taylor 2002: 35). STP is certainly at the heart of, what has become known as, transactional marketing[1] the dominant marketing paradigm for much of the twentieth century, with its supremacy only comparatively recently being challenged with the advent of relationship marketing.

STP
Shorthand for segmentation, targeting and positioning.

Transactional marketing
The traditional marketing or mass-marketing paradigm.

Relationship marketing
To 'identify and establish, maintain and enhance and, when necessary, terminate relationships with customers and other stakeholders, at a profit so that the objectives of all parties involved are met; and this is done by mutual exchange and fulfilment of promises' (Grönroos 1994: 9).

---

[1]Transactional marketing is sometimes referred to as the traditional marketing or mass-marketing paradigm.

SEGMENTATION AND TARGETING

The fundamentals of STP are graphically illustrated in Figure 7.1. In practice segmentation and targeting is all about the division of a large market (defined perhaps geographically or by industry sector) into smaller market segments. Each segment has its own distinct needs and wants and/or may respond to communication stimuli in different ways. For this reason some segments may be more attractive (because they are more practical and/or beneficial) to target than others. Attractive target markets will generally be more profitable because they are:

- closer or more easily reachable than other target markets;
- may prove or have already proven to be more loyal; and/or
- may prove or have proven to be heavy users of the product or service.

Target marketing is where specific segments are selected and marketing plans developed (traditionally based around the manipulation of the **marketing mix** or 4Ps) to satisfy the needs of the potential buyers in chosen segments. In order to ensure communications are coherent, consistent, uniform and successful, it follows that a clear understanding of the segmentation base is vital. For this reason viable segments should meet a number of important criteria (represented by the mnemonic **ADMARS**). They should be:

- **Accessible**: they can be reached through specific media.
- **Differentiated**: different from other segments.

Marketing mix
Otherwise known as the 4Ps (product, place, price and promotion) of marketing.

ADMARS
Segmentation mnemonic Accessible, Differentiated, Measurable, Actionable, Relevant and Substantial.

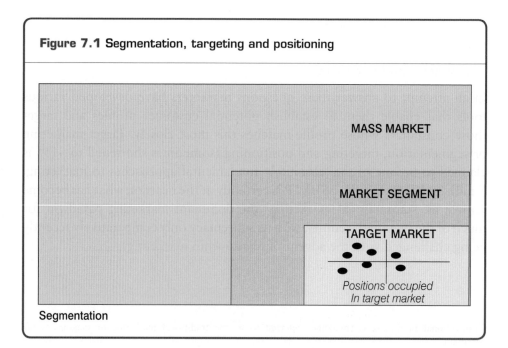

Figure 7.1 Segmentation, targeting and positioning

MASS MARKET

MARKET SEGMENT

TARGET MARKET

Positions occupied In target market

Segmentation

- Measurable: they can be defined and measured to some degree of accuracy.
- Actionable: the company has the resources to reach them.
- Relevant: the product/service is relevant to this segment.
- Substantial: the segment is large enough to warrant targeting.

There are various ways of segmenting the market many of which were discussed previously in Chapter 3 and are summarized in Box 7.1 below.

Often segmentation may take place on the basis of two or more variables. The example shown below (Figure 7.2) assumes that vineyard holidays would be attractive to frequent leisure travellers but even more attractive to frequent travellers who are also wine drinkers. The consumer information required to permit such segmentation may already be available within the organization

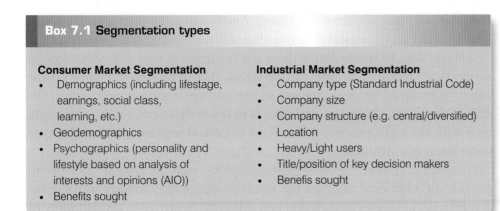

Box 7.1 Segmentation types

Consumer Market Segmentation
- Demographics (including lifestage, earnings, social class, learning, etc.)
- Geodemographics
- Psychographics (personality and lifestyle based on analysis of interests and opinions (AIO))
- Benefits sought

Industrial Market Segmentation
- Company type (Standard Industrial Code)
- Company size
- Company structure (e.g. central/diversified)
- Location
- Heavy/Light users
- Title/position of key decision makers
- Benefis sought

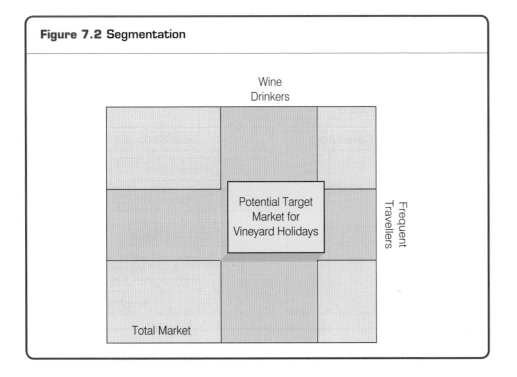

Figure 7.2 Segmentation

Lists
Listings of potential customers with a specific characteristic (e.g. food lovers) available to rent for a specific direct mail, telemarketing or e-mail campaign.

List brokers
Intermediaries between list owners and organizations wishing to rent lists.

Demographic
Statistical data relating to the population and groups within it.

Geodemographics
A method of segregating a market on the basis of social demographics and location.

or be purchased (although strictly each list is rented[2]) as **lists** (see Chapter 13) available from **list brokers** or other commercial sources.

There are numerous ways with which to segment a market, indeed one of the biggest criticisms of segmentation is that marketers define segments to fit their own beliefs and prejudices rather than being reflective of the market. Consultants are frequently criticized for developing customer typologies of dubious practical use. In their defence such professionals argue that it is better to concentrate on one segment rather than no segment at all.

Not only might markets be segmented in many ways but frequently new segments appear as styles change, technology advances and society develops. More recent new segment introductions include MP3 players, palm-top computers, alchopops and off-road vehicles.

Demographic segmentation remains an important classifier. Probably the most often used demographic is gender because large numbers of products and services are either gender specific (e.g. lipstick) or are dominated by a certain gender (e.g. children's clothing). Another obvious demographic is age. The financial services market is one that utilizes demographic segmentation in a major way. In this industry there is a recognition that different financial products are required at different life-stages. As can be seen in Figure 7.3 the need for financial services changes as the average customer gets older. The skill of the financial services marketer is to reach these customers at the right time with the right product at the right price and segmentation of this type contributes towards this.

Geodemographics combine demographic and locational factors to provide an additional slant on the needs of customers. Among well-known commercial examples are Acorn and Mosaic. Acorn is a classification of

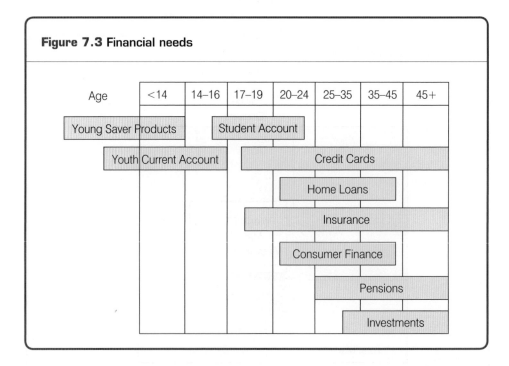

Figure 7.3 Financial needs

[2]Contracts vary but it is usual for organizations to be licensed to use a list for only one campaign.

residential neighbourhoods which is based on the presumption of there being a relationship between the type of home people live in and their purchase behaviour (see Chapter 3).

Consumers however, whatever their particular demographic profile differ in personality and attitude and that a consumer's lifestyle profile is a better behaviour indicator. **Lifestyle segmentation** (often referred to as VALS – values, attitudes and lifestyle) is, therefore, seen as an important segmentation tool. One example of lifestyle segmentation is VALS 2 a second generation values and lifestyles model developed by SRI International with the aim of grouping US consumers into three 'self-orientation' categories depending on whether they are motivated by principles, status or action and then splitting these three categories again depending on the resources they have at their disposal (abundant or minimal). This creates six lifestyle segments plus two segments regarded as outside of the mainstream target markets, one because they are chronically poor and, ironically, one because they are rich enough to indulge whatever they might wish to do. The VALS 2 segmentation by lifestyle model is shown in Figure 7.4.

Elsewhere consumer lifestyles are measured through psychographic techniques including **AIO research** (activities, interests and opinions). Using

Lifestyle segmentation
Values, attitudes and lifestyle analysis (VALS).

AIO research
AIO research uses consumer interviews, statements recorded in focus groups, literature and a little imagination to develop statements associated with clusters of consumers (e.g. Mondeo Man).

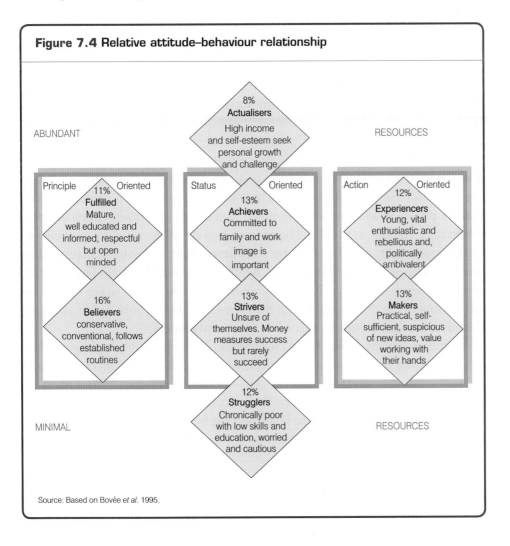

Figure 7.4 Relative attitude–behaviour relationship

Source: Based on Bovée *et al*. 1995.

Take the VALs survey at: **www.sric-bi.com/ VALS.**

consumer interviews, statements recorded in focus groups, literature and not a little imagination they develop statements associated with clusters of consumers.

TARGETING

Targeting of specific segments of a market helps reduce the wastage of resources associated with mass marketing and is likely to increase sales as it is the potentially better customers who are focused upon. Targeting is both a selection of profitable segments and a decision on how these customers can be reached and some media are more wasteful than others. Television has traditionally attracted a wide range of consumers to what were, until relatively recently, a limited number of television channels. The growth of television stations in every developed and many developing markets in the world has helped to a certain extent refine television audiences, particularly those designed for specific audiences (e.g. Home and Leisure, Travel Channel, Nickelodeon, etc.). This has not so much eliminated as reduced **waste**.

Waste
Mass communications that are effectively wasted on non-targeted consumers.

Even the most targeted media, therefore, are liable to waste. The *Sun* newspaper is, for example, a successful newspaper that most observers would see as targeted at the lower end of the social scale. Whilst the majority of *Sun* readers are in the C_2DE socioeconomic groups (see Box 3.1), 30 per cent of its readers are defined as ABC_1. Given that the total circulation[3] of the *Sun* is 3 576 406 there are more ABC_1 readers of that newspaper (approximately 1 073 000) than the total circulation of an obviously ABC_1 newspaper such as the *Financial Times* (715 000). So which newspaper should a provider of up-market products and services use given (unrealistically) these were the only advertising choices available? The answer may lie in the reader's expectation of the newspaper. The *Sun* may be considered light and informative reading on areas such as sport and television, while the *Financial Times* concentration is on business and politics. Readers are more likely to expect to see up-market advertising in the latter rather than the former and this is born out by scanning the advertisements that are placed in these newspapers.

Targeting is far from being an exact science. This is probably highlighted best by considering the airline industry. Many airlines offer three levels of service normally called first class, business class and economy class.[4] All passengers would like the maximum number of benefits (free drinks, maximum legroom, ticket flexability, etc.) but there is a trade-off between these benefits and the cost of a flight. First and business class are normally targeted at the business

[3]Circulation figures are for September 2002 to February 2003.
[4]Over time airlines drop titles such as first-class often to resurrect them at a later date under that or another name.

traveller while economy class (where competition is frequently based wholly on price) is aimed at the personal leisure market. The same business traveller may prefer the additional perks while travelling at the company's expense but be more frugal when it comes to personal expenditure. Alternatively the business person's organization might insist on their personnel flying economy class whereas on holiday that same person may be prepared to pay for added luxury!

There are a variety of different target marketing strategies generally described as:

- Undifferentiated or mass-market targeting
- Differentiated targeting
- Concentrated or niche targeting
- Individualized targeting

Undifferentiated targeting takes place in those markets where the cost of segmenting and targeting is too high or where the product is too generic. In practice, however, there are few examples of truly undifferentiated markets. Even *Campbell's Soup,* a mass marketer in the classic sense, is reported to divide the United States in to 22 geographical regions and formulates its soups to suit regional tastes (Bovée *et al.* 1995). **Differentiated targeting** involves choosing a number of markets, each requiring a particular market positioning and message. A major cycle manufacturer such as Raleigh has many different sectors within the one industry. These are determined by whether the machine is designed for basic travel, leisure pursuits or competitive riding. Each of these different segments require different product benefits and, therefore, different product strategies. There is also a difference, as in most such categories, between occasional and dedicated users. An example of different approaches in marketing a tennis shoe may serve as a good example of different approaches (see Minicase 7.1).

Concentrated or **niche marketing** focuses on one particular segment (e.g. Innocent 'smoothies'), whilst **individualized targeting** invokes the ideas associated with one-to-one marketing. One-to-one marketing, at its extreme, implies that each product or service is crafted specifically for an individual customer and is, therefore, unique to this customer. Examples may include personal services (e.g. hairdressing) or suppliers of bespoke products (e.g. Dell computers), travel (e.g. Expedia.com) or other services (e.g. financial advisors).

The growth of relationship marketing coupled with the advent of data capturing technology has further stimulated organizations to profile customers according to purchasing habits although based on individual requirements. This form of targeting (or **segregation**) departs from the normal, top-down view of segmentation involving as it does the grouping of individual customers with individual requirements albeit that the requirements are not exactly the same. Bringing this level of personalization to what is theoretically the 'mass market' has been called **mass customization**. That is using technology to customize a product whilst still being able to benefit from economies of scale.

Undifferentiated targeting
Takes place in those markets where the cost of segmenting and targeting is too high or where the product is too generic. In practice, however, there are few examples of truly undifferentiated markets.

Differentiated targeting
The selection of a number of target markets each requiring a particular market positioning and message.

Niche marketing
The targeting on one particular, perhaps specialized, segment (also referred to as concentrated marketing).

Individualized targeting
See one-to-one marketing.

Further commentary on mass customization can be found at: **www.managingchange. com/masscust/overview.htm**.

Segregation
The grouping of individual customers with individual requirements although the requirements are not exactly the same.

Mass customization
Using technology to customize a product whilst still being able to benefit from economies of scale.

Nike

Nike placed advertising for its new 'Air Challenge Huarache Tennis Shoe' in the US magazine *Tennis*. It was a very logical move to advertise its high priced, specialist tennis shoe in a magazine targeted at people who liked tennis. But Nike went one stage further by segmenting the *Tennis* magazine audience into those who were

Source: Bovée *et al*.1995: 131.

A less confrontational shoe advertisement from Nike.

serious about the game and those for whom it was a leisure activity or spectator sport. The advertising copy, aimed at the serious players, reads 'You should try on a pair. Or you should take your wood racket and play with your niece.' This gave the impression that only those who were serious about tennis (or aspired to be) should even consider buying the product.

This bottom-up form of segregation is illustrated in Figure 7.5. This bottom-up segmentation has also increased as technology allows companies to capture purchase details from their customers and build up profiles including purchase behaviour (see loyalty).

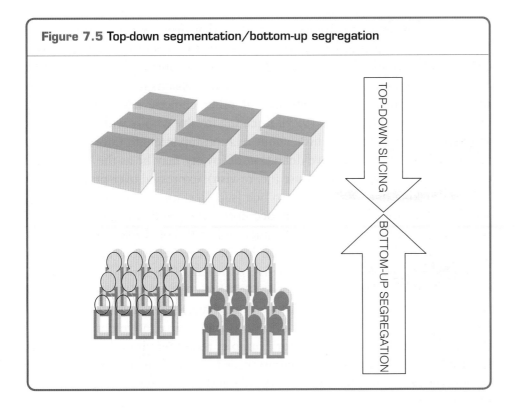

Figure 7.5 Top-down segmentation/bottom-up segregation

LOYALTY

It is almost impossible to discuss targeting without discussing the concept of loyalty. This has become even more important with the advent of loyalty (usually card-based) technologies. Such is its perceived importance that it has been claimed that customer loyalty 'is emerging as the marketplace currency for the 21st century' (Singh and Sirdeshmukh 2000: 150). Technology now enables companies to systematically capture and interrogate customer purchase data leading to significant changes in the application of segmentation and targeting. Tesco (through their subsidiary Dunn Humby) now segment their customer database in reportedly 34 000 ways, building up customer profiles and communicating with and incentivizing individual customers.

The question should, however, be asked 'What is loyalty and how can it help organizations develop their businesses?' There appears to be two main strands of thought on the essence of commercial loyalty (Javalgi and Moberg 1997):

- A definition of loyalty in *behavioural* terms, usually based on the number of purchases and measured by monitoring the frequency of such purchases and any brand switching.

- A definition of loyalty in *attitudinal* terms, incorporating consumer preferences and disposition towards brands to determine levels of loyalty.

The assumption that is frequently made is that, from whatever sources the loyalty is derived, it translates into an unspecified number of repeat purchases from the same supplier over a specified period. The problem with relying on this behavioural definition is that there may be many reasons for repeat patronage other than loyalty, among them lack of other choices, habit, low income, convenience etc. (Hart *et al.* 1999). Equating loyalty wholly with relationship longevity, therefore, tells us little about relationship strength (Storbacka *et al.* 1994). A more comprehensive definition of loyalty may be as the 'biased (i.e. non-random) behavioural response (i.e. re-visit), expressed over time, by some decision-making unit with respect to one [supplier] out of a set of [suppliers], which is a function of psychological [decision-making and evaluative] processes resulting in brand commitment' (Bloemer and de Ruyter 1998: 500).[5]

One way of illustrating the relationship between behaviour and attitude is illustrated in Figure 7.6. When relative patronage (the ratio of return visits to one supplier relative to all suppliers) is high but relative attitude is low then this is **spurious loyalty** and, given the chance, these customers may go elsewhere. In a situation where attitude is high but relative patronage low (for reasons such as accessibility for example) then there is said to be a **latent loyalty** which, given changed circumstances (e.g. opening a new outlet) may result in loyalty. Only when both attitude and patronage are high can it be said the customer is loyal.

Simple repatronage, therefore, is not enough. Loyalty, if it is to have any credence, must be seen as 'biased repeat purchase behaviour' or 'repeat patronage accompanied by a favourable attitude' (O'Malley *et al.* 1998: 50).

Customer loyalty is not always based on positive attitude, and long-term relationships do not necessarily require positive commitment from customers. The distinction is important because it challenges the idea that customer satisfaction (the attitude) leads to long-lasting relationships (the behaviour).

There are other ways of describing loyalty-type and non-loyal customer behaviour. One typology suggested by Uncles (1994), proposes three ways of

Spurious loyalty
High patronage but low attitude to a brand. Customer will probably go elsewhere if another choice becomes available.

Latent loyalty
Low patronage for reasons such as distance but where attitude is high. If the situation changes they are likely to become a loyal customer.

---

[5]Bloemer and de Ruyter were describing 'retail store loyalty' in this definition but it is equally applicable to suppliers in general.

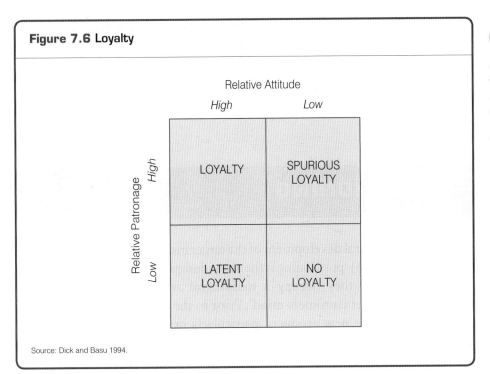

Figure 7.6 Loyalty

Relative Attitude

	High	Low
High	LOYALTY	SPURIOUS LOYALTY
Low	LATENT LOYALTY	NO LOYALTY

Relative Patronage

Source: Dick and Basu 1994.

Customer loyalty, can it be bought? Consider the arguments at: **http://sbinformation. about.com/od/advertisingpr/a/ customerloyalty.htm** and **www.cio.com/ archive/010102/loyalty.html** and **www.thewisemarketer.com/features.**

considering customer repatronizing behaviour:

- **Switching behaviour:** where purchasing is seen as an 'either/or' decision – either the customer stays with you (loyalty) or turns against you (switching).

- **Promiscuous behaviour:** where customers are seen as making a 'stream of purchases' but still within the context of an either/or decision – either the customer is always with you (loyalty) or flits among an array of alternatives (promiscuous).

- **Polygamous behaviour** again, the customer makes a stream of purchases but their loyalty is divided among a number of products. They may be more or less loyal to your brand than any other.

Evidence from consumer research tends to support the view that patterns of promiscuity and polygamy (rather than brand monogomy) are the norm (Uncles 1994). Barnard and Ehrenberg (1997), for example, suggest that many or most consumers are **multi-brand buyers** and that only one tenth of buyers are 100 per cent loyal. This may be because a customer's holistic requirements frequently extend beyond those capable of being effectively fulfilled by a single firm's products and services. Consumers are, therefore, prone to 'mix and match' products and services according to their specific needs (Kandampully and Duddy 1999). There is also doubt over whether loyal buyers are necessarily more profitable than promiscuous or polygamous buyers. Research evidence suggests that loyalists are more often light buyers of products or services in various categories whereas multi-brand (or broad repertoire)[6] buyers are heavier users (East 2000). It is not difficult to perceive

Switching behaviour
Where purchasing is seen as an 'either/or' decision – either the customer stays with you (loyalty) or turns against you (switching).

Promiscuous behaviour
Where customers are seen as making a 'stream of purchases' but still within the context of an either/or decision – either the customer is always with you (loyalty) or flits among an array of alternatives (promiscuous).

Polygamous behaviour
Where customers are seen as making a stream of purchases but their loyalty is divided among a number of products. They may be more or less loyal to one brand than any other.

Multi-brand buyer or Broad repertoire buyer
Buyers who are not particularly loyal to one but are to a number of brands.

[6]See also Chapter 9.

a situation where the less loyal 'heavy' buyer is a more frequent purchaser of a company's products or services (and is consequently more attractive) than a buyer who is one 100 per cent loyal (Uncles 1994).

POSITIONING

Positioning is a natural development of the target marketing process. According to Kotler (1997: 136) 'positioning is the act of designing the company's offering and image so that they occupy a meaningful and distinctive competitive position in the target customers mind'. Prior to the 1970s market growth was the driving force for new products, particularly in the fast moving consumer goods sector. With an expanding market the safest new product launches were me-too products. Thus every category had its market leader and several look-alike brands. The greater competition of the 1970s and later decades coupled with the growing strength of large retailers (many of whom had own-label varieties of these brands) led to over-branding and a rethink about brands positioning in various markets. Most suppliers of both products and services tend now to believe that, in order to avoid direct competition, organizations and brands should take up distinct positions in each marketplace. In order to do this the organization must know what its target customer wants, where its competitors are positioned, where it wishes to compete and then develops marketing and communication strategies to achieve this positioning of its organization and brands in the minds of that target audience.

Me-too products
New products that are similar to existing products already available on the marketplace.

Positioning strategy

There are a number of ways to the development of a positioning strategy, but it is generally accepted that these will incorporate the following:

- Clearly identifying competitors.
- Undertaking an assessment of consumer perception of competitors.
- Determining the relative position of competitors.
- Analysing of consumer preferences.
- Establishing a positioning strategy.
- Implementing the positioning strategy.
- Monitoring the position over time.

First, the organization must identify its major competitors not just in the same product or service category but including competitors that satisfy the same needs in the eyes of the consumer (e.g. air travel versus high-speed rail). Second, the consumers' perceptions of competitive brands should be assessed. What attributes or benefits are important to this market and how do the competitors score on such an evaluation? The third and fourth stages are the determination of the positioning of competitors and analysis of customer preferences through in-depth interviews, focus groups or other qualitative research techniques. A major tool in this process is the perceptual map (or multidimensional map). This consists of two axes each with important attributes or features about the product or service. An example of a perceptual map is shown in Figure 7.7

The perception map in Figure 7.7 shows the main competitors in a fictitious European furniture market where the most important attributes are seen to be style (traditional or contemporary) and quality (luxury or standard). Company A believed they had a reasonably good reputation in the marketplace but research shows that they are seen by their target market as 'stuck in the middle' of a highly competitive part of the marketplace, when they believed their target market would be more receptive to a traditional/luxury positioning. This may result in the adoption of a **repositioning** (or **targeted differentiation**) strategy where the company identifies a specific market position and then redesigns its marketing programme to target it.

Implementing a repositioning strategy would involve adapting the product, price and place (distribution) elements of the mix and communicating this repositioned image (see Figure 7.8) to the target audience as a whole. The marketing imperative is to create marketing mixes which reflect the consumers' subjective, perceptive and cognitive processing of information, their personal lifestyles, values and motivation (Foxall *et al.* 1998).

There are, however, dangers associated with repositioning. Although there may appear to be a gap in a market this does not mean that it represents a good marketing opportunity. EasyCinema was a brand extention designed to

Repositioning or targeted differentiation
The process of recreating or changing the perception of the brand in the consumer's mind.

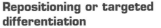

More information on perceptual mapping can be found at: **www.populus.com/ techpapers/map.php** and **www.learnmarketing.net/ perceptualmaps.htm.**

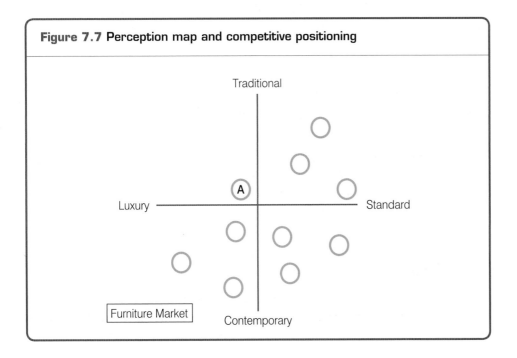

Figure 7.7 Perception map and competitive positioning

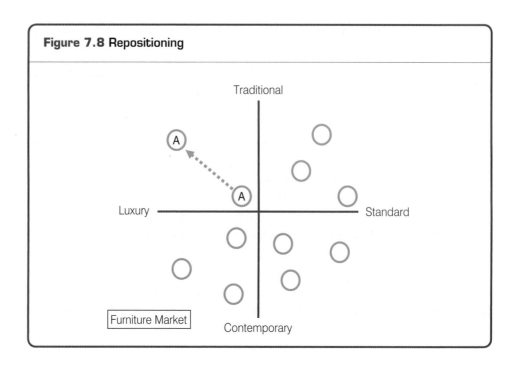

Figure 7.8 Repositioning

fill a 'gap' in the market for inexpensive cinema-going based on the demand model used by its sister company easyJet. It turned out that, in this industry, product quality and originality were more important than price. As easyCinema was effectively frozen out of the major film circuit their 'gap' in the market proved wholly uncommercial.

The final part of the positioning process involves monitoring. Depending on the industry an organization may have to reposition on a regular basis to keep up with the competitive landscape. Some well-known brands have had to reposition significantly based on changes in the competitive landscape. They include:

- IBM formally the world's largest computer manufacturer now repositioned as a 'solutions provider'.
- Kodak withdraws from film production in Europe as the market declines dramatically. Concentration on digital camera production, software and photo-booth technology.
- Lucozade in the 1950s was a drink that you took to sick people in hospital. Today it has successfully repositioned as a drink for healthy sports men and women.
- Aer Lingus faced by competition from airlines such as Ryanair and easyJet has reinvented itself as a no-frills, web-based, competitively priced airline that can compete in the short-haul markets.

All of the above repositioning involved these companies in significant changes in their communication strategies, including rewriting brand messages, restyling brand images and redefining media channels.

Summary

This chapter reviewed the concepts associated with target marketing. It described the criteria necessary for viable segmentation. The importance of targeting was explained and the different targeting strategies, such as undifferentiated, differentiated, concentrated and individual targeting were reviewed. The concept of customer loyalty was addressed and defined on the basis of attitude and behaviour (or patronage). Different 'loyalty behaviours' were also noted. Finally concepts relating to positioning were analysed and positioning strategies discussed.

Review questions

1 What does 'STP' stand for?

2 Expand the mnemonic 'ADMARS'.

3 What is meant by 'geodemographic segmentation'?

4 How would you undertake 'AIO' research?

5 What is the difference between 'niche' marketing and 'individualized' targeting?

6 Explain 'polygamous' behaviour.

7 How exact a science is targeting?

8 Give examples of both differentiated and undifferentiated marketing.

9 Define loyalty in both behavioural and attitudinal terms.

10 What do you understand from the term 'multi-brand buyer'?

Discussion questions

1 What are the differences between consumer and industrial segmentation and how and why do you believe that this is so?

2 What do you understand by the term 'loyalty' and to what extent do you believe that this can be achieved?

3 Take an industry you are familiar with and construct a perceptual map to try and understand how the various operators are positioned. How effective a tool do you believe this to be and why?

Further reading

Bush, V.D., Bush, A.J., Clark, P. and Bush, R.P. (2005) 'Girl power and word-of-mouth behavior in the flourishing sports market'. *Journal of Consumer Marketing*, 22(5): 257–64. Investigating the influence of word-of-mouth (WOM) behaviour among the growing teenage female market segment in the flourishing sports market.

Coleman, L.J., Hladikova, M. and Savelyeva, M. (2006) 'The baby boomer market', *Journal of Targeting, Measurement & Analysis for Marketing*, Apr., 14(3): 191–209. Discusses the maturing of the baby boomer generation and the way this large segment of the population is affecting the workplace and the marketplace.

Dawley, J. (2006) 'Making Connections', *Marketing Research, Summer*, 18(2): 16–22. Offers strategies for incorporating marketing segmentation research into business and marketing practice.

Fletcher, R. (2006) 'The impact of culture on web site content, design, and structure', *Journal of Communication Management*, 10(3): 259–73. Examines the impact of culture on Web site content and emphasizes the need for cultural sensitivity in designing Web sites for communication in a cross-cultural context.

Laiderman, J. (2005) 'A structured approach to B2B segmentation', *Journal of Database Marketing & Customer Strategy Management*, Dec., 13(1): 64–75.

Tuten, T.L. (2006) 'Exploring the importance of gay-friendliness and its socialization influences', *Journal of Marketing Communications*, Jun., 12(2): 79–94. Existing literature on marketing to gay men and lesbians suggests that brands targeting this market should position themselves as gay-friendly. Nevertheless, little is known about consumer perceptions of gay-friendliness, its antecedents or the socialization processes relevant to establishing a brand's gay-friendly claim. This paper attempts to fill this void.

Chapter references

Barnard, N. and Ehrenberg, A.S.C. (1997) 'Advertising: strongly persuasive or nudging?', *Journal of Advertising Research*, Jan./Feb.: 21–3.

Bloemer, J. and de Ruyter, K. (1998) 'On the relationship between store image, store satisfaction and store loyalty', *European Journal of Marketing*, 32(5/6): 499–513.

Bovée, C.L., Thill, J.V., Dovel, G.P. and Wood, M.B. (1995) *Advertising Excellence*, Englewood Cliffs, NJ: McGraw-Hill.

Dick, A. and Basu, K. (1994) 'Customer loyalty: towards an integrated framework', *Journal of the Academy of Marketing Science*, 22: 99–113.

East, R. (2000) 'Complaining as planned behaviour', Psychology and Marketing, 17(12): 1077–95.

Ehrenberg, A. (1997) 'How do consumers buy a new brand?', *ADMAP*, March: 1077–95.

Foxall, G., Goldsmith, R. and Brown, S. (1998) *Consumer Psychology for Marketing*, London: Thomson Learning.

Grönroos, C. (1994) 'From marketing mix to relationship marketing: towards a paradigm shift in marketing', *Management Decision*, 32(2): 4–20.

Hart, S., Smith, A., Sparks, L. and Tzokas, N. (1999) 'Are loyalty schemes a manifestation of relationship marketing?', *Journal of Marketing Management*, 15: 541–62.

Javalgi, R.G. and Moberg, C.R. (1997) 'Service loyalty: implications for service providers', *The Journal of Services Marketing*, Jun.: 11.

Kandampully, J. and Duddy, R. (1999) 'Competitive advantage through anticipation, innovation and relationships', *Management Decision*, 37(1), 51-6.

Kotler, P. (1997) *Marketing Management: Analysis, Planning, Implimentation and Control*, Englewood Cliffs, NJ: Prentice Hall.

O'Malley, L., Patterson, M. and Evans, M. (1998) *Exploring Direct Marketing*, London: Thomson Learning.

Singh, J. and Sirdesmukh, D. (2000) 'Agency and trust mechanisms in consumer satisfaction and loyalty judgements', *Journal of the Academy of Marketing Science*, 28: 150–67.

Smith, P.R. and Taylor, J. (2002) *Marketing Comunications: An Integrated Approach*, 3rd edn, London: Kogan Page.

Storbacka, K., Strandvik, T. and Grönroos, C. (1994) 'Managing customer relationships for profit: the dynamics of relationship quality', *International Journal of Service Industry Management*, 5: 21–38.

Uncles, M. (1994) 'Do you or your customers need a loyalty scheme?', *Journal of Targeting, Measurement and Analysis for Marketing*, 2(4): 335–50.

CASE STUDY 7.1

The child within

January 1966 marked a new development for the toy industry. For the first time ever a 'Toy of the Year' was announced and the winner? A Corgi toy car – the Austin Martin DB5, James Bond car from the film Dr No.

For Corgi this was a major coup. They had been in operation since 1956 and had been simply making copies of commercial vehicles up until 1965, but the tie in with the Bond film represented a significant investment, a calculated risk and an unquestioned commercial success. This was followed with more licensed models over the next few years, from both cinema and TV productions; for example the 'Batmobile' later that same year, the Beatles' 'Yellow Submarine' in 1969 and the Ford Torino used by Starsky and Hutch in 1977.

However, the initial success in the 'Toy of the Year' was not to be repeated. Over the following years the impact of fashion, technology and sheer inventiveness saw the accolade taken by Sindy in 1970, Kites in 1976 and the Rubik Cube in 1980. The next 'car' model was the transformer in 1986, an idea copied in the 2005/6

▶

TV advertising campaign for Citroen and probably conceived by 30-year-old designers who played with them as children?

Teenage Mutant Hero Turtles took the prize in 1990, Barbie and Action Man in 1996 and then, by 2000, technology had taken hold and it was Teksta, the robot dog, which every child wanted. Toy cars had slipped a long way down the popularity list and whilst Corgi remained a profitable company, it had done so by re-evaluating its market and finding new segments. Perhaps a good example of this was a 1993 model of the Inspector Morse Jaguar MkII. Targeted not at the child, but at the more adult, Inspector Morse fan and consciously moving from 'toys' to 'collectables'.

This was followed by a diversification into another 'collectable' area, commercial vehicles, 1994 and the following years saw re-issues of 'Corgi classics' such as the 'Italian Job' minis, giving those who missed them the first time around the chance to recapture their childhood. Ranges expanded to include vintage vans with comic book graphics, D-Day military models, to capitalize on the 1995 50th anniversary celebrations, aeroplanes and specific 'toy' sets, featuring characters such as 'Postman Pat'.

It had become clear that the original toy sector that Corgi had entered in 1956 had changed significantly. No longer was a toy car the preferred toy of every little boy. The market had segmented widely. Both boys and girls were now reflected in the ranges and a new and very valuable sector had emerged – adult collectors.

IDEAL
TEENAGE MUTANT HERO TURTLES
A. PARTY WAGON
For ages 4 years plus.
Figures sold separately.

£22.87

B. MUTATION FIGURES
For ages 4 years plus.

£5.87 Each

C. MUTA CARRIER
For ages 4 years plus.
Figures sold separately.

£29.87 Each

D. MUTA SKI
For ages 4 years plus.
Figures sold separately.

£9.97

E. MUTA BIKE
For ages 4 years plus.
Figures sold separately.

£9.97

Teenage Mutant Hero Turtles took the 'Toy of the Year' prize in 1990.

Typified by the '40 somethings' who had since settled into their adult life, were earning reasonable incomes, possibly had families of their own and alongside the toys for their children they were rebuilding or developing their own collection.

But some buyers were not simply seeking new copies of their childhood toys. In June 2005 a collector of original models, Graham Booth, sent 1000 of his old toy cars to auction alongside the collections of two other enthusiasts. Between them they raised £30 000, which included £290 for a Corgi milk tanker and £260 for four Corgi racing toys. Models that would have cost a few shillings when new.

This particular sale attracted bidders from as far away as New York, Germany and France and Lucy Armstrong, of Halls Fine Arts auctioneers, commented that: 'the most valuable items were usually boxed'. But this figure was quite modest when you consider that the best-known Corgi models, such as its 1965 James Bond Aston Martin DB5 and Monte Carlo Rally Mini Cooper, can sell for thousands of pounds each in mint condition; and even with a bit of wear and tear you could still pay up to £400 for your original, 'boxed' DB5.

For original collectables, condition and 'completeness' are clearly important in relation to value, but for those who cannot afford a few thousand pounds, a new James Bond DB5 would cost just £19.99.

July 2006 saw the company reach its 50th anniversary and, they announced that they would now like to lure a younger generation of toy fans away from their games consoles back to the simple joys of their die-cast models. Understandable, perhaps, when you consider that their new 'collector' segments are mainly the 40–50-year-olds who first collected Corgi models as children in the 1960s and 1970s. As they get older and the next wave of 40–50-year-olds appear, might they not be more interested in Sindy dolls and kites?

Case study questions

1 How many segments is Corgi now operating in and how would you evaluate them in terms of the ADMARS model?

2 Why do you believe that Corgi want 'to lure a younger generation of toy fans away from their games consoles'?

3 What markets do you believe Corgi should target next and why?

Source: Case Study Written by Andy Cropper, Senior Lecturer, Sheffield Hallam University.

CHAPTER EIGHT
CAMPAIGN TACTICS AND MANAGEMENT

LEARNING OBJECTIVES

Having completed this chapter you should be able to:

- Understand the fundamental aspects of campaign planning.
- Recognize the constituent parts of the creative brief.
- Understand the characteristics of communications media.
- Comprehend the value and usage of reach, frequency and gross ratings points.
- Be familiar with various scheduling patterns.

INTRODUCTION

This chapter discusses those elements of the marketing communications plan (as discussed in Chapter 5) that form the tactical campaign. As Figure 8.1 illustrates marketing communications strategies are informed by the marketing communications objectives (see Chapter 5). Given the perceived need for an integrated communications strategy the campaign plan might be seen to represent the whole spectrum of communication tactics. In many organizations, however, there is another layer representing the various marketing communications tools such that independent departments create separate advertising, public relations and other plans. In other organizations it may well be that elements of the communications mix (e.g. public relations and personal selling) are isolated in other parts of the organization (e.g. corporate communications and sales management respectively). The chapter will assume a coordinated campaign but the model can be easily adapted to other organizational formats.

THE CREATIVE BRIEF

The objectives have been set and the strategies developed but this is meaningless unless ways are found to reach the target audience and achieve whatever outcome

Figure 8.1 The campaign process

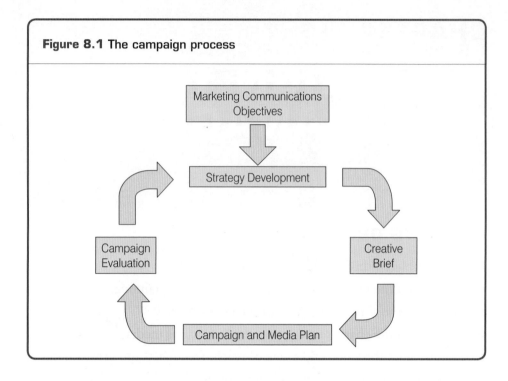

is required. The creative brief outlines the way this will be achieved. It may be an internal document if the bulk of the plan is to be operationalized in-house or created by (or for) one or more agencies (advertising, public relations, etc.) if the bulk of this work is outsourced. In many organizations it will be a mix of internal and outsourced resources and, as such, no one model fits all or even a majority of situations.

The creative brief is something that provides guidance to the creative team, whose task is then to create a piece of communication that is designed to

Box 8.1 The importance of briefs

'Clients generally get the agencies they deserve! The best work flows from client/agency partnerships that are built on mutual respect, integrity and a joint humility of approach which allows the professional perspective of both parties to be recognized and respected.

In working together successfully, clients and agencies need to achieve the commercial equivalent of a "Vulcan mind meld", which can only flow from a clear, open and non-precious communication in both directions.

Establishing a clarity of purpose through the definition of objectives which are outcome focused and measurable is clearly at the heart of the briefing process. Clear briefs are not the only critical success factor in arriving at good advertising and marketing, but without this sound starting point you have little chance of success.'

Andrew Nebel, UK Director of Marketing and Communications, Barnardo's.

Source: ISBA (2006)

actively 'do' something. To effectively penetrate the external noise in order to reach the intended recipient and then to stimulate them to respond in the desired way. It is not one document or the result of one internal or external meeting but a series of iterations. Creative does not only mean clever, original or funny (although it may be some or all of those things) but creating the communication that will do the job it is supposed to do (create awareness, develop interest, sell products/services, etc.) despite communications clutter.

There are essentially two fundamental aspects to a creative brief:

- Direction: clearly defining what the communication needs to achieve and/or the problem that needs to be solved.
- Inspiration: providing the creative team with context, purpose and focus in order to provide a robust starting point for the creative process to begin. This is often called the creative platform.

The process may begin or resume (particularly where agencies are involved) with a company **brief** followed by a briefing session where ideas are explored. The creative brief should have consideration for what went before even if the intension is to change direction. Certain themes, **tag lines** (or **strap line or slogans) lines**, music or visual feature may represent continuity. On the other hand past themes might be at the end of their shelf life and the aim may be to distance the brand (as far as is possible) from what went before. For example *Brylcreem*, a product that kept men's hair under control in the 1950s, has been reinvented as a hair gel for the youth market. Another example is the TSB bank[1] which for many years used the tag line 'The Bank that likes to say YES' a phrase that became (and some might say still is) synonymous with the brand. However, whenever there was a failure in customer service the catch-phrase came back to haunt them as customers invariably used it by way of rebuke. In this instance the expectations created by the creative theme were not being matched by the organization. The importance of matching

@

Creative brief ideas can be found at: **www.adcracker.com/brief/index.htm** and **www.bytestart.co.uk/content/marketing/articles/creative-brief-writing.shtml** and **www.isba.org.uk/isba/documents/Client-brief.pdf#search=%22'agency%20brief'%22.**

Brief
Details of the organization, their brands and all other information pertinent to an agency making a 'pitch'.

Tag line (or strap line or slogan)
Memorable phrases that sum up an important characteristic of the brand.

Box 8.2 Constructive briefs

Gary Duckworth, Chairman and Executive Planning Director, Duckworth Finn Grubb Waters, recounts the following story to illustrate that even the most boring products can have interesting briefing sessions.

'I once heard of an account director who was asked to brief the creative team on a DIY product which filled holes in walls. He walked into the briefing with a hammer, smashed a hole in the wall, and then mixed the product in front of them, using it very successfully to mend the hole in the wall. And then walked out. It's a good story. It doesn't really matter if it's true or not, because it illustrates some great insights. First it was dramatic and entertaining. You wouldn't forget a briefing like that. Second, it gave the creative team a really good idea of what the benefits of the product was. Third, it was a brilliant way to create commitment to the product so the team could feel enthusiastic about solving the advertising problem.'

Source: Duckworth 1999: 155.

---

[1]Prior to its merger with Lloyds Bank.

consumer expectations is a case in point for the importance of the briefing. The briefing session also gives a chance to extend and embellish what was formally set out in the initial brief.

Many agencies have some form of briefing document that aids the briefing discussion. This document usually includes questions such as:

- Why are we communicating?
- Who are we talking to?
- What do they know about the brand?
- What are we saying to them?
- How are we saying it (the tone)?
- What proof can we provide for any claim?
- Are there any other guidelines (things to do/avoid, mandatory requirements, etc.)?
- Are there other requirements (media considerations, timing, etc.)?

Box 8.3 The Levi's 501 campaign

The brief that originated the Levi's 501 campaign is seen as a classic example of how to inspire the creative team. It asked:

What must the advertising say?	501 from Levi's are the right look and the only label.
Why should the consumer believe it?	Because they represent the way jeans should be worn today, and because they are the original jean, indelibly associated with the birth of teenage culture in the 1950s and its finest expression since.
Tone of voice.	Heroic, highly charged, American (but period).

Source: Duckworth 1999.

Why are we communicating?

The answer to this should be to fulfil the marketing communications objectives. As noted in Chapter 5 the objectives may be multi-level (awareness, interest, etc.) but the campaign should be as singular and targeted as possible. A brief résumé of the 'problem' as specified by the brand owner may be appropriate.

Who are we talking to?

There are a number of ways of describing who you are targeting with your message. There are the rather bland demographic descriptors (age: 30–40, BC_1, 80:20 Men:Women, Acorn Areas J–K, median income £45 000, etc.) and the more descriptive VALs (values, attitudes and lifestyles) descriptors (see Chapter 7). Existing customers may be segmented according to recency, frequency and monetary value (**RFM** see Chapter 13) or other descriptors (e.g. loyalty). Who we are taking to is of considerable importance in a campaign as it frequently determines the medium or media through which we might reach these customers.

What do they know about the brand?

What are customers' attitudes to the brand. Is this the one the company seeks? Do they require further information, assurance, or other details. Skoda (see Minicase 15.1) is an example of where consumer knowledge was out of line with the improvements made to the products.

What are we saying to them?

The creative platform is the foundation upon which the campaign message is built. The creative platform for a brand is summarized in a single **positioning statement** (or **proposition**). The positioning statement is designed to incorporate the essence of what the brand stands for in the mind of the target audience in relation to their impression of competitor brands (its position). This can be based on two distinct approaches:

- Functional orientation
- Symbolic/experiential orientation

Functional orientation suggests that the positioning is based on that feature or attribute that is unique (or can be made to appear unique) to that brand (the unique selling proposition or USP). This gives the consumer a distinctly differentiated reason for buying one brand over another. However, USPs can be fleeting as features can often be copied rapidly by competitors. When it was suggested that Gillette's USP for a new razor was that it had three-blades they quite rightly asked what would happen to the campaign if a competitor came up with a four-blade razor! Examples of functional orientation, therefore, tend to be those where the messages have become attached to the brand rather than necessarily its uniqueness such as:

Domestos – kills 99 per cent of household germs
Orangina – shake it to release the taste

Sometimes these 'features' are strictly tongue in cheek for example;

Peperami – it's a bit of an animal
Heineken – reaches the parts other beers cannot reach

Pricing can also be a unique selling proposition (USP) although again its advantages may be fleeting. The entry into the UK banking market of ING with a high interest, internet-based savings account supported by heavy

RFM
Stands for recency, frequency and monetary value: a measure used to establish the value of a direct marketing customer.

Positioning statement
A statement of the brand's positioning in the market.

Proposition
Statement of the brand's central theme or unique selling proposition (USP).

Functional orientation
Where the brand's positioning is based on its features or attributes.

@

Advertising slogan examples can be found at: **www.adslogans.co.uk**.

advertising which made savers aware of their superior rates was quickly followed by other banks offering the same or higher interest. The entry of low-priced competitors into the already crowded low-cost airline and supermarket businesses make it difficult to sustain an image of lower prices without constant promotion. However, this does not seem to have stopped organizations such as Ryanair and ASDA from continuing to keep cost a central theme in their communication campaigns.

Symbolic/experiential orientation is focused on the emotional needs of consumers and is concerned with psychological rather than physical differentiation. This is occasionally referred to as 'the **soft sell**'. It involves using emotional appeals to produce positive feelings that may distinguish and enhance the brand image or, as it is increasingly described, the **brand personality**. This distinct identity or personality is particularly important in categories where there is little physical differentiation (beer, soft drinks, chocolate, cigarettes, fuel, air travel, etc.). Examples of campaigns that use this approach include:

Marlboro – the big country (wilderness, cowboys, etc.)
Land /Range Rover – rugged, unbeatable
Volvic Mineral Water – ancient source of unpolluted, pure water

Many male-orientated campaigns seek to be macho if not seemingly misogynistic such as

Nestlé Yorkie – it's not for girls
XXXX Lager – Australians wouldn't give a XXXX for any other lager.
Nuts (magazine) – women, don't expect any help on a Tuesday

The choice between functional and symbolic orientation is not necessarily a straightforward one. It would be logical to assume that high-involvement decisions (see Chapter 3) are likely to require a more rational, informational emphasis (i.e. highlighting attributes and benefits) whereas low-involvement decision making may require the use of imagery. However, the investment of motor car manufacturers in developing brand status and personality would seem to go against this as would the growing importance of delivering nutritional advice on what would normally be described as low-involvement groceries. As with many maxims associated with marketing communications it is the exception that proves the rule!

There are also a number of additional creative strategies that may be used. These include:

● Resonance strategy
● Emotional strategy
● Generic strategy
● Pre-emptive strategy

Resonance (or **slice-of-life**) **strategies** attempt to match 'patterns' in the message with target audiences' shared experiences. This is frequently expressed in advertising through **indirect address**, where the potential consumer

---

Symbolic orientation
Where the brand's positioning is based on consumers' emotional needs and involves psychosocial rather than physical differentiation (see also experiential orientation).

Soft sell
Using emotional appeals to produce positive feelings for a brand.

Brand personality or branding
The character and essence of a brand. The perceived lifestyle associations and values (e.g. status, fashion, quality, etc.).

View a range of past television advertisements online at: **www. absolutelyandy.com/tvadverts.**

Resonance strategy
Attempt to match 'patterns' in the message with target audiences' shared experiences (also referred to as a **slice-of-life** strategy).

Indirect address
In television or cinema advertising where the potential consumer 'eavesdrops' on, for example, a family, a group of friends, etc. (i.e. the message appears as if it is not directly aimed at the viewer).

The Guinness surfer

One of the most iconic advertisements of the past decade is the Guinness surfer. Among its accolades are that it came top of a Channel 4 poll of the 100 greatest advertisements, it was awarded a Golden Lion at the Cannes Advertising Festival, and received numerous other advertising industry prizes. The agency Abbot Mead Vickers BBDO employed Director Jonathan Glazer to produce what was to become one of the most challenging advertising projects of all time. Enormously detailed planning and complex production work went to create the finished product. It took six months of checking wave projections and meteorological reports to find the perfect time for shooting. The white horses took three-hours of hair and make-up each day, the team listened to over 2000 music tracks over six weeks before making a final choice and the 'voice-over' (Louis Mellis) spent hours repeating the words over and over until he got it right. The production took four and a half weeks to complete with many of the team working around the clock.

The Guinness "Surfer" advertisement was a truly global production: the waves were filmed in Waimei Bay, Hawaii; the horses were Lipizzaner Stallions from the Spanish Riding School of Vienna; and Louis Mellis' voiceover comprised passages taken from Herman Melville's *Moby Dick*.

© IMAGE COURTESY OF THE ADVERTISING ARCHIVES.

Source: '&' (D&AD Magazine) 2006.

Testimonial
A testament to a brand delivered by a personality, an expert or a representative of an average consumer.

Emotional strategies
Appeal to emotions, such as romance, nostalgia, compassion, excitement, joy, heroism, fear, guilt, disgust and regret.

Generic strategies
Where brands are so dominant in a sector that there is (at that time) no need to differentiate the brand from its competitors. Effectively these brands are looking to grow the total market in the knowledge that any increase will disproportionately benefit themselves (e.g. British Telecom's 'It's good to talk').

Pre-emptive strategies
Where the brand asserts its superiority in an undifferentiated market making it difficult for competitors to match such assertions (e.g. 'Carlsberg probably the best lager in the world').

Voice-overs
Commentary over an advertisement.

'eavesdrops' on, for example, a family, a group of friends, etc. Demonstrations may be used to get over important ideas such as ease of use, capability, flexibility or comparison with a named or unnamed competitor. On the other hand the message may be spoken directly to the consumer. This **testimonial** is delivered by a personality, an expert or a representative of an average consumer. Some communications use a mixture of indirect and direct deliveries with the latter often summarizing the benefits outlined in the previous discussions.

Emotional strategies appeal to emotions such as romance (Gold Blend), nostalgia (Werther's Originals), compassion (charities such as Save the Children and NSPCC), excitement (Nike), joy (British Airways), heroism (Peugeot 406), fear (all life insurance), guilt (anti-drink driving campaigns), disgust (Benetton) and regret ('smoking leads to cancer' campaigns).

Generic strategies are associated with brands that are so dominant in a sector that there is (at that time) no need to differentiate the brand from its competitors. Effectively these brands are looking to grow the total market in the knowledge that any increase will disproportionately benefit themselves. Examples of generic advertising[2] include British Telecom's 'It's good to talk' and in the US Campbell's 'Soup is good for you'.

Pre-emptive strategies are those where the brand asserts its superiority in an undifferentiated market, making it difficult for competitors to match such assertions. Examples include:

'Carlsberg probably the best lager in the world'

'Hertz – we're number one'

'British Airways – the World's Favourite Airline'

How are we saying it?

Humour, tension, and other emotions are used in varying degrees to create awareness and interest. The tone of the communication has, however, to be appropriate. It would be questionable for the inclusion of comedy in a campaign against road accidents. On the other hand, health warnings would be out of place (but perhaps appropriate) in a soft drinks commercial. **Voice-overs** can set the required tone as in advertising for Hovis and Kerrygold. As noted in Chapter 2 the accurate transfer and acceptance of messages is highly influenced by the characteristics of the source of the message. Celebrities are often used both to instil confidence and enhance the personality of the brand. Some stars (e.g. David Beckham) no longer have to actively endorse a brand but only have to appear in an advertisement to create meaning. Animated characters are frequently used to convey information often in a humorous way and can become synonymous with the brand (e.g. Jolly Green Giant, the Tetley Tea Folk, Kellogg's Tony the Tiger and Snap, Crackle and Pop).

Creative communicators will often use metaphors, analogies and stereotypes to create extra meaning. Mothers are frequently used as metaphors

[2]Not to be confused with generic advertising often undertaken by sector representatives such as the Wool Council.

for homeliness and fast cars for success. The skill is to find an appropriate metaphor and ensure it means what it is intended to mean (Brierley 2002). Thus Kellogg's Corn Flakes are associated with sunshine, Bird's Eye (frozen peas) with freshness, Andrex's toilet tissue with softness and Organics and Häagen Dazs with sexual expression! Analogies are sometimes used when a message cannot be realistically portrayed for example a hammer striking a peach as a representation of a child in a road accident (*ibid.*).

Stereotypes abound and we use them in everyday conversation, so it is unsurprising that they are used extensively by communicators as a short-cut towards meaning. For example we all *know* men do not consult maps or multi-task while women cannot read maps and are technophobic. Neither statement is true but there is enough truth that most people in society would recognize the stereotype. The communicator will choose those stereotypes that help create and fix meaning in the message. Absent-minded professors, white-van drivers, mothers (usually in a Volvo) on school runs, taxi-drivers, traffic wardens, grease-covered mechanics, over-bearing parents and angst-ridden teenagers all possess and portray meaning which enables us to share a joke at their expense. Stereotypes are frequently used to enhance meaning and instil values for products and services with geographical and cultural connections. Foster's beer advertising plays on the supposed tendencies of the Australian male to prefer his (cold) beer to his women; Caffries Irish beer evokes the fun-loving, congeniality of the 'old country' in the heart of the cosmopolitan city; while American Airways seeks advice from the straight-talking, no-messing, New Yorkers (from the television series *The Sopranos*). Box 8.4 is a well-known example of how stereotyping (however much we might sometimes regret it) was used to get the (sometimes less than subtle) messages across.

Box 8.4 Metaphors

'Often advertisers will create puzzles and metaphors that people will recognise, and the joke will be that we understand it but others do not; it reinforces social cohesion. A TV ad for *Carling Black Label* shows an English tourist beating a group of German tourists to the sunbeds by throwing his Union jack towel down to the swimming pool; after bouncing on the water a couple of times the towel unfolds on a sunbed, beating the clutch of German holiday-makers who are running to the pool. This ad plays on a number of metaphors which English people are meant to share in a common bonding. The most obvious is the holidaying myth that German tourists always get up early to claim the sunbeds around the hotel pool. This has been a popular anti-German joke in Britain for some time. Second there is a metaphor about British war films, specifically the bouncing bomb (dambusters), and third there is a reference to a previous commercial by Carling Black Label which copied the war film and had two well-known comedians in an aeroplane dropping bouncing bombs and a German sentry parrying the bombs like a goalkeeper (references to the 1966 World Cup final). At the same time music from the film *The Dambusters* played in the background.'

Source: Brierley 2002: 145.

What proof can we provide for any claim?

Making a claim that is evidently unbelievable is unlikely to enhance the image and credibility of the brand.[3] Proof is sometimes required in the form of demonstration or comparison.

Executional guidelines and other requirements

Having developed a creative strategy there is a need to decide how it should be executed. The composition of the communication is crucial whether it be advertising, sales promotion, personal selling or any other of the marketing communications tools. What legal requirements do I need to fulfil (see Chapter 21)? If advertising, sales promotion or direct marketing are involved in the campaign, which media will be used (see below)? Should there be colour, smell, movement or sound? Where should it be positioned (in a publication or broadcast)? What size should it be to create the required impact?

MEDIA CHARACTERISTICS

The overall goal of communications management is to design the best message for the most appropriate medium to reach the maximum number of people in the target audience. As such the management of the media mix is crucial. Over the years new mediums have developed which, despite dire predictions, have complemented rather than replaced what went before. Early hand-painted posters were replaced by printed 'bills' with the arrival of the printing press, which ultimately led to the development of newspapers and magazines. The print medium dominated until the 1920s and the advent of radio, which gradually took over the former's prime position. This was also the golden age of the cinema and it too became a vehicle for commercial messages. With the introduction of television both radio and cinema audiences dropped but they still continued to attract a more definable and, therefore, more targetable clientele. In the 1990s direct marketing (both through mail and telephone) was heralded as the future of communication. The development of electronic media (Internet, World Wide Web, emails, etc.) again brought predictions of the total dominance of these channels. In fact, rather than technical evolution making media decisions more straightforward the plethora of choice makes it even more complex than in the past. Very few campaigns rely solely on one medium. The decision which media to use depends upon cost (always a limiting factor), the target audience reached and the characteristics of that medium.

[3]There are notable tongue-in-cheek exceptions to this such as 'Red Bull gives you wings'.

Outdoor media

Despite being perhaps the oldest commercial communication medium (except for word-of-mouth), outdoor media has remained an important tool, indeed it has achieved something of a renaissance in the latter part of the twentieth century. The term outdoor media relates to posters, hoardings, transport (including liveried balloons or blimps, airliners, trains, taxis and buses) and other non-traditional mediums. Examples of the latter include the Ryanair jet painted with the Hertz livery and the Eurostar train decorated with images from the Da Vinci Code which, in 2006, took the stars of that film from London to the Cannes Film Festival. The traditional poster has also been replaced in high traffic locations by rolling presentations, 3D designs (e.g. Xerox light bulbs) and digital presentations. Giant posters, placed through companies such as Blow-up Media and Mega Ltd, now adorn large office buildings or factories in many major cities around the globe. The term ambient media is often associated with outdoor media and it is best described as anything that introduces a 'wow factor'. That is something not done before that is capable of attracting attention and curiosity. In the past this has included projections onto buildings (including the UK House of Commons), buses with white Polo Mint wheels and the 75 foot by 110 foot (approximately 23 m × 33.5 m) *Maxim* magazine cover in the Arizona Desert that can be seen from space. By definition ambient media ceases to be ambient media once it has become popular (i.e. it no longer has the same 'wow factor') although it is often used as a general term for non-traditional outdoor mediums (see Minicase 8.2).

The advantages of poster and other outdoor mediums is that they are relatively inexpensive yet can offer high **frequency** and **reach** (see media buying). Much depends on location with areas of highest traffic having the densest advertising (e.g. Times Square, Piccadilly Circus, etc.). Indeed there are few heavy traffic sites that do not have marketing messages dominating them. It can sometimes appear that every conceivable vantage point has been taken by outdoor media in some central city locations. On the downside the poster is a largely untargeted medium, although you could argue that the position of sites, for example at airports, does offer some segmentation opportunities. By their very nature outdoor media have a very short time in which to get the message across to the passing public. The industry maxim is that it is unlikely to be an effective poster if there are more than six words on it. Although six words is somewhat prescriptive the message certainly must be easily conveyed in the short time in which the audience is exposed. Organizations that have used posters as a central vehicle in their campaigns include *The Economist* and Benetton where the messages (in words and/or pictures) are straightforward and to the point.

Frequency
The number of times the target audience have an opportunity-to-see (OTS) the message.

Reach
The percentage of the target audience exposed at least once to the message during a period (normally four weeks).

Print media

There are two major classifications of print media (other than leaflets, brochures, etc. which are covered in Chapter 13): newspapers and magazines.

Newspapers have been a vehicle for advertising almost since their inception (see Chapter 1). For much of that time they were limited to black on white and limited type size and relied on repetition and blocks of print to create effect (see Chapter 13) In recent years, however, the introduction of colour and improvements in paper and printing quality has gone some way to improving their appeal. Newspapers have short lead times, enabling flexibility and rapid response where required. It is a highly portable medium and individuals can choose when to 'consume' it, but it has a very short shelf life. Newspapers are good at explaining complex issues (in print and pictures) although practical demonstration is more difficult than in a televisual medium. It is not a highly targeted medium (except for specialist publications such as the *Financial Times* or the *Racing Post*), although different national newspapers attract somewhat different demographic groups (see Chapter 7). Regional newspapers and local variations of nationals allow for geographically based campaigns. From a public relations perspective journalistic and editorial content has high credibility but this can also work against as well as for the organization.

Magazines have a number of similar advantages (portability, can handle complexity, consumption choices, credibility, etc.) but generally have a much longer shelf life and an audience generally larger than the number of copies sold (i.e. multiple readership). The production qualities are generally considerably higher than newspapers, consequently lead times are much longer. Dominant publications in the 1960–80 period were often general interest, wide circulation magazines such as the *Radio Times* and *Woman's Own*. Although general interest magazines still exist, many magazines today reflect particular interests and lifestyles making them better vehicles for targeting (e.g. *Hello, OK, Heat, Zoo, Nuts, etc.*).

Radio

Radio was the driving force behind marketing in the USA in the 1930s and 1940s with sponsored programming and **spot advertising**. In the UK, however, commercial radio stations were banned until 1973 when LBC became the first radio station (and Bird's Eye the first advertiser) to broadcast legally. Prior to that Radio Normandy and Radio Luxembourg broadcasting from the continent in the 1940s and 1950s brought commercial advertising to British listeners including the popular (Ovaltine sponsored) 'Ovaltineys'. In the 1960s so-called pirate radio stations, for example Radio Caroline, transmitted from off-shore vessels also paid for by advertising. Although these stations were frequently closed down they eventually created the pressure required to lift the ban on commercial radio.

Radio currently represents around 7 per cent of advertising spend in the UK although growth has been sporadic in recent years. Among the advantages of radio are that it is relatively low cost, it is a portable medium and (because of the targeted audiences) can be usefully segmented. In addition to geographical targeting (for example Capital Radio in London and BRMB in Birmingham)

Spot advertising
Advertising between programming that typically lasts for between 30 seconds and 1 minute.

most radio stations limit their musical and/or spoken output to attract specific audiences (for example XFM, Magic, Classic FM, etc.). Production costs are a fraction of those for television and lead times shorter.[4] In addition radio (unlike television) enables the individual listener to create 'pictures' in their own minds, a device used extensively by both radio programme producers and advertisers. On the other hand, radio lacks the impact of television as it is frequently no more than 'aural wallpaper' alongside other activities (driving, working, cooking, etc.) and as such does not have the prestige of other mediums.

Despite any failings major companies such as Procter & Gamble, BT, Kellogg's, Ford and Vodaphone use radio extensively and find it a cost-effective medium for getting more out of their television and press coverage (Grimshaw 2004).

Television

It was the advent of television in the USA that rapidly expanded the platform for advertising in that country. In the UK, however, commercial television was again a late arrival coming more than a decade after North America. The costs associated with television are high but the CPT[5] (cost per thousand audience exposure) is low because of the large audiences some stations and programmes attract. For example the cost of a spot advertisement during the televising of the US Superbowl is over $2 million but it does reach over 40 per cent[6] of US households. The main advantages associated with television are in the visuals and sound that can be harnessed to produce a powerful and prestigious message. It can also be a good medium for demonstrations but not, given the time restraints, for complex explanation. A high amount of repetition is also necessary if the message is to have a long shelf life.

Television has been the dominant medium since the second half of the twentieth century currently attracting around 45 per cent of advertising spend. It may continue to be influential for some time yet despite the problems associated with the traditional 'spot advertising' format. The introduction of the handset made changing channel during a commercial break (**zapping**) much easier. Evidence from the USA suggests that one-third of the potential advertising audience are lost to zapping activity (Cronin 1995). The introduction of pre-recordable videos and latterly technology enabled personal video players (PVRs) has led to an increase in **zipping** (the fast-forwarding of commercials during pre-recorded programmes) again enabling viewers to bypass spot advertising. It is perhaps no coincidence that many PVRs, for example TiVo, enable fast-forwarding in 30 second chunks, the most popular commercial advertising length. In an ironic twist TiVo may be looking for their own advertising opportunities. It has been reported that

Zapping
Changing channel during a television commercial break.

Zipping
The fast-forwarding of pre-recorded programmes enabling viewers to bypass commercials.

---

[4]Particularly since the introduction of J-ET, an electronic Web-based advertising trading system.
[5]Also called CPM where 'M' is the Latin representation of 1000.
[6]Down from 49 per cent in 1982.

on the new TiVo OS model, when you hit the fast-forward button to skip past the advertisement, you will see instead small banner ads on-screen.

In an attempt to beat the zippers and zappers and in recognition of the growing power of the Internet the US television station ABC announced in April 2006 that it would make key programmes available on the Internet the day after broadcast paid for by advertisements from organizations such as AT&T, Ford, Procter & Gamble and Unilever. While customers will be able to pause, rewind and fast-forward the episodes they will not be able to skip the advertisements which will be custom-made interactive slots (Curtis 2006).

Direct mail and telemarketing

Direct mail
Advertising, through the medium of the mail, to targeted, profiled customers.

Telemarketing
The use of telephony to maintain a relationship with your customer.

Direct response
Media where the customer can respond immediately to the offer.

Off-the-page
Newspaper or magazine offers with a direct response mechanism (e.g. freephone, envelope, etc.).

Junk-mail
Any mailing the customer decides is untargeted and obtrusive.

Spam
Unsolicited, bulk e-mails.

Door-to-door
The household delivery of leaflets, samples, etc.

In-game product placement
The placement of product in video games for the purpose of publicity.

Direct mail (traditional 'snail-mail' or electronic mail) and **telemarketing** are associated closely with direct marketing and are covered in more detail in Chapter 13 together with **direct response** media such as television (dedicated channels such as QVC as well as 'spot' advertising) and **off-the-page**. Although direct mail can be a highly creative and flexible medium it has been criticized for **junk-mail** (or with email **spam**), an image that the industry finds difficult to shake off. Telemarketing too is regarded as an effective but highly intrusive medium. Other direct marketing techniques (including **door-to-door** leafleting or inserts) can be effective in support of other media-led campaigns, particularly when the objective is the trial of a new brand or brand extension. In general terms one of the most difficult issues is that of data protection. As a medium that relies on data, recent legislation has made data acquisition more difficult and data storage more restrictive.

Electronic media

Perhaps the fastest growing area of media, it includes the Internet and World Wide Web[7] (see Chapter 13), mobile telephony, CD-ROMs (which have largely replaced video and may itself soon be replaced by more advanced technology) and others including screen savers and electronic **in-game product placement**. An example of the latter is the deal reached between Cadillac and Microsoft that will bring virtual creations of the CTS-V, STS-V and XLR-V high-performance models to Xbox Live. Microsoft have also recently acquired Massive, a company specializing in in-game advertising as the platform to exploit Xbox Live's advertising space.

Mobile telephones are being extensively used as the medium of choice for participating in competitions or to obtain further product or service information. The Internet enables information for consumers to be presented, questions to be asked and brand or corporate image to be refined

[7]The terms Internet and World Wide Web (WWW) are often used interchangeably but they are not the same as is explained in Chapter 13.

in addition to acting as an advertising poster site. Both mobile telephone and Internet sites are, however, passive mediums, as potential targets have to be attracted to the text number or Internet site. The Internet does offer limited distribution (of software programs, music, tickets, etc.) in addition to being a highly interactive communications medium, thus closing the gap in time that normally exists between message delivery and the purchase of certain product or service types. Its value as an advertising medium (through **banner-ads, pop-ups,** etc.) is questionable and, given the clutter of many websites, may distract from the effectiveness of the sites themselves. According to a study by MSN (see case study) recall of web advertising is lower than that of television. According to Nielsen/Net Ratings the **click-through rate** on such advertising in 2001 was less than half of 1 per cent (Shimp 2003). **Interstitials** (advertisements that appear between Web pages) would appear to gain better results. **Search engines** are also becoming highly influential with companies paying for priority retrieval based on specific key words.

Whereas radio, television and printing media were largely (but not exclusively) utilized by advertisers, electronic media is available to the whole gamut of communication tools including public relations, sponsorship, sales promotions and personal selling. Electronic media holds out the promise of reaching highly targeted audiences but only after the consumer volunteers information and/or tracking technology builds up a profile of purchase and other interests (usually through **cookie** technology – see Chapter 13). The Internet is usually accessible 24 hours a day and seven days a week although responses to queries may only be handled during normal working hours.

Banner-ads
Vertical or horizontal website advertisements.

Pop-ups
Message boxes that 'pop-up' on websites either to add additional information or as advertising.

Click-through rate
The number of times online users 'click-through' or transfer to sponsored websites.

Interstitials
Advertisements that appear between one Web page and the loading of the next.

Search Engines
A portal that enables users to search the Web.

Cookie
A small text file left on the user's PC that identifies their browser so that they are 'recognized' when they revisit a site.

Building wraps
Giant poster advertising (usually on canvas) hung from a large building (or buildings whilst under construction).

For an example of how advertising online operates, look at: **www.bidvertiser.com**.

MINICASE 8.2

Fiat media plan

In 2004 Fiat re-launched an old favourite the Panda.

Objectives: to capitalize on its car's various awards, emphasize its compact shape and strongly communicate that it was a new Panda.

Strategy: target women drivers. Highlight features (storage space, headroom, five-doors) that would be attractive to women. Rather than point out the rational benefits the marketing team chose to communicate these features using an emotional strategy, playing up the charm. It also sought diversity in the campaign to maximize the 'noise level' at the campaign launch.

Execution: an animal theme was adopted with different animals suggesting different vehicle features (giraffe for headroom, kangaroo for storage, rhino for power). Press and poster advertisements (including on public transport and **building wraps**) were used. Fiat also arranged for helicopters to fly around key cities dangling a cage with a Panda (car) in it to gain press coverage. It also turned the Cherhill White Horse in Wiltshire into a panda. Fiat took a multi-agency approach to the campaign using Leo Burnett (advertising), Arc Interactive (direct marketing, promotions and Web design), Starcom Mediavest (media planning and buying) and Poster Publicity (poster planning and buying).

▶

Results: tracking showed recognition of the posters was 20 per cent higher than average for the medium. Four months after launch Fiat had sold 3138 Pandas in the UK achieving 40 per cent of its annual sales target. The success of the Panda enabled Fiat to increase its market share from 2.49 per cent in April 2003 to 2.74 per cent in April 2004.

FIAT MEDIA PLAN

Cars in Cages		
Dealership Promotions		
Microsite		
Press and Posters		
Building Wraps		
January	February	March

☐ Stunt Marketing ☐ In-Store ☐ Online ☐ Advertising ☐ Ambient Media

Source: Murphy, C., 'Fiat Panda', *Marketing*, 19 May 2004: 29.

MEDIA MANAGEMENT

Selecting the right medium for the message depends, therefore, on individual medium characteristics. Each has advantages and disadvantages and the skill in media management is to find the most effective way to fulfil the communications objective. Although simplistic Figure 8.2 suggests that various media, given their particular strengths and weaknesses, are more effective than others as determined by their contribution to fulfilling 'hierarchy of effects' objectives.

Media planners and buyers must also know not only which media might be effective but how many of the target audience they might reach, how many times and the costs associated with this. To do this they use a form of currency to describe the 'value' of each radio or television slot or publication space. These are usually termed **gross rating points**[8] (GRP) and are calculated by multiplying two measures: reach and frequency (see Box 8.5 on page 186).

Gross rating points
An advertising media currency calculated by multiplying 'reach' and 'frequency'.

- Reach: the percentage of the target audience exposed at least once to the message during a period (normally four weeks).

[8]In the UK television industry these are normally referred to as TVRs (Television Rating Points).

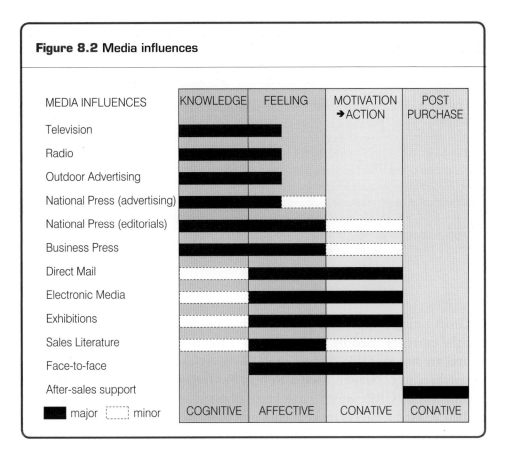

Figure 8.2 Media influences

- Frequency: the number of times (on average) the target audience has the opportunity-to-see (OTS) the message.

'Reach' is an important consideration because it reflects the ability to get through to your target audience. On its own though, this only gives us an insight into who might be exposed, it does not help understand how frequently they need to be exposed for the communication to be effective. 'Frequency' takes us a step closer and is not just about getting the prospective customer to see one media type (e.g. a particular television advertisement) but also reaching them through alternative channels or mediums. Media buyers, therefore, buy space in overlapping media to increase the frequency. But what is the ideal frequency? In the early 1970s Herbert Krugman (1972) presented a paper in the *Journal of Advertising Research* that suggested only three exposures might be needed; the first initiating the response 'What is it?', the second 'What of it?', and the third, and those thereafter, were simply reminders of the first two exposures. An alternative approach to estimating effective frequency is the **efficiency index**. This assumes that with each exposure there is a greater chance of reaching and influencing your audience – up to a point. After this point is reached each exposure no longer adds reach or improves effectiveness. The difficulty in quantifying when the point is reached still makes this theory imperfect and it is effectively left to the experience of the media buyer as the final decision maker as to the required exposure.

Efficiency index
An index that assumes that with each exposure of an advertisement there is a greater chance of reaching and influencing your audience – up to a point. After this point is reached each exposure no longer adds 'reach' or improves effectiveness.

> **Box 8.5** **Reach and frequency and target rating points calculations**
>
> *Reach*
> If 75 per cent of the audience of 12 million *Coronation Street* viewers are C_2DE and the total C_2DE in this particular market is 10 million then the reach is 80 per cent.
>
> | Reach = | $\dfrac{\text{(No. of Target Viewers) x 100}}{\text{(Size of Target Market)}}$ | = | $\dfrac{8 \times 100}{10}$ | = 80 |
>
> *Frequency*
>
> | 10 per cent of target audience exposed 10 times | = | 100 | |
> | 25 per cent of target audience exposed 7 times | = | 175 | |
> | 65 per cent of target audience exposed 1 time | = | 65 | |
> | | | 340 | ÷ 100 = 3.4 |
>
> *Target Ratings Points*
>
> | TRPs = | Reach × Frequency | = | 80 × 3.4 | = 272 |

Target rating points (TRPs)
A variation of gross ratings points adjusted to reflect the chosen target audience.

Rate card
The published cost of media advertising.

Scheduling
The chosen media schedule format (see burst, drip, continuous, pulsing and flighting campaigns).

Burst
Concentrating the campaign 'spend' in a short period to raise awareness and increase reach.

Drip
Extends the campaign over time which increases potential frequency. This is often used for 'reminder campaigns' or when an objective is to change longer-term attitudes.

Reminder campaign
Follows major campaigns and acts as a reminder and reinforcement of the message.

Continuous
Where there is relatively even advertising expenditure over the year.

Pulsing
Continuous advertising campaign which is higher at different times of the year and which may reflect seasonal considerations.

Gross rating points (GRPs), although a product of reach and frequency, are the currency used by media buyers if frequency, distribution and reach figures are not available. For example GRPs are assigned to a 'spot' by media researchers (e.g. Nielsen Media Research). **Target rating points (TRPs)** are a variation of GRPs which have been adjusted to reflect the chosen target audience. Media buyers make media purchases by deciding how many GRPs or TRPs are required to fulfil objectives.

The cost of space in particular media is determined by a number of factors including the size and nature of the audience and what the rest of the market is prepared to pay (Brierley 2002). In the UK the publication *British Rates and Data (BRAD)* is the media buyers' reference book as it lists circulation/audience figures, **rate card** costs,[9] deadlines and other mechanical data (column sizes, etc.). Expenditure is expressed as a 'cost-per-thousand' (CPT or CPM) consumers reached by a particular medium. Some CPT rates include weightings for such things as colour, quality of editorial, etc. There is also an important distinction to be made between the actual CPT and the CPT for reaching a particular target audience.

Choices also need to be made regarding **scheduling**. Is it to be a short, sharp campaign, relatively continuous or any of the myriad of combinations in between? Choices include the:

● **Burst**: concentrating the 'spend' in a short period to raise awareness and increase reach.

● **Drip**: extends the campaign over time which increases potential frequency. This is often used for **reminder campaigns** or when an objective is to change longer-term attitudes.

● **Continuous**: relatively even expenditure over the period.

● **Pulsing**: continuous campaigning which is higher at different times of the year and which may reflect seasonal considerations.

[9]Although the costs shown on rate cards are published these are usually highly flexible.

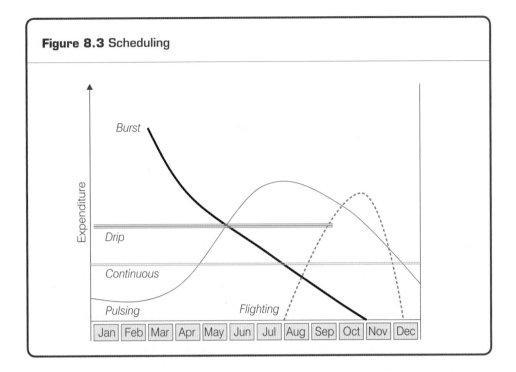

Figure 8.3 Scheduling

- **Flighting**: expenditure concentrated in some periods leaving other periods with zero expenditure

One approach to scheduling proposed by Erwin Ephron, a New York media specialist, is the **recency principle** (or **shelf-space model**) (Shimp 2003). This principle reflects what is known as the '**weak theory**' of advertising discussed further in Chapter 9. The 'weak theory' questions the power of advertising to persuade (as suggested by the **strong theory**) suggesting instead that it acts more as a reminder or gentle nudge toward a particular brand than a highly influential force. The recency principle supposes that:

- A consumer's first exposure to an advertisement is the most powerful.[10]
- Advertiser's primary role is to influence brand choice (when the customer is ready to buy).
- Achieving a high level of weekly reach for a brand should be emphasized over acquiring heavy frequency.

Although the first exposure may be the most powerful, one exposure is probably not enough. However, short-term additional exposure is likely to be wasted on the consumers not in the market for the product or service. This suggests a continuous or near-continuous presence where advertising is used to remind, reinforce or evoke earlier messages rather that teach consumers about benefits or uses. The objective is to reach as high a percentage of the target market audience as possible for as long a period as practical.

Another current trend in media planning is **media-neutral planning** where, rather than base media selection on traditional criteria, market communicators

[10]Shimp (2003) warns that the evidence supporting this is tentative.

Flighting
Campaign expenditure concentrated in some periods of the year leaving other periods with zero expenditure.

Recency principle
A principle which supposes that a consumer's first exposure to an advertisement is the most powerful, that the advertiser's primary role is to influence brand choice (when the customer is ready to buy) and that achieving a high level of weekly reach for a brand should be emphasized over acquiring heavy frequency (also referred to as the shelf-space model).

Weak theory of advertising
Sees advertising power as much more benign than the 'strong theory of advertising'. It questions the power of advertising to persuade, suggesting instead that it acts more as a reminder or gentle nudge toward a particular brand than a highly influential force.

Strong theory of advertising
Where advertising is presumed to have the power to inform, persuade and sell.

Media-neutral planning
A customer-focused review of media based on research, analysis and insight and not habit and/or preference.

see media planning from the consumer's perspective (see case study). Media neutral evaluation is not straightforward as it means using qualitative research to understand the target audience and to understand how they interact. In theory agencies should be assessing all media but many are not structured to be neutral because of the structure of the industry, agency remuneration and long-term habitual behaviour.

Despite the various theories available decision making is frequently down to the media buyer's experience, industry case studies and, above all, an intuitive understanding of the marketplace.

Summary

This chapter continues the marketing planning process by considering campaign tactics and management. It begins by discussing the creative brief and briefing sessions whose objective is to produce directional and inspirational elements for the campaign. Among the principal questions being asked by the creative team are who are we talking to, what are we saying, how are we saying it? Conceptual terms such as the creative platform, positioning, functional orientation (and the USP, unique selling proposition) and symbolic/experiential orientation were discussed as was their contribution to brand image (or brand personality). Other strategies such as resource strategy, emotional strategy, generic strategy and pre-emptive strategy were further defined. The importance of the message source was again reiterated and the contribution of metaphors, analogies and stereotypes highlighted as a means to get across messages. The characteristics of various mediums were discussed including outdoor, print, radio, television and electronic and a definition of ambient media suggested. The concepts of gross rating points, reach and frequency were covered and the merits of burst, drip, continuous, pulsing and flighting scheduling discussed, as was the recency principle and media neutral planning.

Review questions

1 Give an example of a pre-emptive strategy.
2 What are the two main elements of a creative brief?
3 Explain the principle of functional orientation.
4 What is 'the soft sell'?
5 Give examples of outdoor media.
6 How effective do you think banner-ads and pop-ups are, and why?
7 Explain the use of 'TRPs'.
8 What is the difference between 'frequency' and 'reach' in assessing media?
9 What would be your media scheduling options?
10 Explain the principle of media-neutral planning.

Discussion questions

1 Why is the creative brief important, what do you think it should contain and what are the problems that could arise if it is not clear?

2 How would an emotional strategy take its form, and why might it work? Find examples of current advertising campaigns that use this approach and assess their potential impact on the implied target market.

3 Radio advertising has been popular in the past, but now only represents around 7 per cent of UK advertising spend. Why might this be so and, as a potential advertiser, under what circumstances might you consider a radio campaign?

Further reading

Berglind, M. and Nakata, C. (2005) 'Cause-related marketing: more buck than bang?', *Business Horizons*, Sep., 48(5): 443–53. Exploring the concept and practice of cause-related *marketing*, as well as some of its social-ethical complexities.

Holm, H. (2006) 'Integrated marketing communication: from tactics to strategy', *Corporate Communications: An International Journal*, 11(1): 23–33. One conclusion is that there are barriers to developing integrated marketing communications (IMC) from tactics to strategy. The main purpose of this paper is to identify obstacles to further developing IMC

Krieger, A.M. and Green, P.E. (2006) 'A tactical model for resource allocation and its application to advertising budgeting', *European Journal of Operational Research*, May, 170(3): 935–49. Introducing a tactical, short-term model, called SALIENCE, whose purpose is to allocate sales efforts in such a way as to increase the relative importance of attributes for which the sponsoring firm's current product has a (possibly temporary) differential advantage.

Percy, L. (2006) 'Are product placements effective?', *International Journal of Advertising*, 25(1): 112–14. The article comments on the neurological perspective of product placement effectiveness. It explains why implicit learning and memory may not result in changes in brand attitude or behaviour.

Chapter references

Brierley, S. (2002) *The Advertising Handbook*, London: Routledge.

Cronin, J.J. (1995) 'In home observations of commercial zapping behaviour', *Journal of Current Issues and Research in Advertising*, 17: 69–76.

Curtis, J. (2006) 'Revenue channels', *Marketing*, 20 April: 15.

Duckworth, G. (1999) 'Creative briefing' in L. Butterfield (ed.) *Excellence in Advertising*, Oxford: Butterworth Heinemann/IPA, pp. 135–57.

Grimshaw, C. (2004) 'Condé Nast takes 30 plus plunge', *Marketing*, 21 July.

ISBA (2006) 'The Client Brief', Joint Industry Guidelines.

Krugman, H.E. (1972) 'Why three exposures may be enough', *Journal of Advertising Research*, 12(6): 11–14.

Shimp, T.A. (2003) Advertising, Promotion and Supplemental Aspects of Integrated Marketing Communications, 6th edn, Cincinnati: Thomson Learning.

CASE STUDY 8.1

Brand first, medium second

Changes in the consumption of media are giving media buyers a big headache. Conventionally, buyers have sought to spend the bulk of their budgets on terrestrial television to gain the widest reach of any medium, but that model is coming into question as audiences decline and other media open up.

But where should companies go to get the most bang for their buck? They could bung it all on niche cable channels with fewer – but more dedicated – viewers, or splash out on an expensive space in a 'water cooler TV programme' seen by millions. And what of the alternative methods of marketing products, such as product placement deals and mobile phone campaigns? Evolving media habits mean an eclectic mixture of different outlets might be needed to make an impact on target groups.

Hence the trend towards media-neutral planning. According to Tim Ambler of the London Business School, this can be defined as the idea that planners should 'see brand communication from the consumer's point of view and without any predisposition to one medium or another. The marketer should understand the brand, its positioning and the key message first and only then worry about the medium.' Which sounds like plain common sense, really. Surely planners, at least in advertising agencies and within companies, should always have been thinking about the brand first and worrying about the medium afterwards? Yet the way in which the industry has been set up has often discouraged such a holistic view, as different agencies may handle different media for the same client.

Tim Elton, communications planning director at BBJ Communications, says: 'It's very difficult for ad agencies to achieve media neutrality because they tend to have specialisms like TV or print, whereas neutrality is about getting everything together, from point of sale and packaging to posters to TV. It's the Holy Grail.'

The eagerness of some agencies to preserve the distinction between 'above-the-line' and 'below-the-line' marketing has also had an adverse effect on achieving media neutrality. Below-the-line marketing can often be easier to measure, but accurate measurement techniques for media-neutral campaigns, which combine many different platforms, have not yet been developed.

The irony is that while there is more media fragmentation, there is consolidation of media ownership at the top. 'Media buying deals are largely driven by media ownership. This means that fewer overall deals are done at media owner level, but the negotiation emphasis for the media buyer then switches to how they allocate their media buying money across channels within a deal', says Elton.

Media buying itself is now consolidated into fewer hands, with the top seven agencies controlling 77 per cent of the TV advertising market, making them very powerful negotiators, but also showing a bias towards TV that may not be justified as consumers increase their intake of radio, the Internet, and other marketing channels. And consolidation, even in traditional media like print, is not the end of the story. There is a plethora of start-up media owners, swimming against the tide, and buyers have to appraise and set money aside for these new players.

Media neutrality means knowing much more about the customer and therefore the intended audience. This requires better data on what a brand's customers are doing, why and where and more information on media consumption habits, as well as increasingly efficient ways to sort through this data. Some of the media buying techniques required in a media-neutral campaign are actually not that different from ordinary practice. For example, when a buyer is doing a deal with Sky TV, the advertiser needs to be very clear about whether it wants the sports channels, films or Sky One. 'The starting point has to be knowing which individual channels your target audience watches and building the overall deal from there,' says Elton.

As organizations like the Institute of Practitioners in Advertising, which orchestrates the Advertising Effectiveness awards, have thrown their weight behind media neutrality, companies seem more open to the holistic view of planning.

Michael de Kare Silver, chief executive of Web consultancy Modem Media, says: 'You see it a lot more in clients. They've put a lot of thought into the mix of media they want, and they're willing to put a lot of work into how the same campaign and executions can work across those different media.' He encourages clients to set up meetings once a

The idea for his Million Dollar Home Page only took Alex Tew 20 minutes to think up: selling pixels as advertising space with a minimum purchase of US $100 for a 10 x 10 pixel block. By early 2006 he had sold the last square and netted over half a million pounds.

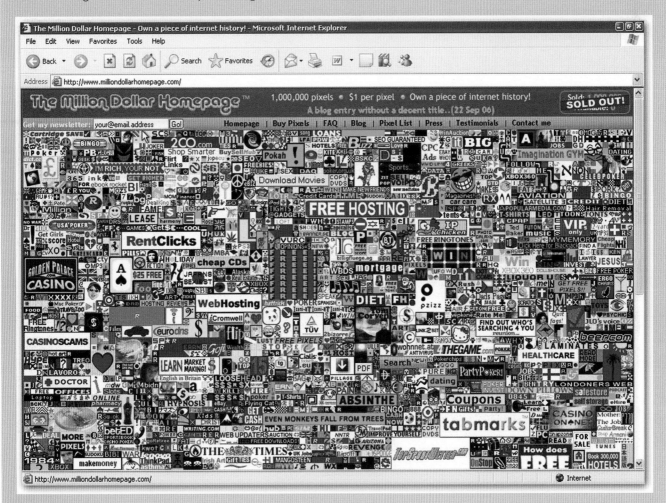

month with all of its agencies and media specialists, so those working on different media can swap ideas and learn what is proving most effective.

The new emphasis means a greater share for niche channels like the Internet and SMS*, which used to simply soak up leftovers in the budget. Evidence is mounting that new media used in conjunction with old can reinforce brand messages more effectively than either alone. For instance, a recent study by MSN found that the use of online advertising added a further 16 per cent audience reach on top of the 48 per cent reach achieved by television, and increased the recall rate. Of those who saw an ad only on the Internet, 4.7 per cent spontaneously recalled it. An ad seen only on TV was recalled by 21.7 per cent of viewers. But recall rates rose to 31.2 per cent if the ad was seen on both media.

However, neutrality cannot succeed unless agencies take on board the need to develop skills in-house to cater to the broad variety of media, or to cooperate more closely with experts in niches, such as SMS and the Internet.

Elton concludes: 'The mainstream advertising community needs to broaden its skill base, because otherwise clients will still have to use four or five different agencies for the same end.'

Case study questions

1 Define, in your own words, the meaning of media-neutral planning.

2 What do agencies need to do to accommodate media-neutral planning?

3 In what ways might marketers collect additional information concerning their customers?

Source: Fiona Harvey, *Financial Times*, 5 May 2003 (used with permission).

* Short Message Service or mobile phone texting.

CHAPTER NINE

ADVERTISING

LEARNING OBJECTIVES

Having completed this chapter you should be able to:

● Understand how advertising developed and the part it played in creating modern consumer markets.

● Recognize and describe the strong and weak theories of advertising.

● Discuss the means by which the advertising industry measures effectiveness and the problems associated with such measurements.

● Describe those characteristics of good advertising.

● Understand how advertising standards are maintained.

● Discuss the factors currently affecting the advertising industry.

INTRODUCTION

Advertising, it has been suggested, is the world's second oldest profession. Certainly, as Chapter 1 illustrated, it can be traced back to the Babylonian, Greek and Roman civilizations. Up until the mid-nineteenth century the term advertising was used widely to refer to any and all forms of promotional activity. However, by the twentieth century it came to be more narrowly defined as paid-for, non-personal form of mass communication from an identified source, used to communicate information and influence consumer behaviour.

This differentiates advertising from public relations or general publicity as it implies paying to place your message, constructed wholly to promote your product or service, in the media (and the position in that media) of your choice. Advertising is also seen as non-personal as it is directed through the mass media at groups of consumers rather than individuals and from an identified source whose product or service is being selectively promoted.

THE GROWTH OF ADVERTISING

Advertising developed considerably in the three hundred years prior to the twentieth century. From the late 1700s through to the nineteenth century was an era when mechanization and factory systems revolutionized industrial output. Mass production demanded mass distribution to mass markets. Prior to the Industrial Revolution trade in other than very basic commodities was largely the preserve of the rich. Most goods were produced locally in quantities suitable for local consumption. With the Industrial Revolution came enormous increases in supply. As we have seen in Chapter 1, advertising essentially emerged as a means of getting an over-production of goods to the wider market. The underlying problem it was addressing, therefore, was that of under-consumption and so advertising was not acting as a mechanism for satisfying wants, as it is seen today. Instead it was concerned with creating that want.

One of the first manufacturers to try to expand his potential market through advertising was Josiah Wedgwood, the founder of the pottery Wedgwood, who in the late 1700s began to target the growing middle class through newspaper advertisements, posters, handbills and shop signs. Other manufacturers of pioneer branded goods also began to recognize the value of advertising, seeing its potential in a number of areas, including:

- Giving information to the consumer.
- Compensating for any weakness in wholesalers.
- Boosting sales efforts in the retail trade.
- Attacking competitive brands.
- Helping to keep aggressive rivals at bay.

The ability to mass produce goods at a vastly reduced cost ensured that they were affordable to a great many more people and advertising was the means by which their availability would be made known to the public at large. Indeed advertising has been credited as one of the main economic factors driving consumer spending and economic growth for the best part of two centuries.

HOW ADVERTISING WORKS

There are countless models and theories which purport to suggest why advertising may work, but these can be categorized into two broad perspectives. In the first, the strong theory of advertising, it is presumed to have the power to inform, persuade and sell. This is the traditional viewpoint taken by academics and practitioners over the past one hundred or more years. Under the 'strong' theory, advertising was seen as an almost irresistible force driving consumption. Such was the belief in the power of advertising that it often attracted hostile criticism. C.P. Snow, speaking in a debate broadcast by the BBC in 1936 claimed (Nevett: 1982: 161)

> *'I see modern advertising as an attempt to impel people to buy what, if it were not for the advertisement, they would never think of buying. Advertising begins by taking our money and ends by depriving us of our freedom.'*

The second theory of advertising sees its power as much more benign. The weak theory questions the power of advertising to persuade, suggesting instead that it acts more as a reminder or gentle nudge towards a particular brand than a highly influential force.

STRONG THEORY OF ADVERTISING

In Chapter 2, hierarchy of effects models were introduced. Hierarchy models are classically 'strong' theory models which suggest a rational, sequential approach to advertising. As noted previously these models (see Figure 9.1) are some of the oldest of all marketing communications models with the first (AIDA) being published in 1898 and further developed by Strong in 1925. Their influence on the advertising sector remained dominant until the 1980s, when challenges to the rigidity of the structure began to appear. It is arguable, however, that despite these challenges, they are still not without influence today. The models purport to describe the outcomes of advertising.

Figure 9.1 Hierarchy of effects models

	KNOWLEDGE	FEELING	MOTIVATION ➔ ACTION
AIDA Strong 1925	*Attention* *Interest*	*Desire*	*Action*
DAGMAR Colley 1961	*Awareness* *Comprehension*	*Conviction*	*Purchase*
Lavidge and Steiner 1961	*Awareness* *Knowledge*	*Liking* *Preference*	*Conviction* *Purchase*
Wells *et al.* 1965	*Awareness* *Perception* *Understanding*		*Persuasion*
	COGNITIVE	**AFFECTIVE**	**CONATIVE**

Cognitive response model
A model that maintains that exposure to advertising elicits different types of response and purports to suggest how these responses relate to attitudes and purchase intentions (Belch and Belch 2001).

Product/message thoughts
(see **cognitive response model**) Those thoughts directed at the product/service and/or the claims made in the advertising.

Source orientated thoughts
Represent those associated (positively or negatively) with the origin of the message (see cognitive response model).

Advertising execution thoughts
Relate to how favourably or unfavourably messages are received (see cognitive response model).

For example DAGMAR (Colley 1961) (which stood for Defining Advertising Goals for Measuring Advertising Results) was promoted as a means of establishing the objectives of an advertising campaign.

The hierarchy of effects models imply that for advertising to be successful it must guide consumers from one stage (e.g. non-awareness) to another (e.g. awareness) and so on until the ultimate goal (the sale) is reached. These models, whilst using different terminology, were largely similar in construction having a cognitive (knowing), affective (feeling) and conative (motivational) dimensions (see Figure 9.1). The objective of any particular campaign (e.g. awareness) then determined the content and form of the advertisement.

Other 'strong' advertising models developed followed a similar linear development. One of the most widely used is the **cognitive response model**. This model (see Figure 9.2) maintains that exposure to advertising elicits different types of response and purports to suggest how these responses relate to attitudes and purchase intentions.

In the cognitive response model the response to an advertising stimulus is one of three 'thought' processes. The first category (**product/message thoughts**) comprise those thought process directed at the product/service and/or the claims made in the advertising. **Source orientated thoughts** represent those associated (positively or negatively) with the origin of the message. **Advertising execution thoughts** relate to how favourably or unfavourably the messages are received. These in turn determine the consumers' attitude toward the advertisement and the brand. Advertisers are particularly interested in consumers' attitudes to particular forms of advertising as studies suggest (e.g. Ambler and Burne 1999) that people who show a positive response to an advertisement are more likely to purchase a product than those whose attitude is neutral. It is attitude which, in this model, affects our purchase intentions.

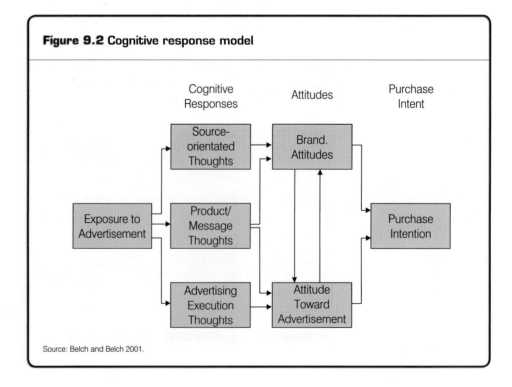

Figure 9.2 Cognitive response model

Source: Belch and Belch 2001.

These 'strong theories' models assume that advertising can ultimately persuade consumers to purchase a particular brand. It underwrites the view of many in the communications industry that it can have a substantial influence on the way we behave. As one prominent practitioner John Bartle[1] (1999) suggests 'I do not think it is too fanciful to talk of the best of advertising, with the greatest powers of transformation, as almost performing *magic*, turning the familiar and similar into the very special and unique.'

The problem with hierarchy of effects and other linear models is there is very little evidence to show that they are predictive. Indeed they appear to be more descriptive of a few rare cases than generalizable across all situations and have been heavily criticized as such.[2] One of the major realizations and a fundamental criticism is that there is no empirical evidence to actually support the argument that consumers pass through each stage in turn. The essence of a hierarchical model is this implied progression yet it is clear that influences can be cumulative and that there will not only be intervention between stages but that post-purchase experience will also be a factor. On this basis one may have assumed that as Crosier (1999: 264) notes 'One might expect these theoretical shortcomings would inhibit practical application of the Hierarchy of Effects as a framework for decision-making. On the contrary case histories show that campaign objectives are repeatedly couched in (these) terms.'

Despite the evident shortcomings there may be some advantages in discussing the hierarchy of effects models and their alternatives (see Chapter 2). To begin with, it is possible to overlook issues of accuracy or predictive ability and draw out an acknowledgement of the importance of the brand. They may also help distinguish between the likely objectives (awareness, etc.) at each stage of a campaign. As Crosier (1999: 264) notes a 'deficient but codified basis for objective formulation is preferable to no common framework at all'. A third value of hierarchy models may be in exploring the relative importance of all the marketing communications tools (including advertising) at various times during the perceived process (see Figure 9.3). As noted in Chapter 2 and illustrated in Figure 2.9, marketing communications tools are regarded as more or less effective depending upon the objective of the campaign. Advertising is seen to be most valuable in long-term brand-building through the generation of awareness and interest but contributes less to the closing of a sale.

There is little doubt that advertising has contributed over time to the creation of very powerful brands such as Nike, Coca-Cola, Microsoft, Sony and Vodaphone. However, whereas it is clear that advertising can inform and contribute to a brand's image over time, its ability to persuade and/or to sell (particularly in the short term) is a more dubious claim. If there is any direct link between advertising and sales it is typically delayed or lagged particularly regarding goods or services that are infrequent purchases (e.g. insurance,

---

[1] Founding partner of Bartle, Bogle, Hegarty and President of the Institute of Practitioners in Advertising from 1995–1997.
[2] See Crosier (1999) for a more detailed criticism of hierarchy of effects models.

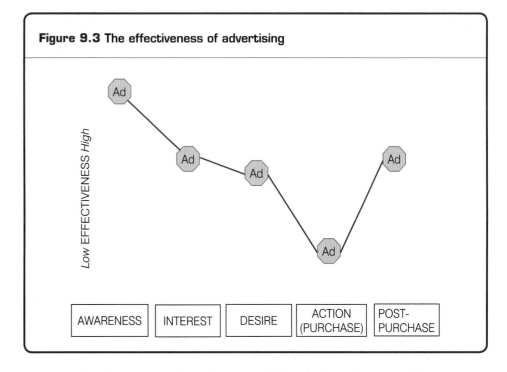

Figure 9.3 The effectiveness of advertising

vehicle sales, etc.).[3] Brierley (2002) suggests, based on industry estimates, that immediate response to an advertisement[4] is as little as 0.01 per cent. To illustrate this consider an advert for Volkswagen (VW) or BMW in the UK. It is highly unlikely that these would generate an immediate, high level of response as the element of the market it can attract is restricted to those who are ready to buy. Other research into television advertising (Wharton 1999) indicates the impact emerges typically within six months, and this draws us to the logical conclusion that the true effects of advertising can only be assessed over time.

Advertising is, however, seen to become important again after the sale. Bovée *et al.* (1995) suggests that in the post-purchase period there is a point when advertising should be used to bolster the customers' sense of satisfaction about the action or purchase (see also cognitive dissonance). The suggestion is that having made a decision to purchase a product or service a consumer looks for reasons to justify their buying decision and that this may be found through advertising and some other communication tools (e.g. public relations, etc.).

In this 'limited benefits' model advertising may be seen to be most effective when it is used to:

- stimulate interest and trial;
- extol features and benefits (pre and post sale);
- create positive brand values and associations (pre and post sale);
- differentiate the brand from the competition (pre and post sale).

[3]What we regard as hard sell (buy now while stocks last, etc.) type communications are not, arguably, advertising as such, rather they have the features of sales promotion. Sales promotion being defined as the use of incentives to generate a specific (usually short term) response.
[4]This distinguishes between advertising as defined in this book and direct marketing which is sometimes called direct response advertising.

WEAK THEORY OF ADVERTISING

Other authors see advertising as less powerful. One explanation for this may be because although advertising allows for a high degree of control over the design and placement of the message it is never either neutral or unbiased and, therefore, may suffer from a low degree of credibility unless accompanied by a high degree of trust. Most products and services are unlikely to be so highly trusted (although there are some notable exceptions). In addition it has been noted that, as the decades have gone by, consumers have become more sceptical and less trusting of advertising messages. Advertising's potential for persuasion may, therefore, be continuing to wane.

With this in mind researchers have proposed alternatives to models such as the hierarchy of effects and other 'strong theories'. Ehrenberg and Goodhart (1979), for example, suggest that the greater part of the buying experience is rooted in past experience as indicated in the ATR (awareness, trial, reinforcement) model (see Chapter 3, Figure 3.3). Having become aware of and eventually trialling a product or service, advertising acts to remind and reinforce the decision made. Ehrenberg (1997) was later to adapt this model further to suggest that the power of advertising was less in persuasion than gentle 'nudging' (see Figure 9.4 below). In this model advertising stimulates trial and subsequently reinforces any positive associations with the brand, gently nudging the consumer toward that brand in the future.

The 'weak' perspective also includes those who suggest that advertising helps maintain a brand within the consumer's repertoire of brands. This viewpoint is generally referred to as the 'portfolio' or 'broad repertoire' view. This perspective suggests that we each generate, through trial, a portfolio of brands from which we make our choice. Advertising keeps the individual portfolio brands front-of-mind, whilst the advertising (or promotion) of other brands may encourage us to try 'new' products which may or may not become part of our portfolio. Rossiter and Percy (1998) suggest that with new products that have been supported by heavy television advertising (such that 90 per cent of the target audience have an opportunity-to-see the

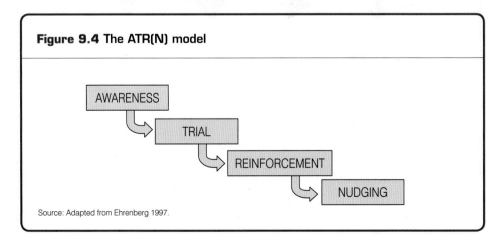

Figure 9.4 The ATR(N) model

AWARENESS

TRIAL

REINFORCEMENT

NUDGING

Source: Adapted from Ehrenberg 1997.

commercial) the advertiser might expect 60 per cent of viewers to be attentive to the advertising. Of these a third may be sufficiently impressed to consider sampling the product or service, the majority of which (70 per cent) may go on to make a trial purchase. From the original target audience approximately 13 per cent may reach the stage of trial purchasing. This supposition is illustrated in Figure 9.5. The similarity to the awareness–loyalty scale in Figure 5.6 should also be noted.

Ehrenberg's (1997) ATR(N) theory appears to be a reasonable explanation for low priced, fast moving consumer goods (FMCG) brands but what about products or services that consumers are unlikely to be able to trial (in the consuming sense), such as a new car or an expensive overseas holiday. In this respect the brand promises (claims associated with a particular brand) become important. These promises are communicated through advertising and may as such replace trial as the reason for including individual brands in the individual consumer's portfolio. This may also be particularly relevant when a new brand is introduced into a category or when a brand is relaunched (Jones 2004). Smith and Taylor (2002) take this portfolio theory a stage further by suggesting various levels of filtering out of brands before making the final purchasing decision as illustrated in Figure 9.6.

Another theory associated with the portfolio or 'weak theory' viewpoint is '**low-involvement theory**'. Low-involvement processing is essentially continual scanning of the environment, regularly, automatically and to a large degree subconsciously in order to identify anything that might be worth consideration in depth. For consumers, advertising serves to remind them of the preferred products, services and brands and to act as a post-purchase reassurance medium. Indeed, the majority of advertisements actually reflect this theory and concentrate around talking points, be they visual or verbal

Low-involement theory
Theory that suggests that consumers scan the environment, largely subconsciously to identify anything worth consideration in depth.

Explore questions of advertising effectiveness at: **www.adcracker. com/theory/feel.htm** and **http://papers. ssrn.com/sol3/papers.ctm?abstract_ id=906662**

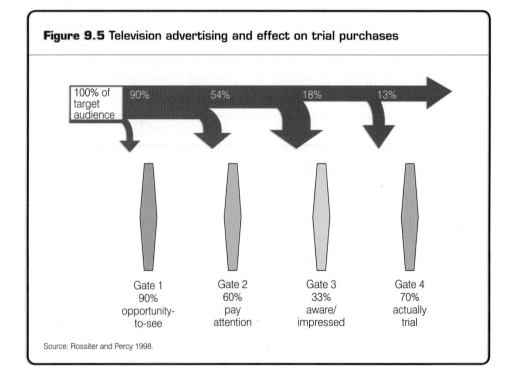

Figure 9.5 Television advertising and effect on trial purchases

100% of target audience — 90% — 54% — 18% — 13%

Gate 1
90%
opportunity-to-see

Gate 2
60%
pay attention

Gate 3
33%
aware/impressed

Gate 4
70%
actually trial

Source: Rossiter and Percy 1998.

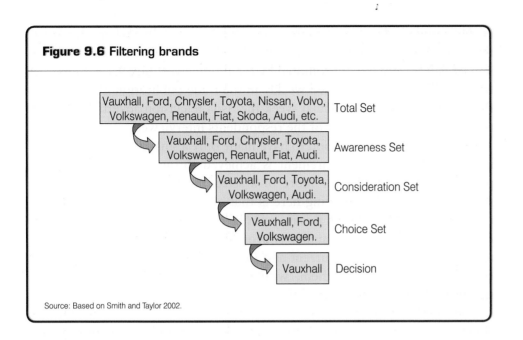

Figure 9.6 Filtering brands

Source: Based on Smith and Taylor 2002.

and designed to bring these to the fore with impact and in a creative way, rather than delivering strong selling propositions. Weak theory, therefore, suggests that advertising works in the same way as strong theory in improving knowledge, but where it differs is that consumers are thought to be selective in the way they decide which advertisements they pay attention to and only acknowledge those which promote products that they either use or have some prior knowledge of. Consequently, advertising, mainly supports existing buyers and helps to reinforce past sales and improve the pattern of repeat buying.

MEASURING ADVERTISING EFFECTIVENESS

Theories, experience and modelling can probably suggest how an advert should work, but none of these will tell you how it does work in practice. Perhaps the old advertising adage[5] 'I know that half my advertising doesn't work, the problem is I don't know which half', sums up best the problem of accurately or even approximately measuring the effectiveness of advertising.

The difficulty of measuring effectiveness has not, however, stopped the industry from developing means by which to gauge advertising's contribution and using these as evidence of advertising effectiveness. In terms of the 'high-involvement' or strong model of advertising, recall has traditionally been the most popular measure. **Day-after recall** was first developed in the USA in the 1930s by George Gallup for Procter & Gamble but it is still much in

Day-after recall
Unprompted recall of previous day's advertising. Developed by Gallop in the 1930s (see also **Advertising recall**).

[5]Attributed variously to Lord Leverhume of Lever Brothers, John Wannamaker, US retail tycoon and Henry Ford.

View the latest advertisements online at:
www.adwatch.tv/.

Precisely wrong
Strictly an incorrect measure. Proxy measures such as brand awareness, recall or recognition, whilst being easy to measure precisely are not directly associated with sales and might be said to be precisely wrong (see vaguely right).

Vaguely right
Actual sales directly related to advertising are almost impossible to gauge accurately but an estimation can be said to be vaguely right (see also precisely wrong).

evidence today. With recall surveys respondents are asked what advertising they remember, as the theory is that only advertising that has made a high impact will be recalled unprompted by the interviewee. Box 9.1 is an extract from recall research published weekly in the trade publication *Marketing*. In the 'adwatch' for this particular week the Asda television advertisement was remembered by 79 per cent of the respondents interviewed.[6]

As advertising is understood to have made only a small impact in the 'low-involvement' model, measurement is achieved through recognition (i.e. a positive response to one or more of a selection of products presented to the interviewee). The thinking here is that as advertising only 'nudges' the consumer toward the brand this may not be remembered unaided but will be remembered when the consumer is prompted. Both recall and recognition testing are used to justify current and future campaigns, but there is a clear cost differential between them, with the recall methodology requiring a significant higher level of expenditure.

Both methodologies are, however, flawed in one important respect. The ability of a consumer to recall or recognize a brand does not mean that a respondent will ultimately buy that brand either now or in the future. Brand awareness, recall or recognition, whilst being easy to measure precisely, is not directly associated with sales and might be said to be strictly an incorrect measure (it is, therefore, **precisely wrong**). On the other hand actual sales directly related to advertising are almost impossible to gauge accurately (but may be said to be **vaguely right**). Thus we have allusions or indirect measures that serve mainly to remind both advertisers and their agencies that absolute dependence upon recall of recognition could be misleading.

Box 9.1 Adwatch, the weekly analysis of advertisement recall, *Marketing,* 10 August 2005 Q: Which of the following TV commercials do you remember seeing?

	Account	Agency/TV Buyer	%
1	Asda	Publicis/Carat	79
2	Churchill Insurance	EBP/MediaCom	72
3	Esure	In-house/Carat	70
4	British Gas	Clemmow Hornby Inge/Carat	63
5=	DFS	Phillipson Ward Longworth Camponi/Brilliant Media	56
5=	Vauxhall Corsa	Delaney Lund Knox Warren/Initiative	56
7	Pampers Kandoo	Saatchi & Saatchi/Starcom	53
8	McDonald's	Leo Burnett/OMD UK	49
9=	Quorn	Farm/Walker Media	47
9=	Tesco Personal Finance	Lowe/ Initiative	47

Source: Adwatch research conducted by NOP Research Group (survey conducted 28/07/05–01/08/05)

[6]Ironically this was the same advertising banned by the *Advertising Standards Authority (ASA)* as discussed in Minicase 9.2.

The contribution that advertising makes to sales can, however, be approximated. This is normally achieved by calculating actual (advertising supported) sales against **simulated sales** (i.e. sales calculated on the basis of no advertising). The means used to establish the value of simulated sales are, however, largely subjective in that no established brand can truly be matched against an impartial control sample. With new introductions, however, the effect of advertising may be measured using different geographical regions and/or different media for the advertising against non-advertised control samples.

In the 1960s new methods of measurement involving usage and attitude came to the fore. Rather than measuring the affect of advertising after a campaign has been launched this suggested measuring consumer attitudes both before and after a campaign. One method is to use an **attitude scale** as illustrated in Figure 9.7. A random selection of consumers are asked to rate each pair of statements to establish their attitude towards the brand. Following the campaign the exercise is repeated using the same or different random sample. The before and after scores show the change in attitude to the brand as a result of the campaign. Some companies (e.g. Intel) use rolling research of this type to monitor attitudes to their brand over time.

Attitude research is, however, expensive and it is worth reiterating that a good attitude toward a brand, although desirable, does not necessarily lead to positive purchase behaviour.

In summary measuring the effectiveness of advertising continues to be a problem in the industry and, in a world of tighter budgets and the requirement to justify costs, this has contributed in no small part to the relative decline in the importance of advertising (see 'The advertising industry').

Simulated sales
Sales calculated on the basis of no advertising, which can then be used to measure the contribution of advertising.

Attitude scales
Scales that measures a respondent's attitude to predefined statements. Examples include nominal scales, ordinal scales, interval scales and ratio scales.

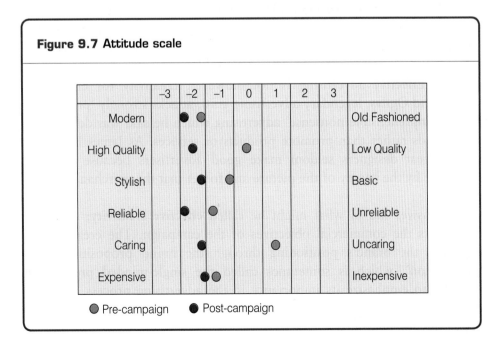

Figure 9.7 Attitude scale

	−3	−2	−1	0	1	2	3	
Modern	●	○						Old Fashioned
High Quality		●	○					Low Quality
Stylish		●	○					Basic
Reliable	●	○						Unreliable
Caring		●		○				Uncaring
Expensive		●○						Inexpensive

● Pre-campaign   ● Post-campaign

ADVERTISING CHARACTERISTICS

Whether working with the 'weak' or 'strong' theories it is recognized that certain advertising characteristics cause us to remember and empathize with some messages over and above others. Any one advertisement, therefore, has to compete with thousands of paid and other messages (i.e. noise) every day. Unless your message catches sufficient of the target customers' (or other influencers') attention, and is relevant to them, it can be said to have been ineffective. To create an advertisement with the power to do this requires creativity.

Creativity

The ability to attract and hold the attention of the target audience through the manner and composition of the advertisement.

Creativity in advertising is the ability to attract and hold the attention of the target audience through the manner and composition of the advertisement. It is an art and not a science (although the industry has built up a body of knowledge on what is likely to be successful) and can be affected by a myriad of factors, each of which can make or break the creative effect.

To begin with, however, the product or service has got to have merit. As Marcel Bleusteun-Blanchet, founder of the Publicis agency in 1926 observed 'you can't have good advertising for a bad product'. Advertising may prompt you to investigate but closer examination (sampling, test-drive, etc.) of a poor (relative to price and function) product or service will restrict sales whatever the level of advertising investment. Similarly advertising may encourage the consumer to trial a particular fast moving consumer good (FMCG) but only if that trial is satisfactory will the consumer consider purchasing it again in the future. Playing around with an existing product, whatever the advertising support, can also lead to dire consequences as Coca-Cola discovered when they reformulated the drink (based upon market research) in 1985 and caused uproar amongst traditional drinkers.

Advertising problem

The reason(s) why an organization is advertising.

Establishing the **advertising problem** (the reason the company is resorting to advertising) is the next stage of the advertising creation process and is derived from the advertising objectives. Much good adverting is based on a creative concept (or creative platform), an idea upon which the campaign is built. Effective advertising is not, however, creativity for creativity's sake. David Ogilvy, legendary advertising guru, attacks strongly 'pretentious and incomprehensible nonsense' advertising which he said was designed to win awards rather than promote products or services. As James R. Adams noted 'great designers seldom make good advertisers because they get overcome by the beauty of the picture and forget that the merchandise must be sold'.

Effective creativity

Creativity that meets the commercial objectives of a campaign.

Single-minded proposition

Brand's unique selling proposition.

The answer lies in what might be called **effective creativity**; creativity that meets the commercial objectives of the campaign. The creative idea expresses the brand's positioning through the brand proposition. This 'proposition', which is sometimes called the **single-minded proposition** in order to emphasize its importance in the advertising process, needs to capture the qualities of the brand and incorporate the right mix of functional properties and emotional characteristics.

The profile of the target audience is also key to the creative platform, upon which the advertisement is based, and the **media strategy**, which defines the means of its distribution (see Chapter 8). It is interesting in this regard to note that product producers frequently use advertising to promote the intangible factors (prestige, reputation, etc.) associated with their brand, whereas service providers often attempt to promote the physical, tangible outcomes (comfort, relaxation, etc.).

Although no strict formula exists experience suggests certain characteristics appeal to the consuming public. To this end good advertising is said to generate the **Waterloo effect**. The Waterloo effect (based on the story in Minicase 9.1) is where the advertising is said to have one or more of the following features:

- uniqueness
- repetition
- relevance

Unique advertising undoubtedly stands out from the rest and gets talked about through 'word-of-mouth' and/or '**media chatter**'. Repetition meanwhile fixes a message in our memory. Popular and memorable tag-lines such as 'Beanz Meanz Heinz' (Heinz), 'the world's favourite airline' (British Airways) and 'probably the best beer in the world' (*Carlsberg*) rely on repetition to become memorable. This is further enhanced by consistency (message, image, storyline, etc.). Relevancy is, however, seen as the strongest influence of all. If advertising is relevant to the consumer's needs, at the time s/he wants to satisfy them (or in the foreseeable future), attention will be paid to the advertisement. For this reason advertisers look to target those consumers (by age, by income, by lifestyle, etc.) who most clearly fit their existing customer profiles in the expectation that the advertising will be most relevant to them.

Media strategy
Decisions on which media to use for a given campaign.

Waterloo effect
Content of good advertising campaigns, namely uniqueness, frequency and relevance.

Media chatter
Subject matter that is discussed by, and in, the media.

Look at the Centre for Interactive Advertising at: **www.ciadvertising.org**.

MINICASE 9.1

The Waterloo effect – uniqueness, frequency and relevance

Long ago an advertising practitioner used the following story to describe what he called the Waterloo effect. He explained that on his way home each night he would pass the time waiting for his train sitting in the bar at Waterloo Station drinking a pint of beer and watching his fellow passengers go by. Occasionally, out of the thousands of people in the station, his gaze would fall upon somebody different from the rest. It might be because of their behaviour or they might be dressed outrageously or be sporting a crazy hairstyle. Because they were different (or *unique*) they stood out from the crowd. At other times he would become aware that the same person kept passing in front of the bar. He might not notice that person the first few times but invariably the more often they passed the more conspicuous they became. Repetition (or *frequency*), therefore, made them stand out from the crowd. On yet other occasions he would be gazing into the crowd when he saw someone he recognized. Out of all those people in the station, this person was *relevant* to him personally and, therefore, attracted his attention. In the same way that these factors made people stand out from the crowd at Waterloo Station then good advertising should incorporate *uniqueness, frequency* and *relevance*.

Impressions
A single instance of an advertisement being displayed.

Stopping power
Advertising that has the effect of attracting complete attention.

Demonstration advertising
Advertising where the effectiveness of the product or service and the way it may be used is demonstrated.

Typical-person endorsement
The use of everday characters (usually played by actors) to endorse a product or service.

Expert endorsement
Advertising which uses known or supposed (from their description or appearance) experts to recommend a product or service.

Celebrity endorsement
Advertising which uses the credibility associated with a celebrity to carry the message. The greater the celebrity's influence on a particular target audience the greater the wish to mimic that celebrity.

Slice-of-life
Advertising that uses simulated 'real-life' situations and where the viewer is encouraged to get involved with the action.

Comparative advertising
Direct comparison of one brand with another, usually its main competitor. This may be to establish the brand's position in the marketplace or to claim price or functional superiority.

In the USA, research suggests people are exposed to between 300 and 1500 advertising **impressions** per day (Jones 2004) and that by the age of 18 the average American will have seen approximately 350 000 commercials (Law 1994)[7]. Advertising, therefore, must aim for **stopping power** whether through uniqueness, repetition or relevancy. To do this advertisers use one or more proven formats including:

- Demonstration advertising: advertising which demonstrates the effectiveness of the product or service (e.g. Shake-n-Vac) and the way it may be used (e.g. 'have a break, have a Kit-Kat) or its use extended (Lea & Perrin's Worcestershire Sauce in spaghetti bolognaise, Kellogg's Corn Flakes in the evening, etc.).

- Testimonials or Typical-person endorsement: where advertisers use everyday-type people (usually actors) to say how good the product or service is and any other messages the advertiser wishes to convey.

- Expert endorsement: advertising which uses known or supposed (from their description or appearance) experts to recommend a product or service. For example a former Police Officer endorsing burglar-alarm equipment. Frequently the 'expertness' is a creation of the advertiser. For example the advertising of products said to include special formulations (haircare, headache relief, etc.) often appear to be based in a laboratory with people in white coats giving the scientific claims more supposed validity.

- Celebrity endorsement: uses the credibility associated with a celebrity to carry the message. The greater the celebrity's influence on a particular target audience the greater the wish to mimic that celebrity. The celebrity, therefore, should be appropriate for both the product/service and target audience. David Beckham endorsing Stenna stair lifts or Thora Hird endorsing Police sunglasses are unlikely to be as affective as the original advertisements have been.

- Slice of life: the use of simulated 'real-life' situations have long been a vehicle for advertising messages. In these the viewer is supposed to get involved with the action either in an everyday setting (e.g. the various incarnations of Katie and the rest of the OXO family), long-running romances (e.g. Goldblend) or dramas (e.g. Ensure, AA, Mini, etc.). These 'slice-of-life' advertisements are in fact 'mini-soaps'[8] or continuing dramas.

- Comparative advertising: the direct comparison of one brand with, usually, its main competitor. This may be to establish the brand's position in the marketplace (e.g. Hertz: 'Number One', Avis: 'We Try Harder') or to claim price or functional superiority over an opponent (e.g. Asda versus Tesco see Minicase 9.2). Limitations exist in some markets as to the level of direct comparison that can be made.

[7] Quoted in Brierley 2002.
[8] An irony because the name 'soaps' came originally from the sponsorship of radio programmes by soap companies in the USA.

Watchdog tells Asda to drop 'cheapest' claim

According to an article in the *Guardian*, 20 August 2005, ASDA, one of the UK's largest supermarket chains has been ordered to stop saying it is the cheapest supermarket after a year-long battle with arch-rival Tesco. Tesco complained to the UK Advertising Standards Authority (ASA) about advertising that hailed Asda as 'officially Britain's lowest priced supermarket'. The ASA agreed with the complainant that this was misleading. Asda had come top in a survey conducted by the trade magazine the *Grocer* but the ASA said that this was only based on 33 product lines and was, therefore, 'too limited' to judge who was the cheapest. Asda provided six other independent surveys that said it was the cheapest store but the ASA said that these either had insufficient product lines or did not compare the retailer with discount chains such as Netto, Aldi or Lidl. Richard Hyman, chairman of retail consultancy Verdict Research considers the price of goods in Tesco, Asda and Morrisons to be similar with 'no meaningful difference between them'. He noted, however, that Netto and other discount chains are significantly lower than the large chains.

Source: Heather Tomlinson, *Guardian*, 20 August 2005.

Within these broad formats advertisers use particular features to enhance the appeal of the advertising. These include:

- Logical appeals: appeals to our sense of logic and reason, for example 'this product out-performs everything else in the market'. Many early advertisers used the 'reason-why', logical appeal, format as the basis for their advertising. This was developed further in the 1920s by US advertising agency boss Rosser Reeves into the unique selling proposition (USP). USP theory assumes consumers can only comprehend one major factor about a brand and that brand's advertising should concentrate on this.

Logical appeal or (reason why) advertising
Appeals to our sense of logic and reason for example 'this product out-performs everything else in the market'.

- Emotional appeals: these develop atmosphere and appeal to an individual's ego, status or sense of worth. As early as 1916 Coca-Cola were running full-colour posters, with little copy and much white space, featuring two young and fashionable women drinking Coke. Far from a logical appeal (e.g. it satisfies your thirst) this advertising sought to establish the drink as youth-associated and fashionable.

Emotional appeal advertising
Advertisements that develop atmosphere and appeal to an individual's ego, status or sense of worth.

Copy
Relates to written material. Advertising copy is the text in an advertisement. Journalistic copy relates to published articles.

- Stereotyping: short-hand notions of what people and places are in order to communicate messages quickly and effectively. Examples include the OXO mum (mother knows best), the Marlboro cowboy (manliness), Audi's German heritage (well engineered) and Foster's Australian men (sexist drinkers who know a good beer). See Chapter 8, Box 8.4.

Stereotyping
Short-hand, generalized characteristics of people and places used in order to communicate messages quickly and effectiveness.

- Humour: according to research, one-third of all global advertising contains humour (De Pelsmacker et al. 2001) and 26 per cent of all positive responses to television advertising are because consumers are 'amused' (Lach 1999). Humour is, as such, a staple of the advertising industry. The reason is because humour attracts our attention and,

Humorous advertising
Designed to attract, through humour, consumer attention. If it is good enough and is memorable it may also generate 'word-of-mouth'.

Creatives

Individuals who work in the creative industries (e.g. designers).

if it is good enough, is memorable and may generate 'word-of-mouth' (as does other highly creative advertising). There is, however, a narrow line between success and failure. Some 'humorous' advertising can, with repetition, become annoying (e.g. Michael Winner in Esure advertisements – see Case study 9.1) although some creatives would argue that mild annoyance is yet another way of keeping a brand at the front-of-mind of the consumer. Although much humour is 'culture-specific' many humorous commercials (especially those based on visual gags) do travel, as witnessed by the increasing number of television shows around the world based on this genre.

Erotica

Where sexual imagery is used to attract attention and enhance stopping power.

- Erotica: 'sex sells' is another old advertising maxim and there is little doubt that it can, at times, yield enormous stopping-power.[9] The use of sexual imagery has, however, changed over the decades. Semi-clad models draped over motor cars are now seen as tacky and dated whereas the erotica associated with the sophisticated advertising of Häagen-Dazs ice cream or Organics shampoo has undoubtedly differentiated these brands in their particularly crowded market places. Levi's 501 advertising has used both sexes in mildly erotic advertising. Advertisements for the Yves Saint Laurent perfume Opium featuring model Sophie Dahl and the Club 18–30 poster campaign[10] (both subsequently banned as potentially offensive) succeeded in generating considerable media comment (media chatter). The Wonderbra 'Hallo Boys' campaign, which cost around £500 000 to produce, was rumoured to have generated additional publicity worth £50 million. There are, however, two ironies associated with much 'erotic advertising'. The first is that although mild erotica is powerful, overt erotica is seen as a turn-off by consumers. The second is that most erotic advertising, that feature naked or part-clad women, appears directed at women consumers (e.g. lingerie and perfumery)!

Shock tactics

Advertising that is shocking but attracts attention.

- Shock tactics: shock advertising techniques aim to make the consumer sit up and think about the message. Benetton have for many years used images such as newborn children, AIDS patients and death-row prisoners to 'promote' a message of international solidarity with their brand. Whatever the ethical issues surrounding the use of such images they have rarely failed to cause comment. In the not-for-profit sector, charities such as Barnado's and the NSPCC (most recently in their 'full-stop' campaign) have used images of child abuse to shock potential contributors to take action. Health campaigns regularly use shock treatment (e.g. interviews with dying cancer patients) to try to change personal lifestyles and road-safety campaigns use horrific

[9]The small number of minor road accidents reported around the Wonderbra 'Hallo Boys' poster sites in Great Britain and Ireland are perhaps evidence of this.
[10]Including such slogans as 'Beaver Espania', 'The Summer of 69' and 'It's not all sex, sex, sex, sex, sex … there's a bit of sun and sea as well.'

Ryanair

Towards the end of the Iraq war budget airline Ryanair ran an advertising campaign which put its main competitors easyJet on the defensive. The advertisement featured Iraq's Information Minister Mohammed Saeed Sahaf, nicknamed 'Comical Ali' who became well known during the conflict for his highly unrealistic view of Iraq's fortunes during the war. Under the heading 'Easyjet's Head of Information' the Minister was portrayed as saying 'We are winning the war! We are beating the Americans! EasyJet has the lowest fares!' EasyJet failed to see the funny side describing the advertisement as 'insensitive'. Samantha Day, spokesperson for easyJet, said 'We haven't lost our sense of humour, but this ad was released on the day the Information Minister was rumoured to have committed suicide and we thought it was distasteful to say the least.'

SOURCE: IMAGE COURTESY OF THE ADVERTISING ARCHIVES.

Easyjet criticized the negative campaign but an unrepentant Ryanair trumpeted it as one of their most successful advertisements ever.

images (e.g. a car crash without seat-belts) to drive messages home. Shocking advertising invariably attracts the attention of the media and often prolonged 'media chatter' and 'word-of-mouth' ensures the brand (or, in the case of health campaigns, the message) is kept forefront in the public mind.

Fear
Advertising that uses fear of something happening (e.g. house fire) as the central theme.

- Fear: again a staple of advertising. The fear can be against the physical well-being of the individual or his or her dependents (e.g. 'what will happen to your family if you die?'), social status (e.g. 'will you be able to afford to retire?') or performance (e.g. 'can't sleep?'). The purpose of this advertising is to offer the consumer a remedy that will reduce the specific fear factor (e.g. insurance, pension funds or sleep aids respectively).

Sensory appeal
Creating fantasy and/or aura to attract attention to the message.

- Sensory appeal: yet another old advertising maxim is that you should be selling the sizzle not the sausages. For many years Marlboro, the world's largest cigarette brand, used the image of the 'cowboy' and 'the big-country' as the setting for all of its advertising. Citroen's fire-raising visuals, complemented by the 'takes my breath away' soundtrack had enormous resonance with audiences. Fantasy, escape and nostalgia are also seen as attractive. For example Bounty tastes of paradise, the National Lottery can make your dreams come true and Hovis is endowed with the supposed qualities associated with a bygone age. British Airways have used the same piece of music in its advertising since 1983. Although the 'Flower Duet' from Delibes' opera *Lakmé* has been adapted and re-scored on several occasions the basic melody is said to express everything the airline wants to say to its customers. It is now so established that in the UK market the playing of the first few bars is instantly associated by most people with the airline. Indeed music often becomes better known and more popular after it has been used in advertising (see Box 9.2).

Box 9.2 Advertising theme tunes.

Advertiser	Title	Artist
Vodafone	Bohemian Like You	The Dandy Warhols
Citroen Xantia	The Passenger	Iggy Pop
Adidas	Peaches	The Stranglers
Rolling Rock	Drinking In LA	Bran Van 3000
Levi's Twisted	Before You Leave	Pepe Deluxé
Gap Denim	Digital Love	Daft Punk
Mercedes Benz	If Everybody Looked The Same	Groove Armada
Guinness	Phat Planet	Leftfield
The Times	Barber's Adagio For Strings	William Orbit
Lynx	Bentley's Gonna Sort You Out	Bentley Rhythm Ace
Miller Genuine Draft	Loco	Fun Lovin' Criminals
Nike	Mas Que Nada	Sergio Mendes

Box 9.2 (Continued)

Advertiser	Title	Artist
Peugeot 306	Can't Take My Eyes Off You	Andy Williams
Diet Coke	Lady Marmalade	LaBelle
Fiat Punto	Don't You Want Me	The Human League
Smile Internet Bank	Smile	The Supernaturals
Levi's 501s	Inside	Stiltskin
Levi's TV	Sarabande (Suite No.4 in D Minor)	Academy of St Martin In the Fields
Kroenenberg 1664	Slip Into Something More Comfortable	Kinobe
Adidas	Beautiful Crazy	Space Raiders
Levi's	Before You Leave	Pepe Deluxé
Grolsch	I'm Bored	Iggy Pop
Levi's	Itchy & Scratchy	Boss Hogg
Carling	Much Against Everyone's Advice	Soul Wax
Baileys	One Way Or Another	Blondie
Levi's	The Second Line	Clinic
American Express	Cars	Gary Numan
Mercedes Benz	If Everybody Looked The Same	Groove Armada
Sainsbury's	Got Myself A Good Man	Pucho & His Latin Soul Brothers
XFM	Yellow Butterfly	Tahiti 80
Carling	6 Underground	Sneaker Pimps
Daewoo	Purple	Crustation
Tic Tac	27 Women	La Honda
Levi's	Death in Vegas	Dirge
BUPA	Cry	Howie B
Citreon Xsara	Rise	Craig Armstrong
Vodafone	Smokebelch	Sabries of Paradise
Guinness	Original	Leftfield
Adidas	Right Here Right Now	Fatboy Slim
Renault Kangoo	Run On	Moby
Virgin Cola	With You	Alex Gopher
Cafffrey's	Clubbed To Death	Rob D
Levi's	Novelty Waves	Biosphere
Compaq	Carrera Rapida	Apolla 440
Levi's	Underwater Love	Smoke City
Guinness	Guaglione	Perez Prado & His Orchestra
Lynx	Chewy Chewy	Ohio Express
Dairylea	Gimme Dat Ding	The Pipkins
McDonald's	Hot Diggity Dog Ziggity Boom	Perry Como
Maxell Tapes	The Israelites	Desmond Dekker
British Gas	Wipeout	The Safris
Lynx	Miniskirt	Esquivel & His Orchestra
Alliance and Leicester	Baby Elephant Walk	Henry Mancini
Guinness	Babarabateri	Beny More/Perez Prado & Orchestra
PPP Healthcare	Boum!	Chales Trenet
Guinness	Incidentally Robert	Tot Taylor

Box 9.2 (Continued)

Advertiser	Title	Artist
Triumph Bras	Va Ba Boom	Edmundo Ros
Nike	Soul Bossa Nova	Quincy Jones
Go! Airlines	Theme From 'The Fox'	Hugo Montenegro & His Orchestra
The *Guardian* newspaper	Dean Fraser	Dick Tracey
Powergen	Green Bossa	Tot Taylor
Halifax	Surfin	Ernest Ranglin
Ariston	Da Da Da	Trio
Maynard's Wine Gums	Hoots Mon	Lord Rockingham's XI
Fiat Bravo	Rubber Biscuit	The Chips
Kellogg's Fruit 'n' Fibre	The Banana Boat Song (Day-O)	Harry Belafonte
Wrangler	Follow The Yellow Brick Road	Victor Young & His Orchestra

Sources: various

For more examples of music used in advertising look at: **http://www. commercialbreaksandbeats.co.uk/**.

- **Shape and colour**: play a part in aiding recognition. The Coca-Cola and Heinz ketchup bottles and the McDonald's golden arches are icons of design and instantly recognizable. Cigarette brands frequently use colour, in some cases to circumvent advertising restrictions. Example include Marlboro's red livery, Silk Cut's purple silk and Benson and Hedges gold. Cadbury (purple), Virgin (red) and McDonald's (red and gold) are other examples of brands with strong colour associations.

In summary advertisers use a wide range of different characteristics individually or in combination to draw the attention of the consumer toward their branded product or service.

THE ADVERTISING INDUSTRY

Undoubtedly advertising was the communications tool of choice for most of the twentieth century. It was endowed with the ability to create and maintain the profile of a wide range of national and international brands and was the backbone upon which the communications industry was built. By the end of the century, however, the ratio of promotional expenditure to advertising was 3 to 1. This distribution of marketing communication funds would have been unthinkable to advertisers and agencies during the 1960s (Jones 2004).

Although advertising spending worldwide has doubled per person in real terms since the 1950s, the year-on-year growth rates have declined substantially. In recent years advertising has recovered slowly from a substantial downturn in 2001 but annual growth rates are still below those of the 1990s. According to the UK Advertising Association advertising expenditure rose by 2.4 per cent in 2003 to £17.2 billion. As this figure took no account of inflation the

Box 9.3 Media spend by top 20 UK advertisers

Rank 2004	Rank 2004	Advertiser	2004		Cinema		Outdoor		Press		Radio		Television	
			Ad Spend £m	% Difference	% of Total	% Difference	% of Total	% Difference	% of Total	% Difference	% of Total	% Difference	% of Total	% Difference
1	1	Procter & Gamble	199.57	**3.8**	1.5	**269.3**	3.4	**−28.9**	13.1	**8.8**	2.6	**−55.8**	79.5	**8.3**
2	2	COI Communications	159.54	**11**	1.9	**−5.2**	8.1	**58.1**	25.9	**17.9**	15.6	**3.9**	48.6	**5.5**
3	4	L'Oréal Golden	95.20	**5.4**	0.1	**−61.2**	6.8	**98.4**	23.9	**15.3**	0.0	**−82.6**	69.2	**−1.6**
4	3	BT	81.56	**−15.8**	0.0	**−X**	14.0	**41.8**	33.6	**−10.3**	9.7	**35.7**	42.7	**−33.2**
5	6	Lever Fabergé Personal	73.42	**4.0**	6.1	**17.7**	20.1	**58.2**	12.6	**2.9**	2.0	**−4.5**	59.2	**−7.4**
6	12	Reckitt Benckiser	70.28	**16.5**	0.0	**0.0**	4.0	**5.2**	2.8	**−40.8**	1.0	**27.8**	92.2	**15.8**
7	10	DFS	69.34	**12.3**	2.7	**−39.2**	5.8	∞	45.1	**11.2**	4.0	**−6.4**	42.4	**6.6**
8	5	Ford	66.32	**−16.3**	0.0	**−X**	17.5	**−10.6**	28.8	**−16.7**	7.5	**−0.6**	46.3	**−19.9**
9	7	Nestlé	65.88	**−5.5**	2.8	**−7.5**	14.3	**−8.6**	13.0	**20.0**	3.8	**15.9**	66.2	**−9.5**
10	21	BSkyB	64.47	**53.4**	4.2	**0.0**	18.2	**54.5**	41.6	**26.1**	7.0	**1.2**	29.0	**69.8**
11	11	Renault	58.89	**−3.5**	9.0	**20.0**	9.8	**1.0**	29.6	**0.0**	7.9	**4.9**	43.8	**−11.3**
12	14	Vauxhall	57.22	**−2.5**	4.6	**235.2**	5.6	**−30.4**	34.6	**−17.5**	8.2	**57.6**	47.0	**2.1**
13	19	Kellogg's	56.35	**28.0**	2.5	**118.5**	4.1	**−42.5**	8.6	**−12.3**	5.5	**17.3**	79.3	**43.3**
14	9	Orange	53.59	**−14.2**	25.6	**11.1**	14.5	**−37.1**	30.7	**31.5**	6.6	**−36.7**	22.7	**−38.4**
15	8	Masterfoods	52.75	**−17.1**	0.7	∞	24.8	**0.9**	13.6	**22.4**	2.2	**−27.9**	58.8	**−22.2**
16	18	Toyota	51.36	**5.6**	4.3	**−22.0**	7.3	**−16.1**	30.6	**16.2**	7.0	**−14.9**	50.8	**10.6**
17	13	Lever Fabergé Home	51.34	**−13.5**	1.5	**−40.9**	39.3	**16.1**	12.0	**−38.6**	5.8	**−50.1**	41.4	**−13.7**
18	27	Tesco	49.77	**34.0**	0.0	**0.0**	9.0	**−32.0**	38.3	**33.1**	3.2	**−22.2**	49.6	**73.2**
19	16	Sainsbury's	49.32	**−0.5**	0.0	**0.0**	6.3	**0.1**	31.7	**67.4**	14.4	**−34.2**	47.6	**−10.8**
20	15	Hutchinson 3G	48.95	**−2.7**	5.0	**−0.9**	14.1	**−36.1**	22.7	**31.2**	19.3	**117.4**	39.1	**−21.2**

Key: X = −100 per cent, ∞ = increase in excess of 1000 per cent

Source: Neilson Media Research ©. Tables cannot be republished without prior written permission from Nielson Media Research.

real growth was a sobering 1.1 per cent in real terms. The press (newspapers, magazines, directories, etc.) accounted for the largest share of advertising expenditure[11] (48.7 per cent) with newspapers and directories growing 3.2 per cent and 4.0 per cent (1.8 per cent and 2.6 per cent in real terms) respectively. Other press advertising expenditure fell. Television advertising rose by 1 per cent to £4,374 million (in real terms a fall of 0.4 per cent). Outdoor and radio advertising, against the general trend, grew significantly in 2003 by 10.4 per cent and 6.8 per cent respectively. Cinema advertising showed no growth whereas Internet advertising grew 61.6 per cent to £376 million according to industry estimates. In 2004, according to Nielsen Media

[11]Advertising expenditure costs include production costs.

Research, the increase in total spend by the UK's top-twenty advertisers was 2.1 per cent over 2003 expenditure[12] (see Box 9.3) again representing almost stagnation in real terms. The top-100 total advertising expenditure was slightly better as total spend rose by 3.3 per cent to £3.6bn although nearly half (43 per cent) cut their above the line spend from 2003. Among the high profile companies who cut year-on-year 'above-the-line' expenditure at that time were Coca-Cola (–31.7 per cent), Unilever (–35.5 per cent), Honda (–27.4 per cent), Boots (–24.6 per cent), Nissan (–24.6 per cent), HSBC (–22.9 per cent) and Wrigley (–19.1 per cent). In the first quarter of 2006[13] advertising actually increased by 4 per cent although all categories except for Outdoor and Transport (+3.6 per cent) and the Internet (+53.6 per cent) actually declined (see Box 9.4).

The reason for the relative decline in advertising is manyfold. They include:

- Consumer markets in relative decline: Much of the success of advertising in the first half of the century was on the back of expanding populations and developing markets. By the 1960s markets were becoming saturated and population growth was stagnant or in decline. When it was recognized that advertising could no longer stimulate growth in market demand the emphasis switched to developing market-share. The advertising industry now claimed that of the power of advertising lay in its ability to build long-term brand loyalty.

- Branding crisis: many branded fast moving consumer goods (FMCGs) came under pressure in the 1970s and 1980s, particularly with the sectoral dominance of a few large supermarket retailers in each of the most developed markets and the growth of own-label brands produced for these stores. Whereas, in earlier years, it had been the norm for medium to large retailers to stock the brand leader and

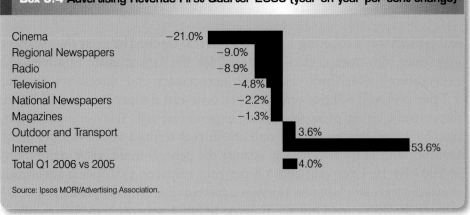

Box 9.4 Advertising Revenue First Quarter 2006 (year on year per cent change)

Cinema	−21.0%
Regional Newspapers	−9.0%
Radio	−8.9%
Television	−4.8%
National Newspapers	−2.2%
Magazines	−1.3%
Outdoor and Transport	3.6%
Internet	53.6%
Total Q1 2006 vs 2005	4.0%

Source: Ipsos MORI/Advertising Association.

[12] 2003 £1.44bn, 2004 £1.48bn.
[13] The latest figures prior to publication.

up to three follower brands in any category, the reality today is the brand leader vies for space on the shelves with other brands alongside the store's own label produce. Individual retailers are less interested in brand advertising (because the brand can be purchased at any of that retailer's competition) and more interested in using promotion (frequently on the basis of price or multiple-pack offers) to attract consumers to their store. To guarantee shelf space brand owners have had to switch much of the money that previously went into 'brand-building' advertising to sales promotion within the stores.

Follower brands
Brands that are not leaders in their category.

- Sector bans: One sector that had traditionally attracted high advertising expenditure is that of cigarettes. In 1965 the UK government banned cigarette advertising on television. The cigarette industry responded by increasing its spending on poster, magazine and cinema advertising in addition to 'point-of-sale' materials and sponsorship. Despite arguments from the industry that advertising did not encourage new smokers and only affected market-share a ban on all tobacco advertising and sponsorship was announced prior to the millennium. For the advertising (and sponsorship) industry this was a blow. Other sectors such as alcohol and medicines, whilst not being wholly banned, are severely curtailed in many markets.

- Media fragmentation: in the nineteenth century mass media advertising, largely through the press and magazines, was cheap and relatively focused. By 2000 the sheer number of different media is a major problem for advertisers. Whereas in the 1950s to 1980s Independent Television (ITV) companies accounted for between 90 per cent and 100 per cent of television advertising, today it represents (despite extra channels) around 40 per cent and still falling. Whereas for many of these years there was only one UK commercial television channel, today the Broadcaster's Audience Research Board (BARB) report figures on over one hundred stations and these exclude overseas channels available to many cable or satellite subscribers. Commercial radio stations have also multiplied. New media (Internet, email, etc.) is fast expanding and offers almost endless opportunities. While the press is one medium where the number of titles has decreased there has been a huge explosion in magazine titles in the past 30 years. With more potential outlets for advertising and fewer consumers seeing individual media the fragmentation of the media has increased substantially the cost-per-thousand (CPT) of individual campaigns.

Media fragmentation
The dilution of TV or radio station audiences due to the proliferation of channels

- Advertising effectiveness: the 1990s and beyond has seen the tightening of purse-strings and a disillusionment with marketing expenditure in general and advertising in particular. For the brand leaders, ironically (given the above discussion concerning cost effectiveness), the UK's high television advertising costs in the 1950s, 1960s and 1970s (due to the ITV monopoly) protected them against new entrants to the market challenging their status. In addition established brands, looking to maintain awareness, do not need to do quite as much advertising as new brands fighting to establish their place. The fragmented media, whilst generally increasing the cost-per-thousand rates have, however, produced a more level playing field particularly for targeted products or services. The modern company, run largely by accountants,[14] look for short-term reward rather than long-term brand building. They are looking for proof, which is not always readily forthcoming, that their advertising expenditure is justified. To the extent that advertising is notoriously difficult to measure accountants have been more willing to invest in direct marketing and sales promotion where success or failure can be easily and quickly measured.

Box 9.5 UK historic advertising spend by media sector

	1954	1974	1994	2002	% 94/02
Newspapers	£76m	£434m	£3.2bn	£4.8bn	50%
Television	–	£176m	£2.5bn	£3.7bn	48%
Magazines	£50m	£158m	£1.3bn	£1.9bn	46%
Outdoor (Posters)	£14m	£34m	£350m	£802m	129%
Radio	£1m	£6m	£243m	£545m	124%
Cinema	£4m	£8m	£53m	£180m	239%
Internet	–	–	–	£197m	∞

Source: Advertising Association.

Summary

This chapter examined the growth of advertising in the twentieth century and suggested two theories (weak and strong) as to why advertising may work. The strong theory of advertising, which suggests it is highly persuasive, has been the dominant viewpoint in the industry for the majority of the twentieth century. The weak theory, however, is probably more realistic in suggesting that the most advertisers can do is 'nudge' consumers towards their products or services. The chapter looked at the means by which advertising effectiveness is measured but recognizes the flaws in such measurements as recall and recognition. It continued by examining those characteristics of good advertising such as uniqueness, repetition and relevance and those other factors that give advertising stopping-power. The chapter concluded by examining the problems faced by the advertising industry over the last five decades.

[14]70 per cent of the top 100 FTSE companies have CEOs who are accountants or come from an accounting background.

Review questions

1 What is the difference between the strong and weak theories of advertising?
2 Describe the processes associated with the cognitive response model.
3 Explain the ATR(N) model.
4 What is low involvement theory.
5 Explain the difference between 'recall' and 'recognition' testing.
6 Describe the phenomenon known as the Waterloo Effect.
7 It is recognized that advertisers need to achieve stopping power. How might they do this?
8 Give an example of a logical appeal in advertising.
9 What is the main assumption of USP theory?
10 Explain what advertising execution thoughts relate to.

Discussion questions

1 If you were to set up a rolling research programme for your brand how might you go about this and what categories might you use in an attitude scale to support this?
2 Shock tactics are often used by advertisers to gain attention. Under what circumstances would you consider these to be inappropriate?
3 Media fragmentation has had a heavy impact upon the advertising industry in recent years. How do you feel this will impact upon advertising campaigns in the next ten years?

Further reading

Calder, B.J. and Malthouse, E.C. (2005) 'Managing media and advertising change with integrated marketing', *Journal of Advertising Research*, Dec., 45(4): 356–61. Defines the integrated marketing process and shows how it can be used to improve advertising.

'Commercial conundrum', *Marketing Management*, Mar./Apr. 2006, 15(2): 6. Discusses consumer attitudes toward television advertising, identifying that television ads may not be reaching their intended targets.

Horsky, S. (2006) 'The changing architecture of advertising agencies', *Marketing Science*, Jul./Aug. 2006, 25(4): 367–83. Exploring the firm's decision process in obtaining the creative and media components and a comparison between specialists or full-service agencies.

Lichtenthal, J.D., Yadav, V. and Donthu, N. (2006) 'Outdoor advertising for business markets', *Industrial Marketing Management*, 35(2): 236. Offering recommendations on when and how to use outdoor advertising based on unique business market characteristics, industrial promotional objectives and business product classification.

Chapter references

Ambler, T. and Burne, T. (1999) 'The impact of affect on ad memory', *Journal of Advertising Research*, March/April: 25–34.

Bartle, J. (1999) 'The advertising contribution', in L. Butterfield (ed.), *Excellence in Advertising*, Oxford: Butterworth and Heinemann, pp. 25–44.

Belch, G. and Belch, M. (2001) *Advertising and Promotion: An Integrated Marketing Communications Perspective*, London: McGraw-Hill.

Bovée, C.L., Thill, J.V., Dovel, G.P. and Wood, M.B. (1995) *Advertising Excellence*, New York: McGraw-Hill.

Brierley, S. (2002) *The Advertising Handbook*, 2nd edn, London: Routledge.

Colley, R.H. (1961) *Defining Advertising Goals for Measured Advertising Results*, New York: Association of National Advertisers.

Crosier, K. (1999) 'Advertising' in C. Fill (ed.), *Marketing Communications: Principles and Practice*, London: Thomson, pp. 264–88.

De Pelsmacker, P., Geuens, M. and Van den Bergh, J.V. (2001) *Foundations of Marketing Communications: A European Perspective*, Harlow: Prentice Hall.

Ehrenberg, A. (1997) 'How do consumers buy a new brand?', *ADMAP*, March.

Ehrenberg, A. and Goodhart, E.J. (1979) *Essays on Understanding Buyer Behaviour*, London: Thomson.

Fill, C. (2001) 'Essentially a matter of consistency: integrated marketing communications', *The Marketing Review*, 1(4): 409–25.

Franzen, G. (1999) *Advertising Effectiveness*, Henley-on-Thames, Oxfordshine: NTC Publications.

Jones, J.P. (2004) *Fables, Fashions and Facts About Advertising: A Study of 28 Enduring Myths, Thousand Oaks*, CA: Sage Publishing.

Lach, J. (1999) 'Commercial overload', *American Demographics*, 21(9): 20.

Lavidge, R. and Steiner, G. (1961) 'A model for predictive measurements of advertising effectiveness', *Journal of Marketing*, Oct.: 61.

Law, J. (1994) *Organizing Modernity*, Cambridge, MA: Blackwell.

Nevett, T. R. (1982) *Advertising in Britain: A History*, London: Heinemann.

Rossiter, J.R. and Percy, L. (1998) *Advertising Communications and Promotion Management*, 2nd edn, Singapore: The McGraw-Hill Companies.

Shimp, T.A. (2003) *Advertising, Promotion and Supplemental Aspects of Integrated Marketing Communication*, Cincinati: Thomson.

Smith, P.R. and Taylor, J. (2002) *Marketing Communications: An Integrated Approach*, 3rd edn, London: Kogan Page.

Strong, E.K. (1925) *The Psychology of Selling*, New York: McGraw-Hill.

Wells, W., Burnett, J. and Moriaty, S. (1965) *Advertising Principles and Practice*, New York: Prentice Hall.

Wharton (1999) 'How and when advertising works', *Knowledge@Wharton*, Wharton College, http://knowledge.wharton.upen.edu.

Yeshin, T. (2006) *Advertising*, London: Thomson Learning.

CASE STUDY 9.1

Calm down, dear

The *esure* insurance brand was launched by the Halifax and Bank of Scotland Group in July 2001 and quickly became one of the UK's fastest growing insurance companies gaining over 700,000 customers by 2004. This was in no small part due to *esure's* marketing communications campaign which from the beginning had been attracting a disproportionate amount of attention and media coverage. The campaign, designed to create awareness of the brand, featured film director Michael Winner, a man known principally for his love of food and somewhat annoying bonhomie. Winner not only starred in the commercials but directed them as well. Despite (or perhaps because of) their amateurish look, apparent poor acting and dire scripts the television commercials were, in marketing terms, highly successful. The advertising campaign's catchphrase: 'Calm down, dear, it's only a commercial' attracted huge attention largely because they were so irritating. According to Tim Gibbon of *Elemental PR* it was 'the marketing equivalent of an unscratchable itch'. To back up the advertising *Carson Digital* developed a Michael Winner website for *esure* (www.calmdowndear.com) where visitors were invited to help in 'shooting Winner down' with exotic foods.

The Winner adverts, despite being infuriating, were recognised as highly effective in achieving awareness of *esure* and achieved industry recognition when they were short listed for the 2003 National Business Awards in the Advertiser of the Year category. Such was their success in generating national awareness that the adverts and their catchphrases started to appear in comedy sketches by Rory Bremner, press and magazine articles and were even quoted in a FA Cup Final commentary. For a catchphrase to become so widely recognised was, according to Francesca Newland of *Campaign* magazine 'the Holy Grail of advertising'.

On 23 May 2005, *esure* launched a new character into its advertising – Mister Mouse described by one commentator as 'a sort of Roland Rat with Bronx lilt'. Ironically the idea of a mouse living inside a computer mouse was a concept introduced by Winner himself in the last of his adverts. The character was developed by *esure's* Chairman and Group Marketing Director, Peter Wood, working with two marketing gurus Chris Wilkins and Sian Vickers who had previously developed the *Direct Line* red phone and the iconic *Cadbury's Smash* Martians. Whereas the Winner commercials had appeared almost home-made the mouse commercials were seen a serious piece of work with stylish animation and witty voice-over ("What? You thought it was electronical micro-chips inside these things?"). Mister Mouse was animated by one of the world's leading 'claymation' studios Vinton in Portland, Oregon and each advert was the product of months of stop frame animation to give the Mister Mouse character and his setting a unique 'real life' feel.

▶

SOURCE: IMAGE COURTESY OF THE ADVERTISING ARCHIVES.

Michael Winner's catchphrase for Esure's advertisements is the equivalent of the 'Holy Grail of advertising'.

Why did *esure* make the change when the Winner campaign was such an evident success? Perhaps, having established themselves in the marketplace they were looking for a more up-market image. So is this the end of Michael Winner's association with *esure*? Don't be so certain. Although the mouse has the potential of being annoying he is seen as unlikely to be as irritating as his predecessor. If the brand requires another awareness campaign expect Winner back calming us down.

Case study questions

1   What was the main objective of the Winner campaign and how did this change (if at all) with the introduction of the new advertising?

2   What part did irritation play in the original campaign?

Sources: BBC News, webtrafficIQ and esure.com

Creating a space online*

Max Flint had originally worked in the insurance business before 'throwing it all in' in the late 1990s to join a friend running an independent record company. The association did not last long but having left the insurance business and entered the more glamorous world of show business he decided this was the life for him. Max was lucky at this time to meet the leader of an up and coming rock group (Fruitcake) who had just parted (on very bad terms) from their long-time manager. Fruitcake offered Max the chance to take over as manager. Max lasted three years before he too left following an argument with the band.

With this experience behind him and with the help of some private backers, Max set up in 2004 Mad Max Co., a publishing company specializing in 'fanzines'. Such was the success of the operation that by 2006 Mad Max Co. had 20 different publications each dedicated to individual 'rock stars' or groups. Not only did Max have exclusive publishing rights for these groups but his company (by now employing 30 people full time plus many more freelance) also had the distribution rights for souvenir merchandise. Magazine sales were split between subscribers (around 60 per cent of the total) and retail (e.g. W.H. Smiths), while gift sales were mainly at concert venues.

MySpace has over 100 million users and represents the potential for a successful social networking website built around music. Subtle banner advertising has been introduced and unsigned bands can sell their music as downloads.

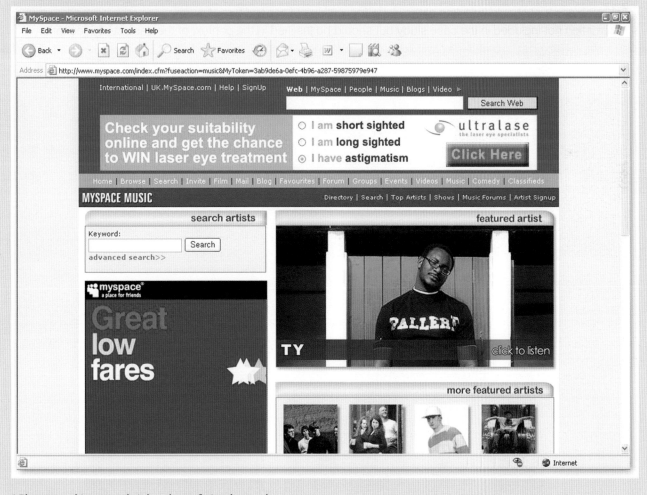

* Please note this case study is based on a fictional example.

'Mad Max Dot Com' (MMDC) was the latest venture from the Mad Max Company. The plan was to give current subscribers password-protected access to the MMDC website where they would find not only current and past issues but substantially more details on each of the groups. Sample tracks could also be played (and downloaded) and talks were already underway with record companies to enable complete tracks to be 'sold' in this way in the future. It was also planned to sell souvenir merchandise direct from the site. Non-subscribers, whilst having limited entry also had the opportunity to review and purchase from the Web catalogue as well as sample tracks and would be offered 'inducements' to subscribe. Max had also sold advertising space to a number of companies on a short-term basis with the option of longer-term agreements if Mad Max Dot Com proved to be a success. Although revenue from merchandise, track and subscription sales would be important it was these latter advertising agreements that could prove to be the biggest money-spinner if all went according to plan.

Max knew that if he was to renew his lucrative contracts then he had to keep the advertisers happy by generating a large volume of 'hits' within a short period after the launch. He recognized that for this venture to be a success there was a need for an intensive, high-visibility, communications campaign. Although Max has some experience in this field he decided that he needed external support. Following 'pitches' from five agencies Max decided to offer the contract to Apple Tree a small agency with both 'above' and 'below the line' experience.

Case study question

1 Assume you are heading the team working on the Mad Max Dot Com campaign. Prepare a marketing communications plan for MMDC for presentation to Max Flint. At this stage a detailed budget is not required although account should be taken of the likely implications of expenditure. Assumptions may be made about information not included in the case study but should be justified in the context of the case study scenario.

CHAPTER TEN
SALES PROMOTION

LEARNING OBJECTIVES

Having completed this chapter you should be able to:

- Distinguish between advertising and sales promotion and between consumer, retail and trade promotions.
- Explain the theories, concepts and generalizations associated with sales promotion.
- Understand the reasons behind the rise of sales promotion relative to advertising.
- Describe the tactics associated with sales promotions and the differences between price promotions and creative promotions (or incentives).
- Analyse the outcomes of sales promotions and their affect on general communication strategies.

INTRODUCTION

Sales promotion has been around for a very long time. Free samples, money-off and additional value (e.g. two for the price of one) have been used by traders for centuries to attract customers. The arrival of newspapers not only saw an explosion in advertising but sales promotion as well. In the *Daily Telegraph*, 4 June 1900, there was a full-page advertisement for Eiffel Tower lemonade ('the largest users of lemons in the world'). Incorporated in the text was an early example of the 'freepost' offers that are so prevalent today.

> *300 Bottles are given away weekly. The firm has adopted the following novel method to induce everybody to try their lemonade. The first 50 letters opened every day will not only have the lemonade sent by return post, but the stamps are also returned to the fortunate applicants.*

There is often confusion between what is advertising and what is sales promotion and many choose not to distinguish between them at all. The *Daily Telegraph* advertisement mentioned above is, from an academic sense, part advertisement and part sales promotion and might be better described as an early example of an integrated marketing communications campaign. Sales promotion is the offering of an incentive to make people act. By its nature it is a tool of 'urgency', designed to encourage buyers to act immediately before it is too late. It has the function of 'acceleration', being designed to increase the volume of sales by directly influencing the decision-making process and influencing the speed of decision. In addition, and in contrast to advertising, which is essentially a long-term tool, best suited to influencing buyer attitude and augmenting brand equity, sales promotion is predominantly a short-term tool that is capable of influencing behaviour rather than changing long-term attitude. Whereas advertising creates value that is intangible (and largely immeasurable), sales promotion adds tangible value to the offering. In terms of the 'hierarchy of effects model' discussed in Chapter 2, sales promotion comes into its own by motivating people to act. This is illustrated in Figure 10.1 below.

Sales promotion comes in four types: consumer, trade, retail and sales force. Sales force promotions are used in many industries to increase sales and generate leads. Sales force promotions will be discussed in more detail in Chapter 14. Consumer and trade promotions are supplier initiated pull and push strategies respectively. Pull strategies are those aimed at 'pulling' consumers to the brand. For example, Walker's Crisps in 2005 ran an instant-win competition with Microsoft i-pods as prizes. The attraction for anyone to purchase and enter the competition was to the brand and not a specific retailer. Retail sales promotions are also pull strategies but in this case the attraction is to the retailer rather than the brand. Push strategies are designed to attract product into the distribution network. Promotions here might include buying allowances, advertising or sales promotion allowances, slotting allowances (slotting-in new products), and others including gifts, training

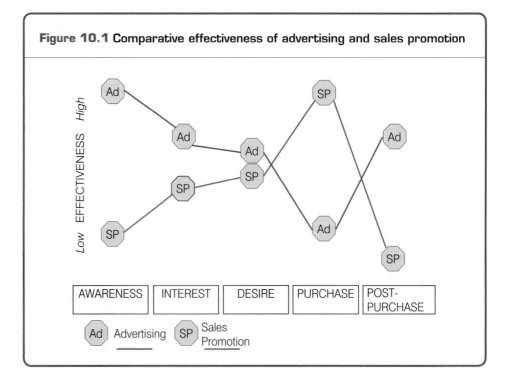

Figure 10.1 Comparative effectiveness of advertising and sales promotion

and other incentives. Figure 10.2 shows the relationship between customer, retail and trade promotions.

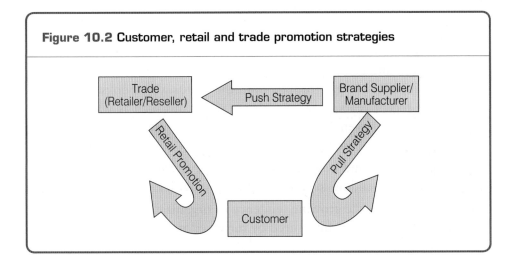

Figure 10.2 Customer, retail and trade promotion strategies

THE GROWTH OF SALES PROMOTION

Over the past few years sales promotion techniques have been introduced in areas such as financial services, media, IT, telecom, travel and leisure and more. Even the UK government are using sales promotion – its agencies have been handing out free condoms and vouchers for fruit and vegetables to promote aspects of a healthier lifestyle. Until the 1980s advertising was commonly 40 per cent of the marketing communications budget. In the intervening period sales promotion has, however, taken over from advertising as the principal marketing communications tool in most developed markets. In the UK, in the years immediately before 2001, it was growing, according to the Institute of Sales Promotion (ISP) at 20 per cent per year although the growth rate has slowed since. Today, advertising typically represents nearer to 20 per cent of marketing communication budgets with sales promotion averaging around 40 per cent. In the FMCG (fast moving consumer goods) sector the figure is much higher. Estimates vary but sales promotion may represent between 60 per cent and 70 per cent of the total communications spend in this sector (Copley 2004). In the UK, in 2004, the ISP estimated that sales promotion was worth £7 billion, although this may exclude promotional 'advertising' (e.g. television commercials that promote added value/incentives to generate action) and the figure may be nearer £15 billion. This is dwarfed by the value of sales promotion in the USA. Consumer directed sales promotion alone

Visit the Institute of Sales Promotion's website at: **www.isp.org.uk**.

doubled there in value to £100 billion between 1991 and 2001 and trade promotion had reached £150 billion by this same date.

The reasons why sales promotion has become so dominant in marketing communications are varied and frequently interconnected. They include:

- Abolition of retail price maintenance (RPM): removed for most consumer goods categories in 1964. Prior to this date all retail prices were fixed and discounting prohibited. One of the few categories that maintained RPM right through until the 1990s were books. It has only been in recent years, therefore, that retail chains such as Waterstones, W.H. Smith or even Amazon have been able to offer 'three-for-two' and other price-based promotions.

- Increased costs and fragmentation in the advertising industry has encouraged spending in 'below-the-line' activities.

- Short-termism: the growing tendency of organizations to want to be seen to be successful (measured by turnover and market-share) in the short term.

- Measurability: sales promotions generally have a specific beginning and end and it is, therefore, easy to measure results. This is in direct comparison to advertising where measurement of results is very difficult particularly in the short term.

- Stagnating markets: reduction in population growth in most developed markets leading to a slow-down in market growth.

- Decline in brand loyalty as products (and to a lesser extent services) have become more similar.

- Spread of own-label (or private-label) and subsequent reduction in the space allocated to brands. It has been estimated that between 1992 and 1995 shelf space for brands in the UK fell by 12 per cent (Laspadakis 1999).

- Increase in repertoire or portfolio buying: the repertoire or portfolio perspective (see Chapter 9) suggests that the majority of the population generate, through trial, a portfolio of brands from which they make their choice rather than being loyal to one particular brand. Based on research, Barnard and Ehrenberg (1997) estimated that only one-in-ten consumers were 100 per cent loyal to any brand.

- Increased power and increased concentration of retailers: retailers are less interested in brand building advertising *per se* because that is not of particular benefit to them alone. Rather they see in-store support for price reductions and other 'extra value' offers as the vehicle for attracting customers and/or increasing customer spend. This is understandable as research suggests as many as 70 per cent of buying decisions are made in-store. At the extreme is **hostaging** where the retailer/reseller is able to exert power over the brand owner in order to provide trade promotions on a more or less permanent basis (Fill 2002).

Hostaging
Where the retailer/reseller is able to exert power over the brand owner in order to provide trade promotions on a more or less permanent basis.

- Increased price sensitivity: it would appear that consumers are more knowledgeable and price sensitive than previously. According to Shimp (2003) sales promotions are in part responsible because they train consumers to search for better deals.

- Improvements in technology: technology has enabled more variation in the types of promotion offered and further simplified the process. Scanning technology means that the operational software can recognize 'multi-offers' and 'price reductions' without human intervention. It also means improved planning for the retailer and the supplier.

SALES PROMOTION THEORY

Sales promotion is giving the customer something extra, rewarding them for their behaviour on this particular purchasing occasion. There are several theories which support the concept of reward as a motivator. In Chapter 3 classical and operant conditioning were discussed. Whereas classical conditioning is largely associated with advertising operant conditioning is seen as an explanation for consumer behaviour in relation to sales promotion. Operant conditioning suggests the response of the individual is likely to be affected by positive reinforcement (reward) or negative reinforcement (punishment), although the affect is likely to cease when these reinforcements are taken away. In commercial terms organizations use reinforcement by stressing the benefits and/or rewards a customer will receive on buying a product or service. The incentive is additional to the basic brand benefits and temporarily changes its perceived value (Shimp 2003). Similarly Edward Thorndike (1927) suggested that the 'law of effect', which had to do with positive and negative consequences of actions, is also relevant to sales promotion. The law states that the consequences of behaviour now will govern the consequences of that behaviour in the future. In other words once

Law of effect
The law states that the consequences of behaviour now will govern the consequences of that behaviour in the future. In other words once a buying pattern is achieved it will continue into the future (Edward Thorndike).

Box 10.1 The prize-winner and the airline

Jane O'Keeffe was the one-millionth Ryanair customer and in 1988, in a prize giveaway publicized by the airline, was to be the lucky winner of free flights for life. Her win had widespread media coverage and O'Keefe used her free flights until 1997 when Ryanair reduced the prize to a maximum number per year. O'Keefe sued for breach of contract.

Ryanair claimed there was no contract but Dublin High Court thought differently and found the airline had breached the terms of its offer. O'Keefe was awarded £43 098 damages.

The ruling demonstrated how critical it is that the terms and conditions of prize draws and competitions used in marketing campaigns are clear, accurate and available to the customer.

Source: Martin Bewick, *The Marketer*, October 2005.

Shaping
Suggests that a final response can be explained as 'appearing after preceding acts which, taken together, constitute a chain of successive approximations' (John Watson).

Chaining
Suggests behaviour emerges from sequences of actions in which the preceding action becomes the discriminative stimulus for the final response (inducement > purchase).

Priming
Suggests that a short exposure to a particular stimulus can evoke an increased drive to consume more of a product.

@

An example of a Sales Promotion Magazine at: **www.salespromo.co.uk**.

Mortgaging effect
That after a promotion, rather than returning to 'normal', sales levels fall back for a period.

a buying pattern is achieved it will continue into the future. John Watson, US psychologist and founding father of American behaviouralism, introduced the concept of shaping. This suggests that a response builds on prior experience and can be explained as 'appearing after preceding acts which, taken together, constitute a chain of successive approximations' (Foxall *et al.* 1998). Shaping breaks the desired behaviour into a series of stages and the parts are learnt in sequence. This is particularly important with new products because trialling involves a complex set of behaviours most notably inducement > trial > repeat purchase. Chaining is a concept that suggests behaviour emerges from sequences of actions in which the preceding action becomes the discriminative stimulus for the final response (inducement > purchase). Priming is yet another theory that suggests that a short exposure to a particular stimulus can evoke an increased drive to consume more of a product (De Pelsmacker *et al.* 2001). All of these different theories offer reasons why you can motivate people to buy more by offering incentives although the continuation of this behaviour is open to doubt.

In purely practical terms Shimp (2003) suggests a number of intuitive generalizations that can be made about sales promotions:

- Temporary price reductions can substantially increase sales.
- The greater the frequency of deals the lower the increased sales.
- The frequency of the deals changes the customer's reference point.
- Higher market-share brands are less 'deal' elastic.
- Advertised promotions increase store traffic.
- Higher quality brands tend to steal sales from lower quality brands.

To emphasize these and other observations about sales promotion Figure 10.3 suggests four possible scenarios that may exist during and after a sales promotion.

Scenario 1

Supports the proposition that price-related sales promotions merely bring forward sales. Ideally sales promotion should generate extra sales that cannot be guaranteed in any other way and should not lead to stocking-up. Jones (1990) suggests there is overwhelming evidence that the sales effect is limited to the duration of the sale and that 'when the bribe stops the extra sales stop'. Another generalized observation is that sales, rather than returning to 'normal', often fall back for a period. This phenomenon, known as the mortgaging effect, suggests that volumes rise (A) and fall below normal sales levels (B) by similar amounts, eventually rising (C) back to normal over time. This implies that regular buyers simply bring forward their purchases. Whereas sales (in volume terms) remain the same profits fall.

Scenario 2

In this scenario there is a diminishing series of returns. Although the sales promotion increases sales it is by an increasing smaller amount perhaps due to the frequency of sales. In addition regular sales are falling.

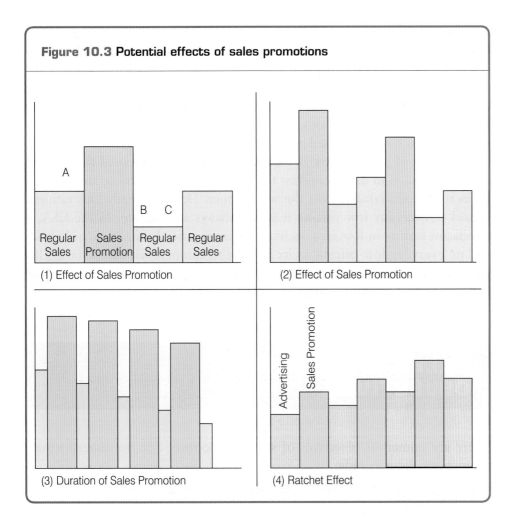

Figure 10.3 Potential effects of sales promotions

(1) Effect of Sales Promotion

(2) Effect of Sales Promotion

(3) Duration of Sales Promotion

(4) Ratchet Effect

Scenario 3

Predicts a situation where the frequency of sales changes the customer's reference point. Sales promotions are so frequent that sales outside those periods fall away. There have been notable examples of this in the past few decades. In the 1980s, for example, it seemed like every piece of MFI furniture was constantly marked-down. Before long customers started to wonder what the real price was (Sclater 2003).

Marked-down
Products or services where the normal retail price is reduced.

Scenario 4

Known as the ratchet effect this predicts the advantages of an integrated strategy that builds credibility through advertising and extra volume through inducements.

Two principal schools of thought exist on the long-term effect of promotions. The first is that they discredit the brand (especially price-led promotions) over time. This is an ongoing debate and something that seems to have a degree of credibility, although there has been little by way of evidence provided to support it. A major study in the UK, USA, Germany and Japan involving dozens of brands in 25 consumer goods categories into the effects

Ratchet effect
Predicts the advantages of an integrated strategy that builds credibility through advertising and extra volume through promotional inducements.

Creative promotions
Promotions that do not rely on price reduction.

Hi-lo pricing (or high-low pricing)
Strategy, prevalent in fast moving consumer goods retailing, where each week a percentage of products are heavily discounted and promoted throughout the store.

Everyday low-prices
Strategy where the emphasis is on low prices across the store (in contrast to the hi-lo pricing strategy).

of price-related promotions (Ehrenberg *et al.* 1994) suggests that promotions have no impact (positively or negatively) on a brand's long-term sales or on consumers' repeat buying loyalty. Sales promotion practitioners represent the second school of thought suggesting that they can actually add to brand value over time particularly through **creative promotions** that exclude discounting. In fast moving consumer goods retailing the strategy of **hi-lo pricing** (or **high-low pricing**) is frequently used as the principal promotion strategy. Each week a percentage of products are heavily discounted and promoted throughout the store. This is in direct contrast to an **everyday low-prices** strategy which looks to spread savings across the whole store. Despite the obvious rational appeal of everyday low pricing it is not always as effective. In the USA, a significant feature in K-mart's decline was its misjudged shift from 'hi-lo pricing' to 'everyday low-pricing' in its attempt to compete with Wal-Mart. This was because K-mart's core customers were 'deal-hunters' and the new value proposition did not satisfy their needs (McGovern *et al.* 2004).

SALES PROMOTION OBJECTIVES

There are numerous objectives of sales promotions. For consumer-focused promotions these include:

- Increased sales: looking to increase or defend market-share or encourage repeat or multiple purchases.

- Stimulate trial: sales promotions can facilitate the introduction of new products, brands or brand extensions.

- Encourage brand switching: encouraging consumers to break any bonds of loyalty to other brands.

- Highlight novelty: bringing the consumer to the realization of change (new, improved, etc.) or the repositioning of a brand.

- Invigorate mature brands: brands that are no longer new and vibrant and/or where the similarity to other brands is high may benefit from sales promotion. For example the retail petrol industry is one where promotions are used to set the brands apart.

- Reward loyal customers: one argument suggests that rewarding your customer for doing what they would do normally is unprofitable. The counter-argument is that without these promotions your customers would go elsewhere for a bargain. There is also a suggestion that customers receive hedonic, non-functional benefits from these programmes, such as a sense of achievement at being a wise shopper, the positive effects of stimulation and variety through trying out new products and the entertainment value associated with certain promotions.

- Locking customers into loyalty programmes: to continue accumulating the reward(s) the customer must remain largely loyal to the same supermarket, airline, petrol supplier, etc.

- Target a specific segment: promotions may be aimed at particular customer types. For example, Guinness have for many years targeted young football and rugby fans during major competitions when many choose to watch the games in public houses or clubs. In exchange for a set number of purchases of Guinness these drinkers can claim hats, tee-shirts or even, as in 1999, an inflatable armchair.

- Moving excess stock: bringing stock levels down where 'normal sales' have not generated required sales or smoothing seasonal fluctuations (for example ice cream in winter).

- Satisfying retailers: as noted retailers have a major preference towards 'below-the-line' promotions that they can control in-store.

- Neutralizing or disrupting the competition: spoiler campaigns designed to thwart the competition. In the 1990s UK tabloid newspapers were continuously running spoiler campaigns (based on cover price, bingo games, scratch cards and other variants) against one another until such time as it became apparent that no one was benefiting from this strategy.

- Build databases: obtaining valuable data on customers. This is now frequently done through loyalty schemes. For example, the widely known Tesco Clubcard scheme has reportedly contributed to saving over £500 million through its generation of customer data, that has subsequently been used by the company to great effect. Alternatively companies may offer gifts or entry to competitions in exchange for information. For example, with the likelihood of a complete ban on cigarette advertising looming the late 1990s Rothmans smokers were encouraged to apply for heavily discounted gifts in order for a database of brand smokers to be developed for direct marketing purposes (see Minicase 10.1).

- Generate publicity: sometimes the magnitude of an offer, for example British Airway's offer of free Concorde tickets, is guaranteed to be newsworthy. In addition the growing number of cause-related promotions (promotions where a charity or other good cause is seen to benefit) are seen as a way of creating a positive image for brands. For example Sainsbury's, in 2005, were one of many brands running obesity campaigns. The ISP award-winning 'bottle hats' campaign by Innocent not only improved sales but raised funds for Help the Aged.

The objectives of trade promotions mirror those directed at the consumer. They are designed to encourage the retailer to facilitate particular goals. These may include:

- Help to introduce new products: new products/brands represent a risk to retailers which, to overcome, may require incentivization. In fast moving consumer goods retailers in particular shelf space is at a premium and to make room for a new product/brand may mean losing currently performing products/brands.

Marlboro's birthday party

In 2005, Marlboro cigarettes turned 50. Despite the cloud of condemnation hanging over cigarettes the brand owners Philip Morris USA Inc. and parent company Altrina Group Inc. pulled out all the stops to celebrate this milestone. The company has plenty to celebrate. Marlboro continues to be the market leader with over 40 per cent of the share of the US market and up substantially on previous years. This is despite the introduction of advertising restrictions in 1998 and a dramatic rise in state excise taxes in 2002. Although the price per pack is still significantly lower than most other developed consumer markets it still maintains a premium price (average $3.28) in the US market.

SOURCE: IMAGE COURTESY OF THE ADVERTISING ARCHIVES.

Chicago advertising agency Leo Burnett personified the Marlboro brand with the rugged, independent cowboy.

Marlboro became the world's most famous cigarette brand the old fashioned way through traditional mass marketing. For many decades Chicago advertising agency Leo Burnett presented the brand with images of freedom and cool living personified by the rugged, horse-riding, Stetson-wearing cowboy. With its traditional advertising route cut off Marlboro's marketers are holding on to first spot through a blend of tactics that fall outside federal restrictions. This includes 'buzz marketing' at live events and in bars that spur Internet chatter, price promotions, trade promotions and direct mail.

Amongst the most successful programmes is one based around its database of 26 million smokers garnered from sign-ups for promotional offers and other sources. This database generates everything from birthday coupons to a chance to attend special events. This year a special booklet of 50 prizes was mailed to the Marlboro faithful. These prizes could be obtained either by collecting Marlboro miles or through sweepstakes. Marlboro also arranged trips to a ranch it owns in Montana where vacationers were showered with gifts, eat five-course meals and enjoyed massages, snowmobiling and horseback riding all courtesy of the company. The members of this smokers' club are, needless to say, devotees who would not miss the opportunity of a discount. They are also a group who often feel victimized by social pressure and growing legal restrictions and may find solace as part of this fellowship.

Anti-smoking advocates may find it ironic that that Philip Morris appears to have become a more deft and efficient marketer as a result of the legal restrictions and the court settlement that sought to cripple the company. By forcing Marlboro to go 'viral', be more aggressive in retail stores and be more creative in its media plan it has put them on a successful path that is being followed by companies such as General Motors (GM) and Audi. It is having a significant effect on profitability. Merril Lynch estimates that operating margins will rise to 28 per cent this year (26 per cent in 2004) as net income grows to $11.4 billion, based on a turnover of $66.3 billion in the USA and overseas.

Source: Nanette Byrnes, 'Leader of the Packs: Marlboro is Still Smokin' at 50, Thanks to Buzz Marketing', 31 October 2005, www.businessweek.com.

- Encourage distribution penetration: increased sales through extended shelf space or improved positioning.
- Encourage special displays (on or off-shelf).
- Thwart the opposition: providing incentives more attractive than the competition.
- Stimulate sales force motivation: for example, certain airlines have, in the past, offered above normal commission to agents encouraging them to divert business that may have gone elsewhere.
- Help overcome stock imbalances: incentives can help move excess stock and/or smooth out seasonal variations.

It is generally recognized that what sales promotion cannot do though is compensate for poor quality of products or permanently halt the decline of a brand.

SALES PROMOTION TACTICS

Historically the marketing literature has bundled together all the sales promotion tools despite them being very different in nature, uses and benefits

Incentives
Extra inducements to purchase.

Combined offers
Joint brand promotion (e.g. free hair-gel with shampoo).

Coupons
Vouchers printed in-store or from packs, magazines, etc. which offer a money-off or other incentive to buy product(s).

Refunds
By way of cash or coupons and may involve one or more purchases and submitting proof-of-purchase by mail or through claims managed via the Internet.

Sampling
Free of charge trialling of products in-store or at other locations.

Direct response
Media where the customer can respond immediately to the offer.

Premiums
Gifts given to consumers either with purchase or, if terms (e.g. collect five wrappers) have to be fulfilled, by other means.

Loyalty schemes
Schemes that reward customers for repurchases over time.

Self-liquidating premiums
Premium (or gift) where the income received covers the out-goings of the promotion.

Loyalty cards
Cards issued to consumers by loyalty scheme organizers to facilitate the management and control of the scheme.

Saving stamps
Now largely defunct method of managing a loyalty scheme where stamps were issued with purchases, collected and ultimately exchanged for gifts of cash. Another form is used in connection with savings clubs in some stores.

(Peattie and Peattie 1993). In essence sales promotion tools can be divided into two types; price promotions and creative promotions (or incentives).

Sales promotion is not, therefore, simply a discount strategy but a wide range of tactical marketing techniques that include:

- Money-off (coupons or at point-of-sale)
- Bonus pack offers (e.g. get 50 per cent extra free)
- Bonus offers (e.g. buy one get one free)
- Refunds
- Combined offers (e.g. buy product A get product B free of charge)
- Sampling
- Premiums and self-liquidating premiums
- Loyalty schemes
- Competitions

Money-off, bonus pack, bonus offers and combined offers are self-explanatory and are in widespread use in retailing. Coupons are still the most popular means of offering targeted customers discounts on selected items. Technology is now such that supermarkets can issue coupons at the point-of-purchase or direct to the home (as part of a loyalty scheme) based on the shopper's buying pattern. So, for example, soft-drink buyers may be enticed to try new brands or flavours or products from an associate category such as snacks. Combined offers are frequently used to introduce a new product or flavour and to create trial of a new product. Refunds (by way of cash or coupons) may involve one or more purchases and may mean submitting proof-of-purchase by mail or (increasingly) claims managed via the Internet. Sampling may take place in-store or at any other location (e.g. train stations) or, if appropriate, may be delivered through a door-to-door distribution. Direct response television and other media campaigns are also used to encourage sampling. Although sampling can be expensive, it is often used when advertising alone is unable to communicate the brand's benefits, when the brand has superior benefits to the competitor, or where the objective is to encourage product switching. Premiums are gifts given to consumers either with the product or, if terms (e.g. collect five wrappers) have to be fulfilled, at some later date. Ovaltine was the reputedly the first company to offer a premium when, in 1930, they distributed a 'de-coder ring' that required the participant to get information from the *Little Orphan Annie* radio show. In the 1950s, Procter & Gamble began offering plastic daffodils in the UK with packets of Daz. Still today, one of their most celebrated promotions ever, its success was perhaps because in those days of post-war austerity the gift was seen as bringing brightness into customers' lives. Some products are offered not free-of-charge but at a much reduced price. If the income received covers the outgoings of the promotion this is known as a self-liquidating premium.

Loyalty schemes may seem a relatively new innovation but they go back over a century. Although the use of loyalty cards is a relatively new introduction, the collection of coupons and saving stamps (in the UK Green Shield were the largest of the saving stamp companies) have always been used to give the customer an extra incentive to shop at the retailers (including at one time Tesco) who distributed them. Even earlier, the Co-operative movement, founded in Rochdale in the nineteenth century, distributed its profits (or dividends) to loyal customers who shopped with them. Many, of a certain age, remember being sent to the Co-op and quoting the 'divi-number' whereby their sale would be entered in a divi-book, which in time would be tallied up and a 'dividend' (cash bonus) distributed. In time this 'divi' book was replaced by saving stamps and ultimately loyalty cards (although in essence they served the same function).

There can be little doubt that we live in the age of the loyalty card. According to Uncles (1994) the espoused view is that customers actively seek an involving relationship with their brand which, in turn, offers psychological reassurances to the buyer and creates a sense of belonging. The goal of these schemes is to establish a higher level of customer retention in profitable segments by providing increased satisfaction and value to certain customers. The reality is that although there is some evidence of first-mover advantage (e.g. American Airlines' Frequent Flyer programme and Tesco's Club Card) when loyalty schemes become the norm potential benefits can turn into the unavoidable costs of doing business. At best, loyalty schemes act as reinforcing mechanisms, since it is often the case that they reward the already loyal rather than anyone else (Ward *et al.* 1998). From the customer perspective many schemes offer 'me-too' benefits, which it would be nice to have (because people like getting something for nothing) but is no guarantee of continued loyalty and are often marginal to their brand choice (Uncles 1994).

Competitive promotions are basically of two types; skill-based **competitions** or **free draws** where the winning is randomized (e.g. scratch cards, entry forms, instant-win packs, etc.). In competitions in the UK the winning of prizes must depend, to a substantial degree, on skill, whereas free draws (if it is not to be deemed a lottery which is strictly licensed in the UK and many countries) must be open to all, including non-purchasers. With competitive promotions the extra value is in the potential of winning the prize. From the brand perspective they promote it without tampering with the price versus quality value-equation and instead adding to the worth of the transaction by

Competitions
In sales promotion terms where the challenge is skill based.

Free draws
Where the winning of a competition is randomized.

Box 10.2 The future of instant wins and prize draws

The future of instant wins and prize draws are thought to be under threat since the formation of the 'Must-win Club' which 'guarantees' its members two prizes in six-months or less. The club, a subsidiary of Competitors Companion, gained 50 000 members within the first four weeks of its launch. The club are taking advantage of the fact that under UK regulations prize draws must be free to enter to everyone regardless of whether or not they have purchased the product and that all prizes must be given away to avoid it being classed as an illegal lottery. So on-pack entry draws and instant win competitions can now expect an additional 50 000 (plain-paper) entries each month and more if membership grows.

Source: ISP 2005.

making the purchase itself the 'ticket' to entering the competition (Peattie and Peattie 1993). Competitive promotions add excitement and are also a popular way of collecting customer data. Peattie and Peattie (1993) define types of customers as to their proneness or otherwise to competitions as follows:

- Non-competitors: people who see competitions as a waste of time and deliberately do not enter competitions for which they are entitled.

- Passive competitors: would enter if qualified (particularly if it were instant win) but would not change purchasing pattern to enter.

- Brand-switchers: would buy a particular brand to enter an attractive competition.

- Product-switchers: would buy a type of product that they would not normally buy to enter a competition.

- Hoarders: will alter their buying behaviour between brands and product types to maximize the chance of winning a competition.

- Dog-fooders: will buy almost anything (even dog-food when they do

@

For examples of sales promotion product suppliers look at: **www.4imprint. co.uk** and **www.britishcompanies. co.uk/promotionalitems.htm** and **www. promotional-merchandise.org.uk**.

Figure 10.4 European sales promotion

	UK	NL	BL	SP	IR	IT	FR	GE	DK
On-pack promotions	✓	✓	?	✓	✓	✓	?	✓	✓
Branded offers	✓	?	?	✓	✓	✓	?	✓	✓
In-pack premiums	✓	?	?	✓	✓	✓	?	✓	?
Multi-purchase offers	✓	?	?	✓	✓	✓	?	✓	✓
Extra product	✓	✓	✓	✓	✓	✓	?	?	✓
Free product	✓	?	✓	✓	✓	✓	✓	✗	?
Reusable/other use packs	✓	✓	✓	✓	✓	✓	✓	✓	✓
Free mail-ins	✓	✓	?	✓	✓	✓	?	✓	✓
With purchase premiums	✓	?	✓	✓	✓	✓	?	?	?
Cross-product offers	✓	✓	✗	✓	✓	✓	?	✓	✓
Collector devices	✓	✓	✓	✓	✓	✓	✓	✓	✓
Competitions	✓	?	?	✓	✓	?	✓	✓	?
Self-liquidating premiums	✓	✓	✓	✓	✓	✓	✓	✓	✓
Free draws	✓	✗	?	✓	✓	✓	✓	✓	✓
Share outs	✓	✓	?	✓	✓	?	?	✓	?
Sweepstake/lottery	?	✗	?	✓	✗	?	?	✓	✗
Money-off coupons	✓	✓	✓	✓	✓	✓	✓	✓	✓
Money-off next purchase	✓	✓	✓	✓	✓	✓	✓	✓	✓
Cash backs	✓	✓	✓	✓	✓	✗	✓	✓	✓
In-store demonstrations	✓	✓	✓	✓	✓	✓	✓	✓	✓

Source: Based on ISP 2005 (correct at 4 November 2005).

Key: ✓ = permitted ✗ = not permitted ? = may be permitted with restrictions.

not have a dog) to enter a competition whether they want it or need the product itself.

Across the world sales promotion is regulated to a greater and lesser degree. What is permissible in one jurisdiction is not necessarily allowable in the next. Figure 10.4 is the current situation in a number of European states. As can be seen, the UK and Spain are amongst the most liberal in attitude whereas France, Belgium and the Netherlands are the most restrictive.

SALES PROMOTION OUTCOMES

The simplest way to promote your product or service is to cut the price. The best way to promote your product, however, is to add value. It follows, therefore, that to add value, sales promotion becomes a strategic tool when it is not utilized for that 'quick-fix', immediate response solution. It needs to becomes a part of a planned set of marketing communications activities over time, with each building upon the other.

The effect on long-term profitability must be regarded as a down-side of sales promotion. The calculation in Box 10.3 below shows the effect of a three-for-two offer based on a gross margin of 15 per cent. This 'loss' may be taken by the manufacturer or retailer[1] and it may be used as a **loss-leader** to stimulate **footfall** thus generating increased sales in other products. The calculation should also be viewed with care because retailers frequently make use of our poor knowledge of prices beyond the basics (bread, milk, etc.).

Loss-leader
A product sold at or below cost to attract customers into a store.

Footfall
Retail jargon for number of customers (e.g. increased footfall = rise in number of customers in a particular store).

Box 10.3 Sales promotion calculation

Non-promotion	Period 1	Period 2	Period 3	Period 4	Totals
Sales (units)	2000	2000	2000	2000	8000
Price	£1.00	£1.00	£1.00	£1.00	
Margin (15%)	£0.15	£0.15	£0.15	£0.15	
Gross Profit	£300.00	£300.00	£300.00	£300.00	£12 000.00
Promotion (period 2)	**Period 1**	**Period 2**	**Period 3**	**Period 4**	**Totals**
Sales (units)	2000	4000	1000	2000	8000
Price	£1.00	£0.66	£1.00	£1.00	
Margin (15%)	£0.15	(£0.19)	£0.15	£0.15	
Gross Profit	£300.00	(£760.00)	£150.00	£300.00	(£10.00)

[1]This is a simple example and could relate to either retailers or brand owners.

The actual saving on any promotion is determined by the original retail price which can vary significantly between retailers. A sales promotion 'trap' develops when the competition start to imitate each other's activities often based upon price reductions.

There is a need for careful planning particularly in relation to competitions and insurance against mishap is now commonplace. When such promotions go well they can be very successful. One of the best-remembered and most profitable was the Shell 'make money' competition, where drivers collected half a note on each visit to the petrol station. Such was its success that the competition has been repeated three times since its original introduction in 1966 and in addition in other formats (e.g. matching cars) too. The dangers are, however, apparent as the examples of two famous sales promotions disasters in Minicase 10.2 reveal.

MINICASE 10.2

Promotional disasters

Two well publicized public relations disasters serve to warn about the potential dangers of planning promotions and insuring against things going wrong.

Pepsi in the Philippines offered one-million pesos (£26 000) to anyone finding a bottle-top with the number 349. Pepsi had paid out £8 million before they realised that thousands of winning tops were appearing everywhere and stopped the payments. In all 500 000 bottle tops were printed with that number which would have cost Pepsi $18 billion. Instead Pepsi reduced the prize money to $19.00 which still cost them $10 million. Following riots and attacks on Pepsi bottling plants, lorries burnt out and three people killed, many Pepsi executives left the country and were later the subject of thousands of lawsuits.

In the UK Hoover offered free flights to the USA in return for purchasing any product over £100. The company wildly underestimated the response because, in the planning stage, they looked at response rates of a two-for-the-price-of-one offer rather than a comparable (if there was one) promotion. The response was huge (100 000 within the first month) with people buying two Hoovers at a time. It was exasperated by the fact that some retailers increased prices of some lines bringing them into the promotion. The agency through which the competition was organized quickly went in to liquidation and Hoover, who were not insured, became liable. Disgruntled customers complained and at least one blockaded a Hoover van and refused to release it until the travel tickets were produced. The promotion cost Hoover £48 million, numerous careers and was a public image disaster.

Sources: Smith and Taylor 2002 and Various.

Summary

This chapter opened with a brief reflection on sales promotions of the past and distinguished sales promotion, as an incentive to people to act, from the brand building qualities of advertising. It further distinguished between consumer, trade and retail promotions and how they interact with general organizational strategy. The growth of sales promotion was highlighted and it was noted that, since 1980, it had replaced advertising as the main medium in the consumer goods field. The reasons behind this were discussed, they included: abolition of retail price maintenance; increased advertising costs; corporate short-termism; the measurability of promotions; stagnating markets; the decline of brand loyalty; the spread of own-label; increased repertoire buying; the increased power and concentration of retailers; increased price sensitivity; and the implications of new technologies. Sales promotions theories were explained in the light of classical and operant conditioning theories, the law of effects, shaping, chaining and priming. Intuitive generalizations and potential scenarios were further discussed and analysed. Sales promotion consumer and trade objectives, including increased sales, trial stimulation, brand switching and rewarding loyalty were analysed and the difference between price and creative promotions highlighted. Outcomes, including the potential downsides to promotions were also discussed.

Review questions

1   What are the four types of sales promotion?

2   What is the difference between positive and negative reinforcement in relation to sales promotion? Give examples for each.

3   Explain 'chaining'.

4   Describe the phenomenon known as the 'mortgaging effect'.

5   What do you understand by the term 'self-liquidating promotion'?

6   Explain the benefits behind undertaking a cause-related promotion.

7   How might a trade promotion differ from a consumer-based promotion?

8   List a range of sales promotion tactics that an organization could use.

9   How might sales promotion activities assist in building or maintaining loyalty?

10   What is a 'dog-fooder'?

Discussion questions

1   What is the difference between advertising and sales promotion and at what point do you believe the two might be the same thing? How might this influence campaign planning?

2   A number of intuitive generalizations can be made about sales promotion. What are these and what might their impact be upon campaign planning?

3   For consumer-focused promotions there can be many sales promotion objectives. List these and discuss how each might be chosen.

Further reading

Alvarez, Begoña Alverez and Casielles, Rodolfo Vázquez (2005) 'Consumer evaluations of sales promotion: the effect on brand choice', *European Journal of Marketing*, 39 (1–2). Providing evidence for the influence that sales promotion has on brand choice behaviour.

Borges, A., Cliquet, G. and Fady, A. (2005) 'Buying association and its impact on promotional utility', *International Journal of Retail & Distribution Management*, 33 (5): 343–52. Even if a sales promotion attracts consumers to the store, performance will be uncertain if these consumers buy only promoted categories, a warning for retailers who need to avoid promoting categories that are frequently bought together in the same promotional action, or be faced with a strong redundancy effect.

Cronin, J. (1993) 'The life cycle of consumer sales promotions', *Journal of Promotion Management*, 1993, 1 (4): 103–11. Explaining that certain types of sales promotions do proceed through a life cycle, and that the consumer promotion life cycle consists of six stages.

DelVecchio, D., Henard, D.H. and Freling, T.H. (2006) 'The effect of sales promotion on post-promotion brand preference: a meta-analysis', *Journal of Retailing*, Sep., 82 (3): 203–13.

Laroche, M., Pons, F., Zgolli, N., Cervellon, M. and Kim, C. (2003) 'A model of consumer response to two retail sales promotion techniques', *Journal of Business Research*, 56 (7): 513–22. A cognitive-affective-behaviour pattern for consumers use of retail sales promotions.

Peattie, K. and Peattie, S. (1995) 'Sales promotion – a missed opportunity for services marketers?', *International Journal of Service Industry Management*, 6 (1): 22–39. This paper attempts to show how promotional competition represents a significant opportunity for services marketers.

Chapter references

Barnard, N.R. and Ehrenberg, A.S.C. (1997) 'Advertising and price', *Journal of Advertising Research*, 37 (3): 27–35.

Belch, G. and Belch, M. (2004) *Advertising and Promotion: An Integrated Marketing Communications Perspective*, London: McGraw-Hill.

Copley, P. (2004) *Marketing Communications Management*, Oxford: Butterworth-Heinemann.

De Pelsmacker, P., Geuens, M. and Van den Bergh, J. (2001) *Marketing Communications*, Harlow: Financial Times/Prentice Hall.

Ehrenberg, A.S.C., Hammond, K. and Goodhart, G.J. (1994) 'The after-effects of price-related consumer promotions', *Journal of Advertising Research*, July/August: 11–21.

Fill, C. (2002) *Communications: Contexts, Strategies and Applications*, 3rd edn, Harlow: F T, Prentice Hall.

Foxall, G., Goldsmith, R. and Brown, S. (1998) *Consumer Psychology for Marketing*, London: Thomson Learning.

Jones, J.P. (1990) 'The double jeopardy of sales promotions', *Harvard Business Review*, Sep.–Oct., 68 (5): 145–52.

Laspadakis, A. (1999) 'The dynamic role of sales promotion', in P.J. Kitchen (ed.), *Marketing Communications: Principles and Practice*, London: Thomson, pp. 289–308.

McGovern, G.J., Court, D., Quelch, J.A. and Crawford, B. (2004) 'Bringing custom to the boardroom', *Harvard Business Review*, November: 70–80.

Peattie, K.J. and Peattie, S. (1993) 'Sales promotion – playing to win', *Journal of Marketing Management*, 9: 225–69.

Sclater, I. (2003) 'Something for nothing', *Marketing Business*, June, Cookham: Chartered Institute of Marketing, pp. 21–3.

Shimp, T.A (2003) *Advertising, Promotion and Supplemental Aspects of Integrated Marketing Communication*, Cincinnati: Thomson.

Smith, P.R. and Taylor, J. (2002) *Marketing Communications: An Integrated Approach*, 3rd edn, London: Kogan Page.

Thorndike, E.L. (1927) 'The law of effect', *The American Jounal of Psychology*, 39 (1/4): 212–22.

Uncles, M. (1994) 'Do you or your customers need a loyalty scheme?', *Journal of Targeting, Measurement and Analysis for Marketing*, 2 (4): 335–50.

Ward, P., Gardner, H. and Wright, H. (1998) 'Being smart: a critique of customer loyalty schemes in UK retailing, *Customer Relationship Management*, 1 (1): 79–86.

Yeshin (2006) *Sales Promotion*, London: Thomson Learning.

CASE STUDY 10.1

Nikon Coolpix Adventure

The compact digital camera market is saturated with many reputable brands, most of which offer the same quality, advantages and product features when compared to competing brands within the same price range. When Nikon produced their new range of Coolpix digital cameras their task was to set this new range apart from the competition as the first choice for consumers and retailers. Five marketing objectives were defined:

● To raise awareness and interest of the Nikon range of Coolpix digital cameras within the trade.
● To incentivize and motivate counter staff to proactively demonstrate and recommend the new Nikon range of Coolpix cameras.
● To drive traffic to participating retailers and give consumers a reason to 'touch' and interact with the Coolpix cameras leading to purchase.

▶

- To collect data for future relationship development and offers.
- To meet or exceed sales targets based on a 10 per cent increase from the previous year.

The strategy involved targeting digital camera buyers and users. Research revealed that 58 per cent of this group were men, mainly between the ages of 35 and 44. Eighty one per cent of the group were married with children and 40 per cent were from households with incomes of over £35k per annum. Concentrations of the target audience needed to be mapped-out in terms of their proximity to the geographical positions of participating retailers in order to enhance sell-in. The strategy also involved creating an overall theme which encompassed a trade incentive and a consumer promotion to encourage interaction with the product range and the brand.

The focused targeting of digital camera users and buyers from affluent families with children was key to the success of the campaign. A 'proximity' model identified these households in relation to potential participating retailers. Leaflets containing a Nikon branded CompactFlash™ card were delivered to half a million of the targeted homes. Each of the memory cards were compatible with any of the Nikon Coolpix digital cameras and recipients were invited to activate the card by visiting their local Nikon retailer and requesting a demonstration. At the store, counter staff would assist consumers to load the CompactFlash card into a digital camera from the Nikon Coolpix range to find out whether they had won an 'adventure' prize. When the camera was switched to 'play' mode, the

The Nikon Coolpix campaign incentivised counter staff by awarding them with the same prize as the winning customer.

LCD screen would indicate whether or not the customer was a winner. A message on the screen would either tell winners their prize or display the message 'NO CARD PRESENT' to indicate that the customer was not a winner.

The total prize fund exceeded £1 million and included adventure activities such as hot air ballooning over Ayres Rock with 14 nights accommodation, discovering Ancient Egypt with 15 nights accommodation and white-water rafting, free entry to Chessington World of Adventure or Madam Tussauds. Counter staff were motivated to demonstrate the cameras, by being awarded with the same prize as the winning customer.

In addition to this, camera purchasers were also invited to enter a competition to win one of 1000 TDK 64Mb memory cards. The competition required the customer to answer three multiple-choice questions relating to the promotion, digital photography and Nikon software. They were also required to complete a 'tiebreaker' by describing their own Coolpix adventure. The promotion was supported by POS (point-of-sale) material, a volume trade incentive and special awards for those retailers who were seen to support the promotion enthusiastically and display the POS material.

The campaign was highly successful. Sales exceeded the target for each month of the promotional period, and the average sales increase over that time was 30 per cent. The 'Nikon Coolpix Adventure' theme had succeeded in encompassing both the consumer offer and the retailer incentive; encouraging consumer interaction with the brand and motivating staff who subsequently responded with interest and enthusiasm.

In 2004, the campaign won two gold awards, plus one silver and one 'Highly Commended' award in the ISP (Institute of Sales Promotion) Award scheme.

Case study questions

1 Which aspects of the campaign involved 'pull' and which aspects involved 'push' strategies?
2 What are the potential downsides or risks associated with this sales promotion campaign?
3 Why not just offer a 'money-off' promotion together with an enhanced sales commission for staff over a limited period of time?
4 How could Nikon extend or enhance this sales promotion campaign?

Source: Case study Written by Nik Mahon, Faculty of Media, Arts and Society, Southampton Solent University.

CHAPTER ELEVEN
PUBLIC RELATIONS

LEARNING OBJECTIVES

Having completed this chapter you should be able to:

- Understand the importance of public relations in the modern organization.
- Describe the purpose of publicity and the importance of media management.
- Recognize the significance of corporate image and the importance of research and counselling as a function of public relations.
- Understand the part played by internal marketing and how organizations manage it.
- Appreciate the importance of specialist areas of public relations such as financial relations, lobbying and crisis management.

INTRODUCTION

Public relations (PR), although considered by some to be a relatively young profession, can like other marketing communications tools be traced back to the earliest times. Edward Bernays, regarded as one of the fathers of modern public relations, has argued that the rulers of ancient Egypt, Sumeria, Babylonia, Assyria and Persia all used techniques that would today be described as public relations. The earliest formal public relations activities were undertaken largely to promote something or to 'spread the faith' – the original definition of propaganda (Grunig and Hunt 1984). Political leaders in particular have always needed to communicate with different **publics** (see Box 11.1) throughout history. Machiavelli, for example, was not only a consummate politician but a public relations practitioner of the highest order. British politician Lloyd George, as Chancellor of the Exchequer, used public relations to promote the old-age pension in 1912 and Sir Steven Tallents (the first President of the Institute of Public Relations) used public relations to promote the Empire Marketing Board between 1926 and 1933 (Baines *et al.* 2004). Public relations' rise to prominence in the commercial sector also began earlier than is often realized. Industrial growth during the

Public relations
The planned and sustained effort to establish and maintain goodwill and mutual understanding between an organization and its publics.

Publics
'Publics' are those people, internal and external to the organization, with whom the organization communicates.

nineteenth century meant that by 1900 powerful business interests in the USA were employing public relations professionals to 'defend their special interests against muckraking journalism and government regulation' (Cutlip *et al.* 1994: 2).

The twentieth century saw public relations somewhat in the shadow of advertising and sales promotion. As one practitioner noted 'PR has long railed against the view that it is the poor relation of marketing communications but, as its practitioners have especially discovered in recent years, the medium seems to be the first on the list for budget cuts' (Barrand 2004: 43). Despite this, public relations has seen enormous growth. UK public relations' expenditure has grown from an estimated £50 million in the early 1960s to £1 billion in the early 1990s and an estimated £6.5 billion by 2005 and the numbers of people employed in the business from 4000 to 48 000 over the same period. According to the world's richest man, Bill Gates 'If I was down to my last dollar I would spend it on PR' (Moloney 2006). Others see public relations' importance continuing to rise, 'as members of the public become increasingly marketing savvy, anecdotal evidence suggests that a more subtle approach to engaging emotions has become the key to successful campaigns' (Siegle 2005: 41).

By the end of the twentieth century the term 'PR' (public relations) had entered everyday language. Public relations jargon had become widely recognized and terms such as **press release**, **image**, **spin doctor**, **soundbite**, **positioning** and **relaunch** had slipped into regular use. The Institute of Public Relations (IPR) became the CIPR as it gained 'chartered status', signalling both its prominence and managerial acceptance. In 1998, *Spectator* magazine even declared public relations as the 'profession of the decade'. Public relations in the new millennium was, it would seem, the new advertising!

PUBLIC RELATIONS DEFINITIONS

Public Relations can be viewed at a number of levels. The Institute of Public Relations[1] (IPR) defined it for many years as (Jefkins 1994: 7): 'the planned and sustained effort to establish and maintain goodwill and mutual understanding between an organisation and its publics'.

A more recent definition expands upon this when it declares PR as (CIPR 2006) as:

the discipline which looks after reputation, with the aim of earning understanding and support and influencing opinion and behaviour. It is the planned and sustained effort to establish and maintain goodwill and mutual understanding between an organisation and its publics.

[1]Now the Chartered Institute of Public Relations (CIPR).

Press release
Newsworthy written announcement distributed to selected media.

Image
A perception of an organization or brand that exists in the minds of customers, stakeholders and publics.

Spin doctor
Public relations jargon for person who 'spins' or creates positive stories (a term often used to ridicule political advisers).

Soundbite
The encapsulation of a message in very few words (for the purposes of television and radio journalism).

Positioning
The process of creating a perception in the consumer's mind regarding the nature of the company and its products relative to the competition (see also benefit positioning, user positioning and competitive positioning).

Relaunch
The reforming of an entity following a dramatic or negative occurrence.

CIPR is the largest public relations institute in Europe: **www.ipr.org.uk.**

These definitions place public relations at the very top of the organization hierarchy. Indeed the increasing popular term **corporate communications** is strongly associated with these definitions. It is not uncommon in many organizations for advertising and sales promotion managers, as well as Public Relations Officers (PROs) and Press Officers, to report to the Director of Corporate Communications rather than the Marketing Director. In this type of organization marketing communications is seen as part of public relations. According to IPR/DTI research, 20 per cent of organizations have public relations decision-makers at board level and a further 47 per cent as a top-line management responsibility.

The alternative argument to this is that public relations is a part of marketing communications. Kotler and Mindak (1978) whilst suggesting that the evolution of corporate communications and **marketing public relations** were different argued that they consisted of overlapping activities and encouraged their integration. This view is not without controversy. One American academic, Martha Lauzen, has argued that by aligning public relations with marketing the latter is attempting to subsume the former through what she calls 'marketing imperialism' (Briggs and Tuscon 1993). Certainly by volume of production there is more marketing public relations than any other type of public relations (Moloney 2006). Public relations as a subset of marketing is often associated with the term **publicity**. With 'publicity' the 'goodwill and mutual understanding' of the earlier definition relates more to building the image of the brand and creating associations between that brand and its publics. In effect the public relations style and function is heavily determined by the organizational type and public relations' recognized role within the organization.

Around the world hundreds of thousands of people work in public relations departments or agencies although many would describe it by other names such as public affairs, public information, communication, community relations or promotion (Grunig and Hunt 1984) or more contemporary titles for example corporate affairs, corporate communications or public affairs (Dolphin and Fan 2000). Despite the difficulties in accurately describing public relations, Public Relations Officer's managers or directors (by whatever title) are usually

Corporate communications
An organizational function that controls all aspects of communication with an organization's publics outside of marketing.

Marketing public relations
Those aspects of public relations directly associated with communication with customers (i.e. publicity).

Useful industry information on public relations can be found at: **www.prweek.com/uk/.**

Publicity
Building the image of the brand and creating positive associations between that brand and its publics.

Box 11.1 Public relations publics

Public relations departments are not concerned with the general public *per se* but in a range of different communities. These are known in public relations circles as 'publics'. The word 'publics' has a very particular meaning and one peculiar to public relations. 'Publics' are those people, internal and external to the organization, with whom the organization communicates (Jefkins and Yadin 1998). These may include (but are not necessarily limited to):

- Customers
- The community
- Existing and potential employees
- Suppliers of goods and services
- Distributors

- Shareholders
- Financial markets
- Media and other opinion formers
- Government and other legislators
- Other stakeholders

involved with one, some or all of the following activities:

- Publicity: positive messages about the organization, its employees or other newsworthy stories designed to improve the image of the brand.
- Media management: sustaining and utilizing long-term relationships with the media.
- Corporate image: publicizing the positive aspects of the organization.
- Research and counselling: monitoring public and other (e.g. government) opinion.
- Internal marketing: managing the organization's relationships with its employees (see Chapter 16).
- Shareholder and other financial relations: informing and maintaining good relationships with shareholders and other stakeholders.
- Lobbying: making the organization's views and arguments known to lawmakers.
- Crisis management: limiting damaging publicity and managing the organization's response.
- Community relations: managing the relationship between the organization and the local community.

This breadth of coverage suggests a wider role than that suggested by the earlier IPR definition particularly in relation to research and monitoring. This aspect was discussed at an international public relations conference held in Mexico City in 1978 and the following definition (which became known as the **Mexico Statement**) issued (cited in Jefkins 1994): 'Public relations practice is the art and social science of analysing trends, predicting their consequences, counselling organisational leaders, and implementing planned programmes of action that will serve both the organisation's and the public interest.'

This statement spells out the full role of public relations and highlights five important responsibilities associated with the broad function of research and monitoring. These are:

- Analysis of trends: to investigate the current situation inside and outside of the organization.
- Predicting the consequences: making determinations of likely outcomes.
- Counselling leaders: giving advice on future strategy and tactics.
- Implementing planned programmes of action: defining the needs and managing the functional aspects of public relations including press relations, internal marketing, etc.
- Serving the public interest: social responsibility and ethical commercialism.

Public relations, therefore, has the potential to be a powerful and complex tool within the organizational armoury. There are, however, no set models applicable to all organizations, rather the organization develops the format it requires determined by its individual needs.

Mexico Statement
Definition of public relations which originated at a public relations conference held in Mexico City in 1978.

PUBLICITY

One of the major functions associated with public relations is that of publicity. Publicity is normally described as a series of positive messages about an organization or its employees designed to improve the image of the organization or brand. Positive brand associations, it is suggested, develop sales over time but, as with advertising, it is almost impossible to measure the effect of publicity in anything but the broadest of terms. As with advertising proxy measures are used to gauge the success of an ongoing publicity campaign. The most extensively[2] used measure is media evaluation. Media evaluation is, according to the Association of Media Evaluation Companies[3] 'the systematic appraisal of a company's reputation, products or services, or those of its competitors, as measured by their presence in the media'. This evaluation (often called a 'clippings service') is carried out either in-house or by media evaluation specialists. Media evaluation of this type has long had its critics but as Hunt and Grunig (1994) note 'if we define the objective of press relations as "getting the proper message on the media agenda" then the clippings service isn't such a bad idea. The clippings show how frequently and in what context the organization has appeared on the media agenda'.

Directly ascribing public relations investment to increased output, however, remains contentious. According to David McLaren[4] of leading public relations agency Hill & Knowlton 'the industry's Achilles heel is its inability to show the relationship between PR output and marketplace effect, affordably'. Indeed, according to research at Henley Management College over half of Public Relations Officer cited 'gut feel' as their primary way of evaluating the success of their campaigns (Siegle 2004).

Although positive publicity is a major public relations objective there is evidence to suggest that even negative publicity can generate potentially valuable awareness. During the 1980s directors of the brewery Guinness went on trial for manipulating the price of the company's shares. During the trial broadcasters and the press covered the case extensively. Despite the negative publicity for the directors it was noted at the time that sales of Guinness actually increased over this period. This was probably because, having brought the product to the attention of the public, more drinkers chose to trial it. This supports the old maxim that 'all publicity is good publicity'. More recent examples of companies for whom negative publicity appears regularly are Ryanair and Benetton. Again adverse comment does not seemed to have harmed these companies' profits, and may well have contributed (through wider exposure) to, increased turnover.

Public relations publicity contributes to the brand in ways similar to those discussed in the chapter on advertising. There are, however, some

Publicity
Building the image of the brand and creating positive associations between that brand and its publics.

Media evaluation
Evaluation of an organization's media coverage over a specific time period.

Clippings service
A service offered to companies who wish to monitor media coverage. The results are frequently used to measure the effectiveness of an organization's public relations efforts.

[2]According to research by Metrica 90 per cent of organizations use media evaluation (Siegle 2005).
[3]Quoted in Theaker 2001: 255.
[4]Quoted in *Marketing*, 19 May 2004.

significant differences. Unlike advertising the organization does not pay to place its message in the media of its choice. In effect the publicized messages (in the form of press releases, speeches, etc.) must compete for attention amongst other newsworthy stories. Even if the story is taken up by one or more media outlets there is no guarantee that the message will be published in the form and with the positive content favoured by the company because journalists will interpret the message in whichever way they wish. Publicity is not, therefore, 'free advertising' (particularly because it involves costs in terms of management and other resources) and there is no guarantee (unlike advertising) of message placement. Another distinction is that whereas the cost of advertising is dictated by the media into which it is placed, the costs involved in public relations are measured largely in terms of the expenditure of personnel resources. Figure 11.1 shows the relationships between public relations publicity and other major marketing communications tools in terms of their brand and image building contribution and the major source of costs.

Another difference between the public relations practitioner and other marketing communication specialists is that their interest goes well beyond that of the consumer. Other 'publics' (see Box 11.1) have to be targeted and the objective may be other than increased sales. In the Guinness trials discussed above other 'publics' of importance to the company (e.g. financiers, shareholders, government regulators, etc.) were receiving messages that would both affect the confidence of shareholders and the company's ability to raise, at competitive rates, funding from financial markets. Here the public relations responsibility would be that of **crisis management** (see page 259). This might include in similar circumstances distancing the company from ex-directors and reassuring shareholders and markets of the organization's current financial probity.

Crisis management
Management of a crisis situation that has the capacity to severely damage the organization.

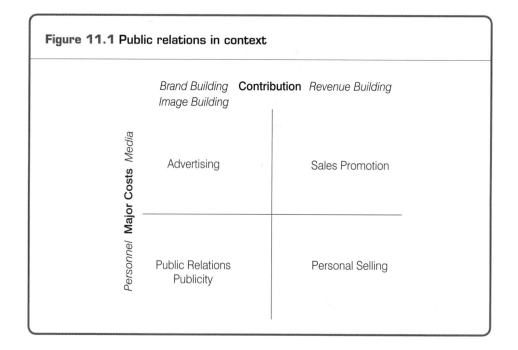

Figure 11.1 Public relations in context

Publicity, like other marketing communication tools, is frequently more effective in combination rather than stand alone (see Chapter 15 'Integrated marketing communications'). Wonderbra advertising, costing £50 000 was said to have generated publicity in excess of £50 million.[5] Camelot's sponsorship of the British Olympic rowing team generated publicity far in excess of the company's investment. When British Airways (BA) ran a promotion offering free Concorde tickets it generated so much publicity that it made headline news in many national newspapers.

In addition to companies wishing to publicize themselves the rise of the 'cult of celebrity' has led to a sub-genre of public relations professionals known as 'publicists'. Most famous amongst these is Max Clifford who has represented the famous and the infamous over his 40-year career. Publicists, in essence differ little from the traditional Public Relations Officers keeping their clients in (or out) of the public eye thus enhancing their celebrity and/or earnings potential.

Publicists
A seeker of publicity on behalf of his/her clients.

MEDIA MANAGEMENT

In terms of the volume of public relations activities, the largest volume is in media relations. The public relations practitioner has been said to serve two masters; the employer and the public interest, with the media essentially forming a bridge between the two. As a consequence, a thorough knowledge of, and a close relationship with, the media are essential elements of good public relations. The terms 'press office' and 'press officer' are still the ones most widely used to describe the unit and personnel responsible for communications with the media despite the extension of their role to cover other news mediums (e.g. television, radio, Internet, etc.). Although there is some evidence of a move to 'media office' and 'media officer' the old titles have largely remained despite the broadening of the role. The Press Officer is there to act positively on behalf of the organization, which means not only reacting to media requests for information but proactively working with the media in creating newsworthy stories.

According to Harrison (2000) the ability to produce and transmit properly written and targeted news releases and the kind of temperament to get on with journalists is crucial. The Press Officer's objective is not, however, sending out press releases (or media releases) *per se* but getting them published. When this works it can be very effective. It has been suggested that 80 per cent of what appears in business pages of newspapers and 40–50 per cent of general news is produced or influenced by public relations practitioners. However, it has been estimated that, in the UK, of the 130 million press releases sent each year 126 million go straight into editors' waste baskets (Smith and Taylor 2002).

Press office or media office
Office which handles press and other media enquiries and issues press releases.

Press Officer or media officer
Representative of the company who handles press and other media enquiries and issues press releases.

---

[5]This type of estimate is based on media monitoring and a calculation of the cost of any coverage in paid-for advertising terms.

Canon Europe: launch of the EOS 350D

In 2005, Canon Europe launched the EOS 350D digital SLR camera as a replacement for the EOS 300D model. At the time of its launch, the EOS 300D was the world's first digital SLR* camera available to consumers at under €1000 and had been responsible for triggering the digital SLR boom. As an upgrade, the EOS 350D lacked the 'big news' value of its predecessor and presented Canon with a public relations challenge: to get strong press coverage without big news.

Key to the success of the public relations campaign, was the need to grab the attention of the media and obtain a dominant 'share of voice' in the press, particularly in comparison to their main competitor, Nikon. One of their objectives was to receive more than five times return on investment, in free editorial.

SOURCE: © CANON (UK) LIMITED (REPRODUCED WITH PERMISSION).

Canon's EOS Safari provided a return of 9 times their investment (for the launch materials and EOS Safari combined) in free editorial.

*Single Lens Reflex.

Press launch events were synchronized to take place at 13 locations around Europe on the 17 February 2005. However, a major phase of the product launch, was the 'EOS Safari' – a trip to the Masai Mara in Kenya for 76 top photographic journalists from Europe and the Middle East, together with a support team from Canon. Almost 3 tonnes of equipment was transported with them, including 115 cameras, 337 lenses and 91 lens accessories. A dedicated Canon immigration desk was organized at Nairobi airport to ease congestion, and a total of 114 tents were erected at two temporary camps on the Masai Mara site.

Over the four day event, groups of journalists were given the chance to take part in four different types of activity, where they had the opportunity to try-out the new camera. A total of 42 activities were organized daily. Guest speakers from Kenya and the local Masai Mara communities hosting the event, addressed journalists on local issues such as sustainability and poaching.

The event received excellent feedback from all of the journalists attending. The EOS 350D alone, received almost twice the volume 'share of voice' received by all Nikon digital SLRs. From February to November 2005, Canon's share in the digital SLR market, was over twice that of Nikon. In addition to this, Canon calculated that in terms of publicity, they had received a return of nine times their investment for the launch materials and EOS Safari combined.

Minicase written by Nik Mahon, Faculty of Media, Arts & Society, Southampton Solent University (Source: www.ipr.org.uk/excellence/casestudies06/category14.asp).

Although the mass media may be important at times, it is particularly important to recognize the importance of targeting 'special interest' mediums. In some quarters it is believed that the media are the 'publics' for an organization, or indeed, by achieving media coverage that, in itself, achieves the goal. The reality is that the media is simply a conduit for accessing the true publics and that coverage in no way ensures that the message will be seen. It is important, therefore, to acknowledge that there are other conduits, such as face-to-face communication, and these too will need to be utilized as appropriate.

In order to develop a newsworthy story the press officer needs good lines of internal and external communication so as to encourage the flow of news and develop the knowledge of where to place it. Mass distributed press releases on subjects unlikely to interest anyone outside of a confined readership (and perhaps not even then) are, quite literally, not worth the paper they are written on. Targeted releases are both much more likely to be published and more cost effective for the organization.

CORPORATE IMAGE AND CORPORATE IDENTITY

The corporate image of an organization is seen as a role managed by the public relations practitioner. Corporate image and corporate identity are terms that are often confused. Although the latter should contribute positively and help define the former they are different concepts. Corporate identity concerns the aims, values and ethos of an organization and a key aspect of this is the visual cohesion and representation, in terms of aspects such as the company name, logo and livery. Corporate identity is physical and is how an organization portrays itself to the outside world. Corporate image is, in contrast, highly subjective. It is what 'publics' see and feel when confronted by the organization and is based on their knowledge and prior experience. Poor image problems can be two-fold. Either the company deserves its image or it has in some way been misunderstood. Misunderstanding can be resolved through communication and it is the responsibility of the Public Relations Officer to implement this. This has been called the **public relations transfer process** (Jefkins 1994). Whatever level of opinion is current the Public Relations Officer is looking to move that further in favour of the organization through knowledge and greater understanding. This is illustrated in Figure 11.2 below.

Public relations transfer process
A theory of public relations that suggests incremental stages between hostility and acceptance.

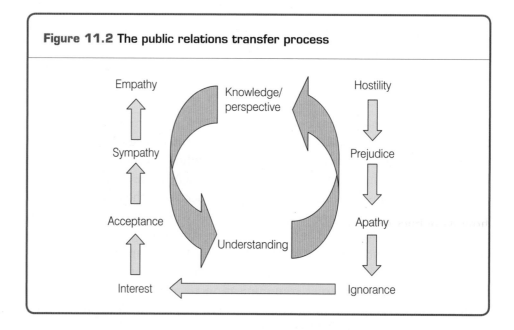

Figure 11.2 The public relations transfer process

An image that is deservedly poor can only be corrected by the organization itself. Frequently attempts to improve an organization's image without dealing with the root cause leads to further negative publicity. The exposure of Nike's use of overseas 'sweat-shops' affected its corporate image significantly and no amount of public relations justification could resolve this until they changed their manufacturing policy.

An organization's image can, of course, mean different things to different publics as well as internally in the organization. Baines *et al.* (2004) describe the different forms of image and their relationship with one another as follows:

Mirror image
How internal management think outsiders see the organization.

Current image
The image held by outsiders based on a consensus of perceptions modelled by their knowledge and experience.

- Mirror image: how internal management think outsiders see the organization. In the mirror held up to the company the image looks rosier than from the outside.

- Current image: the image held by outsiders based on a consensus of perceptions modelled by their knowledge and experience.

- **Multiple image:** where different people see different images dependent on their particular relationship with the organization. For example a customer's view of an efficient supermarket may be excellent whereas its suppliers may be highly critical.

- **Wish image:** the image that the organization might aspire to.

- **Optimum image:** what the company might aspire to may not be possible and so a rather less than perfect image may be sought. For example petroleum companies are unlikely to be admired by the general public and, as such, might seek a more benign and responsive persona rather than being high profile.

An organization wishing to sustain or adapt its corporate image should do this as part of its integrated communications strategy (see Chapter 15). This would include conducting regular **communications audits** (sometimes called **reputation audits**). A communications audit examines a number of aspects, from the functional elements to the specific. Functional aspects include factors such as communication need, channels, technologies, patterns etc. Specific aspects include content and content clarity of the message, its effectiveness, the effective fulfilment and inclusion of the needs of the various parties involved in its construction, the reflection of corporate culture and the wider impact of the communication in terms of organizational motivation and performance.

Figure 11.3 below outlines the process that might be followed when a firm needs to bring about an effective change in its image. The diagram suggests the disparity between how a company would like to see itself (wish image) and how management might regard it (mirror image) and contrasts this with how its publics see it (current image) through a communications audit. The

Multiple image
Where different people see different images dependent on their particular relationship with the organization.

Wish image
The image that an organization aspires to.

Optimum image
The image a company aspires to (wish image) may not be possible and so a rather less than perfect image may be sought.

Communications or (reputation) audits
A communications audit looks at communications' needs, patterns, flow, channels and technologies, examines content clarity and effectiveness, information needs of individuals, work groups, departments and divisions; non-verbal communications and corporate culture issues and communication impacts on motivation and performance.

Figure 11.3 Image management

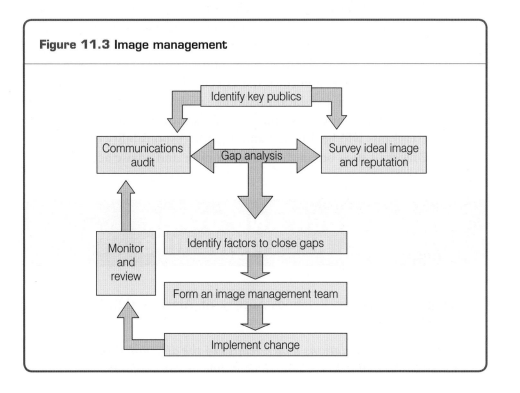

factors contributing to the gap are analysed and the means of closing that gap in perceptions sought.

RESEARCH AND COUNSELLING

Although outlined in the Mexico Statement (see page 248), this element of public relations is often underrepresented particularly in relation to marketing communications. Yet as early as 1922, Edward Bernays, in a book entitled *Crystallizing Public Opinion*, talked about the 'new profession of public relations counsel'. In this he explained that public relations counsellors were different from press agents and publicists of the day and that they were using:

> the knowledge generated by social science to understand public opinion, public motivation, public relations techniques, and methods for modifying group points of view. The objective of the public relations counsel was to interpret the organisation to the public and the public to the organisation. (Grunig and Hunt 1983: 3)

This act of mediation between the organization and its public is an important one. The responsibilities are to evaluate public attitudes and ensure that the policies and procedures of an organization are in line with it. Public attitude may be measured through survey methods or more qualitative methodologies such as focus groups (see Chapter 6). Public attitude may be informed and/or hardened by 'influencers' such as the media. In recent years various media have been responsible for creating reaction to everything from the euro to national team management and much more in between. Public opinion changes and the Public Relations Officer should understand its implications for the organization. For example attitudes to public smoking have changed in the past few years. From toleration many non-smokers have hardened their opposition based on the evidence of the effects of passive smoking and this has led to a proposal for legislation banning smoking in public places. Any organization involved not only in the cigarette sector but businesses such as bars and restaurants will be affected and it is the responsibility of the Public Relations Officer of such organizations to monitor and advise accordingly.

SHAREHOLDER AND OTHER FINANCIAL RELATIONSHIPS

According to the Public Relations Society of America (PRSA 1995: 22) financial public relations is:

> that area of Public Relations which relates to the dissemination of information that affects the understanding of stockholders

(shareholders) and investors generally concerning the financial position and prospects of a company and includes among its objectives the improvement of relations between corporations and their stockholders.

This is probably an oversimplification because it is not only existing shareholders that are important, as financial intermediaries can have a considerable influence on these or indeed future shareholders. The main financial publics are, therefore:

- Current shareholders
- Prospective shareholders
- Financial intermediaries (banks, credit rating agencies, stock-markets, etc.)
- Financial media (specialist financial press such as the *Financial Times* and the *Wall Street Journal* as well as the financial sections of national and international newspapers).

Financial publics are highly active and interested in a company's financial status and react to information on this accordingly. With 'good news' (frequently transmitted through the financial media) existing shareholders may decide to retain or extend their investment whilst new shareholders help stabilize or increase share prices. Organizational stability may attract a favourable **credit rating** from **ratings agencies** such as Dun and Bradstreet and Standard and Poor, which will affect the organization's ability to lend, and the rate on which that loan is based.

Credit rating
Based on the financial integrity of the organization, ratings are set by ratings agencies such as Dun and Bradstreet and Standard and Poor.

Ratings agencies
Organizations which monitor companies and establish credit ratings based on commercial risk. These ratings affect the company's ability to lend, and the rate on which that loan is based.

Shareholders, in public limited companies, are its financial backbone. In essence the primary objective of such organizations should be the creation of maximum shareholder value, although short-term management-driven objectives are often seen to be in opposition to this. Shareholders generally come in two types. The institutional investor who buys and retains shares as a fund-raising device on behalf of pension-funds, unit trusts and other investment mediums. In this instance loyalty to a particular company is small as the institutional investor looks for the best return on behalf of his/her fund or investment trust. At the other end of the scale are the private investors. These investors are also looking for a return on their investment, however, rather than invest in general cross-market funds (e.g. investment trusts) they buy shares from one or more specific organizations. If a publicly quoted company has a large number of private shareholders they can prove to be a very powerful constituency. It is widely believed that Philip Green's failure to take over Marks and Spencer in 2005 was due in large part to the loyalty of private shareholders to the existing management.

The responsibilities under the heading of financial public relations are varied and diverse. They include:

- The preparation and distribution of financial news releases.
- Media placement of newsworthy, positive stories about the organization and ensuring company spokesperson involvement where pertinent.
- Production and circulation of annual reports and the conduct of shareholder meetings.

- The production and distribution of shareholder newsletters and/or the maintenance of shareholder websites.
- In the event of financial activity (e.g. takeover, share issue, buy-back, etc.) the management of news and information to relevant stakeholders.

An in-house Public Relations Officer's (PRO) responsibility for financial public relations may not extend beyond existing shareholder relations and day-to-day contact with the financial media. Other financial public relations functions may be associated directly with the organization's Financial Director. Often specialized agencies (see Box 11.2) are used on a contract basis particularly in relation to complex financial activity.

@

For examples of public relations agencies look at: **www.greenpr.co.uk** and **www. nelsonbostock.com.**

Box 11.2 Selecting a public relations agency

The Public Relations Consultants Association, an industry body representing many public relations agencies has produced a guide to selecting the right sort of public relations agency.

Generalized Benefits
- Agencies who provide the potential to translate key learning/successes from one market to another.
- Agencies who generally have a bigger market and geographical spread and who can reach those audiences required by the organization.
- Agencies who have a bigger base of staff and in-house resources to call upon.
- Agencies that have access to more or higher supplier discounts.
- Generalized agencies who have specialized departments.

Specialized Benefits
- Agencies who have specialist expertise of markets, audiences and/or communication streams.
- Agencies that understand niche markets/audiences and how to communicate with them effectively.
- Agencies who are closely networked with key opinion formers within niche markets.
- Agencies who provide smaller working teams and, therefore, the potential for the development of client–consultancy relationships.
- Agencies reputed to have lower overheads.

Source: Based on *Marketing*, 26 January 2005 and www.prca.org.uk.

LOBBYING[6]

Public affairs
A specialist area of practice within public relations concerned with public policy-making, legislation and regulation that may affect the interests of the organization.

As with financial public relations, lobbying is seen as a specialist area of public relations. In many organizations this is often called **public affairs** to emphasize that it largely involves relationships with governmental organizations and,

---

[6]There is some dispute over the origin of the term. The name derives either from the practice of UK Members of Parliament meeting constituents and others in the lobby of the House of Commons or from the habit of US politicians meeting petitioners in the lobby of the Willard Hotel in Washington.

perhaps, to distance it from the somewhat tarnished reputation of some lobbyists. Public affairs has been defined as 'a specialist area of practice within public relations concerned with those relationships involved in public policy-making, legislation and regulation that may affect the interests of organisations and their operations' (White 1991: 55). Lobbying, meanwhile, has been described as 'the specialist part of public relations that builds and maintains relationships with government primarily for the purpose of influencing legislation and regulation' (Cutlip *et al.* 1994: 17). The differences appear to be more semantic than substantial.

Lobbying is all about knowledge and relationships. The knowledge of how the various levels of government work and how they can be best influenced is coupled with access to those people (not necessarily the final decision-makers) who can best affect it. These may be politicians, civil servants or other influencers. Some lobbyists successfully use the media to put their case and build up public opinion for and against an issue. Such is the specialist nature of lobbying that in all but the largest corporations lobbying is usually undertaken either by trade or management associations (e.g. the Confederation of British Industry (CBI)) or specialist lobbying agencies.

CRISIS MANAGEMENT

Response to crisis situations has become an important function of public relations. According to Hayes (2001) the best way to destroy one's reputation is to be ill-prepared for all types of crises and to fail to take a stand on appropriate issues. A crisis is not a day-to-day problem but one that has the capacity to severely damage the organization. The crisis may be caused by all manner of reasons but it is likely to have one or more of the following characteristics (White and Mazur 1995):

- A high degree of threat to life, safety, or to the continuing existence of the organization.
- Time pressure (ensuring that decision-makers have to work urgently).
- Stress placed upon those responsible for managing the situation.

Examples of possible crises include industrial accidents, environmental problems, hostile takeovers, strikes, kidnapping, product tampering, product recall, security leaks, unethical behaviour, workplace violence, employee fraud and government action (Baines *et al.* 2004; Pearson 2002). Managing the response to the situation is of paramount importance as it may not be the incident *per se* that causes the critical episode but the company's response to it (Stewart 1998). See Box 11.3.

Although crisis management is not a day-to-day activity preparedness should be regularly on the agenda. Active preparedness is described as 'a systematic approach that engages the whole organisation in efforts to avert crises that may affect the firm and manage those that do' (Baines *et al.* 2004: 327). Crisis

> ### Box 11.3 Cadbury
>
> In June 2006 Cadbury announced that salmonella had been reported at one of their production plants and that they were recalling from retailers all the chocolates that might be affected. The recall was announced on a Friday and by the following Monday a Cadbury spokeswoman claimed that the vast majority of affected products had been removed from the shelves but did not indicate what was left to be cleared.
>
> When further details became known Cadbury were criticized for the time taken between when they discovered the outbreak (January 2006) and when it was confirmed to the Food Standards Agency (FSA) and environmental health officials. According to *Marketing* (28 June 2006) questions have been raised as to whether Cadbury withheld information about the contamination until after the key Easter sales period. Cadbury's response was that it did not report the contamination because the levels, which were below the authorized threshold, were low.

@

Getting your message out: **www. prnewswire.com.**

management is dealing with the sporadic, the unlikely and the unpredictable so how can a crisis be foreseen? Although a specific crisis is unlikely to be predictable it is, however, possible to imagine exceptional situations in advance. On a university campus, for example, the possibility of fire, flooding, etc. may cause those responsible for drawing up contingency measures to develop emergency procedures. Similarly the Public Relations Officer may wish to ensure that s/he has important contact details internally and externally to be able to respond to a crisis effectively and responsibly. More unlikely scenarios, such as attack or occupation, may not be considered in detail but the general response to a crisis situation (e.g. the formation of crisis team) can and should be planned for.

Although the media have no right to information, they may often demand it and it is part of crisis decision making as to what information should be released at what time. However, attempts to deny responsibility or conceal information in crisis situations (e.g. Jarvis during the Potters Bar rail crash or Ford's attempt to blame Firestone for a series of accidents in the early 1990s) can often backfire, whereas openness (e.g. New York Mayor, Rudolf Giuliani's handling of the aftermath of the World Trade Center attacks on 11 September 2001 or Transport for London's response to the 7 July 2005 bombings – see Case study 11.1) is, generally, seen as a positive move in most situations.

COMMUNITY RELATIONS

This aspect of public relations acknowledges the importance of the organization maintaining good, or at least respectable, relationships with local, national and wider communities. In addition to wishing to generally avoid 'bad press' there is the likelihood, with consumer goods and services companies in particular, that these communities are, or can influence, your customers. Thus some organizational policies can have considerably wide-ranging effects such as Barclays Bank's involvement in apartheid South Africa or Reebok's purchasing strategy, which both led to calls for a consumer boycott of these organizations. On a more localized note it is likely that current and future employees are going to come from communities influenced by the activities of the organization.

Summary

The heading 'public relations' covers a wide and diverse set of responsibilities that can affect the organization (and its brands) in widely different ways. From encouraging well-being and association through publicity, to lobbying for legislation which will benefit the company and from maintaining or enhancing financial standing to research and counselling the public relations process is at the heart of an organization's marketing communications.

This chapter examined the part public relations plays in the modern organization. In particular it looked at publicity and media management and how this can be managed to the benefit of the organization. It examined the growing importance of the research and counselling function within public relations and analysed the part played by corporate image and how this might be managed. Internal marketing and internal communication were considered and its importance noted. More specialist areas such as financial relations, lobbying and crisis management were examined and the importance of community relations noted.

Review questions

1 How would you define public relations and why?
2 List a selection of public relations' publics.
3 What are the main responsibilities of public relations in relation to research and monitoring?
4 Who are the main financial publics?
5 What is 'lobbying' and what does it entail?
6 Why might public relations be used for community relations?
7 What was the 'Mexico Statement'?
8 Why might a 'clippings service' be of value?
9 Would you consider publicity to be free advertising?
10 What do you associate with the term 'optimum image'?

Discussion questions

1 Public relations is often concerned with managing a company's image. However this means different things to different people. What are the different ways that image could be interpreted?

2 What might be the responsibilities under the heading of financial public relations and under what circumstances might organizations undertake financial public relations activities?

3 How might you select a public relations agency and what might the problems of selection be?

Further reading

Brody, E.W. and Brody, E.W. (2005) 'The brave new world of public relations: a look back', *Public Relations Quarterly*, Winter, 50 (4): 31–4. The article looks at the *history* of public relations and how the field has changed since its inception.

Edelman, D.J. (2006) 'The golden age of public relations', *Public Relations Quarterly*, Spring, 51 (1): 20–1. A discussion on how public relations is beginning to be seen by corporate leaders as an essential part of an advertising and marketing strategy.

Robinson, D. (2006) 'Public relations comes of age', *Business Horizons*, 49 (3). Public relations now employs such techniques as event sponsorship, stunt marketing, charitable activities, and placement and this paper defines contemporary public relations practice and develops rules for successful implementation of these modern approaches to promotion.

Scammell, Alison (2006) 'Business writing for strategic communications: the marketing and communications mix', *Business Information Review*, 23 (1): 43–9. Provides an outline of the role of business writing in the communications strategy and highlights that writing is a fundamental business skill and offers an overview of some of the tools, methods, formats and media available for use in a communications campaign.

Chapter references

Baines, P., Egan, J. and Jefkins, F. (2004) *Public Relations: Contemporary Issues and Techniques*, Oxford: Elsevier Butterworth-Heinemann.

Barrand, D. (2004) 'Promoting change', *Marketing*, 6 October: 43–5.

Briggs, W. and Tuscon, M. (1993) 'Public relations versus marketing', *Communications World*, March, San Francisco, CA: IABC.

Center, A.H. and Jackson, P. (2003) *Public Relations Practice*, 6th edn, Englewood Cliffs, NJ: Prentice Hall.

CIPR (2006) www.ipr.org.uk.

Copley, P. (2004) *Marketing Communications Management*, Oxford: Butterworth-Heinemann.

Crimmins, J. and Horn, M. (1996) 'Sponsorship: from management ego trip to marketing success', *Journal of Advertising Research*, July/August: 11–21.

Cutlip, S.M., Center, A.H. and Broom, G.M. (1994) *Effective Public Relations*, Englewood Cliffs, NJ: Prentice Hall.

Dolphin, R.R. and Fan, Y. (2000) 'Is corporate communications a strategic function?', *Management Decision*, 38/2: 99–107.

Grunig, J. E. and Hunt, T. (1983) *Managing Public Relations*, New York: Holt, Rinehart & Winston.

Grunig, J. and Hunt, T. (1984) *Managing Public Relations*, Cincinnati: Thomson Learning.

Harrison, S. (2000) *Public Relations,* 2nd edn, London: Thomson Learning.

Hayes, R. (2001) 'The importance of crisis management', *Intermedia*, 29 (4): 36.

Hoek, J. (1999) 'Sponsorship', in P.J. Kitchen (ed.), *Marketing Communications: Principles and Practice*, London: Thomson, pp. 361–80.

Hunt, T. and Grunig, J.E. (1994) *Public Relations Techniques*, Fort Worth: Harcourt Brace College Publishers.

Jefkins, F. (1994) *Public Relations Techniques*, 2nd edn, Oxford: Butterworth Heineman.

Jefkins, F. and Yadin, D. (1998) *Public Relations*, 5th edn, London: Prentice Hall.

Kotler, P. and Mindak, W. (1978) 'Marketing and public relations – should they be partners or rivals?', *Journal of Marketing*, 42, October: 13–20.

Moloney, K. (2006) *Rethinking Public Relations*, 2nd edn, London: Routledge.

Pearson, C. (2002) 'A blueprint for crisis management', *Ivey Business Journal*, 66 (3): 63–9.

PRSA (1995) 'Code of conduct', *Public Relations Journal*, June: 22–5.

Siegle, S. (2004) 'PR Leagues Top 100', *Marketing*, 19 May: 41–9.

Siegle, S. (2005) 'PR Leagues Top 100', *Marketing*, 25 May: 41–50.

Smith, P.R. and Taylor, J. (2002) *Marketing Communications: An Integrated Approach*, 3rd edn, London: Kogan Page.

Stewart, K. (1998) 'An exploration of customer exit in retail banking', *International Journal of Bank Marketing*, 16 (1): 6–14.

Theaker, A. (2001) *The Handboook of Public Relations*, London: Routledge.

White, J.B. (1991) 'Japanese auto makers help U.S. suppliers become more efficient', *Wall Street Journal*, 9 September, AI.

White, J. and Mazur, L. (1995) *Strategic Communications Management: Making Public Relations Work*, London: Addison-Wesley/Economist Intelligence Unit.

CASE STUDY 11.1

Media management of the 7 July London bombings

On the 7 July 2005, at 08.50, three simultaneous explosions on the London Underground, were followed by a further explosion just under an hour later on the Number 30 London bus in Tavistock Square. A total of 52 people were killed in what transpired to be one of the most devastating terrorist attacks, the capital city had witnessed. Within 10 minutes of the first explosions, it was clear that this was an incident of international importance and one that would lead the news headlines around the world during the days that followed. By 11.00 that day, over 250 requests for media interviews had been received by the TfL (Transport for London) press office, who by the end of the day, had received around 2000 phone calls. Hits on the press centre website rose from the daily average of 402, to a staggering 56 562 on the following day.

The TfL press team were in charge of crisis communication. Having undertaken crisis exercises in London, UK and overseas, the team were well trained for such an eventuality. However, prior to the bomb attacks the press team had been heavily involved in Live8 and the 2012 Olympic bid, which London won the day before the bombings. In the space of 24 hours, the team had to switch from managing a celebratory national story, to managing an unprecedented crisis. Five crisis communication objectives were established on the day of the incident:

- to inform the public to allow them to make travel decisions
- to support operational staff by reducing the impact of media activity
- to show that TfL, the emergency services, the GLA (Greater London Authority) and government were co-ordinated in their response

The 7 July bombings left the Transport for London press team to deal with massive levels of media attention.

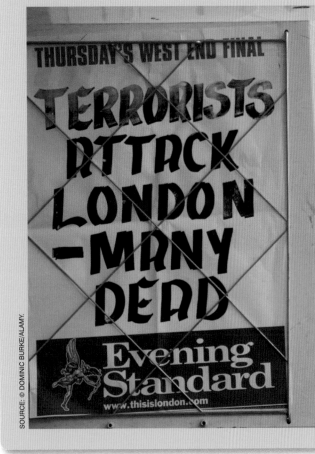 

SOURCE: © DOMINIC BURKE/ALAMY.

- to reinforce Transport for London's key message that passenger and staff safety is the top priority
- to minimize the long-term impact on passenger confidence.

In order to achieve these objectives the press team had to ensure that fast, accurate information was provided to the media, and that the media demand for access, was balanced with operational requirements. It was also imperative that co-ordination was maintained with Mayoral, emergency service and government teams, as well as across TfL itself. The press team also had to ensure that they would be in a position to sustain a professional operation over an unspecified period of time, in demanding circumstances.

After a quick risk assessment, and within 20 minutes of the initial explosions, six press officers were sent, in pairs, to Liverpool Street, Russell Square and Edgware Road tube stations to tackle questions from the media. In order to shorten lines of communication a press officer joined the NCC (Network Control Centre) to act as an information bridge. At 10.30, the first London resilience communications conference call took place.

The initial messages placed the emphasis on operational information and practical advice for travellers. The fast pace of events involved the evacuation of the entire tube network followed by the withdrawal of the London bus fleet and the suspension of the congestion charge. Buses were subsequently re-introduced within a matter of hours and the following day communication focused on the restoration of a full bus service and around 85 per cent of the tube network by the morning 'rush hour'.

Over the days that followed, the press office assisted in the management of three police press conferences, two Mayoral press conferences, two Mayoral visits to stations and two royal visits. It also organized a multi-language briefing for the foreign press association and managed over 270 media broadcast and print interviews. Furthermore, it assisted operational staff by assigning press or British Transport Police officers to stations with large numbers of media, and maintained round-the-clock staffing during this period. Communication aimed to cover three key aspects:

- Security: this included urgent reminders not to leave bags.
- Recovery: it was important for the organization, their passengers and London as a whole that normal services resumed as quickly as possible.
- Professionalism: close liaison with staff, senior management and counsellors ensured that the demand from the media was managed without exposing staff to further trauma.

As a result of the prompt actions taken and the well-considered strategy underlying those actions, recovery was relatively quick, and passenger levels were soon back to normal. The crisis management strategy had not only dealt immediately with the priorities on the day itself, it had looked ahead to the challenges TfL would face in the days and weeks that followed.

The handling of media communication during the crisis earned the in-house team at TfL a high level of critical acclaim from within the public relations industry. It was one of the two top media relations case studies presented at the 2006 PRWeek 'PR and the Media Conference' and won the award for 'Crisis Communications' at the CIPR Excellence Awards 2006.

Case study questions

1 How could the management of TfL's crisis communications be assessed or evaluated?
2 What other activities could have been undertaken to restore passenger confidence as quickly as possible?
3 What lessons can be learned from TfL's handling of the crisis?
4 In the role of TfL press officer, how would you respond to the journalist who asks the question: 'Is it now safe to travel on London's buses and tube?'

Case study written by Nik Mahon, Faculty of Media, Arts and Society, Southampton Solent University (www.ipr.org.uk).

CHAPTER TWELVE

SPONSORSHIP AND PRODUCT PLACEMENT

LEARNING OBJECTIVES

Having completed this chapter you should be able to:

- Understand the place of sponsorship in the marketing communications mix.
- Recognize the reasons behind sponsorship's growth in recent decades.
- Discuss the theory underpinning sponsorship.
- Determine the various sponsorship types and the factors which make them viable.
- Discuss the advantages and disadvantages of sponsorship.

INTRODUCTION

Sponsorship has never been as prominent in the marketing communications mix as it is today. As one industry commentator notes (Duffy 2004: 19):

> some marketers have long held the belief that, with relevantly matched and effectively leveraged sponsorship, brand loyalty can be built between consumers and sponsors; that sponsorship has the power to build strong brands and drive the bottom line better than any other single form of communication.

In spite of its apparent power as a marketing activity, there does seem to be ambiguity about its role (Dolphin 2003). The area of research that incorporates sponsorship is closely associated with both public relations, within whose management remit sponsorship often falls, and advertising, which is commonly an integral part of any sponsorship arrangement. There is a reasonable argument for placing sponsorship within the field of advertising as the most frequent objective of sponsorship activities is that of creating awareness. This, however, excludes the element of philanthropy (which is still sometimes evident) and/or the risk that is associated with some forms of sponsorship. Nevett (1982: 194) writing at a time of great expansion of sponsorship perhaps reflects yet another viewpoint when he suggested 'the future of sponsorship seems to lie not so much in its effectiveness as an advertising medium as in providing a means for companies to parade their social consciences in public'.

Modern sponsorship, however, whilst maintaining in some quarters an element of philanthropy and social consciousness is primarily viewed as a commercial arrangement. For big-name brands who are targeting consumers, sponsorship today is as carefully thought through as any other marketing tool.

WHAT IS SPONSORSHIP?

Sponsorship is about involvement outside of an individual or company's normal range of activities. A sponsor is 'the provider of funds, resources or services to an individual event or organisation in return for some rights and associations usually to be used for commercial advantage' (Copley 2004: 289).

This definition does not necessarily exclude philanthropic support as there is frequently an association between social recognition and commercial advantage albeit a tenuous one. Some sponsors do see sponsorship as 'enlightened self-interest' (Smith 1998). However, as Warner Canto of American Express notes[1] 'if your primary goal is to donate to a cause, the experts say it's a lot less complicated simply to write a check (cheque)'. A cynic might suggest no sponsorship is undertaken without at least the hope of some commercial (or personal) pay-back.

Not withstanding the complex and sometimes personal objectives of some sponsorship, within a marketing communications strategy it is essentially a commercial-based activity wherein access to the target audience of one party is made accessible to another in return for finance, services or resources.

The growth of sponsorship in the last two decades of the twentieth century owed much to difficulties associated with advertising. Not only were the costs increasing but some sectors, notably the cigarette industry, were excluded by regulation from advertising on television, radio and, ultimately, all other media. Brands such as Marlboro, John Player, Benson & Hedges and Silk Cut moved heavily into sponsorship which was not (at that time) subject to such restrictions. Formula 1 and other motor racing events and most snooker championships were soon heavily under the patronage of one or other of the cigarette brands. This coincided, in the UK, with a relaxation in the rules concerning the broadcasting of sponsored sports events. The expansion in the number of such events, partly driven by the growth in available leisure time, further provided more sponsorship opportunities.

In a world of communications, sponsorship was coming to be seen as a cost-effective alternative to traditional advertising. For the majority of sponsors, however, this was not the only or even the main promotional activity undertaken

@

Sponsorship news can be found at:
www.sponsorship.com.

[1]Quoted in Bovée et al. 1995: 510.

by them. Indeed, sponsorship is one marketing communications tool that should never be used in isolation. Rather it is supported by other marketing communications tools including advertising, sales promotion and public relations. In the 2000 Olympics, for example, whereas approximately 20 per cent of the communications expenditure was sponsorship, over 50 per cent was advertising. In general terms it is suggested that whatever the initial cost of a sponsorship deal the sponsor will spend about 150 per cent with other marketing communications tools, again notably advertising (Barrand 2004).

WHY SPONSORSHIP WORKS

Whilst sponsorship clearly creates awareness and may be the basis of trial, there is no direct evidence to suggest that increased awareness leads directly to increased sales, although there is a perceived relationship (see Chapter 5). The building of longer-term associations must also play a part. There are a number of theories as to why sponsorship may work including those associated with the behavioural and cognitive paradigms discussed in Chapter 3. In behavioural terms enjoyment of a sponsored event may act as a reinforcement of previous experiences with the brand. The evidence certainly seems to suggest that consumers do feel some gratitude towards the sponsor of an event but whether this is affective linking, however, is harder to confirm (Blythe 2000). From a cognitive perspective it is believed that sponsorship, as with advertising, works through associations that consumers make with the brand and the event or otherwise being sponsored. Positive brand associations may even be more achievable through sponsorship than advertising as it may be perceived as less commercial. Consumers may make a judgement based on the fit between the event and the sponsorship in that the greater the degree of compatibility the more readily acceptable the sponsorship is likely to be (Fill 2002). Association between the sponsor and sponsored event is, therefore, important but emotional involvement (attitude strength, actual

Box 12.1 Crock of gold

In August 2006 the England cricket team were preparing for the Third NPower Test Match against Pakistan at Headingley without their captain Michael Vaughan who was recovering from a knee operation. On the day before the match began Vaughan visited the training ground to offer help and advice to stand-in captain Andrew Strauss – with the aid of crutches sponsored by NatWest Bank. According to the *Daily Mirror* when it comes to corporate branding Vaughan is 'a crock of gold'.

Source: *Daily Mirror*, 4 August 2006.

purchases and word-of-mouth) is also crucial in terms of recall because of the way attitudes to brands are formed (Copley 2004: 294).

Crimmins and Horn (1996) argue that the persuasive impact of sponsorship is determined in terms of the strength of the links generated between the brand and the sponsorship and the effect on the target audience. They suggest that the persuasion impact (PI) was a combination of the strength and duration of the sponsorship link and the gratitude and perceptual change associated with it and proposed the equation $PI = SL \times DL \times (GL + PL)$. In this model 'strength of link' (SL) refers to how integrated the marketing communications is with the event. For example sponsors who fail to advertise at such events are being less than fully effective at building links with the attending and viewing public. Duration of the link (DL) refers to how long the exposure can be maintained. For example, main sponsors at the Olympic Games may have up to four years association with the event. A feeling of gratitude (GL) may seem far-fetched, however, in a survey 60 per cent of US adults said they try to buy products that support the Olympics and felt they were contributing by buying a sponsor's products (Fill 2002). Finally the change in perception (PL) due to the sponsorship is introduced into the equation. Whilst not suggesting that such a calculative model can truly represent sponsorship it highlights those aspects that are seen as important for a successful sponsorship campaign.

Hoek (1999: 366) offers an alternative model (see Figure 12.1) which emphasizes the advantages of sponsorship from the consumer perspective. This suggests that it will be the consumer's attitude to the event, to the commercialization surrounding the event and their ultimate behavioural outcome (e.g. awareness) that determines the success or otherwise of sponsorship. Again it throws some light upon the perceived processes going on.

@

More information on sports and arts sponsorship can be found at:
www.sports-sponsorship.co.uk and
www.uksponsorship.com/arts1.htm.

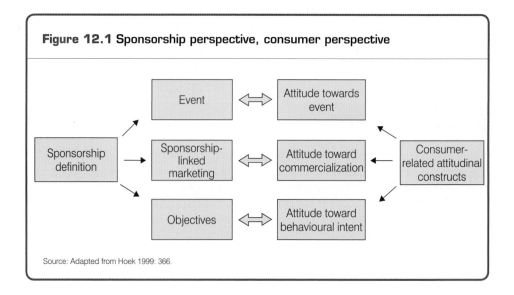

Figure 12.1 Sponsorship perspective, consumer perspective

Source: Adapted from Hoek 1999: 366.

SPONSORSHIP TYPES

Sponsorship may be divided in to several, not exclusively mutual, types. These are:

- Arts sponshorship
- Events sponsorship
- Sports sponsorship
- Broadcast sponsorship (and product placement)
- Cause-related sponsorship

Historically sponsorship was largely directed towards the arts. Personal sponsorship of musicians and artists by ruling families, church dignitaries and the growing number of wealthy traders, could be said to have supported and nurtured fine art and music throughout the centuries. The de Medici family's sponsorship of Michaelangelo and Mozart's support by both church and state are but two examples of a system of patronage that enabled the development of the arts throughout the world. In 1976 the Association for Business Sponsorship of the Arts (ABSA) was founded by a group of business leaders. This organization has been particularly influential in promoting arts sponsorship and today many major corporations are seen to promote the arts. ABSA was also a co-founder of the Comité Europeén pour le Rapprochement de L'Economie et de la Culture[2] (CEREC). Amongst the most recent UK corporate sponsorships of the arts are Barclays' £1.9 million sponsorship of the National Theatre, The British Museum, National Gallery and Tate Britain, Sainsbury's support of the Youth Orchestra series and Awards for Art Education and Lloyds' sponsorship of the BBC's Young Musician of the Year. Sponsorship of the arts, therefore, has clearly moved on from simply being a means of supporting the community to becoming a sophisticated means of targeting and positioning brands as part of the wider communications portfolio. Ernst & Young, for example, follow a wholly arts-based, hospitality associated, sponsorship strategy which, they maintain, offers the firm a personality that differs from that you would normally associate with them. In 2004 the company sponsored exhibitions at the Tate Britain, Tate Modern and the Victoria and Albert Museum. Research would seem to back art sponsorship's effectiveness. In a report by Performance Research over 50 per cent of those with an interest in the arts indicated they would almost always buy from a company that sponsored cultural events (Dolphin 2003).

Events sponsorship might be seen to come in two types; those events organized and supported wholly by the company (e.g. Red Bull's cart races) and the more traditional financial sponsorship of existing or future events (e.g. Millennium Dome sponsorships). Either way, there is a good argument that events are much more memorable and motivating than a more passive brand

[2]The European Committee for Business Arts and Culture.

message. In recent years there has been a growth in an offshoot of events marketing known as experiential marketing. An early example of this was Disney whose theme parks integrated the brand into a consumer experience. A more recent example is the Guinness experience in Dublin. This is not just a museum or showcase but more an interactive theatrical event.

Sports sponsorship has grown incrementally over the past few decades. Its popularity is derived from the ability of some sports at the top level to attract large audiences and extensive media coverage. Demand for top-level sponsorship is high and this is reflected in the costs. For example a title sponsorship of a Formula 1 team ranges from £15 million to £35 million (Gillis 2005). Such is the demand to sponsor some football events that as well as the teams, the ball, the stadiums (e.g. JJB Stadium, Emirates Stadium) and even the referees (by Specsavers in the Scottish Premiership) have been made available for sponsorship. In 2003 Barclays signed a three-year £57 million deal with the Football Association for the top English league to be known as the Barclays Premiership and associated rights. In the same year in the USA, the National Football League (NFL) signed an $18 million three-year deal with IBM. From 2007 to 2014 there will be six top-tier sponsors of football's governing body FIFA events (including the 2010 and 2014 World Cups). They include Sony, Hyundai and Adidas who will pay a total of between £160 million and £180 million each (Gillis 2005).

The largest sporting event in the world is the Olympic Games. In a survey by Sponsorship Research 81 per cent of participants associated the Olympic rings with success and high standards and it inevitably attracts those companies who wish to be associated with these attributes. The first Olympic Games to be televised widely was the 1960 event in Rome when it was broadcast live to 18 European countries, time-delayed to the USA, Canada and Japan and was supported by 46 brands (Britcher 2004). At the Olympic Games in Sydney in 2000 over 3.7 billion people (over half the world's population) saw one

Box 12.2   Top teams by sponsorship income World Cup 2006

Team	Income	Primary Sponsors
1 England	£49.1m	Umbro, McDonald's, Carlsberg, Nationwide, Pepsi
2 Italy	£27.6m	Puma, TIM, Mapei
3 France	£25.5m	Adidas, Caisse d'Eparne, Brioche Pasquier, SFR
4 Japan	£16.6m	Kirin, Adidas, Saison Card, International, Family Mart, Fujifilm, JAL, Nissan
5 Brazil	£16.6m	Vivo, Ambev, Coca-Cola, Nike
6 Germany	£10.4m	Mercedes-Benz, Adidas, Coca-Cola, Lufthansa, McDonald's, Siemems
7 Spain	£8.7m	Adidas, Toyota, Santa Monica Sports, Mahou
8 USA	£7.7m	Budweiser, Gatorade, The Home Depot, Nike, Hyundai, Panasonic
9 Netherlands	£7.3m	ING, Adecco, Heineken, Nuon, Tele2, Staatasloterij, Super de Boer, Nike
10 Switzerland	£1.8m	Sporttip, Swisscom, Puma, Credit Suisse, Carlsberg, Swiss Life

Source: *Marketing*, 10 May 2006.

or more of the events. Control of Olympic Games sponsorship rights lie at various levels: at Olympic Organisation level; National Olympic Association level; and individual sports association level, which can lead to confusion (see ambush marketing). At the highest level are 'The Olympic Partners' (TOPs). Established in 1985, TOP sponsors contract with the Olympic Committee for a period of four years prior to the games. For the 2000 Games TOPs sponsors included Coca-Cola, John Hancock, IBM, Kodak, McDonald's, Panasonic, Samsung, Sports Illustrated/Time Inc., UPS, Visa and Xerox each paying an approximately $50 million for the privilege and raising a total

@ For more information on marketing and London 2012 look at: **www.london2012. org/en/olympic_marks.htm.**

Carlsberg was a primary sponsor for the England football team at the 2006 World Cup.

of $579 million for the Games. The TOPs sponsorship from 2001 to 2004 was $603 million approximately, equivalent to what was spent on tickets for the Games (see Box 12.3). Coca-Cola, who have sponsored every Olympic Games since 1928 and were an original TOP sponsor, use the event as a centrepiece of their brand marketing. At the 2004 Games the company used the Games as a platform to promote a relatively low-key product Powerade on an international stage (Britcher 2004). Sports sponsorship in general is particularly attractive to marketers as it enables the targeting on large numbers of consumers sharing similar characteristics. On the downside it may have reached a point where costs have become so inflated that return on investment must be becoming questionable.

Broadcast sponsorship is when an individual or organization, other than the makers or broadcasters of the programme, sponsor all or part of the production and/or transmission costs in return for the right to promote its brand or other interests. In the USA, broadcast sponsorship is an established communications medium (see Box 12.4) with nearly 90 per cent of network advertising time being sold as participation. In the UK Cadbury's sponsorship of long-running 'soap' *Coronation Street* began in 1996 and is said to cost the company £10 million each year when all promotional materials are taken into account. Other companies notably HSBC and Stella Artois are also getting more involved in programme sponsorship. The market has a considerable way to grow before competing with television commercials. In 2004, the

Box 12.3 Olympic games revenue

	1997–2000	2001–2004
Broadcast	$ 1850 million	$ 2240 million
TOP sponsors	$ 579 million	$ 603 million
Host sponsors	$ 655 million	$ 736 million
Ticketing	$ 625 million	$ 608 million
Licensing	$ 66 million	$ 81 million
Totals	$ 3770 million	$ 4260 million

Source: International Olympic Committee, *Marketing*, 20 September 2005.

Box 12.4 Soap operas

The history of the 'soap opera' in the USA is inexorably tied to sponsorship. In the 1920s daytime radio attracted few advertisers because it was thought that housewives did not have time to listen to the radio. In 1932 the Blackett-Sample-Hummert agency in Chicago began producing long-running, sentimental, human interest stories with continuing characters in daily instalments. One of the most enduring was 'Oxydol's Own Ma Parker' which ran for over 27 years. The association of Oxydol and other detergent manufacturers with these shows led to them being labelled 'soap operas'.

Source: Sivulka (1998).

total UK television sponsorship was estimated at £100 million compared to £4 billion in traditional spot advertising. It is anticipated, however, that this gap will narrow considerably in future years.

Although not strictly sponsorship *per se* product placement is an area of substantial growth and should be discussed alongside broadcast sponsorship. Product placement is defined by the US Association of National Advertisers (ANA)[3] as 'the convergence of advertising and entertainment industries where a brand message is integrated within the appropriate context as part of the interaction', which covers a broad range of potential uses. It is not, however, a new phenomena, with its origins in the 1890s motion picture industry when Lever Brothers placed their soap products in some of the earliest films. In the 1930s Warner Brothers and Buick entered into a ten-film product placement arrangement and in this and subsequent decades US tobacco companies regularly paid movie stars to use their brand on-screen (Hudson and Hudson 2006). It has been since 1982 (when ET followed a trail of Reese's Pieces chocolate, which led to a reported 65 per cent rise in sales) that the number of placements has grown to majestic proportions. The use of Ray-Ban sunglasses in the 1986 film *Top Gun* is credited with turning around the company's performance. In the 1997 film *Tomorrow Never Dies* the automobile company BMW supplied seventeen model 750L vehicles worth an estimated £75 000 each, so replacing the Aston Martin as the traditional mode of transport for James Bond. In addition the film included product placements from Visa, Avis, Smirnoff, Heineken, Omega and Ericsson. In the 2002 film *Minority Report* there were appearances by Lexus, Guinness, American Express, *USA Today*, Pepsi and Gap. More recently still Galaxy chocolate featured prominently in *Bridget Jones: The Edge of Reason* and in Will Smith's film *Hitch* there were reported to be over 50 brands featured. For the communications industry product placement is designed to lead to increased awareness and a more positive attitude towards that brand. According to research by Mediaedge:cia, 61 per cent of film goers said they noticed brands promoted this way and 30 per cent said that they could be persuaded to buy a brand having seen it in a film (Jones 2004).

In the US television industry product placement has been a major revenue earner since its inception. In addition to straightforward endorsement, brand-owners are looking at ways of incorporating the brand into the fabric of programming. Recently, for example, Colgate-Palmolive provided $50 000 budgets for *each* team on the reality television programme *The Apprentice* whose task it was to launch Crest's latest flavoured toothpaste (Hudson and Hudson 2006). **Advertising funded programming (AFP)** is a particular growth area. AFP is where a sponsor part funds the programme in return for product placement. Coca-Cola, BMW and Ford Motor Company have all adopted roles in programme producing.

In the UK the television regulator OFCOM's rules currently prevent brands from blurring the editorial/commercial line (Fry 2004). In Italy 'surreptitious advertising' is frowned upon and in France it is currently illegal (Hudson and

Product placement
The placement of product in films, television shows and video games for the purpose of publicity.

Advertising funded programming (AFP)
Where a sponsor part-funds the programme in return for product placement.

[3] www.ana.net.

Hudson 2006). Given that much satellite, cable and other digital television channels are largely outside the control of European television regulators, however, the likelihood is that the remaining restrictions may ultimately be withdrawn (see Minicase 12.1 below). Indeed the European public are already viewing product placements in US television programmes such as *Sex in the City* (Apple lap-top computers), *24* (Ford), *Friends* (US store Home Depot) and *Desperate Housewives* (Buick).

Product placement has also invaded the video-games industry. It is estimated that the video games business reached $11 billion in 2006 and, as has happened for decades, advertisers have followed audiences. As each game can cost up to $25 million to develop, game producers are anxious to attract revenue from as many sources as possible. The exposure of the brand is in two forms. Traditional advertising as the game downloads and the placement of brands within the game itself. It has been estimated[4] that by 2009 one-third of product placements in video games will be in the form of advergaming, where practitioners create a game around the brand rather than place their brand within a well-known title. On the Internet especially designed story-led commercials for brands such as those for Volvo are in the ascendancy. Consumers are also entreated to visit brand websites for 'extra-value' information and rewards.

Cause-related sponsorship is another growth area. Perhaps closest to the original philanthropic origins of sponsorship, contemporary cause-related marketing is, however, largely based on consumers' positive attitudes to organizations that support good causes. According to research by Business in the Community/Research International CSR 2003:

- 86 per cent of consumers agreed that when price and quality are equal they are more likely to buy a product associated with a cause.

Advergaming
Where a game is created around a brand.

MINICASE 12.1

Pushing the boundaries

The Flood is a made-for-television disaster thriller about a tidal wave hitting London. It is made by Power, the London-based production and distribution company whose credits include television spectaculars such as *Casanova*, *Colditz* and the *Virgin Queen* and funding has come from broadcasters including TF1 in France, RAI in Italy and CBC in Canada. Power's declared aim is to push back the boundaries of advertising involvement in television dramas. According to their Chief Executive Justin Bodles 'there is a clear market for advertisers to be involved in production and distribution of high-end programming and we want to drive that forward'. Mark Dineley, the company's Vice-president of Media Sales added that the potential lay in offering brands the right to use exclusive footage from the production 'to use in marketing and promotion campaigns'. It is assumed that Power will follow the example of US television producers by writing brands into the script.

Source: Meg Carter, *Guardian*, 31 January 2006.

[4] *Financial Post* 2005

- 61 per cent of consumers said they would change retail outlets for the same reason.

- 86 per cent of consumers agree that they have a more positive image of a company if they see that it is doing something to make the world a better place.

Sue Atkins, Director of Business in the Community believes cause-related marketing will grow substantially in the future. She says

people are cash-rich and time-poor so cause-related marketing fits beautifully into the way they go about their daily lives – they're going to the shops anyway and by making a selection for a cause-related marketing product or service, they can also make a contribution. (Murray 2002).

SPONSORSHIP OBJECTIVES

Sponsorship is usually seen as more than patronage, altruism or benefaction, although it can indeed help others whilst simultaneously achieving specific communication objectives (Smith 1998). Commercial sponsorship objectives may, for example, include:

- Awareness: making a target audience aware of the organization.
- Image building: associating the organization with a cause or event.
- Citizenship: developing bonds with a community.
- Alteration of perceptions: change people's attitude about a brand.
- Building trade relationships: extending hospitality (an estimated £750 million market) to clients at sponsored events.
- Motivating employees: building the reputation of the company and, in the case of charity sponsorship, actively encouraging the participation of staff.
- Media attention: leveraging the news value of the sponsorship.
- Shareholder reassurance: associating the organization with success and/or corporate altruism and/or corporate responsibility.

The advantages of sponsorship is that it can be more cost-effective than advertising and can enable organizations to target consumers (usually when they are relaxed and possibly more susceptible) on two levels; those of the immediate audience and those wider audiences to whom it may be transmitted or who come to hear about the sponsorship through other sources. It is difficult to watch or listen to any sports broadcast or read any sports section of a newspaper without the mention of the Barclays Premiership in England or the Bells Premiership in Scotland, the Carling Cup, Coca-Cola Championship, the Emirates and Reebok stadiums and many more. In the arts section, companies such as Bank of Scotland and Ernst & Young sponsor classical concerts. In the case of Ernst & Young it is selective targeting. The company claim they have entertained every FTSE 100[5] Chief Executive during a single season. Musical events targeted at a younger audience are sponsored by Pepsi, Visa and Tennent's and T-Mobile (who have sponsored concert tours by the Rolling Stones and Kylie Minogue). Such is the perceived value of sponsorship that you can now sponsor the possibility of having an event. For example, Granada sponsored Manchester's bid for the 2000 Olympics and BT, British Airways, Virgin Atlantic and EDF Energy each paid £1 million to be premier partners in London's (ultimately successful) 2012 Olympics bid.

Companies also use sponsorship as a differentiator. According to Nicki Major,[6] Head of sponsorship at Ernst & Young 'the majority of the public don't need to know who we are, so we aren't using it to generate mass profile but we are in a relationship-based business in a market where we all offer relatively similar products'. Sponsorship has one further advantage over most other forms of communication. It can overcome the barriers of language and culture. For international brands sponsorship of events that will be broadcast around the world ensure a powerful and consistent brand message.

The disadvantages of sponsorship are that many of the variables (weather, attendance, media coverage, etc.) are uncontrollable. It can also be seen, particularly in the arts, as undermining artistic integrity and/or an act of excessive corporate indulgence. Over-commercialization is a constant charge in the arts world. It is, however, unlikely that many arts venues could continue with their current output without some level of commercial sponsorship. Ethical concerns are also a consideration. In the USA the decision to link Tylenol with arthritis, through the Arthritis Foundation ran into trouble when the media questioned whether it was appropriate for an arthritis charity to be in partnership with one brand of painkiller (Murray 2002). Sponsored events can also become a focus for discontent. In April 2001 action by a group of students who were distributing leaflets reading 'no sweatshops' stopped the inauguration of a Nike-sponsored tournament at a school in Rome (Osmon 2004). There are also particular risks associated with personal sponsorships. In the 1998 World Cup Adidas' sponsorship of England football star David Beckham (and the associated advertising that accompanied it) was halted following Beckham's dismissal in the game against Argentina. Pepsi's sponsorship of Michael Jackson's world tour was immediately halted when he came under police investigation. There is a reasonable argument that there are yet further threats that can be associated with sponsorship, such as **negative association**, over-commercialization, **sponsorship clutter**, and evaluation problems. Negative associations can occur through the sponsorship of a controversial event or group that attracts both highly positive and negative associations. In the latter category the sponsorship of particular football teams can generate negative associations with rival fans. This is particularly

Negative association
The sponsoring of teams, individuals, etc. who engender hostility from some quarters.

Sponsorship clutter
When sponsorship and associated advertising becomes overpowering.

[5] *Financial Times* listing of the top 100 shares on the London Stock Exchange.
[6] Quoted in Gillis 2004: 37

Box 12.5   Who was wearing what at the 2006 World Cup?

Brand	Teams Sponsored	Players Sponsored
Nike	Brazil Holland Mexico Portugal USA Croatia Australia South Korea	Ronaldinho Ronaldo Thierry Henry Ruud van Nistelrooy Wayne Rooney
Adidas	Argentina Germany France Spain Trinidad and Tobago Japan	David Beckham Frank Lampard Arjen Robben Michael Ballack Zinedine Zidane Raúl Juan Roman Riquelme Kaká
Puma	Italy Poland Paraguay Ivory Coast Iran Angola Ghana Czech Republic Switzerland Togo Tunisia Saudi Arabia	Freddie Ljungberg Gabriel Heinze Jamie Carragher
Umbro	England Sweden	Michael Owen
Lotto	Ukraine Serbia and Montenegro	
Marathon	Ecuador	
Joma	Costa Rica	

Source: Owen Gibson 'Gloves off and kits on for football's other battle', *Guardian* 23 March 2006.

true when arch-rivals are involved (e.g. Arsenal and Tottenham Hotspur, A.C. Milan and Inter Milan). Such is the partisanship amongst supporters of Glasgow's Rangers and Celtic teams that for many years the only way to resolve this was to have one main sponsor for both clubs (Carling in the 2005/06 season). 'Sponsorship clutter' acknowledges the preponderance of sponsors particularly in high-profile events such as the Olympic Games, World Cup, the Super Bowl or Formula 1. In all these cases the events and teams seem over-burdened with sponsor's logos and advertising hoardings to the

Ambush marketing
The practice whereby another company, often a competitor, attempts to deflect some of the audience to itself and away from the sponsor.

possible detriment of the individual sponsor. Evaluation problems, seen as a particular problem with sponsorship, will be discussed later in this chapter.

Another threat is so-called **ambush marketing**. The phrase was first coined in the mid-1980s in response to competitive clashes between Kodak and Fuji during the 1984 Los Angeles Olympic Games (Hoek 1999). Meenaghan (1994: 77) defines ambush marketing as 'the practice whereby another company, often a competitor, attempts to deflect some of the audience to itself and away from the sponsor'. Examples of ambush marketing are shown in Minicase 12.2 below.

MINICASE 12.2

Ambush marketing

Ambush marketing is the sponsorship equivalent of a 'spoiler campaign'. The 1992 Olympics in Atlanta, as well as being dubbed the most over-commercialized, had numerous examples of ambush marketing. In the figure-skating event, whereas McDonald's were main sponsors, Wendy's, a fast-food competitor, sponsored US star Kristi Yamaguchi who attracted most attention from the US audience. In subsequent research Wendy's was seen to have generated greater awareness. In the same year the USA's basketball 'dream-team' was officially sponsored by

Dutch supporters pose ahead of their team's World Cup football match against the Ivory Coast at Stuttgart's Gottlieb-Daimler Stadium.

SOURCE: © ADRIAN DENNIS/AFP/GETTY IMAGES

Reebok and the team's tracksuits carried the Reebok logo. Several members of the team, however, endorsed Nike products and at the medal ceremony these players carried US flags to obscure the Reebok logo. Two days before the Men's 100 metres Linford Christie appeared at a press conference wearing contact-lenses with the Puma logo and pictures of this went around the world. This was a coup for Puma particularly as Reebok sponsored the event. Ambush marketing did not stop in Atlanta. In 1998 Adidas paid approximately £20 million to sponsor the football World Cup. Nike, however, sponsored nine of the sixteen teams including the favourites Brazil and, it was rumoured, were willing to spend an equivalent £20 million to highjack the coverage. In Euro 2004 (the European nations' football championship), the tournament was sponsored by Coca-Cola. Pepsi, however, had a £5 million sponsorship deal with David Beckam and a £20 million deal with the England team. David Beckham also had a £3 million personal deal with Adidas whereas he turned out in kit sponsored by Umbro. Wayne Rooney also had deals with Nike and Coke. Michael Owen meanwhile had a deal with supermarket ASDA when the official England partner was Sainsbury's. During the Athens 2004 Olympics, authorities either took down or covered with sheets 'illegal' posters around the Olympic venues. However, they could not catch everyone. Anyone watching the Games in Brazil would have seen spectators wearing clothing with the Banco do Brazil logo even though the bank was not a sponsor. In the 2006 World Cup hundreds of Dutch fans had to watch the Netherlands–Ivory Coast match in their underwear after stewards at the stadium rumbled an ambush marketing ploy. The fans all turned up in bright orange lederhosen displaying the name of Dutch brewery Bavaria. Anheuser Busch's Budweiser was the official beer of the tournament and world football's governing body FIFA fiercely protects its sponsors and ordered that they could not enter the stadium with the lederhosen. According to FIFA they were alert to the kind of ambush marketing Bavaria had attempted. A Bavaria spokesman said it was 'going too far'.

SPONSORSHIP EVALUATION

As with public relations the most common methods of evaluation of sponsorship are through media audits. These calculate sponsorship exposure in terms of advertising costs and awareness, image or behaviour surveys. According to one leading practitioner[7] 'the usual method for sponsorship value measurement is to analyse brand exposure, compare it with (an) advertising rate card, and apply a discount'. Surveys have similar problems, as Hoek (1999: 371) notes:

> the difficulties, either logical, practical or both, in using awareness, image and behaviour as an indication of sponsorship effectiveness inevitably raises the question of whether sponsorship can be evaluated (and may explain why so few managers appear to undertake any formal research).

Nationwide, who are heavily involved in sports sponsorship, track the exposure generated in the major media and judge the return on investment using advertising rates. They then blend them with traditional consumer awareness research to give an overall gauge of the sponsorship effect. According to research by strategic sponsorship consultancy Redmandarin, 12 per cent of organizations who spend money on sponsorship fail to set clear objectives (Collett 2004) making measurement of success or failure even more difficult.

[7] Quoted in Rines 2003: 25.

It is also difficult to separate sponsorship from advertising, promotion, public relations and other marketing communications tools. Where does one element begin and another end? According to Richard Berry, Managing Director of sponsorship research specialists S:Com 'in many respects sponsorship is beginning to be seen as a media buying exercise' (Rines 2003: 24). There are also some signs that investment in sponsorships are not producing the returns of earlier times when perhaps their significance was undervalued. In the sporting field, in particular, inflated figures have made the true value of sponsorships hard to gauge (Rines 2003).

Despite the problems with evaluation and not withstanding the element of risk involved sponsorship is seen as a medium with considerable brand building potential. Dolphin (2003: 184) sums this up when he notes:

> *sponsorship – ambiguous or otherwise – has proved itself to practitioners and scholars alike as a cutting edge marcoms activity; one with the potential to reach specific audiences and to reach them with sharply focused messages and themes – ones capable of achieving and sustaining real competitive advantage. Thus sponsorship has become a global tool in an age when the global village has become a reality.*

Summary

This chapter has discussed the importance of sponsorship and product placement to the marketing communications mix. The different types of sponsorship were discussed including arts sponsorship, events sponsorship, sports sponsorship, broadcast sponsorship and cause-related sponsorship and the features of each reviewed. It analysed the reasons why sponsorship might work with reference to behavioural and cognitive paradigms, the persuasive impact of the sponsorship model and the consumer attitude model. The chapter went on to discuss the objectives behind sponsorship campaigns, including awareness, image building, citizenship, changing perceptions, external and internal relationship building and gaining media attention. The potential disadvantages were also analysed, including negative association, sponsorship clutter, over-commercialization and ambush marketing, and the risks evaluated. Finally the problems surrounding evaluation were highlighted.

Review questions

1 List the various types of sponsorship.
2 What is 'advergaming'?

3 List the key objectives of commercial sponsorship.

4 To what extent can commercial sponsorship be used to motivate employees?

5 What are the advantages of sponsorship?

6 Explain the term 'sponsorship clutter'.

7 Give an example of ambush marketing.

8 How easy is it to evaluate the benefits of a sponsorship campaign?

9 Define sponsorship.

10 What is broadcast sponsorship?

Discussion questions

1 Why do companies engage in sponsorship activities and what are the benefits they seek?

2 Under what circumstances might cause-related sponsorship be of benefit to an organization?

3 List the key disadvantages of sponsorship and discuss how a company might reduce these.

4 Does sponsorship work?

Further reading

Farrelly, F., Quester, P. and Greyser, S.A. (2005) 'Defending the co-branding benefits of sponsorship B2B partnerships: the case of ambush marketing', *Journal of Advertising Research*, Sep., 45 (3): 339–48.

Meenaghan, T. (1998) 'Current developments and future directions in sponsorship', *International Journal of Advertising*, 17 (1): 3–28. Providing insight into the development of sponsorship as a tool.

Pringle, H. and Binet, L. (2005) 'How marketers can use celebrities to sell more effectively', *Journal of Consumer Behaviour*, Mar., 4 (3): 201–14. This paper summarizes the key points about the use of celebrities in advertising and includes a more detailed analysis of the 'celebrity' through case histories.

Chapter references

Barrand, D. (2004) 'Promoting change', *Marketing*, 6 October: 43–5.

Belch, G. and Belch, M. (2001) *Advertising and Promotion: An Integrated Marketing Communications Perspective*, London: McGraw, Hill.

Blythe, J. (2000) *Marketing Communications*, Harlow: Financial Times, Prentice Hall.

Bovée, C.L., Thill, J.V., Dovel, G.P. and Wood, M.B. (1995) *Advertising Excellence*, New York: McGraw-Hill.

Britcher, C. (2004) 'Lessons from Athens', *Marketing,* 2 September: 15.

Collett, P. (2004) 'Sponsorship can prove worth', *Marketing*, 16 February: 33.

Copley, P. (2004) *Marketing Communications Management*, Oxford: Butterworth-Heinemann.

Crimmins, J. and Horn, M. (1996) 'Sponsorship: from management ego trip to marketing success', *Journal of Advertising Research*, July/August: 11–21.

CSR (2003) 'A cause related marketing product is bought every second in the UK', The Corporate Social Responsibility Newswire, http://www.csrwire.com/synd/business-ethics/article.cgi/2206.html, accessed 2 July 2006.

Dolphin, R.R. (2003) 'Sponsorship: perceptions on its strategic role', *Corporate Communications: An International Journal*, 8(3): 173–86.

Duffy, N. (2004) 'Doing it for the fans', *The Marketer*, 6 October: 18–19.

Fill, C. (2002) *Marketing Communications: Contexts, Strategies, and Applications*, 3rd edn, Harlow: Financial Times Prentice Hall.

Fry, A. (2004) 'Ad-funded TV tackles obstacles', *Marketing*, 9 June: 21.

Gillis, R. (2004) 'Alternative invitation', *Marketing*, 4 August: 27.

Gillis, R. (2005) 'FIFA turns the screw', *Marketing*, 20 April: 17.

Hoek, J. (1999) 'Sponsorship' in P.J. Kitchen (ed.), *Marketing Communications: Principles and Practice*, London: Thomson, pp. 361–80.

Hudson, S. and Hudson, D. (2006) 'Branded entertainment: a new communications technique or product placement in disguise', *Proceedings of the Academy of Marketing Conference 2006*, London: Middlesex University.

Jones, H. (2004) 'The silent screen idols', *The Marketer* 6 October: 16–17.

Meenaghan, T. (1994) 'Point of view: Ambush marketing – immoral or imaginative', *Journal of Advertising Research*, 34 (3): 77–88.

Murray, S. (2002) 'Cost-effective philanthropy', *Financial Times*, 4 December.

Nevett, T.R. (1982) *Advertising in Britain: A History*, London: Heinemann.

Osmon, M. (2004) 'When to take a back seat', *The Marketer*, 6 October: 2.

Pickton, D. and Broderick, A. (2001) *Integrated Marketing Communications*, Harlow: Financial Times, Prentice Hall.

Rines, S. (2003) 'Headline deals and half truths', *Marketing*, 27 November: 24–5.

Sivulka, J. (1998) '*Soap, Sex and Cigarettes*', Belmont, CA: Wadsworth Publishing Co.

Smith, P.R. (1998) *Marketing Communications: An Integrated Approach*, 2nd edn, London: Kogan Page.

Common Goal

Those in the know are increasingly using the words 'sponsorship partnership' rather than just sponsorship. Whereas a sponsorship speaks of a one-way relationship – we give you money, you display our logo – a partnership is the way the industry is moving – we work together for a mutual benefit. Partnerships can be struck between brands and individuals, teams, events, buildings, TV programmes, films – in fact almost anything that a brand feels it could exploit to fulfil its objectives. By following a set pattern, most brands can ensure they go into a sponsorship for the right reasons and make a success of it.

Objectives and brand fit

You don't buy a sports car to do the school run. A sponsorship needs to be bought according to your brand's specific requirements and objectives. Sponsorships can fulfil a number of requirements for a brand, ranging from awareness and increased sales to internal motivation and corporate entertaining or, as is most usual, a mixture of all. It would be impossible to buy the right property at the outset without knowing which of these your brand needed. In addition, different properties deliver different audiences – make sure you know your target audience and that the property with which you want to partner hits this demographic. Historically, successful sponsorships have the advantage of great brand fit with the sponsored property – look no further than Carling and football's Premiership, which makes a natural link between football, men and lager. To make a success of any sponsorship there needs to be full buy-in

Mark Cueto scores a try between Royal Bank of Scotland branded goalposts.

SOURCE: © LEO MASON/CORBIS

across the entire business. This is especially relevant in large organizations where major sponsorships require support across their various departments in order to gain full value.

Integration

Royal Bank of Scotland's sponsorship of rugby union's Six Nations Tournament provides a strong example of integrating a group-owned sponsorship across a number of consumer-facing brands. In addition to guiding the sponsorship through all internal marketing channels, processes have been created and facilitated to integrate the sponsorship across RBS's consumer brands including Royal Bank of Scotland, NatWest, Ulster Bank, Direct Line, Lombard, Drummonds, Coutts and Tesco Personal Finance. Some examples of how each subsidiary of the business used the sponsorship include:

Royal Bank of Scotland	RBS Six Nations clothes worn in branch
	RBS Six Nations Trophy toured branches and offices
	Merchandise Offer to all staff
NatWest	Perimeter boards at England games
	ATM 'golden ticket' promotion
Ulster Bank	Perimeter boards at stadium
	Staff incentives
Tesco Personal Finance	Toured the Six Nations trophy to 14 stores and offered customers a chance to meet players and be photographed with the trophy.

It is this type of integration that drives full value from a sponsorship across a number of brands within a group. Through-the-line support is only required if the sponsorship is targeted at a consumer market. If it is, then in an ideal world, this would mean a full through-the-line campaign involving advertising, public relations and marketing support.

Through-the-line support

Sponsorship is your brand in action, whereas advertising is what your brand says – the two complement each other. A successful sponsorship will interest consumers in your brand and an integrated advertising campaign will tell consumers what your brand can do for them. Run side by side, this can be extremely effective. Research shows that Coca-Cola's support of football directly increases the propensity to purchase its product among football fans. Its partnerships with the sport from the domestic to the global stage are always backed up by fully integrated marketing campaigns that are sympathetic to the fans. Of course, not all brands have Coca-Cola's money, but even a basic but creative public relations campaign can bring the sponsorship to life.

Creativity

This brings us to a key factor – creativity. Today, a lot of marketing activity across all sectors reaches an increasingly savvy audience. Marketers are looking for something that is going to provide cut-through – that is going to make their target audience sit up and take notice. Sponsorship can provide this at two levels. The first is fundamental – sponsors become involved to transfer the brand values of the property to their brand.

Mobile phone provider O_2, sponsors of England's rugby team, enjoyed huge, positive brand association when the team won the World Cup in Australia in 2003. The O_2 logo was plastered across players and open-top buses as the team was feted by over a million people on the streets of London. On a smaller scale, ice-cream manufacturers

Ben & Jerry's sponsored wacky events such as the World's Toe Wrestling Championship and Bog Snorkelling to emphasize the brand's position as unconventional.

The second level of cut-through is the element of creativity used within the framework of the sponsorship. Every sponsor is looking for something extra, a certain spark, that takes its property to a wider audience and brings it to life. The Whitbread Book Awards is a long-established sponsorship. Leisure services company Whitbread was looking for an injection of publicity to counter a rather staid image. In 1999, super model Jerry Hall was invited to sit on the judging panel. Her presence on the night of the awards ensured front-page coverage in several national newspapers resulting in a significant image shift for the awards.

Measurement

Measurement and evaluation in sponsorship has become increasingly necessary. Quite rightly, Marketing Directors want to know exactly what bang they are getting for their buck. The key to measurement is to establish the objectives of a sponsorship at the outset. Whether these objectives are met must be measured during and at the end of a sponsorship. It is essential that objectives can be measured against tangible results, whether these are an increase in awareness, sales, public relations value or just ensuring that guests are entertained successfully. Accurate measurement enables a long-term sponsorship to reassess itself on an ongoing basis, making changes as it goes to ensure continuing value for money and a satisfactory sponsorship.

Case study questions

1 What were the objectives and outcomes of the Royal Bank of Scotland sponsorship of the Six Nations?
2 What does the author mean by 'sponsorship is your brand in action, whereas advertising is what your brand says'?
3 What part does creativity play in sponsorship?

Source: Dominic Curran, *The Marketer*, 6 October 2005 (reproduced with permission). Dominic Curran is Director of Karen Earl Sponsorship.

CHAPTER THIRTEEN

DIRECT MARKETING AND E-COMMERCE

LEARNING OBJECTIVES

Having completed this chapter you should be able to:

- Describe the characteristics of direct marketing.
- Explain why direct marketing has grown in prominence in the past decade.
- Differentiate between direct and database marketing.
- Recognize the importance of customer retention and customer acquisition.
- Describe the various direct marketing media and their characteristics.
- Analyse the various components of the direct marketing offering.
- Recognize the importance of testing to direct marketing.

INTRODUCTION

Direct marketing is often characterized as a recent addition to the marketing communications mix because of its association with database technology and, more latterly, the power of the internet. However, the fundamentals of the direct marketing industry have been around for centuries. In 1498 Aldus Manutius produced a book catalogue in Venice, in 1667 William Lucas' gardening catalogue was tempting his customers in London, while Ben Franklin produced his book catalogue in 1774 (Tapp 1998; Kitchen 1999). All of these pioneer catalogues were effectively using direct marketing techniques to promote their products. Notable entrepreneurs such as Josiah Wedgwood, Chippendale and Thomas Edison also used recognizable direct marketing mediums such as flyers (i.e. distributed pamphlets) to generate sales of their wares. In 1872 Chicago-based Montgomery-Ward issued their first flyer and went from there to become a United States institution. The first UK consumer catalogue (Freemans) began life in 1905. In 1891 Avon Cosmetics invented the concept of direct marketing beauty products.

In the 1930s and 1940s, as marketing concepts began to take shape, direct marketing (i.e. the means by which dialogue could be established with a

Flyers
Distributed pamphlets.

potential or actual customer rather than the mass market) became a laudable aim and a logical extension of the ideas surrounding segmentation and targeting. At this time researchers began asking groups of consumers about their likes and preferences but they were without powerful analysing tools to help them. It was not until later in the century that technology developers came up with the tools that could rapidly analyse data and enhance interactivity.

DIRECT MARKETING DEFINITION

The UK Direct Marketing Association (DMA) describes direct marketing as an interactive system of marketing which uses one or more advertising media to effect a measurable response and/or transaction in any location. The introduction of the term 'advertising', however, may confuse (in part because of the way advertising was described and defined in Chapter 9). Whereas advertising builds up the image and personality of a brand in the longer term, direct marketing (in most cases) asks people to act and often incentivizes them to do so. In this regard it is closer to the earlier definition of sales promotion (Chapter 10). A major difference, however, between direct marketing and either sales promotion or advertising is that it targets individual customers rather than market segments.

Direct marketing not only exploits a consumer's wish to acquire goods and services but also to be involved. Relationships are developed over time. It can be argued that, in addition to fulfilling sales objectives, direct marketing can maintain these relationships between sales (sometimes referred to as **affinity marketing** or **loyalty marketing**). For this reason direct marketing is sometimes described as 'through the line' (as opposed to above or below the line) in recognition of the multiple aims.

Direct marketing is also, because of the interactive element, frequently described as the nearest thing to **personal selling**. Given the expense of personal selling and the relative inexpensiveness of direct marketing it is seen as particularly useful in developing a dialogue prior to personal contact. Indeed personalization is a defining feature of direct marketing. According to research by Drayton Bird, a direct marketing specialist, someone's name in a message increases responses by 50 per cent (Bewick 2005). Figure 13.1 illustrates the level of personalization and interactivity associated with the various marketing communications tools.

Affinity marketing or loyalty marketing
Developing customer relationships over time.

Personal selling
An interpersonal tool where individuals, often representing an organization, interact in order to inform, persuade, or remind an individual or group to take appropriate action, as required by the sponsors.

For more information on direct marketing look at the Institute of Direct Marketing's website at: **www.theidm.co.uk**.

DIRECT MARKETING DEVELOPMENT

The growth of direct marketing in the 1980s and 1990s can be traced to a number of different drivers. In addition to the search for better targeting

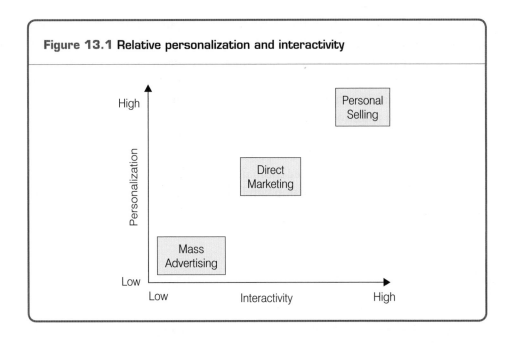

Figure 13.1 Relative personalization and interactivity

and closer customer relationships, the increased cost of advertising and fragmentation of advertising media was undoubtedly an influence on its development. Importantly, however, it was the development of the tools and the technological sophistication to handle the complexity involved with personalized marketing, which is seen as the greatest promoter of direct marketing growth. Among these technological advances were:

- Increased processing power
- Analytical systems development
- Development of telephone technology (e.g. freephone access, voice recognition, etc.)
- Electronic point-of-sale (EPOS) technology
- Smart-card technology
- Interactive television
- Internet and World Wide Web technology

Each played their part in enabling direct marketing to become a powerful proactive tool in the hands of the marketer. In under ten years to 2003, the UK expenditure on direct marketing more than tripled to £13.6 billion (Bold 2004).

Direct marketing has a number of characteristics which make it a valuable tool. In particular it is highly measurable and there is the ability to test the significant variables regularly. It is targeted, cost efficient (especially in relation to personal selling) and flexible, fast and interactive. These are all characteristics which distinguish it from traditional marketing. In addition, whereas traditional marketing relies on reaching mass audiences through mass media, direct marketing aims to communicate with individual customers through personalized messages. Budgets in direct marketing are determined through testing the various components of the offering and generating decision-making data to establish the optimum return rather than being defined by the availability of budget and incomplete segment-based and/or surrogate measures (e.g. recall). Direct marketing also requires specific action(s) to be taken which is then measurable against expected outcomes. The objectives of traditional marketing meanwhile can be unclear and/or long term in nature, making measurement difficult if not impossible. Additionally, whereas traditional marketing campaigns are highly visible and, therefore, vulnerable to competitive spoiler campaigns, direct marketing campaigns are largely invisible even after the campaign launch. These various advantages are summarized in Box 13.1 below.

Box 13.1 Comparisons between general marketing communications and direct marketing

General Marketing Communications	Direct Marketing
• Mass audiences through mass media	• Direct communication with customer
• Impersonal communication	• Personalized
• Controlled by size of budget	• Budget determined through testing
• Desired action unclear or delayed	• Specific action requested
• Incomplete data for decision making	• Database drives promotion
• Analysis at segmentation level	• Analysis at individual level
• Uses surrogate measures (e.g. recall)	• Measurable (and, therefore, controllable)
• Promotions highly visible	• Promotions largely invisible

DATABASE MARKETING

According to an Institute of Direct Marketing (IDM) discussion paper in 2000 'the essence of direct marketing lies in the ability to gather information about customers, analyse it and tailor messages accordingly'. As the direct marketing process involves the identification and qualification of prospects, their attraction to the brand and the conversion and retention of these prospects (Copley 2004), this would be a tedious and highly limited operation if it were not for the development of the computer-accessed database.

Database marketing
The holding and analysing of customer information thereby helping create marketing strategies.

The term most associated with data gathering and processing is database marketing. Although the terms database marketing and direct marketing are often used interchangeably there is a useful distinction to make. Database marketing is seen as the process of holding and analysing customer information, thereby helping to create strategies for marketing, whereas direct marketing focuses upon using that database to communicate (and sometimes distribute) directly to customers so as to attract response (Tapp 1998). In essence the former is all about data capture, storage, analysis, interpretation and application in a manner that discovers patterns and relationships that may be previously hidden in the data (Smith 1998), whereas the latter is the utilization of this information in ways that will elicit responses from current or potential customers.

There are two terms particularly associated with database marketing. **Data warehousing**, as the term implies, is the taking and storing of data from a variety of sources. The data is stored because it may not be seen as currently usable either because its value is not immediately appreciated or because it requires further qualification. **Data mining** is the extraction of this data from the data depositories in a form useful to marketers. Both terms imply that data gathered may not necessarily be used immediately but held until such time as it can generate information useful to the marketer.

The value of a database to direct marketers, therefore, is that it allows the identification of:

- the most profitable customers, for **up-selling** and **cross-selling** activities
- the most profitable potential customers, for new sales
- past customers who are still valid prospects, for reactivation
- the most profitable products and services in the portfolio, to drive merchandising activities
- the most appropriate pricing policies, both that the market will stand and that are competitive
- the most appropriate and effective promotions and media, to assist with planning and implementation of communications campaigns
- new market opportunities for development
- channel efficiency evaluation, to help maximize opportunites
- opportunities to increase profitability through identifying and reducing waste and inefficiency

There are, however, potential downsides that should be considered. Sometimes data is incomplete or out of date rendering it potentially damaging. Some data may be inaccurate through human error or where the source deliberately enters false data (as has been particularly the experience on the Internet). Duplication is also a continuous problem particularly where data is stored using various styles of address (e.g. J. Smith, John J. Smith, J.J. Smith, etc.). Even the same name at the same address is no guarantee of duplication as it may be two members of the same family. Advanced software is used to search for potential duplication so that de-duping can take place although this is far from infallible (see Box 13.2).

Data warehousing
The storing of data from a variety of sources. The data is stored because it may not be currently usable either because its value is not immediately appreciated or because it requires further qualification.

Data mining
The extraction of data from a data depository in a form useful to marketers.

Up-selling
Selling higher quality (and, therefore, higher price) items to existing customer base.

Cross-selling
Selling other items (sometimes from different categories) to existing customer base.

De-duping
The removal of duplicate names from mailing and other lists.

DIRECT MARKETING OPERATIONS

Broadly there are three levels of direct marketing involvement (also see Case study 13.1). These might be described as:

- Integral
- Integrated or
- Peripheral

Box 13.2 Updating databases

Dun and Bradstreet report that 7 per cent of businesses move location annually and Experian report that 5 per cent of businesses have name, address or contact changes per month. In research undertaken by Wegener DM in 2004 of 51 business-to-business databases and a total of 1.53 million records they reported:

- 13 per cent of records had no name present
- 21 per cent had no postcode
- 19 per cent had incorrect or incomplete postcodes
- 19 per cent of records were duplicates
- 3 per cent related to companies that had ceased trading

There are, however, several sources of updated information including directories such as Yell or Thomson or data-gathering companies such as Dun and Bradstreet. In addition to these 'business universe' lists there are others which concentrate on contact details from the UK's largest companies or those in specialist sectors.

Source: Murphy 2005.

Integral (databases)
Where direct marketing is the principal marketing tool.

Integrated (databases)
Where the database plays an important part in the business and direct marketing is one of the company's most important tools in its multi-channel operation.

Peripheral (databases)
Where the database and direct marketing play only a minor role in a company.

Customer acquisition
The process of acquiring new customers.

Customer retention
The process of retaining existing customers.

Lead qualification
Improving the quality of the information known about the customer/prospect.

Customer relationship maintenance
The maintenance of regular contact with the customer.

Leaky bucket metaphor
Metaphor for the dual needs of customer acquisition and retention.

Where the database is integral to the business, direct marketing is the principal marketing tool. Examples include catalogue operations, distance learning, direct insurers and Internet-only retailers. Where the database is integrated it plays an important part in the operation and direct marketing is one of the company's most important tools in its multi-channel operation. Examples include multiple retailers and travel organizations. Organizations where the database and direct marketing play only a peripheral role are harder and harder to find but may include fast moving consumer goods manufacturers or others where personalized communication is not seen as cost effective. Where direct marketing plays a supportive role most customer data is not recorded but direct marketing techniques (e.g. direct mail) may be used to support sales.

There are two principal objectives of direct marketing:

- customer acquisition and
- customer retention

There are also two subsidiary objectives associated with the above which are:

- lead qualification (adding to the information known about the customer/prospect)
- customer relationship maintenance (maintaining contact)

The importance of customer acquisition and retention are illustrated by the 'leaky bucket' metaphor (see Figure 13.2). This suggests that for a company to maintain or increase customer numbers they must either increase the flow (acquire new customers) or stem the leakage (retain more customers). All companies lose customers for competitive (e.g. attracted by a competitor) or non-competitive (e.g. changes location) reasons. In booming markets the loss of existing customers is less than crucial if there are others to take their place. In slow-growth or stagnant markets the acquisition of new customers becomes considerably harder (and more expensive) and retention of existing customers becomes the priority.

The significance of customer acquisition and retention to the direct marketing concept are visualized in the 'wheel of prosperity' as shown in Figure 13.3 (Smith 1998). This 'wheel' illustrates those aspects of direct marketing that contribute to commercial prosperity.

Wheel of prosperity
Model detailing the direct marketing process.

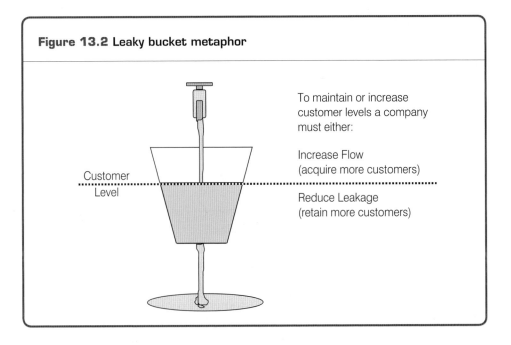

Figure 13.2 Leaky bucket metaphor

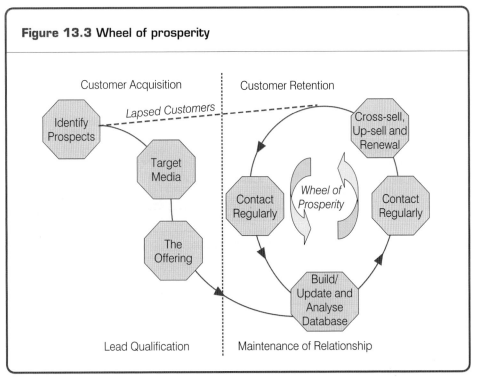

Figure 13.3 Wheel of prosperity

Prospect

A potential customer.

Prospect hierarchy

A hierarchy of potential customers ranging from lapsed customers at the top to 'suspects' at the bottom.

Suspects

Based on geodemographic profiling, values, attitudes and lifestyle profiling (VALs) or previous purchase behaviour which indicates they *may* have the profile of current customers.

Response lists

Lists of prospective customers with identified product interest (IPI).

Identified product interest (IPI)

Customers with an interest in a particular product or service category.

Compiled lists

Lists of individuals with identified characteristics but *not* identified product interest.

House lists

Lists compiled from a company's own database.

List brokers

Intermediaries between list owners and organizations wishing to rent lists.

List exchanges

Exchange of customer data between companies (illegal in certain countries).

Hand-raisers

Prospects who have indicated by their behaviour (e.g. ordering a catalogue) that they *may* want to become customers.

Profiled prospects

Prospects whose general profile suggests they *may* become customers.

Referrals

Those prospects who have been encouraged by existing customers to contact the company.

Enquirers

Prospects who have directly contacted the company for specific information.

IDENTIFY PROSPECTS

As the wheel of prosperity model suggests prospects are first identified. Prospects (i.e. non-customers for whom varying degrees of sales potential can be attached) may be described on the basis of a prospect hierarchy. At the lowest level are the suspects. This category may be based on geodemographic profiling, values, attitudes and lifestyle profiling (VALs) or previous purchase behaviour which indicates they *may* have the profile of current customers. These names may be obtained in the form of commercially available lists. Lists may be divided into three types:

- response lists: individuals with identified product interest (IPI)
- compiled lists: individuals with identified characteristics (but not IPI)
- house-lists: compiled from a company's own database.

Lists (unless in-house) are generally rented on a one-time only basis and the cost-per-thousand (CPT) determined by the quality of the list. Lists are obtained from list compilers (who use house-lists, surveys and other available data), list brokers (who act as brokers between list owners and renters) or through list exchanges with other companies.[1]

Above the level of 'suspects' the details are likely to come from the company's own records or again derived from compiled or response lists. Hand-raisers are those who have indicated by their behaviour (e.g. ordering a catalogue) that they *may* become customers. Profiled prospects are those whose general profile suggests a likelihood of becoming customers. Referrals are those who have been influenced by existing customers to contact the company whereas enquirers have directly contacted the company for specific

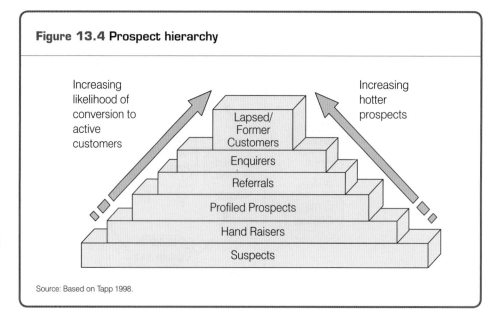

Figure 13.4 Prospect hierarchy

Source: Based on Tapp 1998.

[1]Subject to legal restrictions in many countries.

information. At the top of the prospect pyramid are former or lapsed customers. Customers who have purchased from you before by definition are closest to your customer profile and always the most likely to come back to you again. For this reason organizations may go further in incentivizing these customers than any others (often referred to as win-back strategies). For example 'book clubs' offer substantially reduced prices to lapsed customers to get them back into the monthly cycle of book ordering.

Former (or lapsed) customers
Customers who have previously purchased from the organization but no longer do so.

Win-back strategies
Strategies for winning back former customers.

TARGET MEDIA

The reference to target media on the 'wheel of prosperity' model refers to the media most likely to generate a response from the targeted prospects. In terms of direct marketing, organizations may use interactive media including direct mail, telemarketing or e-marketing to stimulate a response or alternatively use media normally associated with advertising (e.g. television, radio, magazines, posters, etc.) as long as these have a response mechanism (e.g. freephone, freepost, etc.).

Interactive media
Media that interacts with the consumer (e.g. Internet, satellite/cable television).

E-marketing
Marketing using the medium of the Internet.

Direct mail is a flexible communications medium with almost limitless creative potential. It can be effective as both a customer acquisition and/or customer retention tool. For the ten years up to 2004 UK direct mail grew by 87 per cent while expenditure on campaigns grew 118 per cent. On a five-year basis direct mail grew by 42 per cent (compared to 16 per cent for advertising).[2] In 2004 nearly 5.5 billion items were mailed in the UK (Ronay 2005) representing 12 per cent of total media spend in the UK (Holder 2005).

Response mechanism
The means by which a customer responds to an offer, e.g. freephone, freepost, etc.

Direct mail
Advertising, through the medium of the mail, to targeted, profiled customers.

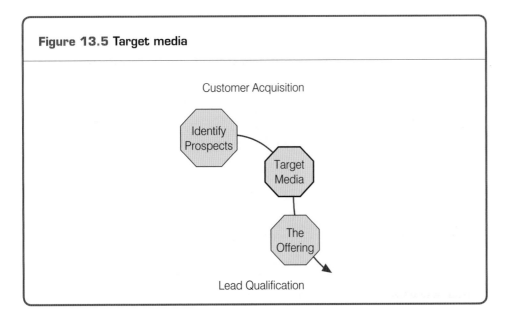

Figure 13.5 Target media

Customer Acquisition

Identify Prospects

Target Media

The Offering

Lead Qualification

---

[2]Figures from www.royalmail.com accessed 2 January 2006.

Junk-mail
Any mailing the customer decides is untargeted and obtrusive.

On the downside the mail order industry has a reputation for junk-mail. In direct mail campaigns responses between 3 per cent and 5 per cent *may* represent a successful campaign (see response rates Box 13.3) which implies, 95 per cent to 97 per cent are disinterested or could not bothered to respond. There are both ethical and ecological factors associated with this level of mass mailing. According to Ecofuture[3] the direct mail industry uses 100 million trees annually and the majority of household waste now consists of unsolicited mail. In general consumers see junk-mail as correspondence they have no interest in whatsoever (particularly when it is repetitive) rather than those they choose not to respond to. As such the actual percentage categorized by consumers as junk-mail is not quite as high as these figures suggest.

In general, however, direct mail is seen as a successful medium which, according to Royal Mail (www.royalmail.com), has a return on investment in the UK of £14.00 for every £1.00 spent on the campaign. In 2003 £26.28 billion was spent by UK consumers with an average spend of £577, as a result of receiving direct mail (Acland 2004). Although in some industries (e.g. low-cost airlines) e-mail has displaced direct mail because its costs are so much lower, the creative potential of direct mail may see its continued use into the future.

Catalogue retailing
A means by which products or services can be purchased from a selection of those on offer in a catalogue.

Mail order
The ability (through selection in a catalogue) to order products for delivery by mail.

Catalogue retailing (or **mail order**) has long been associated with direct mail. In addition to its advantages as a flexible and creative medium, catalogues have the advantage of an extended life as a reference document. On the downside catalogue production and distribution costs can be very high. The history of catalogues has differed in various markets (Blythe 2000). In the USA long distances between towns prompted the generally well-to-do to order catalogue merchandise not available locally. Similarly in Germany, travel difficulties coupled with legal restrictions on retail opening hours prompted the affluent customers to turn to mail order. In Britain, however,

---

Box 13.3 Average direct mail response rates

	Response Rate*	Total Response Rate
Charities	8.6%	12.4%
Automotive	7.0%	12.4%
Travel/Holidays	7.4%	11.7%
Utilities	5.5%	11.0%
Retail	6.5%	10.8%
Luxury Goods	7.6%	9.6%
Mail Order	7.0%	8.5%
Household Appliances	4.8%	8.4%
Financial (loans)	5.5%	5.5%
Financial (savings/investments)	2.9%	4.4%
Financial (credit cards)	3.9%	3.9%

*Response rate in column one excludes campaigns with a 30 per cent response rate or more.

Source: Response 2003 Report, Direct Mail Information Service, *Marketing*, 7 July 2004.

---

[3]www.ecofuture.org.

it was the availability of credit and 'easy-payment terms' that attracted customers largely from lower socioeconomic groups. Even by 1980 over 50 per cent of catalogue customers were in the C_2D socioeconomic category. Following a decline in the 1970s catalogues saw a resurgence in the 1990s with the introduction of more specialist catalogues made possible by lower publishing and design costs. According to the National Directory of British Mail Order[4] 63 000 different catalogues are issued each year.

Telemarketing can be classified as either as in-bound or out-bound. In-bound telemarketing is the use of telephone services to facilitate responses from customers usually via a 'freephone' or local call rate number. These are frequently handled by call-centre operations which may be outsourced nationally or internationally. Out-bound telemarketing is the planned use of the telephone to make unstructured calls to an audience in a measurable and accountable way (Tapp 1998). Telemarketing, where the customer has given permission for the company to contact them, or where the company believes it is in the customer's interest to contact them, is distinguishable (although not always clearly) from telesales, where no such permission is given or implied. Telesales calls (like junk-mail and spam) are based on the annoyance of the many in return for a small percentage (yet profitable) return. Another persistent complaint is about silent calls generated by predictive dialling technology. Designed to speed up agent productivity it frequently leaves customers with a disturbing silence when they answer their telephone. In the UK you can restrict telephone calls and facsimile (fax) messages by registering with the Telephone Preference Service or Fax Preference Service. In the USA the 'Do-not-call registry' provides a similar service. In addition, according to the US Federal Trade Commission's telemarketing sales rules, a consumer can claim $500 from companies who, if they have been told not to call, continue to do so.

Telemarketing has become the basis for what is usually called **customer relationship management (CRM)**. Depending on your source of reference, a number of different aspects are associated with CRM. These include data warehousing, customer service systems, call centres, e-commerce, and Web

@

For an example of how consumers can prevent unwanted mail look at: **www.mpsonline.org.uk/mpsr.**

In-bound telemarketing
The use of telephony to facilitate responses from customers usually via a 'freephone' or local call rate number.

Out-bound telemarketing
The planned use of the telephone to make unstructured calls to a target audience in a measurable and accountable way.

Telesales
Cold-calling (without prior contact or permission) with the objective of making a sale or starting the process towards a sale.

Silent calls
Calls generated by predictive dialling technology designed to speed up agent productivity but which frequently leaves customers with a disturbing silence when they answer their telephone.

Customer relationship management (CRM)
A management process which uses database technology and call centres to maintain customer relationships.

Box 13.4 Junk-mail

Following an agreement with the UK government in 2003, the Direct Marketing Association (DMA) ran a campaign on behalf of the direct marketing industry highlighting the industry's commitment to cutting direct mail wastage, as well as promoting the environmental benefits of recycling. The messages behind the campaign are that consumers can conserve natural resources by recycling and that those who perceive direct mail as 'junk-mail' can sign up to the Mail Preference Service allowing them to opt out of receiving direct mail. In addition to advertising in the UK national press and online, 310 000 postcards were distributed in coffee shops and bars.

Source: *Marketing*, 2 October 2003.

---

[4]Published 1997

marketing together with operational and sales systems (McDonald 2000). According to Kelly (2000) key analytical CRM applications include:

- *Sales analysis*: offering the organization an integrated perspective on sales and enabling the sales function to understand the underlying trends and patterns in the sales data.
- *Customer profile analysis*: allowing the organization to distinguish, from the mass of customer data, the individuals as well as the micro-segments.
- *Campaign analysis*: providing the ability to measure the effectiveness of individual campaigns and different media.
- *Loyalty analysis*: measuring customer loyalty with reference to the duration of the customer relationship.
- *Customer contact analysis*: analysis of the customer contact history of any individual.
- *Profitability analysis*: measuring and analysing the many different dimensions of profitability.

Supporters suggest that CRM seeks to systematically resolve the problems associated with the collection and interpretation of customer data, although even advocates will admit that progress has been slow with data not being harnessed with anything like the degree of sophistication that technology allows (Kelly 2000). McDonald (2000) suggests that the simple truth is that CRM projects will produce enormous amounts of data.

A growing area of communications interest associated with telephony is **mobile marketing**. According to *Marketing Direct* (2005), with over 90 per cent of 15–44 year olds owning a mobile phone and with this demographic owning 80 per cent of the UK's wealth it is seen as an important medium in the future not just in 'text-to-win' competitions but as part of strategic campaigns. Research suggests that this medium holds considerable potential with 94 per cent of messages read and up to 23 per cent shown or forwarded to friends and between a 71 per cent and 96 per cent recall rate on campaigns (*Marketing Direct* 2005). In recognition of the potential abuse of mobile marketing the Institute of Practitioners in Advertising (IPA) have produced guidelines endorsed by the Direct Marketing Association (DMA) regarding opting-out of campaigns and, where necessary, that verifiable parental consent is obtained.

The terms **Internet** and **World Wide Web** (WWW) are often used interchangeably but are not the same. The Internet is a collection of wires, protocols and hardware that allows the electronic transmission of data including e-mails, file transfers and global networking, whereas the World Wide Web exists on the Internet and is comprised of **hypertext** pages viewed by a **browser** (Rayport and Jaworski 2001). Web pages always begin http:// or https:// signifying the content being viewed is hypertext and transferred using the **hypertext transfer protocol**. The Internet, as we know it today, consists of small area networks belonging to individual organizations (local area networks or LANs), networks spread across large geographical areas (wide area networks or WANs) and individual computers (Chaston 2001).

Mobile marketing
Any aspect of marketing using mobile telephone technology.

Internet
A collection of wires, protocols and hardware that allows the electronic transmission of data including emails, file transfers and global networking.

World Wide Web
The World Wide Web exists on the Internet and is comprised of hypertext pages viewed by a browser. Web pages always begin http:// or https:// signifying the content being viewed is hypertext and transferred using the hypertext transfer protocol.

Hypertext markup language
The language used to create Web documents.

Browser
Web viewing programme such as Firefox or Internet Explorer.

Hypertext transfer protocol
The protocol by which Web documents are transferred.

More information on direct marketing can be found on the Direct Marketing Association's website at: **www.the-dma.org** and on the Institute of Direct Marketing at **www.theidm.co.uk.**

In 2003 online marketing grew by 20 per cent representing 8 per cent of total marketing spend (Bold 2004). Four per cent of all retail purchases now take place online but for many more the Web has become the first place to look for information. According to research by AOL, in 2004 almost 80 per cent of people looking for information on a new car used the Internet (Bonello 2004). The search for products and services often begins with a **search engine** of which Google (who get around 6 billion searches per month) is a popular example. Although search engines do trawl the Internet for key words **paid-for placement** (PFP) guarantees top ranking in such listings. Although the Internet has transformed information exchange it is not a new type of marketing or marketing communication. It is simply another medium albeit faster, with more comprehensive 'rich' information, interactive and with instant geographic reach. As Derek Holder of the IDM notes it is 'direct marketing through new media' (IAB 2005). It can, however, be used in novel ways as noted in Minicase 13.1.

Search engine
A portal that enables users to search the Web.

Paid-for placement (PFP)
A paid-for service which, on the basis of certain key words, guarantees top ranking in search engine listings.

MINICASE 13.1

Internet promotion

The Arctic Monkeys are a four-piece indie rock band from Sheffield, UK. They were formed in 2002 but first started to gain widespread public attention when their demos were made available to download from the Internet in late 2004. Their early concerts included many songs that were only available as demos on the Internet. Their appearance on the Carling stage at the 2005 Reading Festival and Leeds Festival was much hyped by the music press particularly NME and their sell-out concert at the London Astoria saw 2000 fans singing along to every song despite the fact

SOURCE: © TIM MOSENFELDER/GETTY IMAGES

The Arctic Monkeys' use of the Internet to gain wider popularity has been so successful that some commentators believe it may change the way new bands achieve recognition.

that the band had only released a single limited edition EP. All the while the band resisted the temptation of signing an album deal going so far as banning record company scouts from their gigs. Lead vocalist Alex Turner declared as 'amazing' their rise to stardom via the Internet. When they did eventually sign for Domino Records in June 2005 their first single sold 38 962 copies and went straight to number one in the UK singles chart. Their long-awaited debut album *Whatever people say I am that's what I'm not*, was released in January 2006 and sold almost 120 000 copies on its first day of sale. According to Phil Penman of HMV 'they're well on their way to having the first million-selling album of 2006'. The album was also on-course to becoming the best-selling debut album in chart history. Such was the band's novel way of getting to number one that the *Guardian* suggested this could signal a change in how new bands achieve recognition.

Source: Rte. ie. Answers.com.

Some innovative marketers are already using the medium of the Internet to involve consumers themselves in the marketing of products and services. Interesting or amusing files, associated with particular brands, are being circulated to friends and relations in a form replicating the spread of a virus (viral marketing). Radical new mediums are also appearing daily. Personalized sites including MySpace, YouTube and Second Life (see Box 13.5) have become overnight sensations. MySpace already has 75 million users with 240 000 new ones joining each day. The X-Men page on MySpace, on which 20th Century Fox chose to spend 8 per cent of its launch budget, has 3 million 'friends' associated with its page (Ritson 2006).

A website, like a catalogue, has to attract customers to its pages for it to be a valuable tool and, therefore, requires widespread advertising and/or publicity. What does work on the Internet would appear to be those sites that exploit the Internet's interactive and creative strengths and intelligent email. It is also highly cost effective. According to Google the average cost-per-lead online is £0.27 compared to around £9.00 for direct mail (IAB 2005). On the downside mass, unsolicited emails (or 'spam')[5] also work because the sheer volume sent produce a small but profitable response.

Box 13.5 Viral marketing

Around the time of the Millennium, Ed Robinson, an advertising executive, carried out an experiment. He spent more than £5000 producing a 12-second humorous video about a man who explodes while inflating a child's raft, attached the firm's Web address and e-mailed it to five friends. By the end of the first week more than 60 000 people had seen the video and within three months Robinson's website received 500 000 hits. Today Robinson's London-based company, The Viral Factory charges $250 000–$500 000 to create ads he guarantees will reach an audience equal to or greater than the original.

Source: *Business Week*, 23 July 2006.

[5]The name is said to be based on the Monty Python 'Spam' sketch. For non-aficionados the sketch was located in a restaurant that sold spam (a ham-based meat product) and nothing else. Spam in this context was a metaphor for lots of what people do not want.

Box 13.6 Jargon busting – guide to the language of online marketing

Ad serving	The process of delivering online ads to a PC through an advertisement management system that allows different audience groups to be targeted across multiple sites.
Affiliate	The publisher/salesperson in an affiliate marketing relationship (see Affiliate marketing).
Affiliate fraud	Bogus activity by an affiliate in an attempt to generate illegitimate unearned revenue.
Affiliate marketing	Revenue sharing between online advertisers/site publishers, whereby commission is paid on performance measures typically sales, clicks, registrations or a hybrid model.
Banner ad	Graphic Web advertisement unit, typically measuring 468 x 60 pixels.
Blogging	The act of creating a Web log – a personal Web space where users can post text, images or pictures.
Click fraud	The act of purposefully clicking on an advertisement listing without intending to buy to cost the advertiser money.
Clickthrough rate (CTR)	The percentage of users to whom a link is displayed who then click on that link.
Contextual advertising	Advertising search terms linked to the content on a Web page being viewed.
Conversion rate	The number of visitors who take a desired action such as buying something compared with those who merely view an ad.
Cookie	A small text file left on the user's PC that identifies their browser so that they are 'recognized' when they revisit a site. It allows information such as a user name to be stored and a website to personalize its offering.
Cost-per-action (CPA)	Online advertising payment model in which remuneration is based soley on a particular action being taken such as a sale.
CPM (CPT)	Cost-per-thousand impressions.
Expandable or extendable ad	An advertisement that begins in a banner or skyscraper format and then expands when the cursor rolls over it.
Frequency cap	Restriction on the number of times a specific visitor is shown an ad.
Interstitial	An advertisement that loads when navigating between two Web pages.
Keyword	A word or phrase that potential customers type into a search engine to find a service or product.
Opt-in email	An email that is explicitly requested by the recipient.
Pay-per-click	Online advertising payment model in which remuneration is based solely on users who have 'clicked through' the ad.
Pay-per-lead	Online advertising payment model in which remuneration is based on leads generated.
Permission marketing	Marketing that requires the customer's consent to be delivered to them. Often used in email marketing.
Podcasting	Making audio or video files available to consumers for use on mobile audio devices.
Pop-up ad	Advertisement that displays in a new browser window above the current page.
Pop-under ad	Advertisement that displays in a new browser window behind the current one.
Search-engine optimization	The process of maximizing the relevancy of a site and its content for both search engines and their users.

Box 13.6 (Continued)

Search-engine marketing	The process of keyword bidding and management to gain placement in the sponsored links delivered with search results. Carried out by SEM (search-engine marketing) agencies, it is sometimes used as a blanket term to cover both paid-search and SEO (search-engine optimization) agencies.
Rich media	Advertising that goes beyond static banners. Can feature audio, video and increased interaction.
Really simple syndication (RSS)	Technology that allows users to receive constantly updated content without having to revisit the website.
Skyscraper	A long, vertical, online advertisement usually found running down the side of a page in a fixed placement.
Sponsorship	Advertising that seeks to establish a deeper integration between advertiser and a publisher, often involving co-ordinated beyond-the-banner placements and integrated content.
Stickiness	Measure used to gauge the effectiveness of a site in retaining its users, usually in terms of visit duration.
Takeover ad	Creative positioned on a layer that covers the entire page for a specific amount of time before it disappears.
User-generated content	Content generated by the user rather than the website publisher.
Viral marketing	Often video or game based, and developed so it can be easily passed on by users, sometimes achieving millions of views in just a few days.
Web 2.0	Collective name for new technologies and online consumer trends. It includes blogs, RSS and podcasting.

Source: *Marketing*, 5 June 2006 (reproduced from *Marketing* magazine with the permission of the copyright owner, Haymarket Business Publications Limited).

More general media (described in an earlier definition as advertising media) include magazines and newspapers (often referred to as off-the-page), television and radio, inserts and door-to-door communications. These are normally used as customer acquisition devices (used to generate leads) rather than retention media and their particular characteristics are covered more generally in Chapter 8. One area of distinct growth of interactive activity, however, is **direct response television**. Television is a medium intertwined with our lives. In 2004 the average Briton spent 223 minutes in front of the television each day yet fewer were watching spot advertising, with the advent of video, enabling advertisements to be bypassed (referred to as zipping), and easy switching to other channels (zapping). Using the ability of television to visually describe the features of products, television channels such as QVC use television as an automated and descriptive catalogue from which customers can purchase by telephone or email. In addition interactivity can be achieved (on satellite or cable television) via the television set itself (iTV). In September 2005 Ofcom (the UK communications regulator) estimated that 65 per cent of UK homes now have 'iTV compatible' sets (Svennevig 2005).

Box 13.7 describes the advantages and disadvantages of the various direct marketing media discussed.

Box 13.7 Direct marketing media comparisons

	Advantages	Disadvantages
Interactive Media		
Direct Mail	• Can generate leads, improve image and sell, up-sell, cross-sell and help build/ qualify databases • Cost effective • Creative opportunities	• Cost-per-thousand (CPT) high compared to advertising • Clutter (junk-mail)
Telemarketing	• In-bound responsive to customer • Out-bound relationship building	• Customer intolerance against cold-calling
Internet marketing	• Inexpensive • Interactive	• Passive medium • Millions of sites
Catalogues	• As Direct mail • Frequently kept as reference	• High production costs
Direct Response	• Interactivity and movement • Explanation of features	• Must, wait for specific offerings to be made
Television	• Immediate ordering facility	
Advertising Media		
Magazines (off-the-page)	• Enables editorial • Enables complex explanation • Relatively long shelf life	• Mass media and, therefore, not highly targeted
Posters	• Relatively inexpensive	• Only very simple messages
Newspapers	• Enables editorial • Enables complex explanation	• Mass media and, therefore, not highly targeted • Short shelf life
Television	• Interactivity and movement • Explanation of basic features	• Difficulty in explaining complexities • Relies on consumer remembering and responding to particular telephone number/address
Radio	• Relatively inexpensive • Atmospheric	• As television
Cinema	• Interactivity and movement • Relatively inexpensive	• As television
Inserts	• Relatively inexpensive	• Easily ignored
Door-to-door	• Relatively inexpensive	• Easily ignored

THE OFFERING

The sales element is comprised of a number of factors which together make up the offering to the customer. These are:

- the list ($\times$ 6.0)
- the offer ($\times$ 3.0)

Offering
A number of factors (product, price, etc.) which together make up the direct marketing offering to the customer.

- the timing ($\times$ 2.0)
- the creative element ($\times$ 1.5)
- the response mechanism ($\times$ 1.2)

Drayton Bird[6] carried out tests to assess the importance of getting these factors right. With respect to the list he calculated a six-times better response between the best and worse he tested. The offer, timing, creative element and response mechanism also showed significant differences between best and worst (these factors are indicated next to each item above). As a whole he calculated that given these variables the difference between the best and the worst response could be as high as fifty-eight-times! This both signifies the need to attend to each aspect of the offer as well as highlighting the importance of testing to direct marketing, a subject that will be referred to again later in this chapter.

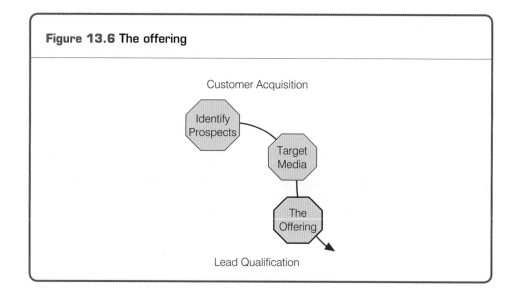

Figure 13.6 The offering

The offer is comprised not only of the main attraction but the pricing and incentivizing elements as well. Regardless of how good the list is or how creatively the offer is presented, unless the main product (or service), together with the incentive, at the price quoted, interests the customer the customer will not respond. A secondary incentive may be associated with a prompt reply within a given time period. This is offered in the knowledge that the longer a customer takes to consider the offer the less likely they are to respond.

The timing of the offer is also crucial as many items are either seasonal or associated with a particular time of the year (e.g. Christmas, Valentine's Day, etc.). Where information is known about a particular anniversary (birthday, insurance renewal date, etc.) appropriate communications can be made with the prospect. It is also generally true that, at different times during our lives, we have different needs. This is particularly true of the financial services

[6]Quoted in Smith and Taylor 2002.

industry. Few teenagers are interested in pensions but may be interested in student loans. Married couples may require substantial loans particularly if they plan to purchase their own property but are unlikely to have money to spare for investments. 'Empty-nesters' (couples whose children have left home), however, may have the funds to invest on their own or their children's behalf.

The creative element of the offer in particular is seen as crucial to its success. Developing a creative strategy means:

- Defining the primary marketing problem.
- Developing key selling concepts.
- Creating message strategies.
- Specifying desired action and the means by which it can be accomplished.
- Including mandatory (i.e. legal) requirements.

The creative element is the 'icing on the cake' and can make the difference between being noticed and acted upon and being ignored.

Finally, but importantly, there is the response mechanism. How easily can the prospect contact you? Initially mail was the preferred media and then the telephone. More latterly the Internet has been promoted to service customer needs effectively and efficiently.

CUSTOMER RETENTION

Once a prospect has become a customer the work of retention begins. Direct marketers build their database and continually qualify (i.e. update and improve) the data over time but, as Clive Humby of Dunn Humby[7] notes 'it is not the detailed transaction data that is of interest but patterns in transactions'. To enable patterns to emerge direct marketers use software frequently based upon three factors:

- **Recency**: how long ago did this customer buy from us.
- **Frequency**: how often does this customer buy from us.
- **Monetary value**: how much does this customer spend with us.

As might be expected it is likely that the customers who have most recently bought from the company and have most frequently spent relatively significant amounts with them, that are most likely to be the most valuable in the future. Profiles can also be based more specifically on customer purchase and price preferences and other details. Once profiles have been established the company *may* wish to contact the customer through newsletters, updates, etc. to maintain contact. Alternatively (or in addition to)

---

[7]Formerly an independent company that helped launch Tesco Club Card now a part of Tesco.

correspondence may be aimed at additional sales or targeted to cross-sell (sell an associated product) or up-sell (sell a higher quality product) increasing the value of that customer to the company. The retention of this customer over time becomes the 'wheel of prosperity' for the organization.

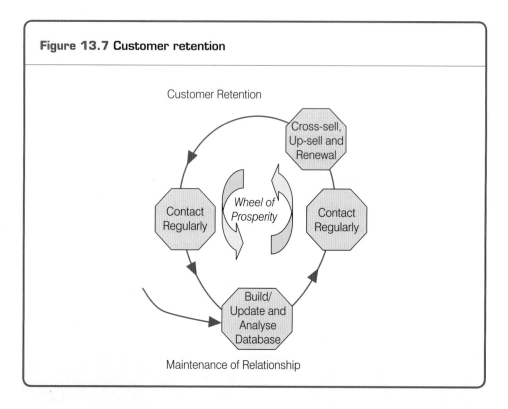

Figure 13.7 Customer retention

On the theoretical front concepts associated with relationship marketing and loyalty marketing encourage the retention of customers, pointing out that in most (but not all) circumstances it was more cost effective to hold on to your customers than to acquire new ones. It was also proposed by Dwer *et al.* (1987), Payne *et al.* (1995), Kotler (1997) and others that customers develop over time (see Figure 13.8) from 'simple' customers to advocates and ultimately partners in the business! In reality very few customers develop beyond the client stage although exceptions might be relationships with charities and sports clubs, where some extreme loyalists may eventually end up as part of the management of an organization.

The advantages associated with loyalty were taken further by Reichheld (1996) who developed a theory that suggested that relationships paid dividends over time. The model (see Figure 13.9) suggested that each year the customer would spend more, lower your costs (because you knew more about them), profit from customers who they refer to you and (by way of gratitude) you can charge them premium prices because they are loyal to you and will not go elsewhere.

As might be suspected this is a highly dubious model. The presumption that each year a customer will spend more is compounded by the other unrealistic assumptions. The likelihood of cost-saving on the basis of customer knowledge is fractional, indeed an important customer may use his or her leverage to elicit discounts or other 'costs' from the organization. Referrals are a dangerous assumption because of the likelihood of referrals away from as well as to the business. The most far-fetched suggestion is that competitive organizations can extract price premiums for any period of time without being found out. The experience of Amazon (see Box 13.8) may act as a deterrent for those who try.

In general, however, customer retention is seen to be positive and organizations go out of their way to maintain relationships. Proactively this

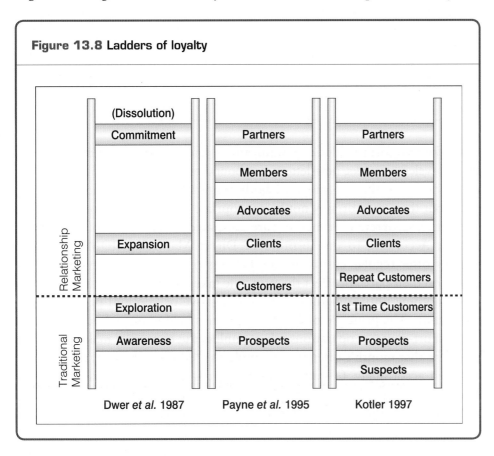

Figure 13.8 Ladders of loyalty

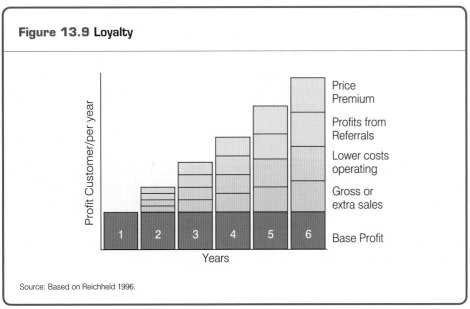

Figure 13.9 Loyalty

Source: Based on Reichheld 1996.

> **Box 13.8 Amazon**
>
> Between May and September 2000 Amazon.com, the world-famous Internet bookseller, tried out a dynamic pricing strategy that varied the prices of products by determining the profiles of existing customers. Regular customers, it was hypothesized, would be more likely to pay more and, therefore, should be charged more for products! Discussions began on message boards and forums (such as DVDTalk.com) and stories began to spread about price differentials between whom Amazon perceived as new and existing customers. Confusion became outrage as customers found out what was going on. An Amazon spokesperson stated that the experiment 'was done to determine customer responses to different price levels'. Ultimately the company admitted its mistake and promised its customers it would not happen again.
>
> Source: Egan 2004, based on Mohammed *et al.* 2002.

Sales communications
Direct marketing with a view to generating a sale.

Non-sales communications
Direct marketing but not with a view of generating an immediate sale (e.g. welcome packs, newsletters, etc.).

Principle of negative option
Offers regular customers the benefits of continuous service without action on their part. In effect the principle takes advantage of our inclination to do nothing until something (often a negative perception) prompts us to take action.

Standing order or direct debit
An order to a bank to make a payment on a regular basis or on demand.

Lifetime value
An approximation of the value of a customer over a lifetime.

Continuous credit
Paying-off mail order costs in instalments.

Continuity series
Where a finite number of items (usually in a series or set) are made available over time (e.g. monthly).

Clubs
Where membership entitles members to certain privileges not available to non-members.

Continuity series
Where a finite number of items (usually in a series or set) are made available over time (e.g. monthly).

Subscriptions
A fee for membership or for the right to receive something (i.e. newspapers) on a regular basis for a set period of time.

may take two forms; **sales communications** and **non-sales communications**, such as welcome packs, newsletters, out-bound telemarketing, etc. Sales communications have the advantage of both maintaining contact and generating profit but these may or may not be appropriate on every occasion.

Another set of retention methods are associated with the **principle of negative option**. According to the Institute of Direct Marketing (IDM)[8] 'negative options offer regular customers the benefits of continuous service without action on their part'. In effect the principle takes advantage of our inclination to do nothing until something (often a negative perception) prompts us to take action. The principle of negative option is behind many book-clubs and other short-contract operations where, unless the consumer makes an effort to refuse that month's offer (for example the 'editor's choice'), they will be invoiced accordingly. Certain financial devices also work on this principle. Once a **standing order** or **direct debit** has been established the customer must actively cancel the instruction before the relationship is ended. Research indicates that these devices substantially lengthen the **lifetime value** of the customer. Such is the value of such devices to organizations that they are frequently prepared to be exceptionally generous in the incentives offered for them to be set up. **Continuous credit** (offered by many mail-order companies) and leasing/rental agreements similarly keep relationships from terminating. Non-financial incentives to loyalty include **clubs** (where membership entitles members to certain privileges), **continuity series** (where a finite number of items are made available over time), **subscriptions** and loyalty programmes.

TESTING

Testing is of central importance to the success of direct marketing. Testing, as noted in Chapter 6, is different from market research. Whereas research may tell

[8] www.theidm.co.uk.

you why something works and suggest a number of alternatives, testing establishes *if* something works and *evaluates* alternatives. Testing can predict, therefore, the outcome of future marketing activities and is crucial to the integrity of direct marketing. Effectively all elements of the offering can be tested including:

- The list: different lists, parts of lists, etc.
- The offer: variations in the offer (including price) or the incentives.
- The timing: varying the timing of the offer, one-shot versus campaign, etc.
- The creative element: varying the creative element including the copy, physical format and media.
- The response mechanism: softening (i.e. making ordering simple through freephone or freepost) or hardening (perhaps where limited quantities are available or a higher quality of customer is required)[9] the offer.

In simple terms tests are made against a control sample usually the existing best variable in the way shown in Box 13.9 below. In this example the response of each audience and each offer can be made.

The reliability of any given test is determined by three statistical concepts relevant to direct marketing[10] These are:

- The sample: how representative it is of the population at large. Thus the sampling error is the difference between the mean of the sample and the mean of the population as a whole. The greater the level of error you can tolerate the smaller the sample can be.
- The **significance**: analysing the differences between the observed and expected results and noting whether they are a real and significant differences.

Significance
The analysis of the differences between the observed and expected results noting whether they are real and significant differences.

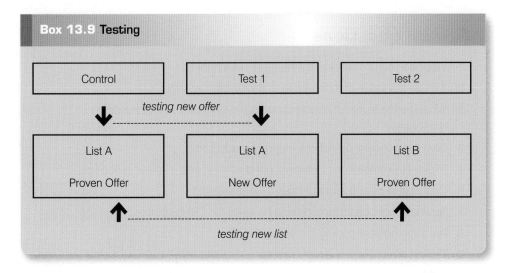

Box 13.9 Testing

Control	Test 1	Test 2

testing new offer

List A	List A	List B
Proven Offer	New Offer	Proven Offer

testing new list

[9]Although fewer potential customers may apply for an offer, catalogue, etc., if it is made more difficult for them to order it is perceived wisdom that they become better quality customers.
[10]Although a brief description appears here full statistical explanations are beyond the scope of this text.

Confidence interval
In market research how different must the
results be before you can be confident of
their significance.

Examples of direct marketing trade
magazines can be found at: **www.
responsemagazine.com/responsemag**
and **www.directmag.com.**

- The confidence interval: how different must the results be before you can be confident of their significance.

Testing is relatively low cost and reliable if properly executed, and can save the organization costs and/or help realize future revenue. It can be analysed and refined over time and help secure competitive advantage over competition. Indeed testing provides information on the likely outcome of future marketing activity.

Summary

This chapter traced the development of direct marketing which it described as an interactive system of marketing. It reviewed the reasons behind the growth of direct marketing, in particular those associated with the development of increased processing power, analytical systems development and other technological advances. It described the characteristics of direct marketing and compared them with traditional marketing, and the outcomes achievable from effective databases. The chapter went on to describe the operation of direct marketing in organizations where the principal objectives are to acquire and retain customers. Using the 'wheel of prosperity' as a model it reviewed the identification of prospects through lists and other sources, the targeting of the media and the offering as 'acquisition strategy'. Once this is achieved the building and updating, cross-selling, up-selling and win-back strategies are part of the maintenance and retention of relationships. In conclusion the importance of testing to direct marketing was highlighted.

Review questions

1. What do you understand by the term 'data mining'?
2. Explain the value of a database to the direct marketer.
3. What are the levels of direct marketing involvement in organizational databases?
4. Give the principal objectives of direct marketing.
5. Explain the differences between 'hand raisers' and 'profiled prospects'.
6. Describe in-bound and out-bound telemarketing.
7. To what extent can telemarketing be used for CRM activities?
8. Are zapping and zipping the same thing?
9. Testing is a feature of direct marketing activities. What can be tested and why would you test at all?
10. Explain the leaky bucket metaphor.

Discussion questions

1 Databases are crucial tools to the direct marketer. What are the problems associated with data capture and storage and how might this impact upon a campaign?

2 Using an existing campaign, analyse it in terms of the wheel of prosperity. What is it trying to achieve and how does it integrate with other communications being undertaken by the same company?

3 Discus the phenomena of junk-mail. Why do companies send it out? What might the advantages be to them? Why is it considered junk and by whom?

Further reading

Chaffey, D. (2000) 'Achieving internet marketing success', *The Marketing Review*, 1(1). Suggesting that for success, the unique characteristics of the digital medium should be exploited through creation of two-way dialogues via the website and email.

Grosso, C., Shenkan, A., Guggenheim, S. and Hobart, P. (2006) 'A reality check for online advertising', *McKinsey Quarterly*, 3: 10–11.

Hoan Cho, C.-H., Kang, J. and Cheon, H.J. (2006) 'Online shopping hesitation', *CyberPsychology & Behavior*, Jun., 9 (3): 261–74. Looking at factors that influence consumer hesitation or delay in online product purchases.

Lagrosen, S. (2005) 'Effects of the internet on the marketing communication of service companies', *Journal of Services Marketing*, 19 (2): 63–9.

Pons, A.P. (2006) 'Biometric marketing: targeting the online consumer', *Communications of the ACM*, Aug., 49 (8): 61–5.

Sipior, J.C., Ward, B.T. and Bonner, P.G. (2004) 'Should spam be on the menu?', *Communications of the ACM*, Jun., 47 (6): 59–63. Discusses the concerns associated with spam, and examines legislative and administrative initiatives intended to balance the interests of consumers and Internet service providers with those of direct marketers.

Chapter references

Acland, H. (2004) 'The value of response', Marketing, 7 July: 37–8.

Bewick, M. (2005) 'Charm School', *The Marketer*, 18 November, Cookham, Berkshire: Chartered Institute of Marketing, pp. 14–17.

Blythe, J. (2000) *Marketing Communications*, Harlow: FT/ Prentice Hall.

Bold, B. (2004) 'Marketers increase direct spend by 15%', *Marketing,* 24 July: 5.

Bonello, D. (2004) 'Car makers find value in the web', *Marketing,* 7 July: 14.

Chaston, I. (2001) *e-Marketing Strategy*, Maidenhead: McGraw-Hill.

Copley, P. (2004) *Marketing Communications Management*, Oxford: Butterworth-Heinemann.

Dwer, R., Schurr, P. and Oh, S. (1987) 'Developing buyer–seller relationships', *Journal of Marketing*, April: 11–27.

Egan, J. (2004) *Relationship Marketing: Exploring Relational Strategies in Marketing*, 2nd edn, Harlow: FT/Prentice Hall.

Holder, D. (2005) 'Marketing goes direct', *The Marketer*, 18 November, Cookham, Berkshire: Chartered Institute of Marketing, p. 25.

IAB (2005) 'The on-line direct marketing guide', Interactive Advertising Bureau, http://www. Iab.net.

Kelly, S. (2000) 'Analytical CRM: the fusion of data and intelligence', *Interactive Marketing*, (3): 262–7.

Kitchen, P.J. (1999) *Marketing Communications: Principles and Practice*, London: Thomson Learning.

Kotler, P. (1997) *Marketing Management: Analysis, Planning, Implementation and Control*, Englewood Cliffs, NJ: Prentice Hall.

Marketing Direct (2005) London: Haymarket Business Publications.

McDonald, M. (2000) 'On the right track,' *Marketing Business,* April, Cookham: CIM, pp. 28–31.

Mohammed, R.A., Fisher, R.J., Jaworski, B.J. and Cahill, A.M. (2002) *Internet Marketing: Building Advantage in the Networked Economy*, New York: McGraw-Hill.

Murphy, D. (2005) 'A clean sweep', *The Marketer,* 18 November, Cookham, Berkshire: Chartered Institute of Marketing, pp. 11–13.

Payne, A., Christopher, M. and Peck, H. (1995) *Relationship Marketing for Competitive Advantage: Winning and Keeping Customers*, Oxford: Butterworth Heinemann.

Rayport, J.F. and Jaworski, B.J. (2001) *E-Commerce*, Boston, MA: McGraw-Hill/Irwin.

Reichheld, F. (1996) *The Loyalty Effect*, Boston, MA: Harvard Business School Press.

Ritson, M. (2006) 'New media are defining marketing', *Marketing,* 26 July, 19.

Ronay, A. (2005) 'Paint your brand', *The Marketer*, 16 September, Cookham, Berkshire: Chartered Institute of Marketing, pp. 6–7.

Smith, P.R. (1998) *Marketing Communications: An Integrated Approach*, 2nd edn, London: Kogan Page.

Smith, P.R. and Taylor, J. (2002) *Marketing Communications: An Intergrated Approach*, 3rd edn, London: Kogan Page.

Svennevig, M. (2005) 'Press the red button', *The Marketer,* 18 November, Cookham, Berkshire: Chartered Institute of Marketing, pp. 22–3.

Tapp, A. (1998) *Direct and Database Marketing*, Harlow: Pearson.

Marketing goes direct

Derek Holder, founder of the Institute of Direct Marketing, shares his views on the future of the industry.

Talking to a Marketing Director from a major financial services company whose entire business is direct to consumers, when confronted with the question, 'What is direct marketing?' he replied, 'Direct marketing is marketing'.

This statement is increasingly true. This particular company has built its brand image and database of prospects/customers entirely through direct response advertising. It has developed measurable cross-sell and up-sell programmes, as well as win-back strategies, while adding new business using the Internet and contact centres. The blurring of the traditional marketing disciplines is exaggerated by the multiplicity of new channels to market and the increasing array of media choice available. If you go back to basics, then the question is: what's the difference between direct marketing and marketing?

In the past the consumer was an anonymous buyer. Until Tesco launched its Clubcard in 1993, it did not really know who its customers were. As author Alan Mitchell says,

The problem with traditional marketing branding, advertising and marketing research were surrogates – brands were a surrogate for the relationships between company and customer; advertising the surrogate for the

SOURCE: © TESCO.

Tesco's Clubcard has provided them with an extensive database of information regarding their customers which can be 'mined' to shape future marketing strategies.

dialogue such a relationship produces and marketing research the surrogate for the learning that takes place with the dialogue.

Direct marketing, however, creates the prospect/customer information that provides the dialogue. The simple difference between direct marketing and mass marketing is that the latter talks only to anonymous buyers, while direct marketers talk to known, identified individuals. The question is, what is a better predictor of a customer's future actions? An awareness/intention to purchase a product, or behavioural information on what a customer has already bought?

The importance of data

Behind all good direct marketing is data and a customer database. A database very simply tells you who bought what, when, for how much and where. Adding marketing research might reveal the 'why' answers as well. The fusion of database information and marketing research today has led to the term 'consumer insight'. Enterprise-wide systems were followed by CRM (customer relationship management) systems and today many companies can provide a single view of the customer, which is critical for handling customers across multiple channels and providing a consistent response.

However, three points continue to irk me. First, the misconception that direct marketing is just direct mail. More than five billion mailing pieces are sent per year. Direct mail accounts for 12 per cent of media spend annually, but it is only one of many communications that direct marketers employ. It can be used for both acquisition and retention of customers, depending on the industry sector. It can also help build brands and has several unique qualities: it is a measurable, personal, timely and cost-effective communication medium.

Different industry roles

Second, direct marketing has three different roles in industry. It works for single channel companies, multi-channel companies and plays a supporting role in certain sectors. In the single channel situation all customers are recorded on the database and sales are at a distance. Direct marketing's roots lie in traditional mail order but the modern-day equivalent are companies such as First Direct, Direct Line, MBNA, Screwfix, Amazon and easyJet. These are all pure direct marketing businesses.

In multiple channel companies such as Barclays, Tesco and British Airways, customers have a choice of channels through which to respond. Here all or most of the customers are recorded on a database. Where direct marketing plays a supporting role, most customers are not recorded, but direct marketing is used to support sales (e.g. fast moving consumer goods companies).

Asking permission is only the first step

Third on my list is the notion of permission marketing. How quickly does the recipient tire of your communications but not let you know? It's far better to perceive all marketing communications as personal and relevant. Getting permission is only the start of a dialogue and, to get permission, means using interruption marketing – the opposite concept!

As we enter an era when digital marketing will assume its proper role as integral to marketing strategy (for example, spend online has just topped £1 billion a year), it forces a rethink on the attributes tomorrow's marketer should possess. In my view, the modern marketer must be digitally able, brand literate, media and channel dexterous, data literate, financially literate and ethically informed. The Institute of Direct Marketing, as an education trust, is working with leading UK business schools to ensure this vision is built into the curriculum. And, finally, to ensure the four Ps of marketing are assigned to the graveyard of the twentieth century.

Questions

1   Elaborate on the comment that 'behind all good DM is data and a database'.
2   What advantages might accrue from having 'a single view of the customer'?
3   Why is permission marketing seen as being important?

Source: *The Marketer*, 18 November 2005 (used with permission).

CHAPTER FOURTEEN

PERSONAL SELLING, POINT-OF-SALE AND SUPPORTIVE COMMUNICATIONS

LEARNING OBJECTIVES

Having completed this chapter you should be able to:

- Describe the strengths and weaknesses associated with personal selling and its importance as part of the marketing communications mix.
- Comment upon the value of field marketing and multi-level marketing.
- Recognize the importance of packaging in point-of-sale decision making.
- Assess the value of point-of-sale materials to marketing communications.

INTRODUCTION

In the last chapter it was suggested that direct marketing was moving communications closer to the customer. This chapter gets closer still by looking at those elements of the marketing communications mix nearest the consumer and, by definition, closest to the point of purchase. We will examine, therefore, personal selling and those features which together are referred to as **point-of-sale (POS)**, or **point-of-purchase (POP)**. The logic behind presenting what at first might appear disparate tools in one chapter are that personal selling has such a wide spectrum of types from the complex negotiator to the supermarket shop-floor assistant. At the latter end of this continuum point-of-sale features assume a more significant role in the purchasing process.

Figure 14.1 illustrates those influences closest to the (physical) point of sale. Advertising, public relations, sales promotion and sponsorship have a distant influence but may create the conditions to prompt a sale. Direct marketing is generally closer as are interactive tools such as the Internet (although it may be argued this too can be at the point-of-sale). Personal selling and point-of-sale materials are at the customer interface and directly influence the purchase.

Point-of-sale or point-of-purchase
In-store materials displayed at the time the customer is making buying decisions.

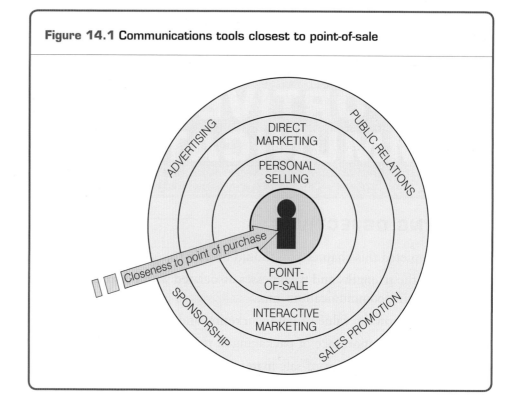

Figure 14.1 Communications tools closest to point-of-sale

PERSONAL SELLING

Personal selling is as old as bartering and much older than any organized monetary system. It evolved from the time when human kind first found themselves with a surplus of a commodity and sought to find others with whom to trade. Despite its traditional place within the 'marketing department' it is not universally accepted that personal selling should be regarded as part of the marketing communications mix. An argument sometimes used is that salespeople are there to sell what already exists (the antipathy of marketing) and/or that it is more to do with customer service than communications. The perspective taken in this text is that salespeople can be persuasive, acting as important communicators and contributing to a successful sale. Perhaps, the term personal communications would describe it better than personal selling.

It is estimated that there are approximately 470 000 professional salespeople in the UK who operate at a cost of around £19 billion (Smith 1998). Although the spectrum of personal selling types is wide, certain important characteristics set it aside from other communications tools. Most importantly the communication is between two (or more) people who interact with each other in 'real-time' and respond to each other's informational needs. This is important because it usually means much less noise (i.e. other distracting communications) and that the customer is involved and, therefore, plays a large part in the buying process. It is frequently, but not always, face-to-face with exceptions being where part or all of the negotiation uses technology (e.g. the telephone, Internet, etc.) as a medium between the salesperson and the customer. Its fundamental aim is to inform, persuade or remind an individual or group to act, in the way desired by the initiator of the contact. The interactivity may, however, be part of a longer term relationship between the salesperson and their customer. In this case current negotiations may be heavily influenced by past experience.

Personal selling is seen as an action-driving tool which is most effective at or near the point-of-sale. As such other longer-term, brand building tools (e.g. advertising, public relations, etc.) are seen as complementary to personal selling. It is a tool that is heavily used in more complex, industrial or business-to-business (B2B) situations, whereas it is less intensely used in business-to-consumer (B2C) marketing. Where personal sales are significant in B2C is in retailing and in the sale of products or services direct to the customer, frequently in their own homes (e.g. Avon) or through personal technology (e.g. telephony) medium.

In the marketing communications effectiveness model (see Chapter 1, Figure 1.6) personal selling's influence is seen to peak at the point of purchase. In business to consumer marketing, many consumer services (e.g. financial services, personal care, etc.) and some retail operations, the importance of personal sales support continues after the transaction and the salesperson may build up a long-term relationship with the customer. In the past this level of relationship might have been with the local insurance salesman or woman (e.g. 'the man from the Prudential'),[1] the local shop-keeper or bank manager. Today this might be with your financial adviser, sales assistant (of your favourite store) or personal shopper. What they all have in common is relationships. The effectiveness of personal selling model (Figure 14.2) is amended to show that, in certain circumstances, the importance of personal salesmanship (or saleswomenship) may extend into the post-purchase period.

Salespeople come in all types and utilize different approaches in their professional lives. There are those who fit the popular stereotype of the pushy, unrelenting, 'foot-in-the-door' individual whose particular skills appear to be a necessary feature of some industries (e.g. second-hand cars). Equally certain is that there are those who are honest, reliable and supportive, characteristics that are particularly important if any trusting relationship is to be built. Credibility also plays a large part. The best salespeople believe in the value of their product/service and are able to transmit this belief to the customer.

Personal selling is most effective when:

- New products are introduced.
- New features are developed.
- The product or service is complex and requires explanation and/or demonstration.
- The product or service is recognized as a long-term expenditure/investment.

[1]'Trust the man from the Pru' was a long running tag line of the Prudential Insurance Company.

- There is a need for negotiation and/or response to feedback.
- Relationship building is part of the marketing strategy.

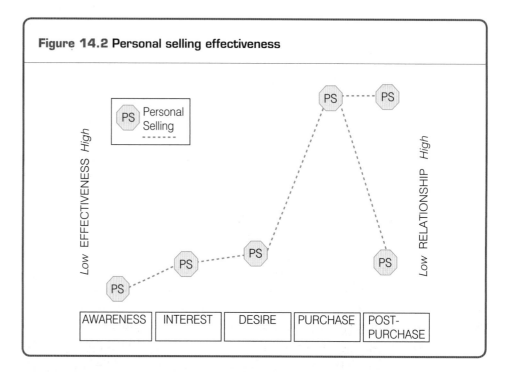

Figure 14.2 Personal selling effectiveness

Personal selling is important in situations where other communication tools are weak, particularly where instant response and complex explanations are needed and where relationship building and maintenance are major factors in the business. Where negotiation is the norm (largely but not exclusively in business to business situations) salesmanship is also an important factor in finalizing the sale. It is also logical to assume that the smaller the number of customers and, consequentially, the greater percentage contribution these customers make to turnover, the more likely the requirement for a relationship-based, personal sales operation.

The value and salience of a product or service also appears to be important. Whereas 80 per cent of car purchases involve buyers searching for information on the internet only 5 per cent of actual sales take place using this medium. Buyers still apparently want some form of human intervention (and the possibility of negotiation) that is not necessarily available through technological mediums. Box 14.1 compares the factors that influence the importance of personal selling as compared with mass marketing tools.

On the downside personal selling has a number of distinct weaknesses notably:

- Cost
- Reach and frequency
- Control

Cost has always been a major factor in the use of personal selling and how it is managed in organizations. There are effectively two types of salesperson,

Box 14.1	Comparisons of personal selling and mass communications	
	Personal Selling	**Mass Marketing**
Information needs	High	Low
Complexity	High	Low
Number of customers	Low	High
Pricing	Negotiable	Set
Order size	High	Low
Value/Salience	High	Low

those located generally in one place and those who normally visit their customers. In business to business marketing salespeople of the latter type spend between 5 and 10 per cent of their time in negotiations with customers. Although a percentage of this time may be involved in relationship building this still represents to many an inefficiency. Organizations may be seen to reduce the impact of these disadvantages through the management of their customer base and/or though the use of technology as a medium. Another suggestion is to encourage customers to come to them at the organization's showroom or an appropriate exhibition. Further Pareto analysis suggests around 80 per cent of orders are generated by 20 per cent of the customer base and this mismatch is observable in most if not all organizations. The importance of the customer to an organization, therefore, acts as a measure of the importance of personal selling relative to other tools. Customers further down the chain may have considerably less personal contact with most of their communications being through other tools (e.g. telemarketing, catalogues, etc.). Even where customers travel to the salesperson (often at a fixed retail location) cost is a factor. There is, therefore, usually a direct correlation between the relative number of salespeople and the profit margins in the sector.

Pareto analysis
The general supposition that business relationships follow an 80:20 ratio (e.g. 80 per cent of business comes from 20 per cent of customers).

According to Albers (2000) factors which affect the efficiency and effectiveness of the salesperson are partly under the control of the individual and partly due to exogenous circumstances. From the salesperson's perspective it is determined by the effort they put in (number of calls, calling time, etc.) and their own personal characteristics (e.g. experience, attitude, aptitude and education). Exogenous factors include the effect of sales management (type of supervision, experience, etc.), the marketing effort of the firm (e.g. advertising), the characteristics of the territory (potential, customer concentration, etc.) and the level of competitive activity they face.

In order to contain personal selling costs back-office administrators will often contact prospects and create sales appointments and organize travel schedules to optimize the effect (and lower the costs) of sales personnel. This begins a process known as the 7Ps of selling, which consist of:

● Prospecting: looking for prospective customers.

● Preparation: customer research, objective setting, etc.

- Presentation: demonstration and discussion.
- Possible problems: foreseeing and handling objections.
- Please give me the order: closing the sale and getting the order.
- Pen-to-paper: recording details accurately.
- Post-sales service: developing the relationship.

The problem of controlling organizational messages with a diverse sales-force is another important potential downside of personal selling (and one shared with public relations – see Figure 14.3 below). However well-intentioned the salespeople may be they may jeopardize the company's image by poor, inconsistent or inaccurate communications. **Over-selling** (i.e. claiming more for the product/service than can be achieved) is a particular problem. Customers do not usually complain if they get what they expect, but not living up to expectations is a major cause of dissatisfaction. Salespeople often have a financial or other stake in a sale. This *may* encourage inaccurate information or highly speculative claims in an attempt to close the sale. For example, the recent heavy fines by the UK financial regulator on organizations whose sales force were involved in over-selling (or **mis-selling**) the features of endowment mortgages. Organizations may attempt to overcome this lack of control over salespeople by regular training and the updating of product/service information but there is always an unpredictability associated with human behaviour.

Another charge against a minority of sales personnel is that they may hustle and cajole customers into a sale. Commonly called the **hard sell** it was not so long ago that this was seen as evidence of salesmanship and that it was up to the customer to beware (*caveat emptor*). Attitudes to this type of practice have changed and legislation has been introduced in most developed markets inserting 'cooling-off periods', during which the customer can withdraw from any commitment made through personal selling. Conversely the term **soft sell** is often used to

Over-selling
Promising more than is available through the sale.

Mis-selling
Selling something based on a falsehood.

Hard sell
Promoting heavily the tangible benefits available from a product or service.

Soft sell
Using emotional appeals to produce positive feelings for a brand.

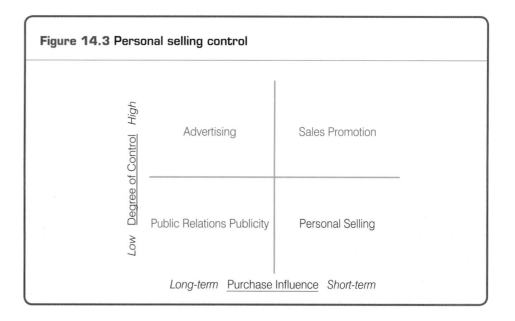

Figure 14.3 Personal selling control

	Long-term Purchase Influence *Short-term*
High Degree of Control	Advertising · Sales Promotion
Low	Public Relations Publicity · Personal Selling

describe selling techniques where the salesperson's candour, perceived honesty and friendliness appear to disarm the customer's natural defences.

In business to business markets sales forces are organized in a number of different ways depending on the industry, customer requirements and/or the history of sales in the organization. Amongst the most common formats are those that are shown in Box 14.2 below.

Box 14.2 Sales force organization

Sales Force Type	Common Titles
Geographically based	Area/regional sales manager
Product or brand-based	Product/brand manager
Market-based	Category manager
Account-based	Account manager

Geographically based sales personnel are the most common and straightforward means of organizing a sales force. It is usually highly responsive and represents the least duplication of calls upon customers. It also concentrates the effort within the designated territory. The disadvantage in a multi-brand organization is that this type of sales force is unlikely to have specialist knowledge about any or all the products and/or services on offer. Product or brand-based sales teams will usually have a greater knowledge of the offering (which may increase credibility) but can involve duplicating the visits of other members of the sales team. Account-based sales teams usually deal with one, or a very few major accounts whilst other customers (of lesser relative importance) are handled in more general ways (e.g. geographically, product-based, etc.). Account managers frequently build up close relationships with their customers and may even be based part or all of the time in the customer's workplace. The major danger associated with getting *too* close to the customer (particularly in business-to-business relationships) is that it may hamper or restrict negotiation and potentially add to overall costs.

IN-STORE SALES

In-store sales people possess many of the same characteristics and personal skills associated with their business-to-business colleagues. As a generality the greater the retail price and margin and the greater the salience, the more experienced sales staff are required to be. At this end of the scale the salesperson at, for example Tiffany, may only have to work with a few customers each day. At the other end, supermarkets have few (if any) dedicated sales staff.

@

For more information on in-store marketing look at *In Store Magazine's* website: **http:// www.instoremagazine.co.uk/.**

Field marketing
Syndicated or shared teams working largely in the fast moving consumer goods sector, who carry out a number of selling and other 'sales' associated tasks on behalf of one or more suppliers.

Not all in-store sales are undertaken by employees of the company. The term field marketing is used to describe syndicated or shared teams who work, largely in the fast moving consumer goods sector, and who carry out a number of selling and other 'sales' associated tasks on behalf of one or more suppliers. Field marketing originated in the 1960s when fast moving consumer goods giants such as Mars sought to increase penetration in the independent stores sector (Benady 2002). The range of activities carried out by field marketing companies have become very wide covering (and in many ways bridging) both personal sales and point-of-sale activities including:

- Sales calls (typically on smaller, independent retailers).
- Sampling and other in-store promotions.
- Merchandising and in-store displays.
- Market research (including as mystery shoppers).
- Event marketing: representing and promoting the brand at major events.

Mystery shoppers
Researchers who visit a store under the guise of a shopper for the purpose of consumer observation.

The advantage to the supplier of utilizing field marketers is in the generally lower outsourced costs of the syndicated teams and the avoidance of high fixed costs associated with employing a sales force. On the downside, as field marketers are not employed directly by the organization the risks associated with controlling inconsistent or inaccurate communications are high.

Multi-level marketing
Selling direct to the public through a network of self-employed salespeople, often at house parties and other private gatherings. The multi-level marketing company initially recruits distributors who in turn recruit more distributors and so on. Earnings come both from a distributor's own sales and the sales of those they recruit (and often even further down the line).

Another form of personal selling that has increased dramatically in the last few decades is multi-level marketing also known as network selling and (particularly when being disparaged) as pyramid selling. The terms broadly describe selling direct to the public, through a network of self-employed salespeople, often at house parties and other private gatherings. The multi-level marketing company initially recruits distributors who in turn recruit more distributors and so on. Earnings come both from a distributor's own sales and the sales of those they recruit (and often even further down the line). The success of building and maintaining such a structure often relies on a form of corporate evangelism, which infects and drives the participants not only to greater sales but (often more importantly) to further recruit other distributors and the dream of significant future income as the 'pyramid' grows. Although some schemes may work well many have unscrupulously exploited distributors through high training fees and the high cost of sample packs, such that legal restrictions have been imposed in many developed markets limiting the charges associated with this form of selling.

Pyramid selling
A form of multi-level marketing where the central purpose is to earn commission (or receive other payments) from those further down the line rather than sales *per se*.

THE FUTURE OF PERSONAL SELLING

The future of personal selling as a major communications (and sales) medium will, as organizations look to curtail costs, be heavily determined by technological advances which are making location of diminishing importance.

Field marketing activities

Field marketing is a form of personal selling that can involve a variety of different activities aimed at end consumers and/or trade outlets.

When Lever Fabergé launched their 'Sunsilk Frizz Control Cream' in 2004, they recruited teams of brand ambassadors to distribute one million samples of the new haircare product in 20 days across the UK. In order to do this they provided motor scooters to half of their team members who completed a full motorbike test enabling them to carry a passenger and tow a trailer. Teams of eight leather clad females on four Sunsilk branded scooters would arrive in town centres to the accompaniment of music such as 'Walking on Sunshine' to underline the key brand insight. The imaginative and dramatic way in which samples were distributed not only turned heads, it also helped to generate excellent brand recognition and awareness as well as reinforcing brand values alongside the above-the-line campaign. (See www.thegalleryuk.com/sunsilk.htm).

When Bosch and Dremel joined forces to promote sales and distribution of their power tool products in B&Q warehouse and Homebase stores throughout the UK, 48 skilled trades people were recruited to demonstrate the products in-store to the end-user consumer. Over a period of ten weeks during the peak Christmas sales period, 700 Bosch demonstration days were organized with a further 200 additional demonstration days for Dremel products. A total of 24 627 demonstrations prompted 6743 sales as a direct result (5463 Bosch and 1280 Dremel products), averaging 9.56 sales per day.

When Interbrew wanted to achieve maximum visibility for their Stella Artois and Tennent's brands and block competitor display during the vital sales period leading to Christmas, they naturally chose to focus their efforts on sales calls and merchandising. Retailers throughout the UK were approached and encouraged to take part in the 'Christmas Space Race'. They were given the responsibility of purchasing key stock to create floor displays which would have to feature a mixture of canned and bottled drinks and include at least five cases of 'six-packs'. Retailers were also encouraged to enhance their displays with appropriate point-of-sale material. Each retailer complying with the display criteria was given a free case of Stella Artois large cans and the best displays in each of the 18 territories were awarded a stocked double-door chiller. The retailer with the best display, not only won a Citroën Relay van, he saw his multi-pack sales rise from zero to an average of 20 cases per week.

Minicase written by Nik Mahon, Faculty of Media, Arts and Society, Southampton Solent University (www.field.dma.org.uk/content/inf-case.asp).

SOURCE: IMAGE COURTESY OF FDS FIELD MARKETING.

The Sunsilk roadshow invovled three teams of eight leather-clad women that toured UK town centres on branded scooters handing out over 1 000 000 samples to a defined target audience.

Where technology can effectively replace the salesperson (as for example in the case of travel agent services and insurance sales) it will inevitably lead to a decline. Electronic point-of-sale (EPOS) technology can calculate sales and order replacements more effectively than any travelling salesperson. Even in the business-to-business sector, where complex contract negotiation has to take place, personal meetings may be replaced by video-conferencing or video telephones. Documentation can be transmitted electronically with electronic signatures removing yet another reason for negotiators to meet face-to-face. In the business-to-consumer sector, traditional person-to-person contact that the customer may have had with his or her bank manager or insurance salesperson are now largely handled by call centres using customer relationship management (CRM) technology.

Despite these advances human beings crave personal contact, as these are the basis of strong relationships. The attempt to use technology to wholly substitute interaction may prove destructive and there is ample evidence of the consuming public's annoyance at call centres.[2]

POINT-OF-SALE

Point-of-sale (POS) or (as favoured in North America) point-of-purchase (POP) has often been regarded as the least glamorous of the communication sectors, yet it is considerably important from a communication and sales perspective. Point-of-sale is particularly important in fast moving consumer goods retailing where point-of-sale materials play the part of the 'silent salesperson'[3] communicating the features, benefits and subtleties associated with the decision to buy. Marketplace research suggests[4] that only 30 per cent of US consumer purchases are specifically planned and that the remaining 70 per cent of decisions are made in-store. Kotler *et al.* (1999) suggest that 53 per cent of all purchases are made on impulse. Research by Point of Purchase Advertising International (POPAI), the industry trade body, also suggests that just under three-quarters of purchase decisions are made without pre-planning on the part of the consumer (Europe 67.2 per cent, USA 72 per cent). Although impressive these figures should be regarded with some scepticism as they ignore the conscious or subconscious influence of other marketing communications (i.e. advertising) on the ultimate purchase. However, this warning aside point-of-sale marketing is significant and should not be underrated.

@

POP Industry Bodies: **www.popai.co.uk** and **www.instoremarketer.org**.

---

[2]In a recent (2004) nationwide telephone poll conducted by the BBC programme 'Brassed-off Britain' call centres came a close third to banks and junk-mail for what annoyed the British most (www.bbc.co.uk/bob). These top three were well ahead of the rest of the field.
[3]The original term 'silent salesman' was coined by Kornblau (1961: 296).
[4]1995 POPAI (Point-of-purchase Adverting International) study quoted in Shimp 2003.

Packaging

The most basic (and often underrated) marketing communication tool is a product's packaging. Attracting various descriptions such as the 'least expensive form of advertising', the 'five-second commercial' and the 'silent salesman', it should not be forgotten that although packaging serves to protect, contain and offer convenience to the purchaser it is also a major communications device. Good packaging in this respect should:

- Gain attention (through attractive or brash or familiar labelling).
- Be distinctive (e.g. Cillit Bang).
- Instruct and inform (e.g. serving suggestions, calorific and ingredient information).
- Signify value for money (e.g. through size, promotion, etc.).
- Help persuade (or 'nudge') the purchaser toward a purchase (e.g. competitions, etc.).
- Reflect the personality of the brand (e.g. Peperami).
- Motivate brand choice.

Packaging (unlike other communications) offers instant gratification, is reasonably cost-effective and can be altered at short notice. It helps 'brand-loyalists' identify the product and, more generally, assists brand choice decisions. Packaging designers talk about the value of **shelf impact** (Keller 1998). It is, however, not just the writing and imagery that contributes to good packaging but shape, for example Cif Lemon, Bovril and Heinz Ketchup, adds to its impact. Brands such as Orangina, Perrier and Coca-Cola are instantly recognizable by the shape of their containers. It is interesting to note that this latter icon of the twentieth century, the Coca-Cola bottle,[5] did not come about by accident. The original design brief from the company was that (Smith 1998):

Shelf impact
The impact of product packaging.

> we need a new bottle – a distinctive package that will help us fight substitutes... we need a bottle which a person will recognise as a Coca-Cola bottle even when he feels it in the dark. The Coca-Cola bottle should be shaped that, even if broken, a person could tell what it is.

Size and or presentation can also be a feature. Normally larger packs communicate better value but this is not always necessarily the case. Returning to Coca-Cola as an example, in the UK consumer goods market three main packages[6] are popular. These are the can, the traditional bottle (often now plastic rather than glass) and the 'family-size' bottle. A quick calculation of prices (in whatever retail type) shows no real correlation between quantity and price. Even though all three sizes may be available at one outlet they are aiming at different marketplaces. The portability and throw-away nature of

[5]Such is the strength of the Coca-Cola imagery that a recent advertising campaign replaced the product name with the campaign tag line relying wholly on the bottle shape and the tag-line typography for recognition.
[6]Although other sizes (e.g. miniatures) also exist.

the can appears to be aimed at the young, whereas the family-sized bottle is aimed (rather obviously) at the home market. The traditional bottle, however, remains associated with the products history and reputation and often sells at a distinct premium from the other sizes. Aficionados might also suggest that the taste is somehow better in a bottle!

Colour has a particular part to play in conveying meaning and emotion to prospective buyers. The degree to which it can have an effect can be quite startling. A study by Tom *et al.* (1987) used three identical vanilla puddings with minor differences in their colour (induced by the addition of food colouring). Of the three shades of brown the majority of interviewees described the dark brown pudding as the richest and with the best chocolate taste whereas the light brown pudding was the creamiest. Ernest Dichter's research (Smith 1998) also suggests that colour affects perception. In this case four containers were presented each with the same coffee but with different colour exteriors. When questioned about the flavour and aroma of the coffee:

- 73 per cent believed the coffee in the dark-brown container was too strong.
- 84 per cent believed the coffee in the red container was richer.
- 79 per cent believed the coffee in the blue container was milder.
- 87 per cent believed the coffee in the yellow container was too weak.

It is understandable, given this information why Nescafé uses colour to distinguish between various flavours.

Of all colours the colour red is amongst the most prominent and the chosen corporate colour for brands such as Coca-Cola, *The Economist*, Virgin and the re-launched Abbey brand. It is described as 'active, stimulating, energetic and vital' (Shimp 2003: 191). Brand expert Professor Leslie de Chesatony notes (Ronay 2005: 6) that.

> 'going back to the early evolution of mankind red was the colour that evoked basic protection instincts. As such it is still a colour that instils a drive in people to take some action'.

Other colours give different messages but these may, however, be culturally specific as noted in Box 14.3.

Point-of-sale materials

Point-of-sale materials are important because they communicate with consumers at the time and place that they are ready to make purchasing decisions. They are designed to inform, remind and encourage customers toward the promoted product. They act as in-store reminder cues which capitalize on previous consumption experiences and/or media advertising. For example the Duracell and EverReady battery brands frequently feature a 'bunny' and 'battery-man' respectfully in their various in-store campaigns. In-store displays (and packaging) carry these themes through to the shop

Box 14.3   The influence of colour

Red	Red is a high-wavelength colour (as are yellow and orange) and generates excitement. It is described as active, stimulating, energetic and vital. It is the colour of prohibition and warning in Europe but it is also associated with love (e.g. Hershey Hearts). Popular in China as it implies good-luck and in India where it is a Hindu symbol of love and generally denotes life, action and gaiety. In Ireland (together with white and blue) and Paraguay (with green and blue) the colour has political connotations.
White	The colour for weddings in Europe and North America, where it generally denotes purity and mildness (therefore, often used for toiletries and soaps, e.g. Dove). In China and South America, however, it denotes mourning and in India it is the most important priestly colour.
Blue	The colour associated with baby boys in the UK, baby girls in Belgium and eastern France and females in Japan. It is seen as trustworthy in Europe and India. It is also associated with coolness and refreshment and is often used in skin products (e.g. Nivea) and spearmint products (e.g. Wrigley). Lighter shades of blue are associated with mildness (e.g. Nescafé, Silk Cut).
Black	The European and North American colour for mourning and funerals. Combined with yellow in nature it means warning and is similarly used in this combination on road signs. Also in this combination it is used for brash, over-the-top, signage associated with downmarket retailers. However, combined with gold, it suggests elegance and superiority (e.g. John Player Special).
Yellow	A high wavelength colour which is the colour of caution in Europe (usually combined with black in hazard warning signage). It is an Imperial Chinese colour which denotes grandeur and mystery. In India it is associated with merchants and second only to white in denoting sanctity. It is the colour of Sultans in Malaysia (and therefore never worn by the common people) and of despair in Brazil. It is the colour of lemons and frequently used if this is an important ingredient (e.g. Cif).
Pink	The colour associated with baby girls in the UK, baby boys in Belgium and eastern France and which is a masculine colour in Japan.
Orange	A high wavelength colour which is the national colour of the Netherlands. In Northern Ireland it is the colour of Loyalists and therefore unpopular with republicans north and south. It is often used, as yellow, for brash, over-the-top, signage associated with downmarket retailers. Orange is the colour of easyJet perhaps reflecting its low pricing.
Green	The colour denoting the environment and environmental issues in Europe and in brands to reflect their environmental concerns (e.g. BP). It is a significant colour for all Muslims and has religious significance in Malaysia. It is the colour most associated with Ireland and often used to express Irish associations (e.g. Kerrygold). It is also associated with abundance, health, calmness and serenity and often used in packaging for beverages (e.g. Heineken, Sprite, Seven-up, etc.) and mint and mentholated products (e.g. Wrigley).
Purple	The colour of royalty in the UK and associated with quality and elegance and associated with superiority (e.g. Cadbury). It is also associated with mourning and sorrow in many countries.

Sources: *Marketer*, 16 September 2005, Shimp 2003 and various.

floor. These characters act as differentiators between these and other brands in the battery market.

To emphasize the effect point-of-sale displays can have on sales, a POPAI (1992) supported research study undertaken in Canada in 80 stores across four major pharmaceutical (drug-store) chains involving the Benylin cough syrup and Listerine mouth wash brands highlights the impact. The stores were put into four groups (a control group plus three others) as described in Box 14.4. The result of featuring these products in prime locations were certainly impressive. Even though the feature price evidently affected sales it was the prominent positioning that showed the highest increases in turnover.

Merchandising
The act of deciding upon store layout and the product mix within it.

Merchandising involves the logical placement of merchandise to fulfil the store's objectives. Increasing the shelf space given to a brand (manufacturer or own-label) and/or placing merchandise at the optimum height (eye-level) both noticeably improve sales. Merchandisers are also responsible for ensuring goods make it rapidly to the shelves. Failure to keep shelves stacked was seen as a major reason for Sainsbury's poor sales in the early part of the millennium.

The way stores are designed can effect the sales of the products within and flow modelling (which takes into account that 90 per cent of people who enter a stores turn to the right) guide customers around to each site (e.g. IKEA). Lighting and signage is used to emphasize and attract potential customers. In-store displays are designed to direct customers toward products and include:

@

For more information on in-store research look at: **www.ddimagazine.com/ displayanddesignideas/design_center/ instore_marketing.jsp**.

- brand display units (supplied normally by brand owner)
- dump bins
- show cards
- posters
- video
- sampling

Technology is also being used to direct customers through in-store design technology (e.g. B&Q), interactive kiosks and coupon dispensers.

@

For an example of a retail activity research company look at: **www.rms-uk.com**.

Proximity to the point of purchase is evidently an important influence on the consumer. The communication opportunities offered by managing point-of-sale materials should be managed as efficiently and effectively as any other marketing communication tools.

Box 14.4 Point-of-sale research

	Pricing	Position	Benylin*	Listerine*
1	Regular Price	Normal Shelf Position	control	control
2	Feature Price	Normal Shelf Position	29% increase	11% increase
3	Feature Price	End of Aisle display	98% increase	141% increase
4	Feature Price	Aisle/Front Aisle display	139% increase	162% increase

Source: Shimp 2003.

*increase is over control sample results.

Summary

This chapter looked at those elements of the marketing communications mix that are nearest the point of purchase. It discusses the strengths and weaknesses of personal selling and the situations where it is deemed important and necessary. As a costly tool it looks at the ways managers may handle a sales force efficiently and effectively and the various ways a sales force can be organized. It reviewed the selling process and emphasized the growing importance of retaining and developing existing customers. Field marketing, where syndicated teams carry out a number of sales and other associated tasks, was discussed as was the sometimes dubious nature of multi-level marketing. Packaging was described as the 'silent salesperson' as it was seen to gain attention through its distinctiveness, instruct and inform and motivate brand choice. The importance of point-of-sale materials were described and the importance of prime display space discussed.

Review questions

1 Is there a difference between POP (point-of-purchase) and POS (point-of-sale)?
2 When is personal selling most effective?
3 What are the 7Ps of selling?
4 Define 'field marketing'.
5 Explain the key weaknesses of personal selling.
6 What is 'pyramid' selling?
7 Explain the difference between a hard and a soft sell.
8 What is 'over selling'?
9 Describe the key promotional roles of packaging.
10 List examples of in-store displays.

Discussion questions

1 Explain the principal differences between personal selling and mass communications and discuss why these might be so. How might companies construct their personal-selling approach to reflect these differences?

2 Why might an organization use mystery shoppers? How would you plan a mystery shopping campaign and what would it entail?

3 It has been shown that consumers respond to colour and make associations to the products that accompany it. To what extent do you believe this to be true?

Further reading

Jaramillo, F., Mulki, J.P. and Solomon, P. (2006) 'The role of ethical climate on salesperson's role stress, job attitudes, turnover intention, and job performance', *Journal of Personal Selling & Sales Management*, Summer, 26 (3): 271–82. A demonstration that an ethical climate results in lower role conflict and role ambiguity and higher satisfaction, which results in organizational commitment and lower turnover intention.

Jones, E., Brown, S.P., Zoltners, A.A. and Weitz, B.A. (2005) 'The changing environment of selling and sales management', *Journal of Personal Selling & Sales Management*, Spring, 25 (2): 105–11. New developments and trends in selling and sales management are creating demands and opportunities that require adaptation and new approaches, this paper summarizes the critical dimensions of change.

Mermelstein, E. and Abu-Shalback Zid, L. (2006) 'Clothes call', *Marketing Management*, Jan./Feb., 15 (1): 6. The findings of a market survey on consumers' decisions on clothing purchases which asserts that point-of-purchase and in-store print information influence final decisions on clothing purchases.

Roper, S. and Parker, C. (2006) 'How (and where) the mighty have fallen: branded litter', *Journal of Marketing Management*, Jul., 22 (5/6): 473–87. This article focuses upon packaging, which has been described as 'the silent salesperson' playing an important role in communicating with the consumer at the point-of-sale.

Sharma, A. (2006) 'Success factors in key accounts', *Journal of Business & Industrial Marketing*, 21 (2): 141–50. Examining the success factors for key accounts within firms, i.e. what factors lead to successful versus unsuccessful key accounts. Design/methodology and approach.

Tom, G., Lopez, S. and Demir, K. (2006) 'A comparison of the effect of retail purchase and direct marketing on the endowment effect', *Psychology & Marketing*, Jan., 23 (1): 1–10. Retail channel of delivery and consumer expectation with the possession of the product at the point-of-purchase leading to a strengthening of the endowment.

Chapter references

Albers, S. (2000) 'Sales-force management' in K. Blois, *The Oxford Textbook of Marketing*, Oxford: Oxford University Press, pp. 292–315.

Benady, D. (2002) 'Fielding discussion', *Marketing*, 19 September: 39–40.

Blythe (2004) *Sales and Key Account Management*, London: Thomson Learning.

De Pelsmacker, P., Geuens, M. and Van den Bergh, J.V. (2001) *Foundations of Marketing Communications: A European Perspective*, London: Prentice Hall.

Keller, K.L. (1998) *Strategic Brand Management: Building, Measuring and Managing Brand Equity*, Harlow: Prentice Hall.

Kornblau, C. (1961) 'Packaging and supermarkets: the package in the marketplace', *Effective Marketing Coordination*, Chicago, IL: American Marketing Association.

Kotler, P., Bowen, J. and Makens, J.C. (1999) *Marketing for Hospitality and Tourism*, Upper Saddle River, NJ: Prentice Hall.

POPAI/Warner-Lambert (1992) *Canada POP Effectiveness Study*, Englewood, NJ: The Point of Purchase Advertising Institute.

Ronay, A. (2005) 'Paint your brand', *The Marketer*, 16 September, Cookham, Berkshire: Chartered Institute of Marketing, pp. 6–7.

Shimp, T.A. (2003) *Advertising, Promotion and Supplemental Aspects of Integrated Marketing Communication*, Cincinnati: Thomson.

Smith, P.R. (1998) *Marketing Communications: An Integrated Approach*, 2nd edn, London: Kogan Page.

Tom, G., Barnett, T., Lew, W. and Selmants, J. (1987) 'Cueing the consumer: the role of salient cues in consumer perception', *The Journal of Consumer Marketing*, 4 (Spring) 23–7.

CASE STUDY 14.1

Innocent fruit drinks

Since the launch of their first fruit smoothie drinks in 1999, Innocent Drinks have seen a phenomenal growth in the popularity of their brand. The company was founded by three London City workers Richard Reed, Jon Wright and Adam Balon, who felt that nutritional-starved Londoners would benefit from their vitamin-rich product. Their initial market research was conducted from a stall they hired at a local jazz festival:

> We put a sign over the stall asking the customers if we should give up our jobs and form a company, providing two bins for the empty bottles, one that said 'yes' and one that said 'no'. At the end of the day the 'yes' bin was overflowing.

Innocent fruit drinks are now a common sight in coffee bars, delicatessens, sandwich shops and supermarkets across the UK. By 2004, the company turnover was in the region of £11 million. At the heart of the company's success was the simple ethos that: if the product was good enough and the communications strategy witty enough, the product couldn't fail. A fundamental part of the witty communication strategy was the packaging of the product.

With only a small budget, the three partners did not have the funds to hire top designers or market research companies. They hired a friend, Dan Germain, to look after the branding and emailed packaging designs to other friends and acquaintances, who were asked for their views and opinions. The partners' general lack of knowledge with regard to the design process or the finer aspects of sourcing and developing the right image, meant that they were forced to keep things simple.

The resulting design for the pack was one that projected simplicity and the basic qualities of the brand itself. The naive approach to the packaging design was totally appropriate for a fruit drink called 'Innocent' and helped to underline the sense of honesty and natural goodness that was key to the brand philosophy. The design brief was to

▶

emphasize the naturalness of the product which is 100 per cent fresh fruit with nothing added. The company also wanted a bottle that sat easily in the hand.

The logo, resembling an apple or a person with a halo, was initially sketched-out on a serviette with a felt tip pen. Germain explains: 'We tried to make everything say instantly that the product is fun and good for you. The bottles are simple and free of gimmickry. They're easy to hold and that's all they need to be.' He adds: 'We didn't have any sophisticated marketing plan. We just wanted to like the way it looked and tasted and for it to stand out on café shelves.'

Innocent understood the importance of communicating its values clearly and consistently through design and supportive communications. At point-of-sale, the design of the bottles projects a clear message to the consumer.

how to make an innocent smoothie

add loads of this

to lots of these

bin the weird stuff

keep it natural

magic

innocent. nothing but nothing but fruit
and a nice bit of sunshine

Packaging which reflected the quality and ethos of the product was at the heart of Innocent Drinks' communications strategy.

Even the copy on the labelling is intended to develop a relationship between the company and the customer, using an informal tone of voice laced with humour. Facts and trivia relating to the brand are presented on the label in a style that is unique to the brand:

> *The deepest well in Europe is 800 metres down. We know this because it's where we got our spring water from. We haven't descended all the way because we're a bit scared, but we found some monkeys who have hats with torches on.*

The label also invites customers to call Innocent on the 'banana phone' or 'pop round to say hello'. Germain says that it's all about 'owning a tone' and making sure that the tone is consistent across everything from labelling to advertising. Witty details on the label, such as '® = Rol poly', or the 'consume by' date on the bottle top being replaced by an 'enjoy by' date, help define that tone and set Innocent apart from their competitors. Innocent even use the label as a recruitment advertisement when they need to hire staff, underlining the role of their packaging design as an advert at point-of-sale.

Innocent continues to extend its product line as it prepares to roll out into different countries. Their design work has won a high level of critical acclaim and in 2004 was nominated for a Silver Award by the D&AD.[7]

Case study questions

1 Why was packaging design so important to the success of the Innocent brand?

2 What problems may the company face as they expand and roll out their product into other countries?

3 How would you define the target market group for this product?

Case study written by Nik Mahon, Faculty of Media, Arts and Society, Southampton Solent University (Source: www.designcouncil.org.uk and presentation by Dan Germain at D&AD Xchange, 3 September 2003).

---

[7]D&AD is an educational charity that represents the global creative, design and advertising communities.
For further information see http://www.dandad.org/about/what-we-do.html.

CHAPTER FIFTEEN

INTEGRATED MARKETING COMMUNICATIONS

LEARNING OBJECTIVES

Having completed this chapter you should be able to:

- Describe the concepts behind integrated marketing communications (IMC).
- Understand the market, industry and media drivers that have promoted integrated marketing communications.
- Recognize the problems associated with integrated marketing communications implementation.
- Assess the potential advantages and disadvantages of integrated marketing communications.

INTRODUCTION

As noted in Chapter 1 integrated marketing communications (IMC) is a concept that has caused considerable debate since its theoretical inception in the late 1980s. Although most academics and practitioners regard integrated marketing communications as a major communications development it is not fully accepted in academia nor fully adopted in the communications industry, largely because of its supposed difficulty to implement. Whilst supporters of integrated marketing communications would argue that under current marketing thinking and in today's markets, effective implementation is critical to success, others would point to the belief that it is an old idea that has little evidence of ever being realized. It is indeed arguable whether integrated marketing communications is a truly new innovation in communications or an old idea revived through the intercession of modern technology. In the early days of commercial communication (see Chapter 1) little if any distinction was made between the marketing communication tools. It was only as organizations expanded and the gap between customers and organizations grew that greater sophistication and specialization was required leading ultimately to the barriers between the marketing communications disciplines.

Despite nearly 20 years of debate most practitioners still see integrated marketing communications as an emerging discipline (Eagle and Kitchen 2000) rather than a fully formed concept. Like many concepts that have yet to fully develop it is subject to varying, and sometimes colourful terminology. Thus '360° Branding', 'Total Branding', 'Whole Egg', 'Seamless Communication', 'New Advertising', 'Orchestration', 'Relationship Marketing', 'One-to-one Marketing', 'Integrated Marketing' and 'Integrated Communications' (Pickton and Broderick 2001; Kliatchko 2005) have all been used to describe all or part of the integrated marketing communications concept prompting the charge that integrated marketing communications is yet another management fad. What most observers agree on is that integrated marketing communications is a good idea in theory but hard to implement in practice. Indeed, even its most fervent supporters would be forced to admit that translating the theory into practice could present organizations with immense problems.

DEFINING INTEGRATED MARKETING COMMUNICATIONS

@

The American Association of Advertising Agencies website can be found at: **www. aaaa.org**.

The Institute of Practitioners in Advertising (IPA) in their criteria for integration use the phrase 'joined-up-thinking' to describe the thread running through a co-ordinated campaign. This concentration on co-ordinating ideas is a theme running through many descriptions of integrated marketing communications. The most often cited definition is that of the American Association of Advertising Agencies (4As) formulated in 1989. This stated that integrated marketing communications was:

> *a concept of marketing communications planning that recognises the added value of a comprehensive plan, that evaluates the strategic roles of a variety of communication disciplines – general advertising, direct response, sales promotion and public relations – and combine these disciplines to provide clarity, consistency and maximum communications impact. (Eagle and Kitchen 2000: 667)*

This sees integrated marketing communications as the process of using promotional tools in a unified way to create synergy (Semenik 2002) and, by taking a holistic view, as an approach that also ensures the continual consideration of a brand's contribution to and inclusion in each and every communication. Here the emphasis is on using the various tools or disciplines and having one communications strategy or plan as the unifying theme and is best summed up by the mantra 'one spirit, one voice, one look' (Kliatchko 2005). Consequently, integrated marketing communications is felt to be concerned with getting all of the various communications messages to work together in order to present a unified message. Ensuring that 'above-the-line' and 'below-the-line' activities are mutually supportive, utilizing consistencies in message and presentation content, duplicating key aspects such as colour, design, straplines and imagery.

Critics have pointed out, however, that there are inadequacies with this definition. If this was all that integrated marketing communications delivered then it was simply describing what many good marketers had been doing for decades. This definition fails to consider factors such as consumer orientation, creativity, measurability, cost-effectiveness and interactivity which are central to the argument for communications integration (Kitchen and Schultz 1999). Under this more holistic viewpoint integrated marketing communications should include *everything* that the organization and its people and brands communicate in their interaction with targets and publics, either deliberately or not (Copley 2004).

Another justification for integrated marketing communications can be found in a theme that has run through this text. Notwithstanding earlier warnings regarding the 'hierarchy of effects' models the varying effectiveness of various marketing communications tools at different stages in the consumption process also supports the notion of synergy and communications impact through integrated marketing communications (see Figure 15.1). Thus advertising can keep the brand 'front-of-mind, public relations maintain the brand's image, while sponsorship helps build associations and sales promotion provides an added incentive to buy.

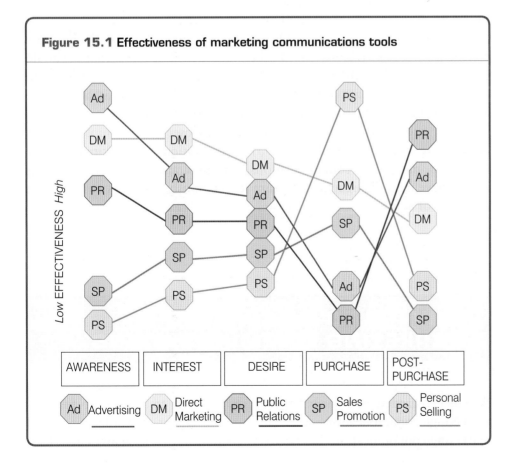

Figure 15.1 Effectiveness of marketing communications tools

Novak and Phelps (1994) suggested that integrated marketing communications, rather than just the co-ordination of marketing communications tools and messages, was based on three conceptualizations:

- One-voice marketing communications: integration which creates a clear consistent image, position, message and/or theme across all marketing communications disciplines or tools.

- Integrated communication: the creation of both brand image and a behavioural response that emanates directly from marketing communications material (e.g. adverts).

- Co-ordinating marketing communications: that associates integration with the concepts of co-ordination of all marketing communications tools to produce a holistic campaign that both develops awareness and builds brand image, at the same time evoking a behavioural response from target audiences. What Smith (1998) describes as wrapping communications around customers and helping them through the various stages of the buying process.

Schultz and Schultz (1998) offer a further definition that expands the theme further. This includes the traditional view of marketing communications tools co-ordination but extends this, not only to all customer contact points but highlights the importance of internal as well as external communications (Kliatchko 2005). This suggests that IMC is a strategic business practice used to plan and implement measurable brand communications programmes over time with all relevant external and internal audiences.

This brings integrated marketing communications in line with the more general concept of 'relationship marketing' when it suggests that it should seek to address all of the organization's relevant publics (or stakeholders) to the organization and not just focus solely on the consumer (Kliatchko 2005). The rationale being that an organization needs to establish relationships both internally and externally, in order to establish closer relationships with and better serve its customers (Berry 1995). Organizations are looking, through integrated marketing communications, to simultaneously consolidate its image, develop a dialogue and nurture its relationship with its customers at all points of contact.

@

For fascinating insights into what industry professionals are thinking look at: www.adverblog.com.

DRIVERS TO INTEGRATED MARKETING COMMUNICATIONS

Whether regarded as a new concept or a return to an earlier form of marketing communications the current movement towards integrated marketing communications has been hastened by dramatic changes in at least three main areas; the marketplace, the organization, and in the media and communications industry.

Market-based drivers

The modern marketplace is highly competitive with low levels of brand differentiation. The result is that organizations must work harder and harder to get their message noticed and appreciated by an audience that is both communications literate and sceptical of the accuracy of claimed benefits. In addition media and audience fragmentation has led to a re-evaluation of mass media and a consequent move towards targeted as opposed to mass communication. This was coupled with a challenge to the traditional transactional marketing paradigm and the subsequent reappraisal of the importance of internal and external relationships.

Media and communications-based drivers

There is no doubt that the media and communications environment has changed significantly in the past two decades. The increased sophistication of the communication industry has been responsible for increased commercial activity and a cluttered environment in which communication has to operate (Copley 2004). These advances have largely been driven by technology which is not only increasing the efficiency of the industry but acting as the catalyst for greater targeting of consumers. On the downside the same technology is creating information overload and clutter, devaluing the power of individual communications. The marketing communications industry in its many formats are 'transitioning through a period of marked, sometimes turbulent, change forcing a re-examination of roles and responsibilities of both marketing and of marketing communications suppliers' (Eagle and Kitchen 2000: 668). There is the implication, however, that the impetus for change in the industry may have had more to do with the problems facing the advertising industry generally rather than any particular or conscious desire for improvement.

Organization-based drivers

Organizations too have been evolving. They are paying more attention to brand development and the need to establish competitive advantage. In respect to the latter some commentators suggest that in today's marketplace marketing communications is the only means of gaining competitive superiority. Organizations are looking to increase profits through improved efficiency meanwhile utilizing managerial time more effectively. On the downside they are increasingly making decisions that produce short-term results. In another development client organizations are looking to set the communications agenda rather than relying on formally powerful agencies to set it for them.

International brands in particular have been looking to establish a clear image of themselves as the media by which it is carried crosses more borders than ever before. Further, the rate of technological advances and most notably the Internet explosion have forced organizations to reconsider their marketing communications options and approaches.

Another organizational challenge is whether integrated marketing communications is right for all types of company and there is some research to suggest that certain organizational types are more likely to implement integrated marketing communications than others (Low 2000). They are:

- Smaller firms (perhaps using less diverse marketing communications tools).
- Firms involved with marketing services rather than products.
- Business-to-consumer (B2C) rather that business-to-business operations.
- Companies whose marketing communications budgets are allocated primarily to advertising (as opposed to trade promotion).
- Firms enjoying higher market shares and realizing greater profits.
- Organizations with experienced marketing communications managers.

Integrated marketing communications has emerged, therefore, for a number of reasons, some proactive and others reactive. Among the most powerful were in reaction to the structural inadequacies of the industry and the realization by clients that their communication objectives could be achieved more effectively and efficiently. As integrated marketing communications pioneer Don E. Schultz (Schultz and Schultz 1998) has noted: 'integration just plain makes sense for those planning to succeed in the twenty-first century marketplace. Marketers, communicators and brand organisations simply have no choice.'

IMPLEMENTING INTEGRATED MARKETING COMMUNICATIONS

Undoubtedly the implementation of integrated marketing communications is an issue that has troubled even its most ardent supporters. Most commentators perceive change itself as a problem as resistance to change is inherent in human beings who seek stability wherever possible. The development of integrated marketing communications requires change, and not simply change within the marketing function but stretching to the 'part-time marketers'[1] and external suppliers (agencies) as well. Given the extent of such upheaval an incremental

---

[1]Gummesson (1990) uses the description 'part-time marketer' to describe non-marketers who have a significant influence on servicing the customer.

approach to implementation is thought most likely to succeed. An example of an integrated marketing communications development model can be seen in Figure 15.2 below. From initial co-ordination of promotional campaigns to functional co-ordination, where different parts of the organisation are introduced to a notion of internal marketing relationships. From here a cultural shift is required if the organization is to move towards stronger customer orientation. Such culture change is not a company-only activity. In research amongst clients and agencies (Eagle and Kitchen 2000) a crucial factor to success was seen to be the ability to match and harmonize client and agency cultures in order to build ongoing relationships.

The perceived complexity in the planning and co-ordination of integrated marketing communication has also been a factor in resisting its introduction. Rather than concentrate on the scope and magnitude of integrated marketing communication implementation, therefore, an alternative approach would be to concentrate on the key aspects of what it entails:

- Customer focus: start with the customer or prospect and work backwards in determining the most appropriate messages (for example customers do not differentiate between public relations and advertising, the website and customer service so why does the organization?).

- Contact: use any form of relevant contact (within reason and efficiency, the more points of contact the better) and be willing to use any communications outlets that are appropriate for meeting the target audience.

- Synergy: achieve synergy through use of marketing communications tools' strengths in support and in co-ordination of a campaign.

- Relationships: build relationships between the brand and the customer.

Progress towards full implementation of integrated marketing communications is regarded as a 'fairly steep learning curve' (Eagle and Kitchen 2000). As with any major change (particularly involving the reorganization of organizational structures) training and staff development programmes are likely to be appropriate. Appointing a 'champion' or 'change agent' may also help direct the organization towards a customer-focused approach. As one respondent in the Eagle and Kitchen (2000: 676) research noted, integrated marketing communications implementation 'requires people whose professionalism is bigger than their ego...skilled and knowledgeable people who will consider all forms of communication'.

@

Integration in practice at: **www.bima.co.uk** and **www.netline.com/newsletter/h/ feature02_02.html.**

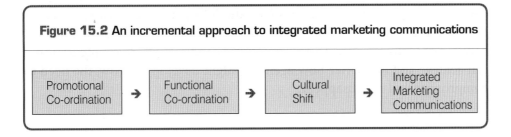

Figure 15.2 An incremental approach to integrated marketing communications

Promotional Co-ordination → Functional Co-ordination → Cultural Shift → Integrated Marketing Communications

Many of these step changes are easier to describe than implement and the route to integrated marketing communications is strewn with pitfalls and barriers. Among those barriers to integrated marketing communications is the structure of the communications industry itself. The first agencies concentrated on advertising and these were well established by the time sales promotion and public relations began to become important. Personal sales too grew as a distinct function. This 'specialization' was further entrenched by the development of trade associations, sometimes with more than one per industry. In the UK organizations such as the Institute of Practitioners in Advertising (IPA), Institute of Sales Promotion (ISP), Public Relations Consultants Association (PRCA), Institute of Public Relations (IPR), Direct Marketing Association (DMA) and Institute of Direct Marketing (IDM) naturally defended their particular 'specialization'. Research and education (including professional awards) are geared towards these specializations and 'turf wars' have been known to break out. This structure has fuelled the functional divisions and expectations of marketing communications managers and industry employees since the Second World War and, once entrenched, has proven difficult to change. On the client side it was (and in many instances still is) no less rigid with traditional hierarchical brand management structures that were slow to change and again focused on specialization. For integrated marketing communications to work, it is clear that communications activities need to be cross-functional in the way they are operationalized.

Even though the concept has been debated for a decade and research suggests a strong commitment on both the client and the agency side to integrated marketing communications, research has further revealed substantial differences in perception between the two groups (Eagle and Kitchen 2000). On the one hand, clients perceive integrated marketing communications as a counter to the structural inadequacies of the communications industry as a whole and the means to rise above these and better meet their underlying objectives. As such, they essentially see integrated marketing communications as offering them a control they had previously lacked. Large agencies, on the other hand, argue that control and co-ordination should be left to them in their capacity as the 'dominant supplier'. Neither perspective though seems to wholly achieve the ambitions of integrated marketing communications.

Total integrated marketing communications is clearly only achievable when all external agencies, outsourcing providers and partners work together with the organization to deliver perceived consistency to customers in terms of the promises given, the actions undertaken and in the overall customer experience. Sceptics, though, might question whether agencies can actually deliver these expectations. Inevitably there will need to be some level of trade-off between the expertise an agency can provide and the degree of integration it can achieve and no matter how agencies might develop or grow, the need to compromise will not disappear.

Skoda: bridging the perception gap

Formerly one of Europe's leading car manufacturers, the Czechoslovakian car company Skoda, had seen the popularity of its brand drop dramatically after the Second World War. In the UK Skoda cars developed a reputation for poor quality and unreliability and by the time that Volkswagen took over the beleaguered company in the early 1990s, the brand had a major image problem. By the late 1990s, the company had one of the world's most efficient car plants and was manufacturing cars which were on par with its competitors in terms of function, style and value for money. However the brand still retained its negative image and was generally being rejected by consumers.

In 2000, Skoda launched a new integrated marketing strategy aimed at bridging the gap between image and reality. The strategy involved confronting consumers' negative preconceptions head-on, with a common theme that was to link all marketing communication: 'We know what you think about Skoda, but think again.' The task was to extend the target market beyond existing Skoda owners to a wider population, and convince them that Skoda had changed.

With a limited annual marketing budget of only £4 million (a fraction of what rival car brands spend), it was important that all marketing communication worked synergistically for maximum effectiveness and cost efficiency. Whilst advertising would play a lead role, it was clear that public relations would be a major component of the campaign.

The initial print advertisements featured the Skoda Fabia, and made brand statements which were accompanied with the strapline: 'The new Fabia, It's a Skoda. Honest'. Subsequent commercials depicted prospective buyers fleeing showrooms in panic or throwing themselves out of the vehicle during a test drive, in fear or worry over the negative perceptions that surround the brand.

Direct marketing also played an integral role. Care was taken to ensure that the creative idea, tone and style of Skoda's advertising was consistent throughout. A mailing to 'cold' prospects, comprised of a boxed Skoda badge for recipients to fix to their existing car, enabling them to test drive the brand before purchase.

In 2000, sales of Skoda grew by 33 per cent year on year in an otherwise flat car market. By 2002, the number of consumers claiming they would never consider a Skoda had fallen from 60 per cent to 40 per cent. The new marketing communications strategy won advertising industry plaudits at a number of awards schemes including the D& AD, and a Gold in the IPA Effectiveness Awards.

SOURCE: IMAGE COURTESY OF THE ADVERTISING ARCHIVES.

A Skoda television commercial showing a prospective buyer fleeing the showroom in panic at the thought of taking a test drive.

Minicase written by Nik Mahon, Faculty of Media, Arts and Society, Southampton Solent University (Source: D&AD 'Creativity Works 2003').

ADVANTAGES AND DISADVANTAGES OF INTEGRATED MARKETING COMMUNICATIONS

Media-neutral
A customer-focused review of media based on research, analysis and insight and not habit and/or preference.

The potential advantages of integrated marketing communications are manyfold. To begin with, the co-ordination of both creative application and production has obvious benefits in terms of cost and performance efficiencies. The increased control and co-ordination of brand-related messages increases the overall synergy of communications even further and, taken together, the impact should result in more effective communication. Research also suggests that although staff and other costs may go up on implementation, these costs fall in the long run (Eagle and Kitchen 2000). Integrated marketing communications also reduces dependence on mass-media advertising, encourages investigation of targeted mediums, heightens demands on agencies to multi-tasking and outsourcing and stimulates efforts to assess the return on investment (ROI) on organizational communications. This viewpoint has become known as being **media-neutral**. This involves a customer-focused review of media based on research, analysis and insight and not habit and/or preference. Integration also offers the potential of reducing the ambiguity of messages coming from the organization and reducing duplication of effort (Blythe 2000). Perhaps one of the strongest arguments of all is that through clear positioning and as a resultant power of synergy the drive for competitive advantage has more chance of success. As Hackley and Kitchen (1998: 233) note 'creatively powerful promotional campaigns may be conceived as something which can slice through the cognitive debris of other half-remembered campaigns, memories of product trials and popular myths to create a new or more persuasive sense of meaning for consumers.'

Every concept has its dark side. Among the potential disadvantages of integrated marketing communications are that it encourages centralization (which may or may not be a good thing) and bureaucracy. It also has the potential to dilute creative opportunities as a result. There is also danger in a strict uniformity of communication (although some authors support this) because this has the potential of boring the consumer. Researchers (Pechmann and Stewart 1990) have found that irritation with a particular repeated message can lead to wearout (see Chapter 2). Doubts have also been raised about the ethical issues of intrusive campaigns, some of which hide under the mantle of 'permission marketing' and whether the resultant (physical and mental) clutter is socially justified. Another major criticism surrounds the ability to measure and evaluate integrated marketing communications effectively (Eagle and Kitchen 2000) although this merely extends a deficiency that has long dogged the industry.

Summarizing the literature to date in the field of integrated marketing communications and highlighting the problems with which it is associated leads us towards a number of questions around whether it:

- May or may not be ethically sound.
- May or may not be an increasing form of social pollution.

- May or may not be increasingly integrative as an organizational function.
- May or may not be in need of radical theoretical and practical re-conceptualization.

It would seem that Integrated Marketing Communication is a concept designed for modern communications but which the communications world has yet to catch up with.

@

An example of integrated marketing communications in action at: **www. mediacampaign.org**.

Summary

This chapter reviewed the literature on integrated marketing communications (IMC), questioning whether its time had come or whether, however well supported in theory, its implementation posed considerable difficulties. The chapter reviewed the popular definitions of integrated marketing communications and suggested it was more than just media and marketing communications tools co-ordination (one voice) but included a dedication to customer focus, creativity, measurability, cost-effectiveness and interactivity. Further, it was seen to extend the organization's marketing communication to all customer contact points and internally, as well as externally, to the firm. Dramatic changes in markets, the marketing communications industry and in organizations were seen as drivers to integrated marketing communications and the factors associated with these discussed. The problems associated with implementation were reviewed and potential barriers assessed including the 'specialist' nature of the industry itself. In conclusion the potential advantages and disadvantages were reviewed.

Review questions

1 What concept has been described as one that evaluates the strategic role of a variety of communication disciplines to provide clarity; consistency and maximum communication?

2 What is the 'mantra' used to sum up the concept of a single communication strategy or plan?

3 In the modern marketplace, what has led organizations to move towards targeted as opposed to mass communication?

4 Describe the driver responsible for the increase in commercial activity and a cluttered environment, in which communication has to operate.

5 What are organizations paying more attention to in order to establish a competitive advantage?

6 What recent technological advance has most contributed towards organizations reconsidering their approach to marketing communications?

7 For integrated marketing communications to work within a company what activity have clients and agents suggested must take place?

8 What might the appointment of a champion or change agent direct an organization towards?

9 Describe two advantages that an organization may experience as a result of implementing integrated marketing communications.

10 What are considered to be the potential disadvantages of integrated marketing communications?

Discussion questions

1 There is much debate around the realities of a company being able to fully implement an integrated marketing communications strategy. What do you feel are the challenges that might be faced and how might they be overcome?

2 All organizations have 'part-time marketers'. What would you need to do to ensure their support and contribution to customer-facing marketing communications activities?

3 When might it be appropriate for organizations not to adopt an integrated approach to their marketing communications activities?

Further reading

Bearden, W.O. and Madden, C.S. (1996) 'A brief history of the future of advertising: vision and lesson from integrated marketing communications', *Journal of Business Research*, Nov., 37 (3): 135–8. If advertising does not take the step into integrated marketing communications, will it ultimately be forced out by other ways of attracting customers? The thinking behind the development of integrated marketing communications in the last ten years.

Cornelissen, J.P. (2003) 'Change, continuity and progress: the concept of integrated marketing communications and marketing communications practice', *Journal of Strategic Marketing*, Dec., 11 (4): 217–34. This article explores whether integrated marketing communications can be considered as a valid theory of contemporary marketing communications management.

Fill, C. (2001) 'Essentially a matter of consistency: integrated marketing communications', *Marketing Review*, Summer, 1 (4): 409. An incremental approach to the way in which integrated marketing communications might develop in organizations.

Hart, R. (2006) 'Measuring success: how to "sell" a communications audit to internal audiences', *Public Relations Tactics*, Apr., 13 (4): 9–19.

Kitchen, P.J. (2005) New paradigm – IMC – under fire', *Competitiveness Review*, 15 (1): 72–80.

Spotts, Harlan E., Lambert, D.R. and Joyce, M.L. (1998) 'Marketing deja vu: the discovery of integrated marketing communications', *Journal of Marketing Education*, Fall, 20 (3): 210–18. Examining the history of integrated marketing communications and its relationship to marketing literature.

Chapter references

Berry, L.L. (1995) 'Relationship marketing of services: growing interest, emerging perspectives', *Journal of the Academy of Marketing Science,* 23 (4): 236–45.

Blythe, J. (2000) *Marketing Communications*, Harlow: Financial Times, Prentice-Hall.

Copley, P. (2004) *Marketing Communications Management*, Oxford: Butterworth-Heinemann.

De Pelsmacker, P., Geuens, M. and Van den Bergh, J.V. (2001) *Foundations of Marketing Communications: A European Perspective*, London: Prentice Hall.

Duncan, T. and Caywood, C. (1996) 'The concept, process and evolution of integrated marketing communications', in E. Thorson and J. Moore (eds), *Integrated Communications: Synergy of Persuasive Voices*, Mahwah, NJ: Lawrence Erlbaum, pp. 13–34.

Eagle, L. and Kitchen, P.J. (2000) 'IMC, brand communications, and corporate cultures: client/advertising agency co-ordination and cohesion', *European Journal of Marketing*, 34 (5/6): 667.

Fill, C. (2002) *Marketing Communications: contexts, strategies, and applications*, 3rd edn, Harlow: Financial Times Prentice Hall.

Gummesson, E. (1990) *The Part-time Marketer*, Karlstad: Centre for Service Research.

Hackley, C.E. and Kitchen, P.J. (1998) 'IMC: A Consumer Psychological Perspectives', *Marketing Intelligence and Planning*, 16 (3): 229–35.

Kitchen, P.J. and Schultz, D.E. (1999) 'A multi-country comparison of the drive for IMC', *Journal of Advertising Research*: 1–17.

Kliatchko, J. (2005) 'Towards a new definition of integrated marketing communications (IMC)', *International Journal of Advertising*, 24 (1): 7–34.

Low, G.S. (2000) 'Correlates of integrated marketing communications', *Journal of Advertising Research*, 40 (May/June): 27–39.

Novak, G. and Phelps, J. (1994) 'Conceptualising the integrated marketing communications phenomenon', *Journal of Current Issues and Research in Advertising*, 16 (1): 49–66.

Pechmann, C. and Stewart, D.W. (1990) 'Advertising repetition: a critical review of wear-in and wear-out', Working paper, Cambridge: Marketing Science Institute.

Pickton, D. and Broderick, A. (2001) *Integrated Marketing Communications*, Harlow: Financial Times, Prentice Hall.

Schultz, D.P. and Schultz, S.E. (1998) *Psychology and Work Today*, Upper Saddle River, NJ: Prentice Hall.

Semenik, R.J. (2002) *Promotion and Integrated Marketing Communications*, London: Thomson Learning.

Shimp, T.A. (2003) *Advertising, Promotion and Supplemental Aspects of Integrated Marketing Communication*, Cincinnati: Thomson.

Smith, P.R. (1998) *Marketing Communications: An Integrated Approach*, 2nd edn, London: Kogan Page.

CASE STUDY 15.1

Stella Artois

In an economy-conscious world where many products and services are marketed on price, Stella Artois has long stood apart as a brand that was not afraid to promote itself as 'reassuringly expensive'. This unique approach had proved highly successful since the brand's launch in 1976 until the beginning of the 1990s, when Stella Artois began to lose market share and volume in the face of a number of entrants in the premium lager sector.

With consumer attitudes having moved beyond price, the 'Reassuringly expensive' slogan seemed inappropriate and the obvious solution to the decline was either to relaunch or reposition the brand. However, Stella Artois

SOURCE: IMAGE COURTESY OF THE ADVERTISING ARCHIVES.

Stella Artois' sophisticated television commercials illustrate the overall aim of their marketing strategy to inexplicitly emphasize price and quality.

refused to abandon consistency and its core product focus. Instead, the vital strategic breakthrough came in a subtle shift in the message that the brand communicated, opting for a non-explicit emphasis on price and quality. This revision essentially relied on the consumer working out for themselves the quality offered by Stella Artois. With this positioning underpinning every piece of strategic thinking and marketing brief for the brand since 1990, Stella Artois has fought back from decline and is now re-established as the biggest premium lager brand in the UK.

Design became a primary communication tool for this approach, with packaging initiatives such as embossing the can and re-designing the crate box in the style of Champagne, promoting the brand's exclusivity. A Stella Artois pint glass was introduced in 2001 and, within 12 months of launch, 66 per cent of UK households possessed at least one glass. Driven by a strong rise in draught sales, distribution growth has also propelled the brand forward, with Stella Artois now being the most widely circulated lager in the on-trade (licensed public houses), available in 52 per cent of all pubs. The brand has focused on three areas of promotion to support its positioning: TV advertising, sponsorship and price promotion in the off-trade (retail). The successes of these campaigns, both in terms of the impact of the creative and the effectiveness of the brand positioning, have had a marked effect on the bottom line. Between 1996 and 2003, Stella Artois has seen volume growth of 217 per cent compared with premium lager growth of 66 per cent over the same period. This rise has made it the third-biggest lager brand in the UK, selling 3495m barrels in 2003. Stella Artois now holds an 8.9 per cent share of the total beer market, more than triple its 1996 share of 2.2 per cent. This compares favourably with a share increase of less than double for the two leading lager brands, Carling and Foster's. Furthermore, Stella Artois is now a top-four grocery brand, behind Coca-Cola, Walker's and Muller, having moved up from 34th in six years.

The brand's success in recent times is undoubted and, despite market pressure to abandon its consistency and product focus, has gone from strength to strength. Few brands would have the courage to take the route less travelled, but to do so successfully is no mean feat, which is why Stella Artois is a worthy winner of the Grand Prix (Marketing Awards 2004).

Case study questions

1 What, in communication terms, were the reasons behind Stella Artois' success?

2 What marketing tools were used by Stella Artois and why?

3 Suggest possible themes for a future Stella Artois campaign.

Source: Marketing: The Marketing Society Awards June 2004 (reproduced from *Marketing* Magazine with the permission of the copyright owner, Haymarket Business Publications Limited).

CHAPTER SIXTEEN

INTERNAL MARKETING

LEARNING OBJECTIVES

Having completed this chapter you should be able to:

- Understand the reasons why organizations are putting more resources into internal marketing.
- Describe the concepts that are involved with internal marketing.
- Discuss ways in which internal marketing can be implemented.
- Assess the potential benefits of an effective internal marketing programme.

INTRODUCTION

In Chapter 11 (public relations) the concept of internal marketing (IM) was introduced but discussion postponed as its importance merited the inclusion of a specific chapter on this concept. Internal marketing has, in recent years, received widespread attention in the academic and professional management literature. This has developed on the back of a widespread realization that there is a basis of competitive advantage to be had through the improvement of organizational capability and delivery of customer services that actually matches customer needs and expectations. This development of interest in the internal workings of the organization has not been restricted to the field of marketing. A number of themes are closely associated in the literature with human resource management (HRM) and trends in organizational structure (Gummesson 1999). However, despite the obvious overlap internal marketing has communications at its core. Communications in this organizational context may be seen to be a means of creating a more democratic, training-oriented organization (Kitchen 1997) which results in greater professionalism and, importantly, greater empowerment.

In the marketing literature, internal marketing is closely associated with developments in relationship marketing and a recognition of the importance of the supplier–customer interface. Whereas traditional marketing focused wholly on the external customer, relationship marketing stressed the additional

Internal marketing
Concerned particularly with internal communications and developing responsiveness, responsibility and unity of purpose in an organization.

significance of the internal customer in successfully establishing relationships (Gummesson 1991). Modern marketing, therefore, calls not only for an external marketing orientation but also for an 'internal marketing' focus on employees (Javalgi and Moberg 1997). It is, according to one marketing consultant,[1] 'the application of marketing inside the organisation to instil customer focused values'.

As with external marketing, internal marketing is dependent upon communications. In communication terms internal marketing seeks to supplement and rationalize the messages and communications which come from the company's employees at the customer interface that are normally difficult to control. It is seen as a means of moderation in what the employee says or does and what images and associations this creates in the mind of the customer. It is not, therefore, simply the managerial benefits that are associated with professionalism and empowerment but a conscious effort to align company communications with those of their staff. As Copley (2004: 264) notes internal communications, 'often seen as the Cinderella subject by some can have a big impact on external communications and relations in terms of the internal feel of the organisation'.

The ideas associated with internal marketing and internal partnerships have had a chequered career. Perhaps the most prevalent view of employees is that they exchange their skills and labour, in relation to tasks performed, for remunerative reward. Not unsurprisingly, therefore, the historic and rather archaic role of internal marketing was felt to be persuading staff to do as the management wished. It was not until the realization that organizations have 'internal customers' within those internal markets that there was a change in mindset, a concept that arose from the idea of having to 'sell jobs' and make them more attractive for employees (Reynoso 1996). The American Marketing Association define internal marketing rather more broadly as 'Marketing to employees of an organization to ensure that they are effectively carrying out desired programs and policies' (AAA 2006). In more recent times internal marketing has become associated with a wide number of concepts, among them:

- The orchestration of staff working together and attuned to the company's mission, strategy, goals (Christopher et al. 1991) and the wider operations of the company with its environment (Hogg et al. 1998).

- Efforts to 'sell' the message of an organization to its internal audience, using similar techniques to those used in the organization's relationship with its external audiences (Palmer 1998).

- Any activity within an organization that focuses staff attention on the internal activities that need to be changed in order to enhance the external marketplace performance (Ballantyne 1997).

- Activities that improve internal communication and customer consciousness among employees (Hogg et al. 1998).

[1]Sybil Sterstic quoted in Duncan (2002: 225).

These ideas converge to suggest the prime constituents of internal marketing. It was this broader concept that Christopher *et al.* (1991: 30) were describing when they noted that internal marketing was 'recognised as an important activity in developing a customer-focused organisation'.

In practice, internal marketing, is concerned with communications, with developing responsiveness, responsibility and unity of purpose. The values transmitted externally to customers, suppliers and distributers through external communications, therefore, need to be both supported and reinforced by the values expressed by employees themselves, and especially those who interact with external stakeholders at whatever level.

@

For an example of a marketing communications company with a specialism in internal marketing look at: **www.frameworks.co.uk**.

CUSTOMER–EMPLOYEE INTERFACE

Recognition of the importance of the employee–customer interface has, in large part, promoted interest in internal marketing. Increased consumer sophistication and choice has meant that consumers are judging quality and value not just in terms of what they buy but also in terms of the 'exchange experiences' themselves. People are an essential part of those experiences and thus the total value package itself. As a consequence, employees' actions are important both in terms of the tangible aspects of service delivery and the intangible ones, such as presentation, attitude and the way in which the service is actualy provided. Research suggests that the quality of relationships a company has with its customers is largely determined by how employees on the front line make customers feel (Barnes and Howlett 1998).

Reputation is based upon quality service and quality service upon employee know-how. Employees individually accumulate know-how (often referred to as knowledge capital because of its value to the organization) over time. This in-company know-how is what turns knowledge into application and adds the extra value to the product or service offered. It is also suggested that whereas the customer–supplier interface is more immediate, the internal climate has a strong impact upon employee satisfaction and customer retention (Payne 2000), although a direct causal linearity between the two cannot be assumed (Ballantyne 1997). In service organizations, internal marketing can be seen to be of the utmost importance. Manufacturing firms, however, may have to rely on mass communication or (increasingly) technology (e.g. call centres) to develop some level of relationship, whereas a service firm's contact with its customers is normally directly through its own employees. This does not exclude manufacturing companies from consideration of internal marketing. In all organizations perception is influenced by the character and personality of the organization as a whole and not just through its traditional paid or unpaid media. With advertising and sales promotion the organization

Knowledge capital
The knowledge held within an organization.

can largely determine the message it wants to convey. Even public relations and sponsorship, although less controllable, are seen to be managed to produced, hopefully, a desirable outcome. With employees, however, the internal market consists of people with needs and wants which must constantly be assessed and, if practical, satisfied. It is this strategic intervention that can directly influence positive and/or negative communications from this source (see Figure 16.1).

Internal marketing also challenges the notion that it is only functional marketing staff who 'own the customer' and that they alone should be concerned with communications with them. Many companies have centralized marketing and sales staff, who might be called 'full-time marketers'. These employees do not, however, represent all the marketers and salespeople the firm has at its disposal (Grönroos 1996). The phrase 'part-time marketers' (PTM) is now widely used to describe these non-marketing specialists who, regardless of their position in the company, are crucial to the company's marketing effort. These part-time marketers include all of those employees who, in any way, influence customer relations, customer satisfaction and the customer's perceived quality (Gummesson 1991). As Grönroos (1996) notes, in many situations their impact on customer satisfaction and quality perception is more important to long-term success in the marketplace than that of the full-time marketer. In building reputation it is often the intangible aspects such as attitude and sincerity rather than the competence of the service provision, that has the most powerful influence.

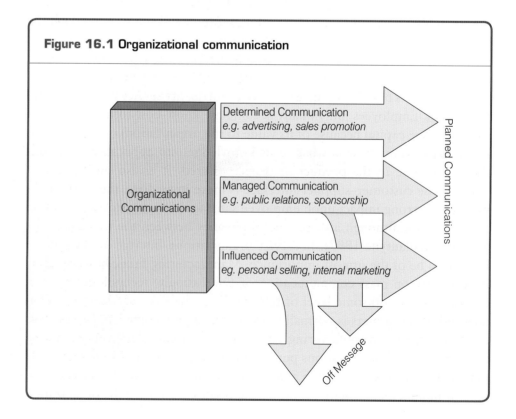

Figure 16.1 Organizational communication

Here today ... gone tomorrow

According to the Department of Trade and Industry (DTI), there were 5700 call centres in the UK in 2005, supporting 581 800 jobs. Future projections vary, but it seems that by 2008 there will be around 6000 centres representing 650 000 jobs. An indication of the increasing reliance that companies are placing on third-party providers.

Outsourcing creates a dependency upon the provider to deliver a consistent quality of service that reflects the image of the company they support. If they fail in this, customers don't see the call centre being at fault but the company itself, and that could have serious consequences for long-term growth.

Good staff, good training and good operational systems are the key to call-centre success. However, a quarter of all call-centre staff are employed by companies who employ less than 100 staff in total and the Consumer Contact Association's research has identified that the average staff turnover in this sector has risen year on year from 13 per cent in 2002 to 20 per cent in 2005, with one company alone experiencing an 82 per cent turnover level.

High turnover means increased recruitment cost and training, increased workloads on remaining staff and more pressure, greater levels of dissatisfaction, confusion and frustration and, ultimately, decreased performance. For UK companies, therefore, this statistical trend is very worrying.

Minicase written by Andy Cropper, Senior Lecturer, Sheffield Hallam University.

Like other businesses, Powergen established call centres in India five years ago citing the financial benefits it brought but then, amongst much publicity in 2006, announced it was moving them back to the UK because it was 'not prepared to achieve savings at the risk or expense of customer satisfaction'.

SOURCE: IMAGE COURTESY OF THE ADVERTISING ARCHIVES.

THE EMPLOYEE PERSPECTIVE

@

For a view on what makes employees happy look at: **www.insightlink.com/What-makes-employees-happy.html.**

Obtaining and understanding the employee perspective is a critical tool in managing customer satisfaction, as it enables managers to exercise internal marketing – in effect meeting the needs of employees so that they can meet the needs of customers (Shershic 1990). Research suggests that employee commitment to the organization requires that they have the opportunity to participate in company decision making and a clear understanding of company values (Varey 2002). Internal marketing, it is claimed, is a relationship development process in which staff autonomy and know-how combine to create and circulate new organizational knowledge that will challenge internal activities that need to be changed to enhance quality in marketplace relationships (Ballantyne 1997). It is built on the premise that employees want to give good service just as customers want to receive it, and managers who make it easier to achieve this will find that both customers and employees are likely to respond positively (Schneider 1980).

At a tactical level internal marketing may include ongoing training and encouragement of formal and informal communications (such as newsletters and social events). Patterns of working and expectations are transmitted through communication mechanisms such as training and socialization programmes which acquaint staff with the norms and expectations the organization holds about marketing and communications (Kitchen 1999). At the strategic level internal marketing extends to the adoption of supportive management styles and personnel policies, customer service training and planning procedures (Hogg *et al.* 1998). There is also a suggestion that implementing an internal customer approach involves a number of processes. These include the creation of internal awareness, the identification of employee expectations, the communication of those expectations to internal management, and the development of measures of internal customer satisfaction and feedback mechanisms.

Internal communications are necessary in order that internal staff are motivated and involved with the brand in such a way that they are able to present a consistent and uniform message to anyone they come in contact with outside the company. The danger inherent in this is that internal marketing may be limited in what it contributes to the wider issues of organizational culture as it all too often defaults to a one-way communications exercise (Meldrum 2000). What is required are proper mechanisms to ensure superior performance which requires support, flexibility and feedback.

Knowledge is a key driver to staff effectiveness (and indeed satisfaction). As Gummesson (1987) notes, all 'contact personnel' must be well attuned to the mission, goals, strategies and systems of the company otherwise they would be unable to handle those crucial 'moments of truth' that occur during the interaction with customers. This is particularly evident in service firms where the interface with the customer is broad and intense but may also be generally true of all companies.

According to Kandampully and Duddy (1999: 321) an internal marketing programme should 'be considered the firm's life-blood – percolating through all ranks, departments, functions and assets of the firm – with the ultimate aim of simultaneously offering and gaining value at all levels'.

INTERNAL MARKETING IN PRACTICE

In many organizations internal marketing has advanced a long way from the days of the corporate newsletter to well-organized systems of internal communication. Research by Richmond Events suggests 75 per cent of UK companies have a department responsible for internal communications but not all can be said to be implementing internal marketing strategies. To do this would require:

- An organization actually recognizing/acknowledging that it needs to set objectives.
- The subsequent formulation of an internal strategy.
- It's implemented through a combination of skills that involve persuasion, negotiation and politics, coupled with their tactical application.
- An evaluation of the process.

There are a number of reasons for this increased emphasis on including internal marketing amongst the strategic processes of the organization. These include (Baines *et al.* 2004):

- A greater requirement for companies to inform their employees about policy and financial affairs including annual reports and accounts.
- Increasing democratization of industry.
- Increasing employee ownership of equity through privatizations, flotations, management buy-outs, share ownership schemes and performance-related pay schemes.
- The availability of new communications technology, making it easier to organize and conduct internal communications.
- Increasing significance of service industries and the consequent importance of the employee/customer interface.

Internally directed communications can be placed under three headings of **downward**, **sideways** and **upward communications** (Jefkins 1990) representing management–employee, employee–employee and employee–management relationships. Downward communication is often through house journals or other printed material. Staff meetings are also used as they are more personal and enable feedback. A number of companies utilize Internet technology to

Downward communications
Management to employee communication often through house journals or other printed material.

Sideways communications
Employee–employee communications.

Upward communications
Employee to management communications.

organize video-newsletters and video-conferencing. Cisco Systems' employees, for example, are addressed regularly by their President via the Internet. Sideways communication (employee to employee) is encouraged in many businesses in the belief that it contributes to staff satisfaction. The organization may, therefore, organize or facilitate employee events to promote collegiality especially across departments. Upward communication has, traditionally, been difficult to encourage even when management wanted to hear the opinion of staff. Some organizations hold regular staff surveys or focus groups to stimulate such debate. Others still rely on middle management to feed back from the front line, a notoriously ineffective strategy. It is generally supposed that the shorter the distance between the top and the bottom of the organizational pyramid the better the communication. In effect, however, it is the systems in place to encourage this communication that determine successful interaction.

INTERNAL MARKETING BENEFITS

It has become increasingly acknowledged that in order to sustain a competitive position in the marketplace organizations must develop and maintain a customer service culture that both allows and encourages employees to give good service. From a management and human resource perspective internal marketing focuses on the three core value-adding activities of innovation, effective processes and customer support, and builds networks which design in quality (Doyle 1995). It involves retaining customer-conscious employees (Grönroos 1990) and the development of employee empowerment to better satisfy the needs of the customer. Internal marketing reflects the belief that if management wants its employees to deliver an outstanding level of service to customers, then they must be prepared to do a great deal for its employees (Reynoso 1996).

From a marketing communication viewpoint this alignment between management and staff considerably improves the chances that the images and perceptions communicated by way of traditional marketing communications media is reflected in the actions of staff. The calculation is that employees who believe that the organization facilitates their performance, aids their career expectations and provides positive supervision will feel enabled to carry out the business' main work of serving customers (Varey 2002).

Effective internal communications, whether they be through personal contact or internal media, may have a positive affect on employees in a number of ways. They can:

- Serve to clarify organizational roles by explaining the way the organization works and the employees' part in it.
- Enable them to make promises that can be delivered through the knowledge of company strengths and limitations of the organization.

- Demonstrate that the organization is ethical and has values by informing them of what the organization has achieved in the local community, nationally and internationally.
- Inprove employee loyalty because well-informed, empowered and satisfied employees are more likely to stay and be generally supportive of the organization.
- Decrease employee turnover as a result of a satisfied and loyal workforce.
- Reduce training costs through reduced employee turnover.

The role of internal marketing can also be seen to be affective to organizations who are going through crisis in helping stabilize the confidence of employees (see Case study 16.1 Inspiring people). However, it can also have a negative effect if:

- Claims are made by the company that employees know are unrealistic and/or undeliverable.
- Company messages are untrue and the workforce realize that this is the case.
- The jobs of employees are unflatteringly portrayed.

@

For advice on building an internal marketing programme look at: **www.brandbuilding. com/best/buildinginternal.htm.**

Summary

This chapter reviewed the concepts and themes surrounding internal marketing. It suggested that internal marketing was receiving widespread attention because of the perceived need for improvement in organizational capability and in the delivery of customer service and traced its development. It suggested that employee interaction is not only important in service delivery but in intangible aspects such as attitude and the way the service is provided and contrasted this with the more or less controllable tools such as advertising and public relations. The chapter discussed internal marketing implementation and how this is delivered in practice. It also discussed the potential benefits which in addition to better customer service include the clarification of roles, capabilities and values and improved loyalty, decreased turnover and reduced training costs. These benefits were contrasted with the potential problems associated with unrealistic or untrue claims and when employees are portrayed unflatteringly.

Review questions

1 What is considered to be the focus of traditional marketing?
2 What concept has been recognized as being an important activity in developing a customer-focused organization?

3   What term is used to describe the accumulation of know-how by employees?

4   What do the initials PTM stand for?

5   What is considered to be a critical tool in managing customer satisfaction?

6   Describe the process required when implementing an internal customer approach.

7   Why are internal communications a necessary part of internal management?

8   Give an example of downward communication.

9   What is considered to be the main factor in sustaining a competitive position?

10   How can internal marketing assist organizations that are going through crisis?

Discussion questions

1   You are tasked with implementing a significant change within your organization that will prove unpopular to some of the older staff. How would you go about minimizing the resistance to change?

2   What means of communicating with staff are available to an organization and how would you evaluate their effectiveness?

3   We now live in an age when text and email contact has become a normal way of communicating. What might the impact of this be in another ten years on internal communication within companies?

Further reading

Cockrill, M. (2006) 'Adapting to cultural diversity', *Strategic Communication Management*, Aug./Sep., 10 (5): 4. An interview with Michelle Cockrill, Director of Communications for UTC Fire & Security in Asia.

De Bussy, N.M., Ewing, M.T. and Pitt, L.F. (2003) 'Stakeholder theory and internal marketing communications: a framework for analysing the influence of new media', *Journal of Marketing Communications*, Sep., 9 (3): 147–61. This paper draws on stakeholder and communication theories to provide a framework for understanding the dimensions of effective internal marketing communications and presents the results of an empirical study on the relationship between these dimensions and the use of new media in the workplace.

Goebel, D.J., Marshall, G.W. and Locander, W.B. (2004) 'An organizational communication-based model of individual customer orientation of non-marketing members of a firm', *Journal of Strategic Marketing*, Mar., 12 (1): 29–56. Results indicate that highly valued interfunctional communications by marketing results in non-marketing members being more customer-oriented and more willing to contribute actively.

Gombeski Jr., William R., Krauss, K., Taylor, J., Colihan, L., Wilson, T. and D'Antonio, M. (2004) 'Harnessing employee marketing power', *Marketing Health Services*, Spring, 24 (1): 49–51. Organizations achieve significant increases in volume by educating employees about their marketing role and training them to help their families, friends and neighbours choose their organization's services and products.

Papasolomou-Doukakis, I. (2002) 'Internal marketing: a means for creating a sales or marketing orientation? The case of UK retail banks', *Journal of Marketing Communications*, Jun., 8 (2): 87–100. The core finding from this exploratory research suggests that there are substantial barriers to the successful implementation of internal marketing

Spitzer, R. and Swidler, M. (2003) 'Using a marketing approach to improve internal communications', *Employment Relations Today* (Wiley), Spring, 30 (1): 69–82. Describes the philosophy and methodology of the employee communications segmentation (ECS) process that adopts proven consumer communications techniques for use to improve corporate internal communications.

Chapter references

AAA (2006) 'Marketing Dictionary', http://www.marketingpower.com/mg-dictionary-view1590.php, accessed 2 October 2006.

Baines, P., Egan, J. and Jefkins, F. (2004) *Public Relations: Contemporary Issues and Techniques*, Oxford: Elsevier Butterworth-Heinemann.

Ballantyne, D. (1997) 'Internal networks for internal marketing', *Journal of Marketing Management*, 13 (13): 343–66.

Barnes, J.G. and Howlett, D.M. (1998) 'Predictors of equity in relationships between service providers and retail customers', *International Journal of Bank Marketing*, 16 (1): 5–23.

Christopher, M., Payne, A.F.T. and Ballantyne, D. (1991) *Relationship Marketing: Bringing Quality, Customer Service and Marketing Together*, Oxford: Butterworth Heinemann.

Copley, P. (2004) *Marketing Communications Management: Concepts and Theories, Cases and Practices*, Oxford: Elsevier.

Doyle, P. (1995) 'Marketing in the new millennium', *European Journal of Marketing*, 29 (12): 23–41.

Duncan, T. (2002) *Using Advertising and Promotion to Build Brand*, New York: McGraw-Hill.

Fill, C. (2002) *Marketing Communications: Contexts, Strategies, and Applications*, 3rd edn, Harlow: Financial Times Prentice Hall.

Grönroos, C. (1990) 'Relationship approach to the marketing function in service contexts: the marketing and organization behaviour interface', *Journal of Business Research,* 20: 3–11.

Grönroos, C. (1996) 'Relationship marketing: strategic and tactical implications', *Management Decisions*, 34 (3): 5–14.

Gummesson, E. (1987) 'In Search of marketing equilibrium: Relationship Marketing versus Hypercompetition', *Journal of Marketing Management*, 13 (5): 421–30.

Gummesson, E. (1991) 'Marketing orientation revisited: the crucial role of the part-time marketers', *European Journal of Marketing*, 25 (2): 60–7.

Gummesson, E. (1999) *Total Relationship Marketing: Rethinking Marketing Management: From 4Ps to 30Rs*, Oxford: Butterworth Heinemann.

Hogg, G., Carter, S. and Dunne, A. (1998) 'Investing in people: internal marketing and corporate culture', *Journal of Marketing Management*, 14: 879–95.

Javalgi, R.G. and Moberg, C.R (1997) 'Service loyalty: implications for service providers', *The Journal of Services Marketing*, Jun., 11 (3): 165–79.

Jefkins, F.W. (1990) *Public Relations for your Business*, London: Mercury Books.

Jobber, D. (1995) *Principles and Practice of Marketing*, Maidenhead: McGraw-Hill.

Kandampully, J. and Duddy, R. (1999) 'Relationship marketing: a concept beyond the primary relationship', *Marketing Intelligence & Planning*, 17 (7): 315–23.

Kitchen, P.J. (1997) *Public Relations: Principles and Practice*, London: Thomson Learning.

Kitchen, P.J. (1999) Marketing Communications: Principles and Practice. London: Thomson Learning.

Meldrum, M. (2000) 'A market orientation', in Cranfield School of Management, *Marketing Management: A Relationship Marketing Perspective*, Basingstoke: Macmillan, pp. 3–15.

Palmer, A.J. (1998) *Principles of Services Marketing*, London: Kogan Page.

Payne, A. (2000) 'Relationship marketing: managing multiple markets', in Cranfield School of Management, *Marketing Management: A Relationship Marketing Perspective*, Basingstoke: Macmillan, pp 16–30.

Reynoso, J. (1996) 'Internal service operations: how well are they serving each other?', in B. Edvardsson, S.W. Brown, R. Johnston, E.E. Scheuing, (eds), *Advancing Service Quality: A Global Perspective*, New York: ISQA, pp. 77–86.

Reynoso J. and Moores B. (1996) 'Internal relationships', in Francis Buttle (ed.), *Relationship Marketing: Theory and Practice*, London: Chapman Schneider, pp. 55–73.

Schneider, B. (1980) 'The service organisation: climate is crucial', *Organisational Dynamics*, Autumn: 52–65.

Shershic, S.F. (1990) 'The flip-side of customer satisfaction research', *Marketing Research*, December: 45–50.

Varey, R.J. (2002) *Marketing Communication: Principles and Practice*, London: Routledge.

Varey, R.J. and Lewis, B.R. (1999) 'A broadened conception of internal marketing', *European Journal of Marketing*, 33 (9/10): 926–44.

Inspiring people

Rosabeth Moss Kanter of Harvard Business School believes that leadership matters most when executives have to bring their companies back from the brink of failure. She also believes that one aspect of this leadership task often goes unnoticed. That is that 'turnaround champions… reverse the cycle of corporate decline by restoring people's confidence in themselves and in one another'. When things start going wrong in an organization it begins what she calls a 'death spiral'. 'After an initial blow to the company's fortunes, people begin pointing fingers and deriding colleagues. The resulting tensions inhibit collaboration and encourage protectionism and secrecy.' Reversing this spiral is crucial. Kanter points to three examples, Gillette, the BBC and Invensys, which show how a chief executive's internal marketing can pull organizations out of this downward spiral.

Gillette in 2001 was a company that had been experiencing years of flat sales, declining margins and loss of market share, despite the success of its Mach3 shaving system. On his first day as chief executive Jim Kilts held a meeting of the operating committee. In this meeting, Kilts outlined his style and leadership philosophy, giving particular prominence to the statement: 'if something bothers you, I want open dialogue'. He established several additional communication channels from weekly staff meetings to a chairman's page on Gillette's intranet, where staff could post questions and receive answers from the chief executive himself. Controversially he began to

Prior to resigning in 2004, Greg Dyke was heralded for helping to restore confidence in the BBC.

SOURCE: © TOBY MELVILLE/REUTERS/CORBIS

share personal performance data among senior managers. The policy in time, however, increased disclosure and communication among colleagues. Eventually, secrecy and denial receded and conversations shifted from individual reports to group dialogue.

Similarly when Greg Dyke took over as Director-General of the BBC in 1999, it was a demoralized organization. Its ratings were in decline and it was being outpaced by its commercial rivals. BBC programme producers complained of a long bureaucratic process that usually ended in their proposals being rejected more than half of the time. Scepticism and cynicism were widespread. Dyke quickly restructured to remove a layer of management that had separated leaders from those responsible for audiences and products. He put producers on the executive committee and gave them a voice in decision making.

When Rick Haythomthwaite took over as Chief Executive in 2001 at the production technology group Invensys, he was, according to Kanter 'conscious of walking a fine line between truth and reconciliation'. The company, who employed more than 50 000 people in the industrial and energy sectors, was close to a debt default. Continuous restructuring had created a 'culture of fear and reduced initiative'. Haythomthwaite made few changes in senior management in his first months, suggesting there was quality to be found among existing staff. By involving about 100 people in strategy formulation development, he gave them a chance to demonstrate their talents. Invensys' new leader looked inside not outside the organization for best practices and to raise the organization's confidence.

According to Kanter putting an organization on a positive path requires leaders who can energize the workforce. The small victories that newly empowered people create are the first signs that a turnround is under way. This is 'the true test of leadership'.

Case study questions

1 What part does leadership play in internal marketing?

2 Explain what Kanter means by 'walking a fine line between truth and reconciliation' and what influence has this on internal communications.

Source: Inspire People to Turn Around Your Business, Rosabeth Moss Kanter, Published 24 August 2003, FT.Com. (used with permission).

CHAPTER SEVENTEEN

MARKETING CHANNELS AND BUSINESS-TO-BUSINESS COMMUNICATIONS

LEARNING OBJECTIVES

Having completed this chapter you should be able to:

- Understand the characteristics of business-to-business (B2B) communications.
- Recognize the similarities and differences between business-to-business and consumer communications.
- Understand the reason for supplier partnerships.

INTRODUCTION

The concept of 'channels' has been inherent in marketing since its inception. A channel suggests a flow. In this case the flow is from the manufacturer or service provider to the consumer either direct or through intermediaries (wholesalers, retailers, catalogue operations, etc.). What also flows along the channel(s) are marketing communications although this can and should be a two-way rather than unidirectional flow. Although Figure 17.1 is a simplification, particularly in our complex, multi-channel, services dominant society, it remains a useful analogy in relation to the business-to-business (B2B) markets.

The consumer may be either another organization or the general public. If the consumer is another business the original supply may be sold-on unchanged (although frequently in less bulk), used in or combined with another product or service (which later re-enters the channel) or is used to enable the company to carry out its main function (e.g. stationery, machinery, etc.). This inter-organizational trade is most commonly known as 'business-to-business'[1] (B2B) marketing and is distinguished from transactions with the public or 'business-to-consumer' (B2C) marketing. Where an organization sells virtually the same products/services to both consumers and businesses (e.g. Dell) this is commonly known as **direct channel marketing**.

Direct channel marketing
Where an organization sells virtually the same products/services to both consumers and businesses (e.g. Dell).

[1] In earlier times it was more generally called Industrial Marketing.

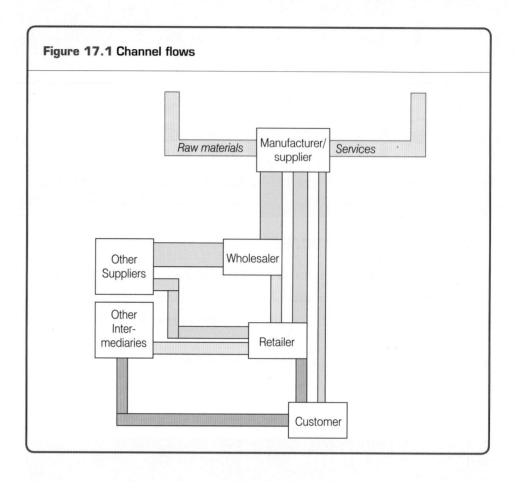

Figure 17.1 Channel flows

Business-to-business markets include the industrial and public sectors, materials, components, consumables and services and the total volume far exceeds that of consumer markets. One feature of the digital age, which initially forecast the demise of intermediaries, is the growing complexity of markets where consumers can be re-sellers (on *ebay*) and where companies encourage customers to participate in the product or service offering. The distinction between business-to-business and business-to-consumer may be becoming less important.

BUSINESS-TO-BUSINESS COMMUNICATIONS

The characteristics of the business-to-business sector are generally regarded as different from those of consumer marketing, although these are sometimes exaggerated to suggest that there is no commonality at all between business-to-business and business-to-consumer. In effect there is little difference in the wants and desires of either sector, although characteristics of the business-to-business sector do influence the form that these communications may take.

The business-to-business characteristics that most affect this application are:

- Larger markets
- Fewer customers
- Higher spend
- Wider geographical spread
- Complex buyer–customer interaction.

The relative complexity and fewer (but higher spending) customers are reasons why personal selling is so important in business-to-business markets. A trained sales executive can demonstrate, answer technical questions and negotiate in real time. Although trade advertising, exhibitions, direct mail and public relations all play their part, these are frequently in support of personal sales particularly in the customer acquisition phase. Once a relationship has been established the communications' dynamic changes. As noted in Chapter 14, most frequently the communication is between two (or more) people who interact with each other in 'real-time' and respond to each other's informational needs. To facilitate these important relationships organizations may appoint **key account managers** to work specifically with one or a limited number of accounts. These interactions frequently lead to long-term and sometimes close relationships between the individuals involved. It is generally accepted that organizations are networks in their own right but these relationships extend outside the organization to other individuals in other organizations, such that complex external networks develop (see Figure 17.2). It is along

Key account managers
Marketing and/or sales executives who work specifically with one or a limited number of accounts.

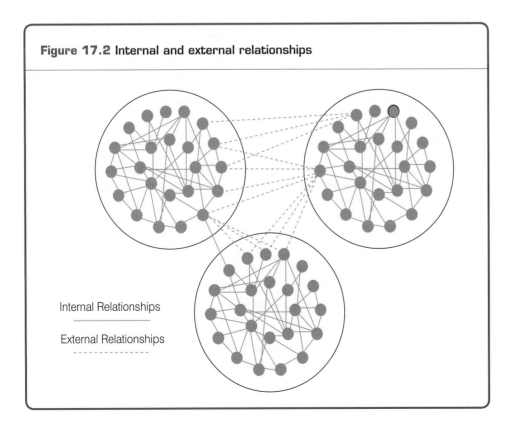

Figure 17.2 Internal and external relationships

Internal Relationships
_____

External Relationships
- - - - - - - - - - - - - - - -

these lines of personal communication that a large volume of marketing messages pass.

In overall communication terms the relative importance of the various tools in business-to-business are almost the inverse to that of business-to-consumer marketing. In business-to-business markets personal selling replaces advertising and sales promotion as the main tool while others trail in relative significance (see Figure 17.3). However, personal selling is expensive and many business-to-business organizations use it as sparingly as possible, utilizing other tools to create awareness, develop interest and ferment desire. Personal selling is then used where it is most effective in closing the sale and developing the relationship.

Trade advertising, as the term suggests, utilizes largely specialist publications including trade journals, newspapers and magazines aimed at a particular industry buyers. Trade press is not the only media outlet. Business-to-business organizations do advertise in mass-media publications for reasons associated with corporate image and brand awareness and development. This is a fast growing trend with 73 per cent of business-to-business advertising in the USA in consumer magazines and on television (Gilliland and Johnston 1997).[2] It is also true that buyers and other decision makers are in themselves consumers, which is important to recognize particularly in resale industries.

According to De Pelsmacker *et al.* (2001) business-to-business advertising tends to:

- be more sexist
- depict fewer people
- give more space given to copy
- mention product characteristics more often
- use psychological appeals less often than rational appeals.

All in all this seems to suggest less creativity and more appeal to basic, rational instincts, a charge frequently associated with this sector in the past.

@

For examples of trade magazines look at: **www.pharmafield.co.uk** and **www.sme.org/cgi-bin/find-issues. pl?&&ME&SME&** and **www.retail-week. com.**

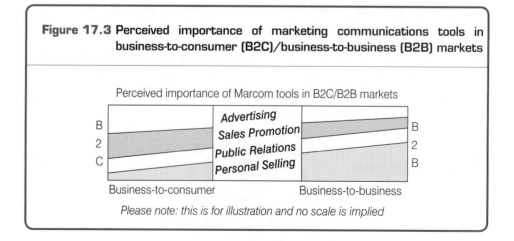

Figure 17.3 Perceived importance of marketing communications tools in business-to-consumer (B2C)/business-to-business (B2B) markets

Perceived importance of Marcom tools in B2C/B2B markets

B2C — Advertising — Sales Promotion — Public Relations — Personal Selling — B2B

Business-to-consumer   Business-to-business

Please note: this is for illustration and no scale is implied

[2]Quoted in De Pelsmacker *et al.* 2001.

However, as is noted later in this chapter, these characteristics may be becoming less destinct.

Web-based advertising and servicing is also growing in importance as business-to-business suppliers vie to create the best websites, with the most interactivity and effective customer care (e.g. order tracking). On the other side of the fence, customers looking to determine the best (in terms of quality and price) supply use the Internet to acquire this knowledge.

Trade promotion at retail level includes buying allowances, advertising or sales promotion allowances, slotting allowances (slotting-in new products, increasing shelf space), and others including gifts, training and other incentives (see Chapter 10). At all levels in the business-to-business sector promotions include discounts or other offers to clear stock, increase sales during slow periods, introduce new products, increase distribution or counter competitive activity. Promotional offers may be targeted at specific buyers or made available to all through trade publication announcements. There is one major difference between business-to-business and business-to-consumer markets regarding one aspect of sales promotion. Whereas in business-to-consumer markets individual customers are incentivized (i.e. bribed) to change their buying behaviour in business-to-business markets this may be considered unethical.

Direct marketing has begun to play a larger part in business-to-business communications. Because of the continually rising costs of personal selling and the falling costs of database management coupled with considerable advances in technology, direct marketing is seen as the 'next best thing' to personal contact. Direct mail (and more recently email) is used to create awareness, enhance image and establish credibility. Telemarketing helps establish and qualify leads, facilitate customer enquires and is even used as

SOURCE: © SAMI SUNI.

Football 'bungs' (illegal payments to football club staff aimed at influencing player purchasing decisions) are a good example of unethical B2B deals.

Cold calling
Contacting consumers without prior knowledge or permission with the objective of making a sale or starting the process towards a sale.

a direct sales channel. As with consumer-based direct marketing there are problems associated with junk-mail, spam and **cold calling** (see Chapter 13).

Public relations (or corporate communications) is a tool utilised in the business-to-business sector. Public relations style and function is heavily determined by the organizational type and public relations' recognized role within the organization. However suppliers of products or services and their customers are naturally keen to ensure 'goodwill and mutual understanding' exists between them and turn to public relations techniques to deliver these messages.

THE BUSINESS-TO-BUSINESS MESSAGE

Business-to-business communications' tactics are a series of activities designed to influence the target audience (usually but not exclusively the buyer) and persuade a percentage of these to ultimately purchase the product(s) and/or service(s). The characteristics of business-to-business have led observers to suggest that the content and targeting of messages is significantly different from business-to-consumer marketing. These differences are shown in Figure 17.4 below.

In business-to-business the decision making unit (DMU) is assumed to involve many functions, relative to consumer marketing, where a purchase decision is made by relatively few. As a generality this is indeed the case although some organizational buyers have considerable personal authority. A business-to-business decision making unit can consist of multiple roles, and a number of models have been developed to demonstrate this. Perhaps the

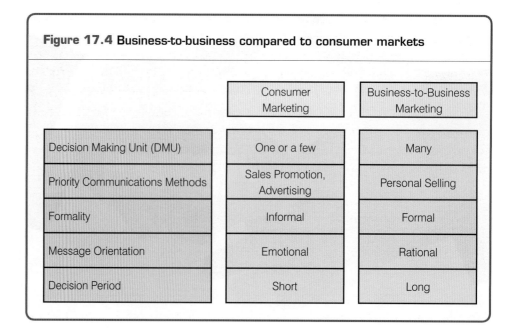

Figure 17.4 Business-to-business compared to consumer markets

	Consumer Marketing	Business-to-Business Marketing
Decision Making Unit (DMU)	One or a few	Many
Priority Communications Methods	Sales Promotion, Advertising	Personal Selling
Formality	Informal	Formal
Message Orientation	Emotional	Rational
Decision Period	Short	Long

most widely used was suggested by Webster and Wind (1972) who identified six roles, which might be performed by different people, or with individuals adopting multiple roles or, in some cases, just by one person. These are users, influencers, deciders, approvers, buyers and gatekeepers. Who to target is, therefore, a major consideration and many companies compile or rent lists of such contacts to use for direct mailing or telemarketing purposes. The downside of this strategy is that individuals change jobs or leave organizations on a regular basis making the upkeep of such lists a burden (see Chapter 13).

As noted above personal selling (or personal contact) is the major conduit in many business-to-business organizations, although again it is the exceptions that make the rule. Organizations such as Viking Direct and Niceday deal with their largely organizational customers through catalogues and some companies, for example Intel, use cooperative consumer advertising in their case to maintain their influence on the computer processor market.

The assumed formality in procedure and rationality in decision making has long been seen as a feature of business-to-business although research (e.g. Naudé and Holland 1996) shows many inter-firm transactions are conducted within enduring business relationships where mutual trust and adaptation are commonplace rather than the then prevailing rational view of inter-firm transactions conducted largely on a contractual basis (Brennan and Turnbull 2001). Buyers, influencers, etc. are all human and sometimes take decisions based not on rationality but emotion. Nevertheless much printed communication (flyers, catalogues, etc.) in particular concentrates more on the features and specifications rather than on emotional appeals. A logical extension of this behaviour is the suggestion that brand image plays less of a part in business-to-business markets. However, as the computer buyer's maxim 'you will never get the sack if you buy IBM' suggests, brand reputation must play a significant part. Indeed, contrary to what is sometimes suggested many business decisions are based on psychological factors such as past performance, trust, flexibility and reliability (De Pelsmacker *et al.* 2001) rather than more basic reasons such as cost.

The length of time between needs recognition and supply are likely to be longer than in business-to-consumer markets. In the fast-moving consumer goods marketplace (i.e. supermarket retailer) this can be counted in minutes. The complexity and/or personalization and/or bulk involved in some business-to-business ordering may extend waiting time into months (or even years in the case of the aircraft industry). If orders are going to tender the ordering time requires extending to cope with short-listing, obtaining tenders, evaluation and selection. In addition strict delivery times may be crucial. For these as well as other reasons continual, often personal contact over long periods is the norm.

For an example of business-to-business and business-to-consumer look at Viking Direct's website: **www.viking-direct.co.uk.**

SUPPLIER PARTNERSHIPS

In terms of marketing communications the format of any trade and cooperation and the inter-organizational relationships that may develop from this will inevitably have a heavy influence on the nature and form of marketing communication activities. When it comes to business-to-business no business is an island (Häkansson and Snehota 1989) thus, by the very nature of the interdependency of most business-to-business markets, business relationships of one sort or another are inevitable. Personal relationships between the employees and owners/directors of companies have for some time been explicitly recognized by both buyer and seller organizations and individuals within those organizations (Blois 1997).

Relational 'bonding' between business-to-business traders is not even a twentieth-century phenomenon. In the pre-industrial revolution world such associations were quite prevalent between traders, partly because of the need, in turbulent, minimally legislated and sometimes dangerous markets, to do business with others you could trust (Sheth and Parvatiyar 1995).

Communication within the supplier–customer channel is determined by three factors;

- Channel structure
- Channel climate and culture
- Balance of power.

Channel structure may range from the traditional large industrial producer to the small, flexible supplier of creative services and organizational climate and culture may be equally diverse. In organizational relationships the 'balance of power' is rarely symmetrical (Gummesson 1999) with one party usually the stronger of the two. During the so-called 'golden age of marketing' from the mid-1950s to the mid-1970s, it was the brand supplier who financed the development of individual brands, largely through mass advertising, and who dominated and manipulated the means of distribution. The observable tension in the distribution chain was evident in relationships between brand suppliers and their retail intermediaries. Only rarely did brand owners and retailers work together to achieve a result that would satisfy both parties. Most often suppliers used 'pull strategies' (see Chapter 5) with the objective of attracting customers 'over the heads' of the retailer. Although 'push strategies' (effectively using trade incentives and promotions to 'push' product through the distribution chain) were used they tended to be one-off tactics rather than strategic cooperative communication activity. The third quarter of the twentieth century saw a change in the balance of power between suppliers and retailers, particularly in the fast-moving consumer goods sector, but as yet little movement towards cooperation. As the power of larger supermarket retailers grew, suppliers were often played off against each other. Information regarding production capacity on one side and sales on the other was regarded as commercially sensitive and distrust of one's supplier or customer was the norm. In the 1990s, however, retailers and suppliers began to recognize that in a relatively stagnant market one of the few opportunities to increase effectiveness was in channel distribution. To facilitate this electronic point of sale (EPOS) systems were introduced which enabled products to be replaced and sales to be monitored on a regular basis. From the marketing communications' perspective electronic point of sale allowed for retailers and suppliers to

Electronic point of sale (EPOS)
Technology at the point of sale that enables transactions to be tracked on a merchandise and customer level.

monitor the effect of changing communications ranging from the effect of moving a solus display to a major advertising campaign.

Another form of partnering involves generic campaigns organized by groups of suppliers. The trend to this type of cooperative behaviour began in the UK in the years between the world wars when the British public were asked to buy British cars, eat more fish and fruit, smoke imported Havana cigars, dress in Harris Tweed, protect woodwork with white lead and send their friends British Christmas cards (Nevett 1982). Cooperative campaigns today range from those for the meat, wool and other basic industries to those of the two major airline groupings of OneWorld and the Star Alliance and many in between.

Visit the Star Alliance website at: **www. staralliance.com.**

Summary

This chapter reviewed the concept of marketing channels and business-to-business communications. It distinguished between business-to-business and business-to-consumer media and the messages they carry and which characteristics affect this. The chapter reviewed the relative importance of marketing communications tools and the importance of relationships. The chapter also discussed supplier partnerships and the changes that have occurred in the past few years.

Review questions

1   Explain what is meant by direct channel marketing.

2   What do business-to-business markets include?

3   Describe the composition of a business-to-business decision making unit.

4   What factors determine communication within the supplier–customer channel?

5   Explain the advantages of an electronic point of sale system

6   What is the difference between business-to-business and business-to-consumer markets?

7   For business-to-business markets, what is the major communications conduit used?

8   What is 'trade advertising'?

9   Which technology allows retailers and suppiers to monitor the effect of changing communications?

10 What do you understand to be the basis under which most business decisions are made?

Discussion questions

1 Personal selling is important in business-to-business markets. Why might this be and what would companies need to do in order to be effective in this area?

2 Sales promotion activities in business-to-business markets risk being considered as unethical. Why is this so and in what circumstances would it be acceptable?

3 It is accepted that the decision making unit within one organization can be complex and bear no resemblance to that of a similar organization. If you were tasked with trying to ensure your communications reached the right person, how would you plan this?

Further reading

Berger, P.D., Lee, J. and Weinberg, B.D. (2006) 'Optimal cooperative integration strategy for organisations adding a direct online channel', *Journal of the Operational Research Society*, Aug., 57 (8): 920–7.

Blythe, J. and Zimmerman, A. (2004) *Business to Business Marketing Management*, London: Thomson Learning.

Ford, D. (2002) *Understanding Business Marketing and Purchasing*, 3rd edn, London: Thomson Learning.

Hutt, M. and Speh, T. (2006): Business Marketing Management, 9th edn, Thomson Learning, Cincinnati.

Spencer-Matthews, S. and Lawley, M. (2006) 'Improving customer service: issues in customer contact management', *European Journal of Marketing*, 40 (1/2): 218–32. This research aims to better understand the issues of why individualized communications should be incorporated into customized customer contact service and how customer contact management should be implemented.

Chapter references

Blois, K.J. (1997) 'Are business to business relationships inherently unstable?', *Journal of Marketing Management*, 13 (5): 367–82.

Brennan, R. and Turnbull, P.W. (2001) 'Sophistry, relevance and technology transfer in management research: an IMP perspective', *Journal of Business Research*, 55: 595–602.

De Pelsmacker, P., Geuens, M. and Van den Bergh, J.V. (2001) *Foundations of Marketing Communications: A European Perspective*, London: Prentice Hall.

Fill, C. (2002) *Marketing Communications: Contexts, Strategies, and Applications*, 3rd edn, Harlow: FT/Prentice Hall.

Gummesson, E. (1999) *Total Relationship Marketing: Rethinking Marketing Management: From 4Ps to 30Rs*, Oxford: Butterworth Heinemann.

Häkansson, H. and Snehota, I. (1989) 'No business is an island', *Scandinavian Journal of Management Studies*, 4 (3/89): 187–200.

Naudé, P. and Holland, C. (1996) 'Business-to-business relationships', *Relationship Marketing, Theory and Practice*, London: Paul Chapman Publishing.

Nevett, T.R. (1982) *Advertising in Britain: A History*, London: Heinemann.

Sheth, J.N., Mittal, B. and Newman, B.I. (1999) *Customer Behavior: Consumer Behavior and Beyond*, Cincinnati: Thomson Learning.

Sheth, J.N. and Parvatiyar, A. (1995) 'The evolution of relationship marketing', *International Business Review*, 4 (4): 397–418.

Webster, F.E. and Wind, Y. (1972) *Organisational Buying Behaviour*, Englewood Cliffs, NJ: Prentice Hall.

CASE STUDY 17.1

Intel

It's been a busy 12 months at Intel Corp. The company ushered in a new CEO, hired a new CMO, reorganized its business structure and overhauled its marketing department. Oh, and also hired a new advertising agency.

McCann Worldgroup took over the account in March and, with years of experience on other big tech accounts, including Microsoft Corp., has quickly picked up Intel's marketing strategy.

'You want to get to the place where your customers look at you as a valued strategic partner and not just a provider of commodity technology. Intel has done a good job of that, and we're going to direct that even more', said Michael McLaren, executive vice-president-director of global accounts at McCann Worldgroup, New York.

McCann's first enterprise campaign for Intel is in the works, and is expected to be ready soon. McCann's first work was a fall ad campaign launched in September promoting Intel's Centrino wireless technology and using celebrities to tout the value of Centrino wireless to entertainment.

Intel continues its long-running and successful 'Intel Inside' programme and will still promote its products as the premier technology inside, also known as 'ingredient branding'. Still, some changes will affect its marketing.

One change that has already had an effect is Intel's move to reorganize its product brands around platforms rather than individual products. That means marketing messages can better address business challenges solved by groups or combinations of products.

Will Swope, vice-president-director of Intel's Digital Enterprise Brand Management, said, 'The future will be messages more about how the integrated processes of Intel move enterprise forward.'

Swope said he is pleased with the way the entire Intel ecosystem, such as personal computer (PC) manufacturers and software vendors, has been included more in marketing under the new system. 'It's reflective of the way business actually works', he said. 'It's a win for the OEMs*, a win for the software vendors and a win for Intel.'

Intel shifted more marketing dollars online, reflecting its importance in research and purchase choices to enterprise customers. 'Network administrators or IT buyers are time stressed and very busy, and that's one of the reasons why the Web is so important. They spend a lot of time on it, and it's where they go for information', McLaren said.

*Original Equipment Manufacture.

▶

SOURCE: © INTEL CORPORATION.

Visitors at a 2006 Intel Developer Forum.

Yet even with the many changes over the last year, Intel continues to use the tried and true marketing methods that work for it, including print, direct and events, such as its Intel Developer Forum, this year held in eight countries around the world. The forums serve as innovation showcases for Intel's work, but also as places to get feedback from developers and begin or expand partnerships.

Case study questions

1   Why would a parts supplier such as Intel be interested in effective communication?

2   What are the objectives of the 'Intel inside' and new campaign?

Source: By Beth Snyder Bulick, 21 October 2005, *Business-to-Business Magazine* (used with permission).

CHAPTER EIGHTEEN

ETHICAL MARKETING AND THE REGULATORY ENVIRONMENT

LEARNING OBJECTIVES

Having completed this chapter you should be able to:

- Understand the problems associated with ethical marketing.
- Detail those ethical breaches associated with the advertising industry and the arguments for and against them.
- Understand the relationship between self-regulation and legislation.
- Comprehend the advertising industry codes relating to misleading or offensive advertising.
- Be aware of the ethical concerns in the sales promotion, public relations, personal selling and direct marketing industries.

INTRODUCTION

The purpose of this chapter is to review the much debated field of marketing ethics and the voluntary or legislative regulation that parallels much of this discussion. Whether justified or not marketing is perceived in some sectors as 'an untrustworthy profession where duplicitous methods are used to sell customers products they do not particularly need or want' (CIM 2006: 11). Although much of the blame can (and should) be attributed to the management of such companies, in general it is the marketing communications specialists who invariably come in for most criticism.

ETHICAL MARKETING COMMUNICATIONS

Ethical marketing
A set of moral principles concerned with social well-being as related to marketing practice.

Ethics, according to the *Oxford English Dictionary* is 'a set of moral principles' (OED 1995). A concise definition of the term **ethical marketing** is as a set of moral principles concerned with social well being as related to marketing practice. Unethical conduct, it is suggested, has negative consequences for the contemporary organization ranging from adverse publicity to diminished corporate reputation, to lower employee morale, customer boycotts and, eventually, legal sanctions. With such a potential downside it might be logically assumed that marketers would avoid such controversy. In the marketing communications industry, however, ethical decision making is sometimes blinded by the need to attract attention to the brand or by crossing the line of 'good taste' in search of a humorous campaign (see Box 18.1).

The problem with applying ethical considerations to marketing is that morals change with both time and place. What was unacceptable in parts of Europe 25 years ago may be quite acceptable today. An advertisement involving an unmarried, co-habiting couple (such as in a recent commercial for BT) would have been condemned in the 1950s or 1960s, indeed it would probably never have reached the screen. It is also true that images of women regarded as inoffensive across Europe and North America would be regarded as highly offensive and would be banned in a state such as Dubai.

If morals are constantly shifting is it the marketers' responsibility to stand behind the moral white line or should they be challenging it? Given that creative communicators by definition push the frontiers of our experience, are they not bound to court controversy? Yet the dangers are evident and potentially costly. It is, therefore, up to each individual to make a stand and not only decide what is right and what is wrong but also be able to justify those personal decisions to critics. As one eminent practitioner Francis Goodman[1] has put it 'we all have our own moral compasses and know right from wrong in what we are doing. It's up to the relative integrity of the person...(and) it's just as important for companies to engender an ethical way of operating' (Miles 2005).

As Malcolm McDonald notes 'much of the criticism levelled against marketing is in fact directed against one aspect of it – advertising'[2] (CIM 2006: 11) and there are some who regard the whole advertising field as inherently unethical. This is not a new charge as the 1962 speech detailed in Minicase 18.1 clearly shows.

Box 18.1 Britain's most complained about television advertisements

Advertiser/Product	Advertisement	Complaints
Wrigley's/Xcite	Man vomits dog	863
Mr Kipling/Cakes	Woman gives birth on stage	570
Velvet/Toilet Tissue	Bare bums	403
Nestlé/Kit Kat	Old lady ignored by meals-on-wheels	318
Toyota/Corolla	Key swop party	236

Source: Campaign Book of Lists 2003.

---

[1]Francis Goodman Director of the Maiden Group quoted in Miles (2005).
[2]Malcolm McDonald is using a broad definition of advertising that almost certainly incorporates sales promotion and direct marketing.

MINICASE 18.1

Advertising to children

The fear of subjecting children to advertising is not new. Nearly 45 years ago at the 1962 Annual Conference of the National Association of Schoolmasters, Mr Terry Casey argued strongly in the following terms.

"Perhaps the most pervasive anti-educational influence is that of modern advertising, for that *exists* to circumvent the reasoning faculty and weaken judgment. Some of it is puerile, but it can be subtle. Of the former kind are the many variants of the *ex parte* claim that 'Bloggs makes the best-whatever it is. This must be so because Bloggs says it is so'. Millions of young minds, which we seek to train to think, are constantly bombarded with this sort of nonsense. Not content with bad logic, resort is had to bad manners. Children themselves are recruited as advertising agents, and are urged to make importunate demands upon their parents to buy this or that product. 'Don't forget my fruit gums, Mum!' is not even prefaced with the little word 'please'.

Under the rough treatment of the 'blurb' writers, adjectives have lost their vitality and almost their validity because of the excessive use of superlatives. In school we try to enrich vocabularies, but many children are reduced to the verbal poverty of using the prepositional prefix 'super' as an all-purpose adjective denoting approbation, thanks to the baleful influence of the 'Ads'. Psychology, the science which we thought was to be the handmaiden of education, has been prostituted to serve the ends of salesmanship, the panjandrum of the inflated economy. If advertising really is necessary to keep the wheels of industry and commerce turning, is it too much to ask that it be presented in ways which do not offend good taste nor affront good sense?"

Source: Nevett 1982.

Over the years, advertising has been accused of a number of ethical breaches, perhaps the majority of which focus on its apparent lack of social responsibility. These include accusations that:

- Advertising promotes materialism
- Advertising wastes resources
- Advertising creates unwanted needs
- Advertising perpetuates stereotyping
- Advertising causes people to use harmful products
- Advertising promotes unethical brands
- Advertising inhibits media coverage
- Advertising targets vulnerable groups
- Advertising delivers subliminal messages

Advertising promotes materialism

There is a widespread belief that advertising bombards consumers with images associated with the 'good life'. Advocates of this viewpoint suggest that advertising promotes the idea that the acquisition of material possessions will lead to contentment, happiness and add to the general joy of living. Over 30 years ago a Green Paper (government consultation document) on advertising castigated advertisers for their 'tendency to over-encourage gross materialism and dissatisfaction and its tendency to irresponsibility' (Nevett 1982). Even earlier George Orwell invoked this image when he described advertising as 'the rattling of a stick inside a swill bucket'. The counter-argument is that materialism promotes consumer spending. For all its faults it is advertising that has driven prosperity to new heights not only in so-called 'Western' markets but emerging economies such as India and China.

Advertising wastes resources

Advertising, it is argued, adds costs to products and services resulting in consumers having to pay more than they should. It may equally be argued, however, that advertising drives competition and acts as a downward pressure on prices.

Advertising creates unwanted needs

This suggests that because advertising exposes the public to products or services that they might not know existed, it creates unnecessary wants and needs. While this is an evident truism it seems to suggest that consumers would be satisfied in their ignorance and ignores their natural curiosity. A further argument against this manipulative affect of advertising can be found in the high rate of failure amongst new products for which advertisers are presumably looking to create such a need. Many new products are supported by huge advertising and marketing budgets yet on average only one in ten succeed (Sheehan 2004). On the other hand some products have become 'must-haves' without the support of any advertising at all, an example of which was the Beanie Baby craze of the late 1990s (*ibid.*)

Advertising perpetuates stereotyping

The major charges here are against gender and ethnic stereotyping. For much of the twentieth century women were portrayed either as home-makers or sex symbols. Advertising for domestic appliances promoted the benefits to the husband of his wife being relieved of the pressures of domestic toil. When it came to looking after the home the OXO housewife always produced a delicious meal for her family, Flash cleaned her floors, Dettol killed 99 per cent of her household germs and Fairy Liquid helped her clean the dishes to the standard required. At the other extreme women were being used as sexual symbols to sell everything from cars to cameras. Ethnic stereotyping has also long existed in advertising. In nineteenth and early twentieth-century America, advertising for Cream of Wheat was accused of perpetuating the stereotype of African-Americans as smiling chefs, minstrels, porters and servants, whilst Rough-on-Rats (rat poison) perpetuated the stereotype of Asians as long-haired, oddly attired people (Sivulka 1998). Stereotyping is indeed used extensively by advertisers as short-cuts to meaning (see Chapter 8). To counter the charge advertisers would suggest that rather than perpetuating stereotypes they were holding a mirror up to the society of the day. That most stereotypes are recognizable at a particular time and in a particular place, and uncomfortable and outlandish in others, suggests some support for this viewpoint.

Advertising causes people to use harmful products

The charge that advertising has promoted potentially harmful products is undoubtedly justified given that for many decades quack-medicinal cures, cigarettes and alcohol were the mainstays of the advertising world. The counter argument is that if a product or service can be sold legally then it should be allowed to be advertised. Cigarette manufacturers have frequently made this case. They have also argued that, in a declining market, they are using advertising not to attract new customers but to gain market share from their competitors!

Advertising promotes unethical brands

The charge here is that advertising promotes brands whose owners have acted unethically in regards to such things as environmental breaches, 'sweat-shop' labour, inhumane regimes, etc. Whilst individuals have every right to object or boycott such brands, it is difficult for an industry to take such a position, particularly when some of the world's most illustrious brands have fallen foul to such breaches over the years. The cost to the companies that are accused is not cheap. Boycotts have, for a time, cost Shell an estimated 20 per cent of its sales, Nestlé $40 million and Nike substantial loss of reputation. In August 2006 a number of UK universities began a boycott of Coca-Cola products on campus because of allegations regarding human rights abuses.[3] The ban was expected to severely dent the company's reputation.

Advertising inhibits media coverage

Another perennial charge is that advertisers use their strength to inhibit free speech or distort information flow. The term 'Chinese Wall'[4] has been used to describe the relationship between the content function (i.e. news, entertainment) and the advertising function (Sheehan 2004). The 'Chinese Wall' should guard against potential conflicts of interest but it is widely suggested the concept fails to live up to its promise. In the 1972 Green Paper the UK newspaper industry was accused of 'excessive reliance on advertising' (Nevett 1982) although it fell short of direct allegations of abuse. Evidence of actual and potential abuse comes largely from the USA. In one US study it was suggested that magazines that relied on cigarette advertising were

Chinese wall
First after the 1929 stock market crash to describe new regulations that provided a separation between brokerage and investment bankers and only later to the separation between editorial and advertising functions.

[3]*Marketing*, 23 August 2006.
[4]The term 'Chinese Wall' was first used after the 1929 Stock market crash to describe new regulations that provided a separation between brokerage and investment bankers and only later to the separation between editorial and advertising functions (Sheehan 2004).

considerably less likely to publish articles about the health hazards associated with smoking (Lipman 1992). In addition magazines consider and often consult their advertisers when developing stories and selecting goods and services on which to report (Sheehan 2004). In another US study of 147 daily newspapers, 90 per cent of editors said they had been pressured by advertisers and more than one-third said advertisers had succeeded in influencing news in their papers (Belch and Belch 2001). Benign censorship may also be evidenced. Large fast moving consumer goods companies such as Procter & Gamble, who spend a huge percentage of their budget on television advertising, have been said to avoid airing commercials in any television programme that they regarded as being controversial (Sheehan 2004). In 1993 Chrysler motor company instituted a prenotification policy which said that any magazine wishing to run its advertising had to provide summaries of articles with sexual, political or social issue content against which such ads might appear (*ibid.*). Advertorials are a further problem that exists both sides of the Atlantic. Advertorials can breach the 'Chinese Wall' between news/entertainment and advertising by blurring the distinction between them, creating potentially higher credibility in the confusion between advertising and editorial comment.

Whilst impossible to justify the charge of media manipulation it is difficult to see how the advertising industry itself could stop such, often covert, acts. Even legislation against such practices would be very difficult, if not impossible, to enforce.

Advertising targets vulnerable groups

The targeting of vulnerable groups is a major issue. Advertising to children is a particularly contentious area and in 2001 Sweden attempted to introduce a ban on television advertising for toys, food and drinks across the European Union. Marketers argued that this was overprotective and that children should, as part of growing up, be exposed to the trappings of a material world. The Swedish attempt to legislate never passed into law but could return at some point in the future. Indeed the debate has been reignited more recently in relation to obesity in children and the advertising associated with fast-food chains. Amongst other vulnerable groups are the poor who are seen to be targeted for financial loans to consolidate debt, to buy lottery tickets or otherwise gamble and/or buy that product or service that would normally financially be out of their reach. Potential or actual alcoholics, shopaholics and gamblers are also seen as targets for advertising's power.

Advertising delivers subliminal messages

That some advertising puts messages into our heads, below the level of our consciousness has been a charge for many years. This idea was popular during the 1950s and 1960s and began to be taken seriously after experiments with cinema goers where messages such as 'drink Coca-Cola' and 'eat popcorn' were interspersed throughout the film (Sheehan 2004). The cinema owners reported that sales of soft drinks and popcorn increased because of the messages but this research was later discredited (Sutherland 1993).[5] Undoubtedly whether you believe that advertising is a highly persuasive force or more a 'gentle nudge' toward a brand (the so-called 'strong' or 'weak' theory of advertising – see Chapter 9), it has *some* affect on potential consumers. That it delivers messages that make consumers act significantly differently or irrationally from normal, as is suggested by the subliminal advertising charge, is highly debatable.

Undoubtedly ethics is such a pluralistic complex and situational phenomenon that it is important for advertisers in particular and all marketing communicators in general to establish boundaries of latitude (Yeshin 2006). The charges of impropriety will not go away but attention to ethical principles, such as those set out in industry codes, may come some way to reducing them.

SELF-REGULATION AND LEGISLATION

Many of the charges levelled against advertising would be very difficult to legislate against and would rely more on advertisers keeping to industry codes and norms. For many years it has been this self-regulation that has been the basis for controlling excesses in the marketing communications industry in the UK. The Advertising Standards Authority (ASA) (discussed in more detail later in this chapter) was set up over 40 years ago to police the rules set down in the advertising codes and works largely on the basis of voluntary restraint although industry sanctions can be applied where necessary. Marketers, through their various trade organizations have argued that self-regulation has advantages. In particular it is much swifter to change a code than enact legislation. This is particularly important when technology is driving marketing and legislators into new areas (e.g. electronic media) they have never been before. It is also true that legislation is nearly always 'black and white', when in the everyday practice of marketing it is sometimes the 'grey' areas that are potential cause for concern.

In the past few years, however, this self-regulatory framework has been challenged with formal legislation. Although much of this new law has a basis in European Union directives, according to Stephen Groom (2005: 10), a specialist in marketing and media law, 'it is a myth that UK marketers are constantly being assailed by wave after wave of changing Euro law'. Rather, public pressure, fuelled by well-publicized examples of dubious marketing practices, has encouraged legislators not only to harmonize legislation across boundaries but to strengthen it. In the UK alone 21 new Acts of Parliament, regulations or amendments affecting marketers were passed in the year to January 2006 with a further ten bills awaiting presentation to Parliament (CIM 2006). This is compounded by laws affecting marketing worldwide. A recently introduced US law forbids companies inside or outside the USA from

The Advertising Standards Authority (ASA)
UK regulatory body for advertising.

@

Look at Advertising Standards Authority's website at: **www.asa.org.uk/asa**.

---

[5]Quoted in Sheehan (2004).

collecting data about minors (defined as children under 13) if that company is a commercial enterprise whether or not the data is eventually used for commercial purposes (*ibid.*). Meanwhile, European Union legislation forbids personal data from inside the EU being transmitted to the USA because the same level of data protection is not available in that market. The law is also being used by companies globally in disputes amongst competitors. In the so-called 'razor-wars' Wilkinson Sword/Schick forced Gillette to withdraw an expensive advertising campaign for its Turbo and Power razors, featuring David Beckham, because a product claim was found to be false and unsubstantiated in a number of major jurisdictions such as Germany and the USA.

Some legislation might be seen to benefit some (but not all) marketers. The 'Olympic' bill (introduced in the UK in preparation for the games in 2012) is designed to combat ambush marketing (see Chapter 12) a phrase that was first coined in response to competitive clashes between Kodak and Fuji during the 1984 Los Angeles Olympic Games (Hoek 1999). This bill will make it illegal to combine words such as 'games', medals', 'gold', '2012', 'sponsor' or 'summer' in any form of communication other than by an authorized sponsor. According to the Legal Director of the Institute of Practitioners in Advertising (IPA) even witty advertising (such as that for an imaginary suntan company 'get bronze in London in 2012') would be illegal (CIM 2006). Although it is understandable that the London 2012 Olympic Committee would want to cut down on ambush marketing it would seem to be somewhat draconian and heavily biased towards the larger sponsors.

There are a number of areas of general concern to the legislators which fall into two sections; those relating to marketing practices and those product categories where potential abuse would be most damaging.

1 Marketing Practices

- Comparative Advertising (see Box 18.2)
- Pricing Claims (see Minicase 9.2)

Box 18.2 Comparative advertising

In 2000 British Airways sued Ryanair for trademark infringement. Two of Ryanair's advertisements compared unfavourably British Airways' prices with their own. BA claimed that the phrase Ryanair used to hammer the price advantage home – 'Expensive BA****DS!' – was offensive, and that the fare comparisons were unfair.

The Court ruled that the use of a trademark in price comparisons was allowed. They also noted that vulgarity didn't amount to trademark infringement or malicious falsehood. Indeed the judge pointed out Ryanair could have gone further in their criticism of BA fares and that the real reason BA didn't like the comparison was that it was true. BA's claims were dismissed and it was ordered to foot the legal bill.

Michael O'Leary, the man who turned Ryanair from a struggling airline into one of Europe's most successful brands has no time for whinging competitors. He believes 'Everyone wants to kick the s**t out of everyone else. We want to beat the crap out of BA. They mean to kick the crap out of us.'

Sources: Martin Bewick, *The Marketer*, October 2005; *Marketing*, 19 July 2006.

- Trademarks and Passing Off (see Box 18.3)
- Product Descriptions
- Promotions
- International Law
- Data Protection
- Marketing to Children

2 Product Categories

- Financial Products and Services
- Food and Drink (including alcohol)
- Medicines
- Cigarettes
- Products Associated with Children

MINICASE 18.2

Selling the cigarette habit

The 1920s in the USA was a decade of delight, decadence, disaster, despair and an enormous rise in the number of smokers. According to Sivulka (1998: 166) the 'selling of cigarettes proved advertising's ultimate triumph of the decade'. Many people before this time regarded smoking as an undesirable habit and employers, such as Henry Ford, deemed smokers unemployable. Others stereotyped smokers as criminals, neurotics and possibly drug addicts.

The First World War and multi-million dollar advertising campaigns, however, were to help cigarettes gain wider acceptance as both returning soldiers and civilians found smoking cigarettes to be 'more convenient, cheaper and more sanitary than chewing gum'. It was into this market that R.J.Reynolds directed its first nationally available brand Camel which quickly gained dominance as an 'upmarket' smoke. Within a short time the American Tobacco Company created Lucky Strike, described as a richer, sweeter product. Camel, Lucky Strike and a third national brand, Chesterfield were to battle for market leadership from 1917 until after the Second World War.

The returning soldiers were, however, all men and American Tobacco Company's owner George Washington Hill, urged on by Albert J. Lasker of the Lord & Thomas advertising agency, wanted to reach an untapped audience – women – who could potentially double the market! Early in the decade women smokers were a controversial issue. Many colleges prohibited women from smoking and they were unable to smoke in railroad diners or in many smoking rooms in stations and on board ships. By the mid 1920s many of these inequalities had been removed. To further fuel this cultural revolution cigarette brands turned to advertising. In 1926 the Newell-Emmett agency daringly presented a poster showing a romantic, moonlit seaside scene and the man lighting his Chesterfield and a women beside him saying 'Blow some my way'. The words shocked many people yet the Chesterfield campaign continued on. Hill and Laskar quickly sensed an opportunity for the Lucky Strike brand and pitched it directly at the female audience. Hill used celebrities from the entertainment world, such as film stars, crooners and jazz musicians to promote Lucky Strike. For the first time women endorsed the product and popularized the image of the fashionable lady who, while she indeed smoked, still appeared stylish and respectable. They even promoted the brand as an aid to keeping a slender figure ('reach for a Lucky instead of a sweet'). Lucky Strike campaigns particularly favoured testimonials from operatic sopranos, actresses and society matrons who all attested to the brand's positive effect.

Source: Sivulka 1998.

For more information on understanding data rights look at: **www.ico.gov.uk.**

Of all the aforementioned it is comparative advertising and pricing claims that most frequently get organizations into trouble (CIM 2006). This is particularly prevalent in the retail sector as Minicase 9.2 indicates. Trademark infringement and 'passing off' is also commonplace and considerably more difficult to enforce in some international jurisdictions (see Chapter 20). The need for international law is growing as unscrupulous companies work from 'off-shore' locations and use the cross-border facility of the Internet.

Data protection is an issue that has grown exponentially alongside the greater use of data by marketers. Legislation has been tightened in past years concerning the collection and use of such data. UK Data Protection legislation demands consumers 'opt-in' if they wish their data used rather than having to 'opt-out' as in the past. Strict rules on what information can be held and for what uses it may be put to are also part of the legislation. Marketing to children, as noted previously, is of uppermost concern and strictly policed because the industry, recognizing the pressures, oppose any formal legislation in this area.

Box 18.3 The confectioner and the copycat

Dutch biscuits and sweets producer Verkade obviously liked the famous Werther's Originals TV ad because they decided to base their own advertising on it. The result was an ad complete with grandpa sitting in his chair reminiscing about his childhood. There was, however, one big difference. In this version grandpa did not give his grandson a sweet. Rather he ignored his grandson and ate all the biscuits himself. As this upset the boy he hit the grandpa on the head with a pan and ran off with the snacks.

Under Dutch law the court ruled that the copycat advertisement was unlawful and found Verkade culpable of a 'tortious act' – that is that it ridiculed the original in a negative and possibly damaging way.

Source: Martin Bewick, *The Marketer*, October 2005.

Particular categories are seen to be particularly important to monitor. Customers of financial products or services rely heavily on trust and the availability of accurate information. Food and drink must not be over-hyped and, in the case of alcohol, drinking should not be associated with attractive human characteristics. Medicines should not claim more than can be scientifically proven. Cigarette promotion, now largely constrained in European markets, continues to be monitored.

In the general field of advertising in the UK (including much of what has been described in this text as sales promotion and direct marketing) the Advertising Standards Authority polices the rules laid down by the advertising code (see Advertising standards below). In November 2004 their remit was extended to cover broadcast advertising[6] (previously handled by Ofcom) but they have limited influence in the area of new media (except email). Other bodies responsible for self-regulation include the Direct Marketing Association (DMA) who, through the Direct Marketing Authority maintain the DMA Code

---

[6]Under the auspices of the British Advertising Standards Association (BASA).

of Practice and adjudicate on complaints against DMA members. The Financial Services Authority (FSA) write, monitor and enforce a set of rules on the content of financial promotions and they have the power to impose financial penalties and sanctions on organizations or individuals (Fleetwood-Jones 2005). This is a field of particular current concern. In a recent (May 2005) survey for Mortgages PLC, one-in-four advertisers of home mortgages were found to be not compliant with the FSA (CIM 2006). The Medicines and Healthcare Regulatory Agency (MHRA) monitors all medical claims. Complaints about an advertisement or any other communication concerning medicines can be made to the MHRA by a customer, a competitor or a patient. The UK watchdog for the collection and usage of data is the Information Commissioner's Office.

UK legislation is, in fact, among the least obstructive in Europe. In Germany a non-compliant marketer can be taken to court not by enforcement bodies but by competitors using the country's wide-ranging unfair competition laws (Groom 2005).

ADVERTISING STANDARDS

In most developed countries advertising, whether on television, radio, the Internet, newspapers and periodicals, posters or elsewhere, is regulated either by government legislation or by industry self-regulation or a combination of the two. In the UK the Advertising Association, founded in 1924, very early on issued a set of ethical codes it encouraged its members to work to. This was encapsulated in the call to advertisers to seek truth, avoid exaggeration, misleading claims and unfair competitive criticism (Brierley 2002). These codes of practice have developed over the years and are still today administered by the industry in the form of the Advertising Standards Authority (ASA) whose role is to 'make sure all advertising,[7] wherever it appears, is both honest and decent' (ASA 2005). The ASA Council is the body that adjudicates on formally investigated complaints. Although industry supported and funded it has an independent chairman and the majority of its members are from outside the advertising industry. The key rules contained in the codes relate to:

- Misleading advertising
- Offensive advertising

Misleading advertising

Advertisements are not allowed to mislead consumers. This means that advertisers must hold evidence to claims that they make about their products or services before the advertisement appears. As the Asda example in

---

[7]One exception to this is political advertising. As this does not fall under the remit of the ASA politicians are excused from the requirement to be honest and truthful.

MINICASE 18.3

Reebok ditches ad

In March 2005 Reebok launched a £12m campaign 'I am what I am' featuring rapper 50 Cent alongside police fingerprint records and the words: 'Where I am from, there is no plan B. So, take advantage of today because tomorrow is not promised.' 50 Cent has been criticized for his supposed feud with rival rapper The Game which involved bullets being fired in a recording studio. The Advertising Standards Authority (ASA) received 55 complaints about the advertising which showed the rapper counting to nine in reference to the number of times he has been shot. The charity Disarm Trust called it 'irresponsible and despicable' and 'preying on young black males'. In a statement Reebok said 'When the 50 Cent television ad' began to air, a small number of the general public found it offensive.' However, with the possibility of a ban Reebok took the decision shortly afterwards to indefinitely stop broadcasting the 50 Cent spot.

Source: *Marketing*, 16 March 2005 and 20 April 2005.

SOURCE: © REUTERS/CORBIS

50 Cent at the 2003 MTV Movie Awards, Los Angeles – a 2005 Reebok ad campaign featuring the singer was dropped after the Advertising Standards Authority received over 50 complaints.

Chapter 9, Minicase 9.2 shows there is a fine line between deliberately misleading consumers and competitive hyperbole.

Offensive advertising

Advertisements are 'not allowed to cause serious or widespread offence' (ASA 2005). Special care is taken regarding the portrayal of gender, race, religion, sexuality and disability but the dividing line between what is offensive and what is not is an ever shifting one, as what offends one person may be regarded as fair comment by another. The ASA considers various factors before deciding whether an advertisement is offensive including the medium in which it appears, the target audience, the particular product or service and, most importantly, what is generally acceptable conduct at the time. This implies that a ban today need not necessarily mean a ban in the future. This has led some observers to suggest that the boundaries of what is acceptable are forever being tested and pushed forward by advertisers.

Other parts of the ASA codes contain specific rules about sales promotions and direct marketing (see Chapters 10 and 13 respectively). There are rules that cover advertisements aimed at children and advertisements for alcohol, health products, beauty products, financial services, employment and business opportunities and gambling. Rules also apply to the types of advertising that can be shown around certain programmes and at certain times (e.g. before the 'nine-o-clock watershed').

Watershed
Denoting a time before which certain advertising (and certain programming) cannot be shown.

Although the ASA codes are not enshrined in legislation the organization can impose sanctions against those who break the rules. If a complaint is upheld the advertiser is requested not to use that advertisement again. The ruling is published on the ASA website and media owners will refuse to take advertising that has been acted against in this way. Misleading advertising or impermissible comparisons can also be referred to the UK Office of Fair Trading for legislative action where appropriate.

Look at the Office of Fair Trading's website at: **www.oft.gov.uk**.

Just one complaint can trigger an ASA investigation and an advertisement being banned. At the other end of the scale just because an advertisement attracts a large number of complaints does not necessarily mean it will be withdrawn. In 2005, KFC's Zinger Crunch Salad TV commercial became the most complained about UK advertisement of all time; not for reasons of sex or nudity, but because the call-centre staff portrayed were singing with their mouths full and complainants felt it encouraged bad table manners (Forbes 2005). The ASA rejected the claim.

Advertising campaigns increasingly cross national boundaries and there is a growing movement to co-ordinate advertising standards particularly across Europe. The European Advertising Standards Alliance (EASA) was formed in 1991 largely to try and circumvent European Union legislation by developing a Europe-wide code of practice for self-regulation of the industry. EASA's membership includes European (Austria, Belgium, Czech Republic, Denmark, Finland, France, Germany, Luxembourg, Netherlands, Portugal, Russia, Slovak Republic, Slovenia, Spain, Sweden, Switzerland, Turkey and the United Kingdom) and four non-European (Canada, New Zealand, South

Look at the European Advertising Standards Alliance's website at: **www.easa-alliance.org**.

Africa and the USA) self-regulating bodies. The organization produce a publication with details on both statutory and self-regulatory rules governing European advertising known as the EASA Blue Book.

OTHER ISSUES

Although advertising has, to date, dominated the ethical and legislative debate other aspects of marketing communications have given cause for concern. In the promotional field the use of incentives (discounts, allowances, etc.) to effectively buy shelf space and keep competitive products out has long been criticized but is a continuing practice. The use of high-cost telephone numbers to enter promotions and/or the misuse of SMS (short messaging service or texting) continue to cause concern (see Case study 18.1). Fraudulent competitions, particular from off-shore locations, would also appear to be on the rise.

In the public relations (PR) field the use of advertorials (promotions masquerading as editorials) is among the practices frowned upon, but still prevalent, in the industry. There is also the dilema posed in public relations between protecting the company and freedom of information. The Institute of Public Relations (IPR) have a code of rules that they ask all member to apply which cover relationships with the media and the public. Fundamental to their code are high levels of integrity, competence, transparency and confidentiality (Baines *et al*. 2004).

Personal selling is an area of potential abuse. Salespeople are exposed to greater ethical pressures because they are largely unsupervised and evaluated and/or remunerated depending on what they sell. According to a *Sales and Management* magazine survey 49 per cent of managers say that their salespeople have lied on sales calls and 22 per cent said they had sold customers products they did not need (Marchetti 1997).

In direct marketing the environmental and personal intrusion arguments against direct mail and telemarketing are heightened by discussion regarding the ethical collection and use of personal data. The commercial incentive to collect, merge, warehouse and sell customer information is enormous, while the safeguards tend to be weak and easily ignored (Prabhaker 2000). In the UK for example, which has significant data protection legislation, there were only 12 successful prosecutions in the year 2004–05. There is little doubt, however, that the UK and European legislation will get tighter in the future. In the knowledge that legislation will ultimately be introduced in some form practitioners are developing techniques for encouraging customers to 'opt in' or 'join' them in their campaigns. This may include the provision of information or services (e.g. online news) in exchange for data. This range of customer authorized data collection strategies has been called 'permission marketing'. There is also some suggestion that customers react badly when they believe their personal details are being indiscriminately passed on, although the practice is difficult to control. On the other side of the coin there is the irony that strictly regulating

Permission marketing
Marketing where you have the explicit permission of the customer to contact them.

the collection of personal information could ultimately limit the quality and level of service that businesses can deliver to their customers (*ibid.*).

Nowhere is this privacy debate more pertinent than with the Internet and the use of 'cookies' to track consumer behaviour. As Prabhaker (2000: 159) notes, from the time an individual interacts with the web s/he leaves behind a trail of extraordinary detailed information about who s/he is, his or her buying habits, financial status, maybe their medical records and other intimate personal details. S/he has very little control over who can have access to this information and what they will do with it. In addition it is unrealistic to expect profit driven businesses not to infringe on consumer privacy in an environment that makes it increasingly profitable and with technology that makes it easier than ever to collect and share personal information.

THE ETHICS SOLUTION?

The legal and ethical minefields in the contemporary marketplace suggests that companies must be aware as never before. According to the CIM (2006: 3) 'companies need to take a more proactive role in order to assist and reinforce self-regulation, to avoid brand damage at best and costly legal proceedings at worst'. There is, therefore, a strong argument in medium-sized and larger companies for the appointment of a Marketing Compliance Officer (MCO) or, in smaller companies, an individual with part-time responsibility for this task. As noted earlier marketers do not have the best of reputations and the appointment of a Marketing Compliance Officer may show that the organization is 'willing to identify and comply with their legal responsibilities, and communicate their actions to the wider business community, government…self-regulatory boards' (CIM 2006: 3) and the general public.

Marketing Compliance Officer
Officer responsible for ensuring the organization complies with laws and regulations.

Summary

This chapter reviewed the ethical and regulatory environment in which marketing communications operates. Recognizing the perception of marketers as untrustworthy the chapter queries whether it is the place of marketers to submit to or push the boundaries of moral welfare and concluded that it was an individual marketer's responsibility to judge where to draw the line.

The chapter reviewed the accusations made against advertising of a number of ethical breaches including that it promotes materialism, wastes resources, creates unwanted needs, perpetuates stereotyping, causes people to use harmful products, promotes unethical brands, inhibits media coverage, targets vulnerable groups and that it delivers subliminal messages and the arguments for and against them. It also reviewed the relationship between self-regulation and legislation and whether the former, despite its advantages, was losing ground as more and more national and trans-national legislation is introduced. It noted that the advertising regulators were particularly concerned about certain marketing practices including comparative advertising, pricing claims, trademarks and passing off, product descriptions, promotions, data protection, international law and marketing to children. They were also concerned with certain product categories including financial products and services, food and drink, medicines, cigarettes, and products and services associated with children.

The chapter looked at the work of the Advertising Standards Agency and other UK agencies and noted that their concentration was against misleading and/or offensive advertising. It also noted that as campaigns increasingly cross national borders so international advertising bodies are colluding in the hope of holding back legislation.

The chapter concludes by looking at ethical issues outside of advertising in the sales promotion, public relations, personal selling and direct marketing industries.

Review questions

1   What do you understand by the term 'ethical marketing'?
2   To what extent might advertising inhibit media coverage?
3   What do you understand by the term 'Chinese Wall'?
4   How would you use an advertorial?
5   To what extent might industry legislators be concerned with marketing practices?
6   What is the difference between 'opt in' and 'opt out' in direct response advertising?
7   Explain the role of the ASA.
8   What constitutes misleading advertising?
9   Define permission marketing.
10 Why might a company appoint a marketing compliance officer?

Discussion questions

1   How do you decide if something is ethical or not?
2   Do you believe that advertising actually wastes resources? To what extent might this be true?
3   What are your views on stereotyping in advertising? Under what circumstances might it not be acceptable?
4   Does self-regulation work?

Further reading

Beckett, R. (2003) 'Communication ethics: principle and practice', *Journal of Communication Management*, Aug., 8 (1): 41–52. This paper concludes by presenting a model of communication ethics that individual managers can use to prescribe a more sensitive and dynamic human-ethical environment.

Capozzi, L. (2005) 'Corporate reputation: our role in sustaining and building a valuable asset', *Journal of Advertising Research*, Sep., 45 (3): 290–3.

'Corporate moral branding: limits to aligning employees', *Corporate Communications: An International Journal*, (2006), 11 (2): 97–108. A critical discussion on the challenges raised for employees as corporate brands increasingly address moral issues.

Dawkins, J. (2004) 'Corporate responsibility: the communication challenge', *Journal of Communication Management*, Nov., 9 (2): 108–19. The paper suggests, in conclusion, that effective communication of corporate responsibility depends on a clear strategy, which evaluates both the opportunities and the risks to the brand and which tailors messages to different stakeholder groups.

Schroeder, J.E. and Borgerson, J.L. (2005) 'An ethics of representation for international marketing communication', *International Marketing Review*, 22 (5): 578–600. This paper offers an ethical analysis of visual representation that provides criteria for and sheds light on the appropriate dimension of marketing communications.

Wenner, L. (2004) 'On the Ethics of product placement in media entertainment', *Journal of Promotion Management*, 10 (1/2): 101–33. This study examines the ethical propriety of current trends in product placement in television and film entertainment

Chapter references

ASA (2005) 'Advertising under control', *Advertising Standards Authority*, http://www.asa.org.uk/asa/about/control, accessed 10 August.

Baines, P., Egan, J. and Jefkins, F. (2004) *Public Relations: Contemporary Issues and Techniques*, Oxford: Elsevier Butterworth-Heiremann.

Belch, G. and Belch, M. (2001) *Advertising and Promotion: An Integrated Marketing Communications Perspective*, London: McGraw-Hill.

Brierley, S. (2002) *The Advertising Handbook*, 2nd edn, London: Routledge.

Campaign (2003) *Campaign Book of Lists 2003*, 19 December, Haymarket Publications.

CIM (2006) *No Marketer is an Island: Marketing and the Law*, Hot Marketing Series Issue 9 January, Cookham, Berkshire: Chartered Institute of Marketing.

Fleetwood-Jones, E. (2005) 'Guardians of good practice', *The Marketer*, 17 October, CIM.

Forbes, C. (2005) 'Be careful what you promise', *The Marketer*, 17 October, CIM.

Groom, S (2005) 'You've never had it so good', *The Marketer*, 17 October, CIM.

Hoek, J. (1999) 'Sponsorship', in P.J. Kitchen (ed.), *Marketing Communications: Principles and Practice*, London: Thomson, pp. 361–80.

Lipman, L. (1992) 'Media content is linked to cigarette ads', *The Wall Street Journal*, 30 January: B5.

Marchetti, M. (1997) 'What ever it takes', *Sales & Marketing Management*, 149 (13): 29–38.

Miles, L. (2005) 'Playing the game', *The Marketer*, 17 October, CIM.

Nevett, T.R. (1982) *Advertising in Britain: A History*, London: Heinemann.

OED (1995) *The Concise Oxford Dictionary of Current Englisth*, Oxford: Oxford University Press.

Prabhaker, P.R. (2000) 'Who owns the online consumer?', *Journal of Consumer Marketing*, 17 (2): 158–71.

Sheehan (2004) *Controversies in Contemporary Advertising*, Thousand Oaks, CA: Sage Publications.

Sivulka, J. (1998) *Soap, Sex and Cigarettes: A Cultural History of American Advertising*, Belmont: Thomson Learning.

Sutherland, M. (1993) *Advertising and the Mind of the Consumer*, St. Leonards, Australia: Allen & Unwin.

Yeshin, T. (2006) *Advertising*, London: Thomson.

CASE STUDY 18.1

Letter of the law

Wherever marketers venture, regulation is sure to follow. Digital marketing is no exception, as the Advertising Standards Authority's (ASA) Committee of Advertising Practice (CAP) has shown by issuing its first set of guidelines for marketing via mobile phones. The increasing number of brands – from Coca-Cola to yoghurt drink Yop – using mobiles as a channel to drive sales and relationships, underlines the necessity of CAP's 'Help Note on Mobile Marketing', which states that consumers must either give their explicit consent or be existing customers to receive mobile marketing.

This is particularly important in view of the limitations of SMS,[8] the predominant form of mobile marketing. The direct and intimate nature of texting is a strength, but coupled with the 160-character limit for a message, it has the potential to be misunderstood and cause offence. Complaints about text messages to the ASA increased by 500 per cent in 2003 to 353, compared with 65 in 2002.

The guidelines are partly a response to this rise in complaints as well as a means of preventing a growth in mobile spam. CAP chairman Andrew Brown says they should ensure the effectiveness of opt-in communication. 'It is important that marketers targeting consumers via their mobiles conduct their business responsibly in this very personal medium', he adds.

Carsten Boers, Chief Executive of mobile marketing company Flytxt, which has run campaigns for Coca-Cola and Orange, points out that the actual number of complaints made about the medium is small. He adds that, unlike email, where problems with spam are well documented, there is a cost associated with sending out texts on a mass scale. 'Mobile spam is not as big an issue as the media coverage suggests because the economics of mobile do not work for spammers.'

---

[8]Short Messaging Service or texting.

Carsten Boers' mobile marketing company, Flytxt, is the lead consultant and technology provider behind the Orange Wednesdays SMS promotion in the UK and Romania.

SOURCE: IMAGE COURTESY OF THE ADVERTISING ARCHIVES.

Peter Larsen, European Managing Director of mobile services provider Enpocket, which has worked with William Hill and the NHS, agrees. 'The technical dynamics of mobile make it easier to nip spam in the bud', he says. 'There is an incremental cost to the spammer not found elsewhere and the sector has been very proactive about the situation.'

Nevertheless, some promotions cross the line inadvertently. Tim Gardner, managing partner of mobile consultancy iris-north, which works with Million-2-1, the holder of a UK permit for SMS lotteries, explains that there is a fine line between gaming regulations and the rules regarding SMS promotions. Many brands, he says, are running SMS prediction promotions and are not even aware that they are potentially breaking the law.

Gardner says marketers must be '100 per cent compliant' to avoid damaging their brands. Million-2-1 has invested more than £500 000 in ensuring it does just this, by working closely with the Independent Committee for the Supervision of Standards of Telephone Information Services (Icstis), gambling addiction support organization Gamcare, Ofcom, the police and the Gaming Board of Great Britain.

Opportune intervention
If prevention is better than cure, the CAP guidelines are timely. As the successes pile up, so the number of brands using mobile will grow. Cadbury cited SMS as a key mechanism for boosting sales in 2003 and newcomers such as Yop have used it in on-pack promotions to boost loyalty and create a database of opted-in consumers for future promotions.

The CAP is not the only body to have produced guidelines; the Mobile Marketing Association (MMA) issued a more comprehensive set last year. But the CAP's profile with marketers who are new to mobile as a marketing channel has lent it credibility. As Flytxt's Boers says: 'Mobile has the potential to grow as a medium. Although companies are increasingly using mobile, there are plenty of brands that may only be familiar with the ASA. The CAP code mirrors the directives and guidelines already in place.'

Enpocket's Larsen agrees: 'The guidelines are a positive step. They match the MMA benchmarks and it is good that a more traditional marketing body is taking a firm position on mobile.' He believes mobile marketing still has more to offer a wider range of brands and the guidelines should help marketers who have yet to try the medium to overcome the 'fear factor'.

Chris Ambler, Managing Director of interactive agency WARL evolution, claims the potential of SMS is self-evident. 'It reaches 80 per cent of the UK population, is read by 94 per cent of recipients, reaches them day and night in the supermarket, the pub, even in bed, and allows them to respond instantly', he says. 'Mobile is no longer a peripheral activity for over-excited teenagers.'

But, Ambler warns, this can be a double-edged sword.

Abuse your invited position in my mobile inbox and I will not respond and may feel worse about your brand as a result. The guidelines – and last year's regulatory changes – are to be welcomed. Hopefully they have arrived in time to save mobile from becoming the discredited medium that email now is.

Punitive measures

Businesses that fail to behave responsibly with mobile marketing have more to worry about than a negative impact on their brands, because the ASA has teeth. 'We don't impose fines, we publicise our findings and ask for the promotion to be stopped. If someone is unwilling to do that, it is referred to the appropriate authority', says an ASA spokeswoman.

For mobile, this includes the regulatory body for premium mobile communications, Icstis. In May it imposed fines totalling almost £500 000 for the sending of spam and scam text messages encouraging consumers to call premium-rate numbers. Six companies were fined £75 000 for breaches of Icstis' Code of Practice, including sending unsolicited text messages, making unsolicited phone calls and using automated calling equipment to leave 'missed calls'. But Boers says the sort of mobile scams that were flourishing 18 months ago, such as offering entry to prize draws, have stopped. 'Returns did not justify the cost of sending them', he explains.

Effective marketing, however, is not just about obeying rules. Ambler says SMS should create value for the recipient each time a brand communicates with them. 'Timely added-value information, sponsored entertainment and instant sales promotions with mobile coupons, can all deliver value', he says.

One example of such a campaign is Yop's SMS promotion. It wanted to boost sales of two flavours – raspberry and strawberry – by 10 per cent over a period of six months last year, and briefed marketing agency Attention, mobile marketing services company Sponge and wireless specialist Netsize to create an SMS-based on-pack promotion across 2.5m bottles. The promotion offered consumers the chance to win 'Trainers for life', as well as bottles of Yop and JD Sports gift vouchers. Consumers entered via SMS using a unique code printed on the drink's label. A return text informed them immediately whether they were a winner.

Overall redemption figures exceeded targets by 53 per cent, according to Netsize. Yop brand manager Olivia Munden says: 'Our aim was to provide a fresh and relevant means of attracting and communicating with our audience. Based on this success, we'd have no hesitation in choosing SMS as an effective and easy-to-manage response mechanism.'

Laying the foundations

Despite this positive example, WARL's Ambler believes more can be done to build on the guidelines. 'The IPA and MMA need to redouble their efforts to ensure that advertisers understand the code and the regulations', he says. 'It would also be good to see the network operators getting involved and encouraging their users to report any unsolicited SMS messages.'

The progression of technology poses further burdens, as well as opportunities, for mobile as a marketing channel. Orange has already started to detail its plans for 3G in the UK, following the launch of vanguard operator 3 some 18 months ago. The rise of camera-phone handsets also offers the allure of combining pictures with words and hence more creative mobile marketing communication.

Larsen believes the guidelines now in place should remain relevant as technologies develop. 'So many different services are developing. There is one- and two-way SMS communication, MMS, Java and 3G. These will move the mobile marketing industry ahead, but the key is to get the permission process in place. Then we can build on that.'

Case study questions

1   What are the suggested benefits of SMS to marketers?

2   Would you support legislation restricting the use of SMS? Explain your reasons why.

Source: Philip Smith, *Marketing*, 4 August 2004 (reproduced from *Marketing* Magazine with the permission of the copyright owner, Haymarket Business Publications Limited).

CHAPTER NINETEEN

THE COMMUNICATIONS INDUSTRY

LEARNING OBJECTIVES

Having completed this chapter you should be able to:

- Understand the history and development of the modern communications industry.
- Comprehend the changes in structure and remuneration systems and what brought them about.
- Understand the basic functions associated with agencies and specialist independent and dependent agencies.
- Be aware of the factors involved in agency selection.

INTRODUCTION

The communications industry might be described as a simple network based upon a tripartite relationship, where the major players are the client, the agency and the media. Traditionally the agency has been seen as an intermediary, first as the agent of the media and then on behalf of the client. The agency/client relationship is said to be 'a dynamic decision-making process in which the participants identify, evaluate and choose appropriate communication strategies and alternatives' (Yeshin 2006: 152). The creative tension that develops is seen to drive the industry forward but is not without its problems. The fact that (in modern times) agencies whilst working for clients were being paid by the media, has also complicated these relationships.

The communications industry today is a complex legacy of developments that continued throughout the eighteenth, nineteenth and twentieth centuries. In the beginning it was the rapid expansion of both newspapers and magazines (seeking clients) and potential advertisers (seeking advertising space) that was the stimulus for this growth. As the numbers grew relationships between both sides became complicated and a need developed in the industry to simplify arrangements. What clients required was someone who could advise on the suitability of a particular medium, write copy if required and simplify accounting (Nevett 1982). What newspaper proprietors needed was a more efficient way of dealing with scores of individual advertisers. As such the latter developed a preference of dealing with specialists who could both offer a professional approach to the placement of advertising and deal with the individual accounts. Advertising agencies, therefore, were the medium that developed to satisfy the needs of both sides of industry. It was the creation of this three-way relationship that first dominated and still influences the communications industry today.

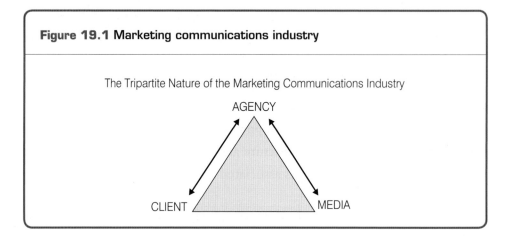

Figure 19.1 Marketing communications industry

The Tripartite Nature of the Marketing Communications Industry

AGENCY

CLIENT   MEDIA

HISTORICAL DEVELOPMENT

As noted in Chapter 1, the earliest agency for which records exist is that of William Taylor who described himself as agent to 'County Printers, Booksellers etc.' and first advertised his services in the *Maidstone Journal* of 1786. Early agents worked not on behalf of the client but for newspaper owners, both collecting news and selling advertising space on their behalf. By 1800 this was beginning to change and in that year James White founded an agency which was not just involved with placing advertisements but in writing copy too. By 1820 the *Edinburgh Review* reported that at the offices of Newton & Co. and Barker & Co., two principal London agents, 'advertisements are received for all county papers without increased charge to the advertiser, the commission of the agent being paid by the newspaper proprietor'. This system of remuneration, based on commissions from media owners, was eventually to become widespread and to dictate the structure of the industry well into the twentieth century.

By the 1830s and 1840s agents were producing lists in the form of reference books which included information on newspapers such as the day and place of publication, political stance and in some cases average circulation. In addition to all the UK newspapers some overseas media were included in these lists. These lists were a direct forerunner of modern industry publications such as *BRAD* (*British Rates and Data*) which catagorizes and lists all UK media together with rates and technical data.

Look at BRAD's website at:
www.brad.co.uk/info/.

As the industry entered the twentieth century competition became intense. Whereas a few decades before it was not unusual to find rival chocolate or soap manufacturers using the same agent, clients were now complaining if there was any sign of conflicting interest. This caused some clients to leave an agency if they took on a rival competitor, while others forced agencies to resign if they had conflicting accounts (Brierley 2002). By 1906 there were 339 advertising agencies in London representing newspapers based in the capital, 22 who specialized in provincial publications and 79 who concentrated on overseas media. Although in the UK London was the main centre for advertising, regional centres in Manchester, Edinburgh and Bristol also began to grow at this time. Commission varied widely with up to 30 per cent in the case of some 'weak and desperate publications' (Nevett 1982). Some media brokers who did not create copy for their clients undercut the main agencies by taking as little as 1 per cent (Brierley 2002).

By the 1920s the mainstream advertising agencies were more clearly defined as intermediaries who managed, created and bought advertising space on behalf of their clients (Brierley 2002). 'Full service' agencies also offered sales support, creative input, research and sometimes product development in addition to purchasing media space. They were, however, continuing to be undercut by media brokers who did not carry the high overheads of the full service agencies and as such there was growing pressure from larger agencies to 'professionalize the industry' to the exclusion of the price-cutters. In 1907 the Incorporated Society of Advertising Agents was formed but it was short-lived, breaking up after continuous disagreements over rebating. In 1917 the Association of British Advertising Agents[1] (ABAA) was formed and in 1921 the London *Times* newspaper signed an agreement with the 60 members of the ABAA restricting commission payments only to recognized agents affiliated to the Association. In 1932 the National Publishers Association produced an accord that formally banned rate-cutting. The NPA agreement was effectively a cartel arrangement between the full service agencies and the media owners that squeezed out any other form of business such as media brokerage or consultancy. Although initially applying only to new agencies it became the accepted norm and from then on dominated advertising remuneration for most of the rest of the twentieth century (Brierley 2002). Under the agreement agencies also had to abide by the IPA (as successor to the ABAA) code of practice reinforcing their role as regulator and effectively a 'closed shop' on industry knowledge (*ibid*.).

During and immediately after the Second World War the main problem facing agencies were related to the management of supply rather than to stimulating demand, indeed, advertising that made the reader want to buy something was actively discouraged in this period (Nevett 1982). By the mid 1950s, however, production and consumption were growing fast and advertisers had a new medium in television. Commission rates were rising. Prior to the 1930s many commission rates were in single figures but by the

Media brokers
Intermediaries who purchase media space (only) without the overheads of a full agency.

Full Service Agencies
An agency that covers a full range of agency disciplines including copy writing, design, media purchase, etc.

Rebating
Giving to the client part or all of the commission paid by media owners.

---

[1]Which later became the Institute of Incorporated Practitioners in Advertising and is now the Institute of Practitioners in Advertising (IPA).

Commercials
Television commercial advertisements.

Media independents
Independent media brokers.

@

Useful information on the history of UK advertising can be found at:**www.hatads. org.uk/links.htm.**

Media dependents
Media brokers that are part of a larger agency group.

1940s these had stabilized at 10 per cent due to the NPA recognition system. On the introduction of commercial television to the UK, station owners offered a 15 per cent commission to help cover the supposed additional costs of TV advertising (*ibid.*). Because of this newspapers also raised their commission rates to 15 per cent.

Changes were, however, in the air. American agencies had begun to establish offices in London during the 1950s and by 1960 there were 36 US agencies in London with 281 offices nationwide, bringing new techniques and a wider range of services to the market (Nevett 1982). When US advertisers wanted to use commercials (commercial advertisements) from their home or other markets and only wanted to buy 'space' and 'time' on the independent television (ITV) network they started to use media independents who, although they received the full 15 per cent commission, 'illegally' rebated 10 per cent to 12 per cent to the client supposedly for 'creative costs' (Brierley 2002). Many of these first media independents operated under 'flags of convenience' for small full-service agencies who in turn got a cut of the commission (*ibid.*).

By the 1970s the recognition system was beginning to break down. The previous decade had shown a decline in business caused by economic uncertainty and unemployment and subsequent increased competition between agencies. In 1976 the UK government introduced the Restrictive Practices Act and in 1978 the Office of Fair Trading (OFT), set up under the act, ruled that fixed commission was anti-competitive. In 1979 the NPA and the Newspaper Society dropped agency recognition. Agencies were forced to negotiate their commission rate individually with media owners and were under pressure from advertisers to rebate some part of this remuneration to them. Agencies that only handled the placement of advertising (media independents) began to openly appear again. Separate media buying was popular with many advertisers as it allowed them to dip in and out of different agencies and pick and choose the services they required. Whereas in 1960 all media buying was controlled by full service agencies by 1980 there were 30 media independents. During the period 1986–91 their share of revenue was to grow by 184 per cent. By 2000 90 per cent of all media expenditure was handled by separate media agencies (*ibid.*).

The response of the full service agencies to the changing marketplace was to begin hiving-off media departments into separate entities in order to compete. By the last decade of the twentieth century it was established practice to have a creative advertising agency, a separate media planning and buying agency and another set of agencies to run direct marketing, sales promotion and public relations campaigns. Agency response to the growth of below-the-line competition was twofold. First, they tried to undermine client decision-making by suggesting that compared with advertising other marketing communications tools were ineffective. Sales promotion was a particular target with advertisers suggesting that it eroded brand values (Brierley 2002). Second, when it became obvious that this ploy was failing, large established agencies began to appropriate existing below-the-line agencies or to create in-house such agencies of their own.

At the turn of the century a number of substantial mergers took place and new 'media dependents' (controlled by parent company agencies) were created such as *WPP's Mindshare* launched in 1997 (Brierley 2002). By 1999 70 per cent of media buying companies were 'media dependents'. Reflecting the move toward integrated marketing communications (IMC) most advertising agencies became subsidiaries of groups usually operating on an international basis who also incorporate specialists in the fields of direct marketing, sales promotion, public relations, sponsorship, etc.

The history of the advertising industry has today, therefore, left it a complex place. Many clients choose not to spend their money through full service agencies. Not only have functions been hived-off but there is a growing number of independent agencies (or group dependents) who operate in narrow fields such as financial services, pharmaceuticals, tourism, business-to-business, etc. Clients as a result may choose two or more agencies to obtain the skills and creativity they need to achieve their objectives.

It is also noticeable that client/agency relationships are not as long-standing as they once were. Long-term relationships (such as the 65-year association between J. Walter Thompson and Kellogg's) are now the exception rather than the norm, with fewer than 25 per cent of major client accounts staying with agencies for ten years or more (Brierley 2002).

MINICASE 19.1

Agency merry-go-round

RHM Foods announced in January 2006 that it was reviewing Mr Kipling cakes' £3 million advertising account. The present incumbent WCRS won it two years ago from Saatchi & Saatchi and were responsible for handling the brand's £5 million re-launch in January 2005. Saatchi & Saatchi lost the account after it created a controversial TV advertisement depicting a woman giving birth during a nativity play (see Box 18.1). Meanwhile in June 2006 McCain ended months of speculation by appointing Beattie McGuinness Bungay (BMB) to handle its £15 million account. This followed a three-way pitch in March in which the former agent TBWA/London declined to take part.

The nativity play advertisement for Mr Kipling was one of the most controversial in 2003 with over 500 viewers complaining.

SOURCE: IMAGE COURTESY OF THE ADVERTISING ARCHIVES.

AGENCY FEATURES

Given their history, agencies have grown up in a variety of types and structures that defy rigid definition. However, a 'typical' agency would have (or have access to) the following functions:

- Account management
- Account planning
- Creative design
- Media management
- Production

Account management

Responsible for liaison with the client, that their needs are being fulfilled by the agency, that timetables are kept and that all work is completed within the budget.

Account planning

Responsible for the changing requirements of the client and advising on the strategic direction of a campaign through pre- and post-campaign research.

The **account management** function is responsible for liaison with the client and ensuring that their needs are being fulfilled by the agency. They are also charged with ensuring that timetables are kept and that all work is completed within the budget.

Account planning is responsible for managing and guiding the changing requirement of the client and advising on the strategic direction of a campaign through pre- and post-campaign research. Account planners would be expected to provide insight and understanding of the consumer and their relationship with the brand and help guide the strategic direction of communications by liaising closely with the creative team.

To call the creative input of an agency a function may appear oxymoronic but as part of a process the creative team has to deliver. Creatives often work in teams and their role is to interpret the creative brief (see Chapter 8) and translate this into effective messages that suits the medium through which they will pass.

Media management

Getting the messages that have been created into the appropriate media at a time and cost that fulfils the objective of the campaign.

Media management involves getting the messages created into the appropriate media at a time and cost that fulfils the objective of the campaign and within the budget allocated. This 'function' has, more recently, been largely separated from agency management with the creation of 'media independents' and 'media dependents'.

Production department

Responsible for ensuring that the creative elements are translated into the right format for the chosen media.

Progress manager

Responsible for ensuring that the various stages of production are completed on time.

Production departments ensure that the creative elements are translated into the right format for the chosen media. In this area **progress (or traffic) managers** ensure that the various stages of production are completed on time.

Although the above represents a typical structure changes are happening very fast. As discussed in Chapter 15 client organisations are looking to set the communications agenda rather than relying on formally powerful agencies to set it for them. The trend towards integrated marketing communications is a principal driver in this regard and has meant significant changes in the industry. Technological advances are yet another reason for organizations to reconsider their traditional modes of marketing communications and re-evaluate their approach. Current industry structures are reflected in these changed requirements. At one end of the scale agency groupings (of dependents) are currently in vogue, whereas at the other small specialist service (media specialists, creative boutiques, etc.) agencies have developed in order to service specialist needs of the industry.

Another dramatic change has been in the way agencies are remunerated. This has been a major cause of friction between agencies and clients for years, particularly as brand owners have sought to get the upper hand over the once-powerful agency cartels. As the power of advertising has declined relative to other marketing communications tools, so brand owners have demanded rebates and set standards to which agencies have been obliged to accede. Contemporary reimbursement options reflect this diversity and now include:

- Traditional commission
- Negotiated commission
- Project fees
- Time-based fees
- Cost-based fees
- Performance-based fees or payment-by-results (PBR)

As noted previously **commission** was the backbone of agency power during most of the twentieth century. Today a mixture of different methods have largely replaced the straightforward 10 per cent or 15 per cent commission payment. Whereas in 1965 media commission accounted for 76 per cent of agency income (the rest was mainly in additional below-the-line services) by 2000 the majority of the top 116 UK 'blue chip' companies pay agencies on a fee basis or payment-by-results (Brierley 2002). **Negotiated commission** maintains some connection to the original system and may involve rebating sometimes on a sliding scale. **Fee payment** is currently the most popular form of remuneration and is based on a quotation for individual projects. Occasionally companies may pay an agency a **retainer fee** to enable them to maintain contact and ensure effective continuity. **Time-based fees** are an established form of recompense in public relations agencies but are also more generally used on special projects. **Cost-based fees** rely on an agreed mark-up on inputs such as media. **Performance-based compensation** or **payment-by-results (PBR)** is based on targets set against a particular campaign (see Case study 19.1). According to the *Incorporated Society of British Advertisers (ISBA)*:[2]

- 40 per cent of creative industry agreements now contain an element of payment-by-results.
- Payment-by-results is most evident in the consumer goods sector, less so in retailing and services.
- The average payment-by-results element is 15 per cent of base remuneration.
- 25 per cent of schemes have a penalty element combining risk and reward.

Commission (agency)
Percentage paid by media owners to agencies in lieu of fees.

Negotiated commission
Commission system which may involve rebating on a sliding scale.

Fee payment
Remuneration based on a quotation for individual projects.

Retainer fee
Fee paid to agency to retain their services on an *ad hoc* basis over time.

Time-based fees
An established form of recompense in public relations but are also used more generally on special agency projects.

Cost-based fees
Remuneration based on an agreed mark-up on inputs such as media.

Payment-by-results (PBR)
Remuneration based on achievement of set targets.

[2]Quoted in Simms (2004).

See the ISBA's website at: **www.isba.org. uk/isba.**

Another major consequence of changes in industry structures and integrated marketing communications is that organizations 'mix-and-match' agencies like never before. It is not unheard of for a company to employ separate creative advertising, media purchasing, promotion, public relations and sponsorship agencies. The key is co-ordination and this is often stipulated in the brief given to the agencies.

CHOOSING AN AGENCY

Apart from the specializations noted above agency structures are rarely that different from each other with any significant innovations quickly being copied by competitors (Brierley 2002). Larger agencies, however, generally have extensive networks in the UK and abroad and will frequently incorporate more extensive research facilities than the small or medium-sized agencies.

A starting point when initially choosing an agency or when a change of agency is considered is whether potential organizations offer the services that the client requires. When selecting (or re-selecting) agencies to pitch for an organization's communication business many are automatically eliminated because of a:

- Requirement for sector experience and specialization (e.g. pharmaceutical, financial, etc.).
- Requirement for a particular agency type (e.g. advertising, promotions, etc.).
- Requirement for particular facilities (e.g. European network, media buying, etc.).
- Client conflict (e.g. existing competitive client).

Where an existing agency already has the company and/or brand brief any consideration to change agency may be because of changed needs (e.g. technological media expertise required, full service agency preferred, etc.) although it is often the result of a breakdown in client/agency relationships. In this event joint-industry guidelines (ISBA 2006b) advise that the client should be clear that it would be in the best interests of the brand or business organization, and enhance shareholder value, to change agency and that efforts should have been made to re-establish a good working relationship. It is evidently not in the interests of industry bodies to encourage agency turnover.

Credentials presentation
Where an agency presents examples of previous work and the personnel who would work on particular assignments.

The initial search may involve consulting trade bodies (e.g. DMA, IPA, ISBA, MCCA and PRCA), industry literature, agency websites and other sources (e.g. recommendation) and could include a pre-pitch **credentials presentation** from candidate agencies, where they present to the client examples of past work. Some companies issue a questionnaire to agencies they are considering to assist shortlisting and to try to ensure that the criteria they establish are met by potential contenders (Yeshin 2006). Even more influential than

For an example of a full service agency look at: **www.principlesagency.co.uk.**

information from the trade bodies or consultancies, word-of-mouth plays a big part in determining who appears on the **pitch-list** (Simms 2004).

The next step is the selection of the candidate shortlist and the issue of a brief which should include a clear indication of the brand and company marketing/communications budget (ISBA 2006b). The creation of a brief is seen as an important part in the selection process that potentially leads to better, more effective and measurable work, a saving in time and money and making remuneration fairer (ISBA 2006a). Industry guidelines strongly suggest that in writing an agency brief companies should think not only 'Where am I now?' but 'Where I need to get to?' (ISBA 2006a). Given the costs involved in preparing a **pitch** some clients will pay agencies a fee for the expense, time and effort involved in making the presentation.

Agencies' responses to a brief will have many implementational consequences, so it is important to bear these in mind when preparing the brief. These fall into three main areas (ISBA 2006a):

- Budgets: clearly stated and, where necessary, broken down into constituent parts in the brief or alternatively a suggested recommended budget to achieve a given set of objectives.
- Timings: what are the key delivery dates?
- Other considerations: are there existing creative ideas to work with? Are there any legal constraints? Are there any brand or corporate guidelines which may affect an agency's work? Are other agencies involved in complementary promotions (for example as part of an integrated marketing communications plan).

Industry norms suggest that up to three agencies should be involved in the final pitch or four if the existing agency is involved (ISBA 2006b). Organizations are encouraged to establish some form of objective assessments against which to measure a pitch presentation (Yeshin 2006). The client organization should make clear in the brief the criteria on which the presentation will be judged, the length of time allowed for the presentation, the facilities available and the location (ISBA 2006b).

Following the decision to appoint a particular agency, joint industry guidelines gives pointers to implementing an agreement and managing the relationship (ISBA 2006b):

- Give losing agencies the courtesy of a full 'lost order' meeting.
- Losing agencies should return all confidential material and information provided for the pitch and the client should return details of the losing agencies' presentations.
- Honour the incumbent agency's contract in relation to agreed notice period and payment of outstanding invoices.
- Ensure incumbent agency fully cooperates in a handover to the new agency.
- Ensure that a new contract is signed with the successful agency covering all aspects of the agreement up to and including termination.

Pitch-list
List of agencies asked to 'pitch' for all or part of an organization's communications business.

Pitch
Agency presentation.

- Arrange for mutual induction meetings between client and agency personnel.
- Agree realistic objectives for brand and corporate communications, put measures of effectiveness in place and report key metrics at CEO/main board level.
- Ensure active management reviews and invest in the relationship through regular brainstorming sessions and 'awaydays'.

The client/agency relationship will always be complex, sometimes fraught and occasionally highly rewarding. Managing the relationship on both sides of the partnership is key to minimizing the pain and maximizing the gain from the experience.

Summary

This chapter looked at the modern communications industry from the perspective of its historical development and the changing needs of the twenty-first century. The industry today, it was suggested, is a complex legacy of developments that took place throughout the previous three centuries. Principal amongst these was the industry remuneration system that ultimately became standardized by agreement between the agencies and media owners and dominated the industry through to the 1970s. The demise of the commission system heralded change from full service agencies to a more diverse system of independent and dependent agencies working within networks. Typical agency services were discussed including account management, account planning, creative design, media management and the production function and contemporary remuneration methodologies were highlighted. The chapter concluded by reviewing the way clients employ agencies with particular emphasis on the importance of the brief.

Review questions

1 What functions would you expect an agency to perform?
2 What is the role of media management?
3 Explain the function of account management.
4 What has been the principal driver to changes in the traditional agency structure and why is this so?
5 How would you describe the function of a retainer fee?
6 How might companies shortlist an agency?
7 List the main agency reimbursement options.
8 Define 'PBR'.
9 What makes up the tripartite nature of the communications industry?
10 Explain what is meant by a full service agency.

Discussion questions

1 If you needed to recruit a new advertising agency, how would you go about it and why? On what basis would you make your decision on who to use?

2 Where do you believe problems might occur between an agency and a company in the development of an advertising campaign?

3 You have a new product to launch. It needs to be kept secret from the competition but you are using an outside agency to do the above the line work. How much do you tell them and why? What might the consequences be of your decision?

Further reading

Daniels, C. (2006) 'Drawing the line', *Marketing Magazine*, 111(25): 11–13. The article offers views of leading business professionals on the importance of ethical issues in everyday business decisions.

Thompson, B. (2006) 'Do the right thing? Not with a rival's inside info', *Advertising Age*, 77(29): 4. This article deals with the online poll conducted by *Advertising Age* magazine on the moral aspects of confidential communication.

Weiner, R. (2006) 'Mind your p's and q's', *Public Relations Tactics*, Jul., 13(7): 7. The article defines several acronyms and media jargons of interest to public relations professionals.

Chapter references

Brierley, S. (2002) *The Advertising Handbook*, 2nd edn, London: Routledge.

ISBA (2006a) 'The Client Brief', Joint Industry Guidelines.

ISBA (2006b) 'The Guide', Joint Industry Guidelines.

Nevett, T.R. (1982) *Advertising in Britain: A History*, London: Heinemann.

Simms, J. (2004) 'You're not paranoid, they do hate you', *Marketing*, 19 May: 32–4.

Yeshin, T. (2006) *Advertising*, London: Thomson Learning.

Should payments be tied to results?

Outstanding work that boosts a client's sales, market share or profits deserves to be rewarded, and it is widely accepted that time-based fees are not a true reflection of creative agencies' contribution. But payment-by-results (PBR), the mechanism that is gradually replacing percentage commission or time-based fees, is not delivering the hoped-for results to either side.

The proportion of companies using some form of payment-by-results in their creative agency agreements will have risen to nearly half next year, up from 40 per cent in 2003, according to the Incorporated Society of British Advertisers (ISBA). While the majority of clients operating such schemes say payment-by-results has increased the level of fees they pay agencies, however, only 56 per cent believe that the agencies' performance has improved accordingly, with some claiming it has actually deteriorated.

ISBA guidelines recommend that clients use three main criteria to assess their agencies' performance: a measure of the relationship, such as service; a measure of advertising success; and an overall business measure, such as market share, profit or sales. In practice, many clients use just one or two of these measures, they do not quantify the elements of 'success' with the agency at the outset and they fail to specify either the scope of the work or the potential rewards the agencies could earn.

Not surprisingly, horror stories abound. It is not uncommon for an agency not to be paid its bonus, even if it has earned it, because the client has failed to budget for it. The base fee is often negotiated down with a 'bonus' top-up giving the agency what it would have earned pre-payment-by-result. Sometimes the bonus is paid, but the client renegotiates fees down the following year. The benchmark for achieving the maximum bonus is frequently too high: only half the agencies in ISBA's 2003 survey received even half of the maximum entitlement. 'There is no point having a relatively modest reward – 10 per cent or 15 per cent, for example – depending on something that needs miracles to achieve it. Agencies need a stronger incentive than that', points out David Wethey, Managing Director of Agency Assessments.

Many believe the very concept of applying payment-by-results to creativity is fundamentally flawed. One reason is that agencies are passionate about what they do and are unlikely to be incentivized by a greater share of the

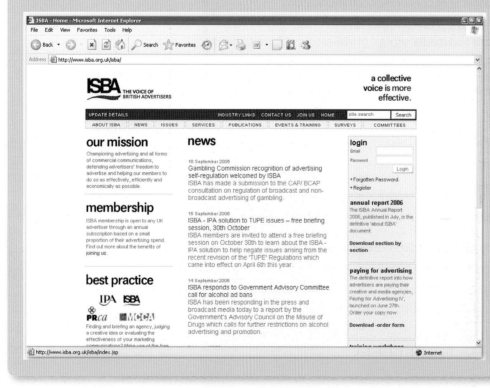

The website (www.isba.org. uk) provides industry news and a host of downloadable publications for members.

spoils. Also, the risk/reward equation is out of balance. 'The principle of PBR is that an agency gets a share in the upside of the client's business, but they are commercially unable to take a share in the downside, so the client has to bear all the risk', points out Andrew Marsden, Category Director of Britvic soft drinks. What's more, sales and profit figures can rise or fall, irrespective of the agency's contribution. In either case, the client might have to pay out if the agency has performed badly, or the agency might be out of pocket even if it has performed well. 'The only way both sides can be happy is if all the metrics are going up – which is unlikely', says one Marketing Director.

In reality, agencies bear the ultimate downside risk – that of being fired, a practice that happens all too frequently, and militates against the kind of long-term client–agency relationships that are traditionally regarded as most conducive to sustained performance on both sides. In a market where supply far outstrips demand, there are always agencies prepared to do work cheaper, and marketing directors, under pressure for greater accountability, are increasingly likely to switch agencies than work to make the relationships they have more productive.

Clare Salmon, marketing director of ITV, believes the fault lies with agencies rather than clients. 'Sometimes agencies become obsessed with the new business process at the expense of their existing client relationships', she claims. Others, including Simon Thompson, Marketing Director of Honda UK, believe the onus lies with clients to nurture agency relationships. 'Firing an agency is easy and tends to be done defensively', he says.

> Notwithstanding the adage that an agency is hired on creative and fired on service, clients should help agencies and move them forward. No one recruits a bad agency, and if the client lets it get away with bad service, that is their fault.

Thompson believes 'clients get the agencies they deserve' and that ensuring there is a shared vision, culture and ambition between the two sides from the outset is critical to constructive relationships. 'Where clients are interested purely in price, or pay on a project basis, they shouldn't be disappointed if the work isn't up to scratch', he says.

Agencies get the clients they deserve too. Libby Child, an independent marketing consultant, says that while many clients admit they do not fairly reward outstanding work,

> they also resent being asked to pay for agency inefficiencies. Agencies need to be more disciplined in the way they manage and report their time, as lawyers and accountants – and, indeed, other marketing agencies – have done for years. Their marketing director clients have to be accountable – so why do they seem to think they are exempt?

The view that agencies need to become more commercial is widely held.

> Advertising has to be the only industry that would celebrate over-manning, as the IPA did recently with its announcement that more people are working in advertising now than ever before. In a highly technological era that is not the mark of a successful industry

says Wethey. Tina Fegent joined ad agency Grey 18 months ago as Commercial Director, charged with managing its cost base and negotiating terms with clients. She was formerly procurement director at Orange. While agencies have 'taken the mickey' in the past, she has also been 'shocked' at the arrogance and rudeness of many of the clients she has come across in her new role. She believes she has brought a new sense of commercial reality to Grey. 'We've cut back on things like the posh biscuits and flower arrangements and the taxis waiting outside. Clients can't afford all this stuff in their own businesses, so why should they end up paying for it at their agencies?', she asks. *Honda's* Thompson adds:

> I would hate my agencies to act like businesses. They are hothouses of creative talent, ideas workshops, and they need the freedom to be able to produce great work. If they produce great ads, I don't mind how many posh biscuits, idling taxis or tables at smart restaurants [they put on expenses]. It is the output that counts.

Thompson's views are unorthodox in today's hard-bitten environment, as is his claim that the results of creativity are easy to measure, over the short as well as the long term. 'It's very simple', he says. 'If customers buy more or pay more, you have success, and you can see that within three months.' Recognizing that both the client and the agency have to be profitable, Honda's payment-by-results scheme uses the same measurement and reward mechanisms for all its agencies, including direct marketing, planning and media, as well as creative. The scores are built around brand equity measures, including price and quality, and the advantage of scoring all the agencies against the same metrics is that it encourages them to work together. The pot of money available and the way in which it is allocated is known to every agency. Two-and-a-half years into the scheme, the results are coming through, says Thompson. 'We pay our agencies more than we did in the past, but we get better output. Despite a falling market, we are more efficient as a business than we were two years ago and we have raised our annual sales from 67 000 cars to 92 000.'

Other marketing directors believe that attempts to simplify payment-by-results are ill-conceived. At Shell, payment-by-results plays a role in all agency relationships apart from creative agencies. 'Since we put our relationship with JWT on a better business footing three years ago we have improved our joint performance', says Raoul Pinnell, Vice-President of global brands and communications.

We identify the scope of work and agree a profit margin. We evaluate it every year against 50 criteria and it does a 360-degree evaluation of us. But full PBR has proved too complicated, and I don't think the industry is mature enough for it yet.

One of the problems, says Pinnell, is that payment-by-results can create a diversion from the critical issue of how to take out structural cost from the agency. Working with Shell, JWT has introduced a digital asset management system that can send work around the world on the company's intranet at very low cost, and has implemented a centre of excellence approach whereby work is carried out in the most cost-effective location globally.

'Agencies need to get more professional, and clients should help them achieve that, but if agencies want PBR they have to accept some of the risk', says Pinnell. 'At the moment, if an ad bombs, it is the client that pays for it.'

There are numerous indications of growing interest in finding better ways to incentivize both sides of the buying equation. For example, the IPA is seeking to implement three-year contracts, and the ISBA, which is due to publish its updated remuneration guide by Easter (2005), will discuss ways of quantifying the value agencies bring at its conference on 8 March (2005). Perhaps the principal issue payment-by-results is supposed to address – rewarding agencies for the value they generate – could be solved by re-establishing the deep relationships with clients that started to be sacrificed some 20 years ago during the transition from full service agencies to à la carte buying. Such a move, even if it meant outsourcing creative work and focusing more energy on strategy, would be rewarded with longer-term loyalty from clients, predicts marketing consultant Mike Sommers. 'What clients need is relevant creative work, and that is largely a product of excellent service levels', he says. Similarly, Nick Smith, Director of marketing and strategy at British Gas, believes agencies add more value at 'the thinking end' of the process, but 'have allowed themselves to be boxed into the delivery end – producing ads – and argue that they can't add value because we don't pay for it'.

If the ideal is longer-term relationships, agencies might do well to look at Tesco, whose success in a ferociously competitive market derives largely from its core purpose of creating value for its customers to earn their loyalty. There is no mention of legislation, no binding contracts, no manipulation of the rules – just a focus on knowing what its customers want and doing a good job of providing it.

Case study questions

1 What are the advantages and disadvantages to clients and agencies of payment-by-results?
2 What factors inhibit the development of payment-by-results?
3 Explain the comment that 'clients get the agencies they deserve'.

Source: Jane Sims, *Marketing*, 2 March 2005, pp. 34–6 (reproduced from *Marketing* magazine with the permission of the copyright owner, Haymarket Business Publications Limited).

CHAPTER TWENTY

GLOBAL MARKETING COMMUNICATIONS

LEARNING OBJECTIVES

Having completed this chapter you should be able to:

- Understand the features and communications patterns of international, multinational, global and transnational companies.
- Be aware of the strategic arguments regarding standardization and local adaptation.
- Comprehend the effect that international branding has had on the communications industry.

INTRODUCTION

There are many drivers to a company deciding to venture abroad. Although international trade has existed since the earliest times it was the Industrial Revolution that created the surpluses that could be exported to other sovereign countries and dependencies. Indeed many British brands became famous and financially successful because they were shipped to all parts of the empire and beyond. Guinness is still promoted in Africa for its strength, a feature born out of its ability to be shipped long distances and still remain drinkable. It was not only one-way traffic. Quaker Oats arrived in Britain from the USA in 1894 and Wrigley's and Palmolive just after the First World War. Since the Second World War there has been an increasing propensity towards the internationalization of brands particularly, but not exclusively, of North American origin.

A common reason for developing overseas markets in the second half of the twentieth century was connected to the saturation of domestic markets and the need to venture abroad or stagnate. A good example of this is McDonald's who (through subsidiaries and franchises) first moved into Western Europe and then, as that market matured too, to Asia and Eastern Europe.

In marketing communications terms international markets provide a significant challenge to the company, ranging from the level of involvement to the development of meaningful brand messages. The skill of international communications management is defining what is optimal for the brand.

@

For an online guide to globalization look at:
www.globalisationguide.org.

INTERNATIONAL AND GLOBAL COMPANIES

There are many ways of describing an organization's level of international involvement, from nil (the wholly domestic) to those organizations that are so globally orientated that their centres of control are no longer necessarily in their country of origin (e.g. IBM). Whatever typology is used there are subtle differences in the way marketing communications operate as determined by their level of international involvement, their degree of centralized control and their choices whether to standardize brand messages or adapt them to individual markets. There are fundamentally four levels of international involvement (Keegan 1989; Bartlett and Ghoshal 1991). These are shown in Box 20.1 and they will determine key messages, management focus (standardization or adaptation), control structures and agency involvement. As the chapter progresses it may become apparent that such a straightforward typology as this may be too simplistic, particularly as we enter the third (and some would suggest global) millennium. It is however a good starting point in recognizing how an organization's involvement with overseas markets leads to changes in its communication strategy.

International company
One whose home market dominates their sales but for whom the export market holds the promise of extra turnover.

An **international company** is one whose home market dominates their sales but for whom the export market holds the promise of extra turnover. It is unlikely that such a company has their own distribution system in overseas markets and may instead ship direct to trade customers, employ an agent, distributor or authorize a licencee to manufacture a product or supply a service on their behalf. As such it is frequently a business-to-business (rather than direct to consumer) transaction where the key messages are based on the product/service features, although the company may sponsor consumer

Box 20.1 International typology

	Home	International	Multinational	Global	Transnational
Communication Stage	Domestic	Export	Multinational	Global	Transnational
Key Message	Product Features	Product/Brand	Corporate and Brand	Corporate and Brand	Corporate and/or Brand
Standardization/ Adaptation	Standardization	Standardization	Standardize/ Adaptation	Regional Adaptation	Global Adaptation
Communications Structure	Centralized	Centralized	Decentralized	Grouped Centralization	Network
Agency Relationship	Domestic	Domestic	Domestic and Foreign Local	Global	Transnational

directed, branded advertising or rely on the agent/distributor to do so on their behalf. Communication messages are likely to be the same as the domestic market although packaging may be adapted to the requirements of the overseas market. Communication to and with potential customers (or agent/ distributors) often takes place at international exhibitions or during overseas sales trips. The international company is unlikely to employ an overseas advertising or other communications agency although their collaborators may use such services. Domestic agencies may, however, support an overseas campaign with resources such as point of sale material.

Multinational companies, as the terms suggests, operate in a number of overseas markets. Although they too may act through agents or distributors they would normally secure more control over them. It may be the case that foreign-based partners are involved and/or that the company has a wholly or partly owned subsidiary. From a communications perspective multinational companies more readily perceive the differences between the markets it serves and often rely on its agent/partner/subsidiary to handle all marketing communications in that area (Yeshin 2006). Although there may be common themes the company is not usually seeking a common transnational message, rather they are looking to the requirements of individual markets.

Global organizations are seen to strive towards commonality of products or services and communication themes normally with some regional adaptations to respond to local pressures (Yeshin 2006). Indeed Michael Perry's[1] (former Chairman of Unilever) definition of a global brand is a 'local brand reproduced many times'. Unilever frequently works with this global-local (glocal) template with toiletry products such as Lynx (UK), Ego (South Africa) and Axe (rest of the world) and frozen food lines Birds Eye (UK), Iglo (Italy) and Findus (rest of Europe) carrying similar packaging, advertising and with comparable line-extensions in each market. Another company with glocal strategies is McDonald's, who offer different menus in different markets[2] accompanied by locally determined messages whilst still retaining a central product offering supported by globally recognized brand themes. Alternatively some global organizations have pulled back from having too many local adaptations. Before 1998 Johnnie Walker, the world's biggest-selling scotch whisky had several different advertising campaigns around the world but since then it effectively uses the same theme around the globe. Today the 'keep walking' campaign uses celebrities to get across the global message and appears in 200 countries worldwide. The Smirnoff 'through the bottle campaign' developed by the agency Lowe Howard Spink ran almost unchanged in 43 countries and BBH's advert for Levi's was also virtually unchanged across the world. Another example is Royal Dutch/ Shell who have used a global theme since 1999. Since then they have worked to achieve consistency across its 45 000 outlets worldwide. They have also slashed their advertising agency roster from 35 to two and use only one global partner (JWT), yet its global messages have been seen in over 140 markets worldwide.

Multinational companies
Operate in a number of overseas markets often through agents or distributors but would normally secure more (relative to international companies) control over them.

Global organizations
Strive towards commonality of products or services and communication themes, normally with some regional adaptations to respond to local pressures.

Glocal
Thinking global but acting local.

---

[1]Quoted in Lewis 2006.
[2]For example 'Croque McDo' (a variation of 'croque monsieur') and Carte Noir coffee in France and fruit salad in the UK.

Transnational organization
An organization whose network structure is such that it is difficult to place their corporate centre (although not their original home). These types of organization utilize the worldwide facilities for production and regards its markets as outlets in a global marketplace.

Transnational organizations make up the fourth category, where the network structure is such that it is difficult to place their corporate centre (although not their original home). These types of organization utilize the worldwide facilities for production and regards its markets as outlets in a global marketplace. Transnational companies may include motor manufacturers such as Ford or General Motors, financial organizations such as American Express and HSBC and fast moving consumer goods companies such as Procter & Gamble, Unilever and Nestlé. The subtle difference between global and transnational is not easy to distinguish and may, from a marketing communication perspective, be a distinction too far given the variety of differing strategies that appear to operate under the global and transnational heading.

STANDARDIZATION vs ADAPTATION

Whether to globally or regionally standardize or locally adapt is a dilemma that consistently arises with marketing in general and marketing communications in particular. Some international and global brands differentiate their product, others the message that is associated with the brand and sometimes both. This is often determined by the product or service characteristics involved. Figure 20.1 based on Hankinson and Cowking (1996) illustrates how the fully global, product adaptive, proposition adaptive and fully adaptive strategies develop as determined by the needs of specific markets.

While global brands are known to drive efficiencies and economies of scale, the practical role of global brand management consists of 'juggling global

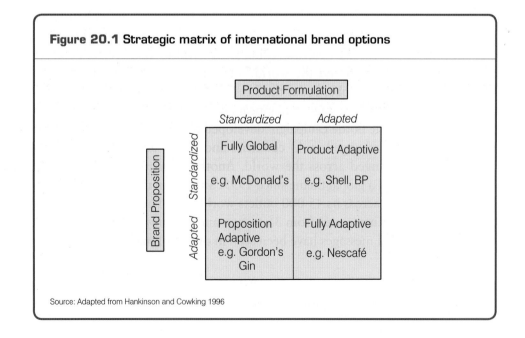

Figure 20.1 Strategic matrix of international brand options

Source: Adapted from Hankinson and Cowking 1996

Lexus

Undoubtedly Lexus is a global brand associated with quality and a consistent message worldwide. Rather than leave the establishment of communications' themes to local markets decisions are made by representatives from key regions who meet in a forum known as the 'global communications council'. According to Paul van de Burgh, General Manager Marketing, Lexus Europe, they work on the basis of 'global consensus'. If there is any opposition from any part of the group then the suggested theme is immediately dropped and they search for another that will gain global support. The local markets do have a contribution to make as each market can add 'local flavour' to the global message and translate advertising headlines. They also choose media schedules relevant to their marketplace. Currently the Lexus global message is going out to 24 markets in 22 different languages.

Lexus' 'global communications council' pursues a universal communications strategy with messages that do not alienate any segment of their market.

Source: Lewis (2006).

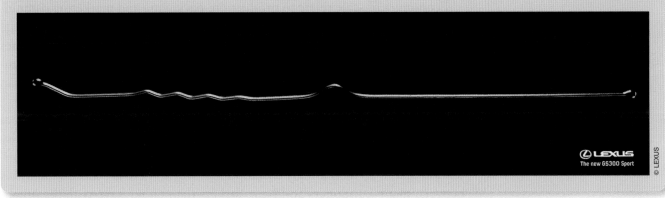

LEXUS
The new GS300 Sport

© LEXUS

priorities with local nuances' and is as such 'fraught with complexity' (Lewis 2006: 7). In a seminal article over 20 years ago Levitt (1983) argued that the world was moving inexorably toward homogenization, globalization and a 'converging commonality'. From a North American viewpoint it may well have appeared that the advent of Galbraithian[3] corporate dominance and the drive for economies of scale made the move toward homogeneity inevitable. Despite the advantages of standardization (discussed below), however, it has become evident that local markets can react poorly (or less than optimally) to both the composition and themes associated with global standardization. Indeed the very term 'globalization' has come to be regarded pejoratively. To wholly adapt to the needs of each market, however, makes little use of potential economies of scale.

As is evident in most debates of this type the answer lies somewhere in-between and is rarely the same for any two organizations. The outcome is normally a mixture of strategies that look to make optimum savings from standardization with the necessary local requirements in terms of

@

For more information on John Kenneth Galbraith look at: **www. johnkennethgalbraith.com.**

---

[3]J.K. Galbraith (1908–2006), Economist.

product/service and messages – what Kenichi Ohmae (1990) summed up as 'think global – act local'. The fundamental essence being that you do not ignore or override differences in culture in order to create mass standardization, instead you work towards building an understanding of what those differences are and where those differences lie and then find ways of accommodating them within your activities so that they can become an integral element of global brand building.

Standardization

The arguments for standardization are rational and largely, but not exclusively, financial. They include:

- Economies of scale.
- Increased homogeneity of markets.

Economies of scale relate to production, packaging and marketing communications. In the latter category the cost of producing a television commercial can be around $500 000 and the development of individual creative themes can run into millions of pounds, euro, dollars or yen. The ability to use campaign themes, commercials or even point-of-sale materials across borders can mean considerably lower costs.

There is also the argument that the world is becoming more of a global village through technological developments and greater consumer mobility and that travelling customers expect more homogeneity. There is also a contention that in an increasingly cosmopolitan world there are more similarities between many Londoners and New Yorkers than either have with the inhabitants of Burnley or Buffalo (although even this cosmopolitan/provincial distinction may also be rapidly disappearing). Certainly luxury goods (Rolex, Gucci, Burberry, Cartier, etc.) and even more commonplace brands (Johnnie Walker, Benson & Hedges, Toblerone, Walker's, etc.) appear to be readily available at virtually every international airport which would suggest that such international segments exist.

One global standardization strategy increasingly used by multinational or global organizations is to unify brand names across markets. Despite considerable investment over time in the original brand name the decision is taken that for it to be recognizable in the international market it requires brand name harmonization. Significant UK brands that have been affected in this way include Marathon (to Snickers), Opal Fruits (to Starburst), Jif (to Cif), Haze (to Airwick), Olivio (to Bertolli) and One-2-One (to T-mobile). Some brands have changed name several times as they sought greater international recognition (e.g. Freeserve to Wanadoo to Orange).

Opportunities do exist for what at first sight would appear as undifferentiated global brand messages in the form of international events. These global (or near global) attractions include the Olympics, the FIFA World Cup and the Formula 1 racing championships. Brands that can afford to appear on the world stage are, however, few and far between. For the 2006 World Cup main sponsors included Philips, McDonald's, Gillette, Emirates, Coca-Cola, Budweiser, MasterCard, Hyundai, Deutsche Telekom, Yahoo and Adidas. In addition to the worldwide publicity, these sponsors look to tie in this coverage with local advertising and promotions. For example, in one part of the UK Coca-Cola used poster advertising to associate the word 'love' (used in a previous poster campaign) but this time in association with the England team and the nationalistic fervour that surrounded the competition. The campaign did not stretch to other constituent parts of the UK not represented in the competition. Local national teams were also heavily sponsored by organizations who wanted to make a statement both internationally and locally. As such sponsors of the top-ten (in terms of income) teams for the same competition meanwhile were a mixture of the main sponsors, rival global sponsors and domestic brands (see Box 12.2).

Adaptation

Despite the potential cost savings there are several barriers to standardization. These include:

- Language
- Culture
- Management issues
- Socioeconomic conditions
- Technological development levels
- Brand status
- Government regulation

Language differences obviously produce difficulties in both packaging and in communicating brand messages. Even variations of the same language can throw up distinct anomalies (e.g. UK, Australian and American English; French and Canadian French) and some markets have two (e.g. Canada, Belgium) or more (e.g. Switzerland, India, South Africa) languages to contend with. Many consumer goods companies cope with the multiplicity of languages by incorporating usage instructions in many regional languages in thick booklets (e.g. Sony, Kodak, etc.) and packaging with as few words as is practical. Fast moving consumer goods, particularly foodstuffs, which are obliged to carry ingredient and other information, are often so full of miniscule, almost unreadable print, that it makes a mockery of any packaging design. In advertising copy and other written communications (e.g. press releases) the most frequent mistakes are in understanding the meaning. Although the translation may be strictly correct the interpretation may not. Most people have come across written communications (for example assembly instructions) that make no sense at all and there have been some notable examples of poor translation from prominent companies in the past (see Box 20.2). Another problem in translating copy, for example for newspaper or magazine advertising, is that some languages require more space to convey the same meaning.

@

For more examples of translation errors look at: **www.mistranslatedsigns.com.**

> ### Box 20.2 Translation examples
>
> Examples of reported mistakes in translation or interpretation.
>
> Parker pens translated 'won't leak in your pocket and embarrass you' as 'won't leak in your pocket and make you pregnant'
>
> Coors' (Beer) slogan was 'Turn it loose' in Spanish read as 'Suffer from diarrhoea'
>
> General Motors introduced the Nova model but it did not go well in Spain. 'No Va' means 'it doesn't go'
>
> Scandinavian firm Electrolux had the following slogan in a US campaign: 'Nothing sucks like an Electrolux'
>
> Perdue 'It takes a strong man to make a tender Chicken' translated in Spanish as 'It takes an aroused man to make a chicken affectionate'
>
> Source: Smith and Taylor 2002.

German requires 25 per cent more space than English and some Arab languages require considerably more.

Some companies have made a virtue of using a one-language tag line in all (or nearly all) markets, for example 'the future's bright, the future's Orange' (Orange) is used by the company in almost all its world markets. It is, however, generally acknowledged that advertising and other communications work better in the recipient's home tongue. Even the increasing international use of English is not always acceptable and sometimes wholeheartedly opposed. It is noticeable that one of the few exceptions to the use of Orange's English tag line is in France.

In many ways all marketing communications are culturally specific. Culture has been defined as 'the values, beliefs, ideas, customs, actions and symbols that are learnt by members of particular societies' (Fill 2002: 414) or perhaps more simply as 'the way things are done at a given place at a given time... a shared understanding we have of the world that surrounds us' (Bewick 2006: 22). Both definitions add something to the marketing communications debate. The first emphasizes that it is a learning experience (nurture not nature) and specific to certain societal groups. The second emphasizes that cultural understanding relates not only to place but to time. A simple commercial example of the latter is in our taste in coffee. Traditionally Latin American and Southern European countries prefer coffee stronger than in the rest of the world. The advent of coffee house chains (*Starbucks, Costa Coffee, Café Nero*, etc.) have started to change the drinking habits of many towards stronger blends and different preparations (e.g. latte, cappuccino, etc.). There is also the constantly changing meaning of language in various societies and particularly amongst the young. English words such as 'fit', 'buff' and 'wicked' have decidedly different meaning in youth culture than in mainstream society and also have the capability of crossing borders.

Cultural differences may be affected by religious belief, moral codes, customs, history, education, work patterns and exposure to outside influences.

This ensures that our interpretation of the colours, symbols and language around us are different in every culture. A particularly difficult area is humour which can be highly culture specific, especially in writing or in speech. It is interesting to note, therefore, that the examples of humour that travel are usually in the form of visual gags rather than metaphors or a play on words.

Consumers respond best to messages that are consistent with their own particular culture. Colours, habits, customs that are taken for granted in one culture can cause misunderstanding and even offence in another. It should, for example, have been easy for such global brands as Unilever and Nestlé to sell ice-cream in Saudi Arabia. However, both companies withdrew from the market in 2001 because they failed to realize that Saudi Arabians view ice-cream as a dessert eaten at home and that female shoppers failed to buy it at supermarkets because they had no driving licences and hence no way to get it home (Lewis 2006).

Country of origin can influence how a particular culture accepts products and services and once again stereotypical behaviour comes to the fore. The French have a decided bias for domestic products whereas in the USA imported goods from beer to clothing and beyond are generally regarded as quality purchases. In the UK and other markets German technology is admired as is Swiss watch-making and Japanese cars. Scotch whisky, Cuban cigars, French Champagne, Italian food and Scandinavian furniture are accepted as brands in their own right around the world. Sometimes the country of origin can be problematical. Undoubtedly many cultures around the world have been influenced by American cinema but many societies openly reject many of the nuances that these films and the culture that it represents contain. Mecca Cola was launched for those who, for political reasons, did not want to associate themselves with American brands Coca-Cola and Pepsi (incidentally hurting sales of Virgin cola which had until then been the preferred alternative). McDonald's is a quintessential global brand that regularly has to put up with attack but not necessarily for the same reason in all markets. In France they are under pressure (and occasionally physical attack) from the farming lobby, in the UK it is from nutritionists and in Israel criticism comes from the religious right. More recently the printing of cartoons offensive to many Muslims has led to a backlash against products from Denmark across the Middle East and beyond.

The level of education and what might be grandly termed 'consumer knowledge' also differs significantly from market to market. There is a view that in 'unsophisticated markets' the emphasis is upon the communication of information whereas in more mature markets the concentration is upon transformational communication. From a communications perspective these are considerably different messages. In Western markets, for example, there is a high level of sophistication both in the use of advertising by organizations and, more specifically, in their interpretation by consumers. Advertising literacy is high, consumers have access to vast amounts of data on the world in which they live and can compare and evaluate wide ranges of brands, products and services with relative ease. The impact of this, however, is an equally high level of cynicism towards the motivations, techniques and activities of

Box 20.3 Low/high consumerization messages

Low Consumerization		High Consumerization
Product Attribute	⇔	Product Benefits
Focus on Product	⇔	Focus on Usage
Rational	⇔	Emotional
Realistic	⇔	Symbolic
Fact	⇔	Metaphor
Maker's Language	⇔	Brand Language
Sales Person	⇔	Consumer
Pack Shot	⇔	Consumption
Left Brain	⇔	Right Brain
Selling	⇔	Buying

Source: Goodyear 1996.

Low consumerism

In global marketing terms, undeveloped or unsophisticated markets.

High consumerism

In global marketing terms, developed or highly sophisticated markets.

Brand's status

The position (e.g. market leader) of the brand in a particular market.

suppliers. In such markets symbols (e.g. Nike ✓, Adidas stripes, etc.) replace words, celebrity associations replace product/service features and entertainment replaces the hard sell. In a similar vein Goodyear (1996) distinguishes between low consumerism (unsophisticated markets) and high consumerism (sophisticated markets) to distinguish between these distinctly different markets and the messages they receive as indicated in Box 20.3.

In low consumerization markets the concentration is on rational, fact-based attributes in sales language and featuring the product. In high consumerization markets the concentration is on emotionally charged benefits delivered in symbolic language and consumer directed metaphors.

A further downside of centralized international communications is in the local management of campaigns. Although standardized communications may offer economies of scale these might prove a false saving as locally placed marketers can often take advantage of opportunities in media placement, react rapidly to competitive activity and understand local nuances and the brand's response to them. Although local control may result in creative and production duplication it may reflect the best opportunities for the brand particularly if the market is significantly different from home and if the brand holds a significantly different status in the overseas market than in the domestic market (see brand status).

The level of education is often, but not always, comparable with the level of socioeconomic well-being in a particular culture (an exception, for example, is Cuba). Put in terms of Maslow's (1954) hierarchy of needs, some economies are fighting for basic survival needs (food, water, etc.) whereas other markets have high numbers for whom self-actualization is the driving force (and every other every level of need in between). This creates segmentation difficulties of huge proportions. Neither is it necessarily intuitive. India, for example, may have many for whom survival is the main priority but there are also more (US dollar) millionaires in that country than any other. Although international and global brands are available in most markets they may be well out of the price range of many. In some markets a McDonald's hamburger[4] may represent a week's wages. This raises the question of whether mass advertising in such markets is socially and morally responsible.

Social nuances also affect the response to commercial messages. The cultural value associated with old age differs significantly from those societies where it is invested with knowledge and good sense to those where the 'grey market' is merely a target segment for investment products, health insurance and stair-lifts. The decision-maker roles may also vary between men and women or a mixture of both depending on the position of women in the society and the importance and extent of family units. The level of class consciousness in particular societies may also affect how brand messages are composed. In such markets aspiration may be a great motivator. Even regional segmentation can prove difficult. Hofstede (1980, 1991) based on a survey of IBM employees around the world, examined cultural differences based on such factors as individualism, authoritarianism (power distance) and risk (uncertainty avoidance). Based upon this he developed a series of national groupings but even they proved an uncertain fit. In terms of culture each market (or subset of a market) has its own profile which frequently defies marketing communication standardization.

The level of technological development in a market can have a great deal to do with the ability to communicate to different audiences. Access to media outlets is paramount and the availability of newspapers, magazines, television and radio has always limited commercial communications. The availability of global media stations (e.g. CNN, MTV, etc.) while perhaps being a vehicle for global brands also need to adapt its messages to the local audience. Certain media may be unavailable especially those driven by new technology (e.g. Internet availability and the wide availability of broadband) or certain media may not be as important in a particular market than in others. The level of technological sophistication may also determine the available media, the level of agency expertise and media specialisms available in the marketplace.

Other problems accompany brands when they enter a market. For example although the product or service may be a major brand or even the market leader in its domestic market this may not be the case overseas. In the new market the brand's status may be different relative to the competition and the desired positioning (e.g. market leader) may be occupied by someone else (Yeshin 2006). Whereas in its own market the brand may have established an unassailable position with the communication strategies which reflect this, in the new market they may have to fight for recognition, prove their credentials and/or encourage sampling, before getting off the ground. Brands such as Hershey and Cadbury may be market leaders in the USA and UK respectively but they are minnows in each other's markets. The strategy may be to work off of the back of existing brands rather than invest the amounts required to attain market leadership even if it were possible.

---

[4]The so-called 'hamburger index' (based on the price of a McDonald's hamburger) is a frequently used measure of economic prosperity.

A final barrier to standardization relates to government regulation. Despite attempts to create international communication legislation (see Chapter 18) it is still rare even within the European Union (Pond 2006). In the area of sales promotion for example Sweden and Norway ban random win promotions whereas elsewhere in Europe it is legal. France, Portugal and Greece insist that a promotion be registered and in Turkey a sum of money has to be deposited as security. An EU sales promotion regulation aimed at harmonizing European legislation was shelved in 2006 because of continuing disagreement. Other examples of differing legislation include tobacco advertising and sponsorship, which is banned across Europe (but not North America) and comparative advertising (common in the USA) which is restricted in Germany. At the other end of the scale some governments do not give enough protection to the integrity of brands in their markets. China has been the home of a great deal of intellectual property abuse in the past although the government is trying to tighten this up in expectation of negotiating with high-profile brands for the 2008 Olympics (Lynd 2006). In 2006 the Chinese government announced its intention to 'strengthen the system for protecting intellectual property rights and intensify law enforcement in this area' (*ibid.*: 16). Already Ferrero, Starbucks and LVMH (Louis Vuitton and other top brands) have successfully pursued counterfeiters through the Chinese courts (*ibid.*).

GLOBAL AGENCIES

As noted in Chapter 19 agencies have played and are playing their part in the international and global communications industry and this is not a recent phenomenon. Quaker Oats' launch in Britain in 1894 was through the London-based Derrick agency, although many other US advertisers, such as American Tobacco, started a trend at the turn of that century of bringing their own agencies with them. These agencies brought new ideas and techniques to the UK market and a new level of account supervision. Lord & Thomas, for example, who brought Wrigley and Palmolive to the UK, reviewed every poster position in London and developed a breakdown of class-structure, whether the site was in a shopping, residential or industrial area and whether the sites were on major transport routes (Brierley 2002). By 1960 there were 36 US agencies in London with 281 offices nationwide (Nevett 1982) and by 1972 US agencies held 86 per cent of declared billings of the top-20 agencies (Brierley 2002). More recent mergers and takeovers have seen the further concentration of agencies, such that the top-10 agencies are estimated to control more than 80 per cent of global markets and the same companies (or subsidiary companies) operating in Europe, America, Africa and Asia where the favoured strategy is a 'glocalisation' hybrid (Yeshin 2006).

Overseas agency development is normally based on one of a number of growth strategies:

- Organic growth (through the creation of overseas subsidiaries).
- Acquisitive growth (through the purchase of an agency in the overseas market).
- Co-ownership (ownership together with a local organization particularly in growth markets such as Eastern Europe).
- Co-operative growth (through networks and strategic alliances).

The advantages of this development into overseas markets include the sharing of creative ideas (with the good ones being replicated), standardized research methods and transnational coverage.

In the age of 'integrated marketing communications' (IMC) agencies should be playing a major part in global integrated marketing communications (GIMC). Global integrated marketing communications has been described as 'a system of active promotional management which strategically co-ordinates global communication in all its component parts both horizontally in terms of countries and organisations and vertically in terms of promotional disciplines' (Grein and Gould 1996). In reality, however, the problems associated with domestic integated marketing communications (see Chapter 18) are often magnified in the international arena. Despite this, global co-ordination is strong with 9 per cent of multinational corporations using totally standardized advertising and 54 per cent a global umbrella strategy which local agencies tailor to individual market needs (Hite and Frazier 1998).[5] Big global brands such as ebay, HSBC, Samsung, Apple and UBS, who were amongst those who reported the largest increase in value in 2005, are amongst those with clear guidelines that are consistent throughout the world.

Summary

This chapter reviewed the problems associated with global marketing communications. It discussed a typology that included international, multinational, global and transnational companies and the key messages, management focus, control structure and agency involvement seen to be associated with such companies. The chapter discussed the principal area of contention in international marketing communications, namely standardization or adaptation not only of the product/service but the brand messages associated with it. The arguments for standardization are based upon potential economies of scale and supported by the proposal that markets are becoming more homogeneous. The arguments

[5]Quoted in Yeshin (2006).

for adaptation are, however, powerful and relate to language differences, cultural nuances, management issues, socioeconomic conditions, technological development, brand status and government regulation. Given the weight of evidence the phrase 'think global – act local' is particularly relevant. The chapter concluded by looking at the internationalization of communication agencies.

Review questions

1 Describe what you understand by the term 'international company'.

2 What are global brands known to drive?

3 What strategy is used by multinational or global organizations to unify brand names across markets?

4 Name three barriers to standardization.

5 What difficulties can language impose on standardization?

6 Despite humour being highly culturally specific and a barrier to standardization, there is one form of humour that can have international appeal. What is it?

7 In markets with high levels of consumerism how are brand benefits delivered to the consumer?

8 What may happen to the status of a brand when it enters an international market?

9 What is the term used to describe a target segment associated with old age?

10 Describe the principal differences between high and low consumerization?

Discussion questions

1 There is evidence to suggest that the country of origin can impact upon the appeal of goods in certain markets. To what extent do you believe this is true? Consider a selection of foreign products you are familiar with and consider to what extent their country of origin impacts upon their promotion and presentation.

2 Redraw the strategic matrix of international brand options, adding your own examples. To what extent have the companies you have categorized as 'standardized' actually done so and why do you think this is?

3 As a product manager, how would you decide on the degree of standardization or adaptation applied to your advertising activities? What data would you gather to help with this decision and why?

Further reading

Aslam, M.M. (2006) 'Are you selling the right colour? A cross-cultural review of colour as a marketing cue', *Journal of Marketing Communications*, Mar., 12 (1): 15–30. Cultural values, marketing objectives and desired customer relationship levels influence the choice of colour in corporate and marketing communications, this paper argues that a cross-cultural perspective of colour research and application is imperative for developing global marketing strategies.

Bulmer, S. and Buchanan-Oliver, M. (2006) 'Visual rhetoric and global advertising imagery', *Journal of Marketing Communications*, Mar., 12 (1): 49–61.

Bulmer, S. and Buchanan-Oliver, M. (2006) 'Advertising across cultures: interpretations of visually complex advertising', *Journal of Current Issues & Research in Advertising*, Spring, 28 (1): 57–71. Pictures are not universal; visual interpretations vary as viewers use culturally sited advertising knowledge and visual signs to interpret commercials. A suggestion that the visual rhetoric approach is useful for interpreting complex communications.

Iyer, G.R., Sharma, A. and Evanschitzky, H. (2006) 'Global marketing of industrial products: are interpersonal relationships always critical?', *Industrial Marketing Management*, Jul., 35 (5): 611–20. For an insight into the value of relationships in business-to-business markets, within a global perspective.

Okazaki, S. (2005) 'Searching the web for global brands: how American brands standardise their web sites in Europe', *European Journal of Marketing*, 39 (1/2): 87–109. Exploring US brands' website standardization in terms of the extent of standardization and the content applied across European markets.

Oosthuizen, T. (2004) 'In marketing across cultures: are you enlightening the world or are you speaking in tongues?', *Design Issues*, Spring, 20 (2): 61–72. Proposing a three-tier core value model to aid marketing and brand communication across different cultures.

Chapter references

Bartlett, C. and Ghoshal, S. (1991) *Managing Across Borders: The Transnational Solution*, Cambridge, MA: Harvard Business School.

Bewick, M. (2006) 'Border Crossing', *The Marketer*, 25, June, Cookham, Berkshire: Chartered Institute of Marketing, pp. 22–3.

Brierley, S. (2002) *The Advertising Handbook*, 2nd edn, London: Routledge.

Fill, C. (2002) *Marketing Communications: Contexts, Strategies, and Applications*, 3rd edn, Harlow: Financial Times Prentice Hall.

Goodyear, M. (1996) Divided by a common language', *Journal of the Market Research Society*.

Grein, A.F. and Gould, S.J. (1996) 'Globally Integrated Marketing Communications', *Journal of Marketing Communications*, 17 (3): 141–158.

Hankinson, G. and Cowking, P. (1996) *The Reality of Global Brands: Cases and Strategies for the Successful Management of International Brands*, New York: McGraw-Hill.

Hite, R.E. and Frazier, C. (1988) 'International Advertising Strategies of Multinational Corporations', *Journal of Advertising Research*, August/September, 9–17.

Hofstede, G. (1980) *Cultures and Consequences: International Differences in Work Related Values*, Thousand Oaks, CA: Sage.

Hofstede, G. (1991) *Cultures and Organisations*, London: McGraw-Hill.

Keegan, W.J. (1989) *Global Marketing Management*, Englewood Cliffs, NJ: Prentice Hall.

Levitt, T. (1983) 'The globalization of markets', *Harvard Business Review*, May/June: 92–102.

Lewis, E. (2006) 'Global vs local', *The Marketer*, 25 June: 7–9.

Lynd, M. (2006) 'Protect your identity', *The Marketer*, 25, June, Cookham, Berkshire: Chartered Institute of Marketing, pp. 16–17.

Maslow, A. (1954) *Motivtion and Personality*, New York: Harper & Row.

Nevett, T.R. (1982) *Advertising in Britain: A History*, London: Heinemann.

Ohmae, K. (1990) *The Borderless World*, London: Collins.

Pond, J. (2006) 'Promotional pitfalls', *The Marketer*, 25, June, Cookham, Berkshire: Chartered Institute of Marketing, p. 37.

Smith, P.R. and Taylor, J. (2002) *Marketing Communications: An Integrated Approach*, 3rd edn, London: Kogan Page.

Yeshin, T. (2006) *Advertising*, London: Thomson Learning.

CASE STUDY 20.1

SABMiller eyes bigger stage

It must be a relief for Nick Fell, the former President of global commercial strategy at Cadbury Schweppes, not to have to worry about the business implications of the salmonella contamination crisis at his previous employer.[6] But on taking up his new role as Group Marketing Director at brewer SABMiller next month, he will find plenty of other challenges to keep him occupied.

SABMiller, whose brands include Pilsner Urquell, Peroni Nastro Azzurro and Miller Genuine Draft, has a presence in more than 60 countries, spread across five continents.

While its sales in some of the mature markets of Western Europe, including the UK, are relatively small, it is undoubtedly a global company with big ambitions, which has been radically transformed in the past four years since

[6]This relates to the discovery of salmonella in a Cadbury's factory and the subsequent withdrawal of product in July 2006. The resulting publicity saw sales of Cadbury's chocolate fall for a period.

it was born out of the merger of South African Breweries and Miller Brewing, bringing the business much-needed scale in a sector rife with consolidation.

In 2003, it acquired Italian beer brand Peroni, last year it purchased South America's second-biggest brewer, Bavaria, and earlier this month it made a smaller, though in some ways no less interesting, acquisition, buying US beer brand Steel Reserve and caffeinated alcoholic malt beverage brand Sparks.

Fell replaces Mark Sherrington, who joined SABMiller in July 2002, and was given the task of re-engineering its marketing department following its takeover of Miller. He resigned last December without a job to go to, but agreed to stay on until a replacement was found.

The recruitment of Fell is based in large part on his impressive international experience. Before joining Cadbury Schweppes, he had spent 15 years at drinks group Diageo in a variety of roles, including Global Brands Director for Johnnie Walker and Global Marketing Director for Guinness.

While Sherrington was brought in to build the group's marketing function, through premium brand directors, for instance, Fell will take the implementation of its international marketing to the next stage. He will oversee the global roll-out of positioning communications for its premium brands as well as being responsible for innovation and bedding-in best practice across the business.

There are potential obstacles to his success. 'The biggest challenge it (SABMiller) has is getting distribution on an international scale", says Canadian alcoholic drinks sector analyst Kevin Baker. 'It has some powerful brands such as Peroni and Pilsner Urquell, but while Pilsner Urquell would be a crown jewel in any portfolio, it just does not have the distribution in the big markets.'

A Merrill Lynch briefing note on SABMiller, published on 12 July, rates the company as a stock to buy, but sounds several notes of caution. 'With between 70% and 80% exposure to emerging markets (South Africa, Africa, Central and Eastern Europe, Russia, China, Latin America), SABMiller does present more risk than its brewing peers, and its share price can be expected to be more volatile', the document reads. 'Our investment case is based on our belief that a strong management team would be able to unlock value longer term, with short-term share price volatility presenting particular buying opportunities.'

Credit Suisse First Boston analyst Michael Bleakley argues that the 'marketing expertise' SABMiller has shown in building local brands in markets such as Central Europe and Africa should be applied to 'reigniting growth' in the USA. 'It has the opportunity to drive premium brand growth harder and improve the proportion of its business from premium brands', he says.

In the UK, SABMiller's four main beer brands account for less than 1 per cent of the market by volume. To address this, a year ago it created Miller Brands UK and put in place a £30m promotional budget to raise the profile of its premium lagers. At the same time, it appointed Jean-Pierre van Lin, formerly Managing Director UK and Ireland for Miller Brewing International, to the top UK marketing role.

Peroni packaging on display at a European warehouse.

SOURCE: © SABMILLER PLC.

A greater UK market share is undoubtedly desirable, but it is not something the company is prepared to secure at any price. The company is aiming to maintain its brands' premium status and margins, and avoid being sucked into the supermarket-driven price-led promotions that have diluted the supposed exclusivity of other 'premium' beer brands.

To this end, Peroni's current 'La Doice Vita' campaign, created by ad agency The Bank, draws on the famous Italian arthouse film of the same name. It associates the lager strongly with Italian style to underline its premium positioning and elevate it beyond the run-of-the-mill beer category. At present, Peroni draft sales are growing quicker than sales of its bottles.

'Gaining share is not necessarily our primary goal at the moment', says SABMiller head of media relations Nigel Fairbrass.

What we are trying to do, especially with Peroni, is grow it at an appropriate rate. We don't want to distribute it in supermarkets; we would rather see it in top-end style-bars and really establish brand equity. Anyone can get volume in the UK by discounting.

SABMiller also has some interesting non-beer brands, such as Brutal Fruit in South Africa, but it claims its innovation focus will remain on beer. Marketing attention will remain concentrated on Peroni, Pilsner Urquell and Miller Genuine Draft and, to a lesser extent, Castle.

Now it is up to Fell to ensure that innovation is translated into international success.

Case study questions

1 What is the next stage in SABMillers international development?

2 What barriers are there to the company's growth overseas?

Source: By Robert Gray, *Marketing*, 19 July 2006, p. 117 (reproduced from *Marketing* magazine with the permission of the copyright owner, Haymarket Publications Limited).

CHAPTER TWENTY-ONE

THE CHANGING FACE OF MARKETING COMMUNICATIONS

LEARNING OBJECTIVES

Having completed this chapter you should be able to:

- Recognize the potential areas of change in marketing communications.
- Be aware of potential technological developments and begin to question the outcome of such advancements.
- Understand the reasons behind potential changes in communication agency structures.

INTRODUCTION

As suggested by the title of this chapter nothing stands still in marketing communications. Although marketers tend to operate on the basis of the here-and-now they have to keep an eye on the future because change can happen fast. This year's success could be next year's failure. It is after all barely 15 years since the introduction of the Internet and who would have forecast then its enormous growth and the influence it would have not just on marketing communications but on all our lives. Its effect on marketing communications has been particularly significant, as Box 9.4 shows (in the latest figures available prior to publication of this text) the only reason advertising is showing an increase in the first quarter of 2006 is the contribution of the Internet (+ 53.6 per cent) and the more modest increase in outdoor poster advertising (+ 3.4 per cent). PriceWaterhouseCoopers[1] estimate that online spending in Europe, the Middle East and Africa will reach $91.7m in 2009 an 80 per cent increase over 2004. All other mediums, including television, which dominated the advertising market through to the second half of the twentieth century, are down by varying degrees. According to ZenithOptimedia[2] television's share of the advertising market peaked in 2004.

[1]Quoted in Grose 2006.
[2]Quoted in Grose 2006.

A rational prediction of the future, therefore, is that technology will play an increasingly prominent part in marketing communications. However, as this text hopefully has indicated, there are lessons to be learnt from the past as well as from our expectations of the future. In addition to technological innovation this chapter suggests other potential changes (particularly in the socio-political area) may also have a great influence on marketing communications.

TECHNOLOGY

As noted the increased sophistication of technology and its increased contribution to marketing communications is perhaps the easiest prediction to make, although its consequences are less immediately clear. For nearly a century, first newspapers, then radio and more recently television, have at various times dominated mass advertising. Although 'direct response television' and more recently 'interactive television' have driven the dream of one-to-one marketing a little closer generally this medium is proving difficult to adapt to the new communications age. Traditional advertising 'spots' are proving less effective (as viewers 'zip' and 'zap' their way past advertising on one of the hundreds of different channels) and despite programme sponsorship becoming more commonplace, advertisers are questioning the medium's viability. Perhaps its salvation lies in the almost inevitable congress of television and the personal computer and/or further developments in hologram technology. Some advertisers are hoping that '**one-pipe convergence**' will remodel the landscape (Grose 2006). This is when a single broadband feed operates television, PCs, DVDs, games consoles and stereo systems.

One-pipe convergence
The movement toward a single broadband feed which supplies television, PCs, DVDs, games consoles and stereo systems.

Other traditional mediums may change through technological development. Outdoor poster sites may be replaced by digital screens that deliver news and entertainment as well as advertising (although there are vehicle safety considerations). The survival of newspapers will depend on their capacity to either continue to raise revenue through advertising or find another revenue-raising model. Classified advertising (which Rupert Murdoch once described as the industry's 'rivers of gold') is fast disappearing. As a new media, the Internet is attracting advertising spend and this budget has to come from somewhere. In Switzerland and the Netherlands, for example, 2006 newspaper advertising revenues are down and there is a suggestion that around half of their classified advertising has been lost to the Internet. On the positive side, the website of the UK's *Guardian* newspaper now has half as many readers in America as it does in the UK. Formats too will change. Newspapers, magazines and catalogues, as well as podcasts, may be downloaded onto hand-held or desk-top devices.

There are likely to be significant developments in point of sale. Point-of-sale technology will continue to become more efficient. This may result in an end to operator-assisted checkouts if 'smart trolley' scanning proves effective.

Audio or video displays may alert shoppers to offers as they pass by and in-store terminals may enable the purchase of more complex services such as insurance. The further extension of Internet ordering and home delivery is likely. Retailers may also use the information they hold about customers more efficiently. Tesco already utilize such customer knowledge to incentivize its Club Card members. It is suggested, however, they currently only use a fraction of the information they collect. Already supermarkets can predict certain customer life-changes from what they purchase. For example folic acid supplement on a till roll is a good indicator that a baby is on the way with all the lucrative trading opportunities that entails. More effective management software and increased processing speeds may produce substantially more detailed information about individuals. Although the possibilities associated with such targeting may excite some marketers there is also considerable ethical considerations associated with such increased knowledge. For example most supermarkets now offer life insurance. Would it be right for such companies to use the data from purchases (which may include cigarettes, alcohol, cholesterol rich and fatty foods, etc.) as part of the life-insurance risk assessment?

@ The future of retailing? Take a look at: **www. future-store.org.**

The growth in Internet usage is a given. Europeans with Internet connection currently spend an average of 10.25 hours per week online, which is a 17 per cent increase over 2004 (Grose 2006). The Internet is still, however, a passive medium requiring constant direction (through advertising and/or promotion) to individual websites. How marketers will attract potential customers to their sites will be a continuing challenge. Cooperative networks of non-competitive suppliers are already cross-referencing (and earning commission) each other's sites, particularly in the leisure and travel industries, and this strategy is likely to develop further into areas such as cross-purchasing and cooperative promotion as these networks stabilize. Virtual communities are another potential platform and the rapid development of sites such as Second Life (see Minicase 21.1) is a likely indicator of further developments. Once consumers reach a website there is still the problem of keeping them interested and involved and stimulating them into action (e.g. purchase) and this will continue to challenge the creative abilities of marketers (see Case study 21.1). Some innovative marketers are already using the medium of the Internet to involve consumers themselves in the marketing of products and services. Interesting or amusing files, associated with particular brands, are being circulated to friends and relations in a form replicating the spread of a virus (viral marketing). On the downside the democratic nature of the Internet enables customers (and others) to post damaging messages. Some brands (e.g. McDonald's) have websites wholly dedicated to attacking them.

The merging of technologies will almost certainly involve more services being available on mobile phones. Internet connection and email facilities are already available, and downloading, albeit currently restricted by size, on third generation equipment. Palm-top computer facilities which support Windows and other software programs are also generally available. Other uses for mobile telephones may include being used for relatively small purchases (mobile phone companies are already charging small amounts to accounts), as a door-opening (or key) device, for entry to multiple locations or even as ticket devices for holding travel, theatre and other bookings. At present these facilities would prove a security risk and much will depend on how quickly such devices can be blocked if they are stolen.

One of the fastest growing areas in marketing communications currently is texting and this is likely to grow significantly. Organizations currently use texting to invite further information and competition entry or to send brand messages. Transnational mobile phone networks (e.g. Vodaphone, O_2, etc.) text messages to travellers and trade fair organizers use texting for reminding visitors of particular events. Even universities are texting potential students with reminders about application procedures and current students with details of their courses and important deadlines, as this method appears more

MINICASE 21.1

Second life

Second Life is a 3D virtual island world owned by the San Francisco company Lindon Lab. It was 'opened' to the public in 2003 and claims to have 300 000 residents, roughly half-and-half men and women with an average age of 33. It is growing at a rate of 12 per cent per month with no marketing.

Residents can buy land to store virtual creations, run businesses and host events for $9.95 a month plus a land fee. Groups too are allowed to own land and resources and run businesses. Commercial activity takes place in 'The Marketplace' using the 'Linden Dollar' which can be traded against the US Dollar at online currency exchanges. Fashion brand American Apparel opened a virtual store recently, Coca-Cola are using it as a marketing medium, the BBC has staged a concert on Second Life island and more than 50 universities own space to trial virtual teaching tools.

Source: *Marketing*, 26 July 2006.

A resident of Second Life – will online environments such as this provide a robust platform for future marketing communications strategies?

effective than email. The trend will continue as advanced technology makes such communication easier and even less costly. The obvious danger is that as costs fall spam email habits will cross over significantly to this medium.

We can, to some extent, forecast the technological changes that will affect the communications industry. What is more difficult is to establish, with any accuracy, how consumers will respond. A current example of innovation through available technology may serve as a warning. Call centres developed as a means of saving customer communication costs but were presented (and continue to be presented) as enhanced customer service. Surveys show general annoyance with call centres in particular the menu options which can at times be completely baffling. Cost savings were extended by transferring many call centres off-shore to parts of the world where the cost of service personnel is low. It is interesting to note that a quiet backlash has caused a number of companies (including NatWest and Direct Line) to bring back domestic call centres and make this repatriation part of their brand message.

An important message for marketers in relation to technological innovation now and in the future is just because technology makes things possible does not imply marketers should use it.

MESSAGE

In technological terms mediums have begun to merge (television programmes and telephone facilities on the Internet, MP3 download facilities and radio on mobile phones and interactivity on television receivers) and this integration is likely to continue. From the marketing communications perspective decisions on how and through which medium to get their messages across will become more crucial. The current 'innovation' of putting across messages while files or programmes download will itself become impractical as the time taken to download shrinks as it surely will. If traditional mediums become more restrictive can sponsorship (of programmes or films) or product placement fully replace mass advertising? How can new brands gain attention or stimulate trial in the new communications era? Although it is now easier to connect with people than ever before, how do you attract their attention with the multiplicity of other messages bombarding the consumer? How do marketing communicators deal with message overload? Traditionally they have used shock (e.g. sex, horror, etc.), emotion (human interest, love, etc.), fear (what will happen if...?) and humour (collectively creativity) to get and maintain attention. Will communicators have to continue to push the boundaries of good taste and moral acceptance to maintain the *status quo* and who, if anyone, should regulate them? It would be doubtful whether industry bodies could keep control in an Internet-dominated environment. Already regulators are having difficulty monitoring activity within their own countries let alone across borders. Increased co-operation between governments is a potential solution but the track-record so far has been poor not only between the USA and Europe but among EU member states themselves. Many in the industry may welcome this continued indecision.

In addition, research shows that consumers are already highly sceptical of the messages from organizations. Advertisers are widely vilified (see Chapter 9) for promoting consumerism and other societal evils. Personal sales assistants are frequently mistrusted (see Chapter 14), direct marketers criticized for spam, junk-mail, telesales (see Chapter 13) and, as noted previously, call centres are generally disliked. Even public relations has not avoided controversy when, according to *PR Week*[3], 'the term PR is giving public relations a bad name'. The growing distrust may be here to stay. In developing markets such as India and China this backlash has yet to begin. It probably took 30–40 years for Western European and North American consumers to reach their current level of 'sophistication' such that they have become antagonistic and less trusting of marketing. It is unlikely that it will take as long in the developing markets.

The creativity behind the message will become even more central to successful marketing communication strategies. Major brands are already replacing the product service 'message' or unique selling proposition (USP) with much more intangible reputation and status 'messages' through association with wholesome activities such as sports, morally justifiable causes and charities and involving themselves in (or responding to) social issues such as childhood obesity and the environment. Whether this will redeem the reputation of marketing communications remains to be seen.

@

Take a look at *PR Week*'s website: **www.prweek.com.**

THE COMMUNICATIONS INDUSTRY

As noted previously, the marketing communications industry prior to the twentieth century was regarded holistically by the term advertising and it was only in that century that specialist functions and singular trade organizations developed (see Chapters 1 and 19). As that century ended, advertising had diminished in importance relative to sales promotion, public relations and sponsorship. In the same period integrated marketing communications (see Chapter 15) became the most talked about, although controversial, subject matter in the industry. Will integrated marketing communications reunite the disparate marketing communications tools and will it be a feature of marketing communications in the new millennium as Figure 21.1 suggests?

As argued in Chapter 15 integrated marketing communications has a powerful range of arguments to support it, although it is not such an easy strategy to implement effectively. One must assume that technology (in the

[3] As quoted in Moloney (2006: 20).

Back to the future

In July 2006 Ryanair launched an advertising campaign promoting its Internet check-in service. It suggested that travellers should 'Avoid Queues. Use Ryanair Web Check-in' above a picture of a seemingly endless queue of would-be flyers. The picture looked familiar because Ryanair were copying one of the most famous advertisements of all time. Saatchi & Saatchi's 1979 Conservative party poster 'Labour isn't working'. According to *Private Eye* magazine 'if one was feeling generous it could be construed as an ironic *homage*'. That is until you noticed that it was the same picture and that all that had been done was 'to scan it, flip it and *Photoshop* it.'

Source: *Private Eye*, 1163, 21 July–3 August, p.11.

Ryanair's homage to the original Conservative Party advertisement.

Figure 21.1 Marketing communications over time

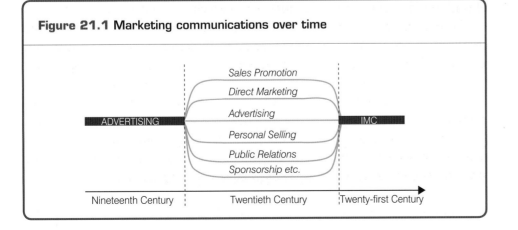

Marketing metrics
The measures used to analyse the success or otherwise of marketing tools and campaigns.

@

Learn more about marketing metrics at: **www.ad-mkt-review.com/public_html/ docs/fs059.html.**

areas of project development, media planning, communications, design and research) will assist those companies and their agencies to develop the capability for integrated campaigns over time. Ironically, rather than create larger and larger full-service agencies to cope, more specialist agencies are likely to become parts of networks (contractually or less formally), albeit large groups may own several specialist agencies in the home market and overseas.

The issue of **marketing metrics** (or how to measure the success or otherwise of marketing tools) will continue to be an issue in the industry. Advances in telephone and Internet technology (e.g. freephone, texting, click-throughs, etc.) have enabled improved estimates to be made of success levels of parts of the communications mix but the outcome of advertising, public relations and sponsorship campaigns will always be largely immeasurable in the short term. There is an old marketing fable that if everyone stopped advertising and promoting brands for a short time nothing much (in turnover terms) would change. Proving this is of course very difficult. A similar challenge faced scientists who were convinced that aeroplane exhaust fumes were contributing to a variation in the earth's temperature but could not prove it. Only after the major tragedy of 9/11, when all planes were grounded over the USA for a few days, were scientists able to prove their calculations to be correct. That any commercial companies (or sectors) would be willing to withdraw from advertising to test the market in this way is an intriguing if unlikely scenario. Future legislation banning, for example, advertising to children, may give more verifiable results of this claim.

In marketing's search for self-justification there is perhaps as much danger in over-measuring or over-researching than being under-informed. Reliance on focus groups or survey research can lead to safe, mundane and/or unadventurous results and can occasionally be highly misleading. In a highly competitive communications market is being 'safe' satisfactory or will the future inevitably require more risk taking? Some companies already launch products without the usual testing and research periods because of the need to get technological innovations quickly to the market. Indeed a number (e.g. Microsoft) have been accused of using customers to 'test-drive' new product. If 'messages' are going to appear fresh and meaningful in a rapidly changing, culturally diverse world perhaps communicators too will see the need to use the market as the testing ground rather than following the path of traditional quantitative or qualitative research.

The industry has a difficult future to which it must adapt. Ignoring the criticism of customers and legislators is no longer a viable alternative but neither is the mundane and safe strategies of the past.

@

Learn more marketing terms at: **www. marketingpower.com/mg-dictionary.php.**

Summary

This final chapter looked at the potential changes in the marketing communications industry. It noted that technical advancements will undoubtedly continue and that new media was already changing the face of the industry. A brief review of potential technological developments was made and the convergence of mediums including television, personal computers and mobile telephones discussed. Communications at the point of sale is also likely to change both how we shop and how we receive information regarding brands. Although technological advances will be central to future change in the industry, the way brand messages are constructed and conveyed is likely to be revolutionized. The traditional ways of attracting consumer's attention may have to be set aside for the more creative and personal approach as the sophisticated consumer looks for attention, stimulation and entertainment. Consumer antagonism against marketers was discussed and the danger of over-measurement considered.

Review questions

1   What developments have driven the 'dream' of one-to-one marketing?
2   Why are traditional advertising spots on TV now proving less effective?
3   How does viral marketing work?
4   What are 'marketing metrics'?
5   Why are consumers highly sceptical of marketing messages?

Discussion questions

1   The development of technology has created choices now that did not exist a few years ago. One of these is new media and the ability to use TV screens to replace traditional poster sites. What advantages does this media offer and to what extent do you think it will develop in the next five years?
2   Press reports from 2006 suggest that the current generation of mobile phone users will, on average, text around four times a day. This represents a growing trend, so to what extent do you think that this change in behaviour will influence the way in which people respond to and interact with traditional forms of marketing communications in the future?
3   How might you cope with message overload?
4   To what extent do you believe that organizations will actually adopt a formal approach to integrated marketing communications and what might the implications of that move be?

Further reading

Bell, GH., Ledolter, J. and Swersey, A.J. (2006) 'Experimental design on the front lines of marketing: testing new ideas to increase direct mail sales', *International Journal of Research in Marketing*, Sep., 23 (3): 309–19.

Boutié, P. (1996) 'Will this kill that?', *Journal of Consumer Marketing*, 13 (4): 49–57. Will new digital media – particularly Internet based – forever change the way companies communicate? A reflection on the thinking that shaped the growth of the Internet.

Clulow, V. (2005) 'Futures dilemmas for marketers: can stakeholder analysis add value?', *European Journal of Marketing*, 39 (9/10): 978–97.

Colauto, G. (2005) 'From in-store TV to narrow casting', *European Retail Digest*, Winter, 48: 28–32. An insight on the results of in-store TV and the case for narrow casting to provide higher sales, higher advertising income and improved branding.

Lagrosen, S. (2005) 'Effects of the internet on the marketing communication of service companies', *Journal of Services Marketing*, 19 (2): 63–9.

Chapter references

Grose, T.K. (2006) 'Ad-ventures online', *Time* (European edition)', 23 August, www.time.com.

Moloney, K. (2006) *Rethinking Public Relations*, 2nd edn, London: Routledge.

CASE STUDY 21.1

Coke taps into brand new Internet craze

Nobody seems sure how the craze started. But for the past several months, teenagers around the world have discovered that Diet Coke and Mentos mints are a volatile combination. Go to any video-sharing website, such as YouTube, and hundreds of amateur films can be found showing bottles of Diet Coke transformed into foaming geysers or home-made rockets when mixed with the mints. The phenomenon has provided millions of dollars worth of exposure for Coke and Mentos. But it has also demonstrated how brands can develop their own online subcultures that companies are powerless to control.

The growing importance of the Internet in shaping perceptions of brands helps explain why Coke last week launched its own interactive website, where users are invited to post home-made video clips similar to those found on YouTube. Coke is the latest in a growing number of companies to experiment with consumer-generated online content, as brand-owners race to adapt their marketing strategies to an increasingly interactive media environment. Last month, Wal-Mart, the US retailer, launched a website called The Hub that allows teenagers to create personal web pages, modelled on 'social network' sites such as MySpace.

'Increased broadband penetration is opening up possibilities that didn't exist even two years ago', says Tim Kopp, Coke's Vice-President of global interactive marketing. On its new website, Coke challenges visitors to make films about a different theme each month, with prizes offered for the best entries. The current brief urges people to submit videos that capture 'the essence of you'. The site is the online dimension of its latest global advertising campaign – using a new slogan: The Coke Side of Life – but the company says it is not looking for home-made commercials. Instead, it wants the site to be a place for consumers to show off their personalities and creativity. 'Advertising can no longer be a one-sided monologue where we are always explaining what Coke is', says Mr Kopp. 'We are trying to develop a dialogue with consumers and learn about how they interact with the brand.'

Coke's experiment with consumer-generated content will be closely watched because the company is one of the world's biggest advertisers, famous for decades of iconic television campaigns. Traditional advertising is losing its potency as media fragmentation makes it harder to reach large numbers of consumers. But Mr Kopp insists the website is designed to complement rather than replace other forms of marketing. 'We need to recognize that online is now an important part of the overall communications mix', he says. 'But we're not saying, "let's take all our advertising off the TV and put it on the web". We need to develop different strategies for each medium.'

Tim Stock of scenario-DNA, a brand consultancy, is sceptical about the ability of large companies to connect with consumers online. 'Coke has a better chance than Wal-Mart because it is a more relevant brand to young people', he says. 'But there's nothing it can do that will match the power of the Mentos craze.' He predicts that the Coke website will attract film and advertising students trying to put their work in the limelight but few of the more spontaneous, rough-edged videos posted by ordinary people on YouTube. His doubts are vindicated by the ten videos loaded on the website so far: all are either arty or quirky, but none of them are likely to generate much buzz beyond the confines of the Coke site. The tame content is perhaps a reflection of the 15 pages of rules and guidelines that warn filmmakers against copyright infringements, vulgarity, defamation and a variety of other outlawed content. Filtering is necessary to bar videos that would damage the Coke brand and to prevent the site being hijacked by its many critics.

Coke's interative website where users are invited to post home-made video clips similar to those found on *YouTube*.

SOURCE: © 2006 THE COCA-COLA COMPANY.

General Motors learned the dangers of uncontrolled consumer-generated content earlier this year when it invited people to create online advertisements for a new Chevrolet sports-utility vehicle. More than 3000 of the responses attacked the company over its safety record and alleged environmental abuses. Mr Kopp says Coke is not trying to become another YouTube or MySpace. 'We are not an online business. We're a beverage business', he says. 'But we have to develop compelling marketing platforms that are relevant to the lives of young people. We're not saying we've got it all figured out. It's a starting point.'

Case questions

1 What are Coca-Cola looking to achieve through this website?
2 What are the potential dangers of such a strategy?

Source: Ward, Andrew, 'Coke taps into brand new internet craze', *Financial Times*, August 7, 2006 (used with permission.

GLOSSARY

4Ps see **marketing mix**

above the line advertising

access panels provide respondents for survey-style information and are made up of targets who have been invited by email to take part with a link to the Web survey

account management responsible for liaison with the client, that their needs are being fulfilled by the agency, that timetables are kept and that all work is completed within the budget

account planning responsible for the changing requirements of the client and advising on the strategic direction of a campaign through pre- and post-campaign research. Account planners are expected to provide insight and understanding of the consumer and their relationship with the brand and guide the strategic direction of communications liaising closely with the creative team

Acorn profiles describes residential neighbourhoods and are based on the approximately 1.7 million postcodes in the UK. The full Acorn profile comprises of 17 distinct categories containing 54 Acorn neighbourhood types

adaptation adapting products and services for specific international markets

ADMARS segmentation mnemonic: Accessible (can be reached through specific media), Differentiated (different from other segments), Measurable (can be defined and measured to some degree of accuracy), Actionable (the company has the resources to reach them), Relevant (the product/service is relevant to this segment) and Substantial (the segment is large enough to warrant targeting)

advergaming where a game is created around a brand

advertising a paid-for, non-personal form of mass communication from an identified source, used to communicate information and influence consumer behaviour with a high degree of control over design and placement but potentially a low degree of persuasion and credibility. It is never either neutral or unbiased

advertising allowances contribution to retailers for advertising

advertising execution thoughts (see **cognitive response model**) relate to how favourably or unfavourably messages are received

advertising funded programming (AFP) where a sponsor part-funds the programme in return for product placement

advertising objectives see **objectives**

advertising problem the reason(s) why an organization is advertising

advertising recall unprompted awareness of recent advertising

advertising recognition prompted awareness of recent advertising

Advertising Standards Authority (ASA) UK regulatory body for advertising

advertorials advertising in the format of magazine or press editorial

affective (see **hierarchy of effects models**) feeling processes

affinity marketing see **loyalty marketing**

affordable (budget) where costs and profit margin are deducted from turnover and the balance invested in marketing and marketing communications

AFP see **advertising funded programming**

agency brief see **brief**

AIDA (see **hierarchy of effects models**) generally attributed to Strong (1925) the model was designed to represent the stages through which a salesperson should take a prospect but was later adopted as a basic framework to explain how persuasive communication (mainly advertising) worked. AIDA stands for attention, interest, desire and action

AIDAS AIDA model with the addition of after-sales service (S)

AIO research (activities, interests and opinions) AIO research uses consumer interviews, statements recorded in focus groups, literature and a little imagination to develop statements associated with clusters of consumers (e.g. Mondeo Man)

allegory where the meaning of message is represented symbolically (e.g. the Irishness of Caffrey's)

alternative media see **ambient media**

ambient marketing see **ambient media**

ambient media often associated with outdoor media and best described as anything that introduces a 'wow factor' capable of attracting attention and curiosity

ambush marketing the practice whereby another company, often a competitor, attempts to deflect some of the audience to itself and away from the sponsor

application (brand identity) attention to other aspects of branding such as corporate advertising, stationery, signage, livery, etc.

arbitrary (budget) a 'build-up' budget approach where senior management arbitrate between different organizational priorities

area cluster sampling where the population is divided into mutually exclusive, distinctly separate, subgroups (or clusters) on a geographical basis. A random selection of clusters is made and a random sample of units taken from these clusters

arousal seeking the motive underlying hedonic consumption is the need to seek arousal. Hedonic consumption refers to the use of products or services for sheer enjoyment rather than problem or need driven

associations see **brand associations**

ATR model Awareness, Trial and Reinforcement. Ehrenberg and Goodhardt (1979) suggest that the greater part of the buying experience is rooted in past experience

ATR(N) model extention of ATR (Awareness, Trial and Reinforcement) model to include Nudging and the proposition that advertising 'nudges' (as opposed to persuades) customers to buy a brand

attention in communications theory attention must be gained before a message can be delivered

attitude see **brand attitude**

attitude scales scales that measure a respondent's attitude to predefined statements. Examples include nominal scales, ordinal scales, interval scales and ratio scales

attitudes strongly felt, not easily changed views. Attitudes form an important part of consumer theory because it is believed to be the link between what consumers think and what they buy in the marketplace

attribution the inference that people draw about events, other people and their own behaviour including such factors as consistency, consensus and distinctiveness

audit data see **syndicated research**

augmented (aspects of a brand) augmented aspects of a brand include packaging/presentation, price/terms, guarantees, extras (for example built-in software) and after-sales support. Any change in augmented characteristics does not alter the basic function or performance but may affect competitive advantage, trust and other subjective measures of the brand's value

autonomic (drive) a motivation or drive felt physiologically and involuntarily

award symbols symbols that represent that a certain level of status has been gained by the brand (e.g. accreditation, awards, etc.)

awareness see **brand awareness**

Awareness Index (AI) a measure of advertising awareness

awareness set those products in a category that the consumer is aware of

awareness to loyalty scale a scale that suggests that although a relatively high percentage of consumers may be aware of a brand, progressively fewer will have a positive attitude, purchase or will be ultimately loyal

B2B markets business-to-business markets

B2C markets business-to-consumer markets

banner-ads vertical or horizontal website advertisements

basic communications model developed by Wilbur Schramm (1955) it is the most commonly used model of mass communication

behavioural learning suggests that an individual develops a pattern of behavioural responses because of the rewards and punishments offered by his/her environment

behavioural paradigm proponents of this paradigm believe it is not possible to study what goes on in the consumer's mind because it is too complex. Instead output is measured following a given stimulus. In effect it is a 'black box' into which stimuli flow and out of which behaviour occurs

below the line the marketing communication tools excluding advertising

benefit positioning positioning on the basis of brand benefits. These can be both functional (e.g. cures headaches) or emotional (e.g. shows status)

bonus offers extra volume incentive (e.g. 2 for the price of 1)

bonus pack extra volume promotional packs (e.g. 50 per cent free)

brand analysis the strength of the brand as perceived by consumers

brand associations those associations built in the consumer's mind between the brand and something else that is important and/or enjoyable (e.g. football)

brand attitude how the consumer feels about the brand

brand awareness how aware a consumer is of the brand

brand benefits what the brand will do for you (e.g. relieve headache, help grass grow greener, etc.)

brand characteristics characteristics (e.g. fun-loving) associated with a particular brand (see also **brand personality**)

brand confusion any misunderstanding concerning brand values and benefits, an outcome of indistinct communication

brand equity the value of owning a particular brand name compared to a generic brand of the same type in the same category

brand experience provision of brand related experiences (e.g. Tango Roadshow, Pepsi Charts, Red Bull Soap Box Derby, etc.)

brand extension Using an existing brand name in a different category

brand identity a composite of those features of a brand (e.g. design) that make it recognizable

brand image see **brand personality**

brand interaction a brand's relationship with their customer (e.g. loyalty, closeness, habit, etc.)

brand knowledge knowledge of the benefits, features, positioning etc. associated with the brand

brand leader the leading brand in a particular category

brand life cycle suggests that brands have different life-stages through which they pass (also see **product life cycle**)

brand personality the character and essence of a brand. The perceived lifestyle associations and values (e.g. status, fashion, quality, etc.)

brand pirates those who seek to pass-off brand characteristics (e.g. package design) as their own

brand promise the promise(s) (e.g. safety, comfort, etc.) associated with a particular brand. Broken brand promises may lead to a reassessment of the brand

brand proposition the brand's central proposition, the focus of the brand campaign

brand recall see **advertising recall**

brand salience the importance and prominence of a brand

brand skills see **brand benefits**

brand values those values associated with a brand (e.g. status, youth, etc.)

branding, brand a collection of physical and emotional characteristics associated with a particular identified product or service that differentiates that product or service from the rest of the marketplace

brand status the position (e.g. market leader) of the brand in a particular market

brief, agency brief details of the organization, their brands and all other information pertinent to an agency making a 'pitch'

briefing explanation of the marketing problem either internally or externally

broad repertoire see **multi-brand buyer**

browser web viewing programme such as Firefox or Internet Explorer

budget modelling various econometric and simulation techniques which seek to model investment and subsequent performance

building wraps giant poster advertising (usually on canvas) hung from a large building (or buildings whilst under construction)

burst (campaign) concentrating the campaign 'spend' in a short period to raise awareness and increase reach

buying allowances cash discounts, increased margins, etc. against goods purchased

buzz marketing see **viral marketing**

carriers see **connectors**

carryover effect see **lagged effect**

catalogue retailing a means by which products or services can be purchased from a selection of those on offer in a catalogue

causal research see **conclusive research**

cause-related marketing an activity in which commercial organizations join with charities or other good causes to market a product, service or the image of the organization, for mutual benefit

cause-related promotions promotions associated with benefiting some charitable or other socially responsible cause

cause-related sponsorship sponsorship associated with benefiting some charitable or other socially responsible cause

celebrity endorsement advertising which uses the credibility associated with a celebrity to carry the message. The greater the celebrity's influence on a particular target audience the greater the wish to mimic that celebrity

chaining suggests behaviour emerges from sequences of actions in which the preceding action becomes the discriminative stimulus for the final response (inducement > purchase)

channel development the development of distribution channels

character-based trust trust in individuals

Chinese Wall first used after the 1929 stock market crash to describe new regulations that provided a separation between brokerage and investment bankers and only later to the separation between editorial and advertising functions

classical conditioning (or respondent conditioning) originally identified by Ivan Pavlov. It describes a largely unconscious process through which we acquire both information and feelings about stimuli

click-through rate the number of times online users 'click-through' or transfer to sponsored websites

clippings service a service offered to companies who wish to monitor media coverage. The results are frequently used to measure the effectiveness of an organization's public relations effort

closure effectively the completion (based on past experience) of something that is incomplete (e.g. part of a name). See **gestalt approach**

clubs (direct marketing) where membership entitles members to certain privileges not available to non-members

cluster sampling where the population is divided into mutually exclusive, distinctly separate, subgroups (or clusters). A random selection of clusters is made and a random sample of units taken from these clusters

co-branding appears in two forms: (1) involves joint marketing of products or services such that both brands benefit in terms of exposure (e.g. Hotpoint and Persil); (2) involves a charitable partner (e.g. NSPCC with Microsoft). See **cause-related marketing**

cognitive (see **hierarchy of effects models**) the process of thinking

cognitive, cognition the act of knowing

cognitive dissonance the mental discomfort that an individual feels if they hold two conflicting cognitions (or views). Individuals will seek to reduce or eliminate this dissonance by either changing one or the other viewpoint or by introducing a third view that will account for and reduce the dissonance

cognitive learning cognitive learning theory suggests that humans store information for different periods of time (see **sensory storage**, **short-term memory** and **long-term memory**)

cognitive paradigm focuses on an individual's thought processes and sees consumer choice as a problem-solving and decision-making series of activities the outcome of which is determined principally by the buyer's intellectual functioning and rational goal-orientated processing of information

cognitive response model a model that maintains that exposure to advertising elicits different types of response and purports to suggest how these responses relate to attitudes and purchase intentions (Belch and Belch 2001)

cold calling contacting consumers without prior knowledge or permission with the objective of making a sale or starting the process towards a sale

combined offers joint brand promotion (e.g. free hair-gel with shampoo)

commercials television commercial advertisements

commission (agency) percentage (usually 10 per cent to 15 per cent) paid by media owners to agencies in lieu of fees

communications audits a communications audit looks at communications' needs, patterns, flow, channels and technologies, examines content clarity and effectiveness, information needs of individuals, work groups, departments and divisions; non-verbal communications and corporate culture issues and communication impacts on motivation and performance

comparative advertising direct comparison of one brand with another, usually its main competitor. This may be to establish the brand's position in the marketplace or to claim price or functional superiority

competitions in sales promotion terms where the challenge is skill based

competitive parity (budget) spending determined relative to the spending of the organization's major competitor(s)

competitive positioning focuses on the relative advantages of the brand relative to its competition. For example Hertz may be 'number one' in car rentals but Avis 'try harder' in direct response to this claim. This type of positioning is often used to establish the profile of a new brand (e.g. Ryanair 'we fly for less') or to distinguish an existing brand in a highly competitive marketplace (e.g. Tesco price comparisons with competitors)

compiled lists lists of individuals with identified characteristics but *not* identified product interest (IPI)

complaints negative reaction reported back to the source (also called customer 'voice')

complementary branding where two brands combine to strengthen an offer (e.g. Braun and Oral B electric toothbrush)

component brand where a brand is incorporated into another product (e.g. Intel, Nutrasweet) also called ingredient brand

conative (see **hierarchy of effects models**) doing, action processes

concentrated marketing see **niche marketing**

concept stage the period when campaign concepts are being developed

conclusive research provides accurate and valid descriptions of the variables (descriptive research) or by determining the relationships between them (causal research), for example between advertising and sales

conditioned response the outcome of a conditioned stimulus. For example the ringing of a bell (conditioned stimulus) means food (unconditioned stimulus) is coming which may cause salivation (conditioned response)

conditioned stimulus something that is associated with something else that is naturally stimulating (e.g. ringing of bell means food is coming)

conditioning see **behavioural learning**

confidence interval in market research how different must the results be before you can be confident of their significance

connectors collective name for opinion formers and opinion leaders and others (e.g. family) who help to carry the message to the consumer

connotative words having meaning unique to the individual

consideration set see **awareness set**

consumer juries a collection of target consumers who are asked to rank in order, ideas or concepts put to them and to explain their choices

content analysis used to attempt to quantify the results of unstructured (qualitative) data. This is a technique for making inferences (or recognizing patterns) from the data

continuity series where a finite number of items (usually in a series or set) are made available over time (e.g. monthly)

continuous (campaign) where there is relatively even campaign expenditure over the year

continuous credit paying off mail order purchases in instalments

control and evaluation the means by which a plan is monitored, controlled and measured

control sample, control the sample which is unaffected by change against which altered variables can be tested

convenience sampling a low-cost 'straw poll' often used in the exploratory stages of a research programme

cookie a small text file left on the user's PC that identifies their browser so that they are 'recognized' when they revisit a site

cooperative branding joint venture schemes (e.g. Ryanair with MBNA on the Ryanair.com credit card)

cooperative strategy (retail) retailers and suppliers working together to develop the business through distribution and other efficiencies

copy relates to written material. Advertising copy is the text in an advertisement. Journalistic copy relates to published articles

core (of a brand) functional characteristics such as basic product/ service, shape/texture, performance and physical capacity. Any changes in the core aspects would directly alter the generic product or service. Also called 'intrinsic' part of a brand

corporate advertising advertising designed to promote and enhance the image of the company amongst its target publics

corporate brand brand which relies heavily on the corporate name, whether or not a sub-brand is used (e.g. Mercedes 320, Renault Clio)

corporate communications an organizational function that controls all aspects of communication with an organization's publics (except consumers)

cost-based fees (agency) remuneration based on an agreed mark-up on inputs such as media

cost–benefit analysis ratio of cost to benefit used to establish whether a project, research, campaign, etc. should proceed

cost-per-thousand a measure for comparing the cost effectiveness of media calculated by dividing the cost of an advertisement in one particular medium by the circulation

coupons vouchers printed in-store or from packs, magazines, etc. which offer a money-off or other incentive to buy product(s)

covert marketing see **guerrilla marketing**

CPT (or CPM) see **cost-per-thousand**

creative brief gives guidance to the creative team who are going to produce a communication

creative platform the creative idea on which a campaign is built

creative promotions promotions that do not rely on price reduction

creatives individuals who work in the creative industries (e.g. designers)

creativity (in advertising) the ability to attract and hold the attention of the target audience through the manner and composition of the advertisement

credentials presentation where an agency presents examples of previous work and the personnel who would work on particular assignments

credit rating based on the financial integrity of the organization, ratings are set by ratings agencies such as Dun and Bradstreet and Standard and Poor

crisis not a day-to-day problem but one that has the capacity to severely damage the organization

crisis management management of a crisis situation that has the capacity to severely damage the organization

CRM see **customer relationship management**

cross-selling selling other items (sometimes from different categories) to existing customer base

current image the image held by outsiders based on a consensus of perceptions modelled by their knowledge and experience

customer acquisition the process of acquiring new customers

customer relationship maintenance the maintenance of regular contact with the customer

customer relationship management (CRM) a management process which uses database technology and call centres to maintain customer relationships

customer retention the process of retaining existing customers

DAGMAR (see **hierarchy of effects models**) DAGMAR (defining advertising goals for measuring advertising results) was Colley's (1961) formula for setting communications orientated objectives

data collection the collection of data for a particular research project

data mining the extraction of data from a data depository in a form useful to marketers

data warehousing the storing of data from a variety of sources. The data is stored because it may not be currently usable either because its value is not immediately appreciated or because it requires further qualification

database marketing the holding and analysing of customer information thereby helping create marketing strategies

day-after recall see **advertising recall**

decay corruption of a message over time

decision (in terms of buyer behaviour) the decision to purchase

decode, decoded translating the message into understandable concepts

de-duping the removal of duplicate names from mailing and other lists

demographic statistical data relating to the population and groups within it

demonstration advertising advertising where the effectiveness of the product or service and the way it may be used is demonstrated

denotative words having meaning for everybody

depth interviews in-depth interviews with a limited number of respondents

descriptive research see **conclusive research**

design elements (of a brand) include the logo, graphic features, typeface, symbols and colours that stimulate the recognition and remembrance of a brand

differentiated targeting the selection of a number of target markets each requiring a particular market positioning and message

differentiation the process of making the organization's brand different from other brands through marketing

diffusion marketing see **viral marketing**

diffusion of innovation the way that new developments (e.g. mobile telephones) enter the market. Rogers' (1983) theory of diffusion suggests that various consumers enter the market at different times and called them innovators, early adopters, early majority, late majority and laggards

direct channel marketing where an organization sells virtually the same products/services to both consumers and businesses (e.g. Dell)

direct debit an order to a bank allowing a company to make withdrawals from an account on a regular basis

direct mail advertising, through the medium of the mail, to targeted, profiled customers

direct marketing seeks to target individual customers with the intention of delivering personalized messages and building a relationship with them based on their responses to direct communication

direct opinion measurement research that directly asks target consumers about aspects such as message clarity, interest, feelings and attitudes

direct response media media where the customer can respond immediately to the offer

direct response television the format or technology that enables viewers to respond to offerings made on television

discriminative stimulus see **operant conditioning**. This is a particular stimulus (e.g. light being switched on) that suggests if you do this (e.g. push a button) you will receive a reward (e.g. food)

door-to-door the household delivery of leaflets, samples, etc.

double-header quality brand on sale in a quality outlet (e.g. Rolex in Harrods)

downward communications management to employee communication often through house-journals or other printed material

drip (campaign) extends the campaign over time which increases potential frequency. This is often used for 'reminder campaigns' or when an objective is to change longer-term attitudes

dummy uncirculated, trial editions of magazines sent to target advertisers or target audiences

early adopters (see **diffusion of innovation**) frequently the opinion leaders. Their entry into the market is significant. They are generally younger with above average education and/or income

early majority (see **diffusion of innovation**) entry of the early majority of customers represent the first move towards general acceptance. The speed of adoption can be seen to have increased considerably

editorial although the term should strictly only be applied to copy written by a newspaper or magazine editor it is frequently used to describe all newspaper or magazine copy

effective creativity (see **creativity**) creativity that meets the commercial objectives of a campaign

efficiency index an index that assumes that with each exposure of an advertisement there is a greater chance of reaching and influencing your audience – up to a point. After this point is reached each exposure no longer adds 'reach' or improves effectiveness

electronic point of sale (EPoS) technology at the point of sale that enable transactions to be tracked on a merchandise and customer level

e-marketing marketing using the medium of the Internet

emotional appeal (advertising) advertisements that develop atmosphere and appeal to an individual's ego, status or sense of worth

emotional strategies (of advertising) appeal to emotions such as romance, nostalgia, compassion, excitement, joy, heroism, fear, guilt, disgust and regret

emotive, emotion strong mental or instinctive feeling (e.g. love, fear, etc.)

encode, encoded (messages) putting the idea into a format (e.g. speech, print, etc.) using a combination of appropriate words, pictures, symbols so that it can be transmitted via a medium (e.g. television)

encoding (memory) the process by which information is symbolically or verbally represented so that it can easily be stored and retrieved (e.g. jingles, tag lines, etc.)

enquirers prospects who have directly contacted the company for specific information

EPoS see **electronic point of sale**

ERG theory (Existence, Relatedness and Growth) Clayton Alderfer's (1972) theory of motivation

erotica (in advertising) where sexual imagery is used to attract attention and enhance 'stopping power'

esteem needs (Maslow's hierarchy of needs) recognition, status, etc

ethical marketing a set of moral principles concerned with social well-being as related to marketing practice

ethnography, ethnographic research where researchers submerge themselves in consumer culture to view consumer dynamics. Photography and video diaries are used by market researchers to delve into consumers' minds

evaluation evaluation of information collected prior to purchase

evangelists see **fashion icons**

everyday low prices strategy where the emphasis is on low prices across the store (in contrast to the hi-lo pricing strategy)

evoked set those products in a category that the consumer has 'front-of-mind' and will make the purchase choice from

exclusive brands brands that, although theoretically independent, trade on an exclusive basis with a single retailer (e.g. Ladybird at Woolworths)

experience (in relation to purchasing) the extent to which the consumer has accumulated prior knowledge of the product or service

experiential learning see **behavioural learning**

experiential marketing brand involvement in events or shows (e.g. Guinness Experience)

experiential orientation see **symbolic orientation**

expert endorsement advertising which uses known or supposed (from their description or appearance) experts to recommend a product or service

expertise expertise includes aptitude, required training and experience and is domain specific

exploratory research initial research designed to establish the parameters of the research problem

extended problem-solving model model where purchase decisions are characterized by their importance (high involvement) and rational decision making

extensive problem-solving model model that reflects important purchase decisions (e.g. higher expenditure) warrant greater deliberation and higher involvement

factor analysis systematic review of the correlation between research variables which groups together those that are highly correlated to reduce a large number of variables to a smaller set that are not correlated

fashion icons celebrity fashion leaders (e.g. David Beckham or Madonna)

fear (in advertising) advertising that uses fear of something happening (e.g. house fire) as the central theme

fee payment (agency) remuneration based on a quotation for individual projects

feedback feedback is the reaction of the receiver having received the message

field marketing syndicated or shared teams working largely in the fast moving consumer goods sector, who carry out a number of selling and other 'sales' associated tasks on behalf of one or more suppliers

field of perception an individual's range of understanding. Overlapping fields of perception enable understanding. Also known as 'realm of perception' or 'realm of understanding'

financial analysis (brand equity) a review of the business earnings contributing to a brand's equity

first-mover advantage advantages associated with being the first organization in the marketplace and which may include experience, distribution channels, etc.

flanker brands where a supplier takes advantage of its market strength to introduce additional brands which compete against the competition brands for shelf space

flighting (campaign) expenditure concentrated in some periods of the year leaving other periods with zero expenditure

flyers distributed pamphlets

fly-posting posters randomly affixed to walls rather than licensed hoardings

FMCG fast moving consumer goods (such as those sold in supermarkets)

focus groups normally consist of a small number (8 to 10) target consumers brought together to discuss elements of a campaign from the initial concept stage to post production

follower brands brands that are not leaders in their category

footfall retail jargon for number of customers (e.g. increased footfall = rise in number of customers in a particular store)

former customers customers who have previously purchased from the organization but no longer do so

free draws where the winning of a competition is randomized

frequency the number of times the target audience have an opportunity to see (OTS) the message

frequency (direct marketing) a measure of how often a customer buys from an organization

front-of-mind-awareness maintaining awareness of the brand in the consumer's mind

frustration–regression principle in Clayton Alderfer's (1972) ERG theory (unlike Maslow's hierarchy of needs) if higher needs remain unfulfilled the person may regress to lower level motivations

fugging fundraising under the guise of research

full-service agency an agency that covers a full range of agency disciplines including copy writing, design, media purchase, etc.

functional orientation where the brand's positioning is based on its features or attributes

generic brands basic, no name or own label range with limited packaging (e.g. Tesco's value range)

generic communications communications designed to expand the sector rather than any individual brand in it

generic strategies (of advertising) where brands are so dominant in a sector that there is (at that time) no need to differentiate the brand from its competitors. Effectively these brands are looking to grow the total market in the knowledge that any increase will disproportionately benefit themselves (e.g. British Telecom's 'It's good to talk')

geodemographic profile combining both geographical and demographic features to provide a profile

geodemographics a method of segregating a market on the basis of social demographics and location

geographical identifiers signs and symbols that suggest a particular geographical location

gestalt approach gestalt (German for 'whole' or 'entirely') and gestalt psychology stresses the fact that perception of a stimulus takes place within a known context and that the individual's reaction is crucially affected by their 'world-view' (see **closure**)

giveaways products distributed (in-store or elsewhere) without cost as a means of encouraging trial

global organizations strive towards commonality of products or services and communication themes normally with some regional adaptations to respond to local pressures

glocal, glocalization thinking global but acting local

goodwill (see **brand equity**) the disparity between the firm's asset value and the true worth of the business

graphic features those features that distinguish a brand (e.g. McDonald's 'golden arches')

gross rating points (GRP) an advertising media currency calculated by multiplying 'reach' and 'frequency'

GRPs see **gross rating points**

guerrilla marketing a term coined by Jay Conrad Levinson and used to describe unconventional marketing intended to get maximum results from minimum outlay

halo effect those aspects of the brand that is portrayed to the outside world through marketing communications. It involves image management and the building up of benefits, brand personality and associations. It is the halo characteristics consumers use to distinguish one brand from another

halo effect (brand extention) when the attributes of one brand are transferred to another in such a way as it affects our judgement

hand-raisers prospects who have indicated by their behaviour (e.g. ordering a catalogue) that they *may* want to become customers

hard sell promoting heavily the tangible benefits available from a product or service

hedonic consumption the use of products or services for sheer enjoyment rather than problem or need driven

heuristic evaluation where evaluation is made based upon extraneous factors such as price (e.g. the higher the price the higher the quality)

hierarchy of effects models models that purport to show how marketing communications can help the buying process. AIDA and DAGMAR are amongst the best known

high consumerism in global marketing terms, developed or highly sophisticated markets

high involvement purchases see extensive problem-solving model

high-low pricing see hi-lo pricing

hi-lo pricing (or high-low pricing) strategy, prevalent in fast moving consumer goods retailing, where each week a percentage of products are heavily discounted and promoted throughout the store

hostaging where the retailer/reseller is able to exert power over the brand owner in order to provide trade promotions on a more or less permanent basis

house-lists lists compiled from a company's own database

html hypertext markup language. The language used to create Web documents

humour, humourous advertising designed to attract, through humour, consumer attention. If it is good enough, is memorable it may also generate 'word-of-mouth'

hypertext see hypertext markup language (html)

hypertext markup language (html) the language used to create Web documents

hypertext transfer protocol the protocol by which Web documents are transferred

hypodermic effect an early model of marketing communications that inferred communication was one way

icon a sign that looks like an object or represents it visually in a way that most people could relate to (e.g. no smoking sign)

iconic (association) developing an association between two or three concepts when there is an absence of stimulus. For example advertisers of certain products that are low value but frequently purchased will try and remind their target audience, repeatedly, of the brand name in an attempt to help consumers learn (effectively learning by rote)

identified product interest (IPI) customers with an interest in a particular product or service category

image a perception of an organization or brand that exists in the minds of customers, stakeholders and publics

image study a study of the organization's image in relation to its competitors

IMC see integrated marketing communications

impressions a single instance of an advertisement being displayed

in-bound (telemarketing) the use of telephony to facilitate responses from customers usually via a 'freephone' or local call rate number

incentives extra inducements to purchase

in-depth interviews a qualitative research technique involving the interviewing of a small number of subjects but in greater depth

index a sign that relates to the object by a causal connection (e.g. yawn relates to boredom)

indirect address in television or cinema advertising where the potential consumer 'eavesdrops' on, for example, a family, a group of friends, etc. (i.e. the message appears as if it is not directly aimed at the viewer)

individualized targeting see one-to-one marketing

industrial markets see B2B markets

influentials see connectors

information search where the customer collects information on a range of products or services prior to purchase

in-game product placement the placement of product in video games for the purpose of publicity

ingredient brand see component brand

innovators (see diffusion of innovation) those customers who are at the forefront of trends particularly in technical innovation. They are likely to have a higher disposable income and willing to pay a high price for being first in the market

institutional trust trust that is based on the rule of law (e.g. minimum standards legislation) or qualification (e.g. doctors, lecturers, etc.)

instrumental conditioning see operant conditioning

integral (database) where direct marketing is the principal marketing tool

integrated (database) where the database plays an important part in the business and direct marketing is one of the company's most important tools in its multi-channel operation

integrated marketing communications (IMC) a concept of marketing communications planning that recognizes the added value of a comprehensive plan, that evaluates the strategic roles of a variety of communication disciplines and combine these disciplines to provide clarity, consistency and maximum communications impact

interactive media media that interacts with the consumer (e.g. Internet, satellite/cable television)

internal marketing concerned particularly with internal communications and developing responsiveness, responsibility and unity of purpose in an organization

international company one whose home market dominates their sales but for whom the export market holds the promise of extra turnover. It is unlikely that such a company has their own distribution system in overseas markets and may instead ship direct to trade customers, employ an agent, distributor or authorize a licensee to manufacture a product or supply a service on their behalf

Internet a collection of wires, protocols and hardware that allows the electronic transmission of data including emails, file transfers and global networking

interstitials advertisements that appear between one Web page and the loading of the next

interval scales attitude scales usually positive or negative values about an arbitrary zero point

interviewer bias where the bias views of the interviewer corrupts the data collection

intrinsic see **core**

involvement (in relation to purchasing) the degree of perceived relevance and personal importance attached to the purchase

IPI see **identified product interest**

iTV interactive television

joint advertising cost of advertising shared between retailer and supplier

judgement sampling where the sample selection is made (by the researcher with or without the advice of experts) based on their relevance to the research project

junk-mail any mailing the customer decides is untargeted and obtrusive

key account managers marketing and/or sales executives who work specifically with one or a limited number of accounts

knowledge capital the knowledge held within an organization

laggards (see **diffusion of innovation**) sometimes technophobic, the last group to take up an innovation

lagged effect (or carryover effect) the time between when a consumer sees an advertisement and when they are ready to purchase.

lapsed customers see **former customers**

late majority (see **diffusion of innovation**) sceptical of new ideas but eventually take up innovations

latent loyalty low patronage for reasons such as distance but where attitude is high. If the situation changes likely to become a loyal customer

law of effect law that states that the consequences of behaviour now will govern the consequences of that behaviour in the future. In other words once a buying pattern is achieved it will continue into the future (Edward Thorndike)

lead qualification improving the quality of the information known about the customer/prospect

leaky bucket metaphor for the dual needs of customer acquisition and retention

learning the human capacity to know and act upon a situation based on some prior experience

legal analysis (brand equity) how well a brand is legally protected

lifestyle segmentation values, activity and lifestyle analysis (VALs)

lifetime value an approximation of the value of a customer over a lifetime

Likert Scale a scale that measures a respondent's attitude to predefined statements where the scores for individual responses are added together to produce an overall result

limited problem-solving model known and familiar purchases (modified or straight rebuys) with medium involvement in the purchase

line extension using an existing brand within a category to introduce new lines within that category (e.g. Persil tablets)

list brokers intermediaries between list owners and organizations wishing to rent lists

list exchanges exchange of customer data between companies (illegal in certain countries)

lists listings of potential customers with a specific characteristic (e.g. food lovers) available to rent for a specific direct mail, telemarketing or email campaign

livery see **signage**. Particularly relates to vehicles

lobbying the specialist part of public relations that builds and maintains relationships with government primarily for the purpose of influencing legislation and regulation

logical appeal (advertising) appeals to our sense of logic and reason, for example 'this product out-performs everything else in the market'

logo an emblem or device used to distinguish an organization or brand

long-term memory information stored for extensive periods of time although constant reorganization and re-categorization takes place as new information is received

loss-leader a product sold at or below cost to attract customers into a store

low consumerism in global marketing terms, undeveloped or unsophisticated markets

low involvement theory theory that suggests that consumers scan the enviroment, largely subconsciously to identify anything worth consideration in depth

loyalty loyalty in behavioural terms is repeated selection of a brand. Loyalty in attitudinal terms incorporates consumer preferences and disposition towards brands

loyalty cards cards issued to consumers by loyalty scheme organizers to facilitate the management and control of the scheme

loyalty marketing developing customer relationships over time

loyalty programmes programmes where customers are rewarded on the basis of general or targeted purchases

loyalty schemes schemes that reward customers for repurchases over time

magic bullet an early model of marketing communications that suggested communication is one way

mail order the ability (through selection in a catalogue) to order products for delivery by mail

MAO factors Petty and Cacioppo (1986) model suggests that it is not only motivation but ability to process information and the opportunity to make it happen that have a role to play in successful communications. The MAO factors are Motivation (a willingness to engage in behaviour, make decisions, pay attention and process information), Ability (refers to resources needed to achieve a particular goal) and Opportunity (the extent to which the situation enables a person to obtain his/her goal)

marcoms a frequently used short-form for marketing communications

marked-down products or services where the normal retail price is reduced

market analysis (brand equity) the percentage of earnings attributed to a brand

market research the study of consumer's needs and preferences

market share the brand's share of the market sector as a percentage of the whole sector

marketing communications the means by which a supplier of goods, services, values and/or ideas represent themselves to their target audience with the goal of stimulating dialogue leading to a better commercial or other relationships

marketing communications mix the tools used in marketing communications such as advertising, sales promotion, public relations, personal selling, direct marketing, etc

marketing communications plan a systematic plan to achieve organizational and marketing objectives relative to marketing communications

Marketing Compliance Officer (MCO) officer responsible for ensuring the organization complies with laws and regulations

marketing metrics the measures used to analyse the success or otherwise of marketing tools and campaigns

marketing mix otherwise known as the 4Ps (product, place, price and promotion) of marketing

marketing public relations those aspects of public relations directly associated with communication with customers (i.e. publicity)

marketing research a collection of 'tools' of assessment, evaluation and measurement which seek to reduce the knowledge 'distance' between the product's or service's manufacturer or supplier and the consumer, primarily through the supply of pertinent information concerning the customer

mass customization using technology to customize a product whilst still being able to benefit from economies of scale

mass media largely untargeted media including newspapers, television, radio etc.

MCO see **Marketing Compliance Officer (MCO)**

measurement techniques those techniques (largely quantitative) which are used when collecting data

media brokers intermediaries who purchase media space (only) without the overheads of a full agency

media chatter subject matter that is discussed by the media

media dependents media brokers that are part of a larger agency group

media evaluation evaluation of an organization's media coverage over a specific time period

media fragmentation the dilution of TV or radio station audiences due to the proliferation of channels

media independents independent media brokers

media management (agency) getting the messages that have been created into the appropriate media at a time and cost that fulfils the objective of the campaign

media office see **press office**

media officer see **press officer**

media release see **press release**

media strategy decisions on which media to use for a given campaign

media-neutral, media-neutral planning a customer-focused review of media based on research, analysis and insight and not habit and/or preference

medium (or media channel) a means of carrying the message

merchandising the act of deciding upon store layout and the product mix within it

message the vehicle by which an idea is transmitted via a medium

metaphor the application of a name or phrase which is imaginatively but not literally applicable (e.g. 'Lenor is like a breath of fresh air')

me-too products new products that are similar to existing products already available on the marketplace

Mexico Statement definition of public relations which originated at a public relations conference held in Mexico City in 1978

minder a person directed to look after a politician to ensure that they do not stray off the Party's official line

mirror image how internal management think outsiders see the organization

mis-selling selling something based on a falsehood

mission the core business of an organization and its ambitions usually normally set out in the company's mission statement

mission statement a statement that asserts the core business of an organization and its ambitions

mobile marketing any aspect of marketing using mobile telephone technology

modelling approach where the consumer through observation and imitation of others (for example in an advertisement) associates it with their lifestyle. Also called observational learning and vicarious learning

monetary value (direct marketing) a measure of how much a customer spends with the organization over a period

money-off (coupons/vouchers) coupons with monetary incentive to buy specific products

mortgaging effect that after a promotion sales, rather than returning to 'normal' levels fall back for a period

motivation inner drives which cause human beings to strive for some level of satisfaction

multi-brand buyer buyers who are not particularly loyal to one but to a number of brands

multi-branding, multi-brand where different brand names owned by one company are used in the same product category (e.g. Procter & Gamble soap powers Dreft, Daz and Bold)

multi-dimensional skills map matrix used to establish a customer's view of the organization relative to its competitors

multi-level marketing selling direct to the public through a network of self-employed salespeople, often at house parties and other private gatherings. The multi-level marketing company initially recruits distributors who in turn recruit more distributors and so on. Earnings come both from a distributor's own sales and the sales of those they recruit (and often even further down the line)

multinational companies operate in a number of overseas markets often through agents or distributors but would normally secure more (relative to international companies) control over them. It may be the case that foreign-based partners are involved and/or that the company has a wholly or partly owned subsidiary

multiple image where different people see different images dependent on their particular relationship with the organization

multistage sampling a form of cluster sampling used where the subgroups are widely dispersed. As with cluster sampling the population is divided into subgroups but a further stage is involved before final sample selection. Techniques may vary but commonly subgroups are selected on a weighted (i.e. proportional to the population of that subgroup) basis and further subdivided, for example on an area (county, city, etc.) basis. The final sample selection is made from these sub-subgroups on a random basis

mystery shoppers researchers who visit a store under the guise of a shopper for the purpose of consumer observation

nature those characteristics we inherit from our forebears

need for attribution see **attribution**

need for cognition a need to understand the world such that it develops curiosity for further information (see **cognitive, cognition**)

negative association (in sponsorship) the sponsoring of teams, individuals, etc. who engender hostility from some quarters

negative reinforcement punishment which reinforces the avoidance of behaviour that led to the punishment

negotiated commission (agency) commission system which may involve rebating on a sliding scale

network selling see **multi-level marketing**

niche marketing the targeting of one particular, perhaps specialized segment

noise anything that interferes with the proper delivery of the message (e.g. competing messages)

nominal scales attitude scales where variables are categorized and used for classification, e.g. age, sex, place of birth, etc.

non-probability techniques techniques which do not adhere to the law of probability and, therefore, the results cannot be generalized across the population. Rather the sample is chosen at the convenience of the researcher or to fulfil the demands of some predetermined purpose

non-sales communications direct marketing but not with a view of generating an immediate sale (e.g. welcome packs, newsletters, etc.)

non-sampling errors those aspects of research (other than sampling errors) that can seriously affect the outcome. These include such factors as misunderstanding and interviewer bias. Non-response is also a factor as it is difficult to know whether those who responded to a particular research programme were in any way different from those who refused to take part

nurture the effect of society upon the characteristics we are born with

objective and task (budget) establishing what needs to be achieved and setting the budget on the basis of achieving those objectives

objectives objectives are what drive an organization. They are the 'where we want to be' of any business. Objectives should be SMART (strategic, measurable, actionable, realistic and timely), communicable and aspirational

observation (research) examining actual as opposed to predicted behaviour. For example an observation of consumers by a researcher interested in the effects of an in-store promotion

observational learning see **modelling approach**

offering a number of factors (product, price, etc.) which together make up the offering to the customer

off-message not keeping to the company, party or other organization's message or official line

off-the-page newspaper or magazine offers with a direct response mechanism (e.g. freephone, envelope, etc.)

oligopolies a market situation in which there are few sellers in the market and where the marketing action of one firm will have a direct effect on the others

omnibus surveys surveys covering a wide range of interests, including those of specific interest to the sponsoring company, are sent to a pre-selected panel of respondents. This type of research enables the costs to be shared with other companies participating in the survey

one-pipe convergence the movement toward a single broadband feed which supplies television, PCs, DVDs, games consoles and stereo systems

one-to-one marketing a concept that proposes that customers can be individually targeted

on-message keeping to the company, party or other organization's message or official line

operant conditioning (or instrumental conditioning) where reinforcement follows a specific response. For example do this (e.g. push a button) and you will receive a reward (e.g. food)

opinion formers people with influence or authority over our lives for example journalists, broadcasters, analysts, politicians, scientists or anyone with some real or imagined status who can be trusted (rightly or wrongly) to impart good advice

opinion leaders may not be formal experts. They do not necessarily provide advice but consumers are prone to follow them. They are often, but not always, from a higher social status than their immediate contemporaries and frequently more gregarious

opportunities-to-see (OTS) a measure used by media buyers to estimate how many times the target audience may see the message

optimum image the image a company aspires to (wish image) may not be possible and so a rather less than perfect image may be sought

ordinal scales attitude scales where objects are ranked in order

OTS see **opportunities-to-see**

out-bound (telemarketing) the planned use of the telephone to make unstructured calls to a target audience in a measurable and accountable way

outdoor advertising/media posters, billboards, transport and other advertising that is located outside

overselling promising more than is available through the sale

own brands see **own label**

own label a retail brand that carries the retailer's name (e.g. Sainsbury's coffee)

paid-for placement (PFP) a paid-for service which, on the basis of certain key words, guarantees top ranking in search engine listings

panel interviews group interviews or focus groups

Pareto analysis the general supposition that business relationships follow an 80:20 ratio (e.g. 80 per cent of business comes from 20 per cent of customers)

parity brand a product or service with little or no intrinsically superior rewards compared with the competition, typically leaving marketers to offer extrinsic rewards to attract patronage

pay-back period (budget) where budget decisions are made based upon the time taken to repay the investment

payment-by-results (PBR) remuneration based on achievement of set targets

percentage of sales (budget) where the communications budget is set at a certain percentage of projected sales. This is widely used as a benchmark in many industries

perception map see **multi-dimensional skills map**

perceptions how we interpret and make sense of the world. The way an individual perceives a situation may be different from how others perceive the same situation

performance-based compensation see **payment-by-results**

peripheral (database) where the database and direct marketing play only a minor role in a company

permission marketing marketing where you have the explicit permission of the customer to contact them

personal selling an interpersonal tool where individuals, often representing an organization, interact in order to inform, persuade, or remind an individual or group to take appropriate action, as required by the sponsors

persuasion shift changes in preferences which occur having seen an advertisement

PEST(L), PEST (or STEP) stands for elements of the macro environment: political, economic, sociological and technological, to which legal (L) is frequently added

PFP see **paid-for placement**

physiological needs (Maslow's hierarchy of needs) hunger, thirst, etc.

pitch agency presentation

pitch-list list of agencies asked to 'pitch' for all or part of an organization's communications business

point-of-purchase see **point-of-sale**

point-of-sale in-store materials displayed at the time the customer is making buying decisions

polygamous behaviour where customers are seen as making a stream of purchases but their loyalty is divided among a number of products. They may be more or less loyal to one brand than any other

POP point-of-purchase (see **point of sale**)

population in marketing research terms population is the group (demographic, geodemographic, users, former customers, etc.) of interest to the marketer

pop-ups message boxes that 'pop-up' on websites either to add additional information or as advertising

portfolio of brands a consumer's basket of brands from which buying decisions are made

POS point of sale (see **point of sale**)

positioning the process of creating a perception in the consumer's mind regarding the nature of the company and its products relative to the competition (see also **benefit positioning, user positioning and competitive positioning**)

positioning statement a statement of the brand's positioning in the market

positive reinforcement reward which reinforces the behaviour that led to the reward

post-purchase dissonance (see **cognitive dissonance**) dissonance (mental discomfort) felt after purchase regarding whether or not the buyer has made the right decision (e.g. is it value for money?)

post-purchase evaluation evaluation of a product or service which may lead to repurchase

post-testing testing after a campaign

prebuttal the planning of a response prior to a negative action or statement

precisely wrong strictly an incorrect measure. Proxy measures such as brand awareness, recall or recognition whilst being easy to measure precisely are not directly associated with sales and might be said to be precisely wrong (see **vaguely right**)

pre-emptive strategies (of advertising) where the brand asserts its superiority in an undifferentiated market making it difficult for competitors to match such assertions (e.g. 'Carlsberg probably the best beer in the world')

premiums gifts given to consumers either with purchase or, if terms (e.g. collect five wrappers) have to be fulfilled, by other means

press office office which handles press and other media enquiries and issues press releases

press officer representative of the company who handles press and other media enquiries and issues press releases

press release (or media release) newsworthy written announcement distributed to selected media

primary data data that is collected specifically for a particular research problem

priming suggests that a short exposure to a particular stimulus can evoke an increased drive to consume more of a product

principle of negative option offers regular customers the benefits of continuous service without action on their part. In effect the principle takes advantage of our inclination to do nothing until something (often a negative perception) prompts us to take action

private-label see **own label**

probability techniques those techniques of selection that are free from personal influence producing a known and non-zero likelihood of any particular subject of the research being included in the sample. They are representative of (but never an exact match with) the population as a whole and a determination is made of their statistical accuracy

problem definition see **problem recognition**

problem recognition (or problem definition) recognition that a purchase must be made to fulfil a need or want

problem-solving models extensive, limited and routinized problem-solving models

process-based trust trust built up over time (i.e. reputation)

product life cycle (PLC) concept that suggests products go through a cycle that includes a period of introduction and growth, a maturity phase and ultimately decline unless the product brand can be reinvented. See also **brand life cycle**

product/message thoughts (see **cognitive response model**) those thoughts directed at the product/service and/or the claims made in the advertising

product placement the placement of product in films, television shows and video games for the purpose of publicity

production department (agency) responsible for ensuring that the creative elements are translated into the right format for the chosen media

profiled prospects prospects whose general profile suggests they *may* become customers

profit optimization (budget) suggests that investment continues as long as the marginal revenue (i.e. each additional unit generated) exceeds the marginal cost (i.e. each additional unit invested to achieve that extra unit generated)

progress managers responsible for ensuring that the various stages of production are completed on time

promiscuous behaviour where customers are seen as making a 'stream of purchases' but still within the context of an either/or decision – either the customer is always with you (loyalty) or flits among an array of alternatives (promiscuous)

promotional mix see **marketing communications mix**

proposition statement of the brand's central theme or unique selling proposition (USP)

proprietary panels online surveys set up or commissioned by a client firm usually made up of customers of that company

PROs Public Relations Officers

prospect a potential customer

prospect hierarchy a hierarchy of potential customers ranging from lapsed customers at the top to 'suspects' at the bottom

proxy measures measures used when the marketing communication effect on sales cannot be directly measured

public affairs a specialist area of practice within public relations concerned with public policy-making, legislation and regulation that may affect the interests of the organization

public relations the planned and sustained effort to establish and maintain goodwill and mutual understanding between an organization and its publics

Public Relations Officers (PROs) employees responsible for reactive and proactive relationships with the media. Also known as Media Relations Officers

public relations transfer process a theory of public relations that suggests incremental stages between hostility and acceptance

publicist a seeker of publicity on behalf of his/her clients

publicity building the image of the brand and creating positive associations between that brand and its publics

publics 'publics' has a very particular meaning and one peculiar to public relations. 'Publics' are those people, internal and external to the organization, with whom the organization communicates

pull strategies strategies which look to influence the end-user and attract these customers (through marketing communications) 'over the heads' of retailers direct to the individual brand

pulsing (campaign) continuous campaign which is higher at different times of the year and which may reflect seasonal considerations

purchase the act of exchange of one commodity for another (usually money)

purposive sampling samples based on certain criteria associated with the research. Therefore, if the research is aimed at gauging the potential impact of a media campaign targeted at, for example, doctors, a purposive sample of doctors may be selected

push strategies strategies designed to influence re-sellers or trade channel intermediaries (e.g. wholesalers, dealers, agents, retailers, etc.) to carry and promote particular brands (i.e. they are 'pushed' into the distribution system)

pyramid selling a form of multi-level marketing where the central purpose is to earn commission (or receive other payments) from those further down the line rather than sales *per se*

qualitative research looking to answer the 'why?' and the 'what?' type of questions qualitative research places greater emphasis on understanding consumer behaviour through insights

quantitative research seeking to answer the questions 'how many?' or 'who?' Research that is looking to measure something

questionnaire research surveys which use structured or semi-structured, personal, mail, telephone and (increasingly) email and Web-based interviews

quota sampling attempts of researchers to mirror the characteristics of the population by selecting on a proportional basis. For example, researchers investigating a new product might base their sample on the demographics (age, sex, etc.) of the target population in proportion to their presence in that population

ratchet effect predicts the advantages of an integrated strategy that builds credibility through advertising and extra volume through promotional inducements

rate card the published cost of media advertising

ratings agencies organizations which monitor companies and establish credit ratings based on commercial risk. These ratings affect the company's ability to lend, and the rate on which that loan is based

ratio scales attitude scales with a predetermined zero point (e.g. percentage of satisfied customers)

reach the percentage of the target audience exposed at least once to the message during a period (normally four weeks)

realm of perception see **field of perception**

realm of understanding see **field of perception**

reasoning where consumers take the information they have about a brand and deduce their own conclusion regarding the brands suitability for purchase and use. Individuals need to restructure and reorganize information already held in long-term memory and combine this with new information. Thus quite complex associations build up (e.g. Silk Cut cigarettes and silk ribbon)

reason-why (advertising) see **logical appeal**

rebating giving to the client part or all of the commission paid by media owners

recall see **advertising recall**

recency (direct marketing) a measure of how long ago a customer bought from the organization

recency principle (or shelf-space model) a principle which supposes that a consumer's first exposure to an advertisement is the most powerful, that the advertiser's primary role is to influence brand choice (when the customer is ready to buy) and that achieving a high level of weekly reach for a brand should be emphasized over acquiring heavy frequency

recognition, recognition tests see **advertising recognition**

reference groups groups with whom consumers associate themselves, e.g. faith groups, social groups, etc.

referrals those prospects who have been encouraged by existing customers to contact the company

refunds (promotion) by way of cash or coupons and may involve one or more purchases and submitting proof-of-purchase by mail or through claims managed via the Internet

rehearsal aids memory. By mentally repeating the information the individual increases the chance that it will be linked to other stored information (i.e. learning by rote)

relationship marketing to 'identify and establish, maintain and enhance and, when necessary, terminate relationships with customers and other stakeholders, at a profit so that the objectives of all parties involved are met; and this is done by mutual exchange and fulfilment of promises' (Grönroos 1994)

relaunch the reforming of an entity following a dramatic or negative occurrence

reminder campaign follows major campaigns and acts as a reminder and reinforcement of the message

renegade marketing see **guerrilla marketing**

repetition repeat exposure to the brand message (also called frequency)

repositioning the process of recreating or changing the perception of the brand in the consumer's mind

reputation trust and confidence built up over time

reputation audits see **communications audit**

research assessment assessing the value of research against the benefits derived from it

research objectives derived directly from the organizational and marketing objectives they may refer to an existing or potential product or service or, specifically in relation to marketing communications, existing or potential campaigns and/or media

research problem what the research is designed to solve

research proposal costed proposal for a particular research problem

re-sellers retailers, wholesalers, distributors

resonance strategy (or 'slice-of-life' strategy) attempts to match 'patterns' in the message with target audiences' shared experiences

respondent conditioning see **classical conditioning**

response lists lists of prospective customers with identified product interest (IPI)

response mechanism the means by which a customer responds to an offer e.g. freephone, freepost, etc.

retainer fee (agency) fee paid to agency to retain their services on an *ad hoc* basis over time

retrieval (of memory) the process where information is returned from the long-term to the short-term memory

RFM (recency, frequency and monetary value) a measure used to establish the value of a direct marketing customer

rolling research research that takes place on a regular basis and asks the same questions so that response comparisons can be made

routine problem solving see **routinized problem solving** model

routinized problem solving repeat behaviour with low involvement, usually low cost and often limited external knowledge

safety needs (Maslow's hierarchy of needs) security, protection, etc.

sales communications (direct marketing) direct marketing with a view to generating a sale

sales promotion the use of incentives to generate a specific (usually short-term) response. Capable of targeting and with a high degree of control over design and placement. Generally regarded as having low credibility although cause-related promotions may have a very positive effect. They are seen to add value for consumers but may bring forward future sales

sales promotion allowances contribution to retailers for promotions

sample error inherent in all research quantified through the application of statistical formulae

sample selection determines the body of individuals involved in a research project

sampling free of charge trialling of products in-store or at other locations

sampling interval when undertaking systematic random sampling the interval between respondents, for example if 200 people are required from a population of 19 000, the sampling interval would be 95

saving stamps now largely defunct method of managing a loyalty scheme where stamps were issued with purchases, collected and ultimately exchanged for gifts of cash. Another form is used in connection with savings clubs in some stores

schedule, scheduling the chosen media schedule format (see **burst, drip, continuous, pulsing** and **flighting campaigns**)

scope (or reach) the boundaries of an organization's operation

search engine a portal that enables users to search the Web

secondary data data which is already available from one or more sources. Secondary data may include internal company data or come from external agencies including research agencies, analysts, omnibus surveys, syndicated research or audit data, trade association reports or departments of local, national and supranational government

sector awareness consumer awareness that a sector (e.g. palmtops) exists

segregation the grouping of individual customers with individual requirements although the requirements are not exactly the same

selective attention the process of screening out information that does not interest us and selectively processing the information that does. Messages that successfully bypass 'selective attention' are likely to be perceived positively

selective distortion the tendency to hear what we want to hear. Distortion may occur because of prejudice or stereotyping

selective exposure where consumers selectively expose themselves to certain messages as opposed to other messages (e.g. by ordering a catalogue)

self-actualization (Maslow's hierarchy of needs) the need for self-fulfilment and a desire to achieve one's own potential

self-liquidating premiums premium (or gift) where the income received covers the outgoings of the promotion

semantics the branch of linguistics concerned with meaning

semiotics the study of signs and symbols in a language

sensory appeal creating fantasy and/or aura to attract attention to the message

sensory storage information that is sensed in our minds for a split-second. If an impression is made this will be transferred to the short-term memory

shaping a behaviouralist theory associated with sales promotion that suggests that a response builds on prior experience and can be explained as 'appearing after preceding acts which, taken together, constitute a chain of successive approximations' (John Watson)

shelf impact the impact of product packaging

shelf-space model see **recency principle**

shock tactics advertising that is shocking but attracts attention

short-term memory maximum number of items stored (perhaps four or five) for short periods of time (perhaps 8 seconds)

sideways communications employee–employee communications

signage the identity applied to buildings, vehicles etc. denoting the organization or its brand(s)

significance (market research) the analysis of the differences between the observed and expected results noting whether they are real and significant differences

silent calls calls generated by predictive dialling technology designed to speed up agent productivity but which frequently leaves customers with a disturbing silence when they answer their telephone

silent communication non-verbal communication, e.g. shrug of shoulders

simile a figure of speech involving the comparison of one thing with another (e.g. 'like Murphy's I'm not bitter')

simple random sampling sampling based on the chance selection from the target population

simulated sales sales calculated on the basis of no advertising which can then be used to measure the contribution of advertising

single-minded proposition brand's unique selling proposition

situation (situational audit) an audit of the current state of the organization often using SWOT and PEST(L) analysis

slice-of-life (advertising) advertising that uses simulated 'real-life' situations and where the viewer is encouraged to get involved with the action

slice-of-life strategy see **resonance strategy**

slogans memorable phrases that sum up an important characteristic of the brand (e.g. the world's favourite airline)

slotting allowances payment in consideration of 'slotting in' a new product into the retailer's merchandise mix

snowball sampling where respondents are initially selected at random and their views sought. Interviewees are then asked to nominate other people who are part of that population and so on

social needs (Maslow's hierarchy of needs) love, belonging, etc.

socioeconomic groupings population classifications such as the National Readership Survey's (NRS) ABC_1C_2DE socioeconomic grouping

soft sell using emotional appeals to produce positive feelings for a brand

soundbite the encapsulation of a message in very few word (for the purposes of television and radio journalism)

source the originator of the message (also refers to the person delivering the message)

source attractiveness how attractive and persuasive the source is and how much the source identifies with the customer

source credibility how much confidence the receiver has that the source can provide an expert and/or objective opinion

source orientated thoughts (see **cognitive response model**) represent those associated (positively or negatively) with the origin of the message

source power where compliance with the request involves a real or perceived reward or actual or apparent avoidance of punishment

spam unsolicited, bulk emails

spin doctor public relations jargon for person who 'spins' or creates positive stories (a term often used to ridicule political advisers)

spoiler-campaign where the competition deliberately introduces competing, conflicting or denigrating messages to counter the message from the source

sponsor the provider of funds, resources or services to an individual event or organization in return for some rights and associations usually to be used for commercial advantage

sponsorship a commercial activity whereby one party permits another an opportunity to exploit a situation with a target audience in return for funds, services or resources

sponsorship clutter when sponsorship and associated advertising becomes overpowering

spot advertisement advertising between programming normally of 30 second to 1 minute duration

spurious loyalty high patronage but low attitude to a brand. Customer will probably go elsewhere if another choice becomes available

stand alone brand brand which is not directly associated with a particular manufacturer or retailer for the purpose of communication (e.g. Persil)

standardization push towards standardizing products for all international markets in order to save on product, packaging and communication costs

standing order an order to a bank to make a payment on a regular basis

statements what is said about the brand and how it is promoted such as copy style and slogans

stereotyping short-hand, generalized characteristics of people and places used in order to communicate messages quickly and effectively

stopping power advertising that has the effect of attracting complete attention

STP shorthand for segmentation, targeting and positioning

storage (of memory) the way the memory is organized

story-boards artistic impressions of a campaign

straight re-buy business-to-business term for re-buying a product without changing the supplier or the specifications

strap lines see **slogans** (also called tag lines)

strategies the 'how we are going to get there'. Communication strategies are the ways an organization chooses to communicate with its customers and other stakeholders

stratified random sampling sample based on the variable percentages as they appear in the population as a whole. Variables may include demographics, income, geography, etc. and should be appropriate to the research taking place

street marketing see **guerrilla marketing**

strong theory of advertising where advertising is presumed to have the power to inform, persuade and sell (see also the **weak theory of advertising**)

subscriptions a fee for membership or for the right to receive something (i.e. newspapers) on a regular basis for a set period of time

suggestions constructive feedback from customers

sugging selling under the guise of research

summated scale where the scores for individual responses are added together to produce an overall result (e.g. Likert scale)

super own label exclusive brands created for emphasis or thematic purposes (e.g. Blue Harbour at Marks & Spencer, George at Asda)

supplier partnerships formal or informal cooperation between organizations

survey research see **questionnaire research**

suspects based on geodemographic profiling, values, attitudes and lifestyle profiling (VALs) or previous purchase behaviour which indicates they *may* have profiles of current customers

switching behaviour where purchasing is seen as an 'either/or' decision – either the customer stays with you (loyalty) or turns against you (switching)

SWOT an analysis of the strengths, weaknesses, opportunities and threats facing an organization

symbol an artificial sign created for a purpose or meaning (e.g. Olympic Rings)

symbolic orientation where the brand's positioning is based on consumers' emotional needs and involves psychosocial rather than physical differentiation (see also **experiential orientation**)

syndicated research (or audit data) carried out by specialist agencies who collect and analyse data on a regular (rolling research) or one-off basis. Clients normally pay a subscription for these services which are available for both retail (e.g. Nielson) and specialist markets

syntactics the grammatical arrangement of words

systematic random sampling an anonymous sample selection based on a sampling interval. If, for example, 200 people are required from a population of 19 000, the sampling interval would be 95 (19 000 ÷ 200). In this example a random starting point (between 1 and 95) is chosen and from that point every 95th unit would be sampled

tactics the operational element of the communications plan and, by definition, short term. The choice may be between different media (including the Internet) or techniques (e.g. direct marketing)

tag lines see **slogans**

target audience a defined group of consumers (demographic, geodemographic, users, former customers, etc.) targeted by the marketer

target marketing the segmentation of markets, targeting of potential customers and the positioning of the organization in the market (STP)

target rating points (TRPs) a variation of gross ratings points adjusted to reflect the chosen target audience

targeted differentiation see **repositioning**

task (budget) see **objective and task**

telemarketing the use of telephony to maintain a relationship with your customer (see 'in-bound' and 'out-bound')

telesales cold-calling (without prior contact or permission) with the objective of making a sale or starting the process towards a sale

television rating points (TVR) a television advertising media currency calculated by multiplying 'reach' and 'frequency' (effectively TV gross rating points)

test markets geographically controlled testing before fully exposing the 'new feature' (product, service, campaign, distribution, etc.) or new brand to a full national or even international launch

testimonial a testament to a brand delivered by a personality, an expert or a representative of an average consumer

testing unlike marketing research testing measures actual behaviour but does not answer the 'why' and 'how' questions

test-screening screening of an advertisement to a sample audience prior to final transmission

time-based fees (agency) an established form of recompense in public relations but which is also more generally used on special agency projects

time–space proximity the time between a stimulus and a response

time-to-market the amount of time it takes an organization to get a product to market from its original inception

tone the feeling or emotion associated with a communication

total set all of the products available in a category

trade channel intermediaries wholesalers, dealers, agents, retailers, etc.

trade promotions promotions designed to develop the brand through the trade (e.g. competitions, demonstrations, etc.)

traffic managers see **progress managers**

trait theory a theory that suggests an individual should be viewed as a composite of several behaviour traits or characteristics

transactional marketing the traditional marketing or mass-marketing paradigm

transfer process see **public relations transfer process**

transformational (advertising) image-dominant, brand building messages

transnational organization an organization whose network structure is such that it is difficult to place their corporate centre (although not their original home). These types of organization utilize the worldwide facilities for production and regard its markets as outlets in a global marketplace

trendsetters see **fashion icons**

trial buying a product for the first time

trial packs new product, frequently in smaller than normal quantity and at a special price to encourage trial

TRPs see **target rating points**

trust a confidence in someone or something. There are three forms of trust: institutional trust, character-based trust and process-based trust

TVRs see **television rating points**

two-step model a model of communications that shows that some messages come by way of others (e.g. opinion formers and opinion leaders)

typeface the style of letters used within an advertisement or other communication

typical-person endorsement the use of everyday characters (usually played by characters) to endorse a product or service

unconditioned response the response (e.g. salivation) to something that is naturally stimulating (e.g. smell of food)

unconditioned stimulus something that naturally stimulates (e.g. smell of food)

under-the-radar marketing see **guerrilla marketing**

undifferentiated targeting takes place in those markets where the cost of segmenting and targeting is too high or where the product is too generic. In practice, however, there are few examples of truly undifferentiated markets

unique selling proposition (USP) the proposition which sets the brand apart from any other brand

up-selling selling higher quality (and, therefore, higher price) items to existing customer base

upward communications employee to management communications

user positioning user benefits relate to the specific profile of the target audience and is commonly accomplished with the aid of demographic and psychographic variables which denote specific lifestyle characteristics

USP see **unique selling proposition**

vaguely right actual sales directly related to advertising are almost impossible to gauge accurately but an estimation can be said to be vaguely right (see also **precisely wrong**)

VALs values, attitudes and lifestyle analysis

values see **brand values**

vampire advertising see **vampire creativity**

vampire creativity (or vampire advertising) occurs when the communication is *too* original, *too* entertaining or *too* involving such that it distracts the consumer from the brand message

vanguard marketing see **guerrilla marketing**

vicarious learning see **modelling approach**

viral marketing marketing spread by word of mouth. Alternatively marketing materials created by the brand owner that are passed on and spread 'virus-like' around the Internet

virtual marketing see **viral marketing**

voice reaction, usually negative, back to supplier (also see **complaints**)

voice-overs commentary over an advertisement

waste   mass communications that are effectively wasted on non-targeted consumers

Waterloo effect   content of good advertising campaigns, namely uniqueness, frequency and relevance

watershed (in advertising)   denoting a time before which certain advertising (and certain programming) cannot be shown

weak theory of advertising   sees advertising power as much more benign than the 'strong theory of advertising'. It questions the power of advertising to persuade suggesting instead that it acts more as a reminder or gentle nudge toward a particular brand than a highly influential force

wearout   consumer boredom and/or irritation at a repeated communication

wheel of prosperity   model detailing the direct marketing process

win-back strategies   strategies for winning back former customers

wish image   the image that an organization aspires to

word-of-mouth   marketing messages that circulate around a marketplace without the aid of marketing communications

world-view   the consumer's view the world (see **field of perception**)

World Wide Web (WWW)   the World Wide Web exists on the Internet and is comprised of hypertext pages viewed by a browser. Web pages always begin http:// or https:// signifying the content being viewed is hypertext and transferred using the hypertext transfer protocol

WWW   see World Wide Web

zapping   changing channel during a television commercial break

zipping   the fast-forwarding of pre-recorded programmes enabling viewers to bypass commercials

INDEX